Lecture Notes
in Business Information Processing 171

Series editors

Wil van der Aalst
Eindhoven Technical University, Eindhoven, The Netherlands
John Mylopoulos
University of Trento, Povo, Italy
Michael Rosemann
Queensland University of Technology, Brisbane, QLD, Australia
Michael J. Shaw
University of Illinois, Urbana-Champaign, IL, USA
Clemens Szyperski
Microsoft Research, Redmond, WA, USA

T0183105

For further volumes:
http://www.springer.com/series/7911

Editors
Niels Lohmann
University of Rostock
Rostock
Germany

Petia Wohed
Stockholm University
Stockholm
Sweden

Minseok Song
Ulsan National Institute of Science
  and Technology
Ulsan
Korea, Republic of (South Korea)

ISSN 1865-1348   ISSN 1865-1356 (electronic)
ISBN 978-3-319-06256-3   ISBN 978-3-319-06257-0 (eBook)
DOI 10.1007/978-3-319-06257-0
Springer Cham Heidelberg New York Dordrecht London

Library of Congress Control Number: 2014938617

Printed on acid-free paper

Springer is part of Springer Science+Business Media (www.springer.com)

Foreword

This volume collects the proceedings of the workshops held on August 26, 2013, in conjunction with the 11th International Conference on Business Process Management (BPM 2013), which took place in Beijing, China. The proceedings are so-called post-workshop proceedings, in that the authors were allowed to revise and improve their papers even after the workshops, so as to take into account the feedback obtained from the audience during their presentations.

The BPM conference is considered the leading research conference in this area, whose practicality appeals to researchers and practitioners alike. As such, BPM is perceived as a premium event to co-locate a workshop with — both by academia and by industry. The 2013 edition of the conference attracted 13 workshop proposals with topics ranging from well-established BPM areas, such as process design and process mining, to recent areas that are gaining growing interest from the research and industry communities, such as security in business processes, artifact-centric BPM, process model collections, and more. Given the high quality of the submissions, selecting candidate workshops and assembling the best mix of workshops was not an easy task. Eventually, twelve workshops were selected for co-location with BPM 2013. As three of these workshops did not receive sufficient submissions, effectively nine workshops took place:

- **9th International Workshop on Business Process Intelligence (BPI'13)** — *organized by Boudewijn van Dongen, Barbara Weber, Jochen De Weerdt, and Diogo R. Ferreira.*

  BPI aimed to bring together practitioners and researchers from different communities such as BPM, information systems research, business administration, software engineering, artificial intelligence, process and data mining with the goal to provide a better understanding of techniques and algorithms to support a company's processes at build-time and the way they are handled at run-time.

- **6th International Workshop on Business Process Management and Social Software (BPMS2'13)** — *organized by Rainer Schmidt and Selmin Nurcan.*

  The goal of the BPMS2'13 workshop was to explore how social software interacts with business process management, how business process management has to change to comply with social software and business processes may profit from social software and social media, and how those new opportunities offered by social software impact the design, development, software support, and continuous improvement of business processes.

- **2nd International Workshop on Data- and Artifact-centric BPM (DAB'13)** — *organized by Marlon Dumas and Richard Hull.*

  The DAB workshop invited researchers from the BPM field as well as from related fields, including data management and information systems engineering. Its objective was the investigation of the tight interplay between data and control flow aspects of BPM and the discussion of the current state of ongoing research, novel approaches to data and process integration and industry needs.

- **1st International Workshop on Decision Mining & Modeling for Business Processes (DeMiMoP'13)** — *organized by Jan Vanthienen.*

  DeMiMoP'13 aimed at discovering and utilizing the decision process. This included the examination of the relationship between decisions and processes, the enhancement of decision mining based on process data, the investigation of decision goals, structures, and their connection with business processes, and to show best practices in separating process and decision concerns.

- **2013 Workshop on Emerging Topics in Business Process Management (ETBPM'13)** — *organized by Nenad Stojanovic, Christian Janiesch, Stefan Schulte, Ingo Weber, Marta Induska, Michael Rosemann, and Michael zur Muehlen.*

  Business Process Management is both, a management approach and an enabling technology. It is neither typical off-the-shelf software nor a preconfigured software solution to solve a particular business problem. As such, BPM technology can be used to solve a number of problems in very flexible ways. Similarly, other enabling technologies and concepts exist which can be combined with BPM to enable even more potential. The design phase of BPM is where it all comes together when a new BPM system is engineered. Consequently, the ETBPM investigated opportunities when designing combined systems of BPM and other enabling technologies, such as the Event-driven Architecture (EDA), Complex Event Processing (CEP), or Cloud Computing.

  In this workshop, also papers of the workshops on Event-driven Business Process Management (EdBPM), Business Process Management in the Cloud (BPMC) and Business Process Design (BPD) where presented. These workshops were accepted, but did not receive sufficient submissions to be hosted on their own.

- **3rd International Workshop on Process-Aware Logistics Systems (PALS'13)** — *organized by Kamel Barkaoui and Zhiwu Li.*

  PALS'13 focused on the design and optimization of global logistics systems, from a business process management perspective. Its topics included exploring and mastering the tools needed for operating, reconfiguring and, in general, making decisions within logistics-based systems, in order to provide the customers and system users with the greatest possible value.

- **4th Int. Workshop on Process Model Collections: Management and Reuse (PMC-MR'13)** — *organized by Remco Dijkman, Marcello La Rosa, Lucinia H. Thom, and Marcelo Fantinato.*

  The PMC-MR'13 focussed on large business process model collections. These models are used to solve a variety of modeling challenges, and they are increasingly published to a large number of stakeholders. In that sense, it may not come as a surprise that many organizations struggle to manage such high volumes of complex process models. Against this backdrop, the aim of this workshop was to discuss novel research in the area of managing business process model collections.

– **2nd Int. Workshop on Security in Business Processes (SBP'13)** — *organized by Rafael Accorsi, Wil van der Aalst, and Raimundas Matulevicius.*

   SBP'13 aimed to bring together researchers and practitioners working toward the reliable security management of business process models in process-aware information systems. SBP 2012 encouraged innovative methods for business process security audit and control along the entire business process life cycle, welcoming contributions beyond the strictly technical character, considering economic, legal, and standardization issues.

– **2nd Int. Workshop on Theory and Applications of Process Visualization (TAProViz'13)** — *organized by Ross Brown, Simone Kriglstein, and Stefanie Rinderle-Ma.*

   TAProViz'13 intended to promote and nurture the development of process visualization topics as continuing research areas. To date, many process model representations have not developed beyond minimally interactive 2D representations of directed graphs. In the workshop, research in computer–human interaction, games, and interactive entertainment was extended toward BPM to engage, provide insight, and to promote collaboration.

With these nine workshops, the BPM 2013 workshop program was rich and stimulating with a variety of topics, and formed an extraordinary and balanced program of high-quality events. BPM 2013 had more than 100 participants including both researchers and practitioners. The papers that were presented in the workshops report innovative and state-of-the-art advancements in the BPM area, spanning from formal to conceptual and empirical research. We are confident the reader will enjoy this volume as much as we enjoyed organizing this outstanding program and assembling its proceedings.

Of course, we did not organize everything on our own. Many people of the BPM 2013 Organizing Committee contributed to the success of the workshop program. We would particularly like to thank the General Chair Jianmin Wang for involving us in this unique event, the Organizing Chair Lijie Wen for the smooth management of all on-site issues, the workshop organizers for managing their workshops and diligently answering the wealth of emails we sent around, and, finally, the authors for presenting their research and work at the BPM 2013 workshops and actually making all this possible.

February 2014
Niels Lohmann
Minseok Song
Petia Wohed

Preface

The following preface is a collection of the prefaces of the workshop proceedings of the individual workshops. The workshop papers, grouped by event, form the body of the volume.

9th International Workshop on Business Process Intelligence (BPI 2013)

Organizers: Boudewijn van Dongen, Diogo R. Ferreira, Barbara Weber, Jochen De Weerdt

Business process intelligence (BPI) is an area that is gaining increasing interest and importance in industry and research. BPI refers to the application of various measurement and analysis techniques in the area of business process management. In practice, BPI is embodied in tools for managing process execution quality by offering several features such as analysis, prediction, monitoring, control, and optimization.

The goal of this workshop is to promote the development of techniques to understand and improve business processes based on run-time data collected during process execution. We aim to bring together practitioners and researchers from different communities, e.g., business process management, information systems, database systems, business administration, software engineering, artificial intelligence, and data mining, who share an interest in the analysis and optimization of business processes and process-aware information systems. The workshop aims at discussing the current state of ongoing research and sharing practical experiences, exchanging ideas, and setting up future research directions that better respond to real needs. In a nutshell, it serves as a forum for shaping the BPI area.

The ninth edition of this workshop attracted 13 international submissions. Each paper was reviewed by at least three members of the Program Committee. From these submissions, the top six were accepted as full papers for presentation at the workshop. The papers presented at the workshop provide a mix of novel research ideas, evaluations of existing process mining techniques, as well as new tool support. The paper by Buijs, Van Dongen, and Van der Aalst proposes an extension of the flexible ETM algorithm allowing users to investigate the trade-offs between different quality dimensions. The paper by Rogge-Solti, Van der Aalst, and Weske is motivated by the need for process models enriched with performance information and suggests an approach to discover different classes of stochastic Petri nets. Popova and Dumas describe a technique that is able to deal with process models structured in terms of sub-process models overcoming the limitations of existing discovery methods that are mainly designed to discover a single process model. Vanden Broucke, Delvaux,

Freitas, Rogova, Vanthienen, and Baesens suggest a methodology to obtain insights on the role of event log characteristics regarding the performance of different process discovery techniques. Bolt and Sepúlveda, in turn, describe a technique for generating recommendations regarding the remaining execution time. Finally, Leemans, Fahland, and Van der Aalst introduce an extension of the inductive miner algorithm to discover sound process models efficiently considering infrequent behavior.

For the third time, the workshop was accompanied by the BPI challenge, a process mining contest based on a real-world event log. This year, an event log from Volvo IT Belgium was made available and participants were asked to extract as much information as possible from this log. We invited the jury to comment on the submissions and our sponsors — Perceptive Software and Fluxicon — provided prizes for the best submission and for all other participants.

In total, 12 submissions were received, all of which were of very high quality. The jury selected the submission by C.J. Kang, Y.S. Kang, Y.S. Lee, S. Noh, H.C. Kim, W.C. Lim, J. Kim, and R. Hong, from Myongji University, Korea, as the winner of the challenge. The jury praised the analysis and the reasoning style, which were easy to follow: "The authors made a point of clearly defining their interpretations and arguing for their assumptions."

The winner received a trophy, designed and handcrafted by Felix Guenther, combined with two tickets to the Process Mining Camp 2014 and licenses for Disco (the process mining tool from Fluxicon) and Perceptive Reflect (the process mining toolset from Perceptive). All other participants also received one or more licenses for these tools. Abstracts of all submissions are included in these proceedings.

As with previous editions of the workshop, we hope that the reader will find this selection of papers useful to keep track of the latest advances in the area of business process intelligence, and we look forward to keep bringing new advances in future editions of the BPI workshop.

Program Committee

Wil van der Aalst	Eindhoven University of Technology, The Netherlands
Ana Karla Alves de Medeiros	Centraal Beheer Achmea, The Netherlands
Boualem Benatallah	University of New South Wales, Australia
Walid Gaaloul	Insitut Telecom, France
Gianluigi Greco	University of Calabria, Italy
Daniela Grigori	University of Versailles St.-Quentin-en-Yvelines, France
Antonella Guzzo	University of Calabria, Italy
Michael Leyer	Frankfurt School of Finance and Management, Germany
Jan Mendling	Wirtschaftsuniversität Wien, Austria
Oscar Pastor	University of Valencia, Spain

Viara Popova	Tallinn University of Technology, Estonia
Manfred Reichert	University of Ulm, Germany
Michael Rosemann	Queensland University of Technology, Australia
Anne Rozinat	Fluxicon, The Netherlands
Domenico Sacca	Università degli studi della Calabri, Italy
Phina Soffer	University of Haifa, Israel
Alessandro Sperduti	Padua University, Italy
Hans Weigand	University of Tilburg, The Netherlands
Mathias Weske	Hasso Plattner Institute at University of Potsdam, Germany

Sixth International Workshop on Business Process Management and Social Software (BPMS2 2013)

Organizers: Rainer Schmidt, Selmin Nurcan

Social software[1] is a new paradigm that is spreading quickly in society, organizations, and economics. Social software has created a multitude of success stories such as wikipedia.org. Therefore, more and more enterprises regard social software as a means for further improvement of their business processes and business models. For example, they integrate their customers into product development by using blogs to capture ideas for new products and features. Thus, business processes have to be adapted to new communication patterns between customers and the enterprise: for example, communication with the customer is increasingly a bi-directional communication with the customer and among the customers. Social software also offers new possibilities to enhance business processes by improving the exchange of knowledge and information, to speed up decisions, etc.

Social software is based on four principles: weak ties, social production, egalitarianism, and mutual service provisioning.

- Weak Ties[2]
  Weak ties are spontaneously established contacts between individuals that create new views and allow for the combining of competencies. Social software supports the creation of weak ties by supporting the creation of contacts in impulse between non-predetermined individuals.
- Social Production[3,4]
  Social Production is the creation of artifacts, by combining the input from independent contributors without predetermining the way to do this. By this means it is possible to integrate new and innovative contributions not identified or planned in advance. Social mechanisms such as reputation assure quality in social production in an a posteriori approach by enabling a collective evaluation by all participants.
- Egalitarianism
  Egalitarianism is the attitude of handling individuals equally. Social software highly relies on egalitarianism and therefore strives to give all participants the same rights to contribute. This is done with the intention of encouraging a maximum of contributors and of getting the best solution fusing a high number of contributions, thus enabling the wisdom of crowds. Social software realizes egalitarianism by

---

[1] R. Schmidt and S. Nurcan, "BPM and Social Software," Business Process Management Workshops, 2009, pp. 649–658.

[2] M.S. Granovetter, "The Strength of Weak Ties," American Journal of Sociology, vol. 78, 1973, S. 1360.

[3] Y. Benkler, The Wealth of Networks: How Social Production Transforms Markets and Freedom, Yale University Press, 2006.

[4] J. Surowiecki, The Wisdom of Crowds, Anchor, 2005.

abolishing hierarchical structures, merging the roles of contributors and consumers, and introducing a culture of trust.

- Mutual Service Provisioning
Social software abolishes the separation of service provider and consumer by introducing the idea that service provisioning is a mutual process of service exchange. Thus both service provider and consumer (or better prosumer) provide services to one another in order to co-create value. This mutual service provisioning is in contrast to the idea of industrial service provisioning, where services are produced in separation from the customer to achieve scaling effects.

To date, the interaction of social software and its underlying paradigms with business processes have not been investigated in depth. Therefore, the objective of the workshop is to explore how social software interacts with business process management, how business process management has to change to comply with weak ties, social production, egalitarianism and mutual service, and how business processes may profit from these principles.

The workshop discussed three topics:

1. New opportunities provided by social software for BPM
2. Engineering the next generation of business processes: BPM 2.0?
3. Business process implementation support by social software

Based on the successful BPMS2 2008, BPMS2 2009, BPMS2 2010, BPMS2 2011, BPMS2 2012 workshops, the goal of the workshop was to promote the integration of business process management with social software and to enlarge the community pursuing the theme.

Four papers were accepted for presentation. In their paper "Enabling Workflow Composition Within a Social Network Environment," Ourania Hatzi, Despina Topali, Mara Nikolaidou, and Dimosthenis Anagnostopoulos introduce a recommendation mechanism, that can automatically discover and combine appropriate gadgets for creating workflows. No predefined workflows or any other knowledge of the available gadgets is required. The proposed mechanism promotes the adoption of social networks as a novel paradigm not only for content sharing and collaboration but also for business process management within the enterprise.

Mohammad Ehson Rangiha and Bill Karakostas propose an idea for driving BPM enactment by social goals in their paper "Towards a Meta-Model for Goal-Based Social BPM." By proposing a goal-based approach toward social BPM, a structured and collaborative model is created for the BPM lifecycle that allows both flexibility and social participation as well as supports the performance of the process within the set business constraints of time and resources. This flexibility and collaboration attempts to overcome the limitations of traditional BPM mentioned above as it engages the users from the early stage of process design and allows them to be part of thedecision making during the enactment of the processes.

David Martinho and Antonio Rito Silva describe an experiment on the capture of business processes tacit knowledge owned by knowledge workers in their paper "An Experiment on the Capture of Business Processes from Knowledge Workers." The experiment hypothesis is that by the guidance of a recommender system, knowledge workers' behavior converge, they label the informational objects with the same set of labels and the reuse of labels increase over time. During the experiment, knowledge workers use a functional prototype to achieve a set of goals described in natural language. To achieve these goals it is necessary to create a set of informational objects.

In the paper of Marco Santorum, Agnès Front, and Dominique Rieu with the title "ISEAsy: A Social Business Process Management Platform," the authors social platform called ISEAsy incorporated into a social network built around organizational processes and participants sharing common interests. ISEAsy can be seen as a social process simulation platform with the addition of game mechanics, including a social interaction system.

We wish to thank all authors for having shared their work with us, as well as the members of the BPMS2 2013 Program Committee and the workshop organizers of BPM 2013 for their help with the organization of the workshop.

Program Committee

Ilia Bider	Stockholm University/IbisSoft, Sweden
Jan Bosch	Chalmers University of Technology, Sweden
Marco Brambilla	Politecnico di Milano, Italy
Piero Fraternali	Politecnico di Milano, Italy
Dragan Gasevic	Athabasca University, Canada
Norbert Gronau	University of Potsdam, Germany
Chihab Hanachi	University of Toulouse 1, France
Ralf-Christian Härting	Hochschule Aalen, Germany
Monique Janneck	Fachhochschule Lübeck, Germany
Rania Khalaf	IBM T.J. Watson Research Center, USA
Ralf Klamma	RWTH Aachen University, Germany
Sai Peck Lee	University of Malaya, Kuala Lumpur, Malaysia
Myriam Lewkowicz	University of Technology of Troyes, France
Bela Mutschler	University of Applied Sciences Ravensburg-Weingarten, Germany
Gustaf Neumann	Unversity of Vienna, Austria
Selmin Nurcan	University of Paris 1 Panthé-Sorbonne, France
Andreas Oberweis	Universität Karlsruhe, Germany
Sebastian Richly	TU Dresden, Germany
Rainer Schmidt	HTW Aalen, Germany
Miguel-Angel Sicilia	University of Alcalá, Spain
Pnina Soffer	University of Haifa, Israel
Karsten Wendland	Hochschule Aalen, Germany
Christian Zirpins	University of Karlsruhe (TH), Germany

The Second Workshop on Data- and Artifact-Centric Business Processes (DAB 2013)

Organizers: Marlon Dumas, Rick Hull

Traditionally, researchers and practitioners in the field of business process management (BPM) have focused on studying control-flow aspects of business processes independently from data aspects. The separation of concerns between control-flow and data has been fruitful and has enabled the development of various foundational theories and methods for BPM. However, the limits of theories and methods built on this separation of concerns are now becoming evident, particularly with the increasing pressure to support ad hoc and flexible business processes, where control-flow is often intermingled with data.

In recent years, various approaches (such as the object-centric, business artifacts, and case management approaches) have emerged that emphasize the integration of data and control as key pillars to support the specification, analysis, and enactment of flexible and rich business processes. From the scientific as well as the practical viewpoint, it is critical to study the fundamental relationships, characteristics, and properties of these emerging integrated perspectives, where data and processes are considered together.

The Data and Artifact-Centric Business Process Management (DAB) workshop series aims at bringing together researchers and practitioners whose common interests and experience are in the study and development of data- and artifact-centric approaches to BPM. In line with the aims of the workshop series, the 2013 edition of this workshop attracted presentations and papers exploring the tight interplay between data and control flow in business processes.

The DAB 2013 workshop consisted of a keynote talk and three paper presentations. The keynote speaker, Jianwen Su, delivered a talk on "Bridging Persistent Data and Process Data," where he discussed the problems that arise due to a lack of explicit specification of the way data manipulated by a business process are stored persistently. Indeed, in most BPM applications, the data manipulated by business processes (BPs) are stored in and managed by database systems (DBs). Even though the artifact BP modeling approach has managed to "weld" together data modeling and activity flow modeling, the relationship between models of persistent data in DBs and data models in BPs has not been clearly explored and captured at the conceptual level. Jianwen Su presented a framework for BP-DB data bindings, and discussed technical issues associated with such bindings.

The technical session included three paper presentations. The first paper by Russo et al. discusses a formal model for artifact-centric business process management, namely, the relational data-centric dynamic systems (DCDS) model. The paper brings evidence of fundamental links between DCDS and rules representation models used by contemporary business rules engines such as Drools, thus opening up the perspective of using such engines as a basis to reason about artifact-centric business process specifications, both at design-time but also at runtime.

The second paper by Eshuis and Van Gorp studies the problem of mapping traditional activity-centric business process models into object-centric models, a problem that arises when artifact or object-centric business process models need to co-exist with activity-centric ones. The paper specifically presents an automated approach that synthesizes an object-centric model captured as a state machine from a business process model captured as an UML activity diagram, lifting certain limitations of previous work along these lines.

The third and final paper by Meyer and Weske also looks at the problem of linking activity-centric process models with object models. Meyer and Weske try to go beyond the idea of mapping one notation to another by sketching a vision and initial results for achieving roundtripping (i.e., model synchronization) between activity-centric and artifact-centric business process models.

The workshop would not have been possible without the valuable contribution of members of the Program Committee, who carefully reviewed and discussed the submissions, and of course the authors who presented their work at the workshop. We also thank the BPM 2013 workshop chairs and the BPM 2013 conference organizers for their support and assistance.

Program Committee

Shuiguang Deng	Zhejiang University, China
Giuseppe De Giacomo	University of Rome La Sapienza, Italy
Rik Eshuis	Eindhoven University of Technology, The Netherlands
Dirk Fahland	Eindhoven University of Technology, The Netherlands
Dragan Gasevic	Athabasca University, Canada
Thomas Hildebrandt	IT University of Copenhagen, Denmark
Lior Limonad	IBM Haifa, Israel
Chengfei Liu	Swinburne University of Technology, Australia
Fabrizio M. Maggi	University of Tartu, Estonia
Fabio Patrizi	Sapienza University of Rome, Italy
Manfred Reichert	University of Ulm, Germany
Hajo A. Reijers	Perceptive Software, Eindhoven University of Technology, The Netherlands
Stefanie Rinderle-Ma	University of Vienna, Austria
Irina Rychkova	University of Paris 1 Panthéon-Sorbonne, France
Farouk Toumani	LIMOS - Blaise Pascal University, France
Hagen Völzer	IBM Zurich, Switzerland
Lijie Wen	Tsinghua University, China
Mathias Weske	Hasso Plattner Institute, Germany

Additional Reviewers

Carolina Ming Chiao
Sira Yongchareon

First International Workshop on Decision Mining and Modeling for Business Processes (DeMiMoP 2013)

Organizers: Jan Vanthienen, Guoqing Chen, Bart Baesens, Qiang Wei

Most processes and business process models incorporate decisions of some kind. Decisions are typically based upon a number of business (decision) rules that describe the premises and possible outcomes of a specific situation. Since these decisions guide the activities and workflows of all process stakeholders (participants, owners), they should be regarded as first-class citizens in business process management. Sometimes, the entire decision can be included as a decision activity or as a service (a decision service). Typical decisions are: creditworthiness of the customer in a financial process, claim acceptance in an insurance process, eligibility decision in social security, etc. The process then handles a number of steps, shows the appropriate decision points, and represents the path to follow for each of the alternatives.

Business decisions are important, but are often hidden in process flows, process activities, or in the head of employees (tacit knowledge), so that they need to be discovered using state-of-the-art intelligent techniques. Decisions can be straightforward, based on a number of simple rules, or can be the result of complex analytics (decision mining). Moreover, in a large number of cases, a particular business process does not just contain decisions, but the entire process is about making a decision. The major purpose of a loan process, e.g., or an insurance claim process, etc., is to prepare and make a final decision. The process shows different steps, models the communication between parties, records the decision, and returns the result.

It is not considered good practice to model the detailed decision paths in the business process model. Separating rules and decisions from the process simplifies the process model (separation of concerns).

The aim of the workshop is to examine the relationship between decisions and processes, including models not only to model the process, but also to model the decisions, to enhance decision mining based on process data, and to find a good integration between decision modeling and process modeling.

Program Committee

Dimitris Karagiannis	Universität Wien, Austria
Xunhua Guo	Tsinghua University, China
Hajo A. Reijers	Eindhoven University of Technology, The Netherlands
Robert Golan	DBmind technologies, USA
Markus Helfert	Dublin City University, Ireland
Leszek Maciaszek	Wroclaw University of Economics, Poland

Pericles Loucopoulos   Loughborough University, UK
Josep Carmona   Universitat Politècnica de Catalunya, Spain
Jochen De Weerdt   Queensland University of Technology, Australia
Seppe vanden Broucke   KU Leuven, Belgium
Filip Caron   KU Leuven, Belgium

International Workshop on Emerging Topics in Business Process Management

Organizers: Christian Janiesch, Stefan Schulte, Ingo Weber

Business process management (BPM) is both a management approach and an enabling technology. It is neither typical off-the-shelf software nor a preconfigured software solution to solve a particular business problem. As such, BPM technology can be used to solve a number of problems in very flexible ways. Similarly, other enabling technologies and concepts exist that can be combined with BPM to enable even more potential. The design phase of BPM is where it all comes together when a new BPM system is engineered.

Consequently, several workshops have been proposed to investigate opportunities when designing combined systems of BPM and other enabling technologies, such as event-driven architecture (EDA), complex event processing (CEP), or cloud computing. In particular, these were:

9th International Workshop on Business Process Design (BPD 2012)

Business process design (BPD) is often seen as the most value-adding stage of the process lifecycle. It is dedicated to the development of improved and compliant business processes. Designing a process that improves corporate performance is a challenging task that requires multi-disciplinary expertise and a plethora of inputs (for example, organizational strategies, goals, constraints, human and technical capabilities, etc.). However, unlike other well-defined and theory-grounded stages of the process lifecycle (e.g., process modeling), process design is scarcely understood and lacks a widely accepted and sound theoretical foundation. The lack of comprehensive research on process design limits the effectiveness of BPM professionals, who currently rely heavily on tacit knowledge and personal experience in the absence of process improvement guidelines or proven practices.

7th International Workshop on Event-Driven Business Process Management (EdBPM 2013)

Event-driven business process management (EdBPM) is an enhancement of BPM by new concepts of service-oriented architecture (SOA), EDA, business activity monitoring (BAM), and CEP. In this context, BPM describes a software platform that provides organizations with the ability to model, manage, and optimize these processes for significant gain. As an independent system, CEP is a concurrently active platform that analyzes and processes events. The BPM and the CEP platforms communicate via events that are produced by the BPM execution engine and by the Web services (if any) associated with the business process steps.

First International Workshop on Business Process Management in the Cloud (BPMC 2013)

Cloud computing is a new paradigm for the on-demand delivery of infrastructure, platform, or software as a service. Cloud computing enables network access to a shared pool of configurable computing and storage resources as well as applications that can be tailored to the consumer's needs. They can be rapidly provisioned and released, and are billed based on actual use, thus reducing investment costs. Not only can individual services be hosted on virtual infrastructures but also complete process platforms. Besides benefits to run-time BPM, during design-time cloud-based services can enable collaboration between geographically dispersed teams and assist the design process in general. Among a number of challenges, there is a lack of conceptualization and theory on BPM with respect to cloud computing. For the most part, the topic of cloud computing has only been implicitly regarded in BPM research when discussing design-time tools.

In order to explore the interconnections between these topics, we decided to combine the best papers from these workshops to form the *2013 International Workshop on Emerging Topics in BPM*. This half-day workshop covered topics from business process design, event-driven BPM, as well as BPM and cloud computing:

- Wang et al. cover the design of a workflow recommender system following the XaaS cloud stack to offer workflow as a service capability.
- Peng et al. focus on the combination of cloud and mobile technology to enable process assignment and execution.
- Bülow et al. bring CEP and EDA to BPM for the purpose of monitoring.
- Bastos et al. research design aspects of semantics and aspect-oriented BPM.

As organizing chairs of the workshop, we would like to thank all involved members of the Program Committee and the chairs of the individual workshops for their quality reviews and decisions as well as the flexibility, which led to the inception of this rather unusual workshop.

Ingo Weber

Program Committee

Arun Anandasivam	IBM Global Business Services, Germany
Soeren Balko	Queensland University of Technology, Australia
Gero Decker	Signavio, Germany
Schahram Dustdar	Vienna University of Technology, Austria
Jan Mendling	Wirtschaftsuniversität Wien, Austria
Hajo Reijers	Eindhoven University of Technology, The Netherlands
Stefanie Rinderle-Ma	University of Vienna, Austria
Ralf Steinmetz	Technische Universität Darmstadt, Germany
Stefan Tai	Karlsruhe Institute of Technology, Germany
Srikumar Venugopal	University of New South Wales, Australia
Xiwei (Sherry) Xu	NICTA, Austria

Third International Workshop on Process-Aware Logistics Systems (PALS 2013)

Organizers: Kamel Barkaoui, Zhiwu Li

This workshop deals with problems related to the design and reconfiguration of complex logistics systems in various domains with an emphasis on the business process and information technology perspectives. It is mainly dedicated to the description, monitoring, and optimization of large-scale logistics systems by making use of process management techniques, analysis of business processes, and information processing. To this end, six research works related to these topics were selected for this third edition of PALS workshop.

Program Committee

Djamil Aissani	Bejaia University, Algeria
Jacky Akoka	Cedric, Cnam, France
Boualem Benatallah	University of New South Wales, Australia
Sami Bhiri	National University of Ireland, Ireland
Hanifa Boucheneb	Ecole Polytechnique de Montréal, Canada
Yufeng Chen	Xidian University, China
Schahram Dustdar	Vienna University of Technology, Austria
Walid Gaaloul	Telecom SudParis, France
Faïez Gargouri	Université de Sfax, Tunisia
Mohand-SaidHacid	Lyon 1 University, France
Mohamed Itmi	INSA-Rouen, France
Kaïs Klaï	LIPN, France
Ding Liu	Xidian University, China
Hamid Motahari	NezhadHPLabs, Palo Alto, USA
Olivier Perrin	Loria, Nancy 2 University, France
Farouk Toumani	Blaise Pascal University, Clermont-Ferrand, France
Long Wang	College of Engineering, Peking University, China
Shouguang Wang	Zhejiang Gongshang University, China
Karsten Wolf	Università Rostock, Germany

Third International Workshop on Process-Aware Logistics Systems (PALS 2013)

Organizers: Ahmed Gaaloul, Zhe Shan

This workshop deals with problems related to the design and development of computer logistics systems in various domains with a particular focus on businesses and standardization.

Program Committee

Forth International Workshop on Process Model Collections: Management and Reuse

Organizers: Lucinéia Heloisa Thom, Marcelo Fantinato, Marcello La Rosa, Remco Dijkman

Nowadays, as organizations reach higher levels of business process management maturity, they tend to collect and actively use large numbers of business process models. It is quite common that such collections of industry-strength business process models include thousands of activities and related business objects such as data, applications, risks, etc. These models are used for a variety of business needs, including requirements analysis, communication, automation, and compliance.

Such large collections of process models introduce both new challenges and opportunities to the area of business process management. On the one hand, it may not come as a surprise that many organizations struggle to manage such volumes of complex process models. This problem is exacerbated by overlapping content across models, poor version management, process models that are used simultaneously for different purposes, and the use of different modelling notations such as EPCs, BPMN, etc. On the other hand, the process models in the collection provide a valuable source of information, which can be reused to facilitate the development of new process models. This reuse will lead to more efficient development of models that are of higher quality and better integrated with the existing models in the collection.

Against this backdrop, the aim of the workshop is to discuss novel research in the area of business process model collections, their management and reuse. To this end, five papers were selected for presentation and a keynote speaker was invited.

As part of the workshop, a process model matching contest was organized. For this contest, researchers submitted their process model matching algorithms, which were evaluated on a sample process model collection provided by the contest organizers. The results of the contest are also presented.

Program Committee

Akhil Kumar	Penn State University, USA
Ana Karla A. de Medeiros	Centraal Beheer Achmea, The Netherlands
Antonio Ruiz-Cortés	University of Seville, Spain
Arnon Sturm	Ben-Gurion University of the Negev, Israel
Artem Polyvyanyy	Queensland University of Technology, Australia
Barbara Weber	University of Innsbruck, Austria
Christoph Bussler	Analytica, Inc., USA
Claudia Cappelli	Federal University of Rio de Janeiro State, Brazil
Fernanda A. Baião	Federal University of Rio de Janeiro State, Brazil
Flávia M. Santoro	Federal University of Rio de Janeiro State, Brazil

George Wyner	Boston University, USA
Gustavo Rossi	National University of La Plata, Argentina
Hajo Reijers	Eindhoven University of Technology, The Netherlands
Jaejoon Lee	Lancaster University, UK
Jan Mendling	Wirtshaftsuniversitä Wien, Austria
Jianmin Wang	Tsinghua University, China
João Porto de Albuquerque	University of São Paulo, Brazil
Luciano A. Digiampietri	University of São Paulo, Brazil
Luciano Garcia-Banuelos	University of Tartu, Estonia
Manfred Reichert	University of Ulm, Germany
Mathias Weske	HPI, University of Potsdam, Germany
Matthias Kunze	HPI, University of Potsdam, Germany
Matthias Weidlich	Technion – Israel Institute of Technology, Israel
Michael Rosemann	Queensland University of Technology, Australia
Minseok Song	Ulsan National Institute of Science and Technology, South Korea
Paulo F. Pires	Federal University of Rio Grande do Norte, Brazil
Shazia Sadiq	University of Queensland, Australia
Sherif Sakr	The University of New South Wales, Australia
Souvik Barat	Tata Consultancy Services, India
Stefanie Rinderle-Ma	University of Ulm, Germany
Stephanie Meerkamm	Siemens, Germany
Uwe Zdun	University of Vienna, Austria
Vinay Kulkarni	Tata Consultancy Services, India
Xiaodong Liu	Edinburgh Napier University, UK
Zhiqiang Yan	Tsinghua University, China

Process Matching Contest Co-chairs

Henrik Leopold	Humboldt Universitä zu Berlin, Germany
Matthias Weidlich	Technion – Israel Institute of Technology, Israel

Second Workshop on Security in Business Processes (SBP 2013)

Organizers: Wil van der Aalst, Rafael Accorsi, Raimundas Matulevi

Despite the growing demand for compliant business processes, security and privacy incidents caused by erroneous workflow specifications are still omnipresent. Prominent examples of failures include, for example, the faulty process at UBS, which led to one of the biggest financial scandals in the bank sector. In fact, often business process management and security issues stand out as separate silos, and are seldom addressed together toward the development of trustworthy and security compliant business processes. The second edition of the Workshop on Security in Business Processes (SBP 2013) brought together researchers and practitioners interested in the management and modelling of secure business processes in process-aware information systems. In particular, SBP 2013 encouraged innovative methods for workflow security modelling, security audit and control along the entire business process lifecycle: from design time verification to online operational support and post-mortem analysis.

The SBP program consisted of one invited speaker, three long papers, and two short papers. The balance of academia and industry authors and the high attendance indicate that the topics addressed in the workshop are of relevance to both communities, suggesting a high potential to transfer research techniques into commercial tools. The workshop was divided into two sessions. This year the workshop's emphasis was placed on the formal methods, modelling, and properties of security in business processes.

During the first session the keynote speech given by Hejiao Huang highlighted the importance of understanding the security properties and of modelling them formally in order to define the security policy within the business processes. The second session paper by Costa et al. emphasized the importance of complying with the properties and non-functional requirements expressed in business processes using a single framework. The mathematical model (a combination of c-semirings, history expressions, and Galois expressions) is defined to support the process orchestration. Jens Gulden completed the session by explaining how business processes could terminate and what the meaning of different termination events is.

The second session started with the study on the importance of process compliance. A study by Ramezani et al. aimed to bridge the gap between the informal description of a precise specification of the compliance requirements. The discussion was resumed by Askavora and colleagues' work, which introduced a framework for the privacy access control model. The final workshop presentation given by Tark and Matulevičius introduced an implementation example where the model-driven security approach is used to secure dynamically created documents.

We wish to thank all those who contribute to making SBP a success: the authors who submitted papers, the members of the Program Committee who carefully reviewed and discussed the submissions, and the speakers who presented their work at the workshop. In particular, we thank the keynote speaker for the enthusiastic and insightful presentation. We also express our gratitude to the BPM 2013 workshop chairs for their support in preparing the workshop.

Program Committee

Anne Baumgrass	HPI, Germany
Achim Brucker	SAP Labs, Germany
Jason Crampton	University of London, UK
Benoit Depaire	University of Hasselt, Belgium
Khaled Gaaloul	CRP Henri Tudor, Luxembourg
Aditya Ghose	University of Wollongong, Australia
Hejiao Huang	Harbin Institute of Technology, China
Michael Huth	Imperial College, UK
Fuyuki Ishikawa	NII Tokyo, Japan
Jan Jürjens	TU Dortmund, Germany
imka Karastoyanova	University of Stuttgart, Germany
Günter Karjoth	IBM Research, Switzerland
Peter Karpati	Institute for Energy Technology, Norway
Seok-Won Lee	Ajou University, Korea
Lin Liu	Tsinghua University, China
Heiko Ludwig	IBM Research, USA
Nicolas Mayer	CRP Henri Tudor, Luxembourg
Per H. Meland	SINTEF ICT, Norway
Marco Montali	Free University of Bozen-Bolzano, Italy
Haralambos Mouratidis	University of East London, UK
Andreas Opdahl	University of Bergen, Norway
Günther Pernul	University of Regensburg, Germany
Silvio Ranise	FBK-IRST, Italy
Stefanie Rinderle-Ma	University of Vienna, Austria
David G. Rosado	University of Castilla-La Mancha, Spain
Shazia Sadiq	Queensland University, Australia
Guttorm Sindre	NUST, Norway
Mark Strembeck	WU Vienna, Austria
Jan M. van der Werf	TU Eindhoven, The Netherlands
Qihua Wang	IBM Research, USA
Nicola Zannone	TU Eindhoven, The Netherlands

Second International Workshop on Theory and Applications of Process Visualization (TAProViz 2013)

Organizers: Ross Brown, Simone Kriglstein, Stefanie Rinderle-Ma

This was the second TAProViz workshop run at BPM. The intention this year was to consolidate the results of last year's successful workshop by further developing this important topic, identifying the key research topics of interest to the BPM visualization community.

More information on the workshop is available at: http://wst.univie.ac.at/topics/taproviz13/

Submitted papers were evaluated by at least three Program Committee members, in a double-blind manner, on the basis of significance, originality, technical quality, and exposition. Two full papers and one position paper were accepted for presentation at the workshop. In addition, we invited a keynote speaker, Hajo A. Reijers, from Eindhoven University of Technology. The papers address a number of topics in the area of process model visualization, in particular:

- Visual Metaphors in Processes
- Visualizing the Process of Process Modeling
- Visualization Techniques for Collaboration and Distributed Processes
- Visual Modeling Languages
- Mobile Process Visualization
- Process Visualization and Sonification

The keynote, "Information Visualization Optimization Applied to Process Mining," by Emiliano Martinez Rivera and Hajo A. Reijers, presented the authors' approach to visual optimization of analysis results delivered by their Perceptive Software process mining tool set.

In his position paper, "Towards Enhancing Business Process Monitoring with Sonification," Tobias Hildebrandt presented an approach for supporting monitoring of business processes by using sonification.

Jorge Cardoso, Stefan Jablonski, and Bernhard Volz presented their full paper, "A Navigation Metaphor to Support Mobile Workflow Systems." This paper reports how they utilized the metaphor of car navigation systems to drive the development of mobile workflow interfaces.

Finally, Joanne Manhães Netto, Flávia Santoro, and Fernanda Araujo Baião, in their full paper "Evaluating KIPN for Modeling KIP," introduced a method for building knowledge-intensive process graphical models called the Knowledge Intensive Process Notation (KIPN).

Program Committee

Ralph Bobrik	Detecon AG, Switzerland
Michael Burch	University of Ulm, Germany
Massimiliano De Leoni	Eindhoven University of Technology, The Netherlands
Remco Dijkman	Eindhoven University of Technology, The Netherlands
Phillip Effinger	University of Tübingen, Germany
Kathrin Figl	Vienna University of Economics and Business, Austria
Hans-Georg Fill	University of Vienna, Austria
Sonja Kabicher-Fuchs	University of Vienna, Austria
Jens Kolb	University of Ulm, Germany
Wendy Lucas	Bentley University, USA
Silvia Miksch	Technical University of Vienna, Austria
Margit Pohl	Technical University of Vienna, Austria
Rune Rasmussen	Queensland University of Technology, Australia
Manfred Reichert	University of Ulm, Germany
Irene Vanderfeesten	Eindhoven University of Technology, The Netherlands
Eric Verbeek	Eindhoven University of Technology, The Netherlands
Günter Wallner	Institute of Art & Technology, Austria

Keynote: Decision Mining:
Are We Looking Under the Streetlight?

Pnina Soffer

University of Haifa, Carmel Mountain 31905, Haifa, Israel
spnina@is.haifa.ac.il

Decision mining in business processes aims at capturing the rationale and guiding decisions that are made in business processes. A basic premise is that decisions are made in a specific context, intending to achieve defined goals. Hence, to understand decisions we should consider three elements: decisions, context, and goals, and the relationships among them. The talk highlights challenges related to each.

Decisions: a major challenge is to gain a complete view of the decisions entailed in a business process. We argue that relying on activity-based process models leads to overlooking decisions that are not explicitly represented in these models. Imperative process models emphasize path selection decisions, represented by choice splits. Declarative models relate to decisions of selecting an activity to perform from the ones available at a given situation. However, many of the decisions made in the course of a business process are embedded within activities. Such decisions become apparent when a state-based view of a process is adopted, so the detailed state that follows an activity reflects decisions that have been made. A state-based view, however, is difficult to manage and visualize, and requires research efforts to produce methods that are computationally efficient and usable for human reasoning.

Context: context plays a major role in decision making. The context of a specific decision would be the detailed state known at decision time. It can reflect previous actions taken through the business process, some initial state and case properties, and events that occurred during the process. The challenge here is twofold. First, given the large amount of data available in business situations, we need to identify the parameters that should be considered as the relevant context of a certain decision. Assuming that different contextual conditions should drive different decisions when striving to achieve specific goals, context identification can rely on mining the decisions and the outcomes achieved by them. Second, even with the large amount of available data, context identification should always take a partial information assumption, since we do not have a complete deterministic knowledge of all the variables that might affect the outcomes of a decision, nor can we assume they are included in the available data.

Goals: decisions are made with the intention of achieving desirable goals. Since a goal can be specified as conditions on the state, a state-based view supports goal specification as well. Three main challenges can be related to goal specification. First, detailed goals might depend on the context, as what would be considered an excellent achievement given some initial state might be considered below expectations with a different starting point. Second, goals can be "hard", namely, their achievement is possible to assess on True/False scale, or "soft", namely goals whose achievement can only be assessed relatively, by comparison of several cases. Decision mining should be able to relate to both kinds of goals. Third, while most business processes have a clear ending point where goal achievement can be assessed, some processes are long-lasting ones without such clear ending. For these processes, means of goal assessment and assessment points need to be defined.

In conclusion, many challenges are still faced by decision mining research. A main issue raised in the talk is the need to anchor decision mining in a state-based process view, since the common activity-based view can only provide a partial understanding. Developing models as well as methods that build upon this view is a main challenge still to be addressed.

Short Biography

Dr. Pnina Soffer is a senior lecturer in the Information Systems Department at the University of Haifa. She received her BSc (1991) and MSc (1993) in Industrial Engineering from the Technion, Ph.D in Information Systems Engineering from the Technion (2002). Her research deals with business process modelling and management, requirements engineering, and conceptual modelling, addressing issues such as goal orientation, flexibility, learning techniques for improving decision making, and context-aware adaptation. Her research has appeared in over 90 conference and journal papers, in journals such as Journal of the AIS, European J of IS, Requirements Engineering, Information Systems, and others. She has served as a guest editor of a number of journal special issues related to various business process topics, and is a member of the editorial board of several journals, including Journal of the AIS. Pnina has served in program committees of numerous conferences, including CAiSE, BPM, ER, and many more. She is a member of the CAiSE steering committee and an organizer of the BPMDS working conference since 2004. She has served in different roles in conference organizing committees, such as Forum Chair and Workshop Chair in CAiSE and in BPM, and leads the organizing team of BPM 2014 in Haifa.

Keynote: Specification and Conflict Detection for GTRBAC in Multi-domain Environment

Ning Bao, Hejiao Huang, and Hongwei Du

Shenzhen Key Laboratory of Internet Information Collaboration,
Harbin Institute of Technology Shenzhen Graduate School, Shenzhen, China
bn_china@163.com, {hjhuang,hwdu}@hitsz.edu.cn

Abstract. Although the development and expansion for the time-based RBAC policy has enhanced the security greatly, there are hardly any paper paying attention to the conflicts that produced by the time feature in multi-domain RBAC model. In this paper, we focus on temporal constraints and the role inheritance constraints that occurred in the interoperation domains based on Petri nets. The approach can check whether an inter-domain access requirement has violated its local RBAC policy or the inter-domain access control policy has improper temporal constraints. In order to illustrate this approach, an applicable example is shown for the specification and conflict detection.

This work was financially supported by National Natural Science Foundation of China with Grants No. 61370216, No. 11071271, No. 11371004 and No. 61100191, and Shenzhen Strategic Emerging Industries Program with Grants No. ZDSY20120613125016389, No. JCYJ20120613151201451 and No. JCYJ20130329153215152. And also Natural Scientific Research Innovation Foundation in Harbin Institute of Technology under project HIT.NSFIR.2011128.

Keynote: Information Visualization Optimization Applied to Process Mining

Emiliano "Max" Martinez Rivera[1] and Hajo A. Reijers[1,2]

[1] Perceptive Software, Research and Development, Piet Joubertstraat 4,
Apeldoorn, The Netherlands
{emiliano.martinezrivera,
hajo.reijers}@perceptivesoftware.com

[2] Eindhoven University of Technology, Department of Mathematics
and Computer Science, Den Dolech 2, Eindhoven, The Netherlands
h.a.reijers@tue.nl

Abstract. This paper accompanies the keynote that was given at the Second International Workshop on Theory and Applications of Process Visualization 2013 (TAProViz'13). In that talk, the visual optimization of analysis results delivered by Perceptive Software's process mining tool set took center stage. In the talk, principles and heuristics underlying this optimization effort were illustrated, in particular, those that were thought to be more generally relevant for the visualization of process-related content.

Keywords: Visualization, Process mining, Industrial software

Summary

Perceptive Software offers various enterprise software tools, among them a sophisticated process mining tool set[5]. Process mining aims at extracting process knowledge from so-called "event logs", which may originate from all kinds of systems [1]. Typically, these event logs contain information about the start/completion of process steps together with related context data (e.g. actors and resources). Insights from process mining can be used by organizations to improve their performance or conformance.

For a process mining tool, as for any information system, it is important that end users find it both useful and usable [2]. This is the reason that Perceptive Software is keen to continually optimize the user experience of its products. In the talk to which this paper is an addendum, the emphasis is on improving the visualization of the results from a *process mining analysis*.

To guide this optimization, two distinct streams of input can be distinguished: a *theoretical* and an *empirical* one. The theoretical stream rests on the *steps* that were presented by Stephen Anderson during his Information Visualization workshop, as

---

[5] See http://www.perceptivesoftware.com/products/perceptive-process/process-mining

held on November 9th in Amsterdam[6]. These include: the framing of the problem to be solved, the filtering of big amounts of data, and massively iterating. Furthermore, they entail the principles that have been outlined by Jakob Nielsen in [3]. Here, one should think of the visibility of a system's status, real-world matching, and consistency. In the talk, both the steps and heuristics have been illustrated by showing how they have guided the evolution of Perceptive Software's process mining tool kit.

The second, empirical stream builds on insights that are gathered through user research. Specifically, in the keynote talk some insights were presented that followed from three successive workshops with end users and managers of one of Perceptive Software's clients. Feedback was gathered on the various user interface components, the visualization of the process model, filter usage, and many other aspects. The talk has illustrated how this feedback shaped the newest versions of the process mining toolkit.

The intent behind the talk was to discuss generally applicable principles and steps to improve the visualization of information, specifically in the context of analyzing business processes. Given the relevance of this topic and the wide attention for process mining, we hope that this talk will inspire researchers and practitioners in this field.

References

1. van der Aalst, W.M.P.: Process Mining: Discovery, Conformance and Enhancement of Business Processes. Springer, Berlin (2011)
2. Davis, F.D.: Perceived usefulness, perceived ease of use, and user acceptance of information technology. MIS Q. **13**, 319–340 (1989)
3. Nielsen, J.: Usability Engineering. Academic Press (1993)

---

[6] See http://www.slideshare.net/stephenpa/quest-for-emotional-engagement-information-visualization-v15

Contents

2nd Workshop on Data- and Artifact-Centric BPM (DAB 2013)

1st Workshop on Decision Mining and Modeling for Business Processes (DeMiMoP 2013)

1st Workshop on Emerging Topics in BPM (ETBPM 2013)

3rd Workshop on Process-Aware Logistics Systems (PALS 2013)

4th Workshop on Process Model Collections: Management and Reuse (PMC-MR 2013)

2nd Workshop on Security in Business Processes (SBP 2013)

2nd Workshop on Theory and Applications of Process Visualization (TAProVis 2013)

9th International Workshop on Business Process Intelligence (BPI 2013)

9th International Workshop on Business Process Intelligence (BPI 2013)

Discovering and Navigating
a Collection of Process Models
Using Multiple Quality Dimensions

J.C.A.M. Buijs[✉], B.F. van Dongen, and Wil M.P. van der Aalst

Eindhoven University of Technology, Eindhoven, The Netherlands
{j.c.a.m.buijs,b.f.v.dongen,w.m.p.v.d.aalst}@tue.nl

Abstract. Process discovery algorithms typically aim at discovering a process model from an event log that best describes the recorded behavior. However, multiple quality dimensions can be used to evaluate a process model. In previous work we showed that there often is not one single process model that describes the observed behavior best in all quality dimensions. Therefore, we present an extension to our flexible ETM algorithm that does not result in a single best process model but in a collection of *mutually non-dominating* process models. This is achieved by constructing a Pareto front of process models. We show by applying our approach on a real life event log that the resulting collection of process models indeed contains several good candidates. Furthermore, by presenting a collection of process models, we show that it allows the user to investigate the different trade-offs between different quality dimensions.

Keywords: Process mining · Process model quality · Process model collection

1 Introduction

The goal of *process discovery* in process mining is to automatically discover process models that accurately describe processes by considering only an organization's records of its operational processes [1]. Such records are typically captured in the form of *event logs*, consisting of cases and events related to these cases. Over the last decade, many such process discovery techniques have been developed [1,5], producing process models in various forms, such as Petri nets, BPMN models, EPCs, YAWL models etc. Furthermore, many authors have compared these techniques by focussing on the properties of the models produced, while at the same time the applicability of various techniques have been compared in case-studies. However, currently no algorithm produces a collection of process models for the user to choose from. Therefore, in this work we extend our genetic discovery algorithm to construct not a single, but a collection of process models. By using the notion of a Pareto front, only the best process models are kept that show different trade-offs between the quality dimensions.

N. Lohmann et al. (Eds.): BPM 2013 Workshops, LNBIP 171, pp. 3–14, 2014.
DOI: 10.1007/978-3-319-06257-0_1, © Springer International Publishing Switzerland 2014

Four quality dimensions are generally used to discuss the results of process discovery [1,5], namely:

Replay fitness quantifies the extent to which the discovered model can accurately reproduce the cases recorded in the log.
Precision quantifies the fraction of the behavior allowed by the model which is not seen in the event log.
Generalization assesses the extent to which the resulting model will be able to reproduce future (unseen) behavior of the process.
Simplicity quantifies the complexity of a process model (e.g. number of nodes).

Surprisingly, many process discovery algorithms only focus on one or two of these dimensions [5]. Therefore, we proposed the ETM-algorithm (which stands for *Evolutionary Tree Miner*) in [5,6] to seamlessly include different quality dimensions in the discovery process. However, until now, weights needed to be given to the different dimensions. Although assigning weights is a common way of aggregating multiple fitness values to a single one, there are some disadvantages. For instance beforehand the impact of a change in the process model on the value in a particular dimension is not known. This makes assigning weights to measures difficult, especially since the sensitivity of each measurement to changes in the process model is different.

The remainder of the paper is structured as follows. Next, in Sect. 2, the Pareto front is explained in more detail and common ways to construct such a Pareto front of candidates are discussed. Then, in Sect. 3, we briefly explain the ETM-algorithm and how it has been extended to build a Pareto front of mutually non-dominating process models. Section 4 then presents a case study where the number of edits from a reference process model is used as a fifth quality dimension. Section 5 concludes the paper.

2   Multi-objective Optimization

Optimizing multiple objectives at the same time is a common challenge in optimization problems [7]. One of the simplest solutions is to use a weighted average over all the quality dimensions to produce a single quality measure. However, this method has several drawbacks:

1. Determining the correct weights upfront is difficult: structural changes on the candidates have unknown effects on the value for a dimension.
2. Values need to be normalized for comparison: a common way to fix the previous issue is by normalizing the values. However, dimensions can still respond differently to changes. Furthermore, a normalized value often provides less information than the absolute value.
3. Only one solution is provided: only the candidate with the best weighted average is presented. However, no insights in the different trade-offs among the dimensions is provided to the user.

The so-called *Pareto* front is often used as an alternative to the weighted sum [7,16]. The general idea of a Pareto front is that all members are *mutually non-dominating*. A member dominates another member if for all quality dimensions it is at least equal or better and for one strictly better, than the dominated member. Since all members in the Pareto front are mutually non-dominating (neither of them dominates another member) they represent different trade-offs in the quality dimensions sacrificing on one quality dimension to improve on another. This concept was originally proposed by Vilfredo Pareto to explain economic trade-offs [11].

An example of a Pareto front in two dimensions is shown in Fig. 1. Each dot in the graph represents a process model with a certain replay fitness and precision value, the two quality dimensions used for this Pareto front. For each dimension a bigger value indicates a better candidate, e.g. the goal is to obtain a process model in the top right corner of the chart. However, often there is no single model that is able to score perfectly on all dimensions. The open dots in the lower middle area of Fig. 1 are non-optimal process models, e.g. one of the dimensions can be improved without reducing the quality in (any of) the other dimension. The closed black dots represent the current estimation of the Pareto front. For these process models there is currently no model known where one dimension has a better score without reducing one of the other dimensions. The bigger dots show the seven most diverse process models in the current front, which can be used to truncate the Pareto front by keeping only one representative for a group of similar process models. The ideal or real Pareto front, as indicated by the curved line, shows that some improvements can still be made.

The construction of a Pareto front has been frequently applied in evolutionary algorithms. As described in [7], an evolutionary multi-objective optimization

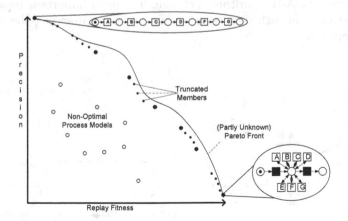

Fig. 1. Pareto front of the two quality dimensions replay fitness and precision. The hollow dots are non-optimal process models, the small black dots are discovered process models representing the current Pareto front and the big black dots are the 7 most diverse among the currently known process models.

(EMO) algorithm aims at both converging close to the real, yet unknown, Pareto front while at the same time maintain a good diversity among the candidates on the current Pareto front. The two most common, state-of-the-art, evolutionary algorithms that build a Pareto front of candidates are the NSGA-II [8] and SPEA2 [18] EMO algorithms. Between the two there is a slight but important difference in the way the fitness evaluation is performed and how the Pareto front is truncated. In short, SPEA2 calculates the fitness using both the dominance and the density of the population. The dominance includes the number of individuals dominated by that candidate. But also the number of individuals dominating the candidate. Furthermore, dominators are given a weight by using the total number of candidates they dominate. The density of the whole population is obtained by first calculating the distances between all candidates, and then considering the distance between a candidate and the k closest candidate. The NSGA-II algorithm defines the fitness of a candidate by the 'non-domination rank' (e.g. the number of candidates dominating the current candidate, candidates with a non-domination rank of 0 are on the 'actual' Pareto front). NSGA-II also has the notion of (crowding) distance which they calculate by taking the distance to the candidate better and the candidate worse in each dimension. These distances are normalized by the total value range of that dimension. The overall crowding distance of a candidate is the average over all dimensions. However, candidates that are at the extremes of a particular dimension, get very low (good) distance values. In this way the extreme candidates are always maintained. Both approaches select the candidates for the new population of the next generation according to a binary tournament using the fitness assignment. They also allow for truncation of the Pareto front using the same fitness function. NSGA-II and SPEA2 have been extensively compared regarding performance but no clear overall winner can be announced [4,10,13]. However, for our particular situation the crowding distance of the NSGA-II algorithm is chosen. The most important reason is the fact that extremes in each dimension are maintained, providing the user with extreme examples.

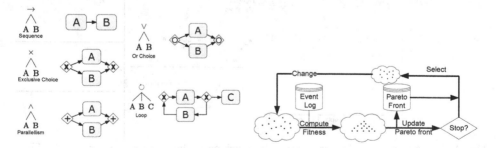

Fig. 2. Process trees operators and their block-structured BPMN translation.

Fig. 3. The different phases of the genetic algorithm.

3   Extending the ETM to Discover a Pareto Front

The ETM (*Evolutionary Tree Miner*) is a flexible evolutionary process discovery algorithm [5]. The ETM-algorithm is able to discover tree-like process models that are sound and block-structured. Examples of the different process tree constructs are shown in Fig. 2. Overall the ETM-algorithm follows the genetic process shown in Fig. 3. The input of the algorithm is an event log describing the observed behavior and, optionally, one or more reference process models. First, different quality dimensions for each candidate in the current population are calculated. Then, for each new candidate, the Pareto front is updated. In the next step, certain stop criteria are tested such as exceeding a time limit or whether the user canceled execution. If none of the stop criteria are satisfied, a new selection of candidates from the Pareto front is made, which forms the new population. The candidates in this population are then changed, the fitness for each of the quality dimensions is again calculated and they are presented to the Pareto front for possible inclusion. This process is continued until at least one stop criterion is satisfied and the current Pareto front is then returned. More details on the ETM-algorithm and the process tree notation used can be found in [5,6].

The ETM-algorithm is able to incorporate different quality dimensions. In general the four standard process discovery quality dimensions of replay fitness, precision, generalization and simplicity are included. However, the ETM-algorithm is also able to incorporate other quality dimensions during discovery. Examples are the conformance of a process model to a given set of rules [3,9,14], the predicted risk [12,15] of a process model, the predicted cost for handling a case with the given process model [17], the overall performance of the process model [2], etc. As long as a quality dimension can be calculated by considering the process model and possibly the event log, and can be influenced by changing the process model, it is valid for inclusion in the quality evaluation of a process discovery algorithm.

In the original ETM-algorithm the weights for each quality dimension, as provided by the user, are used to calculate a single fitness value per candidate and sort them accordingly. Furthermore, when the ETM-algorithm terminates, only the best candidate is returned. In this work the ETM-algorithm is extended with a Pareto front cache that maintains the current Pareto front during the different generations of the ETM-algorithm. At the end of each generation the currently evolved and evaluated population is added to the Pareto front, if they are not dominated by any element currently in the Pareto front. At the beginning of the next iteration a fixed number of candidates is selected from the Pareto front, since the front can grow larger than the desired population size.

In order to select the best candidate from the Pareto front for the population/input of the new generation, a fitness value is calculated. Here we use a fitness calculation inspired by the crowding distance used in the NSGA-II [8] algorithm, as was discussed in Sec. 2. This fitness metric consists of two parts: calculating the number of candidates that dominate the current candidate and calculating the crowding distance of the candidate. The first part of the metric results in an integer value, namely the number of candidates in both the Pareto front and the current population that dominate the particular candidate. The second part of the metric results in a value between 1 and 0 inclusive and represents the 'crowding distance' of a candidate. A value close to 0 indicates that the candidate is not in a crowded area, and a value of 0 indicates the candidate is at one of the extremes for at least one dimension. The crowding distance is calculated per dimension by considering the distance of a candidate with the next candidate that is worse and the next that is better. By normalizing this distance by the overall distance between the worst and best candidate of that dimension, a relative value is obtained. It is important however to assign boundary solutions, e.g. solutions that are best or worst in at least one dimension, a good crowding distance (e.g. a low value) to ensure that they are kept in the Pareto front. The crowding distance thus favors candidates that are diverse, for instance during the selection of candidates for mutation. The ETM with the Pareto front extension is implemented in the ProM framework[1].

4   Application on a Real Life Event Log

In this section we demonstrate our Pareto extended approach using the four quality dimensions of replay fitness, precision, generalization and simplicity. Additionally, we use the edit distance quality dimension as a fifth dimension to evaluate the similarity to a given process model [6]. The ETM-algorithm is started from a given process model and keeps track of the number of edits (add, remove, or update of a single node) made to this model. This allows the user to select a process model that is more or less similar to the reference process model that was provided. We apply the ETM-algorithm as presented in [6] on the same data set used there, but now with our Pareto extension.

The input of the ETM-algorithm is an event log describing the processing of building permits within a municipality. This event log comes from one of the municipalities participating in the CoSeLoG project[2]. The event log contains 1,434 cases with 8,577 events in total and 27 different event classes or activities. The provided reference model, as is shown in Fig. 4, is very detailed with many checks that the employees in practice did not always perform (usually with good reasons). Therefore, the municipality is interested to know where the main deviations are with respect to the reference process model.

The ETM-algorithm was run for 5,000 generations evolving 200 candidates per generation, which took a total of 22 h and 50 min. The experiment was performed on a computation server running Fedora 14 64-bit, with 8 cores running at 2 Ghz and 12 GB memory, of which max. 8 GB was used by the ETM. The four default quality dimensions of replay fitness, precision, generalization and

---

[1] ProM is available for download from http://www.processmining.org/, the ETM algorithm is included in the 'EvolutionaryTreeMiner' package.

[2] More information about the CoSeLoG project can be found at http://www.win.tue.nl/coselog/.

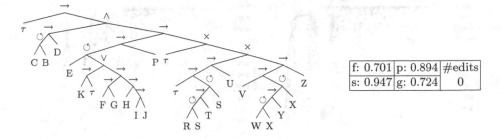

f: 0.701	p: 0.894	#edits
s: 0.947	g: 0.724	0

Fig. 4. Reference model for the case study

simplicity are considered. Additionally, as a fifth dimension, the number of low-level edits made to a provided reference process model is counted as a fitness metric for the similarity dimension. This resulted in a Pareto front containing 2,562 process trees, considering 5 dimensions.

Visualizing five dimensions at once is very difficult, therefore the Pareto front can be viewed using charts where the dimensions can be plotted on the X and Y axes. Figure 5 shows plots using the dimensions replay fitness and precision. The dot plot of Fig. 5a shows the distribution of candidates when considering the dimensions replay fitness and precision. Each dot represents a process model with that particular combination of values for the two selected dimensions. The lines on the top right connect those process models that are on the sub Pareto front, i.e. the Pareto front only considering the dimensions replay fitness and precision. All process models contained in the Pareto front are on a sub Pareto front considering one or more of the quality dimensions. This chart shows that there is not a single process model which has a very good score (i.e. 1.000) for both precision and replay fitness. Currently, the reference process model is selected in the chart, which is indicated by the dotted horizontal and vertical lines.

Additionally, a third dimension could be included in this chart by coloring the dots. This is shown in Fig. 5b where the color indicates the number of edits. A dark color means few edits and the lightest grey color indicates the maximum number of 61 edits observed. Again, the reference process model is selected in this chart. From this enhanced dot plot is becomes clear that the best process models are colored light, meaning that they require more than just a few edits. Furthermore, surrounding the selected reference process model is a 'cloud' of darker dots, indicating that only small changes in precision and replay fitness can be achieved if the process model can only be changed slightly.

Of course, the municipality wants to know how the reference model can be improved. Figure 5c shows a zoomed-in view of the dot plot of Fig. 5a, where only the process models with better scores for precision and replay fitness than the reference model are shown. This plot makes the trade-offs between replay fitness and precision clear. On the bottom right for instance we see the process models which have a good replay fitness, but at the cost of a bad precision

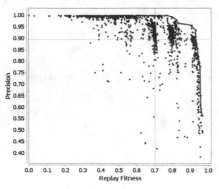

(a) Pareto front on the dimensions replay fitness and precision

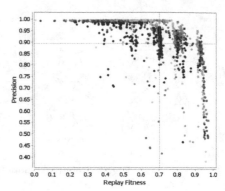

(b) Pareto front on the dimensions replay fitness and precision, colored by number of edits (darker means less edits)

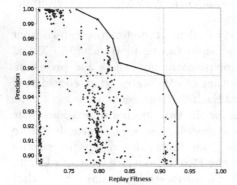

(c) Pareto front on the dimensions replay fitness and precision, showing only models with better scores than the reference model

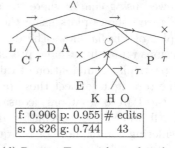

(d) Process Tree with good replay fitness and precision balance

Fig. 5. Views on the Pareto front considering replay fitness and precision

score. The almost straight lines indicate that with only a very small reduction in replay fitness, the precision score can be improved significantly. This trade-off works until a precision of roughly 0.955 is achieved, then precision can only be improved by sacrificing significantly on replay fitness. Which is indicated by the almost horizontal lines between the process models.

Therefore, one of the process models with the best trade-off between replay fitness and precision is the one indicated in Fig. 5c by the dotted vertical and horizontal lines. This process tree is shown in Fig. 5d. The process tree is able to replay most of the behavior observed in the five event logs, with reasonable precision. However, it required 43 edits from the reference process model. The main change is the removal of large parts of the process model, indicating that indeed some activities are skipped often. Furthermore some frequent activities, such as activity L, are added to, or relocated within, the process model.

When looking in more detail at the Pareto front as shown in Fig. 5a it can be observed that most process models are clustered around certain values for replay fitness. For instance there is a cluster of process models around the reference process model. Then there is another cluster or models between a fitness replay score of 0.780 and 0.820, with only few process models in between. Closer investigation of the event log showed that there are six activities (A, C, D, E, L and P) that are executed at least 1,200 times each. The other activities in the event log are executed at most 55 times each. Therefore these clusters consist of process models where one of the six frequent activities are in a particular good control flow construct. Since these activities are observed often, changing the control flow has a relatively large influence on the replay fitness value. The value of replay fitness for these models can still be influenced by repositioning one of the less frequent activities, but this impact is less.

The process model shown in Fig. 5d has little resemblance to the reference process model. Therefore we filter the Pareto front to only contain process models with at most 20 edits from the reference process models. Figure 6a shows the dot plot of the filtered Pareto front on the dimensions precision and replay fitness, using the same scales as in Fig. 5c. It is clear to see that the overall quality of the process models is worse, which can be observed by comparing the size of the area under the lines between the dots. When only 20 edits are allowed less improvements can be made. The trade-offs are also stronger, as is indicated by the almost vertical and horizontal lines between the candidates on this subfront. The process model with the best trade-off in precision and replay fitness is selected and shown in Fig. 6b. With 19 edits, a replay fitness of 0.906 and a precision of 0.955 can be obtained. This is an improvement with respect to the reference process model, especially for replay fitness. Interestingly, this process tree is also on the sub Pareto front as shown in Fig. 5c. However, when more edits are allowed, better quality models are discovered and smaller trade-offs can be made, resulting in a bigger and more detailed Pareto front.

The limitations mentioned in Sec. 2 are all resolved by using a Pareto front. The first issue of determining the weights upfront is solved by only requiring which dimensions to consider, not how to weight them against each other. As shown in Fig. 5, and the related discussion, it is possible to visualize and compare two or three dimensions, even if one is not normalized. This solves the second issue mentioned. The third issue of having only a single result is also clearly solved by presenting a Pareto front. For example between Figs. 5 and 6 it was easy to compare different trade-offs between the number of edits allowed and the resulting scores for replay fitness and precision. These insights were obtained without iteratively calling a discovery algorithm with different parameter settings. Moreover, by inspecting the Pareto front, a selection of process models can be made that satisfy a certain criteria, for instance at least as good precision and replay fitness scores as the reference process model.

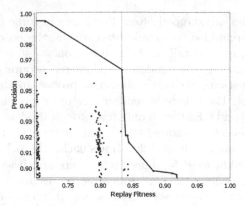

(a) Pareto front with maximum 20 edits

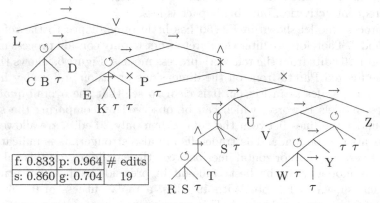

f: 0.833	p: 0.964	# edits
s: 0.860	g: 0.704	19

(b) Best process model with maximum 20 edits allowed

Fig. 6. Pareto front filtered to at most 20 edits from the reference process model

5   Conclusions

In this paper we used the ETM-algorithm to construct a collection of process models that are mutually non-dominating, and thus form a Pareto front. Each of the process models in the Pareto front either scores very good in one of the considered quality dimensions or is able to balance the different quality dimensions well. We applied this extension on a real-life event log. By selecting different views on the Pareto front, we have shown that several insights can be gained and different complementary models can be inspected. This allows the user to decide which process model is best and should be used further. Moreover, the user is aware of the trade-offs to be made rather than giving full control to the discovery algorithm.

Furthermore, by applying the Pareto front, more quality dimensions and metrics can be used by the ETM-algorithm. Since there is no requirement any more to normalize and weight the values, absolute numbers can also be provided.

This makes the ETM-algorithm extendable to use quality dimensions that are not directly related to process discovery. Examples are the discovery of process models that comply to a certain extend to rules, or to discover process models that minimize cost or expected risk.

Another benefit of using the Pareto front is the increase in diversity of the population. Previously the whole population would be focussed towards a specific combination of quality dimensions. However, with the diversity introduced by the Pareto front the ETM-algorithm has a large set of process models to choose from to evolve further. This is especially noticeable in the early generations of the ETM-algorithm where the Pareto front makes quick progress.

In the future we plan to further improve the visualization and navigation options for the Pareto front. It is critical that the user can navigate the collection of process models with ease and quickly gain insights. Moreover we plan to improve the selection of candidates for further evolution. This can be used to speed up the discovery of good process models. It will also help in a quick approach of the estimated Pareto front to the actual Pareto front.

References

1. van der Aalst, W.M.P.: Process Mining: Discovery, Conformance and Enhancement of Business Processes. Springer, Heidelberg (2011)
2. van der Aalst, W.M.P., Adriansyah, A., van Dongen, B.F.: Replaying history on process models for conformance checking and performance analysis. WIREs Data Min. Knowl. Disc. 2(2), 182–192 (2012)
3. Awad, A., Decker, G., Weske, M.: Efficient compliance checking using BPMN-Q and temporal logic. In: Dumas, M., Reichert, M., Shan, M.-C. (eds.) BPM 2008. LNCS, vol. 5240, pp. 326–341. Springer, Heidelberg (2008)
4. Bui, L.T., Essam, D., Abbass, H.A., Green, D.: Performance analysis of evolutionary multi-objective optimization methods in noisy environments. In: Proceedings of the 8th Asia Pacific Symposium on Intelligent and Evolutionary Systems, pp. 29–39 (2004)
5. Buijs, J.C.A.M., van Dongen, B.F., van der Aalst, W.M.P.: On the role of fitness, precision, generalization and simplicity in process discovery. In: Meersman, R., Panetto, H., Dillon, T., Rinderle-Ma, S., Dadam, P., Zhou, X., Pearson, S., Ferscha, A., Bergamaschi, S., Cruz, I.F. (eds.) OTM 2012, Part I. LNCS, vol. 7565, pp. 305–322. Springer, Heidelberg (2012)
6. Buijs, J.C.A.M., La Rosa, M., Reijers, H.A., van Dongen, B.F., van der Aalst, W.M.P.: Improving business process models using observed behavior. In: Cudre-Mauroux, P., Ceravolo, P., Gašević, D. (eds.) SIMPDA 2012. LNBIP, vol. 162, pp. 44–59. Springer, Heidelberg (2013)
7. Deb, K.: Multi-objective optimization. In: Burke, E.K., Kendall, G. (eds.) Search Methodologies, pp. 273–316. Springer, US (2005)
8. Deb, K., Agrawal, S., Pratap, A., Meyarivan, T.: A fast elitist non-dominated sorting genetic algorithm for multi-objective optimization: NSGA-II. In: Schoenauer, M., Deb, K., Rudolph, G., Yao, X., Lutton, E., Merelo, J.J., Schwefel, H.P. (eds.) PPSN 2000. LNCS, vol. 1917, pp. 849–858. Springer, Heidelberg (2000)
9. Governatori, G., Rotolo, A.: An algorithm for business process compliance. In: JURIX, pp. 186–191 (2008)

10. Hiroyasu, T., Nakayama, S., Miki, M.: Comparison study of SPEA2+, SPEA2, and NSGA-II in diesel engine emissions and fuel economy problem. In: The 2005 IEEE Congress on Evolutionary Computation 2005, vol. 1, pp. 236–242 (2005)
11. Pareto, V.: Cours D'Economie Politique, vols. I and II. F. Rouge, Lausanne (1896)
12. Pika, A., van der Aalst, W.M.P., Fidge, C.J., ter Hofstede, A.H.M., Wynn, M.T.: Predicting deadline transgressions using event logs. In: La Rosa, M., Soffer, P. (eds.) BPM Workshops 2012. LNBIP, vol. 132, pp. 211–216. Springer, Heidelberg (2013)
13. Raisanen, L., Whitaker, R.M.: Comparison and evaluation of multiple objective genetic algorithms for the antenna placement problem. Mob. Netw. Appl. **10**(1–2), 79–88 (2005)
14. Ramezani Taghiabadi, E., Fahland, D., van Dongen, B.F., van der Aalst, W.M.P.: Diagnostic information for compliance checking of temporal compliance requirements. In: Salinesi, C., Norrie, M.C., Pastor, Ó. (eds.) CAiSE 2013. LNCS, vol. 7908, pp. 304–320. Springer, Heidelberg (2013)
15. Suriadi, S., Ouyang, C., van der Aalst, W.M.P., ter Hofstede, A.H.M.: Root cause analysis with enriched process logs. In: La Rosa, M., Soffer, P. (eds.) BPM Workshops 2012. LNBIP, vol. 132, pp. 174–186. Springer, Heidelberg (2013)
16. van Veldhuizen, D.A., Lamont, G.B.: Evolutionary computation and convergence to a pareto front. In: Late Breaking Papers at the Genetic Programming 1998 Conference, pp. 221–228 (1998)
17. Wynn, M.T., Low, W.Z., Nauta, W.: A framework for cost-aware process management: generation of accurate and timely management accounting cost reports. In: Asia-Pacific Conference on Conceptual Modelling (2013)
18. Zitzler, E., Laumanns, M., Thiele, L.: SPEA2: improving the strength pareto evolutionary algorithm for multiobjective optimization. In: Proceedings of the EURO-GEN2001 Conference: Evolutionary Methods for Design, Optimisation and Control with Application to Industrial Problems, Athens, Greece, 19–21 September 2001

Discovering Stochastic Petri Nets with Arbitrary Delay Distributions from Event Logs

Andreas Rogge-Solti[1]([✉]), Wil M.P. van der Aalst[2], and Mathias Weske[1]

[1] Business Process Technology Group, Hasso Plattner Institute,
University of Potsdam, Potsdam, Germany
{andreas.rogge-solti,mathias.weske}@hpi.uni-potsdam.de
[2] Department of Information Systems, Eindhoven University of Technology,
P.O. Box 513, 5600 MB Eindhoven, The Netherlands
w.m.p.v.d.aalst@tue.nl

Abstract. Capturing the performance of a system or business process as accurately as possible is important, as models enriched with performance information provide valuable input for analysis, operational support, and prediction. Due to their computationally nice properties, memoryless models such as exponentially distributed stochastic Petri nets have earned much attention in research and industry. However, there are cases when the memoryless property is clearly not able to capture process behavior, e.g., when dealing with fixed time-outs.

We want to allow models to have generally distributed durations to be able to capture the behavior of the environment and resources as accurately as possible. For these more expressive process models, the execution policy has to be specified in more detail. In this paper, we present and evaluate process discovery algorithms for each of the execution policies. The introduced approach uses raw event execution data to discover various classes of stochastic Petri nets. The algorithms are based on the notion of alignments and have been implemented as a plug-in in the process mining framework ProM.

Keywords: Process mining · Stochastic Petri nets · Generally distributed transitions

1 Introduction

Process mining has emerged as a promising technology to gain insights into the actual execution of business processes and has been successfully applied in hundreds of organizations [1]. Besides the discovery of process models, process mining can also be used to enrich existing models with information gathered from event logs. In particular, capturing activity durations and waiting times in the business process is necessary to gain insights into the performance of the process. Further, these enriched models can be used as basis for prediction algorithms to

N. Lohmann et al. (Eds.): BPM 2013 Workshops, LNBIP 171, pp. 15–27, 2014.
DOI: 10.1007/978-3-319-06257-0_2, © Springer International Publishing Switzerland 2014

estimate the time until completion of the process [1]. Estimating the remaining run time of business processes and its activities is an important management task, since it allows to improve the allocation of resources. It also increases the quality of results when clients inquire the status and expected completion of a given business process.

Petri nets have been used widely in the business process domain, either as first class modeling languages, or as basis for verification purposes. There exist mappings for many workflow and business process modeling languages (e.g., BPMN, UML activity diagrams, BPEL, and EPCs) into Petri nets [2], as they are able to capture the most important control flow constructs.

If we have historical observations of a given process, e.g., an *event log* with timing information, it is possible to extract stochastic performance data and add it to the model. These enriched models can be used in a number of use cases. Besides answering questions such as *"How many percent of the process instances take longer than 10 days?"*, they can be used as basis for simulation, e.g., for *what-if* analysis. Moreover, they can be used to get accurate predictions of the remaining time and offer operational support.

Current state-of-the-art performance mining techniques focus only on gathering mean and variance (assuming normally distributed durations) [3,4], or the firing rate (assuming exponentially distributed durations) [5,6] of times. We are interested in automatically learning more fine grained information and want to be able to capture deterministic time-outs, or irregularities, such as multi-modal distributions. This paper investigates performance mining techniques for generally distributed transition stochastic Petri nets (GDT_SPN) that do not restrict distributions to a particular shape.

Multiple execution policies exist for these models that need to be taken into account [7]. In a nutshell, the problem addressed in this paper is to infer the stochastic parameters of a given Petri net, using an event log, and an execution policy. We base our algorithms on the alignment technique originally developed for conformance checking [8]. Our alignment-based approach is more robust than naïve replays of logs on the model, as it guarantees finding a globally best alignment based on a cost function that penalizes asynchronous parts of the replay.

The paper is organized as follows. In Sect. 2 preliminary definitions are provided. The main challenges and the performance mining algorithms addressing them are discussed in Sect. 3. A preliminary evaluation showing the capabilities to restore different kinds of models is presented in Sect. 4. Afterwards, related work is discussed in Sect. 5. Finally, conclusions are presented in Sect. 6.

2   Preliminaries

In order to establish a formal basis and to clarify the difficulties and solution ideas, this section introduces the concepts and techniques used throughout this paper. First, the core concepts of event logs and Petri nets are given.

Definition 1 (Event Log). *An event log over a set of activities A and time domain TD is defined as $L_{A,TD} = (E, C, \alpha, \gamma, \beta, \succ)$, where:*

- E is a finite set of events
- C is a finite set of cases (process instances),
- $\alpha : E \to A$ is a function assigning each event to an activity,
- $\gamma : E \to TD$ is a function assigning each event to a timestamp,
- $\beta : E \to C$ is a surjective function assigning each event to a case.
- $\succ \subseteq E \times E$ is the succession relation, which imposes a total ordering on the events in E.

We use $e_2 \succ e_1$ as shorthand notation for $(e_2, e_1) \in \succ$. We call the ordered sequence of events belonging to one case a "trace". We assume that $e_2 \succ e_1$ implies $\gamma(e_2) > \gamma(e_1)$, i.e., the time ordering is respected.

Definition 2 (Petri Net). *A Petri net is a tuple* $PN = (P, T, F, M_0)$ *where:*

- P is a set of places,
- T is a set of transitions,
- $F \subseteq (P \times T) \cup (T \times P)$ is a set of connecting arcs representing flow relations,
- $M_0 \in P \to \mathbb{N}_0$ is an initial marking.

Over the years, various kinds of extensions to Petri nets have been proposed in order to capture performance criteria. An overview of different important classes of stochastic Petri nets can be found in [9]. For our purposes, we extend the widely known definition of Generalized Stochastic Petri Nets (GSPNs) provided in [10], by allowing durations of the timed transitions to be generally distributed. In terms of the categorization proposed in [9], we use SPN with *generally distributed transitions*.

Definition 3 (GDT_SPN). *A generally distributed transition stochastic Petri net is a seven-tuple:* $GDT\_SPN = (P, T, \mathcal{P}, \mathcal{W}, F, M_0, \mathcal{D})$, *where* (P, T, F, M_0) *is the basic underlying Petri net. Additionally:*

- *The set of transitions* $T = T_i \cup T_t$ *is partitioned into immediate transitions* T_i *and timed transitions* T_t
- $\mathcal{P} : T \to \mathbb{N}_0$ *is an assignment of priorities to transitions, where* $\forall t \in T_i :$ $\mathcal{P}(t) \geq 1$ *and* $\forall t \in T_t : \mathcal{P}(t) = 0$
- $\mathcal{W} : T_i \to \mathbb{R}^+$ *assigns probabilistic weights to the immediate transitions*
- $\mathcal{D} : T_t \to D$ *is an assignment of arbitrary probability distributions* D *to timed transitions, reflecting the durations of the corresponding activities.*

An example GDT_SPN model is depicted in Fig. 1. Here, all weights of transitions are 1, unless otherwise specified, e.g., the weight of the immediate transition leaving the loop t_3 is 0.7. Immediate transitions (t_1, t_2, t_3, t_4) are depicted as black bars and have priority 1. The timed transitions (t_A, t_B, t_C, t_D) are depicted as boxes and have priority 0. The distributions of the probabilistic delays of the transitions D are annotated in a legend in the top left of the figure, e.g., transition t_B has a uniform distribution in the interval [3,14]. Although the transition durations depicted in this example are of parametric shape, it is also possible to specify other distributions, e.g., densities based on nonparametric regression.

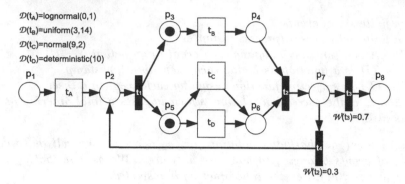

Fig. 1. Example *GDT_SPN* model with two parallel branches, and a conflict between transitions t_C, and t_D.

Note that even though the example model in Fig. 1 is structured and free-choice, the approaches presented in this paper are also applicable for non-structured and non-free-choice models.

The basic semantics of GSPN models [10] are still valid for GDT_SPN models used in this paper, i.e., only the enabled transitions of the highest priority are allowed to fire in the current marking. This ensures that if immediate transitions are enabled, no timed transition can fire. As in GSPN semantics, the choice between multiple enabled immediate transitions is resolved probabilistically in proportion of their weight parameters.

Next to the seven-tuple $GDT\_SPN = (P, T, \mathcal{P}, \mathcal{W}, F, M_0, D)$, an execution policy [7] has to be chosen to resolve conflicts between multiple enabled transitions and to decide upon the *memory* of transitions, i.e., if and how long they store the duration of time passed in enabled state. If more than one timed transition is enabled in a marking of a GDT_SPN, the selection policy defines how the next transition is chosen.

In *preselection* mode, this choice is resolved based on the weights. When using the *race* policy, each enabled transition picks a random sample of its distribution and the one with the lowest sample fires next. The memory policy defines what happens to the transitions that lose the race. There are three options, either (i) *resampling*, which constitutes to losing all progress, (ii) *enabling memory*, where each transition remembers its sampled duration until it becomes disabled or fires, or (iii) *age memory*, where transitions remember their sampled time, even through periods of disabling, until they eventually can fire.

We do not impose restrictions upon the execution semantics in this paper, rather we provide algorithms to reconstruct GDT_SPN models, assuming a particular execution policy. Before that however, we need to introduce the notion of alignments [8, 11], which we base our algorithms upon.

(a) a small log:

tr_1 : ⟨ A, B, D, C, B ⟩
tr_2 : ⟨ B, D, D ⟩

(b) perfect alignment for trace tr_1:

log	A	≫	B	D	≫	≫	≫	C	B	≫	≫
model	A	τ	B	D	τ	τ	τ	C	B	τ	τ
	t_A	t_1	t_B	t_D	t_2	t_4	t_1	t_C	t_B	t_2	t_3

(c) two possible alignments for trace tr_2:

(c.1)

log	≫	≫	B	D	D	≫	≫
model	A	τ	B	D	≫	τ	τ
	t_A	t_1	t_B	t_D		t_2	t_3

(c.2)

log	≫	≫	B	D	≫	≫	≫	D	≫	≫	≫
model	A	τ	B	D	τ	τ	τ	D	B	τ	τ
	t_A	t_1	t_B	t_D	t_2	t_4	t_1	t_C	t_B	t_2	t_3

Fig. 2. Event log and possible alignments for the traces.

2.1 Cost-Based Alignments

Figure 2(a) shows two execution traces (tr_1, tr_2) of the model depicted in Fig. 1, such that each event in the trace corresponds to a transition in the net with matching subscript, e.g., event B belongs to transition t_B. For this example, we assume that immediate transitions are invisible, i.e., they do not appear in the log, and all timed transitions are visible. This must not necessarily be the case in general, as there might be observable immediate transitions or invisible timed transitions as well. Dealing with invisible timed transitions is out of scope of this paper, however. We denote invisible transitions in a model in the alignment with a τ symbol. Note that trace tr_2 does not fit well into the model, so we want to find an optimal alignment between model and log. For this purpose, we reuse the methods developed by Adriansyah et al. in [8], which results in a sequence of movements that *replay* the trace in the model. These movements are either *synchronous moves*, *model moves*, or *log moves*. Figure 2(b) displays a perfect alignment for tr_1 that consists of synchronous, or invisible model moves only.

For trace tr_2 there exist multiple possible alignments, of which two are depicted in Fig. 2(c). The ≫ symbol represents no progress in the replay on either side, e.g., the first step in the alignment in Fig. 2(c.1) is a model move. In fact, for the model in Fig. 1 there exist infinite alignments, as the model contains a loop that could be traversed an arbitrary number of times, resulting in two additional model moves, and three invisible model moves per iteration. The cost based alignment approach in [8] makes sure that alignments containing unnecessary moves get penalized by higher cost and therefore excluded from the optimal alignments. Alignments provide a deterministic firing sequence in the model replaying the traces in an optimal way.

3   Mining GDT_SPN Models

There are multiple difficulties in mining GDT_SPN models from event logs. First, we describe how the alignment technique introduced in Sect. 2.1 helps dealing with noisy event logs, i.e., logs where events might be missing, be at unexpected positions, or be reflecting activities not captured in the model.

3.1   First Challenge: Dealing with Noisy Logs

In order to extract decision and timing information from logs and combine the extracted information with a Petri net to get a GDT_SPN model, each individual trace in the log needs to be *aligned* to the Petri net. That is, the path in the model that was taken in the trace has to be identified. Previous techniques to extend models with performance information, e.g. the work in [3] tries to find the path through a model in a greedy way. Typically, this is done by replaying the model and looking for the best next match(es) between enabled transitions and next events with a given look-ahead. In contrast, the cost-based alignment technique introduced in Sect. 2.1, guarantees to find one of the alignments that is optimal in the sense that it has the least number of asynchronous moves (given that all asynchronous moves are assigned equal costs).

In fact, we add a small cost δ_t based on individual event counts to each transition t in the alignment, such that less frequent events and their corresponding transitions have a slightly higher cost than more frequent ones. This ensures that the alignment algorithm always favors the most frequent option, when there are multiple options to choose a path in the model. This is a simple heuristic that may pick the wrong alignment, but the best guess that can be made based on local frequency-based information. A more accurate option would be to leverage the whole alignment approach to consider the stochastic parameters of the model, which is out of scope of this paper.

The resulting alignments are only usable for our purposes, when most of the observed behavior actually fits the model. If fitness values are very low, a lot of information contained in the event log cannot be mapped to the model, and cannot be used for performance analysis. In this case, we add a preprocessing step before eliciting performance data. In this preprocessing step, the model needs to be adjusted to the log, which can be done by *repairing the model*, cf. techniques presented by Fahland and van der Aalst [12] to add optional subprocesses to models, or alternatively the work by Buijs et al. [13] based on genetic mining.

Figure 3 shows an overview of the elicitation approach proposed in this paper. The inputs to the approach are the Petri net model reflecting the structural behavior of the process, and an event log containing the traces representing actual executed process cases. Further, a configuration is necessary, as GDT_SPN models are flexible in their execution semantics and transition distribution types

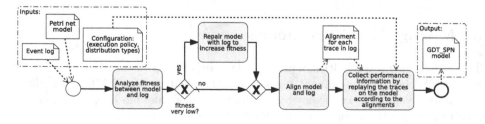

Fig. 3. BPMN model showing the approach to elicit GDT_SPN models.

that will be fitted to the data. The fitness between model and log can be analyzed by the technique described in [8] and implemented in the process mining
framework ProM. If the fitness is under a user specified threshold, e.g., 0.7, first
repair techniques, cf. the work in [12,13], are executed on the model to allow for
the behavior observed in the log. Then, each trace in the event log is aligned to
the model to find one of the optimal paths through the model. With the alignments, the collection of stochastic execution information according to the input
configuration is performed.

3.2 Second Challenge: Collecting the Stochastic Performance Information

With the alignments between model and the traces selected, the collection of
performance information can proceed depending on the configuration of the elicitation algorithm, i.e., execution policies and distribution types. First, we discuss
the common approach that is used regardless of the specific execution policy.

The alignment makes sure that each event is assigned to at most one transition in the model. Based on the alignments, we replay the traces on the model, as
if in a simulation, but instead of sampling random values from the distributions,
we use the observed values extracted from the event log and infer the most likely
stochastic model that explains the observation best. This works well if we can
gather all the information that would also be produced in a simulation, i.e., the
sample values of the transition firings, and the firing ratios for the markings.
The different execution policies (*preselection/race* and in case of a *race* policy
also the memory policy) are complicating matters. For example, races between
simultaneously enabled transitions can only be observed indirectly: the sampled
values of the losing transition of the race cannot be recovered in all cases. Other
reasons for missing information might be noise in the data, e.g., missing events.

Depending on the execution policy of the GDT_SPN model, different
approaches are used to collect the stochastic parameters of the model.

Global Preselection Policy. With the *global preselection* policy, only one
transition can perform work at once, leading to a serialized process execution.
Given this policy, we replay the traces in the model and collect in each visited
marking for each enabled transition the number of times, the transition was
picked. These numbers, when normalized, give us a ratio of the weights of the
transitions in each marking. Note that one transition can be enabled in multiple
markings, i.e., a transition weight needs to fulfill multiple equations and there
may be dependencies. Hence, we solve an optimization problem to find the joint
assignment to the transition weights that minimizes the error in these equations
of each marking. To achieve this, we implemented a gradient descent algorithm
that finds the weight vector that minimizes the individual errors in the process
mining toolkit ProM[1]. The algorithm is guaranteed to converge (if the learning
rate is sufficiently low) to a local optimum. Since the cost function of the errors

---

[1] See the StochasticPetriNet package of ProM (http://www.processmining.org).

is convex by nature and has, similarly to linear regression, no local optima, it finds the best global assignment. Note that if we would extend our model to capture marking dependent weights, we would not need to average the errors out, but could directly estimate the weights as the observed ratio of transition firings in each marking.

The time differences between events in the trace represent the duration of transition firings. Since there is no parallel execution in global preselection, these transition durations can be read from the trace directly. However, special attention needs to be devoted to asynchronous moves in the alignment. The time difference between transitions should only be collected, if the current move is synchronous and the previous is either also synchronous, or a log move. In other cases the difference between the times of events are spanning multiple transitions in the model. If more than one of these transitions is timed, we can use this delay as upper bounds for all involved timed transitions on the path in the alignment between the two events.

Race Selection Policy. In the race selection policy, we also replay the traces in the model according to the path dictated by the alignment. The challenge in the race selection policy is that we can only read the duration sample of the winning transition directly. That duration can however serve as a lower bound for the other transitions that lose their progress. Depending on the memory policy this issue of non-retrievable samples is more or less severe.

With the *resampling* memory policy, we only get exact samples for winning transitions. In the worst case, when a transition loses every race, we have only a lower bound on it's distribution which makes inference on the actual shape or range of it's values impossible. However, this is only a problem for transitions that rarely happen. Note also that this policy is rarely used in practice, as it does introduce dependencies between parallel transitions, i.e., parallel transitions have to restart their work, because another transition was faster.

Of more practical relevance is the *enabling-memory* policy, which allows for transitions that lose a race against non-conflicting transitions to keep their progress. If we have both events for the transition enabling and the one firing the transition, we can calculate the duration of the transition by simple subtraction between these two events. In this policy, we still cannot recover sample durations for transitions that lose a race against a conflicting transition, i.e., a transition that disables it. Thus, we also have to deal with censored data for timed transitions in conflict with other transitions.

Last, the *age-memory* policy even allows to reconstruct the sample duration of timed transitions in conflict, if they are re-enabled, e.g., by another iteration of a loop. We need to collect all enabled periods and take their sum to reconstruct the originally sampled firing duration. This is straightforward by using age variables for transitions and incrementing them by the time spent in enabled state during replay. Note that even in the *age-memory* policy not all duration samples of conflicting transitions can be collected from the event log in general. Recall that a transition does not necessarily become enabled again after being disabled by a conflicting transition.

Thus, we can treat all memory policies for the race policy equally, besides from subtle difference in gathering the samples, i.e., points in time when transition clocks will be reset. In all cases we gather both accurate samples of the unknown distribution that we want to infer, and also lower bounds on the remaining samples, when another transition fired first. In general, we face the problem to infer the probability distribution of a random variable with randomly right-censored data. Approaches to this problem are well-known in statistics, cf. the overview by Padgett and McNichols [14]. We use the method of Kooperberg and Stone [15] that fits log-splines to censored data, and is available in R.[2]

3.3 Third Challenge: Dealing with Special Cases

As claimed in the introduction, allowing for *timeouts* is one important aspect of business process modeling. Therefore, the mining algorithm needs to be capable to detect deterministic durations in a model. In technical terms, once we have gathered the observed samples and censored samples, we can check, whether a transition is deterministic or not, by comparing the observed samples. If the samples are sufficiently close, we define the transition to be deterministic. This can be made more robust against noise, by removing outliers before applying these rules. In the mined model, the deterministic value is estimated as the mean of the observed values.

Another quite important modeling construct are immediate transitions, which fire *immediately* after they have been enabled, provided that they are selected amidst competing immediate transitions. We assumed immediate transitions to be invisible. But if corresponding events exist in the event log, the rule to identify these transitions is to set a threshold and check, whether all observed values are within 0 and that threshold. Note that we cannot give a general rule, as it depends on the domain, e.g., the response time of systems, how large these thresholds should be.

4   Evaluation

To evaluate how well the algorithm works on data, it is necessary to compare its output, i.e., the discovered model, with the model that produced the behavior in the event log. In general however, the theoretical model behind the observable phenomena is not known. Therefore, we rely on a simulation based approach. First, we need a GDT_SPN model. There exist already algorithms that can discover less expressive performance models from data [4,5], which can serve as a starting point, or a hand-made model can be used.

In this evaluation, we focus on the following two questions:

– How many traces do we need to get reasonably accurate results?
– How tolerant is the algorithm towards noise in the log?

---

[2] See package *logspline* in R. (http://www.r-project.org/).

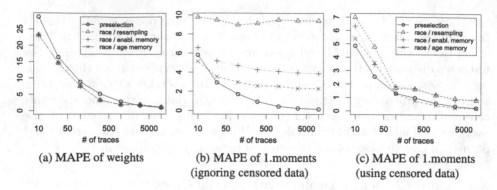

(a) MAPE of weights	(b) MAPE of 1.moments (ignoring censored data)	(c) MAPE of 1.moments (using censored data)

Fig. 4. Effects of trace size on restored model accuracy. Mean average percentage error (MAPE) of weights and MAPE of 1.moments of inferred distributions for timed transitions of the model in Fig. 1. Number of traces drawn in log-scale.

To gain insights into these questions, we ran the following experiment. First, multiple logs are simulated from the GDT_SPN model depicted in Fig. 1 with increasing trace count from 10 traces to 10000 traces. The simulated event logs, the underlying Petri net (P, T, F, M_0) of the GDT_SPN model, and the given execution policy are passed as input to the discovery algorithm. The algorithm produces another GDT_SPN model, which we compare with the original model.

There are several ways to assess the accuracy of a model. To test for the bias that our method introduces in the model parameters, we calculate the mean absolute percentage error (MAPE) of the estimated 1.moment and the original 1.moment of each timed transition's distribution. Note that we omitted the first transition t_A from the calculation, because we cannot calculate its duration, as there is no previous event with a timestamp in the log. Weights are evaluated relatively to each other when selecting an immediate transition, and additionally in *preselection* mode also when selecting the next timed transition. Therefore, we need to compare the weight ratios in each marking of the original and discovered model, where selection of the next transition is based on weights. Because weights are evaluated relatively to each other, we normalize them first, before we calculate the MAPE of the weights in each relevant marking.

Figure 4(a) shows the error of the transition weights between the original model and the inferred model from the log. Note that weight errors of all *race policies* collapse, as their weights are computed in the same way. However, the *preselection* policy has more constraints on the weights, and random behavior of small event logs prohibits discovering the true weights accurately. Figure 4(b) shows the mean average percentage error of the 1.moments, when a simple kernel density estimation is used for estimating the duration of timed transitions. As expected, the *preselection* execution policy does not suffer from bias due to censored data. The *race* with *resampling* method is the most difficult to reconstruct, as many of the samples are discarded. The *enabling memory* policy has less bias, and in the *age memory* policy, the algorithm can restore most of the original sample dura-

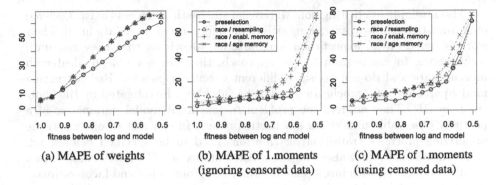

(a) MAPE of weights

(b) MAPE of 1.moments
(ignoring censored data)

(c) MAPE of 1.moments
(using censored data)

Fig. 5. Mean average percentage errors between the model in Fig. 1 and the reconstructed model with increasing amount of noise, i.e., reduced fitness.

tions. Figure 4(c) depicts the error that remains, when the log-spline density estimator [15] is used. Note that this method considers censored data and can correct the bias well. It reduces the biases of the *race* execution policies significantly.

For the second experiment, we keep the trace size at 1000 and run the discovery algorithms with logs of varying degrees of artificial noise, i.e., random addition and deletion of events. Figure 5 depicts the same measures as before, i.e., the MAPE of relative weights in the markings and the MAPE of the 1.moments of the distributions. Observe, how in Fig. 5(b) the MAPE of the 1.moments increases non-linearly with lower fitness values. The quality starts dropping rapidly below a fitness of 0.8 in this example. When dealing with noisy logs, the Petri net models should be repaired first in a preprocessing step, as described in Sect. 3.

As a concluding remark, we caution against drawing general conclusions from these preliminary evaluations. Larger errors are expected for models with bigger state spaces.

5   Related Work

There exists already work on obtaining Petri net models with stochastic performance characteristics from data. Hu et al. propose a method to mine exponentially distributed SPN models from workflow logs in [6] focusing on firing rates of transitions. In contrast, our work allows for generally distributed firing times. Another, quite different approach was proposed by Anastasiou et al. [5] and uses location data to elicit generalized stochastic Petri net (GSPN) [10] models for modeling flows of customers. They fit hyper-erlang distributions to transition durations representing waiting and service times and replace the corresponding transitions with a GSPN subnet exhibiting the same characteristics of the hyper-erlang distribution. They consider every transition in isolation though, which poses no problems in serial processes but parallelism in the processes, especially multiple parallel transitions in conflict, are not covered in that approach.

Also attempts at eliciting non-Markovian stochastic Petri nets exist. Leclercq et al. investigate how to extract models of normally distributed data in [4]. Their work is based on an expectation maximization algorithm that they run until convergence. In comparison to our approach, they are not able to deal with missing data and do not consider different execution policies. Reconstructing model parameters for stochastic systems has also been investigated by Buchholz et al. in [16]. They address the problem to find fixed model parameters of a partially observable underlying stochastic process. In contrast to our work, the underlying process's transition distributions need to be specified beforehand, while our aim is to infer also transition distributions of a GDT_SPN model. In a similar setting, i.e., with incomplete information, Wombacher and Iacob estimate distributions of activities and missing starting times of processes in [17].

In [3], Rozinat et al. investigate how to gather information for simulation models, but rather try to identify data dependencies for decisions and mean durations and standard deviations and do manual replay, which is not guaranteed to find an optimal alignment between model and log. The approach proposed in this paper is capable to deal with noise in a more robust way, by building on the notion of alignments [8,11], which identify an optimal path through the model for a noisy trace. In conclusion, we are not aware of existing work that allows for generally distributed duration distributions, and different execution policies. Moreover, unlike existing approaches, our approach is supported by a publicly available ProM plug-in and can thus be combined with a wide range of control-flow discovery approaches.

6   Conclusion

This paper addresses the challenges that arise when mining performance characteristics for models that can capture distributions other than the memoryless distributions. Unlike earlier work, the paper makes very little assumptions on the event data and underlying process to be mined. Accurate models of process performance are crucial for what-if analysis, predictions, recommendations, etc.

The stochastic model used in this paper extends the popular GSPN modeling technique. To analyze discovered GDT_SPN models, we need to resort to simulation due to the expressiveness of the class of models considered. We discussed different execution policies of GDT_SPN models and have shown how these different semantics can be taken into account when eliciting models. The *preselection* firing policy is the simplest case, which can be learned without problems. All other cases need sophisticated density estimation techniques that are able to cope with randomly right censored data. An implementation producing initial results is made available open source in the ProM framework.

Our next steps include comparing these mined models with other approaches and compare the model accuracy based on a specific use case, such as predicting the duration of a process. Future work also includes extending the alignment approach to align event logs probabilistically to a given GDT_SPN model, such that we can find the alignment with the highest probability.

References

1. van der Aalst, W.: Process Mining: Discovery Conformance and Enhancement of Business Processes. Springer, Heidelberg (2011)
2. Lohmann, N., Verbeek, E., Dijkman, R.: Petri Net transformations for business processes – a survey. In: Jensen, K., van der Aalst, W.M.P. (eds.) Transactions on Petri Nets and Other Models of Concurrency II. LNCS, vol. 5460, pp. 46–63. Springer, Heidelberg (2009)
3. Rozinat, A., Mans, R.S., Song, M., van der Aalst, W.: Discovering simulation models. Inf. Syst. **34**(3), 305–327 (2009)
4. Leclercq, E., Lefebvre, D., Ould El Mehdi, S.: Identification of timed stochastic petri net models with normal distributions of firing periods. In: Information Control Problems in Manufacturing, vol. 13, pp. 948–953 (2009)
5. Anastasiou, N., Horng, T., Knottenbelt, W.: Deriving generalised stochastic Petri Net performance models from high-precision location tracking data. In: VALUE-TOOLS'11, ICST, pp. 91–100 (2011)
6. Hu, H., Xie, J., Hu, H.: A novel approach for mining stochastic process model from workflow logs. J. Comput. Inf. Syst. **7**(9), 3113–3126 (2011)
7. Marsan, M.A., Balbo, G., Bobbio, A., Chiola, G., Conte, G., Cumani, A.: The effect of execution policies on the semantics and analysis of stochastic petri nets. IEEE Trans. Softw. Eng. **15**, 832–846 (1989)
8. Adriansyah, A., van Dongen, B., van der Aalst, W.: Conformance checking using cost-based fitness analysis. In: EDOC 2011, pp. 55–64. IEEE (2011)
9. Ciardo, G., German, R., Lindemann, C.: A characterization of the stochastic process underlying a stochastic Petri Net. IEEE Trans. Softw. Eng. **20**(7), 506–515 (1994)
10. Marsan, M., Conte, G., Balbo, G.: A class of generalized stochastic Petri Nets for the performance evaluation of multiprocessor systems. ACM TOCS **2**(2), 93–122 (1984)
11. van der Aalst, W., Adriansyah, A., van Dongen, B.: Replaying history on process models for conformance checking and performance analysis. WIREs Data Mining Knowl. Discov. **2**, 182–192 (2012). (Wiley Online Library)
12. Fahland, D., van der Aalst, W.M.P.: Repairing process models to reflect reality. In: Barros, A., Gal, A., Kindler, E. (eds.) BPM 2012. LNCS, vol. 7481, pp. 229–245. Springer, Heidelberg (2012)
13. Buijs, J.C.A.M., La Rosa, M., Reijers, H.A., van Dongen, B.F., van der Aalst, W.M.P.: Improving business process models using observed behavior. In: Cudre-Mauroux, P., Ceravolo, P., Gašević, D. (eds.) SIMPDA 2012. LNBIP, vol. 162, pp. 44–59. Springer, Heidelberg (2013)
14. Padgett, W., McNichols, D.T.: Nonparametric density estimation from censored data. Commun. Stat. Theor. Methods **13**(13), 1581–1611 (1984)
15. Kooperberg, C., Stone, C.J.: Logspline density estimation for censored data. J. Comput. Graph. Stat. **1**(4), 301–328 (1992)
16. Buchholz, R., Krull, C., Horton, G.: Reconstructing model parameters in partially-observable discrete stochastic systems. In: Al-Begain, K., Balsamo, S., Fiems, D., Marin, A. (eds.) ASMTA 2011. LNCS, vol. 6751, pp. 159–174. Springer, Heidelberg (2011)
17. Wombacher, A., Iacob, M.E.: Start time and duration distribution estimation in semi-structured processes. Technical report, Centre for Telematics and Information Technology, University of Twente (2012)

Discovering Unbounded Synchronization Conditions in Artifact-Centric Process Models

Viara Popova and Marlon Dumas[✉]

University of Tartu, Tartu, Estonia
{viara.popova,marlon.dumas}@ut.ee

Abstract. Automated process discovery methods aim at extracting business process models from execution logs of information systems. Existing methods in this space are designed to discover synchronization conditions over a set of events that is fixed in number, such as for example discovering that a task should wait for two other tasks to complete. However, they fail to discover synchronization conditions over a variable-sized set of events such as for example that a purchasing decision is made only if at least three out of an a priori undetermined set of quotes have been received. Such synchronization conditions arise in particular in the context of artifact-centric processes, which consist of collections of interacting artifacts, each with its own life cycle. In such processes, an artifact may reach a state in its life cycle where it has to wait for a variable-sized set of artifacts to reach certain states before proceeding. In this paper, we propose a method to automatically discover such synchronization conditions from event logs. The proposed method has been validated over actual event logs of a research grant assessment process.

Keywords: Business process mining · Automated process discovery

1 Introduction

Process mining is concerned with the extraction of knowledge about business processes from execution logs of information systems [1]. Process mining encompasses a wide range of methods, including automated process discovery methods, which seek to extract business process models from event logs.

A common limitation of existing automated process discovery methods is that they are unable to discover synchronization conditions that involve one process waiting for a variable number of other processes to reach certain states. This situation arises for example when one process spawns a variable number of subprocesses and waits for a subset of them to complete before proceeding. In the BPMN notation, a process may contain a multi-instance activity which spawns a number of instances of a subprocess and waits for a subset of these instances to complete based on a so-called *completion condition*. A concrete example is the case where a procure-to-pay process spawns a number of subprocesses to retrieve

N. Lohmann et al. (Eds.): BPM 2013 Workshops, LNBIP 171, pp. 28–40, 2014.
DOI: 10.1007/978-3-319-06257-0_3, © Springer International Publishing Switzerland 2014

quotes from multiple suppliers (determined at runtime) and then waits until a number of quotes have been obtained before proceeding with supplier selection. We hereby call such conditions *unbounded synchronization conditions*.

More general forms of unbounded synchronization conditions are found in artifact-centric process models. In artifact-centric modeling [3,11] a process is decomposed into a collection of artifacts corresponding to business objects with their own life cycles and information models. For example, a conference reviewing process may be split into artifacts *Conference*, *Submission* and *Review*. In this setting, an unbounded synchronization condition is that "a submission can only be evaluated when at least three reviews are completed".

This paper addresses the problem of discovering unbounded synchronization conditions in artifact-centric process models. The contribution is framed in the context of artifact-centric processes represented using the Guard-Stage-Milestone (GSM) notation [6]. GSM divides the life cycle of an artifact into stages that open when their guard conditions become true and close when their milestone conditions become true. A guard condition of a stage of an artifact may refer to milestones of the artifact itself or attributes within the artifact's information model (intra-artifact condition) but it may also refer to the state of other artifacts (inter-artifact condition). The paper addresses the discovery of inter-artifact conditions where the number of artifact instances to be synchronized is not determined at design-time.

The presented methods are implemented as plug-ins in the ProM process mining framework [16] and validated using a real-life log of a research grant assessment process.

The paper is organized as follows. Section 2 gives a brief overview of artifact-centric process modeling using GSMs and a simple scenario that serves as a motivating example. Section 3 presents the proposed method for discovering inter-artifact synchronization conditions. The validation is discussed in Sect. 4. Sections 5 and 6 discuss related work and future research directions.

2   Background: Artifact-Centric Modeling

Artifact-centric modeling is an approach for modeling business processes based on the identification of key objects (artifacts) that encapsulate process-related data and whose life cycles define the overall business process [3,11]. An artifact type contains an information model with all data relevant for the artifacts of that type as well as a life cycle model specifying how an artifact responds to events and undergoes transformations from its creation until it is archived.

The Guard-Stage-Milestone (GSM) meta-model [6] can be used to represent the artifact life cycles which allows a natural way for representing hierarchy and parallelism within the same instance of an artifact and between instances of different artifacts. The key GSM elements for representing the artifact life cycle are *stages*, *guards* and *milestones*. Stages correspond to clusters of activities performed for, with or by an artifact instance intended to achieve one of the milestones belonging to the stage. A stage can have one or more guards and

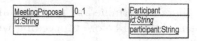

Fig. 1. Artifact types in the motivating scenario: Meeting Proposal and Participant.

one or more milestones. A stage opens when a guard becomes true and closes when a milestone becomes true. Sentries are used in guards and milestones to control when they become true. Sentries contain a triggering event type and/or a condition which may refer to the same or other artifact instances.

As a motivating example we consider the following meeting planning process. An assistant tries to organize a meeting between a group which in our example consists of 6 participants. The assistant proposes time and date. Each participant receives the proposal and considers their availability. If they are not available, they reject the proposal. If available, they consider whether they are prepared to host the meeting and accept the proposal (it is convenient but not prepared to host) or propose to host the meeting. The proposal is successful if at least three participants are available and at least one of them is prepared to host. If it fails, the assistant proposes a new time and date and the process continues until a proposal is successful.

Adopting an artifact-centric modeling approach for this scenario, we can consider two artifact types: Meeting Proposal and Participant (see Fig. 1). One instance of Meeting Proposal reflects the efforts of the assistant to organize a single meeting for specific time and date. One instance of the Participant artifact reflects the activities of one participant for responding to a meeting proposal. Instances of the Meeting Proposal artifact type are identified by attribute id while instances of the Participant artifact type are identified by attribute pair (id, participant). For testing, the scenario was implemented in CPN Tools to generate event logs.

3 Discovery of Synchronization Conditions

The aim of this research is to propose a method for discovering inter-artifact synchronization conditions which can then become part of the guard of the corresponding stage in the GSM model. These conditions reflect the knowledge that the stage can only open when a certain number of instances of another artifact reach a certain state. This state will more specifically be represented by the fact that a milestone of another stage has been reached.

For our meeting planning example such condition can be defined, for instance, for the stage Meeting Successful of artifact Meeting Proposal. Meeting Successful can only open if at most 3 instances of artifact Participant have completed stage Reject Proposal, at least 2 instances have completed stage Accept Proposal and at least one instance has completed stage Host Meeting.

The previously presented methods in [13] provide us with the means to extract the knowledge of which specific instances of an artifact are related to which instances of other artifacts. This information is used when discovering inter-artifact guard conditions. To take advantage of it, a new format for logs is used - *artifact synchronization logs.*

Event logs consist of events which represent executions of activities in the system. Events contain attributes which determine the activity, the time at which the event happened and what business-relevant data values are associated to it.

Definition 1 (Event). *Let $\{N_1, N_2, \ldots, N_n\}$ be a set of attribute names and $\{D_1, D_2, \ldots, D_n\}$ - a set of attribute domains where D_i is the set of possible values of N_i for $1 \leq i \leq n$. Let $\Sigma = \{A_1, A_2, \ldots, A_m\}$ be a set of event types. An event e is a tuple $e = (A, \tau, v_1, v_2, \ldots, v_k)$ where*

1. *$A \in \Sigma$ is the event type to which e belongs,*
2. *$\tau \in \Omega$ is the timestamp of the event where Ω is the set of all timestamps,*
3. *for all $1 \leq i \leq k$ v_i is an attribute-value pair $v_i = (N_i, d_i)$ where N_i is an attribute name and $d_i \in D_i$ is an attribute value.*

All events of an event type A are called event instances of A.

We denote the event type of event e by $A(e)$ and the timestamp of e by $\tau(e)$.

Definition 2 (Trace, log). *A trace L is a sequence of events ordered according to a total order $\leq$ induced by the event timestamps. A set of traces is called a log. An artifact-centric log consists of the traces of its artifact instances. The trace of an artifact instance contains all events affecting the instance in question.*

Let $\mathcal{A} = \{Art_1, \ldots, Art_n\}$ be an artifact system with artifacts Art_i, $1 \leq i \leq n$. Let $\mathcal{L} = \{L_1, \ldots, L_n\}$ be a set of artifact-centric logs of the behavior of the system where log L_i describes the behavior of artifact Art_i and its instances $\{I_i^1, \ldots, I_i^m\}$. For each instance I_i^j, trace T_i^j from log L_i contains all events for this instance. We denote by $I_i^j \mapsto Art_i$ the fact that instance I_i^j is an instance of artifact Art_i. $T_i^j \to I_i^j$ denotes that trace T_i^j describes instance I_i^j.

Let $\mathcal{R}$ be a set of relationships R_{ij} between artifacts of $\mathcal{A}$ in $\mathcal{L}$ such that R_{ij} defines which instances of artifact Art_i are related to which instances of artifact Art_j, $R_{ij} = \{(I_i^t, I_j^s) : I_i^t \mapsto Art_i, I_j^s \mapsto Art_j\}$.

Definition 3 (Artifact synchronization log). *We define an artifact synchronization log L for artifact Art_i with respect to artifact Art_j as the set of traces $\{ST_s\}$ such that ST_s consists of the events of instance I_i^s of artifact Art_i and the events of all instances of artifact Art_j related to that instance: $ST_s = T_i^s \cup T$ where $T_i^s \to I_i^s$ and $T = \{T_j^p : T_j^p \to I_j^p, I_j^p \mapsto Art_j, (I_i^s, I_j^p) \in R_{ij}\}$. Artifact Art_i is called primary or main artifact for L and Art_j - secondary artifact.*

Figure 2 shows a trace in an artifact synchronization log from the example for primary artifact - Meeting Proposal and the secondary artifact - Participant. Note that an artifact synchronization log has the usual structure of a log and can be represented using existing log formats such as XES and MXML.

Using the artifact synchronization logs, the process of discovering inter-artifact conditions (also called *synchronization conditions*) consists of three steps.

```
1970-01-07T03:59:00+02:00 InitiateMeetingPlanning id=769
1970-01-07T04:02:00+02:00 ProposeDateTime          id=769
1970-01-07T04:06:00+02:00 ReceiveProposal          id=769 participant=5
1970-01-07T04:06:00+02:00 ReceiveProposal          id=769 participant=6
1970-01-07T04:06:00+02:00 ReceiveProposal          id=769 participant=4
1970-01-07T04:06:00+02:00 ReceiveProposal          id=769 participant=2
1970-01-07T04:06:00+02:00 ReceiveProposal          id=769 participant=1
1970-01-07T04:06:00+02:00 ReceiveProposal          id=769 participant=3
1970-01-07T04:16:00+02:00 AnswerACCEPT             id=769 participant=6
1970-01-07T04:16:00+02:00 AnswerACCEPT             id=769 participant=4
1970-01-07T04:17:00+02:00 AnswerHOST               id=769 participant=1
1970-01-07T04:22:00+02:00 AnswerACCEPT             id=769 participant=2
1970-01-07T04:24:00+02:00 AnswerACCEPT             id=769 participant=5
1970-01-07T04:26:00+02:00 AnswerHOST               id=769 participant=3
1970-01-07T04:39:00+02:00 ProposalSuccessful       id=769
1970-01-07T04:44:00+02:00 ConfirmMeeting           id=769
```

Fig. 2. Partial artifact synchronization trace from the Meeting Planning process

The first step is to discover which stages should contain such conditions (i.e., are synchronization points). In some cases, the synchronization points of an artifact might be known in advance. For completeness, however, we assume that this is not the case and thus they need to be discovered. For a given synchronization point, at the next step, we discover the best candidates for synchronization conditions. These two sub-problems are discussed in Sect. 3.1. The generated conditions are then assigned a confidence score, allowing the user to rank them and focus on the most likely ones. This is discussed in Sect. 3.2.

3.1   Discovery of Synchronization Points and Conditions

Here we define a simple heuristic which allows us to filter out the points that are most probably not synchronization points. The remaining points are the points for which conditions will be generated. The intuition behind the proposed heuristic is that a synchronization point will sometimes be forced to wait for the synchronization condition to become true (the instances of the other artifact to reach the desired states) even though the instance might be ready to open the stage based on the state of its life cycle alone.

For each occurrence of a candidate synchronization point, we define a window starting at the point in time when it is known that the activity is ready to be executed, based on the state of the instance, until the point in time when it is known that the activity has started.

Definition 4 (Window). *Let L be an artifact synchronization log with primary artifact Art_i and secondary artifact Art_j. Let $T = e_1 e_2 \ldots e_n$ be a trace in L and event type A is a candidate synchronization point for Art_i. Let e_k be an event instance of A in T with timestamp $\tau(e_k)$. For the event instance e_k, a window w is $w = (\tau(e_m), \tau(e_k))$ with starting point $\tau(e_m)$ and end point $\tau(e_k)$,*

$\tau(e_m) < \tau(e_k)$, $\tau(e_m)$ *is the timestamp of event* e_m *of the primary artifact* Art_i *in* T *and there exists no other event* e *of* Art_i *in* T *for which* $e_m < e < e_k$.

Definition 5 (Window activity level). *The activity level in window* $w = (\tau(e_m), \tau(e_k))$ *of event* e_k *in trace* T *is the number of events of the secondary artifact* Art_j *occurring in the window interval in* T.

Finally, we define the activity level for each event type considered as a candidate synchronization point:

Definition 6 (Activity level). *The activity level* $AL(A)$ *of a candidate synchronization point* A *in a log* L *is the average window activity level for the occurrences of* A *in* L.

Activity levels smaller than δ for a sufficiently small δ indicate that the candidate is most probably not a synchronization point. In the experiments $\delta = 1$ was used. This proved suitable in experiments with two real-life and one synthetic log. If longer delays are expected between the time point when the task is ready to be executed and the actual execution, higher values for δ might be more appropriate. For our example, Meeting Proposal has two synchronization points: ProposalSuccessful and ProposalFailed; Participant has one synchronization point: ReceiveProposal. Event type ProposalFailed, on the other hand, has activity level zero and is not considered to be synchronization points.

We now discuss the proposed method for discovering conditions for a given synchronization point. The general form of the discovered conditions is as follows:

Definition 7 (Synchronization condition). *A synchronization condition* $C(S)$ *of a synchronization point* S *is the disjunction* $\bigvee_{i=1..n} C_i$ *such that* $C_i = \bigwedge_{j=1..m}(a_j \, op \, v_j)$ *where* a_j *is a variable that corresponds to an event type* A_j *in the secondary artifact,* $v_j \in \mathbb{N}$ *and* $op \in \{\leq, >\}$.

An elementary condition $a_j \, op \, v_j$ is interpreted as: the number of instances of the secondary artifact where an event instance of A_j was the most recently executed event needs to be at most/greater than v_j for the stage S to open.

In order to discover such conditions, we represent the relevant data as feature vectors which form one dataset for each candidate synchronization point w.r.t. a specific secondary artifact. Let S be a candidate synchronization point in primary artifact Art_1 w.r.t. secondary artifact Art_2. For each event type A_i in Art_2 we construct an integer feature F_i such that, for a specific execution (event e) of S, $F_i(e) = v$ where v is the number of related instances of Art_2 for which the last occurred event at the time of occurrence of e was of event type A_i. Intuitively, v instances were in state "A_i executed" when activity S was executed. We refer to these features as *synchronization features*. More precisely, for the set of instances $\{I_1, \ldots, I_m\}$ of Art_2 appearing in the same synchronization trace as e:

$$F_k(e) = |\{I_i : \exists e_1 \in I_i, A(e_1) = A_k, e_1 < e \wedge (\forall e_2 \in I_i : e_2 < e_1 \vee e_2 > e)\}|.$$

Applying this approach to the artifact synchronization log for Art_1 w.r.t. Art_2, we generate a set of positive examples in the dataset for S.

Definition 8 (Positive example). *Let S be a synchronization point in artifact Art_i for which we are generating synchronization conditions. Let e be an event of event type S in artifact synchronization log L with main artifact Art_i and secondary artifact Art_j. Let $\{F_1, \ldots, F_n\}$ be the synchronization features where F_k is the feature for event type A_k of Art_j, $1 \leq k \leq n$. The feature vector $(F_1(e), \ldots, F_n(e))$ for event e is called a positive example.*

A positive example for synchronization point ProposalSuccessful from the trace in Fig. 2 is the tuple (ReceiveProposal:0, AnswerREJECT:0, AnswerACCEPT:4, AnswerHOST:2) meaning that no related instances of the secondary artifact were in state ReceiveProposal executed or AnswerREJECT executed, four were in state AnswerACCEPT executed and two in state AnswerHOST executed.

Similarly, a set of negative examples is constructed. The difference is that the features do not correspond to executions S but to executions of any activity of the secondary artifact. Intuitively, these are configurations of the secondary artifact's instances which did not trigger the execution of S.

Definition 9 (Negative example). *Let S be a synchronization point in artifact Art_i for which we are generating synchronization conditions. Let e be an event in artifact Art_j in artifact synchronization log L with main artifact Art_i and secondary artifact Art_j. Let $\{F_1, \ldots, F_n\}$ be the synchronization features where F_k is the feature for event type A_k of Art_j, $1 \leq k \leq n$. The feature vector $(F_1(e), \ldots, F_n(e))$ for event e is called a negative example.*

A negative example for synchronization point ProposalSuccessful from the trace in Fig. 2 is the tuple (ReceiveProposal:1, AnswerREJECT:0, AnswerACCEPT:4, AnswerHOST:1) recorded for the event AnswerHOST for participant 3. This means that at some point in time one instance of the secondary artifact was in state ReceiveProposal executed, none in state AnswerREJECT executed, four in state AnswerACCEPT and one in state AnswerHOST and this configuration did not trigger the execution of ProposalSuccessful.

Definition 10 (Dataset). *Let S be a synchronization point in Art_i w.r.t. Art_j and let L be the synchronization log with primary artifact Art_i and secondary artifact Art_j. The dataset for S in L contains one synchronization feature for each event type of Art_j and consists of the following feature vectors:*

- *For each execution of S in L we construct one positive example.*
- *For each execution of event from Art_j we construct one negative example.*

The resulting data set can be used to generate a classifier [19] that distinguishes between the positive and the negative examples. Since we are looking for an explicit representation of the discovered conditions, a natural choice for a classification algorithms is a decision tree algorithm as the tree can be transformed into rules in a straightforward way. We select the rules predicting a positive result (activity S executed) and the conditions (antecedents) of these rules form the synchronization condition as part of the sentry of the guard for stage S.

For example, the synchronization condition discovered for ProposalSuccessful is: "ReceiveProposal ≤ 0 and AnswerREJECT ≤ 2 and AnswerHOST > 0", which is interpreted as: no instances are in state ReceiveProposal executed, at most 2 instances are in state AnswerREJECT executed and at least one instance is in state AnswerHOST executed.

Using this approach can sometimes result in identical feature vectors being both positive and negative examples. In order to avoid this inconsistency, we remove from the set of negative examples any feature vector that corresponds to an event occurring immediately after an execution of S. These record the same configuration as for the corresponding positive example (the execution of S).

3.2   Confidence Score of Synchronization Conditions

After discovering the condition for every candidate synchronization point, we apply additional analysis in order to assign a confidence score to each of them. We consider three factors as part of the confidence score.

First, we consider the quality of the generated decision tree. The intuition here is that the better the classification given by the tree, the higher the confidence score should be. We use the well-known and often-used F-measure [2] to assess the quality of classification given by the generated decision tree. The F-measure combines the precision and recall of the model, defined as follows. Here tp is the number of true positive examples (the positive examples correctly classified by the model as positive), tn is the number of true negative examples (the positive examples correctly classified by the model as negative), fp is the number of false positive examples (negative examples incorrectly classified by the model as positive and fn is the number of false negative examples (the positive examples incorrectly classified by the model as negative).

Definition 11 (Precision). *The precision $P(M)$ of a classification model M is the percentage of true positive examples out of all examples classified as positive by the model: $P(M) = \text{tp}/(\text{tp} + \text{fp})$.*

Definition 12 (Recall). *The recall $R(M)$ of a classification model M is the percentage of true positive examples out of all positive examples: $R(M) = \text{tp}/(\text{tp} + \text{fn})$.*

Definition 13 (F-measure). *The F-measure $F(M)$ for a classification model M is defined as: $F(M) = 2P(M)R(M)/(P(M) + R(M))$.*

The second factor we consider in the confidence score is the size of the tree which we denote by $S(M)$. The intuition behind it is that the conditions used in practice are simple and a larger tree will most probably be a sign of overfitting the data to discover patterns that are not actually present. A decision tree can be built from any data set even a random one. Such a tree will be large to describe every data point. The tree size factor aims at filtering out such cases.

To include in the confidence score, we measure the number of leaves in the tree and then normalize so that the lowest possible size (i.e. 2 leaves) becomes 1 and the highest observed size among all generated trees becomes 0.

Finally, we also use the previously-defined activity level $A(S)$ in the confidence score which is also normalized so that the lowest observed activity level becomes 0 and the highest observed activity level becomes 1.

Definition 14 (Confidence score). *The overall confidence score $C(S)$ for the conditions discovered for model M generated for candidate synchronization point S is defined as:* $C(S) = (F(M) + S(M) + A(S))/3$.

The confidence score calculated for the discovered synchronization rule for ProposalSuccessful was 0.9866.

Note that the confidence score is an arithmetic average, however a weighted average could be used instead. This latter option pre-supposes however that the user has a reason to weigh one factor higher than others.

4   Validation

All methods presented in this section have been implemented within the ProM framework as part of the Artifact Mining package. For decision tree generation, the WEKA suite [5] was used and, more specifically, WEKA's J48 implementation of the C4.5 algorithm [14]. In our implementation, C4.5 was used with 10-fold cross-validation, no pruning and the minimal number of points in a leaf was set to 1. Similar results were obtained for the minimal number of points set to 2. Higher values can result in stopping the splitting prematurely and higher misclassification rate.

In this section we describe the data used for validation and the results received from applying the implemented tools.

The TBM data describes the application and funding process of a funding programme on applied biomedical research - TBM (Toegepast Biomedisch Onderzoek) managed by the IWT agency in Belgium (Flemish region). The data covers project application receipt, evaluation, reviewing, acceptance or rejection, contract signing and payments processing, for the period 2009–2012.

The data was collected from the funding agency's database in the form of three spreadsheets each describing one part of the process: project proposals, reviews and payments. It includes timestamps of events in the life cycles of proposals, reviews and payments as well as relevant data attributes such as project id, reviewer id, reviewer role, partner id, payment number and so on. The data was transformed into a raw log format containing 1472 events and the whole tool chain of methods presented in [13] and this paper was applied. As expected, we discovered three artifact types: Project (121 instances), Review (777 instances) and Payment (50 instances) (Fig. 3).

The Project artifact instances are identified by the projectID and their life cycles cover the process of proposal submission, initial evaluation for adherence to the formal requirements, if approved, then the final decision is taken (based on the received reviews) and, if accepted, the contract is signed. This includes the following event types: ProjectReceived, ProjectAccepted, ProjectRejected, ProjectDecided, ContractIn, ContractOut.

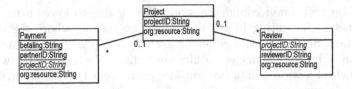

Fig. 3. The discovered ER model for the TBM data.

Primary artifact	Secondary artifact	Synchronization point	Condition	Confidence score
Payment	Project	startApprovalPayment	contractIn > 0	0.97
Reviewer	Project	reviewIN	ProjectAccepted > 0	0.97
Project	Reviewer	ProjectDecided	reviewIN > 4	0.87
Payment	Project	approvalIWA	contractIn > 0	0.64

Fig. 4. The conditions discovered for the TBM data.

The Review artifact instances are identified by attribute pair (projectID, reviewerID) and each instance describes the life cycle of a review for a project proposal by a reviewer. Due to missing data, only one event type belonging to the Review artifact was present in the log - review completion (ReviewIn).

Finally, the Payment artifact instances are identified by the attribute pair (betaling, partnerID) where betaling refers to the number of the payment for this particular project partner. The life cycle includes the event types ApprovalCO, ApprovalWA, SentToBank, StartApprovalPayment, Signing, Payed.

In the model in Fig. 3, the attribute projectID is a foreign key in the Payment and Review entities which establishes the relationship with the Project entity. One project can have multiple reviews and multiple payments. Each review and each payment are for a single project.

Using the raw log and the discovered ER model we generated the artifact synchronization logs - a separate log for each combination of primary and secondary artifact. For each log, we apply the tool for discovering inter-artifact synchronization conditions. Not all logs contain such conditions. For example the log with Project as a primary artifact and Payment as a secondary artifact generates an empty set of synchronization conditions since no activity in the Project artifact is waiting for any activity in the Payment artifact.

Figure 4 shows all synchronization conditions found for the TBM data. The last column gives the number of times the activity was executed in the logs (each execution will generate a positive example in the data set). The features of the data set are equal to the number of event types in the secondary artifact. The first condition says that the approval of payment can only start after the contract has been signed. The second condition says that the review process can only be started after the project has been administratively accepted (i.e. conforms to the formal criteria and is accepted for further evaluation). The third condition says that a final decision on the project can only be taken if at least 5 reviews were completed. The last condition says that an additional approval process for the payment can only be performed if the contract has been signed and is the only condition with lower confidence score. This is due to lower F-measure for the decision tree indicating higher number of exceptions where the condition is not satisfied. Such rules can either be excluded or presented to the user for confirmation. The tool manages to filter out 22 of the candidates which are not real synchronization points (we consider each event type in an artifact as a candidate for a synchronization point w.r.t. each other artifact).

5   Related Work

Process mining [1] methods have been developed in many areas, e.g. process discovery from logs, conformance checking, performance analysis and so on. A number of process discovery methods exist including the heuristics miner [17], the ILP miner [18], etc. Most generate a single flat model, usually a Petri Net and thus cannot represent synchronization based on unbounded number of events as in the case when a process spawns a variable number of subprocesses. A few methods generate hierarchical models (e.g. [4,10,20]) but still do not allow one-to-many relationships between the main process and its subprocess, and thus are not concerned with discovering unbounded synchronization conditions.

In [12] a method was presented for mining artifact-centric models by discovering the life cycles of the separate artifacts and translating them into GSM notation. This method does not consider the question of how artifact instances synchronize their behavior.

The discovery of branching conditions in a single flat model has been addressed in [9,15]. Such conditions determine which branch of the model to choose based on the current values of relevant variables at execution time and are also not applicable for synchronization with unbounded number of processes or sub-processes. The method is based on decision tree mining which is also the approach taken in this paper.

In the area of specification mining, methods exist for mining specifications which carry parameters that are instantiated to concrete values at runtime [8]. Most, however, do not tackle the problem of process synchronization. A method for mining guards for events based on messages received was presented in [7]. It allows to discover some types of guard conditions but is not able to discover conditions of the type: at least n messages of a certain type are received.

To the best of our knowledge, despite the large body of work in the field of process mining, the problem of discovering unbounded synchronization conditions is open and is addressed in this paper.

6   Conclusion and Future Work

The method presented in this paper can be extended in a number of ways. It is possible to consider synchronization with multiple artifacts as well as relative rather than absolute conditions, e.g. "Half of the participants accept the proposal" or "30 % of the reviews are completed". We can also consider the information models of the secondary artifact instances and generate conditions

based also on the data rather than life cycle only, e.g. "At least three participants located in USA and at least one in UK have accepted the invitation and
at least one of them has chosen to be a host".

Another avenue for future work is to adapt and test the proposed method
to discover completion conditions of multi-instance activities in BPMN process
models. Until now, little attention has been given in the field of automated
process discovery to the identification of advanced process modeling constructs
such as multi-instance activities.

Finally, additional testing on real-life event logs would be beneficial in order
to better test the performance of the developed methods and gain insights into
how to tune the δ parameter and how to assign weights for the three components
of the confidence score, which are currently left unweighted.

Acknowledgment. This research is supported by the EU's FP7 Program (ACSI
Project). Thanks to IWT and Pieter De Leenheer for facilitating the logs used in
this research.

References

1. van der Aalst, W.M.P.: Process Mining: Discovery Conformance and Enhancement
   of Business Processes. Springer, Heidelberg (2011)
2. Baeza-Yates, R., Ribeiro-Neto, B.: Modern Information Retrieval. Addison-Wesley,
   Boston (1999)
3. Cohn, D., Hull, R.: Business artifacts: a data-centric approach to modeling business
   operations and processes. IEEE Data Eng. Bull. **32**, 3–9 (2009)
4. Greco, G., Guzzo, A., Pontieri, L.: Mining hierarchies of models: from abstract
   views to concrete specifications. In: van der Aalst, W.M.P., Benatallah, B., Casati,
   F., Curbera, F. (eds.) BPM 2005. LNCS, vol. 3649, pp. 32–47. Springer, Heidelberg
   (2005)
5. Hall, M., Frank, E., Holmes, G., Pfahringer, B., Reutemann, P., Witten, I.: The
   WEKA data mining software: an update. SIGKDD Explor. **11**, 10–18 (2009)
6. Hull, R., et al.: Introducing the guard-stage-milestone approach for specifying business entity lifecycles. In: Bravetti, M. (ed.) WS-FM 2010. LNCS, vol. 6551, pp.
   1–24. Springer, Heidelberg (2011)
7. Kumar, S., Khoo, S., Roychoudhury, A., Lo, D.: Inferring class level specifications
   for distributed systems. In: ICSE 2012, pp. 914–924 (2012)
8. Lee, C., Chen, F, Rosu, G.: Mining parametric specifications. In: ICSE'11, pp.
   591–600. ACM (2011)
9. de Leoni, M., Dumas, M., García-Bañuelos, L.: Discovering branching conditions
   from business process execution logs. In: Cortellessa, V., Varró, D. (eds.) FASE
   2013 (ETAPS 2013). LNCS, vol. 7793, pp. 114–129. Springer, Heidelberg (2013)
10. Li, J., Bose, R.P.J.C., van der Aalst, W.M.P.: Mining context-dependent and inter-
    active business process maps using execution patterns. In: Muehlen, M., Su, J.
    (eds.) BPM 2010 Workshops. LNBIP, vol. 66, pp. 109–121. Springer, Heidelberg
    (2011)
11. Nigam, A., Caswell, N.S.: Business artifacts: an approach to operational specifica-
    tion. IBM Syst. J. **42**(3), 428–445 (2003)

12. Popova, V., Dumas, M.: From Petri Nets to guard-stage-milestone models. In: La Rosa, M., Soffer, P. (eds.) BPM Workshops 2012. LNBIP, vol. 132, pp. 340–351. Springer, Heidelberg (2013)
13. Popova, V., Fahland, D., Dumas, M.: Artifact Lifecycle Discovery (2013). arXiv:1303.2554 [cs.SE]
14. Quinlan, J.: C4.5: Programs for Machine Learning. Morgan Kaufmann, San Francisco (1993)
15. Rozinat, A., van der Aalst, W.M.P.: Decision mining in ProM. In: Dustdar, S., Fiadeiro, J.L., Sheth, A.P. (eds.) BPM 2006. LNCS, vol. 4102, pp. 420–425. Springer, Heidelberg (2006)
16. Verbeek, H., Buijs, J.C., van Dongen, B.F., van der Aalst, W.M.P.: ProM: the process mining toolkit. In: Proceedings of BPM 2010 Demonstration Track, CEUR Workshop Proceedings, vol. 615 (2010)
17. Weijters, A.J.M.M., Ribeiro, J.T.S.: Flexible heuristics miner. In: Proceedings of the IEEE Symposium on Computational Intelligence and Data Mining, pp. 310–317 (2011)
18. van der Werf, J.M.E.M., van Dongen, B.F., Hurkens, C.A.J., Serebrenik, A.: Process discovery using integer linear programming. In: van Hee, K.M., Valk, R. (eds.) PETRI NETS 2008. LNCS, vol. 5062, pp. 368–387. Springer, Heidelberg (2008)
19. Witten, I., Frank, E., Mark, A.: Data Mining: Practical Machine Learning Tools and Techniques, 3rd edn. Elsevier, Burlington (2011)
20. Yzquierdo-Herrera, R., Silverio-Castro, R., Lazo-Cortés, M.: Sub-process discovery: opportunities for process diagnostics. In: Poels, G. (ed.) CONFENIS 2012. LNBIP, vol. 139, pp. 48–57. Springer, Heidelberg (2013)

Uncovering the Relationship Between Event Log Characteristics and Process Discovery Techniques

Seppe K.L.M. vanden Broucke[1]([✉]), Cédric Delvaux[1], João Freitas[1], Taisiia Rogova[1], Jan Vanthienen[1], and Bart Baesens[1,2]

[1] Department of Decision Sciences and Information Management, KU Leuven, Naamsestraat 69, 3000 Leuven, Belgium
[2] School of Management, University of Southampton, Highfield, Southampton SO17 1BJ, UK
seppe.vandenbroucke@kuleuven.be

Abstract. The research field of process mining deals with the extraction of knowledge from event logs. Event logs consist of the recording of activities that took place in a certain business environment and as such, one of process mining's main goals is to get an insight on the execution of business processes. Although a substantial effort has been put on developing techniques which are able to mine event logs accurately, it is still unclear how exactly characteristics of the latter influence a technique's performance. In this paper, we provide a robust methodology of analysis and subsequently derive useful insights on the role of event log characteristics in process discovery tasks by means of an exhaustive comparative study.

Keywords: Process mining · Process discovery · Conformance checking · Benchmarking · Event log characteristics

1 Introduction

The research field of process mining deals with the extraction of knowledge from event logs [1]. One of process mining's main analysis tasks concerns process discovery, which aims to rediscover process models from recorded logs. The field of process discovery and process mining in general has witnessed a tremendous amount of interest from practitioners and researchers alike in recent years, evidenced for example by the large number of process discovery techniques being proposed [1–4].

However, this reality causes a problem for practitioners wanting to use process mining in real-life applications and environments: having so many techniques available, it becomes difficult to choose the most appropriate one for a given situation without possessing a high amount of knowledge about the workings of such techniques. This problem has already been identified in [5,6], where the

N. Lohmann et al. (Eds.): BPM 2013 Workshops, LNBIP 171, pp. 41–53, 2014.
DOI: 10.1007/978-3-319-06257-0_4, © Springer International Publishing Switzerland 2014

creation of benchmarks to compare the performance of different techniques has been labeled as one of the biggest challenges concerning process mining.

To tackle this issue, some authors have proposed frameworks [7] that help to compare the performance of process discovery techniques, whereas others have focused on benchmarking the quality of those algorithms [8]. However, one important aspect to remark is that previous studies focused more on the algorithms themselves together with their general performance, without going into much detail on how they are influenced based on the characteristics of a given event log (the starting point of analysis). In [6], the importance of these characteristics is also mentioned. As such, this paper aims to present a benchmarking study of process discovery techniques which will help to understand the relation between event log characteristics and the performance of a process discovery algorithm and can aid process mining practitioners to make more well-educated choices about the most suitable technique for different scenarios. To do so, an in-depth analysis on the influence that event log characteristics have on the performance of process discovery techniques is presented. In addition, a comparative study between techniques' performances and accuracy in different situations is also carried out.

2   Related Work

The benchmarking of process discovery techniques is a problem that has not been addressed extensively in the literature [6]. This is perhaps partially due to the fact that the research field of process mining is quite young, having seen its bigger boost after the publication of the alpha-algorithm by van der Aalst et al. [1] in 2004. However, the need for such studies is real and motivated by the proliferation of techniques and commercial products that has been occurring recently [5].

The first attempt to come up with a framework that allows to benchmark process discovery techniques was executed by Rozinat et al. [6,9]. These studies aim to reach a "common evaluation framework" which, under the assumption that the log reflects the original behavior, enables the comparison of a discovered model with the event log from which it has been induced by means of conformance analysis. After the groundwork had been set by these publications, other authors utilized similar procedures to construct their frameworks. Weber et al. [10] design a procedure that evaluates the performance of process mining algorithms against a "known grounded truth", referencing to the original process models, with known constructs, that are used to generate the event logs used for the conformance analysis. Although having introduced concrete experiments on artificial process models, which allowed the comparison between the performances of different mining algorithms, only a small number of techniques and models were evaluated (also taking into account a relatively small number of structural properties).

After arguing that the procedure proposed to that date was time consuming and computationally demanding (as this effort is proportional to the number of algorithms and metrics considered), Wang et al. [7,11] suggest a different approach. Their proposed methodology allows for a more scalable method as the evaluation of the algorithms' performance is done on a fraction of the process models of a given company, making it possible to choose the most suitable technique without having to mine all processes available. Finally, De Weerdt et al. [8] include real-life event logs in their study, thus being the first authors to consider such kind of logs. In addition, they propose the "F-score" metric as a valid approach when evaluating the combination of different accuracy dimensions.

3   Methodology

As stated before, the motivation for our study is to understand the effect of the characteristics of event logs on the performance of process discovery techniques, allowing us to pinpoint practical guidelines that helps one making problem-tailored decisions when opting for a process discovery technique.

An experiment was designed comprising of the following phases:

Phase 1 Creation of synthetic process models and generation of event logs.
Phase 2 Mining of generated event logs using broad collection of process discovery techniques.
Phase 3 Evaluation of the quality of the mined models according to the four process model quality dimensions [6], using a collection of published conformance checking metrics.

Before presenting the results of the study, the three phases in the experimental setup are discussed in more detail in the following subsections.

3.1   Phase 1: Synthetic Model Construction and Event Log Generation

Eight process models with increasing complexity levels were designed. The following structural patterns, ordered by complexity, were taken into account: sequence, choice (XOR split/join), parallelism (or: concurrency, AND split/join), loops (repetitions, recurrence), duplicate tasks (activities in the model bearing the same label), non-free choice constructs (i.e. history dependent choices) and finally, nested loops. For each characteristic listed above, a process model was constructed containing this characteristic, together with all characteristics from less complex models, meaning that model eight (shown in Fig. 1), the most complex model designed, contains all listed characteristics.

Artificial event logs were generated using CPNTools[1] based on the eight designed process models with different non-structural characteristics, namely presence of noise (removed events, swapped events and inserted events) and the size of the event log. Table 1 shows an overview of the properties of the generated event logs for each process model.

---

[1] See: http://www.cpntools.org

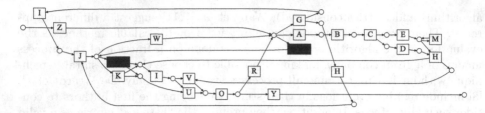

Fig. 1. Eight process models with increasing complexity levels were designed for use in the benchmarking study. The process model shown here is the most complex and contains all included characteristics.

Table 1. For each designed process model, four event logs were generated of different size, with and without noise to represent real-life scenario's.

	Small	Medium	Medium with noise	Large with noise
Number of events:	500	5000	5000	50000
Noise:	No	No	Yes	Yes

3.2 Phase 2: Process Model Discovery

Twelve process discovery techniques are examined: Alpha Miner [1], Alpha Miner+ [12], Alpha Miner++ [13], Heuristics Miner [3], Genetic Miner [4], DT (Duplicate Tasks) Genetic Miner [14], DWS Miner [15], AGNEs Miner [16], the Evolutionary Process Tree Miner [17], Causal Miner [18], ILP Miner [19] and TS (Transition System) Miner [20]. The list of mining algorithms was constructed in such way so that all included process discovery techniques satisfy the following requirements. First, their result should be represented in the form of a Petri net or be transformable into one for the sake of clear and unambiguous comparability. Second, algorithms should be publicly available and implemented in the tools used for research, i.e. ProM 5 and ProM 6 [21], which were applied to mine the models from the constructed event logs.

Concerning configuration options, parameters for each discovery technique were mostly kept to the default options. However, modifications were made for the Heuristics Miner and Causal Miner. More precisely, the option "mine long distance dependencies" was enabled for both, in order to enable to discovery of these constructs. Also, both for Genetic Miner and DT Genetic Miner, the "population size" was set to 10 and 100 for high and small/medium complexity logs respectively, as to keep running time under control. For the Process Tree Miner – another evolutionary algorithm – "population size" was also set to 10 and the "maximum number of generations" to 50.

3.3 Phase 3: Conformance Checking and Statistical Analysis

In the third and final phase of the experimental setup, an exhaustive conformance analysis is performed using a large amount of conformance checking metrics in order to assess the quality of different mined process models in respect with the generated event logs based on four quality dimensions. Next, the results are analyzed and compared using an exhaustive set of statistical tests.

Conformance Checking. Conformance checking techniques demonstrate the representativeness of the discovered process model and the behavior presented in the event log. Conformance is typically measured across the following four quality dimensions [6]:

- Fitness: the discovered model should allow for the behavior seen in the event log;
- Precision: the discovered model should not allow for behavior completely unrelated to what was seen in the event log;
- Generalization: the discovered model should generalize beyond the example behavior seen in the event log;
- Simplicity: the discovered model should be as simple as possible.

An overview of conformance checking metrics included in this study for each quality dimension is provided in Table 2. The CoBeFra conformance checking benchmarking suite was applied in order to facilitate the execution of the conformance checking phase in our study [22]. It is important to note that virtually all metric included in the study return a result in the range of [0, 1]. Most simplicity metrics, however, except for Advanced Structural Appropriateness, return an absolute value, indicating for instance a count. Therefore, we normalize these values before performing the statistical analysis so that 0 corresponds with the minimum (lowest) score obtained and 1 with the maximum (highest score).

Statistical Analysis. After conformance analysis is performed between all mined models and event logs, a set of statistical techniques is applied to evaluate the results, enabling a robust and mathematical rigorous way of comparing the performance of different process discovery techniques (both in general and taking into account specific event log characteristics).

In a first step, a one-way repeated measures ANOVA (Analysis of Variance) test is executed, which is used to analyze the differences between the metrics results for each quality dimension, that is, to assess whether the different metrics "agree" on their result.

Next, a regression analysis is performed to discover the relation between structural process model and event log properties and the performance of process discovery techniques, this for each discovery technique in each quality dimension, so that we can uncover main "driving factors" behind each process discovery technique. Depending on the results of the previous ANOVA test, different response variables are used in the regression test: if the null hypothesis was accepted (no difference in means of metric results), the average of all metrics for one dimension was used as the independent variable (with the different characteristics of logs and models as dependent variables). If the null hypothesis was rejected, the independent variable is based on the result of a carefully selected

Table 2. Overview of conformance checking metrics included in the experimental setup.

Name	Authors	Quality dimension
Fitness	Rozinat et al. [23]	Fitness
Proper Completion	Rozinat et al. [23]	
Alignment Based Fitness	Adriansyah et al. [24]	
Behavioral Profile Conformance	Weidlich et al. [25]	
Behavioral Recall	Goedertier et al. [16, 26]	
Advanced Behavioral Appropriateness	Rozinat et al. [23]	Precision
ETC Precision	Muñoz-Gama et al. [27]	
Alignment Based Precision	Adriansyah et al. [28]	
One Align Precision	Adriansyah et al. [29]	
Best Align Precision	Adriansyah et al. [29]	
Behavioral Precision	De Weerdt et al. [30]	
Alignment Based Probabilistic Generalization	Adriansyah et al. [28]	Generalization
Advanced Structural Appropriateness	Rozinat et al. [23]	Simplicity
Average Node Arc Degree	Sánchez-González et al. [31]	
Count of Arcs	Sánchez-González et al. [31]	
Count of Cut Vertices	Sánchez-González et al. [31]	
Count of Nodes	Sánchez-González et al. [31]	
Count of Places	Sánchez-González et al. [31]	
Count of Transitions	Sánchez-González et al. [31]	
Weighted P/T Average Arc Degree	Sánchez-González et al. [31]	

metric (or metrics) for the four quality dimensions, as it would be unfeasible to incorporate all metrics together with each discovery technique.

Finally, a third test aims to compare the performance of different process discovery techniques in a robust manner. We apply a non-parametric statistical approach towards the comparison of process discovery techniques as outlined in [8,32], encompassing the execution of a non-parametric Friedman test followed by an appropriate post hoc test. These non parametric tests assume ranked performances rather than actual performance estimates, calculating the average ranks per treatment, under the null hypothesis of no significant differences between treatments, i.e. process discovery algorithms. If the null hypothesis of equal performance across all treatments is rejected by the Friedman test, we proceed with a post hoc Bonferroni-Dunn procedure, comparing one treatment (the control treatment) to all others. This test thus compares the different process discovery techniques to the best performing one and assesses whether or not the performances are similar.

4   Results

In this section the results derived from the different analysis that were performed are presented and dissected in order to come up with two major contributions: first, an understanding of the correlation between event log characteristics and technique's performance and second: a comparative performance assessment of available process discovery techniques.

4.1   Statistical Results

First, the results of the included statistical tests are provided. This allows both to address the major goals of this research and to check the significance analysis of the results. A ranking of process discovery techniques according to their conformance performance will be presented, followed by an analysis of run time performance. Finally, the outcome of this benchmarking study is exposed as a set of practical guidelines that are listed at the end of this section.

Comparing Conformance Checking Metric Result Similarity: ANOVA. The first statistical test performed was a one-way repeated measures ANOVA (analysis of variance) test, with the goal of evaluating if the different metrics within the same dimension provide similar results. The null hypothesis is that averages of all metrics (within one dimension) are equal, i.e. meaning that the metrics within this quality dimension "agree" with one another. This hypothesis was rejected for all dimensions; all p-values were below a significance level of 0.05. A Mauchly test for sphericity [33] was performed followed by Greenhouse-Geisser [34] and Huynh-Feldt [35] corrections to obtain valid F-ratios.

Driving Factors Behind Process Discovery Algorithms: Regression. A linear regression analysis was performed to find the correlation between conformance checking metrics (dependent variable) and characteristics of both event logs and models (independent variables) for each of the four quality dimensions and for every process discovery technique. As the previous test showed that there was a significant variation between results from different metrics, we decide on conformance checking metrics for each of the four quality dimensions to configure the dependent variable. This decision was driven by the following criteria: first, the conformance metric should not result in too many missing values, indicating errors during execution or exceeding a run time limit of 24 hours. Second, the metric should not always result in very high or low values. Third, metrics which are described in more recent literature are preferred above earlier approaches. Based on these criteria, the following metrics were chosen to represent each quality dimension:

- Fitness: *Alignment Based Fitness* (symbol used: F^a, Adriansyah et al. [24]) and *Behavioral Recall* (symbol used: F^b, Goedertier et al. [16,26])
- Precision: *One Align Precision* (symbol used: P^a, Adriansyah et al. [29]) and *Behavioral Precision* (symbol used: P^b, De Weerdt et al. [30])
- Generalization: *Alignment Based Probabilistic Generalization* (symbol used: G^a, Adriansyah et al. [28])
- Simplicity: *Weighted P/T Average Arc Degree* (symbol used: S, Sánchez-González et al. [31])

The results show that the values obtained by the conformance checking metrics are indeed correlated with several event log characteristics. Table 3 provides a summarized overview of the driving characteristics for all process discovery algorithms for the four quality dimensions.

Table 3. Results of regression analysis, indicating the manner by which the different process discovery techniques are influenced by event log and process model characteristics.

Characteristic	Alpha Miner	Alpha Miner+	Alpha Miner++	Heuristics M.	Genetic Miner	DT Genetic M.	DWS Miner	AGNEs Miner	TS Miner	ILP Miner	Causal Miner	Process Tree M.
Choice:	$S\downarrow$	$P^b\downarrow$ $S\downarrow$	$F^b\uparrow$ $P^b\uparrow$	$P^b\downarrow$	$F^a\downarrow$ $P^a\downarrow$	$F^a\uparrow$ $P^b\downarrow$ $G\uparrow$	$F^a\downarrow$ $F^b\uparrow$		$P^a\uparrow$ $S\downarrow$	$F^a\uparrow$ $P^a\uparrow$ $G\uparrow$		
Parallelism:		$P^b\downarrow$	$P^b\uparrow$	$P^b\uparrow$			$F^b\uparrow$					
Loop:	$F^a\downarrow F^b\downarrow$ $P^b\downarrow$ $S\uparrow$	$F^b\downarrow$ $S\uparrow$	$F^a\downarrow F^b\downarrow$ $P^a\downarrow P^b\downarrow$ $G\downarrow$ $S\uparrow$	$S\uparrow$	$F^a\uparrow$ $P^a\uparrow$	$F^b\uparrow$	$F^a\uparrow$ $P^b\downarrow$ $S\uparrow$	$S\uparrow$	$F^a\downarrow F^b\downarrow$ $P^a\uparrow P^b\uparrow$ $S\downarrow$	$F^a\downarrow$ $P^a\downarrow P^b\downarrow$ $G\downarrow$		$S\uparrow$
Invisible tasks:												
Duplicate tasks:				$F^a\downarrow$ $P^a\downarrow$		$F^a\uparrow F^b\uparrow$ $P^a\uparrow P^b\uparrow$ $G\downarrow$	$F^a\downarrow$ $P^a\downarrow$	$P^b\downarrow$	$F^a\uparrow F^b\uparrow$ $P^b\downarrow$ $S\downarrow$	$F^a\downarrow$ $G\downarrow$		
Non-free choice:	$P^a\downarrow P^b\downarrow$ $G\downarrow$ $S\uparrow$	$P^b\uparrow$ $F^b\uparrow$		$F^a\downarrow F^b\uparrow$ $P^a\uparrow$	$F^a\uparrow$ $S\uparrow$		$F^a\uparrow F^b\uparrow$ $P^b\downarrow$ $S\uparrow$	$F^b\downarrow$ $P^b\downarrow$	$P^a\downarrow P^b\downarrow$ $S\uparrow$	$F^b\downarrow$ $P^a\downarrow$ $G\downarrow$	$F^a\downarrow F^b\downarrow$ $P^b\downarrow$ $S\uparrow$	$S\uparrow$
Nested loop:	$F^a\downarrow F^b\downarrow$ $P^a\uparrow$ $S\uparrow$	$F^b\downarrow$ $S\uparrow$	$F^b\downarrow$ $P^b\downarrow$ $S\uparrow$	$F^a\downarrow$			$F^a\uparrow F^b\uparrow$ $P^b\downarrow$ $S\uparrow$	$F^b\downarrow$ $S\uparrow$	$P^b\downarrow$ $S\uparrow$	$F^a\downarrow$ $P^a\downarrow$ $G\downarrow$	$S\uparrow$	
Number of traces:					$F^a\uparrow$ $P^b\downarrow$	$F^a\uparrow$ $G\uparrow$ $P^a\uparrow$ $S\downarrow$		$F^b\uparrow$				$S\uparrow$
Number of distinct traces:		$P^a\uparrow$			$F^a\uparrow$		$F^a\uparrow F^b\downarrow P^b\downarrow$ $P^b\downarrow$	$P^a\uparrow$ $S\uparrow$	$F^a\uparrow$	$G\uparrow$ $S\uparrow$	$F^a\uparrow$	
Number of events:			$P^b\uparrow$		$F^a\uparrow$ $P^a\downarrow$	$F^a\downarrow F^b\uparrow$ $G\uparrow$ $S\uparrow$	$F^b\uparrow$ $P^a\uparrow$					$S\uparrow$
Minimum trace length:	$F^a\downarrow$ $P^a\uparrow$ $S\uparrow$	$F^b\downarrow$ $P^b\downarrow$ $S\uparrow$	$F^b\downarrow$ $P^b\downarrow$ $S\uparrow$		$F^a\uparrow$ $P^a\downarrow$	$F^a\uparrow F^b\downarrow$ $G\uparrow$	$F^a\uparrow F^b\downarrow$ $P^a\downarrow P^b\downarrow$ $S\uparrow$	$F^b\downarrow$	$F^a\downarrow F^b\downarrow$ $P^a\uparrow P^b\downarrow$ $S\uparrow$	$F^a\downarrow$ $P^a\downarrow$ $G\downarrow$ $S\uparrow$	$F^a\uparrow$	
Average trace length:	$F^a\uparrow F^b\uparrow$ $P^a\downarrow$ $S\downarrow$	$F^b\uparrow$ $P^b\downarrow$ $S\downarrow$	$F^b\uparrow$ $P^b\uparrow$ $S\downarrow$	$F^a\downarrow$	$P^a\downarrow$		$F^a\downarrow F^b\uparrow$ $P^b\uparrow$ $S\downarrow$	$F^b\uparrow$		$F^a\uparrow$ $P^a\uparrow$ $G\uparrow$ $S\downarrow$	$F^a\downarrow$	
Maximum trace length:	$F^b\uparrow$ $S\downarrow$	$F^b\uparrow$ $S\downarrow$	$F^b\uparrow$ $S\downarrow$	$F^b\downarrow$		$F^b\downarrow$			$S\downarrow$	$S\uparrow$	$S\downarrow$	
Noise:	$S\uparrow$	$F^b\downarrow$ $P^b\downarrow$	$S\uparrow$	$F^b\downarrow$ $P^b\downarrow$ $S\uparrow$	$F^a\uparrow$		$P^a\downarrow$ $S\uparrow$			$P^b\downarrow$ $S\uparrow$		
Number of activities:	$F^a\downarrow F^b\downarrow$ $P^a\uparrow$ $S\uparrow$	$F^b\downarrow$ $P^b\downarrow$ $S\uparrow$	$F^b\downarrow$ $P^b\downarrow$ $S\uparrow$	$F^a\downarrow$ $P^b\downarrow$ $S\uparrow$	$P^a\uparrow$	$G\downarrow$	$F^a\downarrow F^b\downarrow$ $P^a\downarrow P^b\downarrow$ $S\uparrow$	$F^a\uparrow F^b\downarrow$ $P^b\downarrow$ $S\uparrow$	$F^b\downarrow$ $S\uparrow$	$F^a\downarrow$ $P^a\downarrow$ $G\downarrow$ $S\uparrow$	$F^a\uparrow$ $S\uparrow$	$S\uparrow$

Comparative Performance Analysis of Process Discovery Algorithms: Friedman and Bonferroni-Dunn. A Friedman test is applied in order to determine whether there is a significant difference in the performance of the discovery techniques, based on the ranking of their quality results, using the same conformance checking metric for each quality dimension as for the regression analysis. The results show that techniques do not perform equivalently (null hypothesis rejected), this for all four quality dimensions (using a 95 % confidence level and using the conformance checking values obtained by the metrics selected in Subsect. 4.1 to establish the rankings). We thus perform post hoc Bonferroni-Dunn tests for all quality dimensions.

Table 4 depicts an overview of the obtained results. For each quality dimension, the average rank for each process discovery technique is depicted (a higher rank indicates better performance), with the best performing technique shown in bold and underlined. Techniques which do not differ significantly at the 95 % confidence level from the best performing technique are shown in bold. From this table, a tradeoff between fitness/generalization on the one hand and simplicity/precision on the other hand becomes apparent for many discovery techniques. These results point to the difficulty of having process discovery techniques which perform well for all four quality dimensions [36]. In addition, observe the differences between the rankings obtained by different conformance checking metrics within the same quality dimension. This again points to the fact that metrics do not necessary agree on the way they perform their quality assessment. As such, many opportunities for improvement and further research remain in this area.

Evaluation of Run Time. Although not explicitly included in this study, for many real-life applications, the time required to perform a discovery procedure is a critical issue. Motivated by this fact, the run time for each algorithm was recorded. Although the running time was not included in a statistical test as is, the average speed of each discovery technique was taken into account to formulate the practical guidelines below.

4.2 Recommendations Towards Choosing a Process Discovery Technique

Taking into consideration both general performance results (from the Friedman and Bonferroni-Dunn tests), the influence of event log and process model based characteristics (from the regression analysis) and timing issues, general recommendations for choosing an appropriate process discovery technique are formulated.

After considering all quality dimensions from an overall perspective, the following process discovery techniques are recommended. First, Heuristics Miner, which offers fast run time with acceptable quality results. Next, DWS Miner, which was found to be somewhat slower but also offers good quality results. Third, ILP Miner offers high quality levels but comes with very high run times and memory requirements as event logs become more complex. Finally, AGNEsMiner also presents a slower run time for large models, but is also able to reach good quality levels.

Naturally, it is possible to fine tune the selection of a discovery algorithm in case the quality dimension of interest (or quality priorities) are known beforehand, this even more so when the conformance checking metric which will be applied is known to the end user as well. Since we do not assume such prior knowledge, we limit our recommendations to a general listing only. Similarly,

Table 4. Bonferonni-Dunn rankings for process discovery techniques. For each quality dimension, the average rank for each process discovery technique is depicted (1 being the lowest rank). Techniques which do not differ significantly at the 95 % confidence level from the best performing technique (bold and underlined) are shown in bold.

Fitness *Alignment Based Fitness*	*Behavioral Recall*	Generalization *Alignment Based Pr Generalization*
ILP Miner (9.75)	**ILP Miner (11.11)**	**AGNEs Miner (9.36)**
AGNEs Miner (9.64)	**Heuristics Miner (9.61)**	**ILP Miner (9.34)**
Causal Miner (9.31)	**Alpha Miner+ (9.45)**	**TS Miner (8.53)**
DWS Miner (8.72)	**AGNEs Miner (8.89)**	**Heuristics Miner (8.42)**
Heuristics Miner (8.59)	**DWS Miner (8.77)**	**DWS Miner (8.28)**
TS Miner (8.48)	TS Miner (6.69)	**Causal Miner (7.95)**
Region Miner (6.80)	Genetics Miner (6.56)	**Alpha Miner (7.22)**
Process Tree Miner (6.34)	Alpha Miner (6.28)	**Process Tree Miner (7.06)**
Alpha Miner (6.30)	Alpha Miner++ (6.17)	Alpha Miner++ (6.28)
Genetics Miner (5.77)	Causal Miner (5.28)	Genetics Miner (6.00)
Alpha Miner++ (5.11)	DT Genetics Miner (4.77)	Region Miner (5.83)
DT Genetics Miner (4.83)	Region Miner (4.08)	DT Genetics Miner (4.80)
Alpha Miner+ (1.36)	Process Tree Miner (3.34)	Alpha Miner+ (1.92)
Simplicity *Weighted P/T Average Arc Degree*	*One Align Precision*	Precision *Behavioral Precision*
Alpha Miner+ (11.07)	**AGNEs Miner (10.34)**	**DWS Miner (10.09)**
DT Genetics Miner (8.52)	**DWS Miner (9.20)**	**AGNEs Miner (9.38)**
AGNEs Miner (7.12)	**Alpha Miner (8.75)**	**Causal Miner (8.97)**
Causal Miner (6.93)	**ILP Miner (8.67)**	**Alpha Miner (8.78)**
DWS Miner (6.72)	**Heuristics Miner (8.61)**	**Heuristics Miner (8.44)**
ILP Miner (6.72)	**Causal Miner (7.83)**	**ILP Miner (8.27)**
Alpha Miner++ (5.43)	**TS Miner (7.78)**	Alpha Miner++ (7.45)
Region Miner (5.26)	Alpha Miner++ (7.48)	TS Miner (7.11)
Heuristics Miner (5.24)	Region Miner (6.20)	Genetics Miner (6.30)
Alpha Miner (4.79)	Genetics Miner (5.52)	Process Tree Miner (5.14)
Genetics Miner (4.41)	Process Tree Miner (5.09)	Region Miner (4.11)
Process Tree Miner (4.09)	DT Genetics Miner (4.33)	DT Genetics Miner (4.09)
TS Miner (3.59)	Alpha Miner+ (1.19)	Alpha Miner+ (2.88)

if the characteristics of the event logs are known beforehand, it also useful to identify which techniques are best able to handle these properties, based on the results shown in Table 4.

5   Conclusion and Future Work

This paper outlines a benchmarking study of process discovery techniques in which event log characteristics are considered as determining factors of a technique's performance. A large set of mining algorithms and conformance checking metrics was included and a robust statistical framework was utilized in order to reach a set of general guidelines towards choosing a process discovery technique.

Some suggestions remain towards future work. First, the included process discovery techniques were selected based on their capacity of producing Petri nets or other representations that can be transformed into Petri nets. These kinds of structures are considered as the most appropriate for benchmarking studies, since the majority of process discovery techniques is able to fulfill this condition. Also, most conformance checking metrics are tailored for a Petri net representation. Nevertheless, a valid suggestion for future work encompasses the inclusion of non-Petri net based algorithms. Second, as the scope of this benchmarking study was placed on the quality performance of various miners as driven by various event log characteristics, less emphasis was put on the scalability of included discovery techniques, so that their run times were only considered during the formulation of general recommendations. A follow-up study can thus include this "quality perspective" as well, requiring, however, an experimental setup containing sufficient repeated experiments (for each miner on each event log) to reach stable average timing results. Finally, the possibility exists to include real-life logs in the experimental set, although it is remarked that the value of doing so will be limited based on the availability of designed, underlying process models. If no reference model can be provided for a real-life event log, the list of included characteristics will be limited to non-structural event log characteristics only, without being able to incorporate structural, process model based properties.

Acknowledgment. We would like to thank the KU Leuven research council for financial support under grand OT/10/010 and the Flemish Research Council for financial support under Odysseus grant B.0915.09.

References

1. van der Aalst, W.M.P., Weijters, T., Maruster, L.: Workflow mining: discovering process models from event logs. IEEE Trans. Knowl. Data Eng. **16**(9), 1128–1142 (2004)
2. Günther, C.W., van der Aalst, W.M.P.: Fuzzy mining – adaptive process simplification based on multi-perspective metrics. In: Alonso, G., Dadam, P., Rosemann, M. (eds.) BPM 2007. LNCS, vol. 4714, pp. 328–343. Springer, Heidelberg (2007)
3. Weijters, A.J.M.M., Ribeiro, J.T.S.: Flexible heuristics miner (fhm). In: [37], pp. 310–317
4. de Medeiros, A.K.A., Weijters, A.J.M.M., van der Aalst, W.M.P.: Genetic process mining: an experimental evaluation. Data Min. Knowl. Discov. **14**(2), 245–304 (2007)
5. van der Aalst, W.M.P., et al.: Process mining manifesto. In: Daniel, F., Barkaoui, K., Dustdar, S. (eds.) BPM Workshops 2011, Part I. LNBIP, vol. 99, pp. 169–194. Springer, Heidelberg (2012)
6. Rozinat, A., de Medeiros, A.K.A, Günther, C.W., Weijters, A.J.M.M.T., van der Aalst, W.M.P.: The need for a process mining evaluation framework in research and practice. In: ter Hofstede, A.H.M., Benatallah, B., Paik, H.-Y., et al. (eds.) BPM Workshops 2007. LNCS, vol. 4928, pp. 84–89. Springer, Heidelberg (2008)
7. Wang, J., Wong, R.K., Ding, J., Guo, Q., Wen, L.: On recommendation of process mining algorithms. In Goble, C.A., Chen, P.P., Zhang, J. (eds.) ICWS, pp. 311–318. IEEE (2012)

8. Weerdt, J.D., Backer, M.D., Vanthienen, J., Baesens, B.: A multi-dimensional quality assessment of state-of-the-art process discovery algorithms using real-life event logs. Inf. Syst. **37**(7), 654–676 (2012)
9. Rozinat, A., Alves De Medeiros, A.K., Günther, C.W., Weijters, A.J.M.M., van der Aalst, W.M.P.: Towards an evaluation framework for process mining algorithms. BETA working paper series 224, Eindhoven University of Technology (2007)
10. Weber, P., Bordbar, B., Tino, P., Majeed, B.: A framework for comparing process mining algorithms. In: 2011 IEEE GCC Conference and Exhibition (GCC), pp. 625–628 (2011)
11. Wang, J., Wong, R., Ding, J., Guo, Q., Wen, L.: Efficient selection of process mining algorithms. IEEE Trans. Serv. Comput. **PP**(99), 1 (2012)
12. Alves de Medeiros, A.K., van Dongen, B.F., van der Aalst, W.M.P., Weijters, A.J.M.M.: Process mining: extending the alpha-algorithm to mine short loops. BETA working paper series 113, TU Eindhoven (2004)
13. Wen, L., van der Aalst, W.M.P., Wang, J., Sun, J.: Mining process models with non-free-choice constructs. Data Min. Knowl. Disc. **15**(2), 145–180 (2007)
14. Alves de Medeiros, A.K.: Genetic Process Mining. Ph.D. thesis, TU Eindhoven (2006)
15. Greco, G., Guzzo, A., Pontieri, L., Saccà, D.: Discovering expressive process models by clustering log traces. IEEE Trans. Knowl. Data Eng. **18**(8), 1010–1027 (2006)
16. Goedertier, S., Martens, D., Vanthienen, J., Baesens, B.: Robust process discovery with artificial negative events. J. Mach. Learn. Res. **10**, 1305–1340 (2009)
17. Buijs, J.C.A.M., van Dongen, B.F., van der Aalst, W.M.P.: A genetic algorithm for discovering process trees. In: 2012 IEEE Congress on Evolutionary Computation (CEC), pp. 1–8, June 2012
18. van der Aalst, W., Adriansyah, A., van Dongen, B.: Causal nets: a modeling language tailored towards process discovery. In: Katoen, J.-P., König, B. (eds.) CONCUR 2011. LNCS, vol. 6901, pp. 28–42. Springer, Heidelberg (2011)
19. van der Werf, J.M.E.M., van Dongen, B.F., Hurkens, C.A.J., Serebrenik, A.: Process discovery using integer linear programming. Fundam. Inform. **94**(3–4), 387–412 (2009)
20. van der Aalst, W.M.P., Rubin, V., Verbeek, H.M.W., van Dongen, B.F., Kindler, E., Günther, C.W.: Process mining: a two-step approach to balance between underfitting and overfitting. Softw. Syst. Model. **9**(1), 87–111 (2010)
21. van der Aalst, W.M.P., van Dongen, B.F., Günther, C.W., Rozinat, A., Verbeek, E., Weijters, T.: Prom: the process mining toolkit. In: de Medeiros, A.K.A., Weber, B. (eds.) BPM (Demos). CEUR Workshop Proceedings, vol. 489. CEUR-WS.org (2009)
22. vanden Broucke, S., Weerdt, J.D., Baesens, B., Vanthienen, J.: A comprehensive benchmarking framework (cobefra) for conformance analysis between procedural process models and event logs in prom. In: IEEE Symposium on Computational Intelligence and Data Mining, Grand Copthorne Hotel, Singapore. IEEE (2013)
23. Rozinat, A., van der Aalst, W.M.P.: Conformance checking of processes based on monitoring real behavior. Inf. Syst. **33**(1), 64–95 (2008)
24. Adriansyah, A., Sidorova, N., van Dongen, B.F.: Cost-based fitness in conformance checking. In Caillaud, B., Carmona, J., Hiraishi, K. (eds.) ACSD, pp. 57–66. IEEE (2011)
25. Weidlich, M., Polyvyanyy, A., Desai, N., Mendling, J.: Process compliance measurement based on behavioural profiles. In: Pernici, B. (ed.) CAiSE 2010. LNCS, vol. 6051, pp. 499–514. Springer, Heidelberg (2010)

26. vanden Broucke, S.K.L.M., De Weerdt, J., Baesens, B., Vanthienen, J.: Improved artificial negative event generation to enhance process event logs. In: Ralyté, J., Franch, X., Brinkkemper, S., Wrycza, S. (eds.) CAiSE 2012. LNCS, vol. 7328, pp. 254–269. Springer, Heidelberg (2012)

27. Muñoz-Gama, J., Carmona, J.: A fresh look at precision in process conformance. In: Hull, R., Mendling, J., Tai, S. (eds.) BPM 2010. LNCS, vol. 6336, pp. 211–226. Springer, Heidelberg (2010)

28. van der Aalst, W.M.P., Adriansyah, A., van Dongen, B.F.: Replaying history on process models for conformance checking and performance analysis. Wiley Interdisc. Rew: Data Min. Knowl. Disc. **2**(2), 182–192 (2012)

29. Adriansyah, A., Munoz-Gama, J., Carmona, J., van Dongen, B.F., van der Aalst, W.M.P.: Alignment based precision checking. In: La Rosa, M., Soffer, P. (eds.) BPM Workshops 2012. LNBIP, vol. 132, pp. 137–149. Springer, Heidelberg (2013)

30. Weerdt, J.D., Backer, M.D., Vanthienen, J., Baesens, B.: A robust f-measure for evaluating discovered process models. In: [37], pp. 148–155

31. Sánchez-González, L., García, F., Mendling, J., Ruiz, F., Piattini, M.: Prediction of business process model quality based on structural metrics. In: Parsons, J., Saeki, M., Shoval, P., Woo, C., Wand, Y. (eds.) ER 2010. LNCS, vol. 6412, pp. 458–463. Springer, Heidelberg (2010)

32. Demsar, J.: Statistical comparisons of classifiers over multiple data sets. J. Mach. Learn. Res. **7**, 1–30 (2006)

33. Mauchly, J.W.: Significance test for sphericity of a normal n-variate distribution. Ann. Math. Stat. **11**(2), 204–209 (1940)

34. Greenhouse, S.W., Geisser, S.: On methods in the analysis of profile data. Psychometrika **24**(2), 95–112 (1959)

35. Huynh, H., Feldt, L.S.: Estimation of the box correction for degrees of freedom from sample data in randomized block and split-plot designs. J. Educ. Stat. **1**(1), 69–82 (1976)

36. Buijs, J.C.A.M., van Dongen, B.F., van der Aalst, W.M.P.: On the role of fitness, precision, generalization and simplicity in process discovery. In: Meersman, R., Panetto, H., Dillon, T., Rinderle-Ma, S., Dadam, P., Zhou, X., Pearson, S., Ferscha, A., Bergamaschi, S., Cruz, I.F. (eds.) OTM 2012, Part I. LNCS, vol. 7565, pp. 305–322. Springer, Heidelberg (2012)

37. Proceedings of the IEEE Symposium on Computational Intelligence and Data Mining, CIDM 2011, part of the IEEE Symposium Series on Computational Intelligence 2011, April 11–15, 2011, Paris, France. IEEE (2011)

Process Remaining Time Prediction
Using Query Catalogs

Alfredo Bolt[1]([⊠]) and Marcos Sepúlveda[2]

[1] School of Engineering, Universidad Finis Terrae,
Pedro de Valdivia 1509 Santiago, Chile
abolti@uft.edu
[2] Computer Science Department, School of Engineering,
Pontificia Universidad Católica de Chile,
Vicuña Mackenna 4860 Santiago, Chile
marcos@ing.puc.cl

Abstract. A relevant topic in business process management is the ability to predict the outcome of a process in order to establish *a priori* recommendations about how to go forward from a certain point in the process. Recommendations are made based on different predictions, like the process remaining time or the process cost. Predicting remaining time is an issue that has been addressed by few authors, whose approaches have limitations inherent to their designs. This article presents a novel approach for predicting process remaining time based on query catalogs that store the information of process events in the form of partial trace tails, which are then used to estimate the remaining time of new executions of the process, ensuring greater accuracy, flexibility and dynamism that the best methods currently available. This was tested in both simulated and real process event logs. The methods defined in this article may be incorporated into recommendation systems to give a better estimation of process remaining time, allowing them to dynamically learn with each new trace passing through the system.

Keywords: Process mining · Process remaining time prediction · Query catalogs

1 Introduction

When dealing with service processes, a commonly asked question is: when will this case finish? Most companies give their customers general answers, such as "this process usually takes between 3 or 4 weeks". Unfortunately, in many cases this answer is not sufficient for the customers, as it is just an average cycle time plus an expected variation. It is simple, but it lacks precision and it does not consider the activities that have already been executed to give a more accurate prediction. In this article, we present a novel approach to make remaining time predictions, with a better precision than previous approaches and the ability to adjust the remaining time predictions based on new information about the process execution that is being stored by the information systems that support the process.

N. Lohmann et al. (Eds.): BPM 2013 Workshops, LNBIP 171, pp. 54–65, 2014.
DOI: 10.1007/978-3-319-06257-0_5, © Springer International Publishing Switzerland 2014

During the last decades, information systems have been enabling organizations to improve and change their processes. Today, process-aware information systems (PAIS) [1] are able to store data of daily process operations. This information is stored as process events in an event log. When an organization has a PAIS, in most cases the information stored in these event logs is never used. In some cases, supported by specific vendors, the information is used to obtain general process information, such as some business metrics. In a few cases, non-trivial information is extracted using process mining techniques. The extracted information sometimes can be very useful for analyzing and understanding the structure and behavior of a process.

Process mining covers a wide range of techniques, from process discovery to making predictions and recommendations, many of them with a lot of applications [2]. To build recommendation services such as [3], certain predictions must be made to suggest the way forward.

The remaining time of a process instance is an important prediction for any recommendation system. Another valuable use of this prediction is to relate it to a business rule, in order to provide important information for decision making or to modify a process behavior. The approach presented in this article focuses on making process remaining time predictions using query catalogs, overcoming the inherent limitations of other approaches, such as the annotated transition system used in [4] and the regression model used in [5], providing accurate estimates using a flexible and dynamic structure.

2 Related Work

Several works have addressed the task of predicting remaining time, however most were not designed to deal with the complexities of real business processes, but were oriented to more limited contexts and focuses, For example [6] focuses in on predicting cycle times in a semiconductor factory using data mining techniques. However, there are two generic approaches that were designed to predict the remaining time of any process instances: one using annotated transition systems [4] and the other using non-linear regressions [5]. Both methods outperformed simple heuristics (like the difference between the elapsed time of a process instance and its average cycle time) on the accuracy of their results, but both have limitations inherent to their design in terms of its flexibility, dynamism and ability to analyze unstructured processes.

The advantage of using annotated transitions systems [4] is that they simplify the calculation logic, and they achieve a good accuracy. The disadvantage is that the optimal selection of parameters (comparison types and horizon) cannot be known a priori, so it is bound to constant trial and error. In addition, to incorporate new knowledge into the system, e.g., a trace with an event that has never happened before.

The advantage of using non-linear regression models [5] is that it is abstracted from a process structure, and use historical data to predict the remaining time with relatively good accuracy. This allows introducing the concepts of flexibility and dynamism in the calculation models, which had not been addressed yet. However, the disadvantage of this approach is the same as [4] mentioned above.

3 Proposal

This article presents an approach that incorporates useful elements from annotated transitions systems [4] and creates a collection of annotated "partial trace tails" (described in Sect. 4.4) named Query Catalogs.

For this purpose, query catalogs will be created considering all possible combinations of events for all traces of an event log. This schema allows reducing the amount of processing capacity used when calculating remaining time, but it requires more memory usage.

4 Definitions

4.1 Event

An event is an action stored in a log, for example, start, completion or cancelation of an activity for a particular process instance. An event can be described by various attributes, but for the purposes of this article, we need only three, which must be present to properly use the methods proposed.

Let E be an event log and e an event. We define trace_id(e) as the identifier of the trace associated with the event e, act_name(e) the name of the activity associated with the event e, timestamp(e) the timestamp of event e, and remtime(e) the remaining time after the event e. Then, notice that an event log E is a sequence of events sorted in ascending order by their timestamp attribute.

4.2 Trace

A trace can be described through a sequence of n events T_n, with n > 0 which contains all the n events that have the same trace_id(e), sorted in ascending order by their timestamp(e) attribute. Notice that there cannot be two or more traces with the same trace_id(e).

For all the events e of the trace T, the remaining time remtime(e) can be calculated as: $remtime(e_i) = timestamp(e_n) - timestamp(e_i)$.

4.3 Partial Trace

A partial trace PT_m is a sequence that contains the first m elements of a trace T_n, where m is the length of the partial trace and $m \leq n$ and m > 0.

4.4 Partial Trace Tail

A partial trace tail PTT_h is a sequence that contains the last h elements of a partial trace PT_m where h is the partial trace tail **horizon**, and $h \leq m$ and h > 0.

Then, the remaining time of a partial trace tail, remtime(PTT_h), is defined as the remaining time after its last event.

4.5 Comparison Types

For purposes of calculating the remaining time of a new partial trace tail, it's necessary to compare it to the partial trace tails stored in the query catalogs, then identify the similar ones to make an estimation.

First, the equivalence of two events must be defined. Let e_1 and e_2 be two events. e_1 and e_2 are defined as equivalent if they correspond to the same activity: act_name(e_1) = act_name(e_2).

Now, to define the equivalence between partial trace tails, the comparison type that will be used to establish the equivalence must be specified:

Sequence: Two partial trace tails are equivalent as a sequence if they have the same ordered sequence of equivalent events, e.g. a partial trace tail with 3 events $\langle A, B, C \rangle$ is only equivalent as a sequence to another partial trace tail with the events $\langle A, B, C \rangle$.

Then, the function **SequenceEquivalent**(PTT, PTT') is defined to verify if two partial trace tails are equivalent as a sequence.

Multiset: Two partial trace tails are equivalent as a multiset, if they have the same amount of equivalent events, regardless of their sequence. e.g. a partial trace tail with 3 events $\langle A, B, C \rangle$ is equivalent as a multiset to the following partial trace tails: $\langle A, B, C \rangle, \langle A, C, B \rangle, \langle B, C, A \rangle, \langle B, A, C \rangle, \langle C, B, A \rangle, \langle C, A, B \rangle$.

Then, the function **MultisetEquivalent**(PTT, PTT') is defined to verify if two partial trace tails are equivalent as a multiset.

Set: Two partial trace tails are equivalent as a set if each event in a partial trace tail has at least one equivalent event in the other partial trace tail and vice versa, regardless of their sequence and how many times the events had occured. For example, a partial trace tail with 3 events $\langle A, B, C \rangle$ is equivalent as a multiset to the following partial trace tails: $\langle A, B, C \rangle, \langle A, C, B \rangle, \langle B, C, A, B \rangle, \langle C, C, A, B \rangle$, etc.

Then, the function **SetEquivalent**(PTT, PTT') is defined to verify if two partial trace tails are equivalent as a set.

5 Description of the Query Catalog Approach

With all previous definitions made, we can now describe the structure and algorithms that define the query catalog approach, and how it is used to predict remaining times.

5.1 Query Catalog Structure

A query catalog Q is a group of non-equivalent partial trace tails from all traces that have occurred in an event log, and additional information about each partial trace tail.

In order to simplify search operations, three catalogs are used, one for each comparison type. Along with every partial trace tail PTT_i stored in each catalog, the number of times it has occurred(q_i) and the sum of its remaining times(s_i) are also stored in each catalog. It is then straightforward to calculate the average remaining time for each partial trace tail. So, the structure of every query catalog containing n partial trace tails will be: $Q_{sequence/multiset/set} = \{(PTT^1, q_1, s_1), \cdots, (PTT^n, q_n, s_n)\}$.

Notice that the same partial trace tail can exist in more than one catalog, but it cannot exist more than once inside the same catalog.

5.2 Creating/Updating Query Catalogs

This article considers the existence of 3 query catalogs: $Q_{sequence}$, $Q_{multiset}$ and Q_{set}. In order to simplify the following definitions, Q is defined as the generalization of the 3 query catalogs mentioned above.

Function **ExistsPartialTraceTail**(PTT, Q) is defined to verify if the partial trace tail being has an equivalent partial trace tail in the query catalog by checking every partial trace tail in the query catalog. This algorithm returns the position of the PTT' found in the query catalog Q.

Function **AddPartialTraceTail**(PTT, Q) is defined to add a new PTT to the query catalog Q. The new element added is $(PTT, 1, remtime(PTT))$.

Function **UpdatePartialTraceTail**(PTT, Q, i) is defined to update the information (q_i and s_i) of existing PPT^i in the query catalog Q with the information of the newPPT. This algorithm updates the element (PPT^i, q_i, s_i) in the catalog as follows: $q_i = q_i + 1$ and $s_i = s_i + remtime(PTT)$.

So finally, Function **UpdateCatalog** $(T, Q_{seq}, Q_{multi}, Q_{set})$ is defined to update query catalogs with the new information contained in trace T.

Algorithm UpdateCatalog $(T_n, Q_{seq}, Q_{multi}, Q_{set})$
For every partial trace $PT_m \subseteq T_n$ (with $m \leq n$ and $m > 0$):
For every partial trace tail $PTT_h \subseteq PT_m$(with $h \leq m$ and $h > 0$):
Being i = **ExistsPartialTraceTail**(PTT_h, Q_{seq})
if ($i \geq 0$) **UpdatePartialTraceTail**(PTT_h, Q_{seq}, i)
else, **AddPartialTraceTail**(PTT_h, Q_{seq})
Being i = **ExistsPartialTraceTail**(PTT_h, Q_{multi})
if ($i \geq 0$) **UpdatePartialTraceTail**(PTT_h, Q_{multi}, i)
else, **AddPartialTraceTail**(PTT_h, Q_{multi})
Being i = **ExistsPartialTraceTail**(PTT_h, Q_{set})
if ($i \geq 0$) **UpdatePartialTraceTail**(PTT_h, Q_{set}, i)
else, **AddPartialTraceTail**(PTT_h, Q_{set})

Algorithm 1: UpdateCatalog $(T_n, Q_{seq}, Q_{multi}, Q_{set})$

5.3 Remaining Time Estimations for a Single Partial Trace Tail

Let PTT_h be a partial trace tail with length h for which we want to calculate its remaining time. The estimation basically consists of comparing the partial trace tail PTT_h with its equivalent partial trace tail in the catalog, to calculate the average remaining time of the partial trace tails that matched PTT_h.

Now, the algorithm used to calculate the remaining time of a single partial trace tail PTT_h using one catalog is defined as following:

Algorithm CalculateRemTime(PTT_h, Q)

  Output: The calculated remaining time of PTT_h using query catalog Q

  Being i = ExistsPartialTraceTail(PTT_h, Q)

  (1) if ($i \geq 0$) then **return** s_i / q_i

  (2) else, do the following:

  (3)   Being $PTT_h = \langle e_1, \cdots, e_h \rangle$, $PTT_{h-1} = \langle e_1, \cdots, e_{h-1} \rangle$ is defined as a partial trace tail equal to PTT_h, but without the last element e_h.

  (4) $\Delta = timestamp(e_h) - timestamp(e_{h-1})$ is defined as the time difference between the last two events of PTT_h

  (5)   **return CalculateRemTime(PTT_{h-1}, Q) − Δ**

Algorithm 2: CalculateRemTime(PTT_h, Q)

Steps (3), (4) and (5) are necessary when a partial trace tail PTT_h does not have an equivalent partial trace tail in the catalog, checked in (1). If this is the case, the algorithm takes a step back to the previous state of the partial trace tail (by removing the last event) until it finds at least one equivalent partial trace tail in the query catalog.

Then it calculates the remaining time, compensating it for the steps it took back. This feature allows this algorithm to calculate the remaining time of partial trace tails that contains events that never had happened before, giving flexibility and robustness to this approach.

5.4 Remaining Time Estimations for a Partial Trace

Now that these definitions are made, the main issue that motivates this article will be covered. To calculate the remaining time of a partial trace, we have defined three new methods. These will be compared to the approach used in [4] and to a simple heuristic.

Simple heuristic method: For a partial trace $PT_m = e_1, \cdots, e_m$, the calculated remaining time with simple heuristic (SH) will be:

$$SH = Max\{AverageCaseTime - |timestamp(e_m) - timestamp(e_1)|, 0\}$$

Annotated transition system method: This method, defined in [4], consists on the generation of a transition system and then annotates it with the time information contained in a training log. Then, partial traces are evaluated as it goes through the annotated transition system. The experiments conducted with this method in this article will use only *set* as comparison type and a horizon of 1 event, to create, annotate and evaluate the transition system.

Notice that these parameters were the most common and successful parameters used in [4].

Proposed Method 1: Average catalog: This method consists in evaluating a partial trace by estimating each remaining time for each partial trace tail possible contained in it, within each query catalog defined, then calculate the average of all of these estimations and return a single value.

Being $PT_m = e_1, \cdots, e_m$ and $PTT_h \subseteq PT_m, h \leq m$, the calculated remaining time RT will be:

$$RT = \frac{1}{m} \sum_{h=1}^{m} \frac{\text{CalculateRemTime}(PTT_h, Q_{seq}) + \text{CalculateRemTime}(PTT_h, Q_{multi}) + \text{CalculateRemTime}(PTT_h, Q_{set})}{3}$$

The advantage of this method is that is less likely to over-fit the estimations than any method that uses only one match or equivalence.

Proposed Method 2: Best horizon and catalog: This method uses recommendations about the *horizon* and *comparison type* by minimizing expected error, defined for each partial trace length. These optimal horizon and comparison types are calculated as follows.

The event log is separated into a training log and a test log. The training log is used to create the 3 query catalogs mentioned in Sect. 5.1 using the algorithms described in Sect. 5.2. Then the test log is used to calculate the remaining time of each PPT contained in the log and compare them to the real remaining time recorded in each PPT. So then, for all PPT that have the same length, one horizon and comparison type is selected: the one that has the minimum expected error, considering the differences between its calculated and real remaining times. So if the longest PPT in the training log has a length of n, for each length between 1 and n there is one recommended horizon and comparison type. So, the calculated recommended remaining time RRT for a PT_m will be: $RRT = \text{CalculateRemTime}(PTT_{h_m}, Q_{g_m})$, where PTT_{h_m} is the partial trace tail of length m and Q_{g_m} is the query catalog, and (h_m, g_m) are the horizon and catalog combination recommended for a partial trace length m.

Proposed Method 3: Default horizon and catalog: To be able to make a fair comparison between annotated transition systems [4] and query catalogs, they must be executed using the same parameters (horizon and comparison type). In this case, the parameters will be the same as the annotated transition system method defined in [4]: *set* as a comparison type and *1* as horizon. So, the calculated default remaining time DRT will be: $DRT = \text{Calculate}(PTT_1, Q_{set})$.

5.5   Evaluating Estimations

In order to determine the quality of the different estimation types, the log is divided into two parts; a training log and a test log. The training log is used to create the query catalogs, while the test log si used to calculate remaining times, and then comparing them to the real remaining times. To compare the methods defined above, 3 indicators were selected to measure a method's error (difference between calculated and real remaining times): Being b_i^e be the remaining time estimation of an element i. Being b_i^r be the real remaining time of an element i, and n be the number of elements analyzed:

Mean absolute error (MAE): Mean absolute error measures the average distance between both measurements.

$$MAE = \frac{1}{n} \sum_{i=1}^{n} |b_i^e - b_i^r|$$

Mean absolute percentage error (MAPE): Mean absolute percentage error measures the average percentage distance between both measurements.

$$MAPE = \frac{1}{n} \sum_{i=1}^{n} \frac{|b_i^e - b_i^r|}{b_i^r}$$

Root mean square error (RMSE): Rooted mean square error measures the root of the average squared distance between both measurements.

$$RMSE = \sqrt{\frac{1}{n} \sum_{i=1}^{n} (b_i^e - b_i^r)^2}$$

MAE measures the real difference between the estimation and the real value; instead, MAPE considers the percentage difference, giving an equivalent significance to all measurements regardless of its absolute value. On the other hand, using RMSE is a good way to include measurement's variability into the analysis.

Cross validation [7] was used to homogenize results. In a K-fold cross-validation, sample data is split into K equal sized sub-groups. One of the sub groups is used as test data, while the rest (K − 1 sub-groups) are used as training data. The cross validation procedure is repeated K times, each time using a different sub-group as test data. Finally, the arithmetic average of all results is calculated to obtain a single result. This procedure is very accurate, because it makes evaluations from K test and training data combinations. In practice, the number of iterations depends on the size of the original data set. The most common value used for K is 10.

To analyze the flexibility of the new methods introduced in this article, they were tested in two ways, each way will correspond to the same synthetic model; the first was to generate and analyze an event log that has no errors, the second was to generate an event log with 10 % of its traces containing errors.

6 Experiments

To analyze the results of the methods described above, tests were run using different synthetic and real event logs.

In order to generate synthetic event logs, a software named Process Log Generator (PLG) [8] was used, which generates petri nets [9] from certain pattern probability defined by the user. Once the petri net has been generated, then the event log is created from it using simulation techniques. Several synthetic models were evaluated, but for a matter of length, only one synthetic model could be included in this article. The synthetic model used in the tests is shown as a petri net as follows in Fig. 1.

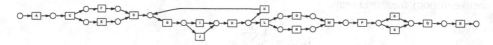

Fig. 1. Synthetic model

This model is fairly simple, but contains most common process patterns: decisions, parallelisms and loops.

Log with no errors: This log was generated based on the synthetic model above and it has 500 traces. Trace durations go from 202 to 432 h, with an average of 272 h and a standard deviation of 64 h. The experiment results are as follows in Table 1.

Table 1. Results for a synthetic event log without errors

Method	MAE (h)	MAPE (%)	RMSE (h)
Simple heuristic (SH)	52,97	52,11	65,27
Annotated transition system	34,06	20,71	47,72
Default horizon and catalog (DRT)	30,96	17,75	**45,62**
Average catalog (RT)	30,91	17,75	45,66
Best horizon and catalog (RRT)	**30,56**	**17,26**	46,14

The new methods and the annotated transition system seems to be better than the simple heuristic and the new methods outperform the annotated transition system, but the difference between the new methods and the annotated transition system is too low to make a conclusion.

Log with errors: Then, we proceed to analyze the synthetic event log generated from the same synthetic model as the previous log, but this time having 10 % of its traces with errors. An error in a trace represents any anomalous behavior that cannot be described by the petri net of the model it is based on, from changes in the order and number of events to new parallelisms, decisions or loops. This log has 500 traces. Trace durations go from 201 to 410 h, with an average of 263 h and a standard deviation of 49 h. The experiments results are as follows in Table 2.

Table 2. Results for synthetic event log with errors

Method	MAE (h)	MAPE (%)	RMSE (h)
Simple heuristic (SH)	40,60	42,57	50,18
Annotated transition system	36,86	32,18	50,77
Default horizon and catalog (DRT)	32,87	29,63	46,17
Average catalog (RT)	**28,76**	**20,60**	**40,35**
Best horizon and catalog (RRT)	37,98	28,70	54,53

We can observe that when using all information available (average catalog method) the difference with all other methods is significant.

Moreover, we can observe that when using the best horizon and catalog method, the rooted mean squared error (RMSE) is higher than in all the other methods. This might be caused by the over-fitting of this method for a model that does not have a rigid structure (because of the incorporated errors). In this trace, all the information used by the average catalog method avoids over-fitting the model.

Real model log: This log was extracted from a Chilean telecommunication company's systems. The analyzed process in this log is a "Technical issues resolution process", which consists in solving technical issues detected by customers, who call the company and request a solution for their issues.

This log has 261 traces. Its durations go from 3.3 h to 58 days, with an average of 18 days and a standard deviation of 21 days. Notice that there is a **significant variability** in the data. The experiment results are as follows in Table 3.

Table 3. Results from real event log

Method	MAE (days)	MAPE (%)	RMSE (days)
Simple heuristic (SH)	19,04	104,56*	20,19
Annotated transition system	17,09	195,52	19,06
Default horizon and catalog (DRT)	15,76	148,24	**18,02**
Average catalog (RT)	**15,57**	**146,83**	**18,02**
Best horizon and catalog (RRT)	15,83	154,05	18,43

We can notice by looking only to the MAPE metric that the simple heuristic (*) has a better performance than all the other methods, but this is not the case, because when calculating the remaining time, the simple heuristic method presents irregularities when the trace elapsed time is more than the average cycle time, if so, the remaining time estimation will be 0. For example, if all remaining time estimations are always 0, MAPE will be 100 %. This is even better than all the MAPE metrics calculated with the three other methods, but it does not make sense from a business or customer point of view. So in high variability scenarios is better to use MAE and RMSE to make conclusions. We can notice that, on high variability scenarios the average catalog method is better than all the other methods presented, but the results with all methods are not good enough from a business point of view, this might be caused by the high variability that exists in this process. These methods should be tested in more real-life logs to make better conclusions.

In this real process, the flexibility provided by the three new methods probably influenced the overall precision, giving them an advantage over previous existing methods. In real life, if any of these three new methods was implemented, new information could be added to the catalogs, and obsolete information could be removed, to maintain only the important information needed to estimate remaining times.

7 Conclusions

In this article we have introduced three new methods for calculating remaining time for partial traces, all of them based on a new approach based on the usage of query catalogs. In both synthetic and company-extracted real event logs, the new methods had better results than other existing methods, measured through three different error metrics. Then it is possible to conclude that these new methods based on query catalogs are more precise than the previous ones. The new approach based on query catalog usage not only allows improving estimation's precision, but also delivers more flexibility and dynamism, allowing to continuously improve estimations based on new information being collected. For example, we could determine the obsolescence of certain partial trace tails or the integration of new ones without needing to reprocess all the previous data, just deleting the obsolete information or adding the new information to the catalogs, both with low computational cost. We can observe that based on the results, the average catalog method behaves better with high variability processes, while the best horizon and catalog method behaves better with low variability processes. Nevertheless, more detailed experiments are required to make a better conclusion about which method is better in different circumstances.

8 Future Work

As future work, we want to establish two parallel roadmaps: implementation and algorithm improvement. In the implementation roadmap, we are developing a plugin for the process mining tool ProM [10], to make this knowledge available to the process mining research community. In the algorithm improvement roadmap, we identify three improvement focuses. The first is about analyzing the behavior of the algorithms with different process patterns (decisions, parallelisms and loops), in order to adapt the strategies used for each one, thus improving the overall estimations. We think that a good starting point is to analyze process segments, allowing us to isolate patterns and analyze them individually, and then regroup results for calculating a single estimation. The second improvement focus is about analyzing the behavior of these methods in processes with different variability, in order to define the best method for each scenario. The third improvement focus is to dynamically select methods depending on the degree of advance of a trace; it is possible that when a trace is starting a method will be more adequate, while when it is close to ending, another method could behave better. Another interesting study subject is to analyze other possible catalog usage, e.g., to establish recommendations, namely show the most probable ways to go for the rest of the trace, and for each one calculate the remaining time estimation. This would allow us to use the query catalog approach to improve in a more comprehensive way actual recommendation systems.

References

1. Dumas, M., van der Aalst, W.M.P., ter Hofstede, A.H.M.: Process-Aware Information Systems: Bridging People and Software Through Process Technology. Wiley, New York (2005)

2. van der Aalst, W.M.P., Reijers, H.A., Weijters, A.J.M.M., van Dongen, B.F., de Medeiros, A.K.A., Song, M., Verbeek, H.M.W.: Business process mining: an industrial application. Inf. Syst. **32**(5), 713–732 (2007)
3. Schonenberg, H., Weber, B., van Dongen, B.F., van der Aalst, W.M.P.: Supporting flexible processes through recommendations based on history. In: Dumas, M., Reichert, M., Shan, M.C. (eds.) BPM 2008. LNCS, vol. 5240, pp. 51–66. Springer, Heidelberg (2008)
4. van der Aalst, W.M.P., Schonenberg, M.H., Song, M.: Time prediction based on process mining. Inf. Syst. **36**(2), 450–475 (2011)
5. van Dongen, B.F., Crooy, R.A., van der Aalst, W.M.P.: Cycle time prediction: when will this case finally be finished? In: Meersman, R., Tari, Z. (eds.) OTM 2008, Part I. LNCS, vol. 5331, pp. 319–336. Springer, Heidelberg (2008)
6. Backus, P., Janakiram, M., Mowzoon, S., Runger, G.C., Bhargava, A.: Factory cycle time prediction with a data-mining approach. IEEE Trans. Semicond. Manuf. **19**(2), 252–258 (2006)
7. Kohavi, R.: A study of cross-validation and bootstrap for accuracy estimation and model selection. In: Proceedings of the Fourteenth International Joint Conference on Artificial Intelligence, pp. 1137–1143 (1995)
8. Burattin, A., Sperduti, A.: PLG: a framework for the generation of business process models and their execution logs. In: Proceedings of the 6th International Workshop on Business Process Intelligence (BPI 2010), pp. 214–219. Springer, Heidelberg
9. Peterson, J.L.: Petri Nets. ACM Comput. Surv. (CSUR) **9**(3), 223–252 (1977)
10. van der Aalst, W.M.P., et al.: ProM 4.0: comprehensive support for *real* process analysis. In: Kleijn, J., Yakovlev, A. (eds.) ICATPN 2007. LNCS, vol. 4546, pp. 484–494. Springer, Heidelberg (2007)

Discovering Block-Structured Process Models from Event Logs Containing Infrequent Behaviour

Sander J.J. Leemans[(✉)], Dirk Fahland, and Wil M.P. van der Aalst

Eindhoven University of Technology, Eindhoven, the Netherlands
{s.j.j.leemans,d.fahland,w.m.p.v.d.aalst}@tue.nl

Abstract. Given an event log describing observed behaviour, process discovery aims to find a process model that 'best' describes this behaviour. A large variety of process discovery algorithms has been proposed. However, no existing algorithm returns a sound model in all cases (free of deadlocks and other anomalies), handles infrequent behaviour well and finishes quickly. We present a technique able to cope with infrequent behaviour and large event logs, while ensuring soundness. The technique has been implemented in ProM and we compare the technique with existing approaches in terms of quality and performance.

Keywords: Process mining · Process discovery · Block-structured process models · Soundness · Fitness · Precision · Generalisation

1 Introduction

Process mining techniques aim to support organisations in improving their business processes. Event logs of historical behaviour can be used to discover process models of the real processes as present in the organisation, as opposed to manually created models that reflect wishful thinking, should-be or as-it-was-two-years-ago behaviour. Auditing of discovered models can prove compliance with organisational and governmental regulations [3], and replay of historical behaviour on the discovered model can reveal social networks and bottlenecks [4,15,17].

The challenge in process discovery is to find the 'best' process model given recorded historical behaviour. Which process model is 'best' is typically evaluated using several quality criteria. Four important quality criteria are fitness, precision, generalisation and simplicity. An un*fitting* model cannot reproduce all behaviour recorded in the log. An im*precise* model allows for too much additional behaviour that is not described in the log and

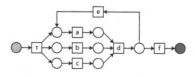

Fig. 1. Unsound process model.

in the log. A non-*general* model only describes the behaviour in the log and

N. Lohmann et al. (Eds.): BPM 2013 Workshops, LNBIP 171, pp. 66–78, 2014.
DOI: 10.1007/978-3-319-06257-0_6, © Springer International Publishing Switzerland 2014

therefore might disallow future behaviour absent in the log. A non-*simple* model needs a lot of places, transitions and arcs to express its behaviour and might be hard to read.

Another important quality criterion is *soundness*: all process steps can be executed and some satisfactory end state, the *final marking*, is always reachable. For instance, the Petri net in Fig. 1 is not sound as it contains a deadlock from which the final marking with only a single token in the final place can never be reached. An unsound process model can still be useful, but applying tasks such as evaluation, auditing, finding social networks and bottlenecks can be difficult if not impossible. Therefore, for most use cases an unsound process model can be discarded without even considering the event log it is supposed to represent.

Traces in a log might follow many different paths through the process. In most real-life event logs, some paths are taken infrequently, or traces only differ by occurrence of infrequent activities. Such logs contain *infrequent behaviour* and challenge discovery algorithms, as a process model scoring well on all quality criteria might not exist. If infrequent behaviour is included in the model, simplicity might be sacrificed, if infrequent behaviour is excluded from the model, fitness might be sacrificed. Fortunately, the Pareto principle (also known as the 80-20 rule) often applies to event logs. Typically, 80 % of the observed behaviour can be explained by a model that is only 20 % of the model required to describe all behaviour. The *80 % model* shows the "highways" in the process. Hence, it is more intuitive, but can also be used as a starting point for outlier detection [2].

To obtain an 80 % model, a classical approach is to globally filter the log before discovering a model. This has numerous disadvantages, as it is difficult to identify infrequent behaviour, and even when infrequent behaviour is filtered out, discovery algorithms (α [6], B' [16], ILP [21]) might still produce undesirable models. Other approaches were designed to ignore infrequent behaviour and can produce an 80 % model but may perform less on other quality criteria: genetic approaches [5,9] have long run times and a heuristic approach [20] produces unsound models.

As of today, no technique has been proposed that *discovers a sound 80 % model, does that fast and is able to filter infrequent behaviour*. Several existing approaches apply divide-and-conquer techniques [10, 16, 22], in which the event log is split and a model is constructed recursively. In this paper we present an extension of such an approach, IM, called *Inductive Miner - infrequent* (IMi), that aims to discover a sound 80 % model fast. We introduce infrequent behaviour filters in all steps of IM, such that infrequent behaviour is filtered locally.

IMi is implemented in the InductiveMiner package of the ProM framework [14]. To evaluate IMi, we compare its performance and its discovered models to other discovery algorithms by means of the quality criteria using real-life logs.

The remainder of this paper starts with a description of logs, process trees and IM. In Sect. 3, IMi is introduced. In Sect. 4 IMi is compared to existing mining algorithms. Section 5 concludes the paper.

2   Preliminaries

Event Logs. An *event log* is a collection of traces. Each *trace* is a sequence of *events* that represent occurrences of *activities* of a process execution in the respective order. Note that a trace might appear multiple times in an event log. The trace without events is denoted with ϵ.

Process Trees. The block-structured process models discovered by IM, ETM and IMi are process trees. A *process tree* is an abstract representation of a sound block-structured workflow net [6]. A tree represents a language, a leaf describes the singleton language of an activity, and a non-leaf node is an operator that describes how the languages of its children are combined. In this paper, we will consider four operators: $\times$, $\rightarrow$, $\wedge$ and $\circlearrowright$. The $\times$ operator denotes the exclusive choice between its children, $\rightarrow$ the sequential composition and $\wedge$ the interleaved parallel composition. The $\circlearrowright(m_1, m_2 \ldots m_n)$ has two groups of children: m_1 is the loop *body* and $m_2 \ldots m_n$ is the loop *redo* part. A trace in the language of $\circlearrowright(m_1, m_2 \ldots m_n)$ starts with a trace from m_1, followed by a repetition of a trace from any $m_2 \ldots m_n$ and a trace from m_1 again. For instance, the language of $\circlearrowright(a, b, c)$ is $\{\langle a \rangle, \langle a, b, a \rangle, \langle a, c, a \rangle, \langle a, b, a, c, a \rangle \ldots\}$.

Another example of a process tree is $\times(\rightarrow(a, b), \wedge(c, d), \circlearrowright(e, f))$, denoting the language $(ab)|(cd)|(dc)|(e(fe)^*)$. For a formal definition, please refer to [16].

Inductive Miner. In this paper, we extend an existing divide-and-conquer approach to process discovery. Divide-and-conquer has been used in process discovery before. For instance, [10] combines it with transition systems and regions; [22] combines it with trace alignments. In this paper we extend the Inductive Miner (IM) [16], of which we first give its basic algorithmic idea and illustrate it with a running example.

IM works by recursively (a) selecting the root operator that best fits L, (b) dividing the activities in log L into disjoint sets and (c) splitting L using these sets into sublogs. These sublogs are then mined recursively, until a sublog contains just a single activity. We first introduce how IM selects an operator and an activity division, and illustrate it with a running example.

Consider log L: $[\langle a, b, c, a, b, e, f \rangle^{50}, \langle a, b, f, e \rangle^{100}, \langle d, e, f \rangle^{100}, \langle d, f, e \rangle^{100}]$. In a *directly-follows graph*, each node represents an activity and an edge from node a to node b is present if and only if a is directly followed by b somewhere in L. The *frequency* of edge (a, b) is how often this happens. Figure 2a shows the directly-follows graph of L. IM searches for a characteristic division of activities into disjoint sets, a *cut*, of the directly-follows graph. Each operator ($\times$, $\rightarrow$, $\wedge$ or $\circlearrowright$) has a characteristic cut of the directly-follows graph. If such a characteristic matches, IM selects the corresponding operator. Otherwise, a *flower model*, allowing for all sequences of activities, is returned.

The dashed line in Fig. 2a is a $\rightarrow$ cut: all edges crossing it go from left to right. Using the cut $\{a, b, c, d\}, \{e, f\}$, IM splits the log by splitting each trace corresponding to the cut: $L_1 = [\langle a, b, c, a, b \rangle^{50}, \langle a, b \rangle^{100}, \langle d \rangle^{200}]$ for the left branch, $L_2 = [\langle e, f \rangle^{150}, \langle f, e \rangle^{200}]$ for the right branch. Then, IM recurses. We first consider L_1. Figure 2b shows its directly-follows graph, the dashed line denotes

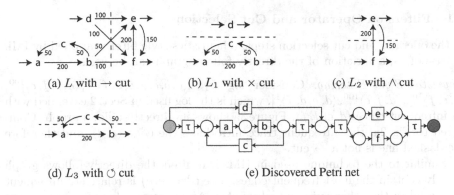

(a) L with → cut   (b) L_1 with × cut   (c) L_2 with ∧ cut

(d) L_3 with ↻ cut   (e) Discovered Petri net

Fig. 2. Directly-follows graphs. Dashed lines denote cuts. Edges have their frequencies denoted. (e) is the mined Petri net.

an × cut, as no edge crosses the cut. The log L_1 is split in $L_3 = [\langle a, b, c, a, b \rangle^{50}$, $\langle a, b \rangle^{100}]$ and $L_4 = [\langle d \rangle^{200}]$. L_4 consists of only a single activity, so for L_4 IM discovers the leaf d. The discovered process tree up till now is →(×(..., d),...).

IM recurses further. Figure 2c shows the directly-follows graph of L_2 with its ∧ cut, which splits L_2 into $L_5 = [\langle e \rangle^{350}]$ and $L_6 = \langle f \rangle^{350}$. Figure 2d shows the directly-follows graph of L_3 with its ↻ cut. IM splits L_3 into $L_7 = [\langle a, b \rangle^{200}]$ and $L_8 = [\langle c \rangle^{50}]$. The complete process tree discovered by IM is →(×(↻(→(a, b), c), d), ∧(e, f)). Figure 2e shows the corresponding Petri net. For more details, see [16].

3   Extending IM

In this section, we introduce *Inductive Miner - infrequent* (IMi) by adding infrequent behaviour filters to all steps of IM. For each of the operational steps of IM it is described how infrequent behaviour affects the step and how distinguishing frequent and infrequent behaviour can be used to improve discovery of the 80 % model. In each recursion step, IMi first applies the steps of IM unaltered. Only if this fails and IM would return a flower model, the filters are applied.

Frequencies of traces and events are ignored by IM but are taken into account by IMi in order to distinguish frequent and infrequent behaviour. In the operator and cut selection steps, two techniques are applied: filtering the directly-follows graph for infrequent edges and using a variant of the directly-follows graph for selection of →. Filters are added to base case detection to filter accumulated artifacts of filtering over recursions. In the following, k denotes a user-defined threshold value between 0 and 1 to separate frequent and infrequent behaviour. Filters on the operator and cut selection steps are described first, followed by filters on base cases, and filters on log splitting.

3.1   Filters on Operator and Cut Selection

In the operator and cut selection steps, a heuristics-style filter is applied by IMi. In case of →, a variation of the directly-follows graph can be used.

Heuristics-Style Filtering. Consider log L_1: $[\langle a, b, c, a, b, e, f\rangle^{50}, \langle a, b, f, e\rangle^{100},$ $\langle d, e, f\rangle^{100}, \langle d, f, e\rangle^{100}, \langle d, e, d, f\rangle^1]$, which is the log used in Sect. 2 extended with an infrequent trace $\langle d, e, d, f\rangle$. Figure 3a shows its directly-follows graph. Compared to Fig. 2a, the infrequent trace introduces the edge (e, d), and therefore the dashed line is not a → cut.

Similar to the technique used in HM, IMi filters the directly-follows graph to only contain the most frequent edges. The edge (e, d) is relatively infrequent compared to the other outgoing edges of e. An outgoing edge of a node is too infrequent if it has a frequency of less than k times the frequency of the strongest outgoing edge of that node. All too infrequent edges are filtered out in IMi before cuts of ×, → and ↻ are detected.

Eventually-Follows Graph. Despite heuristics-style filtering, infrequent edges might remain in the directly-follows graph. Consider log $L_2 = [\langle a, c, d, e, b\rangle,$ $\langle a, b, a, e, d, c\rangle, \langle a, e, c, b, d\rangle, \langle a, d, b, c, e\rangle]$. The second trace is the only trace containing two as: the second a is infrequent. Figure 3b shows the directly-follows graph of L_2. The dashed line in Fig. 3b is not a sequence cut as edge (b, a), introduced by the infrequent a, crosses it in the wrong direction. As all outgoing edges of b have frequency 1, no value of k could filter edge (b, a).

Similar to a technique used in [19] ("weak order relation"), IMi uses the *eventually-follows graph*, which is the transitive closure of the directly-follows relation: an edge (a, b) is present if and only if a is followed by b somewhere in the log.

The eventually-follows graph of L_2 is shown in Fig. 3c. In this graph, all outgoing edges of b are amplified, except the infrequent edge (b, a), which can then be filtered out.

In this example, using the eventually-follows graph allows IMi to deal with infrequent behaviour.

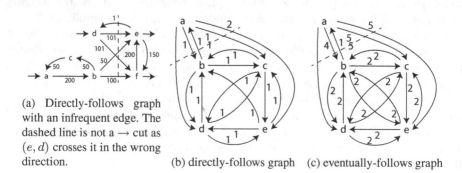

(a) Directly-follows graph with an infrequent edge. The dashed line is not a → cut as (e, d) crosses it in the wrong direction.

(b) directly-follows graph   (c) eventually-follows graph

Fig. 3. Directly and eventually follows graphs.

An infrequent occurrence of an activity still increases frequency of infrequent edges, but adds at most 1 to each of them. The eventually-follows graph amplifies all other behaviour, so using the eventually-follows graph for $\rightarrow$ cut detection increases robustness against infrequent behaviour. IMi uses a filtered eventually-follows graph to detect $\rightarrow$ cuts and if it finds one, selects $\rightarrow$ as operator.

3.2 Filters on Base Cases

In addition to the single-activity base case in IM, as an artifact of filtering it is possible that traces without events, ϵ, remain. On both base cases filters are introduced.

Single Activities. Assume the following two logs:

$$L_1 = [\epsilon^{100}, \langle a \rangle^{100}, \langle a, a \rangle^{100}, \langle a, a, a \rangle^{100}]$$
$$L_2 = [\epsilon^{1}, \langle a \rangle^{100}, \langle a, a \rangle^{1}, \langle a, a, a \rangle^{1}]$$

Both L_1 and L_2 consist of a single activity, cannot be split further and are base cases. Given the representational bias of IMi, for both logs either a flower model or a single activity a can be discovered. In L_1, all traces are frequent and a flower model is obviously the best choice. In L_2 however, only $\langle a \rangle$ is frequent and a best represents the frequent behaviour.

Choosing either option influences quality dimensions: discovering a for L_1 sacrifices fitness, while discovering a flower model for L_2 sacrifices precision. a is only discovered by IMi if the average number of occurrences per trace of a in the log is close enough to 1, dependent on the relative threshold k.

Empty Traces. Assume the following log: $L = [\langle a, b, d \rangle^{100}, \langle a, c, d \rangle^{100}, \langle a, d \rangle]$. In the first recursion, IMi selects the $\rightarrow$ operator and splits L into $L_1 = [\langle a \rangle^{201}]$, $L_2 = [\epsilon^{1}, \langle b \rangle^{100}, \langle c \rangle^{100}]$ and $L_3 = [\langle d \rangle^{201}]$.

Consider L_2. A fitting solution for the empty trace in L_2 would be to mine $\times(\tau, \ldots)$ and recurse on $L_2 \setminus \{\epsilon\}$. For L_2, ϵ is infrequent and discovering $\times(\tau, \ldots)$ would sacrifice simplicity. This is a tradeoff, but for L_2 clearly $\times(\tau, \ldots)$ is preferred. To overcome this problem, IMi only discovers $\times(\tau, \ldots)$ if ϵ is frequent enough compared to the number of traces in the log and with respect to k. If ϵ is not frequent enough, IMi filters ϵ from L_2 and recurses on $L_2 \setminus \{\epsilon\}$.

3.3 Filters on Log Splitting

Assuming the operator and cut have been selected, some infrequent behaviour in the log might not fit the chosen operator and cut. If not filtered out, this unfitting behaviour might accumulate over recursions and obscure frequent behaviour.

This section describes how infrequent behaviour can be filtered during log splitting. It is assumed that the operator and cut are correctly selected and that any behaviour that violates this selection is infrequent. For each operator, we describe the types of violations that can be detected and how they are filtered by IMi, illustrated by an example. In these examples, $\Sigma_1 = \{a\}, \Sigma_2 = \{b\}$ is the chosen cut and L_1, L_2 are the sublogs to-be-created.

× Behaviour that violates the × operator is the presence of activities from more
  than one subtree in a single trace. For instance, the trace $t_1 = \langle a, a, a, a, b, a,$
  $a, a, a \rangle$ contains activities from both Σ_1 and Σ_2. Σ_1 explains the most activities, is most frequent. All activities not from Σ_1 are considered infrequent
  and are discarded: $\langle a, a, a, a, a, a, a, a \rangle \in L_1$.
→ Behaviour that violates the → operator is the presence of events out of order
  according to the subtrees. For instance, in the trace $t_2 = \langle a, a, a, a, b, b, b, b,$
  $a, b \rangle$, the last a occurs after a b, which violates the →. Filtering infrequent
  behaviour is an optimisation problem: the trace is to be split in the least-
  events-removing way. In t_2, the split $\langle a, a, a, a \rangle \in L_1$, $\langle b, b, b, b, b \rangle \in L_2$
  discards the least events.
∧ A parallel operator allows for any sequence of behaviour of its subtrees.
  Therefore, no behaviour violates ∧ and infrequent behaviour can be neither
  detected nor filtered while splitting the log.
↺ Behaviour that violates the ↺ operator is when a trace does not start or end
  with the loop body: For instance, $\circlearrowright(a, b)$, is violated by all traces that do
  not start and end with an a. For each such invalid start or end of a trace,
  an empty trace is added to L_1 to increase fitness of the resulting model.
  Considering the trace $t_3 = \langle b, a, b \rangle$, then $[\epsilon^2, \langle a \rangle^1] \subseteq L_1$ and $[\langle b \rangle^2] \subseteq L_2$.

In each recursion step, first the operator and cut selection steps of IM are
performed by IMi. If that would result in the flower model, the procedure is
applied again, with the infrequent behaviour filters in operator and cut selection,
base cases and log splitting, such that in all steps of IM filters are applied by
IMi. In the next section, IMi is compared to existing process discovery mining
techniques.

4   Comparison to Other Discovery Algorithms

In this section, we compare IMi to existing mining algorithms on performance
and quality criteria of discovered models, using ideas from [11,18]. We first
describe the experimental setup and the used logs, and finish with a discussion
of the results.

4.1   Experimental Setup

We compare the mining algorithms IM, IMi, HM, ILP and ETM using the following quality criteria: we compare performance and measure soundness, fitness,
precision, generalisation and simplicity. To provide a baseline, we include a flower
model (FM), allowing for all sequences of activities. and a trace model (TM)[1].
Figure 4 gives an overview of the experimental setup.

Preprocessing. As a preprocessing step, we add artificial start and end events to
the logs. Mining algorithms might require single start and end events, and these
events help to determine soundness.

---
[1] A trace model allows for all traces in the event log, but no other behaviour.

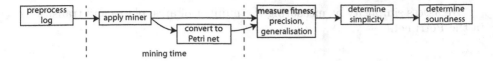

Fig. 4. Experimental setup

Mining. Secondly, the miners are applied: IM IMi, ILP, HM, ETM, FM and TM. We compare all mining algorithms using their default settings. Like in [11], parameter optimisation is outside the scope of this paper. HM and ETM do not produce a Petri net. Therefore the output of each of these miners is converted to a Petri net, measured mining time includes this conversion. We report an indicative mining time on a dual Intel Xeon E5-2630 hexacore, having 64 GB of RAM, running 64-bit Windows 7. As we want to mine models fast, we set a maximum mining time of two hours. ILP is stopped abruptly after this bound, ETM is allowed to finish its round of genetic steps.

Measuring. We are permissive in the soundness check: we add obvious final markings to the discovered models if the mining algorithm does not provide it, and each reasonable final marking in the discovered models is considered to be a valid final marking to be reached by the process.

To measure fitness [7], precision [8] and generalisation [1] of the mined models we use the *PNetReplayer* package in the ProM framework [14]. For these measures, first a projection of the log on the discovered model is computed, an *alignment*. The technique described in [7] provides an alignment that shows the least deviation between log and model.

For computation of the alignment, the final marking to be reached is relevant. On the models discovered by miners that do not provide a final marking, we compute the alignment assuming that every marking is a final marking. For fitness, this yields an upper bound[2]. Experiments show that the upper bound is not necessarily tight: we found differences of 0.3 in fitness between measured with and without final marking. In the results, we denote these upper bound fitness values using *italics*.

From the alignment, a graph of reached and reachable markings, and edges between them is computed. On the markings in this graph, the number of edges that is never used in the alignment is a measure for precision [8], while the frequency of the edges used in the alignment is a measure for generalisation. The values of precision and generalisation highly depend on the chosen optimal alignment. Therefore, the results with and without final marking should not be compared for precision and generalisation. Experiments show that the values are quite close: we found differences with a maximum of about 0.1 in precision when there is no final marking, and 0.005 for generalisation. We denote values obtained without final marking in *italics*.

---

[2] We adapted the fitness computation in the PNetReplayer package to achieve this.

We assess simplicity by measuring the number of arcs, places and transitions in the Petri nets.

4.2 Logs

To compare the mining algorithms, we use 12 real-life event logs. Table 1 characterises the different logs. A process from the gynaecology department of an academic hospital is logged in the BPIC'11 log [12]. The BPIC'12 log [13] originates from an application process for a personal loan or overdraft within a global financial organisation. Furthermore, we use non-public logs of a building permit approval process in five municipalities, resulting from the CoSeLog project[3]. We include these five both untouched, WABO 1 through 5, and filtered to contain only activities common to all five, WABO 1_c through 5_c.

4.3 Results

Table 1 shows the results. ✗ indicates an unsound model, ✓ a sound. A dash (-) indicates that the miner did not produce a result, an empty space indicates that measurement could not be obtained on our machine due to memory restrictions. For some experiments, mining took longer than two hours. This is denoted with (1). The experiments for which a final marking had to be guessed are denoted with (2).

A model with a deadlock is denoted with (10). (11) denotes that the model contains a dead transition, (12) that the model contains either an unbounded or an unreachable transition. The simplicity of the returned models, i.e., the number of arcs, places and transitions in them, is shown in Table 2.

4.4 Discussion

First observation is that for all logs a model was discovered within two hours by IM, IMi, FM and ETM. IMi was for all logs a bit slower than IM, while taking a lot less time than ILP, ETM and TM. A noticeable difference exists between ETM and IMi; ETM took much longer for each log. Second observation is that, not considering FM and TM, no miner has a log on which it performs best on all fitness, precision and generalisation. Tradeoffs have to be made (Table 1).

IM and ILP did not manage to discover a good 80 % model: to achieve perfect fitness, IM sacrifices precision, while ILP sacrifices precision and simplicity. An 80 % model was discovered for most logs by HM, but were less simple, not sound, and for some logs discovery took a long time. ETM, with its default settings as tested, focuses on precision and therefore achieves a lower fitness. Moreover, discovery took a long time. IMi discovered sound 80 % models quickly in all cases. Regarding precision, two groups of event logs can be identified:

- *BPIC'11 and WABO 1 to WABO 5.* On these logs, IMi produces 80 % models with better precision than IM and the baseline FM. Fitness of IMi on all these

---

[3] See http://www.win.tue.nl/coselog/wiki/start

Table 1. Log sizes and results.

		BPIC'11	BPIC'12	WABO 1	WABO 1_c	WABO 2	WABO 2_c	WABO 3	WABO 3_c	WABO 4	WABO 4_c	WABO 5	WABO 5_c
traces		1143	13087	434	434	286	286	481	481	324	324	432	432
events		150291	262200	13571	9287	10439	6898	16566	11846	9743	6650	13370	8752
activities		624	36	173	44	160	44	170	44	133	44	176	44
remarks	IM												
	IMi												
	HM	(1)	(2)	(2)	(2)	(2)	(2)	(2)	(2)	(2)	(2)	(2)	(2)
	ILP	(1)		(1)				(1)	(1)	(1)			
	ETM												
	FM												
	TM	(1)	(1)										
soundness	IM	✓	✓	✓	✓	✓	✓	✓	✓	✓	✓	✓	✓
	IMi	✓	✓	✓	✓	✓	✓	✓	✓	✓	✓	✓	✓
	HM	-	(12)✗	(10)✗	(11)✗	(10)✗	(11)✗	(12)✗	(12)✗	(12)✗	(12)✗	(12)✗	(12)✗
	ILP	-	(12)✗	-	(12)✗		(12)✗	-	-	-	(12)✗	(12)✗	(12)✗
	ETM	✓	✓	✓	✓	✓	✓	✓	✓	✓	✓	✓	✓
	FM	✓	✓	✓	✓	✓	✓	✓	✓	✓	✓	✓	✓
	TM	-	-	✓	✓	✓	✓	✓	✓	✓	✓	✓	✓
mining time (s)	IM	68.3	5.6	0.8	0.2	0.6	0.2	0.9	0.3	0.4	0.1	0.6	0.2
	IMi	182.3	8.1	5.1	0.4	1.7	0.6	1.8	0.5	0.8	0.6	1.3	0.6
	HM	7200.0	2519.2	1.9	0.2	2.5	2.1	2.1	1.9	0.2	1.1	2.0	2.3
	ILP	7200.0	5085.3	7200.0	319.8	1343.5	123.3	7200.0	7200.0	7200.0	1406.2	1452.4	185.1
	ETM	7220.7	51.1	7261.7	2189.1	6018.9	2539.8	5524.2	7282.5	7260.2	2998.1	4268.5	4828.4
	FM	1.1	0.0	0.1	0.0	0.1	0.0	0.1	0.0	0.0	0.0	0.1	0.0
	TM	7200.0	7200.0	320.6	27.9	252.6	25.1	361.3	87.1	115.8	16.8	131.1	19.4
fitness	IM	1.000	1.000	1.000	1.000	1.000	1.000	1.000	1.000	1.000	1.000	1.000	1.000
	IMi	0.698	0.931	0.756	0.780	0.977	0.888	1.000	0.874	0.993	0.757	0.990	0.833
	HM	-			0.940		0.957				0.979		0.960
	ILP	-	1.000	-	1.000		1.000	-	-	-	1.000	1.000	1.000
	ETM	0.158	0.022	0.372	0.709	0.464	0.616	0.520	0.593	0.403	0.698	0.562	0.680
	FM	1.000	1.000	1.000	1.000	1.000	1.000	1.000	1.000	1.000	1.000	1.000	1.000
	TM	-	-		1.000		1.000		1.000		1.000		1.000
precision	IM	0.009		0.040	0.090	0.034	0.077	0.035	0.075	0.070	0.090	0.038	0.083
	IMi		0.300		0.637	0.042	0.465	0.078	0.599	0.091	0.605	0.058	0.644
	HM	-			0.744		0.725				0.489		0.622
	ILP	-	0.306	-	0.537		0.413	-	-	-	0.352	0.324	0.391
	ETM	0.927	1.000	0.937	0.913	0.973	0.994	0.920	0.952	0.961	0.890	1.000	0.895
	FM	0.002	0.051	0.011	0.043	0.009	0.037	0.010	0.040	0.012	0.040	0.009	0.039
	TM	-	-		1.000		1.000		1.000		1.000		1.000
generalisation	IM	1.000		0.999	1.000	1.000	0.999	1.000	1.000	0.999	0.999	0.999	1.000
	IMi		0.999		1.000	0.999	1.000	0.999	1.000	0.999	0.999	0.998	1.000
	HM	-			0.998		0.998				0.923		0.895
	ILP	-	0.997	-	0.803		0.916	-	-	-	0.824	0.690	0.784
	ETM	1.000	1.000	1.000	0.999	1.000	1.000	1.000	0.998	1.000	0.992	1.000	0.992
	FM	1.000	1.000	1.000	1.000	1.000	1.000	1.000	1.000	1.000	1.000	0.999	1.000
	TM	-	-		0.046		0.039		0.035		0.050		0.044

logs is, as expected for 80 % models, higher than ETM, but lower than IM. A manual inspection of the resulting models shows that IMi returns a sequence of activities, whereas IM returns a flower model. Still, some sequential elements are flower models, causing the low precision. Figure 5b shows a part of the model discovered by IMi for WABO 4.

– BPIC'12 and WABO 1_c to WABO 5_c. On these logs, IMi discovers good 80 % models that can keep up with other miners. Figure 5 shows the results of three miners on the WABO 2_c log. The model discovered by ETM contains

Table 2. Simplicity (#arcs,#places,#transitions).

	IM	IMi	HM	ILP	ETM	FM	TM
BPIC'11	1256,5,628	1290,27,645	-	-	16,7,8	1256,3,628	-
BPIC'12	80,7,40	166,41,81	90375,76,16737	919,88,38	2,2,1	80,3,40	-
WABO 1	368,12,184	474,97,237	1071,350,496	-	32,15,16	354,3,177	19582,9513,9791
WABO 1_c	96,5,48	122,37,61	249,92,121	802,73,46	72,32,35	96,3,48	6056,2890,3028
WABO 2	336,8,168	406,43,202	870,324,419	4560,215,162	56,28,26	328,3,164	17340,8454,8670
WABO 2_c	120,16,60	112,25,56	235,92,116	770,62,46	44,21,22	96,3,48	5754,2766,2877
WABO 3	378,18,189	358,14,179	946,344,459	-	50,24,23	348,3,174	20128,9813,10064
WABO 3_c	122,15,61	116,32,58	279,92,135	-	42,21,18	96,3,48	10604,5116,5302
WABO 4	304,23,152	290,21,145	764,270,362	-	34,16,17	274,3,137	12186,5907,6093
WABO 4_c	100,7,50	108,33,54	230,92,114	1239,80,46	78,35,31	96,3,48	4742,2255,2371
WABO 5	368,8,184	392,30,196	910,356,451	5479,233,178	46,22,22	360,3,180	12628,6136,6314
WABO 5_c	96,5,48	116,36,58	254,92,122	786,60,46	64,32,27	96,3,48	5052,2418,2526

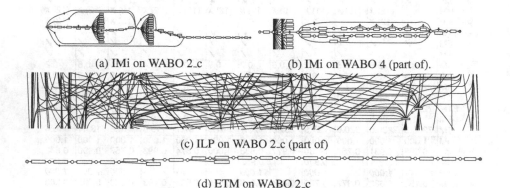

(a) IMi on WABO 2_c   (b) IMi on WABO 4 (part of).

(c) ILP on WABO 2_c (part of)

(d) ETM on WABO 2_c

Fig. 5. Results of discovery.

the least number of transitions and is obviously the simplest model, but its
fitness (0.506) is considerably lower than of IMi (0.946). The main difference
is that IMi adds two flower submodels not discovered by ETM, giving a precision of 0.430 for IMi and 0.994 for ETM. For generalisation, both models
have the perfect score. Of the 44 activities in WABO 2_c, 23 are not in the
model discovered by ETM and only 2 are not in the model discovered by IMi.
Therefore, a future trace is more likely to be accepted by the IMi-model than
by the ETM-model. Also, note that IMi returned a model in 0.1 s and ETM
needed 42 min, showing that IMi can achieve better results in significantly
less time.

5   Conclusion

In this paper, we presented the Inductive Miner - infrequent (IMi), an extension
of the Inductive Miner (IM, called B′ in [16]) that filters infrequent behaviour
locally in each algorithmic step of IM: selecting an operator and a cut, splitting
the log and the base cases of the recursion.

Unlike other approaches, IMi can create the so-called 80 % model using the Pareto principle while guaranteeing to return a sound process model in a short time. We compared IMi to several existing techniques using performance and soundness, fitness, precision, generalisation and simplicity of the discovered models. IM, HM, ILP and ETM were applied to twelve real-life logs. Compared with IM, models discovered by IMi have a lower fitness, higher precision, equal generalisation and comparable simplicity. IMi always returned a sound 80 % model fast, and on all logs scores good on all quality criteria except precision. Results for precision are twofold: on half of the logs, IMi discovered sound 80 % models fast, having a lower precision due to discovery of flower models early in the recursion. Note that for many logs, a model scoring well on all quality criteria doesn't exist: process discovery is a tradeoff. On the other half of the logs, IMi discovered better 80 % models faster than any other discovery technique, showing the potential of the constructive approach.

Future Work. The parallel operator ∧ remains problematic in operator and cut selection, as none of the features proposed in this paper can filter infrequent behaviour and incompleteness related to this construct. Efficient detection of non-complete parallel logs remains a subject of further research.

References

1. van der Aalst, W.M.P., Adriansyah, A., van Dongen, B.F.: Replaying history on process models for conformance checking and performance analysis. Wiley Interdiscip. Rev. Data Min. Knowl. Discov. **2**(2), 182–192 (2012)
2. van der Aalst, W.M.P., et al.: Process mining manifesto. In: Daniel, F., Barkaoui, K., Dustdar, S. (eds.) BPM Workshops 2011, Part I. LNBIP, vol. 99, pp. 169–194. Springer, Heidelberg (2012)
3. van der Aalst, W.M.P., van Hee, K.M., van der Werf, J.M.E.M., Verdonk, M.: Auditing 2.0: using process mining to support tomorrow's auditor. Computer **43**(3), 90–93 (2010)
4. van der Aalst, W.M.P., Song, M.S.: Mining social networks: uncovering interaction patterns in business processes. In: Desel, J., Pernici, B., Weske, M. (eds.) BPM 2004. LNCS, vol. 3080, pp. 244–260. Springer, Heidelberg (2004)
5. van der Aalst, W.M.P., de Medeiros, A.K.A., Weijters, A.J.M.M.: Genetic process mining. In: Ciardo, G., Darondeau, P. (eds.) ICATPN 2005. LNCS, vol. 3536, pp. 48–69. Springer, Heidelberg (2005)
6. van der Aalst, W.M.P., Weijters, T., Maruster, L.: Workflow mining: discovering process models from event logs. IEEE Trans. Knowl. Data Eng. **16**(9), 1128–1142 (2004)
7. Adriansyah, A., van Dongen, B.F., van der Aalst, W.M.P.: Conformance checking using cost-based fitness analysis. In: 2011 15th IEEE International Enterprise Distributed Object Computing Conference (EDOC), pp. 55–64. IEEE (2011)
8. Adriansyah, A., Munoz-Gama, J., Carmona, J., van Dongen, B.F., van der Aalst, W.M.P.: Alignment based precision checking. In: La Rosa, M., Soffer, P. (eds.) BPM Workshops 2012. LNBIP, vol. 132, pp. 137–149. Springer, Heidelberg (2013)
9. Buijs, J., van Dongen, B.F., van der Aalst, W.M.P.: A genetic algorithm for discovering process trees. In: 2012 IEEE Congress on Evolutionary Computation (CEC), pp. 1–8. IEEE (2012)

10. Carmona, J.: Projection approaches to process mining using region-based techniques. Data Min. Knowl. Disc. **24**(1), 218–246 (2012)
11. De Weerdt, J., De Backer, M., Vanthienen, J., Baesens, B.: A multi-dimensional quality assessment of state-of-the-art process discovery algorithms using real-life event logs. Inf. Syst. **37**, 654–676 (2012)
12. van Dongen, B.F.: BPI Challenge 2011 Dataset. http://dx.doi.org/10.4121/uuid: d9769f3d-0ab0-4fb8-803b-0d1120ffcf54 (2011)
13. van Dongen, B.F.: BPI Challenge 2012 Dataset. http://dx.doi.org/10.4121/uuid: 3926db30-f712-4394-aebc-75976070e91f (2012)
14. van Dongen, B.F., de Medeiros, A.K.A., Verbeek, H.M.W., Weijters, A.J.M.M.T., van der Aalst, W.M.P.: The ProM framework: a new era in process mining tool support. In: Ciardo, G., Darondeau, P. (eds.) ICATPN 2005. LNCS, vol. 3536, pp. 444–454. Springer, Heidelberg (2005)
15. van Dongen, B.F., Adriansyah, A.: Process mining: fuzzy clustering and performance visualization. In: Rinderle-Ma, S., Sadiq, S., Leymann, F. (eds.) BPM 2009 Workshops. LNBIP, vol. 43, pp. 158–169. Springer, Heidelberg (2010)
16. Leemans, S.J.J., Fahland, D., van der Aalst, W.M.P.: Discovering block-structured process models from event logs - a constructive approach. In: Colom, J.-M., Desel, J. (eds.) PETRI NETS 2013. LNCS, vol. 7927, pp. 311–329. Springer, Heidelberg (2013)
17. Mans, R.S., Schonenberg, M.H., Song, M., van der Aalst, W.M.P., Bakker, P.J.M.: Application of process mining in healthcare–a case study in a Dutch hospital. In: Fred, A., Filipe, J., Gamboa, H. (eds.) BIOSTEC 2008. CCIS, vol. 25, pp. 425–438. Springer, Heidelberg (2009)
18. de Medeiros, A.K.A., Weijters, A.J.M.M., van der Aalst, W.M.P.: Genetic process mining: an experimental evaluation. Data Min. Knowl. Disc. **14**(2), 245–304 (2007)
19. Smirnov, S., Weidlich, M., Mendling, J.: Business process model abstraction based on synthesis from well-structured behavioral profiles. Int. J. Coop. Inf. Syst. **21**(01), 55–83 (2012)
20. Weijters, A.J.M.M., van der Aalst, W.M.P., de Medeiros, A.K.A.: Process mining with the heuristics miner-algorithm. Technische Universiteit Eindhoven, Technical report WP 166 (2006)
21. van der Werf, J.M.E.M., van Dongen, B.F., Hurkens, C.A.J., Serebrenik, A.: Process discovery using integer linear programming. Fundamenta Informaticae **94**, 387–412 (2010)
22. Yzquierdo-Herrera, R., Silverio-Castro, R., Lazo-Cortés, M.: Sub-process discovery: opportunities for process diagnostics. In: Poels, G. (ed.) CONFENIS 2012. LNBIP, vol. 139, pp. 48–57. Springer, Heidelberg (2013)

Report: Business Process Intelligence Challenge 2013

B.F. van Dongen[1]([✉]), B. Weber[2], D.R. Ferreira[3], and J. De Weerdt[4]

[1] Eindhoven University of Technology, Eindhoven, The Netherlands
b.f.v.dongen@tue.nl
[2] Universität Innsbruck, Innsbruck, Austria
barbara.weber@uibk.ac.at
[3] Technical University of Lisbon, Lisbon, Portugal
diogo.ferreira@ist.utl.pt
[4] Queensland University of Technology, Brisbane, Australia
jochen.deweerdt@qut.edu.au

1 Introduction

For the third time, the Business Process Intelligence workshop hosted the Business Process Intelligence Challenge. The goal of this challenge is twofold. On the one hand, the challenge allows researchers and practitioners in the field to show their analytical capabilities to a broader audience. On the other hand, the challenge (and it's data) allows for researchers to prove that their techniques work on real-life data sets.

Every year, the challenge organizer's look for a real-life event log which contains event-data of one or more operational business processes of an organization. This data is provided to the participants as-is, without any pre-processing or filtering (other than anonymization). The logs are made publically available and are given a DOI for future reference.

In contrast to authors of scientific papers, challenge participants are not asked to write scientific descriptions of algorithms, techniques or tools, nor are they asked to provide scientifically well set-up case studies. Instead, the participants are asked to analyze the provided log data using whatever techniques available, focusing on one or more of the process owner's questions or proving other unique insights into the process captured in the event log.

A jury consisting of academic and industry members with a strong background in business process analysis assesses the submitted reports on completeness of the analysis, presentation of the results and on originality. Finally, the jury decides on a winner who receives a prize offered by one of the challenge's sponsors:

Fluxicon - Process mining for professionals. *The process mining technology in Fluxicon's products can automatically create smart flow diagrams of your process. All you need are event logs that are already on your IT systems. Because our products work with this objective information, you no longer need to rely on belief or hearsay you will know what's going on.*

N. Lohmann et al. (Eds.): BPM 2013 Workshops, LNBIP 171, pp. 79–87, 2014.
DOI: 10.1007/978-3-319-06257-0_7, © Springer International Publishing Switzerland 2014

Perceptive Software. *Through the recent purchase of Pallas Athena, Percep-*
tive Software has become a world-leading Business Process Management Soft-
ware (BPM) and Solutions provider. Their innovative software platforms and
user-friendly designs are well known and recognized throughout the industry.

2   The Event Log of Volvo IT Belgium

For the 2013 edition of the BPI challenge an event log was provided by Volvo IT
Belgium. The log contains events from an incident and a problem management
system called VINST. The primary goal of the incident management process
is restoring a customer's normal service operation as quickly as possible when
incidents arise ensuring that the best possible levels of service quality and availability are maintained. The problem management system includes the activities
required to diagnose the root cause(s) of incidents and to secure the resolution
of those problems to enhance the quality of ITservices delivered and/or operated
by Volvo IT.

The data contained events related to the two processes as well as different
organisational entities and was separated into three event logs:

Incidents [1]. A log of 7554 cases containing 65533 events pertaining to the
incident management process.
Closed Problems [2]. A log of 1487 cases containing 6660 events pertaining
to closed problems in the problem management process.
Open Problems [3]. A log of 819 cases containing 2351 events pertaining to
open problems in the problem management process.

The process owner was particularly interested in four different questions.

Push to Front (incidents only). Is there evidence that cases are pushed to
the 2nd and 3rd line too often or too soon?
Ping Pong Behavior. How often do cases ping pong between teams and which
teams are more or less involved in ping-ponging?
Wait User abuse. Is the "wait user" substatus abused to hide problems with
the total resolution time?
Process Conformity per Organisation. Where do the two IT organisations
differ and why?

3   Submissions

While the first BPI challenge in 2011 attracted only three submissions and the
second BPI challenge in 2012 attracted six, a total of 12 submissions were
received for assessment by the jury this year. In this section, all submissions
are presented. For each submission, a short abstract is included followed by a
selection of the jury's comments on that submission in italics.

M. Arias and E. Rojas, Pontificia Universidad Católica de Chile, Chile [4]

This essay focusses on a couple of the process owners questions. The authors of [4] present an analysis realized through applying different kinds of tools and process mining techniques. They provide an analysis, which discoveres behavior characteristics associated with products, resources and organizational lines.

The Jury: *This is a solid analysis covering many details of the analysis. The report illustrates the method of analysis coming from general to more refined questions that are answered step by step, typically through filtering and process discovery or other kinds of analysis. The report also highlights problems with existing tools and how they have been resolved.*

A. Bautista, S. Akbar, A. Alvarez, T. Metzger and M. Reaves, CKM Advisors, USA [5]

The goal of this study is to identify opportunities that improve operational performance of information technology incident management at Volvo, Belgium. Findings are derived exclusively from computational analysis of the event logs. Improvements that increase resource efficiency and reduce incident resolution times and subsequently customer impacts are identified across the following areas: service level push-to-front, ping pong between support teams, and Wait-User status abuse. Specific products, support teams, organizational structures, and process elements most appropriate for further study are identified and specific analyses are recommended.

The Jury: *It is very interesting to analyze the data at product and country granularities, in order to suggest possible candidates as root causes of bottlenecks. In general, the number of variables taken into account is remarkable and this suggests long and accurate work on actual data.*

S. vanden Broucke, J. Vanthienen and B. Baesens, KU Leuven, Belgium and University of Southampton, UK [6]

This report presents results related to the following investigations. First, an open-minded exploratory analysis of the given event logs and second, answering the four specific questions posed by the process owner. To do so, the authors utilize both already existing as well as dedicated developed tools, and heavily combine traditional data analysis tools and process-oriented techniques. They indicate the existence of a gap between these two categories of tools and as such emphasize the importance of a hybrid approach in a process intelligence context throughout the report.

The Jury: *I particularly liked how carefully and consistently the potential biases were revealed, and that interpretations (particularly concerning individual employees) were given with caution. It's very important to keep in mind that the actual root cause of what can be observed behind a process often lies outside of the data analyst's view (e.g., "Is this team slow or just deals with the more complicated cases?").*

E. Dudok and P. van den Brand, Perceptive Software, The Netherlands [7]

This paper describes the results of the exploratory process mining efforts on the incident management process. Specific areas of interest provided by the process owner are analyzed as well as some additional areas of interest that qualified for further investigation based on the information provided. Interesting results include uncovering specific support teams and products for which specified unwanted behavior such as lack of push to front, ping pong, and wait user abuse was prominent. Also some interesting relations were found, e.g. between the wait user abuse and incident impact category, and the hypothesis that a correlation exists between the number of handovers and total resolution time was proven.

The Jury: *The submission addresses all questions of the process owner in a convincing and very detailed manner. This report goes deep into the different questions and presents findings in such a way that that they are accessible to readers without deep process mining knowledge. In addition, conclusions are explained not at a technical level, but a business level. Most important conclusions are briefly summarized at the end of each question. In addition, an executive summary is provided at the end of the document summarizing the main insights and outlining potential additional directions of analysis. In addition to the questions of the Process Owner an additional area of analysis (Resolution Verification) is added.*

F. van Geffen and R. Niks, Rabobank, The Netherlands and O&I Management Consultants, The Netherlands [8]

Process mining is an accessible technique to visualize and analyze process variation and to yield improvements. The authors experienced that Process Mining can help to overcome some of the barriers of the Six Sigma DMAIC cycle in improvement projects. This results in a significant acceleration to complete such a cycle.

The Jury: *The report is less of a classical solution to the BPI challenge, but a case study on conducting a DMAIC (Define, Measure, Analyze, Improve, Control) Analysis from the Six Sigma Toolkit in a faster and more objective way through the use of Process Mining tools. The BPI challenge data is used as an* *exemplary case study to support this idea. The paper is a nice testimonial about the usefulness of process mining techniques in the context of BPM improvements efforts such as Six Sigma.*

J. Hansen, ChangeGroup, Denmark [9]

The purpose of this document is to answer the questions raised by Volvo IT Belgium. In addition, an attempt is made to capture the incident and problem management processes in the form of BPMN models.

The Jury: *The submission addresses all questions of the process owner using Disco, Excel, Word and Enterprise Architect. The report does not comprise any additional analyses, but provides process documentation in form of BPMN models.*

J. Hevia and C. Saint-Pierre, Pontificia Universidad Católica de Chile, Chile [10]

In this work, the authors tried to give response to the client concerns and provide analysis based on the data, with proposals to improve the performance of the processes in the company. The paper attempts to identify the impact of various failures and the organizaton of the process so that in the future Volvo can correct and thus, provide a better service to it's customers.

The Jury: *In general, this report tends to make excessive use of process mining techniques even when simple data analysis would suffice to answer the clients questions. However, in one particular instance, such approach allowed the authors to discover unexpected behaviour which may be important for the client to know (regardless of their initial questions). This is the case of the push-to-front question, where the authors discovered an escalation of some incidents from level 1 directly to level 3, which might not be desirable.*

C. J. Kang, Y. S. Kang, Y. S. Lee, S. Noh, H. C. Kim, W. C. Lim, J. Kim and R. Hong, Myongji University, Korea [11]

Recently, there has been a strong interest in the application of innovative process mining techniques to promote evidence-based understanding and analysis of organizations business processes. Following the trend, this report analyzes the challenge logs. To create relevant datasets for answering the given questions, the logs are pre-processed with the help of PL-SQL and Java. The datasets are analyzed using ProM's and Disco's state-of-the-art process mining capabilities, SQL, and traditional spreadsheet-based techniques. The authors provide evidence-based answers to the questions and demonstrate the potential benefits of process mining-based understanding and analysis of business processes.

The Jury: *I liked the analysis and found the reasoning style easy to follow. The authors made a point of clearly defining their interpre-tations and arguing for their assumptions. The graphs were mostly well-explained. The solution to process conformity per organization is perfect as far as I know.*

J. Martens, Capgemini, The Netherlands [12]

A professional application of Process Mining has been established in the context of a methodology as defined by a consultancy firm. The results of the research show where in the context of consultancy Process Mining is used and how clients can benefit from expertise and standardized work.

The Jury: *This report attempts to diligently answer, one by one, all questions from the client. I appreciate a consultant taking time to perform such a report, and I do encourage the author to continue in this direction.*

Z. Paszkiewicz and W. Picard, Poznan Unviersity of Economics, Poland [13]

In this paper, the authors provide answers to all the process owner's questions using process mining and social network analysis techniques, and they state the existence of hidden support lines degrading the overall performance of incident handling, little localized ping-pong behavior and wait-user misuse, and various levels of conformity across organizations.

The Jury: *The authors frequently state an hypothesis and then prove or disprove it. This is very good. There is an interesting mix of tools deployed, data inconsistencies are addressed, and assumptions are clearly stated. It's a detailed and good-quality analysis. The chord diagrams are an innovative and interesting contribution.*

S. Radhakrishnan and G. Anantha, SolutioNXT Inc., US [14]

The goal of this paper is to identify some key actionable patterns for improvement. The authors have used a combination of process discovery tools (such as Disco) and reusable scripting on MS Excel to perform their analysis. The focus of their approach is to discern findings and encapsulate them within real world perspectives. The authors brought this real world perspective by reclassifying the given dataset into (a) All cases (b) Incidents only (b) Incidents escalated to problems and (c) Problems only. They assessed (a) wait status abuse, (b) ping -pong behavior across levels and across teams and (c) general case flow pattern. They uncovered interesting finding and captured a set of clear recommendations based on these findings.

The Jury: *All the analyses are performed with Disco and a graphical fuzzy model is used to respond to all questions. The work finishes with three interesting business-level suggestions.*

P. Van den Spiegel, L. Dieltjens and L. Blevi, KPMG Advisory, Belgium [15]

The incident and problem management process forms an essential part in every organization. Since businesses rely heavily on IT, each outage, issue or user service request should be dealt with as quickly as possible in order to minimize its impact on operations. The authors of this report objectively verified the efficiency and effectiveness of the underlying process. The analysis was performed by means of a of a combination of process mining and data mining techniques and tools, including Disco, ProM, Minitab and MS Excel. As part of the exercise, aspects such as total resolution times of tickets, actual resolution process being followed, ping-pong behavior between the different helpdesk lines, differences between distinct support teams etc. are investicated. Finally, recommendations to improve the current process and increase integration between incident and problem management are provided.

The Jury: *I like the mapping of statuses on the standard flow. This really bridges the gap between the data in the event log and the provided process model. Furthermore, the authors make good use of their experience in the business domain and include interpretations from a business level perspective beyond the questions asked by the process owner in the case description. Overall, it's a solid contribution with a good focus on business level insights.*

4 The Winner

Using the jury's scores as initial ranking of the 12 submissions, we obtained a clear top three:

- A. Bautista, S. Akbar, A. Alvarez, T. Metzger and M. Reaves, CKM Advisors, USA
- E. Dudok and P. van den Brand, Perceptive Software, The Netherlands
- C.J. Kang, Y.S. Kang, Y.S. Lee, S. Noh, H.C. Kim, W.C. Lim, J. Kim and R. Hong, Myongji University, Korea

All these submissions were praised for their thoroughness, completeness and presentation. However, one winner had to be selected and the decision was made to select, as winner of the BPI Challenge 2013:

C.J. Kang, Y.S. Kang, Y.S. Lee, S. Noh,
H.C. Kim, W.C. Lim, J. Kim and R. Hong,
Myongji University, Korea

Their report was found to be complete, repeatable and thorough, while maintaining a proper mix between general data analysis techniques and real business process intelligence techniques. During the BPI workshop 2013, the prizes were handed over to the first author of the submission as shown in Fig. 1.

Fig. 1. Award ceremony at BPI'13 showing Prof. Kang (right) receiving the BPI 2013 trophy from the organizers.

5 Conclusion

The BPI challenge has proven to be a succesful way to let practitioners and researchers come together and share their capabilities and techniques. The various reports have significantly increased in quality over the years and this year's result shows how mature the business process intelligence field has become.

With the help of the community, we hope to organize many succesful challenges in the future.

References

1. BPI Challenge 2013, incidents. Ghent University. Dataset. http://dx.doi.org/10. 4121/uuid:500573e6-accc-4b0c-9576-aa5468b10cee
2. BPI Challenge 2013, closed problems. Ghent University. Dataset. http://dx.doi. org/10.4121/uuid:c2c3b154-ab26-4b31-a0e8-8f2350ddac11
3. BPI Challenge 2013, open problems. Ghent University. Dataset. http://dx.doi.org/ 10.4121/uuid:3537c19d-6c64-4b1d-815d-915ab0e479da
4. Arias, M., Rojas, E.: Volvo incident and problem management behavior analysis. In: Proceedings of 3rd BPI Challenge BPIC'13, Beijing, China, CEUR-WS.org, August 26 2013. http://www.CEUR-WS.org/Vol-1052/paper1.pdf

5. Bautista, A., Akbar, S., Alvarez, A., Metzger, T., Reaves, M.: Process mining in information technology incident management: a case study at Volvo belgium. In: Proceedings of 3rd BPI Challenge BPIC'13, Beijing, China. CEUR-WS.org, August 26 2013. http://www.CEUR-WS.org/Vol-1052/paper2.pdf

6. vanden Broucke, S., Vanthienen, J., Baesens, B.: Volvo IT Belgium VINST. In: Proceedings of 3rd BPI Challenge BPIC'13, Beijing, China. CEUR-WS.org, August 26 2013. http://www.CEUR-WS.org/Vol-1052/paper3.pdf

7. Dudok, E., van den Brand, P.: Mining an incident management process. In: Proceedings of 3rd BPI Challenge BPIC'13, Beijing, China. CEUR-WS.org, August 26 2013. http://www.CEUR-WS.org/Vol-1052/paper4.pdf

8. van Geffen, F., Niks, R.: Accelerate DMAIC using process mining. In: Proceedings of 3rd BPI Challenge BPIC'13, Beijing, China. CEUR-WS.org, August 26 2013. http://www.CEUR-WS.org/Vol-1052/paper5.pdf

9. Hansen, J.: Analyzing Volvo IT Belgium's incident and problem management data using automated business process discovery. In: Proceedings of 3rd BPI Challenge BPIC'13, Beijing, China. CEUR-WS.org, August 26 2013. http://www.CEUR-WS.org/Vol-1052/paper6.pdf

10. Hevia, J., Saint-Pierre, C.: Analyzing Volvo information with process mining. In: Proceedings of 3rd BPI Challenge BPIC'13, Beijing, China. CEUR-WS.org, August 26 2013. http://www.CEUR-WS.org/Vol-1052/paper7.pdf

11. Kang, C.J., Kang, Y.S., Lee, Y.S., Noh, S., Kim, H.C., Lim, W.C., Kim, J., Hong, R.: Process mining-based understanding and analysis of Volvo IT's incident and problem management processes. In: Proceedings of 3rd BPI Challenge BPIC'13, Beijing, China. CEUR-WS.org, August 26 2013. http://www.CEUR-WS.org/Vol-1052/paper8.pdf

12. Martens, J.: Professional use of process mining for analyzing business processes. In: Proceedings of 3rd BPI Challenge BPIC'13, Beijing, China. CEUR-WS.org, August 26 2013. http://www.CEUR-WS.org/Vol-1052/paper9.pdf

13. Paszkiewicz, Z., Picard, W.: Analysis of the Volvo IT incident and problem handling processes using process mining and social network analysis. In: Proceedings of 3rd BPI Challenge BPIC'13, Beijing, China. CEUR-WS.org, August 26 2013. http://www.CEUR-WS.org/Vol-1052/paper10.pdf

14. Radhakrishnan, S., Anantha, G.: Process improvement focused analysis of VINST IT support logs. In: Proceedings of 3rd BPI Challenge BPIC'13, Beijing, China. CEUR-WS.org, August 26 2013. http://www.CEUR-WS.org/Vol-1052/paper11.pdf

15. Van den Spiegel, P., Dieltjens, L., Blevi, L.: Applied process mining techniques for incident and problem management. In: Proceedings of 3rd BPI Challenge BPIC'13, Beijing, China. CEUR-WS.org, August 26 2013. http://www.CEUR-WS.org/Vol-1052/paper3.pdf

6th Workshop on Business Process Management and Social Software (BPMS2 2013)

6th Workshop on Business Process Management and Social Software (BPMS2 2013)

Enabling Workflow Composition Within a Social Network Environment

Ourania Hatzi$^{(\boxtimes)}$, Despina Topali, Mara Nikolaidou,
and Dimosthenis Anagnostopoulos

Department of Informatics and Telematics,
Harokopio University of Athens, Athens, Greece
{raniah,it20737,mara,dimosthe}@hua.gr

Abstract. Social networks have emerged as a new paradigm for everyday communication, as well as for promoting collaboration within enterprises and organizations. Using current technology, social network participants not only exchange information but also invoke external applications in the form of gadgets. In order to provide enhanced, complex functionality to participants, enabling them to complete a specific business task, workflow composition based on gadget combination could be supported. In such case, gadgets executed in the context of a user profile may add or update information stored in it, while the profile owner is responsible to combine them. In this paper, we explore how to support such features, based on a recommendation mechanism, which automatically produces gadget composition plans, based on intelligent techniques. This context-driven process provides efficiency in cases when a large number of gadgets is available in a social network. The main contribution of the proposed framework lies in the fact that users are only expected to state the content to be added in their profile; the recommendation mechanism can then automatically discover and combine the appropriate gadgets, proposing a solution; no predefined workflows or any other knowledge of the available gadgets is required. The proposed mechanism supporting gadget composition promotes the adoption of social networks as a novel paradigm not only for content sharing and collaboration but also for business process management within the enterprise.

Keywords: Social BPM · Social network · Enterprise 2.0 · Recommendation mechanism · Workflow composition

1 Introduction

Social networks have emerged as a new model for communication and interaction between individuals, as well as among members of enterprises, communities or organizations [1]. Currently, there are numerous social network platforms, enabling user communication in everyday social life and competing with each other in terms of popularity, by continuously offering enhanced functionality, advanced features, external service invocation and integration with other social networks [23, 24]. At the same time, not only individuals but also enterprises and organizations incorporate

N. Lohmann et al. (Eds.): BPM 2013 Workshops, LNBIP 171, pp. 91–103, 2014.
DOI: 10.1007/978-3-319-06257-0_8, © Springer International Publishing Switzerland 2014

novel interaction models based on private social networks, serving a specific community, for knowledge dissemination, communication and collaboration between their members [2, 10, 16].

Collaboration in a typical social network is performed through exchange of information and notifications in a distributed fashion. In addition to sharing content, the social network model also supports the provision of functionality in the form of *gadgets*, which are external applications executed in the context of the social network, able to access participant's data stored in their profiles. Usually a gadget implements the invocation of an external application, commonly in the form of web services and is executed in the context of a specific user profile, often using as input data stored in the user's profile, as for example age or gender. Thus, gadgets in most social networks are able to read data from the user profile, while writing in it is prohibited to minimize complexity and simplify security enforcement.

To support BPM in a social network environment, a participant should be able to achieve a specific task by composing a workflow based on available gadgets, possibly in co-operation with other participants. In order to be combined, gadgets should be allowed to both use and alter the content of the user profile, e.g. to read and to write or update data stored in it. Such a feature can be easily supported in private social networks, where participants belong in a specific organization/community and can be authorized to access or share specific content, based on their role/position in the community. An example of such an environment is Unity private social network, developed by the authors to support collaboration in a University community [26].

Workflow composition can be facilitated by allowing social network participants to execute specific gadgets based on the context of their profile, which in turn is enriched by gadgets outputs. A gadget can be executed when its input data is missing, which may be produced by the execution of other gadgets, which, in turn, might require more data, leading to the execution of additional gadgets, and so on. As the number of available gadgets increases, this process becomes burdensome and inefficient; therefore, the ability to automatically determine and recommend gadget combinations that fulfils the participants' needs to support workflow is essential. Furthermore, in many case a participant may be aware of the content he/she wishes to be added in their profile, but has no knowledge of the workflow to produce it. Instead, the only truly feasible solution is automated composition, aided by intelligent techniques; such techniques enable the provision of appropriate composition plans, which represent workflows for task completion. Supporting automated gadget composition in a social network may enable service provision and lead to the accommodation of business process management through the social network paradigm [4, 5, 6, 9, 15, 21].

This paper concerns (a) the exploration of the dynamic composition of workflows in a social network by network participants and (b) the development of a recommendation mechanism to assist participants to determine workflows based on alternative gadget combinations and the content of their profile, using intelligent techniques. The produced solutions enable social network participants to achieve specific goals by adding the desired content in their profile, possibly in collaboration with other participants. The proposed recommendation mechanism utilizes existing methods and tools and has been integrated and tested within Unity private social network platform. The rest of the paper is structured as follows: Section 2 provides some background information concerning the social network collaboration paradigm and systems in the area of service composition through intelligent techniques. Section 3 elaborates on the proposed mechanism, while Sect. 4 provides case studies. Finally, Sect. 5 concludes the paper and proposes future directions.

2 Background and Related Work

Social network platform functionality, offered in the form of gadgets, has been utilized to enable the completion of specific tasks within collaborative communities, including organizations or enterprises, which are supported by private social networks [26]. For collaboration purposes, processes can be treated as business goals reached after completing specific tasks, which may be performed by a specific participant and may involve the invocation of external services to be completed. Each task corresponding to a specific process step is handled by a gadget, which may only be executed in the participant's profile.

In order for collaborative processes to be supported, inter-gadget communication must be enabled. Based on available social network technology, gadgets may access and store data in a specific area of the profile they are executed on, as well as in external profiles as well, under certain conditions. For communication purposes, gadgets are described in terms of their inputs and outputs – represented as concepts; a concept may serve as both the input of a specific gadget as well as the output of another. A gadget is allowed to start its execution only when all input data is available.

Generally, each gadget is supposed to implement a simple, basic task, thus promoting reusability; more complex tasks can be achieved by the combination of more than one gadgets. Business process modeling can be achieved by representing each business process as a task, implemented by a simple gadget – in order for the entire process to be completed, a combination of gadgets has to be achieved.

In the case where the number of available gadgets increases, it is difficult – if not practically impossible – for a participant to know which gadget to execute to produce a specific output they wish to be added in their profile. In many cases, there is more than one gadget that could potentially produce this output. Moreover in many cases this gadget cannon be executed unless other gadgets are executed first, most probably in a specific order. This indicates the need to establish a recommendation mechanism, which enables a social network participant to efficiently utilize an existing gadget repository supported by the social network to achieve a specific goal, e.g. to add specific data to their profile. Automatic workflow specification, based on gadget combination, can be performed through intelligent techniques; this paper proposes a mechanism for automatically generating such workflows using AI Planning.

The problem of automatically determining workflows that satisfy enhanced functionality by combining functional components in highly dynamic environments has emerged and has been studied in the past, in the form of web service composition. At the same time, research in this area has shown that we can take advantage of well defined and long studied techniques from artificial intelligence, and apply them to solve problems from different domains. During the design of the proposed recommendation mechanism, similarities between gadgets and web services were identified;

therefore, it was possible to use the same intelligent techniques proposed for web service composition and adapt them to the gadget & social network environment.

To the extent of our knowledge, gadget composition through intelligent techniques has not been presented in the literature; however, composition of functional units, such as components as web services, has been extensively studied [3, 6, 11, 25, 28, 30]. Therefore, the remainder of this section presents related approaches as a foundation for the proposed recommendation framework.

Automated approaches typically involve representation of the composition problem in such a way that well-defined and long-studied AI techniques can be utilized to obtain solutions to the problem [25, 28, 29]. A critical evaluation of the related systems reveals that the utilization of AI planning for automated web service composition provides significant advantages, including the independence of problem representation from problem solution [22, 27, 29], increased interoperability by conformation to current standards [13], and increased scalability, as indicated in [19, 20]. AI Planning has been extensively utilized to provide solutions in similar problems where component composition is performed based on inputs and outputs; such frameworks can benefit from both the solid foundation as well as the ongoing research advances in this area. At the same time, external independent planning tools are available and accessible over the web, communicating using XML based standards, as the Planning Domain Definition Language (PPDL) [13], promoting interoperability. This permits the proposed approach to utilize existing tools.

3   Proposed Framework

The framework proposed in this paper concerns a mechanism which utilizes intelligent techniques to automatically produce recommended gadget composition plans. This process is context-driven and accommodates user requirements for complex functionality. In particular, the recommendation mechanism is employed in the social network, when a user wishes to complete a goal by identifying the content required to be added to their profile. To do so, they should select to perform certain tasks (e.g run gadgets), out of a large variety of available ones. In this case, participants know *what* they want to do (the result) but not exactly *how* to do it (process steps). Both user requirements and available gadgets are described in terms of data exchanged; therefore, the recommendation mechanism is able to match user requirements to gadget inputs and outputs, and formulate a composition plan that might include serial and/or parallel steps, each step representing a gadget execution.

Evidently, the recommendation mechanism needs to be aware of all available gadgets in the social network; more specifically, it requires knowledge of their inputs and outputs. Currently, there is not a commonly accepted standard for describing gadgets in a social network; to overcome this, the proposed framework includes an extension to the standard OpenSocial / Shindig database, depicted in Fig. 1. This extension accommodates the creation of a gadget registry, where the definition of concepts is separated from their use as gadget inputs and outputs; this representation is indicated for cases when developers need to use a common vocabulary (e.g. an ontology) for defining gadgets.

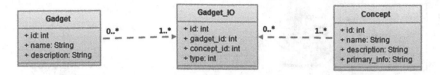

Fig. 1. OpenSocial Database extension implementing gadget registry.

The recommendation mechanism utilizes intelligent techniques, namely AI planning, in order to accommodate reusability and scalability. The problem of combining gadgets in order to come up with a composition plan of a workflow that fulfills users' needs can be transformed into an AI Planning problem and solved using existing domain independent planning systems. Thus, it ulilizes existing tools available in the Internet.

A planning problem is modelled according to STRIPS (Stanford Research Institute Planning System) notation [12] as a tuple $<I,A,G>$ where I is the Initial state, A is a set of available actions and G is a set of goals. States in STRIPS are represented as sets of atomic facts. Set A contains all the actions that can be used to modify states. Each action A_i has three lists of facts containing the preconditions of A_i (noted as $prec(A_i)$), the facts that are added to the state (noted as $add(A_i)$) and the facts that are deleted from the state (noted as $del(A_i)$). An action A_i is applicable to a state S if $prec(A_i) \subseteq$ S. If A_i is applied to S, the successor state S' is calculated as $S' = S \setminus del(A_i) \cup add(A_i)$. The solution to a planning problem is a sequence of actions, which, if applied to I, lead to a state S' such that $S' \supseteq G$.

In order to acquire solutions, a planning problem can be forwarded to external planning systems, as the one presented in [18].

In order to solve a gadget composition problem as a planning one, the required steps are as follows:

Step 1. The gadget composition problem must be transformed into a planning problem.
Step 2. The planning problem must be encoded in a planning standard, such as PDDL; as a result, the planning domain and problem are produced.
Step 3. The planning problem will be forwarded to external planning systems, which will produce as a solution a composition plan.
Step 4. The composition plan must be reversely transformed into the social network domain, the corresponding gadgets must be located and possibly visualized.

The aforementioned steps are depicted in Fig. 2.

Step 1 of the process discussed above, which includes the representation of a gadget composition problem in planning terms, requires gadgets to be viewed as actions, and compositions to be viewed as plans. More specifically, the representation of the gadget composition problem to a planning problem can be performed by applying the following rules:

- The set of all available inputs that the user can provide to the social network formulates the initial state I of the planning problem. In order to release the user

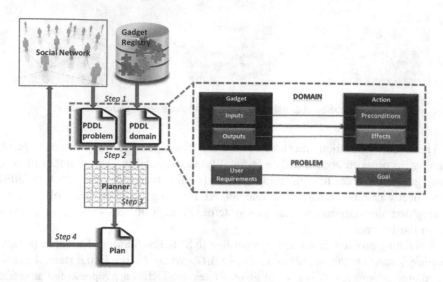

Fig. 2. Proposed recommendation framework utilizing planning

from the obligation to provide a list of every available piece of information that they could potentially provide, we can safely assume that this list can be automatically populated by all inputs of available gadgets that cannot be produced as outputs from other available gadgets.

- The set of all available outputs that the user requires to receive by the desired functionality formulates the goal state G of the planning problem.
- The set of all available gadgets in the social network formulates the set A of actions of the planning domain. More specifically, each gadget is transformed into an action; the inputs of the gadget serve as the preconditions of the action, while the outputs of the gadget serve as the results of the action.

The produced plan will enable to determine the combination of gadgets that can be executed to perform the requested collaborative task. In case when alternative plans exist, due to the fact that certain outputs are produced by more than one gadgets, the planner is able to produce all of them. Also, in case when certain inputs do not exist in the social network the proposed framework is able to produce partial plans and indicate that certain gadgets which would be required to complete the process are missing.

4 Case Studies

The proposed mechanism can be employed in a variety of cases with the following characteristics:

- Highly dynamic environments, where available gadgets change, as new gadgets are added in the social network while other become unavailable.
- Social networks with a large number of available gadgets from different developers, where it is difficult to be aware of all of them and locate suitable ones.

- Cases where user requirements for functionality are complex but not predefined; that is, environments where users require services on demand.
- Social network environments which integrate a variety of external software systems as gadgets; such social networks concern for example e-administration [17] or e-government [8].

The proposed recommendation mechanism application and evaluation was accommodated by Unity, an academic social network implemented at the Department of Informatics and Telematics of Harokopio University of Athens to promote collaboration within faculty, staff and students of the Department [17, 26]. Unity features discrete roles for participants and different kinds of relations between them, based on these roles. The Unity social network incorporates functionality in the form of gadgets; each gadget is an application that can be installed on a participant profile and gain read & write access rights to their profile data. In many cases, the gadget can also gain access to data in the profiles of other participants, in order to promote collaboration. The installation and execution rights of each gadget, as well as the permissions for data access are governed by a security mechanism based on a set of rules which take into account the participants roles and relations between them. Each gadget corresponds to a specific task that a participant can perform. Members of the academic community can receive electronic services through the Unity platform by requesting certain data to be added to their profiles. In case this data is produced not by a single gadget, but a combination, the proposed recommendation mechanism is employed. The recommendation mechanism was incorporated as a component in the Unity social network, facilitating users in determining gadgets compositions which fulfill their needs.

Unity implementation is based on the extension of OpenSocial API and Apache Shindig. A screenshot of the interface of the academic social network constructed using the Unity platform is depicted in Fig. 3. The left part of the profile contains the participant role and their connections with other participants, while the middle part includes all notifications about activities. Finally, the right part of the profile is reserved for gadget execution.

Fig. 3. Screenshot of an example profile of the Unity academic social network.

As an example, the graduation application process is considered. In order to be eligible for graduation, a university student must fulfill the following requirements:

- All courses have been successfully completed.
- The degree thesis has been submitted to the University Library.
- All books borrowed from the University Library have been returned.
- The student ID, transportation card and thesis certificate have been returned.

The student can subsequently fill out a graduation application form and submit it to the Department Secretariat, who confirms that all requirements are valid and notifies the student of the graduation ceremony date.

When the user attempts to perform this task through the Unity academic social network, he or she is not expected to be aware of all these requirements; they are just expected to ask for their graduation date to be added on their profile; this data is produced by the corresponding "Graduation Apply" gadget. Since this specific gadget requires input not already present in the student profile, the recommendation mechanism is employed. Student requirements are viewed as a gadget composition problem and transformed into a planning problem (Step 1). Consequently, the planning problem is encoded in PDDL (Step 2); the corresponding PDDL files (problem & domain) are depicted in Figs. 4 and 5 respectively.

```
(define (problem gadgetproblem)
(:domain states)
(:objects aaa)
(:init (block aaa)
 (Name aaa)(Lastname aaa)(Library_Username aaa)(RN aaa)
(Identification_Card_Number aaa)
(Social_Security_registration_number aaa))
(:goal  (Date_Graduation_Apply aaa)))
```

Fig. 4. PDDL problem file for the problem of graduation application.

The planning problem is the fed to the LPG-td planning system [14] (Step 3), which produces the plan presented in Fig. 6.

The plan is consequently reversely transformed into the gadget domain and visualized with JQuery (Step 4), as depicted in Fig. 7.

To explore the applicability for the e e-government case, the recommendation mechanism is incorporated in the social network model proposed in [7]. As an example, consider the following scenario.

An employer wishes to pay the insurance tax for their employees through web banking, and receive an electronic receipt for the payment. The employer does not need to know neither the prerequisites for this process, nor all the available gadgets that produce these prerequisites and the rest of the required information. The employer only needs to specify their needs; the recommendation mechanism will take over the rest of the process, locate the appropriate gadgets and inform the employer of the produced workflow, which includes the following steps:

- The amount of insurance for each specific employee is calculated based on their identification data and their social security number; for security purposes, redundant data is required.

```
(define (domain states)
(:predicates (block ?b)
(Name ?b) (Lastname ?b)
(Library_Username ?b) (RN ?b) (No_Dept_Books ?b)
(Thesis_Submitted ?b) (None_Remaining_Courses ?b)
(Graduation_Documents_Submitted ?b) (Date_Graduation_Apply ?b)
(Identification_Card_Number ?b) (Social_Security_registration_number ?b)
(Calculation_Contribution_Valid ?b) (Insurance_Number_Valid ?b)
(Taxpayer_Identification_Valid ?b) (Calculated_Amount_Paid ?b)
(Wage_Period_Valid ?b) (Electronic_Contribution_Valid ?b)
(Code_Retrieval_Payment_Receipt ?b))
(:action Library_Book_Account
   :parameters (?b)
   :precondition (and (block ?b) (Name ?b) (Lastname ?b)
      (Library_Username ?b) (RN ?b))
   :effect (No_Dept_Books ?b))
(:action Library_Thesis_Submission
   :parameters (?b)
   :precondition (and (block ?b) (Name ?b) (Lastname ?b)
      (Library_Username ?b) (RN ?b))
   :effect (Thesis_Submitted ?b))
(:action Remaining_Courses
   :parameters (?b)
   :precondition (and (block ?b) (Name ?b) (Lastname ?b) (RN ?b))
   :effect (None_Remaining_Courses ?b))
(:action Graduation_Documents
   :parameters (?b)
   :precondition (and (block ?b) (Name ?b) (Lastname ?b) (RN ?b))
   :effect (Graduation_Documents_Submitted ?b))
(:action Graduation_Apply
   :parameters (?b)
   :precondition (and (block ?b) (None_Remaining_Courses ?b)
      (No_Dept_Books ?b) (Thesis_Submitted ?b)
         (Graduation_Documents_Submitted ?b))
   :effect (Date_Graduation_Apply ?b)))
```

Fig. 5. PDDL domain file for the problem of graduation application.

```
0:    (REMAINING_COURSES AAA) [1]
0:    (LIBRARY_BOOK_ACCOUNT AAA) [1]
0:    (LIBRARY_THESIS_SUBMISSION AAA) [1]
0:    (GRADUATION_DOCUMENTS AAA) [1]
1:    (GRADUATION_APPLY AAA) [1]
```

Fig. 6. Gadget composition plan, produced by LPG-td.

- The employer needs to locate his Employer Identification Number, his Social Security number, and state the amount of insurance payment, as well as determine the time period that this amount corresponds to.
- If all gadgets required in the previous step are executed successfully, the gadget that integrates the bank web service is activated and the payment takes place.
- Finally, another gadget produces the payment receipt and provides it to the employer profile.

The produced gadget composition, transformed back into the social network domain, and represented as specific gadgets along with their inputs and outputs is depicted in Fig. 8.

The case studies in this section indicate the applicability of the approach as far as social networks that conform to contemporary OpenSocial standard are concerned. More specifically, the case studies demonstrate the representation of the available

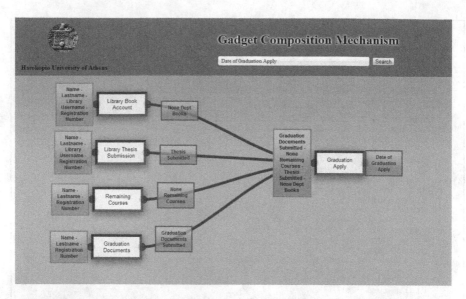

Fig. 7. Gadget composition visualization.

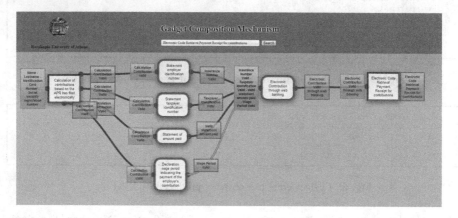

Fig. 8. Gadget composition for the electronic insurance payment case.

gadgets in the social network, the way participants are able to express their requirements for service provision or task completion, and the way gadget compositions are provided automatically as a solution to the problem at hand. The Unity case study validates the feasibility of the approach, since it was implemented in a real-world academic environment, accommodating processes that take place in the University. The e-government case study, on the other hand, expands the application area of the proposed recommendation mechanism and provides insight its usability for highly dynamic, heterogeneous environments. The case studies also demonstrate that the incorporation of the proposed recommendation mechanism in a social network promotes gadget development while relieving users from the obligation to manually discovering and combining functionality.

5 Conclusions and Future Work

As social networks become a widespread paradigm for collaboration and service provision, a requirement for more elaborate methods to manage and discover functionality offered through gadgets emerges. The proposed recommendation mechanism relieves users from the obligation to manually search among all available gadgets and consequently construct a workflow, thus contributing to increased efficiency when utilizing a social network for service provision, for example in an e-administration or e-government context.

The applicability of the approach has been demonstrated by incorporating the recommendation mechanism to Unity existing social network. Participants only need to specify their requirements, in terms of desired outputs added in their profile as content; the recommendation mechanism transforms the gadget composition problem into a planning problem and uses external planning systems to obtain solutions.

A major issue that needs further exploration in the future is gadget descriptions semantic interoperability. Currently, in order for the planning system to be able to match gadget inputs to gadget outputs successfully, syntactic interoperability must be guaranteed; in other words, the concepts used for describing gadget inputs and outputs much be exactly the same. This was guaranteed in the aforementioned examples, since all gadgets were developed by the same party, using the same vocabulary. However, in a more general case, it cannot be expected that all gadget developers will use the same vocabulary; therefore, interoperability between semantically related by syntactically different concepts must be ensured. Ontologies, Taxonomies and Lexical Thesauri, such as WordNet, could prove potentially useful for establishing such interoperability.

Future work also includes refinement of the mechanism to take into account additional restrictions, imposed by security rules that allow the execution of gadgets based on participant roles and relations between them. In such cases, the proposed composition should include different stakeholders, depending on the participant that should execute each gadget. Finally, future goals include more extensive evaluation of the recommendation mechanism in intensive social network environments, where previous recommendations may be used to facilitate efficiency.

References

1. Acquisti, A., Gross, R.: Imagined communities: awareness, information sharing, and privacy on the Facebook. In: Golle, P., Danezis, G. (eds.) Proceedings of 6th Workshop on Privacy Enhancing Technologies, pp. 36–58. Robinson College, Cambridge (2006)
2. Bermejo, J.A.A., Bravo, C.B., Mateos, M.J.R., Piera, J.R.: Social networks in the higher education framework - understanding the University as an organization: inlumine, our study case. In: Handbook of Research on Business Social Networking: Organizational, Managerial, and Technological Dimensions, pp. 805–824. IGI (2012)
3. Bucchiarone, A., Gnesi, S.: A survey on service composition languages and models. In: 1st International Workshop on Web Services Modeling and Testing (WsMaTe 2006) (2006)

4. Bruno, G., Dengler, F., Jennings, B., Khalaf, R., Nurcan, S., Prilla, M., Sarini, M., Schmidt, R., Silva, R.: Key challenges for enabling agile BPM with social software. J. Softw. Maint. Evol. Res. Pract. 23(4), 297–326 (2011)
5. Bruno, G.: an approach to defining social processes based on social networks. In: Handbook of Research on Business Social Networking: Organizational, Managerial, and Technological Dimensions, pp. 272–286. IGI (2012)
6. Chen, Q., Hsu, M.: Inter-enterprise collaborative business process management. In: Proceeding of 17th International Conference on Data Engineering (2001)
7. Dais, A., Nikolaidou, M., Anagnostopoulos, D.: OpenSocialGov: a web 2.0 environment for governmental e-service delivery. In: Andersen, K.N., Francesconi, E., Grönlund, Å., van Engers, T.M. (eds.) EGOVIS 2011. LNCS, vol. 6866, pp. 173–183. Springer, Heidelberg (2011)
8. Dais, A., Nikolaidou, M., Anagnostopoulos, D.: Facilitating business to goverment interaction using a citizen-centric web 2.0 model. In: The Proceedings of IFIP International Conference of e-business, e-goverment and e-society 2009 (I3E 2009). Springer (2009)
9. Dengler, F., Koschmider, A., Oberweis, A., Zhang, H.: Social software for coordination of collaborative process activities. In: Muehlen, M., Su, J. (eds.) BPM 2010 Workshops. LNBIP, vol. 66, pp. 396–407. Springer, Heidelberg (2011)
10. DiMicco, J., Millen, D.R., Geyer, W., Dugan, C., Brownholtz, B., Muller, M.: Motivations for social networking at work. In: CSCW '08 Proceedings of the 2008 ACM Conference on Computer Supported Cooperative Work, pp. 711–720. ACM New York, USA (2008)
11. Dustdar, S., Schreiner, W.: A survey on web services composition. Int. J. Web Grid Serv. 1(1), 1–30 (2005)
12. Fikes, R., Nilsson, N.J.: STRIPS: a new approach to the application of theorem proving to problem solving. Artif. Intell. 2, 189–208 (1971)
13. Ghallab, M., Howe, A., Knoblock, C., McDermott, D., Ram, A., Veloso, M., Weld, D., Wilkins, D.: PDDL – the planning domain definition language. Technical report, Yale University, New Haven, CT (1998)
14. Gerevini, A. Saetti, A., Serina, I.: LPG-TD: a fully automated planner for PDDL2.2 domains. In: ICAPS-04 (2004)
15. Goble, C.A. De Roure, D.C.: myExperiment: social networking for workflow-using e-scientists. In: Proceedings of the 2nd Workshop on Workflows in Support of Large-Scale Science (WORKS '07) (2007)
16. Grasso, A., Convertino, G.: Collective intelligence in organizations: tools and studies. Comput. Support. Coop. Work 21, 357–369 (2012)
17. Hatzi, O., Nikolaidou, M., Katsivelis-Perakis, P., Hudhra, V., Anagnostopoulos, D.: Using social network technology to provide e-administration services as collaborative tasks. In: Kő, A., Leitner, C., Leitold, H., Prosser, A. (eds.) EDEM 2012 and EGOVIS 2012. LNCS, vol. 7452, pp. 216–230. Springer, Heidelberg (2012)
18. Hatzi, O., Vrakas, D., Bassiliades, N., Anagnostopoulos, D., Vlahavas, I.: A visual programming system for automated problem solving. Expert Syst. Appl. 37(6), 4611–4625 (2010). Elsevier
19. Hatzi, O., Vrakas, D., Bassiliades, N., Anagnostopoulos, D., Vlahavas, I.: The PORSCE II framework: using AI planning for automated semantic web service composition. Knowl. Eng. Rev. 28, 137-156 (2013). doi:10.1017/S0269888912000392
20. Hatzi, O., Vrakas, D., Nikolaidou, M., Bassiliades, N., Anagnostopoulos, D., Vlahavas, I.: An integrated approach to automated semantic web service composition through planning. IEEE Trans. Serv. Comput. (2012) (To appear)

21. Johannesson, P., Andersson, B., Wohed, P.: business process management with social software systems – a new paradigm for work organisation. In: Ardagna, D., Mecella, M., Yang, J. (eds.) Business Process Management Workshops. LNBIP, vol. 17, pp. 659–665. Springer, Heidelberg (2009)
22. Klusch, M., Gerber, A., Schmidt, M.: Semantic web service composition planning with OWLS-XPlan. In: AAAI Fall Symposium on Semantic Web and Agents, USA (2005)
23. Kossinets, G., Watts, D.J.: Empirical analysis of an evolving social network. Science 6 **311**(5757), 88–90 (2006)
24. Kumar, R., Novak, J., Tomkins, A.: Structure and evolution of online social networks. In: Proceedings of 12th International Conference on Knowledge Discovery in Data Mining. pp. 611–617. ACM Press, New York (2006)
25. Milanovic, N., Malek, M.: Current solutions for web service composition. IEEE Internet Comput. **8**(6), 51–59 (2004)
26. Nikolaidou, M., Hatzi, O., Katsivelis-Perakis, P., Hudhra, V., Anagnostopoulos, D.: Utilizing social network technology to support collaborative tasks. Computer Supported Cooperative Work, Springer (2012) (under revision)
27. Pistore, M., Marconi, A., Bertoli, P., Traverso, P.: Automated composition of web services by planning at the knowledge level. In: Proceedings of the 19th International Joint Conference on Artificial Intelligence (IJCAI 05), Edinburgh, UK (2005)
28. Rao, J., Su, X.: A survey of automated web service composition methods. In: Cardoso, J., Sheth, A.P. (eds.) SWSWPC 2004. LNCS, vol. 3387, pp. 43–54. Springer, Heidelberg (2005)
29. Sirin, E., Parsia, B., Wu, D., Hendler, J., Nau, D.: HTN planning for web service composition using SHOP2. J. Web Semant. **1**(4), 377–396 (2004)
30. Srivastava, B., Koehler, J.: Web service composition - current solutions and open problems. In: Proceedings of ICAPS 2003 Workshop on Planning for Web Services (2003)

Towards a Meta-Model for Goal-Based Social BPM

Mohammad Ehson Rangiha$^{(\boxtimes)}$ and Bill Karakostas

Dept. of Computer Science, School of Mathematics,
Computer Science and Engineering, City University London, London, UK
{Mohammad.Rangiha.2,Bill.Karakostas.1}@city.ac.uk

Abstract. The traditional approach towards BPM has proven to have a number of limitations such as the processes being imposed on the user and therefore do not benefit from first hand user experience in the process discovery stage. In recent years, proposals to integrate BPM and Social Software have promised to overcome these limitations. One such idea proposed in this paper is driving BPM enactment by social goals. This paper presents a goal-based approach to social BPM that combines flexibility with the element of collaboration as found in social software.

Keywords: BPM · Social software · Goal-based modelling · Social BPM · Social goals · Process enactment

1 Introduction

Business Process Management (BPM) provides a platform to manage business processes throughout their lifecycle; by employing a systematic approach of management, measurement and improvement [2]. Recent research has started to introduce elements of social software into the BPM lifecycle [1, 3, 5, 6, 10].

Social BPM (SBPM) is the intersection of social software and BPM, where elements of social software are incorporated in the BPM systems to enhance their efficiency. Richardson [20] defines social BPM as a "methodology for bringing more and diverse voices into process improvement activities".

This papers proposes a goal-driven approach towards SBPM and is structured in the following way: firstly some basic concepts of SBPM are explained and a number of limitations and potentials found in SBPM are briefly presented (Sect. 2). In Sect. 3, a goal-based approach towards SBPM is presented, proposing a preliminary model on how SBPM would work. Finally Sect. 4 of the paper overviews the proposed framework and draws some final conclusions.

2 Social BPM

BPM is a discipline which aims to manage and optimise business processes within an organisation. "BPM includes concepts, methods, and techniques to support the design, administration, configuration, enactment, and analysis of business processes" [8].

N. Lohmann et al. (Eds.): BPM 2013 Workshops, LNBIP 171, pp. 104–112, 2014.
DOI: 10.1007/978-3-319-06257-0_9, © Springer International Publishing Switzerland 2014

In short, BPM attempts to create a platform where processes are managed and monitored. Numerous models for the BPM lifecycle and the different stages it consists of has been proposed, however for the purpose of this paper we have adapted the 4 stage model by Aalst et al [9] shown in Fig. 1, this is due to the model's simplicity and comprehensiveness.

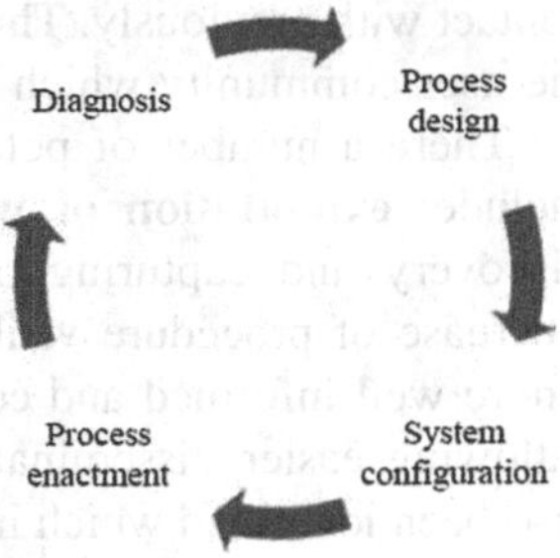

Current state of BPM practice has many limitations, including:

Diagnosis → Process design

Process enactment ← System configuration

Fig. 1. Van Der Aalst et al.'s BPM model [9]

- Lack of Information Fusion: The traditional BPM model follows a top-down approach where processes are designed and imposed on the users to follow [10, 14].
- Model-Reality Divide : Users not having a say in the process design stage results in them not using the processes; this in turn creates a gap between what the process actually is and what happens in real life [4, 10, 14].
- Information Pass-On Threshold and Lost Innovation: Valuable feedback from users regarding the processes remains unused due to hierarchical controls which can prevent sharing of knowledge [4, 10].
- Strict Access-Control: In traditional BPM systems strict access control for the users is quite common and only actors which have been chosen and given specific access are allowed to execute them [11].

2.1   Overview of SBPM

Social BPM is the integration of social software and BPM that is designed to "transform the way organizations identify, manage and resolve issues within their processes" [24]. Gartner emphasizes on the collaborative nature of social BPM stating that it is a concept which describes collaboratively designed and iterated processes [13]. Most of the definitions related to social BPM primarily concentrate on the role of social software during the design stage of the BPM lifecycle and neglect the other stages such as enactment which is a major step in BPM.

In social BPM, the users are involved in the designing of the processes right from the outset and are part of a wider user community group. This is contrary to the traditional BPM model where the processes are designed by a specific group of experts and then imposed on the users to follow. There has been limited research so far regarding what the model for social BPM should be. The current view of SBPM proposes that the developers should use social software in order to improve their experience to design processes. This however, on the one hand ignores collaboration and the use of social elements during runtime and on the other still does not overcome the limitations of traditional BPM model such as model-reality divide. In SBPM everyone contributes to the design of the processes, not just a specific group of experts [7]. According to Palmer [14] the potential of social BPM is reached by making use and engaging the skilled business users whom we may not necessarily have had any contact with previously. This will allow access to the tacit knowledge present amongst the user community which had previously been unknown.

There a number of potential benefits which SBPM can produce, some of these include: **exploitation of weak ties and implicit knowledge** [1, 3] (allowing the discovery and capturing of tacit and informal knowledge), **transparency** [3, 5] (increase of procedure visibility in the organisation), **decision distribution** [3, 16]: (more well-informed and collective decision making), **knowledge sharing** [3, 5, 16] (allowing easier dissemination of knowledge). Potential limitations of SBPM have also been identified which include: **learning effort** [1, 4] (major cultural shift required in the organisation), **security** [4, 5] (access rights given to many people can create an insecure environment), **quality** [4] (the quality of the content could be reduced as input is received from different people), **difficulty to evaluate** [5] (due to scattered benefits of SBPM it is difficult to evaluate them), **process management** (due to the flexible nature which exists it becomes a challenge to manage the interaction and overall processes).

2.2   SBPM at Enactment/Runtime

Kemsley [1] defines enactment or runtime collaboration as the modification of the processes during execution to include and cater for unplanned participation and also in order to complete the execution of the process more effectively; however currently there are no proposals as to what and how the runtime behaviour of SBPM should be. Additionally, the rigid and sequential flow of the processes in the traditional BPM system limits collaboration and flexibility during runtime. Figure 2 captures a summary of the current state of SBPM at the different stages the lifecycle and identifies the gap in the research. We can see that social medium has only been used as a means

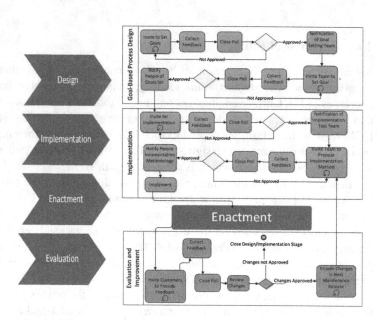

Fig. 2. Integration of social software at the different stage of BPM lifecycle

for designing processes, implementing them and evaluation which in practice has not achieved a total integration, flexibility, transparency and collaboration.

2.3 SBPM at Process Design

The first area in which social software starts benefiting BPM is the initial stage of process design phase and this is the area where the current researches have been mainly addressing. In the design stage the user community, stakeholders and end users are involved in the process discovery stage [1]. Brambilla et al. [6] have proposed an extension of the BPMN which includes some features of social software, what has been proposed is only making use of social technology in order to design processes. The meta-model in the design stage of BPM in Fig. 2 has been derived from an example model proposed by Brambilla et al. [3]. In this model the processes are also predefined and given to the users to follow, which could potentially result in the same limitations found in the traditional BPM model.

3 Goal-Driven Modelling

This research has been inspired by collaborative approaches to Information systems development, such as the Scandinavian approach to participatory design. Participatory Design (PD) enables collaboration amongst a wide range of users in defining problems and proposing potential solutions in designing [16]. Collaboration assumes the setting and agreement of common (or at least not incompatible) goals amongst the stakeholders. Goal definition allows the capturing of the 'why' without specifying the 'how'. Goals are defined as objectives or a state that should be achieved or reached by the system and its environment [17].

Goal-oriented modelling approaches such as *i** (iStar) [29] have been used extensively to support requirements engineering [21]. Even though most process modelling languages do not use goals as an integral elements of their model [23], goals are the core element of all business process. Goal-based approach could be a potential way forward to overcome the rigid nature of the current sequential processes in BPM and allow participation and flexibility during the design stage as well as execution of the processes.

Goal-based modelling approach has been proposed in this paper as a potential way forward for filling in the gap in the research in SBPM at runtime. The following sections elaborate on this idea further, and propose a preliminary model towards a goal-based approach in the context of Social BPM.

3.1 Goal-Driven Social BPM

In social BPM, the flow and sequence of actions should not be enforced upon the user, but rather it should allow and support the enactment of the processes exploring the sharing of knowledge and the business best practices [5] by enabling collaboration and flexibility.

According to Nurcan et al. [5], in order to achieve flexibility during the runtime of the processes based on experience and knowledge, models with rigid sequences of actions would not work. Therefore, to reach a balance between having a flexible and collaborative process on the one hand and the satisfaction of key business constraints, regarding resources, performance and so on, we propose goal-based SBPM enactment.

The very reason a business process exists, is to achieve a set business goals [22]. The goals define 'what' has to be done and the steps illustrate 'how' it has to be or has been done [20]. When the steps are completed and the desired outcome has been achieved, the state of the goal is changed to accomplished, in order words the conditions for the goal to be satisfied have been met and the state of the goal has changed. Initially there can be high-level goals each having a number of sub-goals that need to be satisfied in order for the general goal to be achieved. According to Markovic et al. [18] "the more clearly the goals are formulated, the easier it is to design a corresponding business process that achieves the goal." The user may interact with the customers or any other stakeholder, during any of the execution steps, and based on that, can improve their user experience and incorporate it in the future and share with other users.

The goals set, need to be measurable, attainable and time-bound (there is a time limit to achieve the goal) [18]. According to Nurcan et al. [5] what usually happens after a few iteration and accomplishment of goals based on the actors knowledge, experience or creative way of thinking of achieving the particular goal, the process gradually takes shape and becomes more structured.

3.2   Social Goals

Many authors have proposed the concept of social goals, including Dowson [25] and McInerney [26] who were influenced by Urdan and Maehr [28]. Their work helped categorize social goals into following five groups [27]:

Social affiliation goals: Social affiliation goals involve goals related to belonging to a certain group or community.

Social approval goals: Social approval goals focus on goals that are concerned with gaining praise from others, for example.

Social concern goals: Social concern goals involve goals that aim to help others.

Social responsibility goals: Social responsibility goals may, for example, centre on the pursuit of fulfilling social role obligations.

Social status goals: Social status goals include a focus on the attainment of a social position or a certain level of social status [26].

We propose that social goals such as the above which are related to the user should guide the behaviour of the SBPM system. They will in fact become meta-goals that steer the behaviour of the BPM system during enactment by the user.

While the users of the SBPM system are free to explore alternative routes to realise the technical goals of the process, social meta-goals such as the above can lead to patterns for user tasks and user-customer interactions. Kemsley [1] argues that Social BPM may change the very nature of process modelling, so depending on the approach taken during the enactment, the process design approach might also need to be changed. Social software enhances this process of process/goal evaluation and improvement with the online advanced IT tools present in the market which will be incorporated into the Social BPM lifecycle [10].

Once the goals are set, the user can start the enactment, during which (s)he follows a number of steps or mini-processes [1, 15]. These are not rigid system driven tasks, but intuitive sequences of (SBPM system guided) interactions with the customer that seek to maximise the mutual goal achievement in a win-win situation. This is in contrast to the traditional procedural based BPM systems [15] in which performers are bound to follow a set of predefined rigid series of steps. The steps related to a specific goal are aligned to a business process in order to know which business process contribute to a particular goal. If one goal is modified, its respective business process is easily detectable and analysable.

The proposed goal-oriented model presented in Fig. 3 allows SBPM users the autonomy to follow their own process steps within a dialogue with the customer that is guided by the overall social (meta) goals. Organisation set constraints ensure that the process finishes within a reasonable time and does not require more resources (including customer time/attention) than necessary. SBPM guides the user consciously (rather than blindly) catering for the achievement of such goals, during process enactments. SBPM does not enforce 'box ticking' nor saturates the user (and customers) with a huge number of goals to consider, but un-intrusively supports actions and interactions that are social goal maximising.

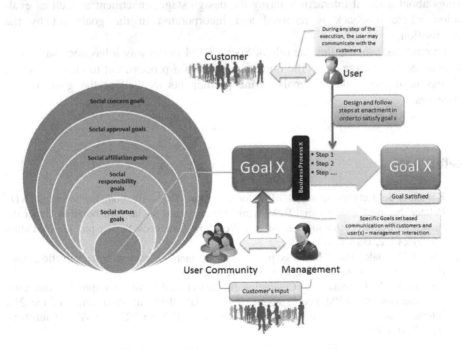

Fig. 3. A goal-based approach to social BPM

4 Conclusions and Future Research

This process of setting process goals presents several challenges, such as ensuring there is no conflicting, contradictory or overlapping goals and identifying interdependent and complementary goals [19]; these are however beyond the remit of this paper which need to be addressed in future works. The goals could be reviewed and refined based on the feedback from the users and the customer to allow improvement of the defined goals and subsequently of the processes and steps performed for achieving those goals. One of the limitations of the proposed approach, as previously mentioned, relates to the complex and time consuming task of identifying and modelling the goals. The other point to note is that this model of setting goals and designing flexible processes would not be feasible in processes where there is an existing monolithic IT implementation, as the steps to follow has already been hard coded and therefore should be followed.

By proposing a goal-based approach towards Social BPM, a structured and collaborative model is present in the BPM lifecycle which allows both flexibility and social participation as well as supports the performance of the process within the set business constraints of time and resources. This flexibility and collaboration attempts to overcome the limitations of traditional BPM mentioned above as it engages the users from the early stage of process design and allows them to be part of the decision making during the enactment of the processes. The goals to be achieved are set collaboratively and are predefined, however the steps for achieving those goals are left to the user to select in a number of steps which could be grouped within a certain process and it is aligned to the respective goal which it aims to satisfy. This model brings about a social interaction during the design stage, enactment as well as evaluation where feedback is received and incorporated in the goals set by the organisation.

Overall, we propose that the role of Social BPM in the way it has been suggested is no longer to enforce a specific implementation of a process, but to ensure that the process is aligned with the goals of the participants as well as the goals of the processes.

References

1. Kemsley, S.: Leveraging social BPM for enterprise transformation. In: Swenson, KD., Palmer, N., et al. (eds.) Social BPM Work, Planning and Social Collaboration Under the Impact of Social Technology. BPM and Workflow Handbook Series, pp. 77–83. Future Strategies Inc, USA (2011)
2. Lee, R.G., Dale, B.G.: Business process management: a review and evaluation. Bus. Process Manag. J. 4(3), 214–225 (1998). MCB UP Ltd
3. Brambilla, M., Fraternali, P.: Combining social web and BPM for improving enterprise performances: the BPM4People approach to social BPM. In: Proceedings of the 21st International Conference Companion on World Wide Web, pp. 223–226. ACM Publishers, New York (2012)

4. Filipowska, A., Kaczmarek, M., Koschmider, A., Stein, S., Wecel, K., Abramowicz, W.: Social software and semantics for business process management alternative or synergy? J. Syst. Integr. **2**(3), 54–69 (2011)
5. Erol, S., Granitzer, M., Happ, S., Jantunen, S., Jennings, B., Koschmider, A., Nurcan, S., Rossi, D., Schmidt, R., Johannesson, P.: Combining BPM and social software: contradiction or chance? J. Softw. Maintenance Evol. Res. Pract. **22**, 449–476 (2010). John Wiley & Sons, Ltd
6. Brambilla, M., Fraternali, P., Vaca, C.: BPMN and design patterns for engineering social BPM solutions. In: Daniel, F., Barkaoui, K., Dustdar, S. (eds.) BPM Workshops 2011, Part I. LNBIP, vol. 99, pp. 219–230. Springer, Heidelberg (2012)
7. Swenson, K.: Who is Socializing in Social BPM? 12 May 2010 [Blog Entry], Collaborative Planning & Social Business. http://social-biz.org/2010/05/12/who-is-socializing-in-social-bpm-2/ (2013). Accessed Mar 2013
8. Weske, M.: Business Process Management, Concepts, Languages, Architectures. Springer, Berlin (2007)
9. Van der Aalst, W.M.P.: Business process management: a personal view. Bus. Process Manag. J. **10**(2), 744–791 (2009). (Emerald Group Publishing)
10. Schmidt, R., Nurcan, S.: BPM and social software. BPM 2008 International Workshops. 17, pp. 649–658. Springer, Berlin (2009)
11. Wohed, P., Henkel, M., Andersson, B., Johannesson, P.: A new paradigm for work organization. Business Process Management Workshops. LNBIP, pp. 659–665. Springer, Berlin (2009)
12. Richardson, C.: Is social BPM a Methodology, A Technology, Or just a lot of Hype? 20 May 2010 [Blog Entry]. Forrester. http://blogs.forrester.com/clay_richardson/10-05-20-social_bpm_methodology_technology_or_just_lot_hype Accessed Apr 2012
13. Gartner, Social BPM: Design by doing, Apr 2010 Sinur, J., Social BPM is Design by Doing: Really? 4 Jul 2011 [Blog Entry], Gartner: http://blogs.gartner.com/jim_sinur/2011/07/04/social-bpm-is-design-by-doing-really/ (2012). Accessed Apr 2012
14. Palmer, N.: The role of trust and reputation in social BPM: In: Swenson, KD., Palmer, N., et al. (eds.) Social BPM Work, Planning and Social Collaboration Under the Impact of Social Technology, BPM and Workflow Handbook Series, pp. 35–43. Future Strategies Inc, USA (2011)
15. Pucher, M.J.: How to link BPM governance and social collaboration through an adaptive paradigm. In: Swenson, K.D., Palmer, N., et al. (eds.) Social BPM Work, Planning and Social Collaboration Under the Impact of Social Technology, BPM and Workflow Handbook Series, pp. 57–75. Future Strategies Inc, USA (2011)
16. Kensing, F., Bloomberg, J.: Participatory design: issues and concerns. Comput. Support. Coop. Work **7**, 167–185 (1998). (Kluwer Academic Publishers, Netherlands)
17. De la Vara, J.L., Sanchez, J.: Business process – driven requirements engineering: a goal-based approach. In: BPMDS 2007, Trondheim, Norway (2007)
18. Markovic, I., Kowalkiewicz, M.: Linking business goals to process models in semantic business process modelling. In: 12th International IEEE Enterprise Distributed Object Computing Conference, pp. 332–338. IEEE Computer Society (2008)
19. Kueng, P., Kawalek, P.: Goal-based business process models: creation and evaluation. Bus. Process Management J. **3**(1), 17–38 (1997). MCB University Press
20. Nurcan, S., Etien, A., Kaab, R., Zouka, I.: A strategy driven business process modelling approach. J. Bus. Process Manag. **11**(6), 628–649 (2005)
21. Kavakli, E.: Goal-driven requirements engineering: modelling and guidance. http://www.ct.aegean.gr/people/vkavakli/publications/pdf_files/PhD/kavakli_chapter2.pdfhype (2013). Accessed May 2013

22. Penker, M., Eriksson, H.-E.: Business Modeling with UML: Business Patterns at Work. Wiley, Fall (2000)
23. Soffer, P., Rolland, C.: Combining intention-oriented and state-based process modelling. http://mis.haifa.ac.il/~mis/userfiles/file/spnina_files/publications/ER%20Map%20GPM. pdf (2013). Accessed May 2013
24. Weeks, D.: The Future of social BPM, Jul 2010 [Blog Entry]. OpenText. http://www. becauseprocessmatters.com/the-future-of-social-bpm (2013). Accessed May 2013
25. Dowson, M., McInerney, D.M.: Psychological parameters of students' social and work avoidance goals: a qualitative investigation. J. Educ. Psychol. **93**, 35–42 (2001)
26. Dowson, M., McInerney, D.M.: What do students say about their motivational goals? Towards a more complex and dynamic perspective on student motivation. Contemp. Educ. Psychol. **28**, 91–113 (2003)
27. Dowson, M., McInerney, D.M.: The development and validation of the Goal Orientation and Learning Strategies Survey (GOALS-S). Educ. Psychol. Meas. **64**, 290–310 (2004)
28. Urdan, T., Maehr, M.L.: Beyond a two-goal theory of motivation and achievement: a case for social goals. Rev. Educ. Res. **65**, 213–243 (1995)
29. Yu, E.S.: Social modeling and *i**. In: Borgida, A.T., Chaudhri, V.K., Giorgini, P., Yu, E.S. (eds.) Conceptual Modeling: Foundations and Applications. LNCS, vol. 5600, pp. 99–121. Springer, Heidelberg (2009)

An Experiment on the Capture of Business Processes from Knowledge Workers

David Martinho[1](✉) and António Rito Silva[2]

[1] Instituto Superior Técnico – UL, Lisboa, Portugal
[2] ESW- INESC-ID, Lisboa, Portugal
{davidmartinho,rito.silva}@ist.utl.pt

Abstract. This paper describes an experiment on the capture of business processes' tacit knowledge owned by knowledge workers. During the experiment, knowledge workers used a functional prototype to achieve a set of goals described to them in natural language. To achieve these goals, they needed to create a set of informational objects. By inspecting these objects, it is possible to decide on the success of a business process instance. The experiment hypothesis states that by enhancing the tool with a recommender system, the nomenclature used by the knowledge workers converges. The experiment took 13 subjects and a confederate. Results show that the proposed approach, empowered with a contextual recommender system, allows work practices to converge, and thus, tacit knowledge to be captured using a practice-oriented strategy.

Keywords: Recommender systems · Ad-hoc workflows · Empirical study

1 Introduction

Capturing knowledge workers' tacit knowledge concerning the organization's business processes is a current problem of the social BPM community [1]. Most organizations execute informal business processes using email instead of formal workflow systems. This happens because the business rules driving the execution of such business processes only exist in the knowledge workers' *heads*, and email provides the necessary flexibility to handle such executions informally.

Traditional requirement engineering techniques focus on the capture of such knowledge, but are known to be time consuming, and to produce biased results due to communication, social or political factors, pondering the cost-benefit of automating such processes. Our goal is to mitigate these problems by providing information about the actual execution of business processes to process experts before they meet with knowledge workers for the first time.

We propose an approach [3,4] to capture tacit knowledge during the execution of business processes. The approach follows a practice-oriented strategy [2], focusing on what knowledge workers actually do, rather than on what they say they do, or on what they ought to be doing. To do so, we developed a modeless

N. Lohmann et al. (Eds.): BPM 2013 Workshops, LNBIP 171, pp. 113–124, 2014.
DOI: 10.1007/978-3-319-06257-0_10, © Springer International Publishing Switzerland 2014

workflow system, with foundations on conversational speech acts [6]. With such foundations, we can structurely capture the knowledge workers' interactions, while still providing the necessary flexibility to continue executing informal business processes with no model constraining their actions. The application allows knowledge workers to address requests to one another and exchange data objects within them. However, since there are no models, knowledge workers must label such requests and data objects in order to tell them apart, i.e. associate some semantic value to them.

With no model constraining a particular nomenclature, an unguided execution is likely to cause divergence on the captured knowledge representation as different knowledge workers can attain the same business goal following different paths of execution, and using different, yet semantically equivalent, labels when refering to requests and data objects. To deal with this problem, we proposed a recommendation algorithm [5] that fosters the reuse of labels used to identify both requests and data objects. Consequently, the algorithm converges knowledge workers' behavior by recommending previously used labels appropriate in similar contexts of execution.

This paper describes an experiment of the approach, demonstrating that the recommender system actually promotes nomenclature convergence among knowledge workers. Although we identified some threats to the experiment's validity, it provides important feedback to enhance both the approach and the tool, improving the outcomes of future experiments.

In Sect. 2 we describe our approach for the non-intrusive capture of tacit knowledge and the tool that implements it. Then, in Sect. 3, we describe the experiment, highlighting its design and analysis. The paper concludes in Sect. 4 with a synthesis of the results and a description of the next steps in our research work.

2   Approach

Setting conversational speech acts as a theoretical foundation, we implemented a modeless ad-hoc workflow system that empowers knowledge workers to send requests to one another, fostering the exchange of business data artifacts in a structured way. The structure consists on keeping track of causality between requests, as well as abstracting and saving the contexts of creation, provision and response of data objects within such requests.

Whenever a new request is created, different contextual information is gathered, and saved in the form of a request template. The request templates are used as the past memory to recommend future requests and data object labels. Finally, when a business process instance is marked as completed, the overall set of data object labels used in that process instance represents the business process goal attained by that process instance. We say that two process instances achieve the same goal when they produce data objects that have the same labels.

With these entities of process goal and request template, we developed a recommender system that is goal-driven as it computes its recommendations based on previously attained goals that best fit the current execution context. Based on that comparison, the algorithm uses the computed set of missing data object labels, and recommends the best fitting request templates that will produce such missing labels.

Since the approach is goal-driven, it only focus on what data objects are produced, instead of how they are produced. This is because different combinations of request templates' executions may produce the same data objects. Therefore, our approach falls better in data-driven approaches, e.g. [7], rather than to activity-centric approaches[1].

2.1 Recommender System

The recommender system recommends both request and data object labels, whenever the knowledge worker initiates a new request or creates a new data object, respectively.

To provide request label recommendations, the recommender system considers three different metrics: goal match, request template fitness and support. The goal match metric ranges between 0 and 1 considering how conform the data labels of the current process instance are to a previously attained process goal. By computing this value for all previously attained process goals, the recommender system then values request templates that drive the process instance towards the achievement of such goals. To do this, the recommendation algorithm analyzes previously captured configurations of requests that created data object labels missing in the process instance. Such analysis results in the request template fitness metric that considers 5 different contexts, which are explained with the required detail in [5]. The request templates that produce data object labels leading the process instance to attain the most conforming process goals are then recommended based on their fitness with the evolving context: who is initiating the request, what data labels existed at that time, what data labels will be created if the request is executed.

Concerning the recommendation of data object labels, the recommender system attempts to find the most matching request template with the current executing request (the one with the higher request template fitness), and recommends the creation of missing data objects based on the creation context captured in the request template.

The use of recommendations in workflow systems is not new [8–11]. However, our approach differs essentially in not relying on a pre-existing process model, even if a probabilistic one. Rather than looking into activity traces, our recommender system considers mainly the data objects created and exchanged within those activities. Additionally, such research work focus on process execution assistance considering a particular performance strategy, whereas our approach addresses the elicitation of business processes.

---

[1] BPMN-like approaches: http://www.bpmn.org/.

2.2 Workflow System

To promote the non-intrusive quality of the approach, the tool follows an email-like experience where requests are assigned to boxes: Inbox, Executing, and Completed. A user accepts requests located in her Inbox, which are move to the Executing box until they are responded. To respond to a request, the executor replies to the request initiator with a set of new data objects, known as the output data objects. These data objects may have been created in the context of that request, or received from a sub-request the executor sent to another co-worker. A business process results in a causal tree of requests, along with information about the data objects provided, produced, and responded to request solicitations, as well as the organizational roles played by the request initiators and executors.

Figure 1 shows a request (Workshop Trip) being executed by Jane Doe (Secretary), which was originally sent by David Martinho (Employee). On the top-right, Jane has two buttons that allow her either to create new sub-requests or reply to the current executing request. Bellow these buttons, there is the request she is executing (Workshop Trip), and one of the sub-requests (Trip Authorization) she sent to António Silva (Supervisor). In the left side of both the request and sub-request detailed views there is a thread of conversation. The top thread allows Jane to chat with the initiator of the Workshop Trip request, i.e. with David Martinho, while the bottom thread allows conversations with the executor of the Trip Authorization sub-request, i.e. with António Silva. In the right side of both detailed views, Jane identifies which data objects were provided as input to her, and those that she provided to the sub-request. That box shows data

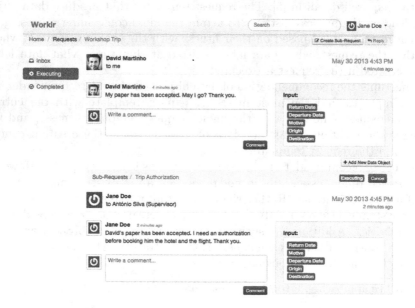

Fig. 1. The tool interface for a request with an opened sub-request

objects that were received with the request, created in its context, and received from its sub-requests.

3 Experiment

3.1 Design

This experiment involved 13 participants, all members of a software development team. Before the experiment, the subjects did not know the business process, neither had interacted with the tool. Only in the day before the experiment, the subjects received instruction about the tool in a common demonstration session, which took about 20 min. During such demonstration, the subjects asked questions about the tool functionalities, but did not discussed their experiment script because they only received it after the demonstration session ended.

Different roles were randomly assigned to the subjects, and each subject only received the description of his competences. Therefore, none of the subjects knew the complete process, neither what roles were played by the other subjects. The confederate was responsible to start the business process instances, address the first request, and receive the last response. Consequently, he could analyze the complete process and decide wether or not the business process instances achieved one of the expected goals.

The experimental case was a simple travel request process, where an employee, played by the confederate, sends a request to his secretary including, as input data objects, the travel motivation, the destination, and both the departure and return dates. The secretary is then responsible for getting two approvals, an operational and a financial, and confirm the hotel and flight bookings. To do so, she must contact three travel agencies to get three different tenders for the trip, and choose the cheapest one. She also interacts with the operational and financial managers to get the respective operational and financial authorizations.

In what concerns to role distribution, six subjects played the secretary role, two the operational manager, another two the financial manager, and three played the travel agencies, one for each agency.

Overall, a process instance may attain one of three expected goals: one where the travel is approved and the employee receives both authorizations, and consequently the hotel and flight information; another two where the travel is denied, either for financial or operational reasons. Although there are only three expected goals, these goals can be achieved through the production of more than three groups of data object labels. This is because the subjects may use different labels for the data objects or may interpret their script differently. These differences will be identified and analyzed in the next subsection.

During the experiment, 16 business process instances were executed and completed. The recommendation system was only activated after the 5th execution, and the operational and financial managers were asked to only authorize 4 of each 5 instances in order to generate all three expected goals.

3.2 Analysis

Given our approach hypothesis, we analyze the experiment results from different perspectives. In the first perspective, we are interest in investigating whether there is convergence in the usage of data object labels. Hence, we want to study the number of data object labels, their frequency (the number of data objects associated to each label), and their usage evolution (how the frequency changes with time). Does a label become popular? Does its frequency increase, or does it become unused instead? To do so, we analyzed each one of the emerged data object labels and grouped them according to semantic similarity. For instance, VÔO and VOO (the Portuguese word for flight written with a selling error in the second case) will be under the same semantic group. This will allow us to identify the more popular labels.

Figure 2 presents the eleven data object labels semantic groups created during the experiment. For each group it is depicted, using different patterns, the variations of labels inside the group. For instance, for the HOTEL NAME group there are five different data object labels with their frequency, NOME HOTEL:20, NÚMERO HOTEL:15, HOTEL:3, HOTEL ESTADIA:2 and N. RESERVA HOTEL:1. The analysis of this diagram shows that for most of the semantic groups, one data object label was predominantly used. Note that the data object labels created by the confederate are not included in the figure, and that the TOTAL PRICE semantic group has a single instance and corresponds to a situation where a secretary decided to create a data object with the sum of the hotel and flight prices to send to the financial manager.

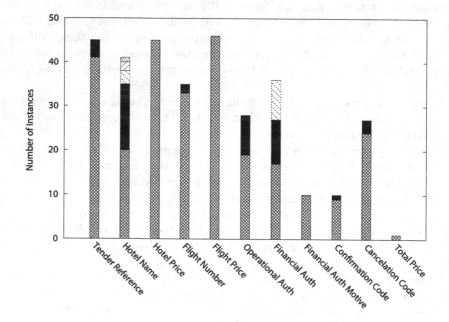

Fig. 2. Data object label semantic groups

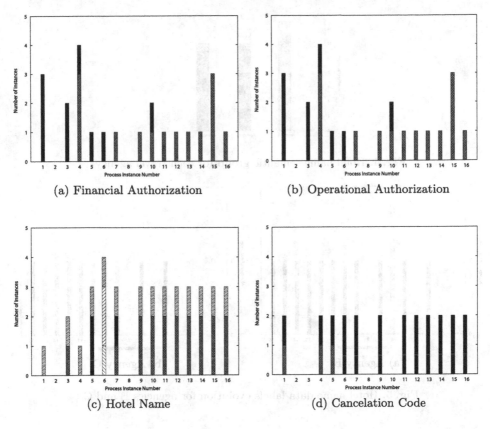

(a) Financial Authorization   (b) Operational Authorization

(c) Hotel Name   (d) Cancelation Code

Fig. 3. Evolution of data object label

Although Fig. 2 suggests that there may exist convergence of data object labels, we want to effectively know whether the predominant data object labels become popular as the recommender system is warmed-up by past executions of business process instances. Figure 3 shows, for the four semantic groups that have more variations, that there is convergence on the use of data object labels.

It shows the usage frequency of data labels for each of the business process instances. Business process instances with a higher number occurred latter in time. Note that, in the HOTEL NAME semantic group, only one of the travel agencies does not follow the recommendation that has a higher rate.

It is also important to analyze whether subjects changed their behavior during the experiment due to the recommendations received by the tool. Note that, it is not surprisingly that a subject commits to the same behavior, and repeats the names of the labels she already used. Such behavior can also be explained by the autocomplete facility of a browser. Nevertheless, it is is interesting to know whether the user accepts recommendations of labels used by co-workers, changing her behavior.

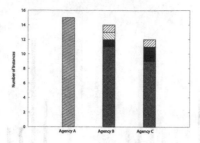

Fig. 4. Hotel name semantic group for each travel agency

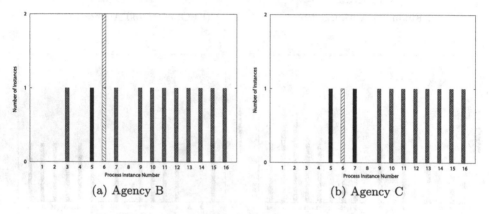

(a) Agency B   (b) Agency C

Fig. 5. Hotel name data labels evolution for agencies B and C

To answer this last question, we analyze the labels used by the travel agencies for the HOTEL NAME semantic group because each agency was played by a single subject. Figure 4 shows that Travel Agency A always use the same data object label while Travel Agencies B and C used different object labels.

If we look more detailedly to these agencies (see Fig. 5), we observe a convergence of data object labels after the 6th process instance as the agencies started to use the same data object label to refer to the hotel name. We can conclude that recommendations fostered the subjects to change their behavior.

After analyzing data object labels convergence, we want to measure the similarity between the achieved goals of the same expected goal. An achieved goal is represented by the labels of data object produced by the business process instance, and it also includes the number of times a particular label was used in the process. For instance, it may be the case that the responses received by the secretary from different travel agencies contain different data objects with the same label, e.g. (HOTEL PRICE). We also want to consider the number of variations among the achieved goals of an expect goal. These variations fit into two aspects: semantic variation and interpretation variation. In the former, two achieved goals contain different labels but they belong to the same semantic group, whereas in the latter the two achieved goals denote different interpretations of the scripts by the

AG1	100%											
AG2	89.41%	100%										
AG3	86.36%	88.89%	100%									
AG4	93.02%	96.20%	92.68%	100%								
AG5	85.71%	96%	92.31%	92.31%	100%							
AG6	74.42%	81.01%	85%	78.05%	84.21%	100%						
AG7	89.89%	92.68%	96.39%	96.39%	88.89%	81.93%	100%					
AG8	79.07%	86.08%	78.05%	85%	82.05%	68.29%	81.93%	100%				
AG9	54.17%	53.93%	56.52%	57.78%	54.55%	47.82%	55.91%	59.09%	100%			
AG10	68.97%	70%	67.47%	74.07%	65.82%	62.65%	71.43%	75.95%	59.77%	100%		
AG11	68.69%	59.57%	57.73%	57.73%	55.91%	60.22%	61.22%	57.73%	37.38%	58.33%	100%	
AG12	64.65%	68.42%	59.26%	65.82	64%	62.34%	63.41%	60.76%	44.94%	71.79%	65.12%	100%
	AG1	AG2	AG3	AG4	AG5	AG6	AG7	AG8	AG9	AG10	AG11	AG12

Fig. 6. Achieved goal matrix for approved travel

subjects. For instance, a secretary created a data object, TOTAL PRICE, that sums the hotel and flight prices, to send to the financial manager, while other forwarded the two data objects received from the travel agency. These measures will allow us to analyze goal convergence according to these two aspects.

Figure 6 shows the comparison of the achieved goals for the expected goal: APPROVED TRAVEL. It compares all the achieved goals, from AG1 to AG12, where achieved goals with lower number were achieved by the latter business process instances, after the recommender system warmed-up.

The similarity measure for two achieved goals, AG_i and AG_j, is computed with the formula:

$$\frac{nEqual(AG_i, AG_j)}{nEqual(AG_i, AG_j) + nSem(AG_i, AG_j) + 1.5 \times nInter(AG_i, AG_j)}$$

where $nEqual$ represents the number of shared data object labels between the two achieved goals, $nSem$ represents the number of data object labels belonging to the same semantic group, and $nInter$ the number of data object labels that are not semantically equivalent.

The analysis of this matrix shows that there is convergence between the goals that were achieved latter, top-left part of the matrix, and divergence between the goals that were achieved earlier, bottom-right part of the matrix. This data reinforces our analysis on the convergence of data object labels as the recommender system warms-up and subjects start following recommendations.

For the second perspective on convergence, we analyzed the use of request labels: Did subjects reuse the request labels? To analyze this hypothesis we group request labels in semantic groups, as we have done with data object labels, and measure the variations within each group.

Figure 7 shows divergence of request labels. For instance, the TENDER REQUEST semantic group has 18 variations. This result is not surprising given the recommendation algorithm emphasis on goal achievement, and the definition of a goal being based on data objects production. It may be the case that if the experiment had took longer, request labels may eventually converge. This will be one the research issues to be addressed in future experiments.

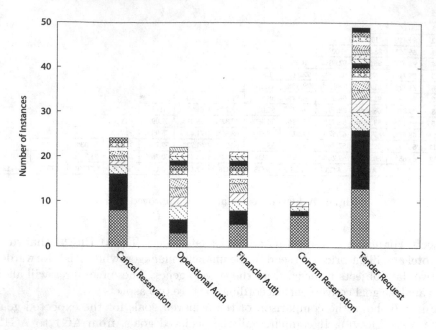

Fig. 7. Request label semantic groups

3.3 Threats to Validity

The subjects received a guided demo of the tool before the experiment, and a script with its responsibilities written in natural language, where there is not an explicit reference to request labels or data objects labels. The business process case fits into the kind of knowledge processes the approach wants to address.

However, we identified some threats to validity of the experiments. The subjects, although being knowledge workers, belong all to the same group, they are software developers, whereas in a business process usually participate different kind of knowledge workers, from technical professionals to administrative staff. On the other hand, the experiment took place in a shared common room, and, although we restricted the communication among subjects during the experiment, it was impossible to completely avoid it during the two hours of experimentation.

These threats were essentially due to logistic limitations, and we were aware of them before the experiment. However, the goal of this first experiment was to receive feedback about the approach and the tool, which will be useful for their improvement and tuning, and to design a new experiment where the identified threats will be dealt with.

As a final note on the threat to validity and the results achieved: from the analysis we can conclude that there is convergence on the goals whereas the same is not true for request labels. In some sense, it confirms our hypothesis that business process goals achievement can be driven by the production of data objects, and that the subjects behavior was not biased because there is divergence in the request labels. They were not aware whether we were studying data object labels convergence or request labels convergence, and if any communication occurred among subjects it makes no sense that it had only impact on the data object labels.

4 Conclusions

In this paper, we present the first experiment of our approach to non-intrusively capture the tacit knowledge of knowledge workers. The experiment addresses the main open issue: can the approach foster the convergence of knowledge workers' behavior during the capture of their knowledge? This issue is particularly relevant because one of the challenges of requirements engineering activities is mutual agreement between stakeholders. This agreement ranges from the terminology of the domain to the goals of the business.

Our hypothesis, i.e. design-by-doing approach performs better on the convergence of behavior, stems from the fact that while performing their daily work, knowledge workers may be more isolated from the social and political factors occuring during requirements elicitation sessions and that are responsible for divergence or requirements misalignment.

To test our hypothesis, we considered that the business process goal is represented by a set of data object labels that are produced during the execution of a process instance, and that it is not so relevant how they are produced, inline with existing workflow data-driven approaches. Therefore, we developed a recommender system and integrated it with an ad-hoc workflow system based on conversational acts. We used these tools in a first experiment, where a group of 13 subjects participated in a travel request process. The results of this first experiment are promising as they show convergence on the data object labels and process goals, despite the divergence in the request labels, which is according to what was postulated by our hypothesis. Although we identified some threats to the validity of the experiment, related to the group composition and environment of the experiment, due to time and logistic restrictions, it gave us good hints on how to pursue our research and design the next experiment.

For the next experiment we will integrate the recommendations presentation with the browser auto-complete to avoid subjects to be confused between our recommendations and the browser auto-completion suggestions. Moreover, we will limit the number of presented recommendations to up to N (we need to identify the threshold value) in order to reduce the noise and allow subjects to carefully choose between a small number of potential recommendations. One of the emphasis of the next experience is to analyze when request labels converge, if they do.

Acknowledgment. We would like to thank the thirteen members of the development team that gently participated in the experiment as subjects. This work was supported by national funds through FCT Fundação para a Ciência e a Tecnologia, under project PEst-OE/EEI/LA0021/2013.

References

1. Bruno, G., Dengler, F., Jennings, B., Khalaf, R., Nurcan, S., Prilla, M., Sarini, M., Schmidt, R., Silva, R.: Key challenges for enabling agile BPM with social software. J. Softw. Maintenance Evol.: Res. Pract. **23**(4), 297–326 (2011)
2. Pickering, A.: From science as knowledge to science as practice. Science as practice and culture 4 (1992)
3. Silva, A., Rosemann, M.: Processpedia: an ecological environment for BPM stakeholders' collaboration. Bus. Process Manage. J. **18**(1), 20–42 (2012)
4. Martinho, D., Silva, A.R.: Non-intrusive capture of business processes using social software. In: Daniel, F., Barkaoui, K., Dustdar, S. (eds.) BPM Workshops 2011, Part I. LNBIP, vol. 99, pp. 207–218. Springer, Heidelberg (2012)
5. Martinho, D., Silva, A.R.: A recommendation algorithm to capture end-users' tacit knowledge. In: Barros, A., Gal, A., Kindler, E. (eds.) BPM 2012. LNCS, vol. 7481, pp. 216–222. Springer, Heidelberg (2012)
6. Winograd, T.: A language/action perspective on the design of cooperative work. Hum.-Comput. Interact. **3**(1), 3–30 (1987)
7. van der Aalst, W., Reijers, H., Liman, S.: Product-driven workflow design. In: 2001 The Sixth International Conference on Computer Supported Cooperative Work in Design, pp. 397–402. IEEE (2001)
8. Barba, I., Weber, B., Del Valle, C.: Supporting the optimized execution of business processes through recommendations. In: Daniel, F., Barkaoui, K., Dustdar, S. (eds.) BPM Workshops 2011, Part I. LNBIP, vol. 99, pp. 135–140. Springer, Heidelberg (2012)
9. Burkhart, T., Werth, D., Loos, P., Dorn, C.: A flexible approach towards self-adapting process recommendations. Comput. Inform. **30**(1), 89–111 (2011)
10. Dorn, C., Burkhart, T., Werth, D., Dustdar, S.: Self-adjusting recommendations for people-driven ad-hoc processes. In: Hull, R., Mendling, J., Tai, S. (eds.) BPM 2010. LNCS, vol. 6336, pp. 327–342. Springer, Heidelberg (2010)
11. Schonenberg, H., Weber, B., van Dongen, B.F., van der Aalst, W.M.P.: Supporting flexible processes through recommendations based on history. In: Dumas, M., Reichert, M., Shan, M.-C. (eds.) BPM 2008. LNCS, vol. 5240, pp. 51–66. Springer, Heidelberg (2008)

ISEAsy: A Social Business Process Management Platform

Marco Santorum$^{(\boxtimes)}$, Agnès Front, and Dominique Rieu

Grenoble CNRS, Grenoble Informatics Laboratory, Grenoble University, F-38041
Grenoble, France
{marco.santorum,agnes.front,dominique.rieu}@imag.fr

Abstract. In today's rapidly changing environment and constant development of new technologies, organizations must be operationally efficient
and agile to respond efficiently and evolve their processes to changing
requirements.

Specialists argue that BPM business process management provides
the base that enables the business to adapt, optimize and evolve. Our
research suggests that stakeholders recognize the importance of creating,
sharing, collaborating and maintaining process maps, but no-one seems
to be ready and motivated to become genuinely involved and to invest
the corresponding time and effort. Moreover, the multidisciplinary team
of actors involves professionals in different domains who use different
vocabularies, and their lack of a common language results in communication problems.

This paper presents a BPM approach incorporated into a social network built around organizational processes and participants who share
common interests. We exploit the motivational characteristics of, participative end-user modeling, gamification and social media tools in order
to motivate and encourage people to perform process formalization and
analysis, process modeling or simulation.

Keywords: Business process · Social · Social media tools · Serious
games · Game mechanics · Gamification · ISEA · BPM

1 Introduction

The ability of an organization to flexibly adapt to changing business requirements
is a key factor to remain competitive. In the modern business environment, the
challenges are to improve process efficiency and quality, to introduce a continuous
process evolution and to improve the stakeholders' satisfaction.

Over the years, specialists argued that BPM technologies [1,2] provide the
base that enables the organisation to adapt, optimize and evolve. They built
tools to manage business processes. These tools offered process management
capabilities but fell short of expectations giving a real solution to the true problem: modeling the business is usually a difficult, complex and exhausting task,

N. Lohmann et al. (Eds.): BPM 2013 Workshops, LNBIP 171, pp. 125–137, 2014.
DOI: 10.1007/978-3-319-06257-0_11, © Springer International Publishing Switzerland 2014

which is often undertaken by business analyst experts, especially if the organization does not have formal and clear process description documents or if the stakeholders work mechanically without a real awareness of the task. Additionally a lack of motivation and ability makes difficult to formalize and maintain an orderly process. Aware of the fact that business processes are complex, sometimes redundant and really not documented, we adopted an iterative approach and user-centered design approach to involve functional actors of specific business processes throughout the design and development of a participative method. The resultant method called ISEA, is presented in Sect. 2.

Thus, the remainder of this paper is structured as follows. Section 2, describes the participative approach ISEA. Section 3 presents the main proposition of this paper: the integration of social media tools and game design techniques with ISEA in a software platform called ISEASY. Section 4 describes a preliminary evaluation of the platform ISEASY. Section 5 briefly compares ISEA to some related works concerning the use of social media tools and game design techniques in the business process domain. Finally, Sect. 6 concludes the paper and describes the follow-up work to be carried out.

2   ISEA Method

The *ISEA* method (See Fig. 1) is composed of four original phases: *I*dentification, *S*imulation, *E*valuation, *A*melioration, and three classical phases: modeling, execution, optimization.

Identification phase aims to identify all the functional actors in a process and to establish a map of the actors of a process. It is the starting point of the method.

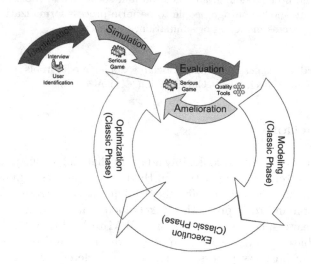

Fig. 1. The ISEA method.

Simulation phase is the most important and innovative phase of the method. All functional actors follow a participative approach in order to collectively elaborate the description of the conducted activities and the exchanged documents in a business process.

Evaluation phase aims to detect the difficulties during the process simulation and thus propose potential improvement actions.

Amelioration phase (or improvement phase), has the objective to "replay" the process according to the proposed improvement actions. Several iterations "simulation - evaluation - amelioration" may be needed.

This early process improvement, of course, does not eliminate the "classical" phases of the BPM life-cycle, but can significantly reduce it: the objective of the modeling phase, as usual, is to document the organizational practices using a business process modeling language such as BPMN [1]. These BPMN models may be partially deducted from the results of the simulation phase. Execution and optimization phases are the same as in traditional life cycles of BPM approaches.

ISEA was defined and designed based on user experiments [13,14]. The purpose of these experiments was to gradually design and evaluate the modeling language and the activities proposed during the phases.

3   ISEAsy: A Participative, Social and Gamified Platform Support to ISEA

In this section, we propose, to insert the tool support of ISEA inside a social network built around organizational processes and participants who share common interests and activities. We thus propose to integrate the motivational characteristics *social media tools* and *game design techniques* (see Fig. 2) with a *participative approach* in order to motivate and encourage people to perform chores that they generally consider boring, such as process formalization and analysis, process modeling or simulation. This tool support is called ISEAsy.

Fig. 2. ISEAsy: combining participative, social and gamified approaches in ISEA

3.1 A Participative Approach for End User BP Modeling

A participative approach involving all stakeholders is widely accepted as a good practice that brings multiple benefits [3]. Firstly, the quality of a process model is enhanced if created in collaboration between stakeholders, rather than resulting from one specialist's interpretation of interviews. Secondly, consensus is better enhanced when a participative approach is adopted. Thirdly, a participative approach involves stakeholders in the decision making process, facilitating the achievement of acceptance and commitment.

In the ISEAsy tool and more generally in the ISEA method, all stakeholders are involved, and more particularly the *end-users*, who are the domain experts and possess the necessary knowledge of how the process should operate, which tasks have to been carried out, which business rules need to be enforced, validation checks to perform, etc. End-users will collaborate around the creation and maintenance of existing process cartographies.

This participative process modeling approach is based essentially on two aspects: a domain specific language adapted to business process modeling and a role-playing simulation game [13,14].

Game Rules. ISEAsy, is essentially a role-playing simulation game where participants assume a role and act out a real-life situation in order to get a description of their daily activities during a specific process in a participative way.

Each participant plays the same role as he fills in real life. He uses a set of graphic elements (see Fig. 3) with which he represents the actions performed during real life. For example the participant places a virtual post-it on the workspace to represent an activity he accomplishes during the process and draws one or more arrows letting the turn to the next participant. Participants take their turn, one after the other, depending on the situation, as would occur in real life. For our example, the game begins with the missionary, who needs to establish a mission request. An activity may be made up of several actions. An action consists of a verb conjugated in the first person singular (e.g. "I ask") and a medium (e.g. "by email") or document if needed (e.g. "a quote") (see Fig. 3). Document creation is a specific action. In this case, the participant uses a document symbol to represent a document associated with this activity. He completes a short description (document name, abbreviation) and chooses a color (a single color coding label to identify each document). If a participant needs a document previously created, he drags the respective color coding label into his post-it. If the intervention of an external actor is necessary, the facilitator plays this role by dragging a pink post-it (different from the internal actors). No action is noted on this post-it, only documents may move or appear on it. The end of a participant's intervention is indicated by placing a STOP sign on his last post-it.

The current version of ISEAsy, developed in JavaScript using the open source JQuery library as a web application. ISEA has been used successfully on a large variety of university processes: the travel expense reimbursement process management of the Grenoble Informatics Laboratory (LIG), the management of overtime pay process at Ensimag School of engineering in Informatics and applied

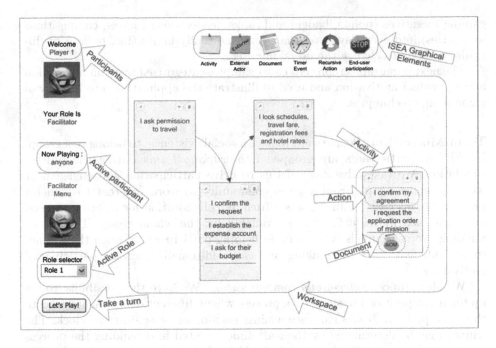

Fig. 3. A business process representation with ISEAsy.

mathematics of Grenoble INP, the application and admission process in MIAGE at Joseph Fourier University. Due to the request of the leaders' committee of the Pierre Mendès France and the Information Systems vice-Presidency of the Universities to participate in the formal representation and risk evaluation of their internal processes. The different projects conducted showed that ISEA method effectively works, it is particularly useful for existing business processes and ISEA method has proved to be easy to use and very advantageous in terms of time. Additionally, ISEA provides conversion rules from ISEA models to BPMN basic models that will be completed by a specialist if it is necessary to assure compatibility with existing tools. ISEA and ISEAsy have now reached a satisfactory level of maturity. ISEAsy is currently the subject of a technology transfer with an IT company.

3.2 Gamification to Make BPM More Fun and Engaging

Gamification is one of the top trends in information technology [9]. According to Deterding et al. [10–12], Gamification can be described as a situation where game techniques are introduced to influence the people evolving within a system; Gamification can potentially be applied to any domain to create fun and engaging experiences, converting users into players.

Gamification uses wide sets of techniques that can be applied to any user experience in order to enhance peoples' motivation. We take advantage of these techniques to make the business process design more attractive. By inserting gaming incentives (points, badges and ranks, leaderboards, levels, competitions and prizes) into everyday tasks that would normally be routine, tedious or difficult, we hope to change the users' mindset.

The next paragraphs represent case examples categorized by team motivation and individual motivation and used to illustrate the application into ISEAsy of game design techniques.

Team-Motivation. People want to have a social existence, to belong to a group. In ISEAsy, participants are grouped into *working teams* during the process simulation. We take advantage of this to drive participation and engagement while grouping people from a given community to work together to model a process. In this case, "Fun" means a friendly collaboration for meeting targets, in which each individual's skill is available for the whole group. This team-building process game is very useful in helping participants to open their mind, to use different ways of thinking and can additionally increase participants' motivation.

We also propose *inter-group communication*. We have the possibility to set up team competitions to simulate a process where different departments execute the same process. Teams can race against each other or against the clock. The winner may be determined by the least time invested into building the process representation or by the best representation of the process, for example. The competition game incentive is used here for motivation, but our purpose is rather to make the different groups exchange on their solutions after the competition. Indeed, explaining one's solutions to others is part of the meta-cognition process, which results in a better acceptance of the group solution after having explained it to others.

Individual Motivation. Individual motivated is enhanced by different things: each individual being motivated in a different way may expect to be able to personalize his/her workspace, tools, and the way the rewards are presented to him/her. A user's individual motivation within a group is also enhanced if the group recognizes his/her individual skills.

ISEAsy offers a flexible user interface allowing personalization. It is possible for a user to customize his/her workspace and avatar. Moreover, a wizard trainer is proposed based on users' abilities, and provides a reward mechanism by giving experience points.

The *acquisition of expertise* is another possibility. The user can acquire new skills in the environment. Some users thus become highly skilled in one particular domain and the system can give them a reward by adding them new rights.

Using a wizard trainer and experience points, ISEAsy offers different levels of challenges allowing users to progress with their skills. When a game participant has earned enough experience points, he increases his level and is offered new abilities that for example allow him to play as a facilitator and create its own simulation game.

3.3   Social Media Tools Applied to BPM

ISEAsy uses social media tools to create a community around the process in order to promote stakeholders collaboration on the process evolution. The social network is built around organizational processes and participants who share common interests and activities. ISEAsy is a social process simulation platform that for example provides participants with the ability to interact with other participants, to share resources between stakeholders and to allow participants to collaborate and identify themselves as roleplayers simplifying the identification phase of ISEA. Additionally ISEAsy includes a social media plugin that allows community members login using Facebook account, share status updates, invites Facebook friends and publish activities to Facebook.

The next paragraphs illustrate some benefits of social media tools applied to ISEAsy.

Communication Exchange. One of the most promising techniques to drive engagement, encourage participants and increase users' participation, is to facilitate the interactions and exchanges among participants. That's why ISEAsy provides participants with the ability to interact with each other using a chat, messaging and discussion groups. Participants may also use a forum to discuss each process simulation, to ask/answer questions about the process, to get feedback or for general announcements, peer review processes or for themes they would like to develop.

Resource Manager. During the simulation game, valuable information is generated about the activities, tasks, documents, and resources involved in the process. ISEAsy offers a "share content" repository where these resources are automatically stored and participants are able to include more detailed information on all the activities, tasks and documents for which documentation is required. Administrators are also able to specify some limits on resources availability and access control.

Stakeholder Collaboration. ISEAsy (see Fig. 4) allows to create a community of users who have participated in the process simulations, which facilitates collaboration between process stakeholders. ISEA participants (the process stakeholders) work together during a simulation game. They can be part of the same or different structures (organizational departments). This feature corresponds more to stable groups that people want to set up in virtual worlds, as in real life. These features are now well known, since they are used as central features in social networks. An invitation system is thus included into ISEAsy to be able to send invitations to contacts within the organization or to external contacts with limited access. Participants have to decide whether or not to register in ISEA and can accept or decline the invitation.

As we said in subsect. 3.1, ISEAsy is currently the subject of a technology transfer with an IT company. In the context of this paper we presents the results

Fig. 4. A screenshot of ISEAsy implementing individual motivation.

of a preliminary evaluation of the social techniques used by ISEAsy. In fact, we have evaluated our social network prototype, this evaluation allows us to derive useful information for further evaluation and optimization of the method and the tool.

4   ISEAsy: Preliminary Evaluation

We have set up a small experiment with the people that were involved in the formalization of different processes using the first version of ISEAsy and the social techniques in order to gather participants' opinions and feedbacks about the applicability and usability of the method and its impact on the motivation. All the participants were interested in being part of the evaluation except two of them (the oldest people in the group that told us that they didn't like this kind of tool and preferred not to participate in this experiment). In this experiment, the analysis of the qualitative evaluation data is based primarily on a evaluation questionnaire, completed by a dozen of participants at the end of the experiment. Basically the following remarks appeared:

- Concerning the method: the first phase of the ISEA method has been considerably simplified. ISEAsy allows participants to identify themselves as roleplayers; they can create, join, leave and manage common-interest user groups simplifying the identification and assignment of roles. Additionally participants can discuss and establish priorities for process modeling: they are able to determine which processes are critical.
- Concerning the ergonomics: participants found the tool intuitive and easy to use. They appreciated the fact that no training was necessary to effectively use the tool.
- Concerning personal motivation: The personalization features are feasible, useful with an attractive user interface but are not sufficient to motivate people. Other incentives may be necessary: some of them proposed for example to have a group quest concerning the promotion of their processes.
- Concerning the game incentives: some participants were frustrated because they did not become an ISEA expert. They found it difficult to become "highly skilled" and didn't get any rewards. It seems that even if the incentive were good, it would have been better to have intermediate rewards in order to keep the users motivated.
- Concerning the Social Network: the participants appreciated the social environment provided. ISEAsy is equipped with the described functionalities and works effectively offering a meeting place for regular communication between stakeholders.

Even if good remarks were extracted from this evaluation, we are aware of the fact that a larger experiment is needed in order to gather a wider range of feedback from various users.

5   Related Works

In our knowledge, no previous work combines a BPM participative approach with gamification and social techniques. In [16], Noyé proposes a Participative approach to process improvement characterized by a user orientation, but it employs classic quality improvement tools to simplify the user participation.

The SimLab business process simulation method [15] is a participative method involving different actors to create knowledge towards indirect influence on policy. SimLab creates a process knowledge sharing community, where the visualized process flow is simulated through joint discussion based on personal experience and joint imagination. The method simulates business processes where the knowledge intensity and human communication are central.

Some professional and industrial tools have started to use more game-like visual simulations for analyzing the impact of changes in processes. For example Arena3D[1] [5,6] provides a graphical animation functionality that according to

---

[1] "www.arenasimulation.com"

Table 1. Process improvement approches and tools summary

Process improvement approaches and tools				
Approach	Goal	Participative techniques	Games techniques	Social techniques
Noyé (1997)	Process improvement	Tools for quality improvement, stakeholder collaboration		
SimLab (2006)	Process improvement	Knowledge base, stakeholder collaboration	Simulation tool	
ARENA (2000)	Simulation and process improvement		Simulation tool	
INNOV8 (2010)	Simulation and communication	Stakeholders collaboration	3D simulation game	
Brown et al. (2011)	Communication	Stakeholders collaboration	3D virtual world	
VIPROSA (2009)	Communication and process improvement		Role simulation game	
Koschmider (2008)	Process modeling	Stakeholders collaboration, collaborative modeling		Social network
ISEAsy (2009)	Process modeling, process improvement	Stakeholders collaboration, quality improvement tools	Serious role playing simulation game	Social network

Arena3D's creators, allows to gain further insight into the process dynamics. Moreover, animation is of great benefit in enticing each stakeholder in the organization to be interested in process improvement.

IBM has also produced a business game called INNOV8[2]. But INNOV8 is an interactive, 3-D business simulator designed to teach the fundamentals of business process management and is used as a method to train students and employees and accelerate the development of new skills.

Another 3D simulator is proposed in [7], where Brown et al. propose a three-dimensional (3D) environment for collaborative process modeling, using virtual world technology. They provide a visualization approach to strengthen the communication channels between business analysts and stakeholders, before any improvement and optimization activity.

---

[2] "www-01.ibm.com/software/solutions/soa/innov8"

VIPROSA (VIsual PROcess Simulation and Analysis)[8], is a game-like tool proposition for business process simulation and analysis that offers a way to inform the workers about the ongoing work, and to let them test their own ideas about improvements on the current situation. VIPROSA combines a serious game with BPMN models to achieve collaboration between business analysts and stakeholders.

Finally, a recommendation-based modeling system is presented by Koschmider, Song, and Reijers [4]. It exploits the information that can be derived from a recommendation modeling history of a community of users. A social network is generated in order to guide the users towards a selection of process fragments that resembles earlier decisions of their peers. Authors promote the Collaborative Modeling of people building on the modeling experiences of others.

To conclude, we can say that each process improvement approach has a different way of conducting the different phases and uses different types of tools. Table 1 summarizes tools and techniques used by the different BPM approaches presented in this section.

6   Conclusion and Future Works

Considering that Business Process Management (BPM) has become a higher priority for all organizations, the ISEA method allows all the actors of an organization to collaborate around the creation and maintenance of existing process and to propose consensual improvements to the processes. ISEA is a user-centered method driving actors' engagement and encouraging and increasing user participation.

This paper presents the social platform called ISEAsy that we have developed as a support of ISEA. ISEAsy can then be seen as a social process simulation platform with the addition of game mechanics, including a social interaction system with profile pages, groups, messaging, file sharing, and a discussion forum. ISEAsy also combines team motivation and individual motivation using a wizard trainer and experience points awarded to participants who achieve better performance. ISEAsy aims to become a community area where participants are connected to design business processes in a participative way and to exchange about them.

ISEAsy does not replace a traditional business process analysis tools, but tries to explore how business process management may profit from social and gaming techniques.

The next step is to conduct user experiments in order to evaluate the acceptability and usability of ISEAsy and to validate our premise that such a social professional network will encourage users participation and motivation. In addition to the tool itself, it is also planned to extend the ISEA approach itself with creativity techniques, with the aim of encouraging innovation and creativity for business process management and more generally for information systems engineering. In particular, we hope to use ISEA for the discovery of services innovation processes in an inter-organizational context. ISEAsy may indeed help to expose and quickly distribute new information and become not only a platform for process optimization, but also a platform for innovation.

Additionally, we will use the ISEA method as a starting point for user interfaces (UI) design. ISEA will allow participants to represent organizational processes as a set of activities that represents users tasks while interacting with systems. These tasks will be used to discover the real-world concepts, their interactions as understood by users and the operations that are possible on these concepts. The goal will be here to design in a participative way the appearance and behavior of a UI from these elements that can be perceived by users who start simulating a process with ISEAsy.

Acknowledgments. The authors thank the Government of Ecuador (SENACYT - EPN) and the University Pierre Mendès France for funding this research.

References

1. OMG, Specification: Business Process Model and Notation (BPMN) Version 2.0, Object Management Group (2011)
2. Gillot, J.N.: Business Process Transformation Or a Way of Aligning the Strategic Objectives of the Company and the Information System Through the Processes, NeoVision Group (2007)
3. Persson, A., Stirna, J.: An explorative study into the influence of business goals on the practical use of enterprise modelling methods and tools. In: Harindranath, G., Gregory Wojtkowski, W., Zupančič, J., Rosenberg, D., Wojtkowski, W., Wrycza, S., Sillince, J.A.A. (eds.) New Perspectives on Information Systems Development, pp. 275–287. Springer, New York (2002)
4. Koschmider, A., Song, M., Reijers, H.A.: Social software for modeling business processes. In: Ardagna, D., Mecella, M., Yang, J. (eds.) Business Process Management Workshops. LNBIP, vol. 17, pp. 666–677. Springer, Heidelberg (2009)
5. Jansen-Vullers, M., Netjes, M.: Business process simulation – a tool survey. In: Workshop and Tutorial on Practical Use of Coloured Petri Nets and the CPN Tools, Aarhus, Denmark, October 2006
6. Notice, Trademark: Rockwell Software, Arena User's Guide. Rockwell Software, Milwaukee (2005)
7. Brown, R., Recker, J., West, S.: Using virtual worlds for collaborative business process modeling. Bus. Process Manag. J. **17**(3), 546–564 (2011). Emerald Group Publishing Limited
8. Liukkonen, T.N.: VIPROSA – game-like tool for visual process simulation and analysis. In: Kankaanranta, M., Neittaanmäki, P. (eds.) Design and Use of Serious Games, vol. 37, pp. 185–206. Springer, Netherlands (2009)
9. Gartner, I.: Gartner says by 2015, more than 50 percent of organizations that manage innovation processes will gamify those processes. http://www.gartner.com/it/page.jsp?id=1629214 (2013). Accessed 9 March (2013)
10. Deterding, S., Dixon, D., Khaled, R., Nacke, L.: From game design elements to gamefulness: defining gamification. In: Proceedings of the 15th International Academic MindTrek Conference: Envisioning Future Media Environments, pp. 9–15. ACM, September 2011

11. Deterding, S., Khaled, R., Nacke, L. E., Dixon, D.: Gamification: toward a definition. In: Proceedings of the 2011 Annual Conference Extended Abstracts on Human Factors in Computing Systems. ACM, New York (2011)
12. Deterding, S., Sicart, M., Nacke, L., O'Hara, K., Dixon, D.: Gamification: using game-design elements in non-gaming contexts. In: PART 2 Proceedings of the 2011 Annual Conference Extended Abstracts on Human Factors in Computing Systems, pp. 2425–2428. ACM, May 2011
13. Santorum, M.: A serious game based method for business process management. In: 5th IEEE International Conference on Research Challenges in Information Science (RCIS'11) (2011)
14. Santorum, M., Front, A., Rieu, D.: Approche de gestion des processus basée sur les jeux. Revue ISI (2011)
15. Smeds, R., Jaatinen, M., Hirvensalo, A., Kilipio, A.: Multidisciplinary research on simulation methods and educational games in industrial management. In: Proceedings of the 10th International Workshop on Experimental Interactive Learning in Industrial Management, pp. 11–13. Norway, June 2005
16. Noyé, D.: L'amélioration participative des processus. M. français pour la qualité, INSEP éditions (1997)

2nd Workshop on Data- and Artifact-Centric BPM (DAB 2013)

2nd Workshop on Data- and Artifact-Centric BPM (DAB 2013)

Towards a Reference Implementation for Data Centric Dynamic Systems

Alessandro Russo[1]([X]), Massimo Mecella[1], Marco Montali[2], and Fabio Patrizi[1]

[1] DIAG, Sapienza Università di Roma, Rome, Italy
{arusso,mecella,patrizi}@dis.uniroma1.it
[2] KRDB Research Centre, Free University of Bozen-Bolzano, Bolzano, Italy
montali@inf.unibz.it

Abstract. Data- and artifact-centric business processes are gaining momentum due to their ability of explicitly capturing the interplay between the process control-flow and the manipulated data. In this paper, we rely on the framework of Data-Centric Dynamic Systems (DCDSs), which has been recently introduced for the formal specification and verification of data-centric processes, showing how it can be lifted towards run-time execution support. In particular, we focus on the problem of database update as induced by the action execution, introducing a set of patterns that allow for an incremental management of the update. At the same time, we discuss the natural correspondence between DCDSs and state-of-the-art rule engines, e.g., JBoss Drools, which paves the way towards a reference implementation for data- and artifact-centric processes, where the model used for analysis and verification is fully aligned with the one adopted for the execution.

1 Introduction

Most of the current approaches to Business Process Management (BPM) adopt a procedural and imperative point-of-view, based on an explicit specification of the tasks to be performed and the execution relationships between them that define the overall flow of control. The modeling perspective is *activity-centric* and the main driver for run-time process progression is given by activity completions that enable subsequent tasks according to the control-flow. Languages such as BPMN and YAWL follow this imperative activity-centric paradigm and mainly focus on the control-flow perspective. Approaches aiming at producing *executable* process specifications should not only be limited to the control-flow perspective, but should also consider the *data perspective*, describing data elements consumed, produced and exchanged during process executions, and the *resource perspective*, describing the operational and organizational context for process execution in terms of resources (i.e., people, systems and services able to execute tasks) and their capabilities (i.e., any qualification, skill, equipment, property etc. relevant for task assignment and execution), along with the policies and rules used to assign tasks to resources for execution. Declarative *constraint-based* approaches,

N. Lohmann et al. (Eds.): BPM 2013 Workshops, LNBIP 171, pp. 141–154, 2014.
DOI: 10.1007/978-3-319-06257-0_12, © Springer International Publishing Switzerland 2014

such as Declare [9], for modeling, enacting and monitoring processes are an initial attempt to increase flexible modeling capabilities, through the specification of a (minimal) set of control-flow constraints to be satisfied (or not violated), defined as relationships among tasks that implicitly define possible execution alternatives by prohibiting undesired execution behaviors. Resulting models have no rigid control-flow structure, but they still focus on tasks/activities and provide limited support for data-oriented modeling and execution.

The root cause of many of the limitations of activity-centric approaches (based either on imperative procedural models or on declarative constraint-based specifications) is often identified in the lack of integration of processes and data [6]. In such models, the information perspective includes a set of data objects and the data flow between activities, along with the definition of which activities may read/write data elements as I/O parameters, but the information and data flows are hidden in the model [7]. To support the enactment of these models, activity-centric process-aware information systems basically distinguish between (i) application data, managed out of the scope of the process by application services invoked during activity executions; (ii) process-relevant data, represented as process variables that are read and updated by the activities and are used by the system to evaluate transitions and path choices (as routing conditions) within process instances; (iii) process control data, that define the current state of a process and its execution history. According to [4], this separation between process data/variables and external data sources leads to an "impedance mismatch" problem between the process layer and the data layer in a typical process-oriented information system. In addition, a recent work [8] has considered the role of data in twelve process modeling languages. The evaluation shows that the general level of data support is low: while in most of the cases the representation of data objects is supported, complex data relationships and their role in process modeling and execution are not considered.

To overcome the limitation of activity-centric approaches, *data-centric*, *object-aware* and *case management* approaches have recently emerged. The PHIL-harmonicFlows framework and prototype enables object-aware process management on the basis of a tight integration of processes, functions, data and users [6]. Process modeling and execution relies on two levels of granularity that cover object behavior (or life-cycle) and object interactions. The framework enables the definition of object types and object relations in a data model, while object behavior is expressed in terms of a process whose execution is driven by object attribute changes.

In data-centric methodologies, as the *business artifacts framework* [5], the data perspective is predominant and captures domain-relevant object types, their attributes, their possible states and life-cycles, and their interrelations, which together form a complex data structure or *information model*. This data model enables the identification and definition of the activities that rely on the object-related information and act on it, producing changes on attribute values, relations and object states. The general artifact-centric model does not restrict the way to specify artifact life-cycles, and constraints can be defined in terms of: (i) abstract procedural process specifications, e.g., expressed as state machines or transition systems, as in SIENA [3]; (ii) logical/declarative formalisms (e.g., temporal or dynamic logics) or as a set of rules defined over the states of the artifacts, as in the Guard-Stage-Milestone (GSM) model [5] supported by the Barcelona GSM environment [13].

Such recent research efforts that focus on data-centric process management are often framed within the wider discussion that opposes BPM with *adaptive case* management (ACM) [12], a paradigm for supporting unstructured, unpredictable and unrepeatable business cases. released a first standard version of the Case Management Modeling Notation (CMMN)[1]; rather than an extension of BPMN, indeed CMMN relies on GSM constructs (guards, stages, milestones and sentries), with the additional possibility to unlink milestones from specific stages, define repetition strategies for stages and tasks, and enable late modeling/planning by introducing discretionary elements to be selected at run-time.

Several works have provided a theoretical foundation to the artifact-centric paradigm, with specific focus on the possibilities to perform verification tasks on the models. We refer the reader to [2] for a comprehensive discussion of the relevant literature. in [1], referred to as Relational Data-Centric Dynamic Systems (DCDSs), that considers both the case in which actions behave deterministically and the case in which they behave nondeterministically, so being still more realistic in modeling external inputs (either from human actors or services). Syntactic restrictions guaranteeing decidability of verification are shown for both cases. In [11] it is shown how to reduce a GSM schema to a DCDS schema. Thus DCDSs are capable of capturing concrete artifact-centric models (being GSM at the core of the CMMN standard) and it gives a procedure to analyze GSM schemas: verification of GSM schemas is, in general, undecidable, but once traduced in a DCDS it is possible to exploit the results in [1] for decidability of verification. A syntactic condition that is checkable directly on a GSM schema is presented and that, being subsumed by the conditions for DCDSs, guarantee decidability of verification.

From a practitioners' point of view, an important missing piece is the availability of process management systems enacting artifact-centric process models. In particular, a kind of reference/core implementation would be beneficial for rapid prototyping purposes, as well as for further research aiming at assessing their practical use, with the need of evaluating the related paradigms and methods in concrete settings. realization of such a reference implementation for DCDSs. Such an ambitious aim poses several challenges, which will be discussed in this paper as well, and has interesting outcomes, i.e., the seamless use of the specification model also as effective run-time of the process instances themselves. It is particularly interesting that the same model used for analysis and for verification is then used for the enactment, and this property is not guaranteed by other formalisms/approaches. Notably, the reduction from GSM to DCDSs [11] produces a DCDS model that resembles an execution engine based on forward rules, and requires to realize some "tricks" and supportive relationships that are

---

[1] http://www.omg.org/spec/CMMN/1.0/Beta1/

very similar to those ones that would serve precisely to manage the execution. We will discuss how to base a reference implementation on state-of-the-art rule engines, e.g., JBoss Drools.

2   Background and Basic Concepts

2.1   Data Centric Dynamic Systems

Data Centric Dynamic Systems (DCDSs) [1] are systems that fully capture the interplay between the data and the process component, providing an explicit account on how the actions belonging to the process manipulate the data. More specifically, a DCDS S is a pair $\langle \mathcal{D}, \mathcal{P} \rangle$ formed by two interacting layers: a *data layer* $\mathcal{D}$ and a *process layer* $\mathcal{P}$ over $\mathcal{D}$. Intuitively, the data layer keeps all the data of interest, while the process layer reads and evolves such data.

The data layer is constituted by a relational schema $\mathcal{R}$ equipped with (denial) constraints, and by an initial database instance $\mathcal{I}_0$ that conforms to the schema and satisfies the constraints. Constraints must be satisfied at each time point, and consequently it is forbidden to apply an action that would lead the data layer to a state that violates the constraints.

The process layer defines the progression mechanism for the DCDS. The main idea is that the current instance of the data layer can be arbitrarily queried, and consequently updated through action executions, possibly involving external service calls to get new values from the environment. More specifically, $\mathcal{P}$ is a triple $\langle \mathcal{F}, \mathcal{A}, \varrho \rangle$, where: $\mathcal{A}$ is a set of *actions*, which are the atomic update steps on the data layer; $\mathcal{F}$ are *external services* that can be called during the execution of actions; and ϱ is a set of condition-action rules that provide a declarative modeling of the *process*, and that are in particular used to determine which actions are executable at a given time.

Actions. Actions are used to evolve the current state of the data layer into a new state. To do so, they query the current state of the data layer, and use the answer, possibly together with further data obtained by invoking external service calls, to instantiate the data layer in the new state. Formally, an *action* $\alpha \in \mathcal{A}$ is an expression $\alpha(p_1, \ldots, p_n) : \{e_1, \ldots, e_m\}$, where: (i) $\alpha(p_1, \ldots, p_n)$ is its *signature*, constituted by a name α and a sequence $p_1, \ldots, p_n$ of *parameters*, to be substituted with actual values when the action is invoked, and (ii) $\{e_1, \ldots, e_m\}$, denoted by EFFECT(α), is a set of *specifications of effects*, which are assumed to take place simultaneously. Each e_i has the form $q_i^+ \wedge Q_i^- \rightsquigarrow E_i$, where:

- $q_i^+ \wedge Q_i^-$ is a query over $\mathcal{R}$ whose terms are variables, action parameters, and constants from ADOM$(\mathcal{I}_0)^2$, where q_i^+ is a union of conjunctive queries, and Q_i^- is an arbitrary first-order formula whose free variables are among those of q_i^+. Intuitively, q_i^+ is applied to extract the tuples used to instantiate the effect, and Q_i^- filters away some of such tuples.

---

^{2} ADOM$(\mathcal{I}_0)$ is the set of constants/values mentioned in the initial database instance $\mathcal{I}_0$.

- E_i is the effect, i.e., a set of facts over $\mathcal{R}$, which includes as terms: terms in $\text{ADOM}(\mathcal{I}_0)$, free variables of q_i^+ and Q_i^- (including action parameters), and in addition Skolem terms formed by applying a function $f \in \mathcal{F}$ to one of the previous kinds of terms. Each such Skolem term f represent a call to an external service identified by f, and are typically meant to model the incorporation of values provided by an external user/environment when executing the action.

Process. The process is used to determine which actions can be executed at a given time, and with which parameters. To do so, it relies on condition-action rules, which constitute a flexible, declarative way of specifying the process, and can be used to accommodate more "concrete" process specification languages. condition-action rules of the form $Q \mapsto \alpha$, where α is an action in $\mathcal{A}$ and Q is a first-order query over $\mathcal{R}$ whose free variables are exactly the parameters of α, and whose other terms can be either quantified variables or constants in $\text{ADOM}(\mathcal{I}_0)$.

Example 1. In this work, we rely on the example presented in [1], where an audit system that manages the process of reimbursing travel expenses in a university is modeled as a DCDS. In particular, we report selected parts of the *request subsystem* that manages the submission of reimbursement requests by an employee. A reimbursement request is associated with the name of the employee (represented in the data layer as a relation Travel $=$ ⟨eName⟩) and comprises information related to the corresponding flight and hotel costs (Hotel $=$ ⟨hName, date, price, currency, priceInUSD⟩ and Flight $=$ ⟨date, fNum, price, currency, priceInUSD⟩ relations). In addition, the data layer keeps the state of the request subsystem (Status $=$ ⟨status⟩ relation, holding the fact Status(*'readyForRequest'*) in the initial state), which take three different values: *'readyForRequest'*, *'readyToVerify'*, and *'readyToUpdate'*, and a list of approved hotels (ApprHotel $=$ ⟨hName⟩ relation).

The process layer includes a set of service calls, each modeling an input of an external value by the employee (e.g., INENAME() for the name of the employee, INHNAME() for the hotel name, INHDATE() for the hotel arrival date, etc.). In particular, the DECIDE() service call models the decision of the human monitor, returning *'accepted'* if the request is accepted, and *'readyToUpdate'*if the request needs to be updated by the employee. The set of actions includes *InitiateRequest*, *VerifyRequest*, *UpdateRequest*, and *AcceptRequest*. When a request is initiated (action *InitiateRequest*), the system status is set to *'readyToVerify'*and the employee provides travel details (her name and hotel and flight details), as modeled by the subset of action effects

true $\rightsquigarrow$ Travel(INENAME())
true $\rightsquigarrow$ Hotel(INHNAME(), INHDATE(), INHPRICE(), INHCURRENCY(), INHPINUSD())

Action *VerifyRequest* models the preliminary check by the monitor. Travel event, hotel, and flight information are copied unchanged to the next state. If the hotel is on the approved list, then the request is automatically accepted and the system status is set accordingly. Otherwise, the request is handled by a human monitor (cf. DECIDE()). Action *VerifyRequest* includes as effects

$$\mathsf{Hotel}(x_1, \ldots, x_5) \wedge \mathsf{ApprHotel}(x_1) \rightsquigarrow \mathsf{Status}(\text{'}accepted\text{'})$$
$$\mathsf{Hotel}(x_1, \ldots, x_5) \wedge \neg\mathsf{ApprHotel}(x_1) \rightsquigarrow \mathsf{Status}(\mathrm{DECIDE}())$$
$$\mathsf{Travel}(n) \rightsquigarrow \mathsf{Travel}(n), \mathsf{Hotel}(x_1, \ldots, x_5) \rightsquigarrow \mathsf{Hotel}(x_1, \ldots, x_5)$$
$$\mathsf{Flight}(x_1, \ldots, x_5) \rightsquigarrow \mathsf{Flight}(x_1, \ldots, x_5), \mathsf{ApprHotel}(x) \rightsquigarrow \mathsf{ApprHotel}(x)$$

In case of rejection,the action *UpdateRequest* is triggered and the employee needs to modify the information regarding hotel and flight, moving the status to '*readyToVerify*'. Finally, action *AcceptRequest* returns the system in the state '*readyForRequest*'. The overall process is defined by condition-action rules that guard the actions by the current system's state and include (among the others): $\mathsf{Status}(\text{'}readyToVerify\text{'}) \mapsto VerifyRequest$, $\mathsf{Status}(\text{'}accepted\text{'}) \mapsto AcceptRequest$.

2.2   Process and Action Execution

To understand the potential of DCDS models as key enablers towards a model-driven process execution and management approach, we define an abstract execution semantics for condition-action rules and actions that determines the actual behavior of an abstract execution engine for DCDSs. Basically, given an instance $\mathcal{I}$ of the data layer and a process specification ϱ, the engine undertakes a set of steps that lead to instantiate the data layer in a new state. The approach is in accordance with the formal execution semantics defined in[1].

Rules Evaluation and Executable Actions. For each CA rule $Q \mapsto \alpha$ the corresponding query Q is executed over the data layer. Whenever a tuple $\vec{d}$ of values is returned by issuing Q over the current database instance, then the condition-action rule states that α is executable by fixing its parameters according to $\vec{d}$. Basically, the eligibility of a rule corresponds to the executability of the corresponding action, under one or more bindings for its parameters. In general, at a given time multiple actions are executable, and the same action can be parametrized in several ways. Notice that this approach provides a notion of concurrency tailored to the one of interleaving, as typically done in formal verification.

Action Execution. Among the executable actions, a strategy has to be implemented to select which action to pick. As pointed out in [10], many possible strategies can be implemented on top of a process-aware information system to allocate actions to resources. These strategies are orthogonal to the execution semantics, and can be therefore seamlessly realized on top of the abstract execution engine described here.

When an action α with parameters σ is chosen, the engine is responsible for the application of the action. In particular, the execution of α instantiated with σ corresponds to evaluating and applying the corresponding effects, according to the following steps:

1. The effects of α are partially instantiated using the parameter assignment σ.

2. The left-hand side of each effect is evaluated by posing the corresponding query over the current relational instance, obtaining back a result set that consists of all possible assignments $\theta_1, \ldots, \theta_n$ that satisfy the query.
3. The right-hand side E_i is considered, so as to obtain, for each θ_i, the set of facts instantiated with σ and θ_i, denoted as $E_i\sigma\theta_i$.
4. $E_i\sigma\theta_i$ may contain service calls. In this case, the engine handles the interaction with such services, so as to obtain the result values for each call[3]. Notice that how these values are obtained is orthogonal to the abstract execution semantics, and could be managed by the execution engine in several different ways, such as interaction with external web services, or with human stakeholders via forms.
5. The new instance of the data layer is obtained by putting together the results obtained from the application of effects and the incorporation of service call results.

3   Basic Effect Patterns for a Reference Implementation

The DCDS semantics described above intuitively defines the execution of an action as a two-step process consisting in: *(i)* the generation of all the facts implied by an action's effects, and *(ii)* the construction of the successor data-layer instance, containing exactly such facts. It is not hard to see that a direct, naïve implementation of this semantics yields, in general, a waste of computational resources. For instance, for an action with effect specifications $e_1 : R(\vec{x}) \rightsquigarrow R(\vec{x})$ and $e_2 : q^+(\vec{x}) \rightsquigarrow R(\vec{x})$, the construction of the successor instance requires to evaluate both $R(\vec{x})$ and $q^+(\vec{x})$ against the current instance $\mathcal{I}$, and then define the successor instance $\mathcal{I}'$ as the union of the obtained facts. However, since the action only adds new facts – those generated by e_2, there is no need to generate the facts that persist from $\mathcal{I}$ – those generated by e_1. That is, according to the the common sense law of inertia, the transition can be efficiently realized in an incremental fashion.

What we do next, is to propose a modeling approach for DCDS that facilitates this incremental approach, by offering specific constructs for actions that only add, update or delete facts from the current instance. For more complex cases we still assume a direct implementation, and leave the analysis of these cases for future investigation.

From a practical perspective, supporting the specification and the execution of actions in terms of create, delete and update operations brings several advantages: 1. The way of specifying DCDS fits the usual attitude of designers and their familiarity with manipulating data through CRUD[4] operations. 2. CRUD operations enable automated techniques for a model- and data-driven generation of user forms for supporting the execution of actions that involve human

---

[3] We assume here two-way blocking service calls.

[4] Notice that the read operation is in fact already supported through queries over the data layer.

performers. 3. Action executions can be efficiently realized through incremental changes over the current instance.

We start by discussing the specification patterns that capture the effects corresponding to create, delete and update. Specifically, we isolate three syntactic patterns that can be used to define the usual create, delete and update operations, and for each of them, we provide an actual syntactic construct. We also introduce a further construct update$^+$, meant to capture a more general form of update where the new values to assign to existing facts can be obtained by answering generic queries over the current instance. This construct, though, needs an additional semantical requirement, in order to guarantee an incremental implementation of action effects. The intended goal of these constructs is to allow DCDS designers to produce action specifications whose effects can be incrementally applied on the current instance. All constructs are detailed below.

In order to be able to define generic DCDS effects, we also introduce the set construct, defined as:

$$\texttt{set } \vec{t} \texttt{ for } R \texttt{ if } q^+ \wedge Q^-,$$

where $\vec{t}$ is a tuple of terms that can be either action parameters, terms from ADOM($\mathcal{I}_0$), Skolem terms (as discussed in previous section), or free variables from $q^+ \wedge Q^-$. This construct corresponds to the effect specification $q^+ \wedge Q^- \rightsquigarrow R(\vec{t})$.

Next, we detail the constructs introduced above. To guarantee the possibility of applying incremental changes, we require that the effect specification of every action α is such that for every relation R, either: (i) only insert's are present that add facts to R; or (ii) only one delete is present that deletes facts from R; or (iii) only one update is present that updates facts in R; or iv) only sets are present that set R. In addition, all relations R_i for which no effects are defined are preserved unchanged, i.e., we add the effect $R_i(\vec{x}) \rightsquigarrow R_i(\vec{x})$. Notice that the unrestricted use of set's guarantees the full expressive power of DCDS, although it may negatively affect the efficiency of execution.

Adding Tuples to a Relation. A create (or ADD) operation that instantiates new facts to add to a relation R corresponds to the definition of the following effect specifications:

$$\textsc{Add}: \big\{q^+ \wedge Q^- \rightsquigarrow R(\vec{t}), R(\vec{x}) \rightsquigarrow R(\vec{x})\big\}$$

The effect specification $q^+ \wedge Q^- \rightsquigarrow R(\vec{t})$ corresponds to the generation of a set of facts to be used to instantiate the relation R in the new state, and no specific restrictions are imposed with respect to the general effect specification form. Specifically, the terms $\vec{t}$ can include constants in ADOM($\mathcal{I}_0$), action parameters (recall that effect specifications occur within action's), free variables of q^+ and function calls that represent external service invocations. The effect specification $R(\vec{x}) \rightsquigarrow R(\vec{x})$ ensures the persistence of existing facts in the relation. The new instance of R can thus be incrementally built from R by adding the set of facts $R(\vec{t})$ obtained according to the general effect execution procedure. The ADD specification pattern is specified by the following construct:

$$\texttt{insert } \vec{t} \texttt{ into } R \texttt{ if } q^+ \wedge Q^-,$$

where $\vec{t}$ and $q^+ \wedge Q^-$ are as defined before. Notice that multiple ADD operations for the same relation R are allowed as effect specifications in an action α. The corresponding effect specifications are of the form:

$$q_1^+ \wedge Q_1^- \rightsquigarrow R(\vec{t_1}), \ldots, q_n^+ \wedge Q_n^- \rightsquigarrow R(\vec{t_n}), R(\vec{x}) \rightsquigarrow R(\vec{x})$$

where each effect specification of the form $q_i^+ \wedge Q_i^- \rightsquigarrow R(\vec{t_i})$ corresponds to the generation of a set of facts to be added to the relation R , and the effect specification $R(\vec{x}) \rightsquigarrow R(\vec{x})$ ensures the persistence of existing facts in the relation.

Deleting/Retaining Tuples From a Relation. Intuitively, deleting from a relation R a set of tuples that match a condition, requires to copy to the next instance (i.e., retain) all the existing tuples in the relation that do not match the deletion condition. To achieve this, we can exploit the explicit distinction made in DCDS effects between q^+ and Q^-, by defining an effect such that: (i) q^+ selects all the tuples in the relation; (ii) Q^- filters away the tuples to be deleted; (iii) the resulting tuples are used to instantiate the new set of facts for the relation.

A delete operation that removes a set of tuples from a relation R can be represented as a DCDS effect of the form

$$\text{RETAIN}: \quad R(\vec{x}) \wedge Q^- \rightsquigarrow R(\vec{x})$$

The effect retains all the tuples in R that satisfy Q^-, or, equivalently, deletes all those that do not satisfy Q^-. The new instance of R can thus be incrementally built from R by deleting all the tuples that satisfy $R(\vec{x}) \wedge \neg(Q^-)$. Notice that the specification restricts the terms $\vec{x}$ to be only variables, i.e., constants in ADOM($\mathcal{I}_0$), action parameters and, for the right-hand side of the effect specification, function calls are not allowed, although constants and action parameters can still be used as terms in Q^-, according to the general effect specification form. The **delete** construct is defined as:

$$\textbf{delete from } R \textbf{ where } Q^-,$$

where Q^- has to fulfill the requirements discussed above. Notice that this corresponds to the effect specification: $R(\vec{x}) \wedge \neg Q^- \rightsquigarrow R(\vec{x})$, which is in the same form as the RETAIN pattern above. As already mentioned, only one DELETE operation for R can be defined in the set of effect specifications, for an action α. Notice, however, that multiple retain/delete conditions over the tuples of R can alway be properly combined in the Q^- part of a single DELETE operation.

Updating Tuples in a Relation. An update operation corresponds to the following effect specifications:

$$\text{UPDATE}: \big\{ R(\vec{x}) \wedge Q^- \rightsquigarrow R(\vec{t}), R(\vec{x}) \wedge \neg(Q^-) \rightsquigarrow R(\vec{x})$$

The effect specification $R(\vec{x}) \wedge Q^- \rightsquigarrow R(\vec{t})$ selects from R all the tuples that match the update condition Q^-, and for each of them a tuple $\vec{t}$ for R is instantiated. As in the general case, constants in ADOM($\mathcal{I}_0$), action parameters, free variables of q^+ (i.e., $R(\vec{x})$) and function calls are allowed in the right-hand side of the effect specification. The effect specification $R(\vec{x}) \wedge \neg(Q^-) \rightsquigarrow R(\vec{x})$ selects from

$R(\vec{x})$ all the tuples that do not match the update condition Q^-, and copies them unchanged to the next state, so as to ensure their persistence. The new instance of R can thus be incrementally built from R by updating each tuple that matches the update condition. The update construct we provide is defined as:

$$\text{update } R \text{ set } \vec{t} \text{ where } Q^-,$$

where $\vec{t}$ and Q^- are as discussed above. Analogously to the DELETE operation, we constrain the specification so that only one UPDATE operation for R can occur in EFFECT(α) for action α. Multiple update conditions over the tuples of R can still be combined in the Q^- part of a single UPDATE.

Updating Tuples in a Relation – Update$^+$. In the UPDATE operation defined above, the updated tuples are generated using constants in ADOM($\mathcal{I}_0$), action parameters, function calls and free variables of the q^+ part (i.e., $R(\vec{x})$). We provide here an extended version of the operation, called UPDATE$^+$, that under specific conditions allows updating tuples in a relation R also with values obtained by querying the current instance of the data layer. The UPDATE$^+$ operator is defined by the following effect specifications:

$$\text{UPDATE}^+ : \{q^+ \wedge Q^- \rightsquigarrow R(\vec{t}), R(\vec{x}) \wedge \widetilde{Q}^- \rightsquigarrow R(\vec{x}), \text{ where}$$
$$q^+(\vec{x}, \vec{y}) = R(\vec{x}) \wedge q(\vec{z}, \vec{y}), \text{ with } \vec{z} \subseteq \vec{x}, \text{ and } \widetilde{Q}^- = \neg \exists \vec{y} \, (q(\vec{z}, \vec{y}) \vee Q^-(\vec{x}, \vec{y})).$$

Intuitively, the answer of $Q(\vec{x}, \vec{y}) = q^+(\vec{x}, \vec{y}) \wedge Q^-(\vec{x}, \vec{y})$ produces a result set where each tuple consists of two sub-tuples: one, the projection over $\vec{x}$, is the R-tuple to update, and one, the projection over $\vec{y}$, contains the values needed to instantiate the updated fact $R(\vec{t})$. Notice that $\vec{t}$ can include free variables of q^+ (i.e., variables from $\vec{x}$ and $\vec{y}$), as well as constants in ADOM($\mathcal{I}_0$), action parameters and function calls. The effect specification $R(\vec{x}) \wedge \widetilde{Q}^- \rightsquigarrow R(\vec{x})$ ensures persistence of the tuples in R not subject to updates. Indeed, it is easy to check that its answer contains all the R-tuples not occurring as sub-tuples in the answer of $Q(\vec{x}, \vec{y})$.

In this case, the new instance of R can be incrementally built from R by updating a subset of its tuples only if the answer given by evaluating $Q(\vec{x}, \vec{y}) = q^+(\vec{x}, \vec{y}) \wedge Q^-(\vec{x}, \vec{y})$ over the current instance of the data layer is such that $\vec{x}$ functionally determines $\vec{y}$, i.e., for each pair of tuples in the answer having the same values for $\vec{x}$, the corresponding values for $\vec{y}$ are the same. Intuitively, this condition ensures that for each tuple in R (i.e., a tuple with values for $\vec{x}$) to be updated, there is a single tuple with values for $\vec{y}$ to be used in the update. We can thus provide an update+ operator defined as

$$\text{update+ } R \text{ set } \vec{t} \text{ where } q^+(\vec{x}, \vec{y}) \wedge Q^-(\vec{x}, \vec{y})$$

where $\vec{t}$ and $q^+(\vec{x}, \vec{y}) \wedge Q^-(\vec{x}, \vec{y})$ are as above. Also in this case, we constrain the specification so that only one UPDATE operation for R can be defined in the set of effect specifications EFFECT(α) for an action α.

In the general case no syntactic restrictions can be imposed on $Q(\vec{x}, \vec{y})$ to ensure the existence of the functional dependency from $\vec{x}$ to $\vec{y}$, which can only be checked at query execution time. If the required functional dependency is violated, the new instance of R cannot be incrementally built from R by updating a subset of its tuples. However it can still be constructed by resorting to the general semantics. In this case, though, the intended semantics of the update is not preserved in general, as the resulting instance of R may contain additional tuples, namely those generated by "updating" an R-tuple with different sets of values.

4   Towards a Rule-Eengine Based Implementation

The executable nature of DCDS models, coupled with the efficient implementation induced by the operators defined above, makes them well suited for the realization of a support system for rapid prototyping of data-centric processes. In particular, state-of-the-art rule engines, such as the open-source Java-based Drools Expert rule engine[5] at the heart of the following discussion, represent a viable technological solution for supporting the declarative specification of a DCDS and for providing the run-time environment that supports the DCDS operational semantics of CA rules and actions.

Data Modeling. The relational schema at the heart of the data layer can be directly mapped to an object-oriented representation of the application domain. In particular, each relation schema is represented as a class having as name the name of the relation and as instance variables the attributes defined in the relation schema, so that each object instance of such a class is considered as a fact and corresponds to a tuple of a relation. representing Java beans), or the Drools type declaration language can be exploited for defining fact types and their attributes.

Example 2. In the travel reimbursement example, the Hotel relation can be represented by the following fact type declaration:

```
declare Hotel
    hName:String        date:Date            price:double
    currency:String     priceInUSD:double
end
```

Actions Modeling and Implementation. DCDS action specifications serve as a basis for driving their implementation, and declarative specifications of action effects can be mapped into a concrete procedural implementation of the action. As the Drools framework provides support for the definition of named queries over the data model, the query part of each effect specification is directly represented by a corresponding Drools query. Queries are used to retrieve fact

---

[5] http://www.jboss.org/drools/

sets based on patterns[6], and a query has an optional set of parameters that we exploit for binding query parameters that refer to action parameters.

Basically, executing an effect requires to execute the corresponding query and the use the query result set according to the specific operation associated with the effect. For `insert`, `delete` and `update/update+` operations, objects representing facts are respectively inserted, deleted and updated in the engine's working memory, by exploiting the `insert()`, `retract()` and `update()` methods provided by the engine. For a `set` operation, existing facts are first retracted, and generated facts are then inserted in the working memory.

Example 3. The effect $\mathsf{Hotel}(x_1, \ldots, x_5) \land \mathsf{ApprHotel}(x_1) \rightsquigarrow \mathsf{Status}(\text{'}accepted\text{'})$ defined in the example, corresponds to a `set` operation of the form

$$\texttt{set } \text{'}accepted\text{'} \texttt{ for } Status(status) \texttt{ where } \mathsf{Hotel}(x_1, \ldots, x_5) \land \mathsf{ApprHotel}(x_1)$$

whose query is mapped to the Drools query

```
query "Hotel Approved"
  Hotel($x1:hName,$x2:date,$x3:price,$x4:currency,$x5:priceInUSD)
  ApprHotel(hName == $x1)
end
```

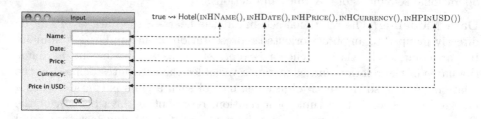

Fig. 1. Form-based user involvement in action executions.

For effects defined as `insert`, `set` and `update/update+` operations, the instantiation/update of new/existing facts may require to obtain new data from the external environment. In general, each functional term can be mapped to a method call, that may consist in a user-defined piece of code, may correspond to a remote method invocation or Web service call, or it may implement the specific logic for generating an input dialog so as to get user's input. updating a fact can be grouped in a single user form, automatically built from the type or class definition (Fig. 1). Attributes whose values are given by the user are shown as input fields, while attributes whose value is already defined (e.g., by a constant/action parameters) are shown as non-editable fields.

Process Modeling. The modeling of a DCDS process as a set of CA rules is directly represented as a set of rules defined in the Drools Rule Language (DRL).

---

[6] Conditions defined in a query or in CA rules are referred to as *patterns*, and the process of matching patterns against the data is called *pattern matching*.

For each condition-action rule of the form $Q \mapsto \alpha$, a corresponding named rule is created, as `rule "ruleName" when` Q `then` $execute(\alpha)$ `end`.

Example 4. In the travel reimbursement example, the condition-action rule represented as Status(*'readyToVerify'*) $\mapsto$ *VerifyRequest* is mapped to the following rule

```
rule "Verify Request"
    when    Status(status == StatusEnum.READY_TO_VERIFY)
    then    Executor.perform(new VerifyRequest());
end
```

Process Execution. The insertion of new data (as well as the update or deletion of existing data), either when the data layer is first instantiated or as a result of action executions, acts as a trigger for the rules evaluation process. and adopts a forward chaining data-driven approach in the process of matching new or existing facts in working memory against the rules, to infer conclusions which result in actions. Rules whose condition part is fully matched become eligible for execution, and the evaluation process can result in multiple eligible rules, i.e executable actions. and according to a conflict resolution strategy determines a single rule activation to be executed. According to our rule definitions, the firing of a rule activation results in the creation and execution of an action instance with a binding for its parameters. The execution of an action results in the insertion, deletion and update of facts in working memory, and the engine starts a new match-resolve-act cycle, where previously activated rules may be de-activated (as their condition is no longer matched by the actual facts) and removed from the agenda, and new instances may be activated, resulting in a new set of executable actions.

5   Conclusions

The DCDS framework induces a data-centric process management approach, where models (i) rely on a complete integration between processes and data, and (ii) are both *verifiable* and *executable*. As a first step towards a reference implementation for DCDSs, we proposed a modeling approach for DCDSs that, on the basis of specific constructs for specifying actions' effects, enables an efficient implementation of action executions, through incremental changes over the current instance of the data model. While rule engines can be exploited for rapid prototyping of DCDSs, several aspects still need to be considered. In particular, the resource perspective must be incorporated into the picture. Data-centric models are able to support an integrated modeling of human resources and data, by combining classical role-based organizational meta-models with a fine-grained modeling of users and their domain-specific roles in relation to data elements. At a process specification level, in line with the well-known resource patterns, this allows declaratively defining possible bindings between actions and human performers on the basis of both user- and data-aware conditions that guard the executability of actions, going beyond simple role-based assignment policies. Similarly, run-time user involvement in the selection of executable actions has to be considered, investigating both the link with classical worklist-based approaches and the possibility of supporting knowledge workers with decision-support features.

Acknowledgments. This work has been partially supported by the SAPIENZA grants TESTMED, SUPER and "Premio Ricercatori Under-40", and by the EU FP7-ICT Project ACSI (257593).

References

1. Bagheri Hariri, B., Calvanese, D., De Giacomo, G., Deutsch, A., Montali, M.: Verification of relational data-centric dynamic systems with external services. In: Proceedings of PODS (2013)
2. Calvanese, D., De Giacomo, G., Montali, M.: Foundations of Data-Aware Process Analysis: A Database Theory Perspective. In: Proceedings of PODS (2013)
3. Cohn, D., Dhoolia, P., Heath III, F., Pinel, F., Vergo, J.: Siena: from powerpoint to web app in 5 minutes. In: Bouguettaya, A., Krueger, I., Margaria, T. (eds.) ICSOC 2008. LNCS, vol. 5364, pp. 722–723. Springer, Heidelberg (2008)
4. Dumas, M.: On the convergence of data and process engineering. In: Eder, J., Bielikova, M., Tjoa, A.M. (eds.) ADBIS 2011. LNCS, vol. 6909, pp. 19–26. Springer, Heidelberg (2011)
5. Hull, R., Damaggio, E., De Masellis, R. et al.: Business Artifacts with Guard-Stage-Milestone Lifecycles: Managing Artifact Interactions with Conditions and Events. In: Proceedings of DEBS '11 (2011)
6. Kunzle, V., Reichert, M.: PHILharmonicFlows: towards a framework for object-aware process management. J. Softw. Maint. Evol.: Res. Pract. **23**(4), 205–244 (2011)
7. Kunzle, V., Weber, B., Reichert, M.: Object-aware business processes: fundamental requirements and their support in existing approaches. Int. J. Inf. Syst. Model. Design (IJISMD) **2**(2), 19–46 (2011)
8. Meyer, A., Smirnov, S., Weske, M.: Data in business processes. EMISA Forum **31**(3), 5–31 (2011)
9. Pesic, M., Schonenberg, H., van der Aalst, W.M.P.: DECLARE: Full support for loosely-structured processes. In: Proceedings of EDOC (2007)
10. Russell, N., ter Hofstede, A.H.M., Edmond, D., van der Aalst, W.M.P.: Workflow data patterns: identification, representation and tool support. In: Delcambre, L.M.L., Kop, Ch., Mayr, H.C., Mylopoulos, J., Pastor, Ó. (eds.) ER 2005. LNCS, vol. 3716, pp. 353–368. Springer, Heidelberg (2005)
11. Solomakhin, D., Montali, M., Tessaris, S., De Masellis, R.: Verification of artifact-centric systems: decidability and modeling issues. In: Basu, S., Pautasso, C., Zhang, L., Fu, X. (eds.) ICSOC 2013. LNCS, vol. 8274, pp. 252–266. Springer, Heidelberg (2013)
12. Swenson, K.D. (ed.): Mastering the Unpredictable: How Adaptive Case Management Will Revolutionize the Way That Knowledge Workers Get Things Done. Meghan-Kiffer Press, Tampa (2010)
13. Vaculin, R., Hull, R., Heath, T., Cochran, C., Nigam, A., Sukaviriya, P.: Declarative business artifact centric modeling of decision and knowledge intensive business processes. In: Proceedings of EDOC 2011 (2011)

Synthesizing Object-Centric Models from Business Process Models

Rik Eshuis[✉] and Pieter van Gorp

Eindhoven University of Technology, P.O. Box 513,
5600 MB Eindhoven, The Netherlands
{h.eshuis,p.m.e.v.gorp}@tue.nl

Abstract. Business process models expressed in UML activity diagrams can specify the flow of multiple stateful business objects among activities. Such business process models implicitly specify not only the life cycles of those objects, but also their communication. This paper presents a semi-automated approach that synthesizes an object-centric system design from a business process model referencing multiple objects. The object-centric design can be used to perform the process in a flexible way.

1 Introduction

The classic way to model business processes is to specify atomic activities and their ordering in a flowchart-like process model. In recent years, data-centric modeling paradigms have increasingly grown popular in research and industry as alternative to the classic, process-centric paradigm. Data-centric modeling approaches aim to have a more holistic perspective on business process [1,2] and support semi-structured, knowledge-intensive business processes [3].

These two paradigms are often positioned as alternatives, each having their own modeling techniques and implementation technologies. Data-centric approaches use for instance state machines [1,2,4,5] or business rules [6] as modeling techniques, while process-centric approaches use process flow models such as UML activity diagrams [7] or BPMN [8], where each modeling technique is supported by dedicated engines.

In practice, however, the strengths of both approaches should be combined. Process-centric models show clearly the behavior of the process, while in data-centric models the expected behavior is difficult to predict, either since the global process is distributed over different data elements or since the behavior is specified in a declarative, non-operational way such as with the Guard-Stage-Milestone approach [6]. Whereas data-centric approaches support more flexible ways of performing business processes than process-centric approaches [9].

We envision that process modeling techniques will be used to specify the main "default" scenarios of a process whereas a data-centric approach is actually used to realize the approach, adding additional business rules for exceptional circumstances. This allows actors to perform the process in the prescribed way for a default scenario, but respond in a flexible way to exceptional circumstances

N. Lohmann et al. (Eds.): BPM 2013 Workshops, LNBIP 171, pp. 155–166, 2014.
DOI: 10.1007/978-3-319-06257-0_13, © Springer International Publishing Switzerland 2014

not covered by the default scenarios, which is one of the strengths of object-centric process management [9].

This paper outlines a semi-automated approach for creating an object-centric design from a business process model that specifies the main scenarios in which these objects interact. The approach uses synthesis patterns that relate process model constructs to object life cycle constructs. The resulting object-centric design can be refined with additional "non-default" behavior such as exceptions.

The approach uses UML, since UML offers a coherent notation for specifying both process-centric and data-centric models. We specify business process models that reference objects in UML activity diagrams with object flows. We use UML statecharts (state machines) to model communicating object life cycles, which specify an object-centric design.

The remainder of this paper is structured as follows. Section 2 summarizes a previously developed approach for synthesizing one object life cycle from a business process model that references the object. This paper extends that approach to the case of multiple objects that interact with each other. Section 3 presents coordination patterns between multiple object life cycles that realize object-flow constraints from the activity diagram. Section 4 presents execution patterns between multiple object life cycles that realize control-flow constraints from the activity diagram. Section 5 discusses various aspects of the approach. Section 6 presents related work and Sect. 7 ends the paper with conclusions.

2   Preliminaries

We assume readers are familiar with UML activity diagrams [7] and UML statecharts [7]. Figure 1 shows an activity diagram of an ordering process that we refer to in the sequel.

2.1   Synthesizing Statecharts from Activity Diagrams

In previous work [10], we outlined an approach to synthesize a single object life cycle, expressed as a hierarchial UML statechart, from a business process model, expressed in a UML activity diagram. This paper builds upon that approach. To make the paper self-contained, we briefly summarize the main results here.

Input to the synthesis approach is an activity diagram with object nodes. Each object node references the same object but in a distinct state. An activity can have object nodes as input or output. An activity can only start if all its input object nodes are filled, and upon completion it fills all output object nodes [7]. If an activity has multiple input or output object nodes that reference the same object, the object is in multiple states at the same time; then the object life cycle contains parallelism. Object nodes are exclusive: if multiple activities require the same object node as input, only one activity can read (consume) the object node.

The synthesis approach consists of two steps. First, irrelevant nodes are filtered from the activity diagram. Object nodes are relevant, but activities are

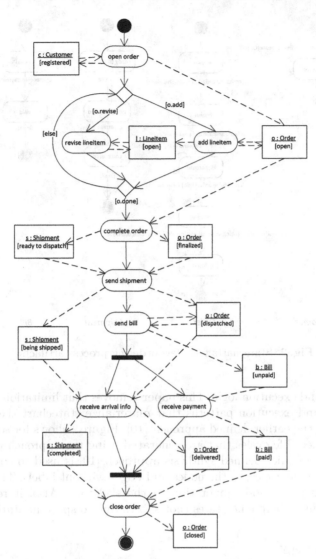

Fig. 1. Activity diagram of ordering process

not. Control nodes are only relevant if they influence the object nodes. Second, the filtered activity diagram is converted into a statechart by constructing a state hierarchy that ensures that the behavior of the statechart induced by the state hierarchy is equivalent to the behavior of the filtered activity diagram.

A limitation of that approach is that it assumes that an activity diagram references exactly one object. If an activity references multiple different objects, for each object a different version of the activity diagram specific to that object can be created. While this ensures that for each object a statechart skeleton can be created, the generated statechart skeletons are not yet executable, lacking

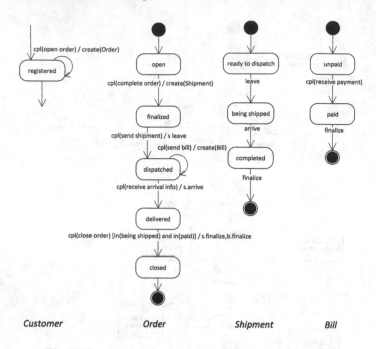

Fig. 2. Statecharts for a few ordering process artifacts

coordination and execution logic. This paper removes that limitation by defining coordination and execution patterns that materialize statechart skeletons synthesized using the earlier defined approach [10]. Figure 2 shows for some objects part of the object life cycles that are generated using the approach proposed in this paper. The earlier defined synthesis approach [10] is used to construct the skeletons of the life cycles, so the nodes and edges without labels. The approach defined in this paper adds annotation to the skeletons. Also, it refines some atomic states into compound states (not shown due to space limitations).

2.2 Terminology

To simplify the exposition, we introduce the following terminology for UML activity diagrams with objects. Let A be an activity (action node) and let $o:O[s]$ be an object node representing object o of class O where o is in state s. Node $:O$ represents an anonymous object of class O.

A *finalizes* $:O$ if there is an object flow from $:O$ to A but not from A to $:O$.
A *creates* $:O$ if there is an object flow from A to $:O$ but not from $:O$ to A.
A *accesses* $:O$ if there is an object flow from $:O$ to A and from A to $:O$. There are two kinds of *access*-relation:
>   A *reads* $:O$ if there is an object flow from $:O[s]$ to A and from A to $O:[s]$.
>   A *updates* $:O$ if there is an object flow from $:O[s]$ to A and from A to $O:[s']$ for $s \neq s'$.

3   Coordination Patterns

Coordination Patterns specify how different objects interact with each other. They derive from the object flows of an activity diagram. Coordination Patterns are not executable, since the patterns do not consider external event triggers. Section 4 presents executable patterns.

3.1   Roles

For each pattern, we identify two different roles for objects: coordinator and participant. Each activity that accesses an object has exactly one coordinator. Performing the activity typically causes a state change with the coordinator. This implies that the activity updates the coordinator. Any object that the activity updates can play the role of coordinator.

If A does not access any object, there is no coordinator. We consider this as a design error that can be detected automatically and fixed via additional user input. If A accesses multiple objects, the user has to decide which object is responsible for coordinating $:P$. Alternatively, from a process model with object flows a priority scheme on object classes can be automatically derived, for instance based on the dominance criterion [4]. The object class with the highest priority can be made the default coordinator of $:P$.

In the sequel, we present patterns for which we assume each activity has one coordinator, which is either derived automatically from the activity diagram or designated by the user.

3.2   Creation

Activity A creates an object of type P under coordination of object $:O$. Figure 3 specifies the creation pattern: Since $:O$ is coordinator, A changes the state of $:O$ from $S1$ to $S2$. When coordinator $:O$ moves from $S1$ to $S2$, an object of type P is created with action $create(P)$. Coordinator $:O$ moves state in task A, but task execution details are not considered for coordination patterns, only for the execution patterns.

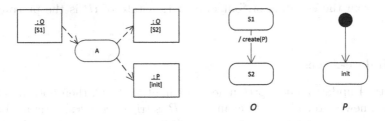

Fig. 3. Creation pattern

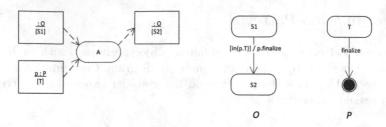

Fig. 4. Finalization pattern

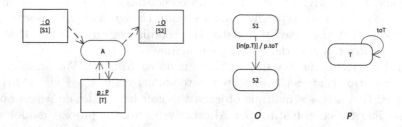

Fig. 5. Read-access pattern

3.3 Finalization

Activity A finalizes object $p{:}P$ by moving $:P$ into its end state; finalization does not mean that the object is destroyed, The finalization is realized (Fig. 4) by sending a special event *finalize* to $p{:}P$ that moves the life cycle to the end state, provided $:P$ is indeed in the expected state $T1$. It might be that the life cycle has multiple end states; in that case, the other branches of the life cycle can still continue after this branch has been finalized.

3.4 Read-Access

If activity A reads object $p{:}P$, then $:P$ does not change state but is accessed. To model this, we use a self-loop from and to the state of $:P$ (Fig. 5) that is triggered an event from the coordinator, but only if the state of $:P$ is the precondition for A.

3.5 Update-Access

If activity A updates object $p{:}P$ under coordination of $:O$, then both $:O$ and $:P$ move to a new state. The state change of $:P$ is triggered by $:O$. Figure 6 shows that $:O$ generates an event that triggers $p{:}P$ to move to its next state, but only if $p{:}P$ is currently in the state that is precondition for A.

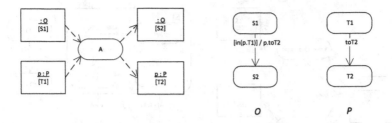

Fig. 6. Update-access pattern

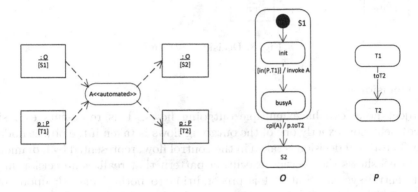

Fig. 7. Task pattern

4   Execution Patterns

Coordination Patterns only capture the object-flow constraints from activity diagrams. To capture the control-flow constraints, we use execution patterns based on control-flow constructs in activity diagrams.

4.1   Task

A task is invoked in an activity node. A typical distinction is between manual, automated, or semi-automated tasks. For this paper, we only consider automated tasks, but we plan to study other task types in future work. Figure 7 shows how a task invocation can be specified in object-centric design. The coordinator $:O$ is responsible for invoking task A; there its precondition state $S1$ is decomposed into two states, where *busy* A denotes that activity A is being executed. Upon completion, the coordinator moves to $S2$ and informs the other object $:P$ that it has to move to new state $T2$. In Fig. 7, the underlying coordination pattern is the update-access pattern, but the task pattern can be combined with any coordination pattern or none.

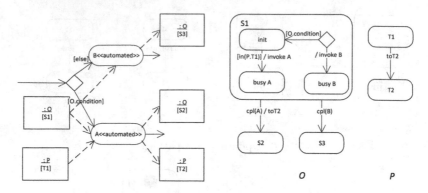

Fig. 8. Decision pattern

4.2 Decision

An object node can have multiple outgoing flows. This represents exclusive (choice) behavior: exactly one of the outgoing flows is taken if the object node is active. The actual decision is taken in the control flow, represented by a diamond.

Figure 8 shows the decision execution pattern that realizes a decision in an object-centric system. State $S1$ is precondition to both A and B; upon completion of either A or B object :O moves to $S2$ or $S3$. As in the case of the task-pattern, the precondition state $S1$ is hierarchical. In this case, $S1$ contains the decision logic to decide between A or B; note that this decision logic comes from the control flow.

4.3 Merge

As in the previous case, an object node with multiple incoming edges represents exclusive behavior: if one of the edges is activated, the object node is entered. Again, the actual behavior is governed by control flow. The resulting merge pattern is symmetric to the decision pattern and omitted due to space limitations.

4.4 Fork

So far, we have seen only sequential state machines that do not contain any parallelism. However, an object can be in multiple states at the same time. Parallelism is created by an activity node that takes the object in a certain state as input and outputs the object in two distinct states, to the activity has two output object nodes that reference the same object. Since activity nodes activate all outgoing edges, both output object nodes are filled.

Figure 9 shows how the resulting fork pattern is specified. The state hierarchy is constructed using the approach we developed previously [10]. The two concurrent states model the two parallel branches started upon completion of A. The state hierarchy for $S2$ and $S3$ derives from the task pattern. The state hierarchy for $S1$ is not shown to simplify the exposition.

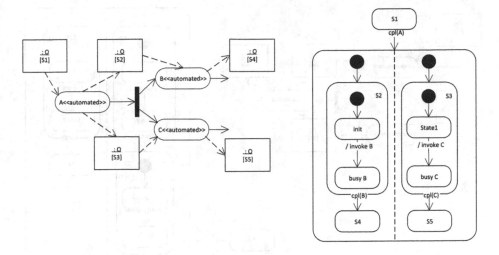

Fig. 9. Fork pattern

Note that if the object node with state $S1$ referred to another object, say $:P$, a create pattern would be present and no state hierarchy would be needed for the object life cycle of $:O$. In that case, the concurrency is expressed implicitly by having two object life cycles ($:O$ and $:P$) active at the same time.

4.5   Join

The join pattern is symmetric to the fork pattern (Fig. 10). Complicating factor is how to invoke the activity C that actually synchronizes the parallel branches. Using the task pattern, the parallel branches are only left if C completes. This implies that C needs to be invoked in one of the parallel branches, but only if the other branch is in the state that is precondition to C, i.e. $S4$. Which parallel branch is chosen to invoke C is arbitrary.

5   Discussion

Order example. To obtain the statecharts in Fig. 2 from the activity diagram in Fig. 1 all four coordination patterns are required. Next, the task, decision and merge patterns are used. Using these patterns introduces compound states which are not shown due to space limitations.

Multiple start states. If an object life cycle has multiple start states that are active in parallel, the synthesis approach will create multiple create actions. This results in multiple objects rather than a single object with parallelism.

We consider multiple start states as a design error: two parallel actions that create the same object $:O$ suggests that $:O$ is created synchronously while the two activities operate independently from one another. This error can be repaired

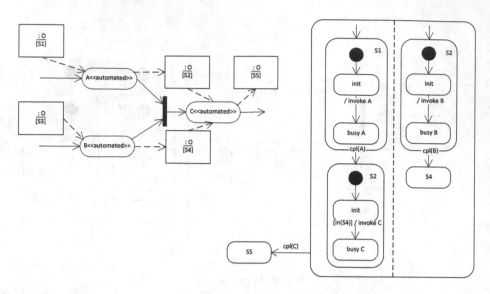

Fig. 10. Join pattern

by merging the activities that create the object. Another option is to insert an initial state that leads to the start states.

Refining. The object-centric design generated using the approach can be further refined, for instance to incorporate human-centric behavior. Suppose the company of the order process wishes to allow that a customer cancels a finalized order that has not yet been paid by rejecting bill. Extending the global process model of Fig. 1 results in a complex diagram with a lot of additional edges. In the object-centric design, only a few local changes are required: extending the life cycle of bill and order with additional cancelled states that can be reached if the cancel event occurs. Note the guard condition on the transition from delivered to closed in Fig. 2 prevents that a cancelled order is closed.

6   Related Work

As stated in the introduction, the last years a lot of research has been performed in the area of data-centric process modeling approaches such as business artifacts [1,4,5,11], case management [3,12], data-driven process models that are executable [2,9,13] and process models with data flow [14–16]. Sanz [17] surveys previous work on integrating the data and process perspective in the field of entity-relation modeling in connection to data-centric process modeling. This paper uses UML activity diagrams with object flows as data-centric process modeling notation.

More related to this paper are approaches that distinguish between process and data models and bridge the gap by deriving a process model that is coherent with a predefined data model [18,19] or object behavior model [20–22]. This paper takes the opposite route: it considers a process model with data (object) flow and derives object behavior models that realize the process model.

Wahler and Küster [16] define an approach that resembles this paper most closely, and we therefore discuss this work in more detail. They too consider process models that manipulate stateful business objects, where each step in a process model can lead to a change in one or more business objects. The setting is a static set of predefined business objects that need to be "wired" together, where the process model is used to derive the wiring relation. They study how to design the wiring in such a way, by changing the process model, that the resulting wired object design has a low coupling. In contrast, this paper studies the problem of deriving an object-centric design from a process model with object flows. The problem is then defining the set of business objects and their behavior, which are both given in the approach of Wahler and Küster.

7 Conclusion

We have presented a semi-automated approach that synthesizes an object-centric system design from a business process model that references multiple objects. The approach distinguishes between coordination patterns that realize object-flow constraints and execution patterns for control-flow constraints. The patterns heavily use the state hierarchy for the object life cycles to establish a clear link with the process model constructs. The resulting object-centric design can be used to perform the process in a flexible way [22].

The approach is defined in the context of UML [7], but we plan to define a similar approach for BPMN [8], which supports a similar object flow notation as UML activity diagrams, though the BPMN semantics appears to be different.

We are currently implementing the patterns in a graph-transformation tool [23]. We plan to apply the prototype to different examples from the literature [16] and from student projects.

References

1. Nigam, A., Caswell, N.S.: Business artifacts: an approach to operational specification. IBM Syst. J. **42**(3), 428–445 (2003)
2. Künzle, V., Reichert, M.: Philharmonicflows: towards a framework for object-aware process management. J. Softw. Maintenance **23**(4), 205–244 (2011)
3. Swenson, K.D.: Mastering the Unpredictable: How Adaptive Case Management Will Revolutionize the Way That Knowledge Workers Get Things Done. Meghan-Kiffer Press, Tampa (2010)
4. Kumaran, S., Liu, R., Wu, F.Y.: On the duality of information-centric and activity-centric models of business processes. In: Bellahsène, Z., Léonard, M. (eds.) CAiSE 2008. LNCS, vol. 5074, pp. 32–47. Springer, Heidelberg (2008)
5. Yongchareon, S., Liu, C., Zhao, X.: An artifact-centric view-based approach to modeling inter-organizational business processes. In: Bouguettaya, A., Hauswirth, M., Liu, L. (eds.) WISE 2011. LNCS, vol. 6997, pp. 273–281. Springer, Heidelberg (2011)

6. Damaggio, E., Hull, R., Vaculín, R.: On the equivalence of incremental and fixpoint semantics for business artifacts with guard-stage-milestone lifecycles. Inf. Syst. **38**(4), 561–584 (2013)
7. UML Revision Taskforce: UML 2.3 Superstructure Specification. Object Management Group, OMG Document Number formal/2010-05-05 (2010)
8. White, S., et al.: Business Process Modeling Notation (BPMN) Specification, Version 1.1. Object Management Group. http://www.bpmn.org (2008)
9. Redding, G., Dumas, M., ter Hofstede, A.H.M., Iordachescu, A.: A flexible, object-centric approach for business process modelling. SOCA **4**(3), 191–201 (2010)
10. Eshuis, R., Van Gorp, P.: Synthesizing object life cycles from business process models. In: Atzeni, P., Cheung, D., Ram, S. (eds.) ER 2012 Main Conference 2012. LNCS, vol. 7532, pp. 307–320. Springer, Heidelberg (2012)
11. Hull, R.: Artifact-centric business process models: brief survey of research results and challenges. In: Meersman, R., Tari, Z. (eds.) OTM 2008, Part II. LNCS, vol. 5332, pp. 1152–1163. Springer, Heidelberg (2008)
12. van der Aalst, W.M.P., Weske, M., Grünbauer, D.: Case handling: a new paradigm for business process support. Data Knowl. Eng. **53**(2), 129–162 (2005)
13. Müller, D., Reichert, M., Herbst, J.: Data-driven modeling and coordination of large process structures. In: Meersman, R., Tari, Z. (eds.) OTM 2007, Part I. LNCS, vol. 4803, pp. 131–149. Springer, Heidelberg (2007)
14. Meyer, A., Weske, M.: Data support in process model abstraction. In: Atzeni, P., Cheung, D., Ram, S. (eds.) ER 2012 Main Conference 2012. LNCS, vol. 7532, pp. 292–306. Springer, Heidelberg (2012)
15. Sun, S.X., Zhao, J.L., Nunamaker, J.F., Sheng, O.R.L.: Formulating the data-flow perspective for business process management. Inf. Syst. Res. **17**(4), 374–391 (2006)
16. Wahler, K., Küster, J.M.: Predicting coupling of object-centric business process implementations. In: Dumas, M., Reichert, M., Shan, M.-C. (eds.) BPM 2008. LNCS, vol. 5240, pp. 148–163. Springer, Heidelberg (2008)
17. Sanz, J.L.C.: Entity-centric operations modeling for business process management - a multidisciplinary review of the state-of-the-art. In: Gao, J.Z., Lu, X., Younas, M., Zhu, H. (eds.): SOSE, pp. 152–163. IEEE (2011)
18. van Hee, K.M., Hidders, J., Houben, G.J., Paredaens, J., Thiran, P.: On the relationship between workflow models and document types. Inf. Syst. **34**(1), 178–208 (2009)
19. Reijers, H.A., Limam, S., van der Aalst, W.M.P.: Product-based workflow design. J. Manag. Inf. Syst. **20**(1), 229–262 (2003)
20. Fritz, C., Hull, R., Su, J.: Automatic construction of simple artifact-based business processes. In: Fagin, R. (ed.): ICDT, ACM International Conference Proceeding Series, vol. 361, pp. 225–238. ACM (2009)
21. Küster, J.M., Ryndina, K., Gall, H.: Generation of business process models for object life cycle compliance. In: Alonso, G., Dadam, P., Rosemann, M. (eds.) BPM 2007. LNCS, vol. 4714, pp. 165–181. Springer, Heidelberg (2007)
22. Redding, G., Dumas, M., ter Hofstede, A.H.M., Iordachescu, A.: Generating business process models from object behavior models. IS Manag. **25**(4), 319–331 (2008)
23. Van Gorp, P., Eshuis, R.: Transforming process models: executable rewrite rules versus a formalized Java program. In: Petriu, D.C., Rouquette, N., Haugen, Ø. (eds.) MODELS 2010, Part II. LNCS, vol. 6395, pp. 258–272. Springer, Heidelberg (2010)

Activity-Centric and Artifact-Centric Process Model Roundtrip

Andreas Meyer[⊠] and Mathias Weske

Hasso Plattner Institute at the University of Potsdam, Potsdam, Germany
{Andreas.Meyer,Mathias.Weske}@hpi.uni-potsdam.de

Abstract. Currently, two major process modeling paradigms exist: activity-centric and artifact-centric. They focus on different first class modeling constructs and therefore, they are eligible for different scenarios. Nevertheless, both paradigms compete for users raising the own capabilities over the other's ones neglecting that both paradigms are compatible to each other such that one can transform one into the other one. In this paper, we provide a set of algorithms to allow these transformations as roundtrip, ie from an artifact-centric process model to an activity-centric one and back and vice versa. To this end, we utilize a synchronized object life cycle as mediator between both paradigms. We show applicability of our algorithms by discussing them in combination with an example.

Keywords: Process modeling · Activity-centric · Artifact-centric · Object life cycle · Model transformation

1 Introduction

Since the 1990s, workflow modeling received much attention, because of the need to specify organizations' workflows and business processes structurally and to use this representation for analysis, improvement, control, management, and enactment of the processes [1]. Today, two process modeling paradigms are of major importance: activity-centric and artifact-centric process modeling. structures (gateways) as first class modeling constructs and regards data objects in specific data states as pre- and postconditions for activity enablement or as main decision indicator at exclusive gateways. The main representative and industry standard is the Business Process Model and Notation [2]. The usage of one data object in different data states in combination with multiple activities allows to derive a so-called object life cycle, which describes the manipulations performed on a data object [3,4]. Artifact-centric process modeling [5–8] regards data objects and their object life cycles as first class modeling constructs and multiple data objects synchronize on their data state changes, ie data state changes in different object life cycles need to be performed together. The synchronization information is stored with the object life cycles instead of a control

N. Lohmann et al. (Eds.): BPM 2013 Workshops, LNBIP 171, pp. 167–181, 2014.
DOI: 10.1007/978-3-319-06257-0_14, © Springer International Publishing Switzerland 2014

unit. Subsequently, the order of activities is not modeled explicitly, but can be extracted by analyzing the artifact-centric process model.

Currently, both process modeling paradigms compete for users, where especially the artifact-centric one lacks major evidence of applicability. It is proved to be useful if the process flow follows from data objects as, for instance, in manufacturing processes [7]. In contrast, in many domains, eg accounting, insurance handling, and municipal procedures, the process flow follows from activities, which need to be executed in a predefined order. While most research only considers one paradigm, we present a set of algorithms allowing the transformation of process models of one paradigm into the other one via a synchronized object life cycle–a set of object of life cycles with their transitions synchronized indicating which data state changes need to occur simultaneously. Liu et al. transform an activity-centric process model into a synchronized object life cycle utilizing the notion of data object dominance [9]. However, the authors have a restricted view on the usage of data objects, because only objects written by an activity are considered for data state determination. Implicit state transitions resulting from, for instance, underspecified process models are missing. The algorithms presented here consider paths of process models to handle underspecification properly. We also discussed this issue recently [10].

The remainder of the paper is structured as follows. Section 2 introduces four types of process models, ranging from artifact-centric to activity-centric process models before we discuss the algorithms to transform one process model type into another one by ensuring a roundtrip from one of the mentioned paradigms to the other and back. Finally, we discuss related work in Sect. 4 and conclude the paper in Sect. 5.

2   Types of Business Process Models

In the context of artifact-centric and activity-centric process models, we identified four different types of process models (cf. Definitions 2 to 5). Thereby, object life cycles describe the allowed data object manipulations and the interdependencies of multiple data objects in the course of process model execution. These can be combined in a synchronized object life cycle, which acts as mediator between activity- and artifact-centric process models as both require to align to this data flow specification. Further, an activity-centric process model may exist in two variations: with and without information about attribute types. Below, we introduce each process model type. But first, we start with the definition of a data object and data object class. Both concepts are the major connection between the artifact-centric and the activity-centric modeling paradigm.

Definition 1 (Data object and data object class). A *data object class* $C = (\mathcal{P}, S, i, S_F)$ consists of a finite set $\mathcal{P}$ of attributes, a finite non-empty set S of data states ($\mathcal{P}, S$ are disjoint), an initial data state $i \in S$, and a non-empty set $S_F \subseteq S$ of final data states. A *data object* $D = (s, P)$ consists of a data state $s \in S$ and a finite set $P \subseteq \mathcal{P}$ of attributes. Each data object D is an instance of a data object class C such that $\varphi(D) = C$, where $\varphi : \mathcal{D} \rightarrow \mathcal{C}$ with $\mathcal{D}$ denoting the finite set of all data objects and $\mathcal{C}$ denoting the finite set of all data object classes.   ◇

The concept of business artifacts [6,11] has been established based on the initial work of Nigam and Caswell [5]. We define an artifact-centric process model – closely related to existing work [11] – as follows.

Definition 2 (Artifact-centric process model). An *artifact-centric process model* $ACP = (Z, V, B)$ consists of a schema $Z = (\mathcal{C}, \lambda, \kappa)$ with a finite non-empty set of data object classes $\mathcal{C}$, the *in-state* function $\lambda : \mathcal{C} \times S \rightarrow \{true, false\}$, and the *defined* function $\kappa : \mathcal{C} \times P \rightarrow \{true, false\}$, a finite set V of tasks, and a finite set B of business rules. Functions λ and κ evaluate to true or false depending on the existence of a data object of class C being in a data state s or containing a value for the attribute p respectively. A task $v = (label, O)$, $v \in V$, consists of a label and a finite set $O \in C$ of data object classes referring to data objects being manipulated by this task. A business rule $b = (pre, post, W)$ consists of a precondition *pre*, a postcondition *post*, and a finite set $W \subseteq V$ of tasks manipulating data objects to meet the postcondition. A pre- as well as a postcondition comprises a set of in-state and defined functions connected by operators $\wedge$ and $\vee$. Thereby, a defined function may only contain a data object class, which is used in at least one in-state function.   ◇

Artifact-centric process models focus on the data objects involved in the process with each object having a life cycle and being synchronized by their state transitions. Following, a commonly used visual representation of such artifact-centric process model is a synchronized object life cycle, which also describes the execution semantics of such process model. We define a synchronized object life cycle as follows.

Definition 3 (Synchronized object life cycle). A *synchronized object life cycle* $\mathfrak{L} = (\mathcal{L}, SE)$ consists of a finite set $\mathcal{L}$ of object life cycles and a finite set SE of synchronization edges. An object life cycle $L = (S, i, S_F, T, \Sigma, \eta)$, $L \in \mathcal{L}$, consists of a finite set S of data states, an initial data state $i \in S$, a non-empty set $S_F \subseteq S$ of final data states, a finite set $T \subseteq S \times S$ of data state transitions, and a finite set Σ of actions representing the manipulations on data objects. Function $\eta : T \rightarrow \Sigma$ assigns an action to each data state transition. Each object life cycle L corresponds to a data object class C such that $\psi(L) = C$, where $\psi : \mathcal{L} \rightarrow \mathcal{C}$ with $\mathcal{C}$ denoting the finite set of all data object classes. A synchronization edge $e = (t_1, t_2)$, $e \in SE$, connects two object life cycles $L_1, L_2 \in \mathcal{L}$ by assigning an edge between data state transitions $t_1 \in T_{L_1}$ and $t_2 \in T_{L_2}$ being part of object life cycles L_1 and L_2 respectively.   ◇

For a data state transition from state $s1$ to state $s2$ we refer to $s1$ as source and to $s2$ as target. The second process modeling paradigm focuses on the partial order of activities, but also requires data flow information for execution, which is comprised as second class modeling artifact. Therefore, the correct usage of data objects needs to be verified by checking them against the allowed manipulations specified in the corresponding object life cycles. We define such activity-centric process model as follows.

Definition 4 (Activity-centric process model). An *activity-centric process model* $M = (N, \mathcal{D}, Q, C, F, type, \mu, \xi)$ consists of a finite non-empty set $N \subseteq A \cup G \cup E$ of nodes being activities A, gateways G, and Events $E \subseteq E_S \cup E_E$ comprising start and end events, a finite non-empty set $\mathcal{D}$ of data objects, and a finite non-empty set Q of activity labels ($N, \mathcal{D}, Q$ are pairwise disjoint). The set of attributes P of a data object $D \in \mathcal{D}$ is suppressed in this type of process model such that $P = \emptyset$. $C \subseteq N \times N$ is the control flow relation, $F \subseteq (\mathcal{D} \times A) \times (A \times \mathcal{D})$ is the data flow relation representing read respectively write operations of activities with respect to data objects; $type : G \rightarrow \{xor, and\}$ assigns to each gateway a type, $\mu : A \rightarrow Q$ assigns to each activity a label, and $\xi : (G \times (A \times G)) \nrightarrow D$ assigns data conditions to control flow edges having an xor gateway as source. $\diamond$

In this paper, we refer to read data objects as *input* and to written data objects as *output* data objects. We call a gateway $g \in G$ an *xor* (*and*) gateway if $type(g) = xor$ ($type(g) = and$). An xor (and) gateway with two or more outgoing edges is called split (fork) and an xor (and) gateway with two or more incoming edges is called join (merge). As usual, we assume process model M to be structural sound, i.e., M contains exactly one start and one end event and every node of M is on a path from the start to the end event. Further, each activity of M has exactly one incoming and one outgoing control flow edge. Finally, we define an activity-centric process model with attribute definitions as extension to M as follows.

Definition 5 (Activity-centric process model with attribute definition). An *activity-centric process model with attribute definition MX* is an activity-centric process model M, where the set of attributes P of a data object D is regarded. $\diamond$

For all notions, we use subscripts, e.g., C_{ACP}, S_L, A_M, and D_{XM}, to denote the relation of the sets and functions introduced above to one of the process models. Subscripts are omitted where the context is clear. Attributes are considered to be flat for all process model types, ie attribute nesting is not in scope of this paper.

3   Roundtrip

In this section, we introduce five algorithms to transform the different types of process models defined in Sect. 2 into each other. Figure 1 shows allowed transformations and aligns the corresponding algorithm to

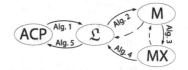

Fig. 1. Transformations between different types of process models

---

Algorithm 1. Transformation of an artifact-centric process model $ACP = (Z, V, B)$ into a synchronized object life cycle $\mathfrak{L} = (\mathcal{L}, SE)$

1: create object life cycle for each data object class
2: for each business rule, add (if not existing yet) states used as precondition respectively postcondition and
corresponding transitions labeled with the task name of the business rule to the respecting object life cycle
3: add synchronization edges between transitions of different object life cycles extracted from the same business rule
4: identify initial and final state in each object life cycle

---

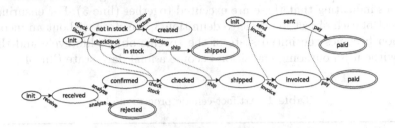

Fig. 2. Synchronized object life cycle

each of them. Algorithm 1 transforms an artifact-centric process model ACP into a synchronized object life cycle $\mathfrak{L}$, which in turn can be transformed into an activity-centric process model M by using Algorithm 2. The enrichment of a process model M with data object attribute information towards MX is described in Algorithm 3. Required information about the attributes is derived from the respecting ACP. For the opposite transformation, we do not provide an explicit algorithm, because it suffices to remove the attribute information to derive M from MX. Further, Algorithm 4 allows the transformation of a process model MX with attribute definition into a synchronized object life cycle $\mathfrak{L}$. It can be easily adapted to use M as its basis. Finally, Algorithm 5 transforms a synchronized object life cycle $\mathfrak{L}$ into an artifact-centric process model ACP by considering information about attributes taken from MX. All algorithms will be explained in detail and supported by brief algorithm representations; fully detailed algorithm representations are provided in our technical report [12].

We start with Algorithm 1. First, the single object life cycles to be comprised by the synchronized one are initialized, one for each data object class used in the business rules of the respecting artifact-centric process model (line 1). Then, we analyze the business rules to extract the data object states and the transitions and dependencies between them. For each business rule, first, the data states used as precondition or postcondition are extracted and added to the set of states of the corresponding data object class if they are not yet present in the respecting set of states. Next, for each data object class, we add a transition from each state used in the precondition to each state used in the postcondition where both states belong to that data object class. Afterwards, the tasks of each business rule are extracted and the tasks labels are assigned to priorly added data state transitions. Thereby, multiple tasks used in one business rule are combined such that their labels are concatenated with + as operator due to the semantics of activity-centric process models, where all activities changing the input data objects into the output data objects are comprised by one single activity instead of multiple tasks affecting different state transitions as allowed for artifact-centric process models (line 2). Finally, after identifying all data state transitions for all data object classes used in one business rule, we synchronize the different object life cycles with respect to these data states by adding a synchronization edge between each two transitions belonging to different object life cycles indicating that these are executed together (line 3). For ensuring the alignment of each object life cycle to definition 3, the state without an incoming transition becomes the initial state of the specific object life cycle and the all states without an outgoing transition become a final data state (line 4).

Table 1. Artifact-centric process model

Data object classes:	order, product, invoice
Set of tasks:	receive, analyze, checkStock, manufacture, stocking, ship, sendInvoice, receivePayment, setPayed
Business rules:	b1, b2, b3, b4, b5, b6, b7, b8

b1: Organization receives order from customer	
Precondition:	$\lambda(\text{Order}, \text{init})$
Tasks:	receive(Order)
Postcondition:	$\lambda(\text{Order}, \text{received}) \wedge \kappa(\text{Order}, \text{CustomerNumber}) \wedge \kappa(\text{Order}, \text{ReceiveDate}) \wedge \kappa(\text{Order}, \text{Products})$

...	...

b3: Organization checks warehouse stock for product availability	
Precondition:	$\lambda(\text{Order}, \text{confirmed}) \wedge \lambda(\text{Product}, \text{init})$
Tasks:	checkStock(Order, Product)
Postcondition:	$(\lambda(\text{Product}, \text{inStock}) \vee \lambda(\text{Product}, \text{notInStock})) \wedge \lambda(\text{Order}, \text{checked})$

...	...

b8: Organiazation receives payment for order from customer	
Precondition:	$\lambda(\text{Order}, \text{invoiced}) \wedge \lambda(\text{Invoice}, \text{sent}) \wedge \kappa(\text{Invoice}, \text{Amount})$
Tasks:	receivePayment(Invoice)
	setPayed(Order)
Postcondition:	$\lambda(\text{Order}, \text{paid}) \wedge \lambda(\text{Invoice}, \text{paid}) \wedge \kappa(\text{Order}, \text{PaymentDate})$

Table 1 shows an extract of an artifact-centric process model describing a simple order and delivery process consisting of three data object classes, nine tasks, and eight business rules, where three of them are completely presented. Due to space requirements, the others are omitted. Based on Algorithm 1, this process model can be mapped into the synchronized object life cycle shown in Fig. 2 consisting of three object life cycles corresponding to the data object classes. Based on business rule *b3*, transitions from data state *init* to *in stock* respectively *not in stock* labeled with the *checkStock* are added to the life cycle of data object *Product* and a transition from *confirmed* to *checked* also labeled *checkStock* is added for the life cycle of *Order*. Additionally, both transitions of the product life cycle are synchronized with the one from the order life cycle.

In Algorithm 2, the transformation of a synchronized object life cycle into an activity-centric process model without attribute definitions (cf. definition 4), the first step is the identification of data state transitions, which are executed together. Therefore, all transitions with the same label are grouped into a combined transition; more specifically, a combined transition comprises the transitive closure over all transitions of the synchronized object life cycle being connected by a synchronization edge. Next, the activity-centric process model is created with a start event as only node (lines 1 to 2).

Then, we iteratively create the process model until no more nodes can be extracted from the synchronized object life cycle (lines 3 to 8). With respect to the nodes of the process model, we distinguish whether it has already been checked for succeeding nodes or not. Each node needs to be checked exactly once. Therefore, in each iteration, we start with the nodes that have not been checked yet, i.e., the nodes added to the process model in the previous iteration. For each such not yet checked node n, we derive the set of combined transitions of the synchronized object life cycle, which are enabled after termination of that node. Additionally, we derive the set of all combined transitions, which might be enabled after termination of that node. Therefore, we determine the combined transition and the corresponding transitions t executed by node n and collect all combined transitions of the synchronized object life cycle, which contain a transition having the target state of t as source state. We call these combined transitions *potentially enabled transitions*. For each such potentially enabled transition, we check whether it becomes enabled after termination of all enabled nodes. If not, we remove that combined transition from the collection. If the node contains output data objects reaching the final state of the corresponding object life cycle, we add an activity labeled *nop : state* to the process model, where *state* refers to the actual final data state. This activity does not contain any data association. Additionally, a corresponding combined transition is added to the set NOP_n of no operation activities of the specific node n such that this activity gets directly marked as checked for combined transitions. Before checking the next node, the currently one is marked as checked for combined transitions (line 4).

Next, we create for each enabled or potentially enabled combined transition an activity and define the corresponding data object accesses, where the source states of all transitions grouped in the respecting combined transition are read while the target states are written. Third, the activity gets assigned the action names of the transitions as activity label. Thereby, the names of multiple transitions are concatenated by using the +. In post processing, a stakeholder may adapt the activity labels (line 5).

Next, we establish the control flow of the activity-centric process model first focusing on sequences, splits, and forks before we focus on joins and merges. If, for a node, the number of combined transitions being enabled equals one, we add a control flow edge from that node to the activity created for the combined transition relating to the node. If the number exceeds one, we either add a split if the set NOP_n of no operation activities of node n is empty or we intersect the combined transitions to determine the split respectively fork for cases where

---

Algorithm 2. Transformation of a synchronized object life cycle $\mathfrak{L} = (\mathcal{L}, SE)$ into an activity-centric process model $M = (N, \mathcal{D}, Q, C, F, type, \mu, \xi)$

1: group transitions executed together, i.e., identically named ones, into combined transitions
2: create activity-centric process model with a single start event
3: **repeat**
4:    identify enabled combined transitions for all not yet checked nodes of the process model
5:    for each identified combined transition, create an activity with input data objects conforming to the source
      states and output data objects conforming to the target states of the transitions comprised in the respecting
      combined transition; the label corresponds to one of the transition actions
6:    add control flow edges to process model (if there exist several combined transitions for one node, an xor
      gateway with respecting edge conditions respectively an and gateway is added as well)
7:    for activities with more than one incoming control flow edge, an xor respectively and gateway is added
      preceding that activity and the control flow is rerouted accordingly
8: **until** all nodes have been checked for enabled combined transitions
9: combine all paths of the process model with an xor gateway (if necessary) and route them towards a single end
   event also added to the process model

NOP_n is empty. If the intersection reveals at least one data object class being used in all combined transitions, we create an xor gateway (split), otherwise we create an and gateway (fork). Then, control flow edges from the node to the created gateway as well as from the gateway to each activity being created for respecting combined transitions are added to the process model. For splits, we also add the edge conditions to the corresponding edges by assigning the data object being input to the activity the edge targets to and being output of the activity being the predecessor of the edge's source, the split. The added gateway gets marked as checked for combined transitions as we processed all paths with above described actions (line 6). Afterwards, all activities having more than one incoming control flow edge are adapted by adding an xor respectively an and gateway, which consumes all these control flow edges. Further, a control flow edge connects that gateway with the activity. To distinguish the type of gateway, we retrieve the combined transition for each activity being the first preceding one of the activity with multiple incoming control flow edges. We intersect these combined transitions as described above. Data object classes used in all combined transitions indicate an xor gateway, otherwise we set the gateway type to and. Again, the added gateway is marked as checked for combined transitions (line 7).

We finalize the process model by adding a single end event. If there exists exactly one node, or more specifically one activity, without an outgoing control flow edge, either this node is connected to the end event via a control flow edge, if it is commonly labeled, or the control flow edge targeting the node is rerouted towards the end event and the node is removed from the process model, if it is labeled with $nop : state$. In case there exist multiple nodes without an outgoing control flow edge, an xor gateway is also added, which connects to the end event. Each such node being labeled with $nop : state$, the control flow edge targeting the node is rerouted to target the added xor gateway while the node gets removed

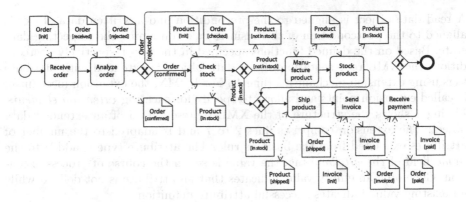

Fig. 3. Activity-centric process model

Algorithm 3. Transformation of an activity-centric process model $M = (N, \mathcal{D}, Q, C, F, type, \mu, \xi)$ into an activity-centric one MX with attribute definition

---

1: extract XML representation of activity-centric process model
2: **for all** data objects of the activity-centric process model **do**
3:     extract attribute types from business rules of corresponding artifact-centric process model
4:     extend XML representation of the data object accordingly to Listing 1
5: **end for**

---

from the process model. For all other such nodes, the node is connected to the xor gateway via a control flow edge (line 9).

Figure 3 shows the activity-centric process model resulting from the synchronized object life cycle given in Fig. 2 after applying Algorithm 2. After termination of activity *Analyze order*, the combined transition comprising all transitions labeled *checkStock* and the one representing a no operation path for the *reject* case are enabled. As there are two combined transitions enabled with one being a no operation path, we add an xor gateway and control flow edges to the corresponding activities *nop:reject* and *Check stock*. The latter one has two input (*Order* in state *confirmed* and *Product* in state *init*) and three output data objects (*Order* in state *checked* and *Product* in states *in stock* and *not in stock* respectively). The *nop:reject* activity has no associated data objects and gets removed while integrating all paths into the single end event.

The first step towards the activity-centric process model with attribute definition is to extract the XML representation from the activity-centric process model as noted in line 1 of Algorithm 3. This extraction aligns to standard XML extractions as, for instance, aligning to the one described in the BPMN specification [2]. Afterwards, all data objects used in the process model are determined (line 2). For each data object, the attribute types are extracted from the business rule of the respecting artifact-centric process model, because the attribute information is only available there (line 3). The correct business rule is identified via the data object and its state as well as the type of access, i.e., read or write.

A read data object is aligned to the precondition and a written data object is aligned to the postcondition of the business rule containing the respecting data state. Based on the defined functions specified in the pre- respectively postcondition, the XML representation of the data object is extended with attribute tags using extension mechanisms (line 4). For BPMN, the extension mechanism is called extension points and allows to specify for each tag *extension elements*. Listing 1 shows the structure of the XML representation of an extended data object. The extension comprises lines 2 to 7 and is adapted to the number of attributes extracted from the business rule. The attribute type is added to the *name* field of the *attribute* tag; the value is set in the course of process execution. Generally, an empty value indicates that an attribute is not defined while an existing value indicates successful attribute definition.

Based on business rule *b1* from Table 1, data object *Order* being output to activity *Receive order* in Fig. 3 gets extended with the attributes *CustomerNumber*, *ReceiveDate*, and *Products*; on model level, each has an empty value.

```
1  <dataObject id="" name="">
2    <extensionElements>
3      <attribute id="" name="">value</attribute>
4      ...
5    </extensionElements>
6    <dataState id="" name="" />
7  </dataObject>
```

Listing 1. Extended XML representation of data object comprising attribute information

---

Algorithm 4. Transformation of an activity-centric process model MX with attribute definition into a synchronized object life cycle $\mathfrak{L} = (\mathcal{L}, SE)$

1: create object life cycle for each data object class
2: **for all** traces through the activity-centric process model with attribute definition **do**
3:    **repeat**
4:      **if** node is an activity **then**
5:        add input data states of node to corresponding object life cycle and connect them via τ-labeled
         transitions to respecting previous states
6:        synchronize transitions belonging to different object life cycles
7:        add output data states of node to corresponding object life cycle and connect them via transitions to respecting previous states considering succeeding xor blocks; the label of the node is mapped to the action of the transition
8:        synchronize transitions belonging to different object life cycles
9:      **end if**
10:   **until** trace has no next node
11: **end for**
12: identify initial and final state in each object life cycle

---

The extraction of a synchronized object life cycle from an activity-centric process model is described in Algorithm 4. First, all data object classes used in the activity-centric process model are identified before for each of them, the corresponding object life cycle consisting of the initial state only is created and the distinct data states are determined. Both information is stored in the corresponding sets of data object classes and data states; the latter one exists separately for each class (line 1). Next, we extract all traces from the start event to the end event of the process model (loops are reduced to a single trace). Then, we handle each trace separately (lines 2 to 11). Thereby, we first create the object life cycle specific collections K_C, which will be used to store data states relating to data objects of the corresponding class. The initial state of the object life cycle is added to each collection. Then, all nodes of the trace are checked for their type and processed accordingly (line 4).

If the node is an activity, the set of input data objects is received grouped by data object classes. Afterwards, if not existing yet, the identified input data states are added to the corresponding object life cycle and the transitions between them are specified; from each entry of the data state collection K_C to each data state identified for the data object class, one transition is added to the object life cycle, if source and target are different states. Each of these transitions gets assigned τ as action, which requires adaptation from the stakeholder in post processing, because these transitions cover implicit data state transitions of the process model. The last step in this regard is to replace the content of collections K_C with the data states valid for the current node (line 5). Adding a synchronization edge between each two transitions just added and belonging to different object life cycles (representing a combined transition) finalizes the processing of the input data objects of the current node (line 6). Next, we process the output data states of the node again grouped by data object classes. After extracting the output data states, they need to be filtered whether they are used as edge condition on outgoing control flow edges of an succeeding split such that not all outgoing data states are utilized in this trace. If a data object class is part of such edge condition, all data states not matching the condition are removed from the set of identified output states. The remaining data states are added to the set of states of the corresponding object life cycle and the new transitions are specified. Comparably to the input data objects, one transition is added from each data state currently stored in data state collection K_C to each remaining output data state independently from source and target state. Following, differently to the input data objects, self-loops are allowed. Afterwards, each newly added transition gets assigned the activity label as action. Transitions being skipped for addition due to existence get their action extended by the label of the current node. Again, the action labeling can be adapted by the stakeholder in post processing (line 7). The output state processing closes with the replacement of data states as discussed for the input data objects before synchronization edges are added between each two transitions being added or skipped above and belonging to different object life cycles (line 8).

If the node is a split, the collection of data states for the data object class used in the edge condition on the outgoing control flow edges is adapted. It is set to the state of the data object used in this trace. After processing all traces, we finalize Algorithm 4 by specifying each state without an incoming transition

Algorithm 5. Transformation of a synchronized object life cycle $\mathfrak{L} = (\mathcal{L}, SE)$ into an artifact-centric process model $ACP = (Z, V, B)$

1: group transitions executed together, i.e., identically named ones, into combined transitions
2: for each object life cycle, create data object class with respecting sets of states and final states and the initial state
3: for each data object, extract the attributes from the activity-centric process model with attribute definition
4: create business rules with information from combined transitions (tasks, in-state functions) and the attributes (defined functions)
5: build artifact-centric process model with a schema comprising all data object classes, the business rules, and the set of tasks utilized in the business rules

---

as initial and each state without an outgoing transition as final state of the respecting object life cycle (line 12).

Activity *Check stock* from the activity-centric process model with attribute definition (visual representation in Fig. 3) adds the states *init*, *in stock*, and *not in stock* with transitions from *init* to the other two states to the *Product* life cycle and adds state *checked* with a transition from *confirmed* to *checked* to the *Order* life cycle. The latter transition is synchronized with the others. All transitions get assigned the action *checkStock*.

Finally, the transformation of an synchronized object life cycle into an artifact-centric process model is described in Algorithm 5. This transformation requires information about the attributes of the data objects, which are taken from the corresponding activity-centric process model with attribute definition. Similarly to Algorithm 2, we first group the transitions of the synchronized object life cycle into combined transitions. Two transitions are executed together if they are connected by a synchronization edge (line 1). Next, for each object life cycle of the synchronized one, we create a corresponding data object class, which gets the states, the initial state, and the final states from that object life cycle. Additionally, for each object life cycle, we create an empty K_C map, which stores for each data state concatenated with a unique identifier a collection of defined functions (line 2). Then, we extract the attribute information from the activity-centric process model with attribute definition. Thereby, we parse the XML structure and for each data object, the set of attribute types is extracted and added to map K_C as well as the set of attributes of the respecting class (line 3). Afterwards, the combined transitions that have been determined in beginning are processed. For each combined transition, one business rule is created. The task affected by the business rule is derived from the action of the transitions (they are equal for all transitions comprised by one combined transition) and added to the business rule. Then, we derive the in-state and defined functions for both the pre- and postcondition of the business rule. An in-state function consists of the data object class the respecting transition belongs to and the source respectively target data state of that transition. The defined functions are taken from map K_C of the data object class the respecting transition belongs to depending on the source respectively target data state of that transition. The assignment of these functions to the pre- and postcondition of the business rule requires

a grouping of them with respect to both conditions as well as the corresponding data object class. The elements within one group are connected by the ∨
operator while different groups belonging to the same condition are connected by
the ∧ operator. Based on the condition, these two statements are added to the
pre- respectively postcondition of the business rule (line 4). Finally, the actual
artifact-centric process model consisting of a schema comprising all data object
classes, a set of business rules, and a set of tasks utilized in the business rules is
created (line 5).

Transformation of the synchronized object life cycle presented in Fig. 2 to the
artifact-centric process model partly shown in Table 1 is achieved by applying
Algorithm 5. Considering the combined transition comprising transitions with
label *paid*, a new business rule is created (cf. *b8*) with the source states being
added to the precondition and the target states being added to the postcondition for both affected data object classes. Differently to the representation in
Table 1, the corresponding task is summarized in one task with both classes as
arguments: *pay(Order, Invoice)*. $\kappa(Order, PaymentDate)$ is extracted from the
corresponding data object of the activity-centric process model with attribute
definition. The data object classes are *order*, *product*, and *invoice*.

For both algorithms with required external information, we utilize this information if it is present. Otherwise, the algorithms ignore the corresponding parts
resulting in incomplete process models. Algorithm 3 results in a plain XML representation of the input activity-centric process model, ie for all data objects,
there do not exist any attribute tags. Algorithm 5 results in an artifact-centric
process model, where the set of attributes is empty for all data object classes.
Subsequently, no defined function exists in any business rule for resulting the
process model.

4   Related Work

Activity-centric business process modeling emerged from workflow modeling and
is described extensively in several works, e.g., [1], with BPMN being the widely
used industry standard [2]. The artifact-centric modeling paradigm was initiated
by IBM research [5] and further formalized by several researchers [6,11]. Additionally, deviations of this paradigm have been developed and process engines
executing such process models have been established [7,8]. Both paradigms compete each other although they only provide different views on the same business
processes putting either activities or data objects in focus. Instead of keeping both paradigms separated, we combined them with a set of transformation
algorithms. First steps towards an integration have been taken by extracting
unsynchronized [3,4] and synchronized [9] object life cycles from activity-centric
process models as well as by extracting activities statically from processing paths
through data objects [13] or goals [14] or dynamically from data dependencies
on missing data [15]. All mentioned approaches provide means to partly support
one of the five transformations introduced in this paper. Liu et al. [9] provide an
approach closely related to Algorithm 4 without attribute consideration. Additionally, they also assume that each data object written in a specific state is also

read in this state, if the object gets read again. Besides considering data object attributes, we also allow the read of a previously written object, if there exists a path between the respecting states in the object life cycle (cf. [10], where we discussed the issue of underspecification).

5   Conclusion

We presented a set of five algorithms allowing to transform artifact-centric process models into activity-centric ones and vice versa via an synchronized object life cycle acting as mediator between both process modeling paradigms. We showed applicability of these algorithms by applying them to a simple order and delivery process. In future work, we will implement the algorithms to allow interested stakeholders to transform their processes from one paradigm into another; e.g., transforming an artifact-centric process model into an activity-centric one to apply existing analysis techniques.

References

1. Weske, M.: Business Process Management: Concepts, Languages, Architectures, 2nd edn. Springer, Berlin (2012)
2. OMG: Business Process Model and Notation (BPMN), Version 2.0 (2011)
3. Ryndina, K., Küster, J.M., Gall, H.C.: Consistency of business process models and object life cycles. In: Kühne, T. (ed.) MoDELS 2006. LNCS, vol. 4364, pp. 80–90. Springer, Heidelberg (2007)
4. Eshuis, R., Van Gorp, P.: Synthesizing object life cycles from business process models. In: Atzeni, P., Cheung, D., Ram, S. (eds.) ER 2012 Main Conference 2012. LNCS, vol. 7532, pp. 307–320. Springer, Heidelberg (2012)
5. Nigam, A., Caswell, N.S.: Business artifacts: an approach to operational specification. IBM Syst. J. **42**(3), 428–445 (2003)
6. Cohn, D., Hull, R.: Business artifacts: a data-centric approach to modeling business operations and processes. IEEE Data Eng. Bull. **32**(3), 3–9 (2009)
7. Müller, D., Reichert, M., Herbst, J.: Data-driven modeling and coordination of large process structures. In: Meersman, R., Tari, Z. (eds.) OTM 2007, Part I. LNCS, vol. 4803, pp. 131–149. Springer, Heidelberg (2007)
8. Künzle, V., Reichert, M.: PHILharmonicFlows: towards a framework for object-aware process management. J. Softw. Maint. **23**(4), 205–244 (2011)
9. Liu, R., Wu, F.Y., Kumaran, S.: Transforming activity-centric business process models into information-centric models for soa solutions. J. Database Manag. **21**(4), 14–34 (2010)
10. Meyer, A., Polyvyanyy, A., Weske, M.: Weak conformance of process models with respect to data objects. In: Services and their Composition (ZEUS) (2012)
11. Yongchareon, S., Liu, Ch., Zhao, X.: A framework for behavior-consistent specialization of artifact-centric business processes. In: Barros, A., Gal, A., Kindler, E. (eds.) BPM 2012. LNCS, vol. 7481, pp. 285–301. Springer, Heidelberg (2012)
12. Meyer, A., Weske, M.: Activity-centric and artifact-centric process model roundtrip. Hasso Plattner Institute at the University of Potsdam, Technical report (2013)

13. Wang, J., Kumar, A.: A framework for document-driven workflow systems. In: van der Aalst, W.M.P., Benatallah, B., Casati, F., Curbera, F. (eds.) BPM 2005. LNCS, vol. 3649, pp. 285–301. Springer, Heidelberg (2005)
14. Vanderfeesten, I., Reijers, H.A., van der Aalst, W.M.P.: Product-based workflow support. Inf. Syst. **36**(2), 517–535 (2011)
15. van der Aalst, W.M.P., Weske, M., Grünbauer, D.: Case handling: a new paradigm for business process support. Data Knowl. Eng. **53**(2), 129–162 (2005)

1st Workshop on Decision Mining and Modeling for Business Processes (DeMiMoP 2013)

1st Workshop on Decision Mining and Modeling for Business Processes (DeMiMoP 2013)

Automatic Generation
of Business Process Models
Based on Attribute Relationship Diagrams

Krzysztof Kluza[✉] and Grzegorz J. Nalepa

AGH University of Science and Technology, al. A. Mickiewicza 30,
30-059 Krakow, Poland
{kluza,gjn}@agh.edu.pl

Abstract. Attribute-Relationship Diagrams (ARD) aim at capturing
dependencies between attributes describing an information system. They
were proposed to prototype rule bases in an iterative manner. In the
paper, we propose to apply the ARD method to business processes. We
describe a technique of automatic generation of a BPMN model with
decision table schemas for business rule tasks and form attributes for
user tasks from the ARD diagram. In our approach, processes and rules
are generated simultaneously. Thanks to this, they are complementary
and can be directly executed using our hybrid execution environment.

1 Introduction

A Business Process (BP) can be defined as a collection of related tasks which
produce a specific service or product for a customer [1]. In practice, BPs are
modeled using the graphical Business Process Model and Notation (BPMN).

However, the detailed aspects of the modeled systems, such as decision rules
or constraints, can not be covered by BP models. In this case, the Business
Rules (BR) approach is often a good choice. Although there is a difference in
abstraction levels between BP and BR, these two concepts are complementary.
Most often, BR are used for the specification of rule task logic in processes.

BP and BR are mostly designed manually. Although a simplified process
model can be generated using process mining tools [2] or from natural language
text using NLP techniques [3], they are not directly suitable for execution. In
our approach (see Fig. 1), we propose to generate an executable BPMN model
with decision table schemas for business rule tasks and form attributes for user
tasks from Attribute Relationship Diagrams (ARD) [4,5].

The ARD method allows an expert to identify gradually the properties of a
rule-based system being designed. Having the properties identified and described
in terms of attributes, the proposed algorithm can automatically generate an
executable BPMN model with the corresponding BR tasks.

The paper is supported by the HiBuProBuRul Project funded from NCN (National
Science Centre) resources for science (no. DEC-2011/03/N/ST6/00909).

N. Lohmann et al. (Eds.): BPM 2013 Workshops, LNBIP 171, pp. 185–197, 2014.
DOI: 10.1007/978-3-319-06257-0_15, © Springer International Publishing Switzerland 2014

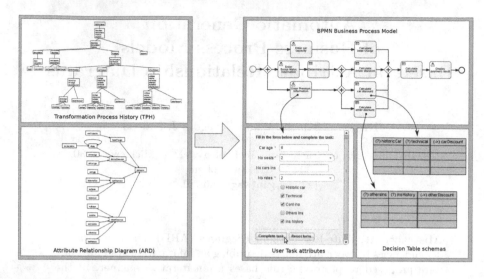

Fig. 1. The outline of our approach

There are several approaches similar to ours, such as Product Based Workflow Design (PBWD) [6,7] or Decision Dependency Design (D3) [8,9]. The comparison with them is provided in the related work section of the paper.

The paper is organized as follows. In Sect. 2 we present the motivation for our research. Section 3 presents the ARD method, and Sect. 4 describes the proposed algorithm. In Sect. 5, we give a design example that uses our method. The execution issues are presented in Sect. 6. Section 7 provides a short overview of related approaches and Sect. 8 summarizes the paper.

2   Motivation

Modern business applications require advanced modeling solutions to deal with the complexity of the stored knowledge. They often use process models for describing workflows (or control flows in general) and rules for detailed business logic specification (e.g. for specification of task logic).

Although such a separation of processes and rules is consistent with the BPMN 2.0 specification, which clarifies that BPMN is not suitable for modeling such concepts as rules, it causes two challenges:

1. the *modeling challenge* – because of the difference between processes and rules, they are often developed and modeled separately;
2. the *execution challenge* – due to the fact that processes and rules can be not well matched, in the case of execution they have to be additionally integrated.

In our research, we address these two problems dealing with BP and BR by proposing the integrated method for holistic modeling BP with BR, which is extremely important in order to ensure the high quality of the system [10]. Moreover, we support the development of the hybrid execution environment for such integrated models [11].

The main contribution is a description of the algorithm for automatic generation of BPMN model in which processes and rule schemas are generated at the same time, so they are complementary. A BPMN model is generated from ARD with decision table schemas for business rule tasks and form attributes for user tasks. Thus, after filling decision tables in BR tasks with rules, the model can be executed directly using our hybrid execution environment.

3   Attribute Relationship Diagram

Attribute Relationship Diagram (ARD) [4,5] is a simple method that allows an expert to gradually identify the properties of a rule-based system being designed.

The ARD method aims at capturing relations between attributes, which denote certain system properties, in terms of Attributive Logic [12,13]. The ARD diagram captures functional dependencies among the properties; thus it indicates that particular system property depends functionally on other properties. Such dependencies form a directed graph with nodes being properties.

Let us present a short, more formal description of ARD [5], on which the algorithm description in Sect. 4 is based.

3.1   Formal Description of the ARD Method

Definition 1. *An **attribute** $a_i \in A$ is a function (or partial function):*

$$a_i \colon P \to \mathbb{D}_i$$

where

- *P is a set of properties,*
- *A is a set of attributes,*
- *$\mathbb{D}$ is a set of attribute values (the domains).*

An example of an attribute can be the `carAge`, which denotes the age of a car, and the attribute value is within the domain $\mathbb{D}_{carAge} = [0, \inf]$.

Definition 2. *A **generalized attribute** $a_j \in A$ is a function (or partial function) of the form:*

$$a_j \colon P \to 2^{\mathbb{D}_j} \setminus \{\emptyset\}$$

where $2^{\mathbb{D}_j}$ is the family of all the subsets of $\mathbb{D}_j$.

An example of a generalized attribute can be the `ownedInsurances`, which is a set of the customer insurances, and the attribute value is a subset of the domain $\mathbb{D}_{ownedInsurances}$, which consists of the possible insurances that a particular customer can possess.

In the case of abstraction level, the ARD attributes and generalized attributes can be described either as conceptual or physical ones.

Definition 3. *A **conceptual attribute** $c \in C$ is an attribute describing some general, abstract aspect of the system.*

Conceptual attribute name starts with a capital letter, e.g. `BaseRate`. During the design process, conceptual attributes are being *finalized* into, possibly multiple, physical attributes (see Definition 9 for the ***finalization*** description).

Definition 4. *A **physical attribute** $a \in A$ is an attribute describing a specific well-defined, atomic aspect of the system.*

Names of physical attributes are not capitalized, e.g. `payment`. A physical attribute origins from one or more (indirectly) conceptual attributes and can not be further *finalized*.

Definition 5. *A **simple property** $p_s \in P$ is described by a single attribute.*

Definition 6. *A **complex property** $p_c \in P$ is described by multiple attributes.*

Definition 7. *A **dependency** $d \in D$ is an ordered pair of properties (f, t), where $f \in P$ is the **independent property** and $t \in P$ is the **dependent property** that depends on f. For simplicity $d = (f, t) \in D$ will be presented as: $dep(f, t)$. If $f = t$ the property is called **self-dependent**.*

Definition 8. *An **ARD diagram** R is a pair (P, D), where P is a set of properties, and D is a set of dependencies, and between two properties only a single dependency is allowed.*

To illustrate the ARD concepts, a fragment of an exemplary ARD diagram with two properties and the dependency between them is presented in Fig. 2. The diagram should be interpreted in the following way: `payment` depends somehow on `carCapacity` and `baseCharge` (either on value or existence). Note that in other modeling languages the dependency is often modeled inversely, i.e. as an arrow pointing from a dependent object to an independent one, e.g. in UML [13].

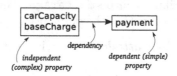

Fig. 2. An example of the ARD diagram

The core aspects of the ARD method are diagram transformations (***finalization*** and ***split***), which regard properties and serve as a tool for diagram specification and development. Transformations are required to specify additional dependencies or introduce new attributes for the system. For the transformation of the diagram R_1 into the diagram R_2, the R_2 is more specific than the R_1.

Definition 9. *Finalization* *is a function of the form:*

$$\text{finalization} : p_1 \rightarrow p_2$$

that transforms a simple property $p_1 \in P$ described by a conceptual attribute into a property $p_2 \in P$, where the attribute describing p_1 is substituted by one or more conceptual or physical attributes describing p_2, which are more detailed than the attribute describing a property p_1.

Definition 10. *Split* *is a function of the form:*

$$\text{split} : p_c \rightarrow \{p^1, p^2, \ldots, p^n\}$$

where a complex property p_c is replaced by n properties, each of them described by one or more attributes originally describing p_c. Since p_c may depend on some other properties $p_o^1 \ldots p_o^n$, dependencies between these properties and $p^1 \ldots p^n$ have to be stated.

To illustrate the ARD transformations, exemplary *finalization* and *split* transformations are presented in Fig. 3. The simple property BaseRate (described by a single conceptual attribute) is *finalized* into a new complex property described by two physical attributes carCapacity and baseCharge. Next, this complex property is *split* into two simple properties described by these attributes.

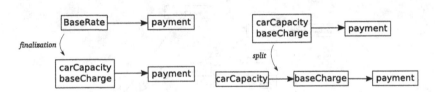

Fig. 3. Examples of the ARD finalization (left) and split (right) transformations

During the design process, upon splitting and finalizing, the ARD model is more and more specific. This can be depicted as a hierarchical model of transformations, in which consecutive levels make a hierarchy of more and more detailed diagrams describing the designed system. Such a hierarchical model is called Transformation Process History (TPH) [5]. A TPH forms a tree-like structure, denoting what particular property is split into or what attributes a particular property attribute is finalized into. Originally [4], the ARD method was proposed as a simple method for generating a knowledge base structure in a similar way as the relational data base structure (tables) are obtained from the ERD diagrams; an alternative to the classic approaches [14].

Based on the ARD dependencies, it is possible to generate decision tables [5], which can be further filled in with rules by a domain expert (see Fig. 4).

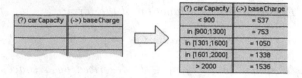

(?) car Capacity	(->) base Charge
< 900	= 537
in [900;1300]	= 753
in [1301;1600]	= 1050
in [1601;2000]	= 1338
> 2000	= 1536

Fig. 4. Decision table schema generated from the obtained ARD dependencies (left) and the same table filled in with rules (right)

3.2 Polish Liability Insurance Case Study

To clarify the ARD method, let us present an illustrative example of the Polish Liability Insurance (PLLI) case study, developed as a benchmark case for the SKE approach for rule-based systems [13]. This is a case, in which the price for the liability insurance for protecting against third party insurance claims is to be calculated. The price is calculated based on various reasons, which can be obtained from the insurance domain expert.

The main factors in calculating the liability insurance premium are data about the vehicle: the car engine capacity, the car age, seats, and a technical examination. Additionally, the impact on the insurance price have the driver's age, the period of holding the license, the number of accidents in the last year,

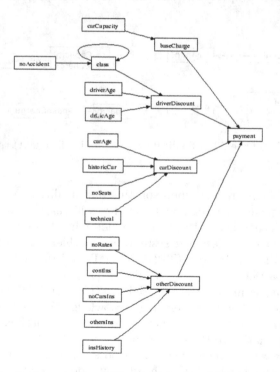

Fig. 5. A complete ARD model for the PPLI example

and the previous class of insurance. In the calculation, the insurance premium can be increased or decreased because of number of payment installments, other insurances, continuity of insurance or the number of cars insured. All these pieces of data, obtained from an expert, can be specified using the ARD method and presented using the ARD diagram (see Fig. 5). As specification of ARD is an iterative process, the history of transformations can be depicted as well[1].

The algorithm described in the following section takes advantage of the existing features of the ARD diagram.

4 Algorithm for BPMN Model Generation from ARD

Input for the algorithm: An ARD diagram consisting of simple properties containing only physical attributes, additionally the TPH diagram can be used.

Output of the algorithm: A partially rule-based BPMN process model.

Goal: The goal of the algorithm is to automatically build a BPMN process model on the basis of Attribute-Relationship Diagram (optionally supported by Transformation Process History). Our algorithm generates both User Tasks with form attributes for acquiring particular pieces of information from a user and Business Rule Tasks with prototypes of decision tables.

Algorithm steps:

1. Select the set A consisting of the ARD input attributes (the attributes which occure only as independent or self-dependent properties in the set of dependencies) and the set D consisting of dependencies with these attributes.
2. Loop for each dependency $d \in D : dep(f,t), f \neq t$.
3. Select all independent properties (other than f) that t depends on.
   Let $F_t = \{f_t^i : dep(f_t^i, t), f_t^i \neq f\}$.
   Remove the considered dependencies from the set: $D := D \setminus F_t$.
4. Select all dependent properties (other than t) that depend only on f.
   Let $T_f = \{t_f^i : dep(f, t_f^i), t_f^i \neq t, \not\exists f_x : (dep(f_x, t_f^i), f_x \neq f)\}$.
   Remove the considered dependencies from the set: $D := D \setminus T_f$.
5. Based on F_t and T_f create *Business Rule tasks* and add them to the B set. Develop BR tasks in the following way:
   (a) if $F_t = \emptyset, T_f = \emptyset$, create a *BR task* "Determine[2] $name(t)$", where $name(t)$ is a name of the t attribute, and associate the task with the following decision table schema: $f \mid t$.
   (b) if $F_t \neq \emptyset, T_f = \emptyset$, create a *BR task* "Determine $name(t)$" and associate the task with the following decision table schema: $f, f_t^1, f_t^2, ... \mid t$.

---

[1] The corresponding TPH diagram can be accessed at (in Polish): http://ai.ia.agh. edu.pl/wiki/student:msc2008_bizrules_cases:hekate_case_ploc.

[2] For user-friendliness of task names, if the attribute t is of the symbolic type or derived one, the word "Determine" should be used in the task name. In other cases (i.e. numeric types), one can use the word "Calculate" instead.

(c) if $F_t = \emptyset, T_f \neq \emptyset$, create a *BR task* "Determine $name(T_f \cup \{t\})$", where $name(T_f)$ is a name of the lower-level conceptual attribute from which all the $T_f \cup \{t\}$ attributes are derived[3], and associate the task with the following decision table schema: $f \mid t, t_f^1, t_f^2, ...$.

(d) if $F_t \neq \emptyset, T_f \neq \emptyset$, create two *BR tasks* "Determine $name(t)$" and "Determine $name(T_f)$", and associate them with the following decision table schemas respectively: $f, f_t^1, f_t^2, ... \mid t$ and $f \mid t_f^1, t_f^2, ...$.

6. End loop.

7. Based on the A set of input attributes and the TPH model, select the set C of high-level conceptual attributes from which these input attributes are derived, and for each conceptual attribute $c \in C$ create a *User task* "Enter $name(c)$ information"[4], and connect it using control flow with the proper *BR tasks* that require these input attributes (with *AND gateway* if necessary[5]).

8. Connect the *Start event* with all *User tasks* using control flow (with *AND gateway* if necessary).

9. Select the set D consisting of all dependencies that have no input attributes in their properties and the set A consisting of all the attributes occurring in these dependencies, and repeat steps 2 – 6 based on this set.

10. Using control flow connect the *BR tasks* from the B set one another (with *AND gateway* if necessary) according to the following rule:
two *BR tasks* $b^1, b^2 \in B$ should be connected if a decision table schema of b^1 contains at least one attribute a as an input attribute which is an output attribute of the b^2 decision table schema.

11. Select a subset B_{out} of B, consisting of *BR tasks* that have no outcoming control flows[6] Select the high-level conceptual attribute c from which the output attributes of task from B_{out} are derived. Add a *User task* "Display $name(c)$ result" and connect the selected task from B_{out} with it[7].

12. Connect the *User task* with an *End event*.

In the following section we will use the selected design example – the Polish Liability Insurance case – to illustrate how this algorithm works in practice.

5   Design Example: Algorithm Applied to the PLLI Case

Let us present the algorithm applied to the PLLI case study described in Sect. 3.2. For simplicity, the algorithm steps have been grouped into the phases ❶–❺, which are described below and illustrated in Fig. 6.

---

[3] The conceptual attribute name can be found in the corresponding TPH model, if it is available for the algorithm. In other case, in the task name the names of all the attributes from the T_f set can be used.

[4] If a particular conceptual attribute covers a single input attribute, create a *User task* "Enter $name(a)$" instead.

[5] The *AND gateway* is necessary if there are more than one *BR tasks* to be connected.

[6] This subset of output BR tasks should not be empty.

[7] If there is only one output attribute, its name should be used instead of $name(c)$.

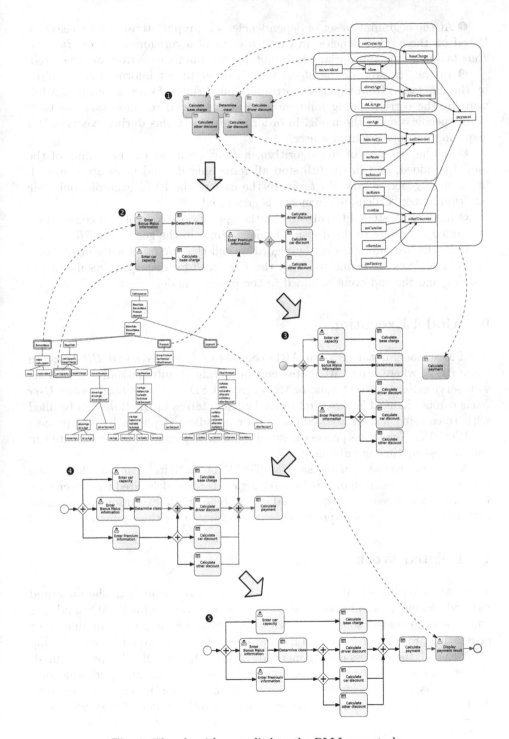

Fig. 6. The algorithm applied to the PLLI case study

❶ At the beginning, a set of dependencies with input attributes are selected. Based on these dependencies, in the 2–6 steps of algorithm, a set of *Business Rule tasks* and the appropriate decision table schema for each task are generated.

❷ In the 7th step of the algorithm, in order to get information (required by the *BR tasks*) from the user, corresponding *User tasks* are generated. Additionally, the corresponding input attributes are added to these tasks in their XML-specification of the model in order to provide forms during execution for acquiring information from a user.

❸ In the 8th step of the algorithm, a *Start event* at the beginning of the model is added; and in the 9th step all remaining dependencies are explored, in order to generate new *BR tasks*. In the case of the PLLI example, only one additional task "Calculate payment" is generated.

❹ In the 10th step of the algorithm, the appropriate control flow connections are added according to the decision table schemas in the generated *BR tasks*.

❺ In the last two steps of the algorithm, all the *BR tasks* without outcoming control flows are connected with the *User task* for displaying results of the process, and the end event is added to the process model.

6   Model Execution

A BPMN model obtained from ARD consists of *User tasks* and *BR tasks*. In some cases, where input attributes can be obtained automatically from some web services (e.g. current time or the current USD exchange rate), some *User tasks* can be changed into *Service tasks*. Decision tables in *BR tasks* can be filled with rules using a dedicated editor [15] or a dedicated plugin for the process modeler [16]. Then, the process is specified detailed enough to be executed in the process runtime environment.

Although process engines, such as jBPM[8] or Activiti[9], can handle process execution, the execution of the *BR task* logic has to be delegated to rule engine. In our previous research, we developed a prototype hybrid execution environment [11], which can serve as a specific execution example for this approach.

7   Related Work

There are several approaches which can be considered related to the presented method. As our method allows for automatic generation of a BPMN model, it could be compared in some ways with such approaches as process mining [2] or generating processes from text in natural language (based on NLP methods) [3].

Although the process mining methods [2] allow for very flexible process models generation, and in some cases do not require any human superintendence, their results are very general processes, which can not be executed directly. To be an executable model, it has to be significantly enhanced and refactored.

---

[8] See: http://www.jboss.org/jbpm/
[9] See: http://www.activiti.org/

Although generating processes from text description in natural language [3] can have practical results and allows for generating a BPMN model, it requires an NLP system for recognizing the meaning of the text; thus, the method is imprecise as much as imprecise is the process description in natural language. In fact, our approach is slightly different, as it is based on the carefully prepared ARD diagram and is applicable mainly to rule-based manufacturing systems.

However, there are approaches which are more similar to the method proposed in this paper, such as generating process models from Bill Of Materials (BOM) [6] and the derived approach, Product Based Workflow Design (PBWD) [7,17], based on Product Data Model (PDM), as well as generating BPMN models from Decision Dependency Design (D3) [8,9].

Although on first sight our approach is very similar to generating processes from the BOM/PDM or D3 representations, there are significant differences. Firstly, our approach is partially rule-based [18] and more holistic, as the generated BPMN model has associated decision table schemas for all the *BR tasks* in the model, and the algorithm assures that the required input attributes will be obtained from the user while executing *User tasks* in the process. This makes the BPMN model data consistent with the rule engine requirements for data.

Secondly, our approach considers the ARD model which is a simple model that can be obtained much faster, as it does not require to precise the dependency semantics, and the method can be used when there are not many pieces of information available. Although this limitation of ARD can be seen as a drawback, the main focus of this method is on simplicity. However, the ARD method can also be extended, e.g. there can be used some mining technique to acquire attributes and dependencies among them. This requires additional research yet. There has been trials of mining such attributes from text in natural language [19].

Finally, our method is not as flexible as process mining techniques, as it requires the input structured using the ARD method, but it produces a BPMN model which is executable and provides support for Business Rule tasks.

8 Concluding Remarks

The original contribution of this paper is an algorithm for automatic generation of a BPMN process model, which is partially rule-based [18] due to supporting *Business Rule tasks*, from Attribute Relationship Diagram. As an input, the algorithm takes the ARD diagram that shows dependencies among system attributes. Additionally, for better task labelling, the history of ARD transformations can be also used. On the output, we get a fully specified BPMN model with the specification of decision table schemas for *BR tasks* and form attributes for *User tasks*. Such a model can be treated as a structured rule base that provides decision tables schemas (rule templates for rule sets grouped in decision tables) and explicit inference flow determined by the BPMN control flow.

Contrary to other approaches, the proposed solution addresses both challenges dealing with BP and BR: separation between processes and rules in the modeling phase as well as the problem of the execution of such separated models, which usually require some additional integration or configuration in the execution environment. In our approach, a process and corresponding rule schemas are generated at the same time. Although they are separated, what enables better decision management, they are complementary and can be directly executed using a hybrid execution environment [11].

As future work, we plan to extend the presented approach in order to take advantage of more advanced BPMN elements and structures. Moreover, the algorithm does not optimize the model; thus, some optimization techniques can be specified, in order to improve the quality of models. As the ARD method is inspired by ERD, there is a possibility of extending it in the similar way [20], or enriching with relations from the similar methods [6–9,17].

References

1. Lindsay, A., Dawns, D., Lunn, K.: Business processes - attempts to find a definition. Inf. Softw. Technol. **45**(15), 1015–1019 (2003)
2. van der Aalst, W.M.P.: Process Mining: Discovery, Conformance and Enhancement of Business Processes, 1st edn. Springer Publishing Company, Incorporated (2011)
3. Friedrich, F., Mendling, J., Puhlmann, F.: Process model generation from natural language text. In: Mouratidis, H., Rolland, C. (eds.) CAiSE 2011. LNCS, vol. 6741, pp. 482–496. Springer, Heidelberg (2011)
4. Nalepa, G.J., Ligęza, A.: Conceptual modelling and automated implementation of rule-based systems. In: Software Engineering: Evolution and Emerging Technologies. Frontiers in Artificial Intelligence and Applications, vol. 130, pp. 330–340. IOS Press, Amsterdam (2005)
5. Nalepa, G.J., Wojnicki, I.: ARD+ a prototyping method for decision rules. method overview, tools, and the thermostat case study. Technical report CSLTR 01/2009, AGH University of Science and Technology, June 2009
6. van der Aalst, W.: On the automatic generation of workflow processes based on product structures. Comput. Ind. **39**(2), 97–111 (1999)
7. Vanderfeesten, I., Reijers, H.A., van der Aalst, W.M.P.: Case handling systems as product based workflow design support. In: Filipe, J., Cordeiro, J., Cardoso, J. (eds.) ICEIS 2007. LNBIP, vol. 12, pp. 187–198. Springer, Heidelberg (2009)
8. Wu, F., Priscilla, L., Gao, M., Caron, F., De Roover, W., Vanthienen, J.: Modeling decision structures and dependencies. In: Herrero, P., Panetto, H., Meersman, R., Dillon, T. (eds.) OTM 2012 Workshops. LNCS, vol. 7567, pp. 525–533. Springer, Heidelberg (2012)
9. de Roover, W., Vanthienen, J.: On the relation between decision structures, tables and processes. In: Meersman, R., Dillon, T., Herrero, P. (eds.) OTM 2011 Workshops. LNCS, vol. 7046, pp. 591–598. Springer, Heidelberg (2011)
10. Nalepa, G.J.: Proposal of business process and rules modeling with the XTT method. In: Negru, V., et al. (eds.) SYNASC Ninth International Symposium on Symbolic and Numeric Algorithms for Scientific Computing, pp. 500–506. IEEE Computer Society, IEEE, CPS Conference Publishing Service, Los Alamitos, California, Washington, Tokyo, 26–29 September 2007

11. Nalepa, G.J., Kluza, K., Kaczor, K.: Proposal of an inference engine architecture for business rules and processes. In: Rutkowski, L., Korytkowski, M., Scherer, R., Tadeusiewicz, R., Zadeh, L.A., Zurada, J.M. (eds.) ICAISC 2013, Part II. LNCS, vol. 7895, pp. 453–464. Springer, Heidelberg (2013)
12. Ligęza, A.: Logical Foundations for Rule-Based Systems. Springer, Heidelberg (2006)
13. Nalepa, G.J.: Semantic Knowledge Engineering. A Rule-Based Approach. Wydawnictwa AGH, Kraków (2011)
14. Vanthienen, J., Wets, G.: From decision tables to expert system shells. Data Knowl. Eng. **13**(3), 265–282 (1994)
15. Nalepa, G.J., Ligęza, A., Kaczor, K.: Formalization and modeling of rules using the XTT2 method. Int. J. Artif. Intell. Tools **20**(6), 1107–1125 (2011)
16. Kluza, K., Kaczor, K., Nalepa, G.J.: Enriching business processes with rules using the oryx bpmn editor. In: Rutkowski, L., Korytkowski, M., Scherer, R., Tadeusiewicz, R., Zadeh, L.A., Zurada, J.M. (eds.) ICAISC 2012, Part II. LNCS, vol. 7268, pp. 573–581. Springer, Heidelberg (2012)
17. Vanderfeesten, I., Reijers, H.A., van der Aalst, W.M.P., Vogelaar, J.: Automatic support for product based workflow design: generation of process models from a product data model. In: Meersman, R., Dillon, T., Herrero, P. (eds.) OTM 2010 Workshops. LNCS, vol. 6428, pp. 665–674. Springer, Heidelberg (2010)
18. Goedertier, S., Vanthienen, J.: Rule-based business process modeling and execution. In: Proceedings of the IEEE EDOC Workshop on Vocabularies Ontologies and Rules for the Enterprise (VORTE 2005). CTIT Workshop Proceeding Series, pp. 67–74 (2005) (ISSN 0929–0672)
19. Atzmueller, M., Nalepa, G.J.: A textual subgroup mining approach for rapid ARD+ model capture. In: Lane, H.C., Guesgen, H.W. (eds.) FLAIRS-22: Proceedings of the Twenty-Second International Florida Artificial Intelligence Research Society Conference, FLAIRS, Sanibel Island, Florida, USA, Menlo Park, California, pp. 414–415. AAAI Press Menlo Park, 19–21 May 2009 (to be published)
20. Chen, G., Ren, M., Yan, P., Guo, X.: Enriching the er model based on discovered association rules. Inf. Sci. **177**(7), 1558–1566 (2007)

Enriching Business Process Models with Decision Rules

Semra Catalkaya, David Knuplesch[✉], Carolina Chiao, and Manfred Reichert

Institute of Database and Information Systems, Ulm University, Ulm, Germany
{semra.catalkaya,david.knuplesch,carolina.chiao,
manfred.reichert}@uni-ulm.de

Abstract. Making the right decisions in time is one of the key tasks in every business. In this context, decision theory fosters decision-making based on well-defined decision rules. The latter evaluate a given set of input parameters and utilize evidenced data in order to determine an optimal alternative out of a given set of choices. In particular, decision rules are relevant in the context business processes as well. Contemporary process modeling languages, however, have not incorporated decision theory yet, but mainly consider rather simple, guard-based decisions that refer to process-relevant data. To remedy this drawback, this paper introduces an approach that allows embedding decision problems in business process models and applying decision rules to deal with them. As a major benefit, it becomes possible to automatically determine optimal execution paths during run time.

Keywords: Business process modeling · Decision support · KPI

1 Introduction

Making the right decisions during the execution of business processes is crucial for any company to achieve its business objectives [1,2]. When choosing the wrong alternatives and execution paths during process execution, in turn, unnecessary costs or other disadvantages might result.

For instance, consider the make-or-buy process in Fig. 1 as an example of a decision-making process. Regarding this process, a manager must decide whether to produce goods locally or to outsource the production. In order to make the right decision, strategic information is required, like, for example, the time required to produce (and potentially to deliver) the goods or the production costs. However, as can be observed in the context of this example, respective information is usually not made explicit, i.e., it does not become transparent at the process model level. Hence, the manager must either query this information outside the scope of the respective process-aware information system (e.g., in an external database or application) or rely on his personal expertise.

This work was done within the research project C³Pro funded by the German Research Foundation (DFG), Project number: RE 1402/2-1.

N. Lohmann et al. (Eds.): BPM 2013 Workshops, LNBIP 171, pp. 198–211, 2014.
DOI: 10.1007/978-3-319-06257-0_16, © Springer International Publishing Switzerland 2014

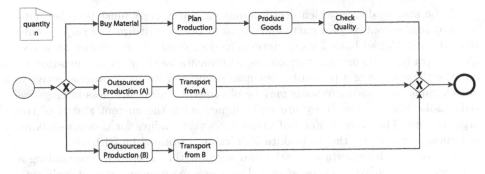

Fig. 1. Make-or-Buy process

In management science, *decision theory* deals with the identification of factors relevant for solving particular decision problems [3]. Thereby, a *decision problem* corresponds to a problem the decision maker (i.e., organization) faces and for which decision theory is intended to provide an answer or relevant information [4]. In particular, to solve a decision problem, *decision rules* may be applied. In turn, a decision rule corresponds to a mathematical function that, given a set of parameters (e.g., production costs, time, and logistics costs), computes the best alternative based on the criteria important for a particular decision. Therefore, integrating such decision rules into business process models will make decisions in the course of a process more explicit and allow process participants to select the best alternative at a certain decision-making point.

When adding decision rules to business process models, a number of requirements must be met. First, it becomes necessary to identify the parameters that must be taken into account for a particular decision-making point (i.e., the parameters of the respective decision rule). Second, the values of these parameters have to be determined. Third, these values must be up-to-date; i.e., they must reflect the current situation of the organization, e.g., the production costs must be in accordance with current material costs. Fourth, a method is required for embedding decision rules into process models. In turn, the use of this method should be intuitive for process participants, which means that embedding and visualizing these rules within a process model must not be a complex task.

There exist very few approaches that have already applied decision theory or process mining for optimizing decision-making in the context of business processes [5–7]. However, none of them meets all of the aforementioned requirements. In general, these approaches neither provide a generic method for embedding decision rules into business process models nor do they allow for dynamic updates of parameter values required for evaluating decision rules.

The approach presented in this paper aims at overcoming these drawbacks and provides a comprehensive method for embedding decision rules into business process models. For this purpose, we introduce a modified XOR-split gateway, which we denote as *r-gateway*. The latter allows process modelers to define decision problems and decision rules directly in process models. In particular, to each r-gateway a specific decision rule may be assigned.

To be able to decide which decision-making parameters must be taken into account in the context of a particular decision rule, we utilize *key performance indicators* (KPI) as basis for our approach; e.g., costs of performing an activity. Generally, KPIs are quantifiable measurements used by an organization to analyze the success of a particular business process or business process activity. For example, such measurements may be obtained by using business intelligence (BI) tools. Furthermore, they are well aligned with the current status of the organization. Therefore, instead of manually setting values for decision-making parameters, we utilize the up-to-date KPI values obtained by BI tools.

Moreover, it is important to take into account that a branch representing a particular alternative in a process model may comprise various sets of activities. In our approach KPI values are associated with a single activity, but not with an entire execution branch of a process model. Therefore, a decision rule associated with a r-gateway computes the best alternative by aggregating all KPI values corresponding to the activities of a branch. The approach presented in this paper constitutes work-in-progress. In particular, a proper evaluation, including experimental results and a deeper investigation of potential drawbacks of our approach will be done in future work.

The remainder of this paper is structured as follows. In Sect. 2, fundamentals of decision theory are presented, which are required for a better understanding of this paper. Our approach is discussed in Sect. 3. First, an architecture of a process-aware information system is presented outlining the system components required in the context of our work. Second, we introduce the *(decision) rule-based XOR-split gateway (r-gateway)*, which allows process modelers to explicitly embed decision rules in business process models. Third, the formal semantics of the r-gateway is described. In Sect. 4, we illustrate the use of our approach along a simple example. Related work is discussed in Sect. 5. Then, Sect. 6 concludes the paper with a summary and an outlook.

2   Backgrounds on Decision Theory

In decision theory, three kinds of decision problems are distinguished, depending on the available knowledge [8,9]:

- decision problems under certainty
- decision problems under risk
- decision problems under uncertainty

Generally, decision theory offers a wide range of decision rules that allow determining the best alternative, while taking different viewpoints (e.g., optimistic and risk-averse decision making). In the following, we summarize basic characteristics of decision problems under certainty, uncertainty and risk. Furthermore, we provide examples of decision rules (see [10] for a detailed description of these decision rules).

Decision problem under certainty. Regarding decision making, this problem presumes the presence of alternatives with deterministic effects [8,11]. The *Lexicographical Order* is an examples of a decision rule addressing decision problems under certainty [11]. It chooses an alternative by considering the most important KPI for decision-making [12]. If two alternatives are equal with respect to the primary KPI, the second most important KPI will be considered as well, and so forth.

Decision problem under risk. A decision problem under risk is characterized by knowledge related to the potential effects of applying the available alternatives and to the probabilities of these effects. As opposed to a *decision problem under certainty*, the alternatives have nondeterministic behavior. The *Bayes Rule* constitutes an example of a decision rule that may be applied to decision problems under risk [9,13]. It chooses the alternative with maximum expected value of the KPIs of the different execution branches [14].

Decision problem under uncertainty. A decision problem under uncertainty is characterized by knowledge related to the potential effects of applying the available alternatives. As opposed to a *decision problem under risk*, the probabilities of these effects are unknown [15,16]. Decision rules like *MaxiMax*, *MaxiMin*, *Hurwicz's* and *Savage-Niehans* are options to solve decision problems under uncertainty. Regarding decision-making, the *MaxiMax* Rule chooses the alternative with the maximal best-case value of a particular KPI [17]. In turn, the *MaxiMin* Rule chooses the alternative with the maximal worst-case value of a particular KPI [15]. The *Hurwicz's Rule* combines MaxiMax and MiniMax. More precisely, for each alternative it sums up the weighted values of the worst and best case with respect to a particular KPI. Then, the alternative with the maximum sum is chosen [18]. The *Savage-Niehans Rule* (also called *MiniMax Regret Rule*) needs two steps for decision making. First, it calculates the regret values for all cases. Thereby, a regret value corresponds to the difference between the maximum value of a particular KPI for respective consequence and the value of a particular alternative for the same consequence. Following this, the rule chooses the alternative showing the smallest maximum regret value [19].

3   Embedding Decision Rules in Process Models

This section presents our approach for capturing and configuring decision problems within business process models. First, we describe components of a process-aware information system relevant in our context. Second, we show how to specify decision rules in business process models. For this purpose, we introduce a XOR-split gateway, which is associated with decision rules. Furthermore, we show how to configure such a gateway with a particular decision rule. Finally, we define the semantics of the particular XOR-split gateway at run-time.

3.1   Architecture

To enable the application of decision rules in a process-aware information system (PAIS), the latter must be able to access and process knowledge concerning the alternatives that exist in the context of a particular decision problem. However, the architecture of a PAIS enabling the use of decision rules, comprises standard components, like a process model editor, process engine, and repository (e.g., for storing activities, process models, process instances, and event logs). In our context, the process model editor must be extended to embed decision rules into process models. In turn, the BI tool analyzes process logs and stores statistical data and run-time information related to actual process execution in a respective repository (e.g., KPIs of activities, probabilities of events), i.e., *process statistics*. Finally, the process execution engine is enriched with a plug-in component evaluating decision rules at run-time. Figure 2 outlines this architecture for decision rule support in PAIS.

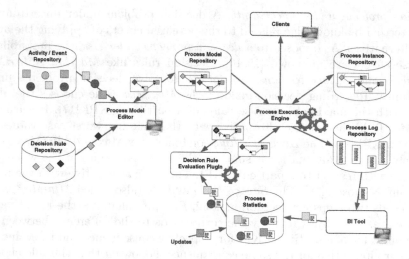

Fig. 2. Architecture of a PAIS integrating decision rules

3.2   Embedding Decision Rules in Process Models: The r-Gateway

This section introduces our approach for capturing decision problems in business process models. More precisely, respective decision problems must be annotated with a corresponding decision rule within the process model. For this purpose, we introduce the (decision) rule-based XOR-split gateway (cf. Fig. 3).

Figure 3 illustrates how the make-or-buy decision problem from Fig. 1 can be modeled by the use of a rule-based XOR-split gateway (r-gateway). Similar to common XOR-split gateways, the r-gateway allows expressing when a decision must be made. The *configuration artifact* defines the specific decision-rule, which first computes the various KPIs of the existing alternatives, and then determines

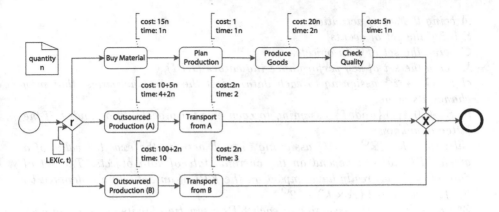

Fig. 3. Make-or-Buy process

the optimal alternative. In our example, the configuration of the r-gateway refers to the Lexicographical Order (LEX). Further, Fig. 3 highlights the KPI values of the different activities. Note that these annotations can be added automatically (cf. Sect. 3.1). A more precise description of Fig. 3 is presented in Sect. 4.

3.3 Formal Framework

This section provides a set-based formalization of process models. For the sake of simplicity and to set a focus, we only consider well-structured process models in this paper. Since well-structured process models can be always represented as a *process structure tree* (PST) [20], our formalization is based on the latter (cf. Definition 2).

Process Domain. First of all, we formally introduce the notion of *process domain* (cf. Definition 1). It defines the main building blocks for modeling business processes (e.g. process fragment types, activities, events, and data objects). A process domain further comprises functions for describing relations between activities, KPIs and data objects on one hand and for accessing probabilities of events and KPI values, stored in the process statistic repository (cf. Sect. 3.1), on the other. Finally, the process domain provides functions Z^s and Z^+ to allow for the computation of KPI values of alternatives composed out of multiple activities and nested gateways.

Definition 1 (Process Domains). *A process domain $\mathfrak{D}$ is a tuple $\mathfrak{D} = (\mathcal{T}, \mathcal{A}, \mathcal{E}, \mathcal{O}, \mathcal{K}, chg, p, val, Z^s, Z^+, \epsilon_F)$ with*

- *$\mathcal{T} := \{s, +, d\times, e\times, r\times, dr, er, A\}$ the set of process fragment types, whereby s corresponds to a sequence, + to a parallel gateway, $d\times$ to a data-based xor-split, $e\times$ to an event-based xor-split, $r\times$ to a rule-based xor-split, dr to a data-based repetition, er to an event-based repetition, and A to an activity execution.*

- $\mathcal{A}$ being the set of activities
- $\mathcal{E}$ being the set of events,
- $\mathcal{O}$ being the set of data objects,
- $\mathcal{K}$ being the set of key performance indicators (KPI),
- $chg : \mathcal{O} \to 2^{\mathcal{A}}$ assigning to each data object the set of activities, that may change its value.
- $p : \mathcal{E} \to [0,1] \cup \{undef\}$ assigning to each event a probability or $undef$ if the latter is unknown,
- $val : (\mathcal{A} \times \mathcal{K} \times \mathbb{R}^{\mathcal{O}}) \to \mathbb{R}$, assigning to each activity the expected value of a given KPI that can depend on the current state of data objects. The set of data objects that really have impact on the KPI of an activity are denoted by the function $imp : (\mathcal{A} \times \mathcal{K}) \to 2^{\mathcal{O}}$
- $Z^s : \mathcal{K} \to (\mathbb{R}^+ \to \mathbb{R})$ assigning to each KPI a function for its aggregation over fragments or activities arranged in sequence (e.g., for KPI duration Z^s might return a function that computes the sum of the parameters passed),
- $Z^+ : \mathcal{K} \to (\mathbb{R}^+ \to \mathbb{R})$ assigning to each KPI a function for its aggregation over fragments or activities arranged in parallel (e.g., for KPI duration Z^+ might return a function that computes the maximum of the parameters passed),
- ϵ_F the empty fragment.

Process Model. Based on process domain, we now introduce the notion of process model using the process structure tree [20]. According to Definition 2, a process model is composed out of fragments of different types and properties:

Definition 2 (Process model). *Let $\mathfrak{D} = (\mathcal{T}, \mathcal{A}, \mathcal{E}, \mathcal{O}, \mathcal{K}, chg, p, val, Z^s, Z^+, \epsilon_F)$ be a process domain. Any well-structured process model can then be represented as a tuple $P = (F, \lessdot, rf, type, class, evt, grd, cnf, f_r)$ with*

- *F being the set of fragments and f_r the root fragment.*
- *$\lessdot \subseteq F \times F$ being the sub-fragment relation, i.e. $g \lessdot f$ means that g is a direct sub-fragment of fragment f. Thus, $(F, \lessdot)$ is a tree with root node f_r. Based on $\lessdot$ we define*
  - *$\lessdot \subseteq F \times F$ as the transitive closure of $\lessdot$.*
  - *$|.| : F \to \mathbb{N} : f \mapsto |f| := |\{f'|f' \lessdot f\}|$ assigning to each fragment the number of its direct sub-fragments*
- *$type : F \to \mathcal{T}$ assigning to each fragment its type (cf. Definition 1). Based on such a type, for each $\circ \in \mathcal{T}$, we can define the set $F^{\circ} := \{f \in F|type(f) = \circ\}$ and $F^{\lessdot\circ} := \{f \in F|\exists g \in F : f \lessdot g \wedge type(g) = \circ\}$, thereby $\bigcup_{\circ \in \mathcal{T}} F^{\circ} = f_r \cup \bigcup_{\circ \in \mathcal{T}} F^{\lessdot\circ}$ are partitions of the fragment set F.*
- *$rf : F^{dr} \cup F^{er} \to F$ assigning to each repetition the repeated fragment, i.e. $rf(f) \lessdot f$.*
- *$grd : F^{dx} \cup F^{dr} \cup F^{dr} \to \mathfrak{G}$ assigning a guard to each branch/fragment of a data-based xor-fragment. Further, grd assigns a guard to each data-based repetition fragment and the corresponding repeated fragment. Thereby, $\mathfrak{G}$ corresponds to the set of guards and a particular guard $g \in \mathfrak{G} := (\mathbb{R}^{\mathcal{O}}) \to \mathbb{B}$ constitutes a function. The latter depends on the values of data objects and decides whether or not a branch is chosen. Thereby, a guard is a function*

that depends on the values of the data objects and returns either **true** *or* *false.*

- *class* : $F^A \rightarrow \mathcal{A}$ *assigning to each activity fragment an activity class.*
- *evt* : $F^{\leq ex} \cup F^{\leq er} \cup F^{er} \rightarrow E$ *assigning an event to each branch/fragment of an event-based xor-fragment. Further, evt assigns an event to each event-based repetition fragment and the corresponding repeated fragment.*
- *cnf* : $F^{rx} \rightarrow \mathfrak{R}$ *configuring each rule-based xor-split with a particular decision rule. Thereby, $\mathfrak{R}$ corresponds to the set of decision rules. A particular decision rule $r \in \mathfrak{R} := \mathbb{R}^\mathcal{O} \times (2^F - \{\emptyset\}) \rightarrow F$ constitutes a function that selects one fragment out of a set of fragments based on KPIs of the fragments. Since some KPI depend on the values of data objects, a decision rule may depend on the values of the data objects as well.*

Further, we define

- $uses_O : \mathfrak{G} \rightarrow 2^\mathcal{O}$ *that assigns to each guard the set of data objects used by the guard.*
- $uses_K : \mathfrak{R} \rightarrow 2^\mathcal{K}$ *that assigns to each decision rule the set of KPIs used by the rule.*

Decision Problems. As described in Sect. 2, decision theory distinguishes between decision making under certainty, uncertainty, and risk. Accordingly, we define formal criteria for certainty, uncertainty, and risk:

Definition 3 (Criteria for Decision Problems). *Let $\mathfrak{D} = (\mathcal{T}, \mathcal{A}, \mathcal{E}, \mathcal{O}, \mathcal{K}, chg, p, val, Z^s, Z^+, \epsilon_F)$ be a process domain and $P = (F, \lessdot, rf, type, class, evt, grd, cnf, f_r)$ be a process structure tree, then:*

- $f^c \in F^{rx}$ *defines a decision problem under certainty,*
  iff $\forall f \lessdot f^c : type(f) \in \{s, +, dx, A\}$
- $f^u \in F^{rx}$ *defines a decision problem under uncertainty,*
  iff $\forall f \lessdot f^u : type(f) \in \{s, +, dx, ex, A\}$.[1]
- $f^r \in F^{rx}$ *defines a decision problem under risk,*
  iff $\forall f \lessdot f^r : type(f) \in \{s, +, dx, ex, er, A\}$ and probabilities of the used events are known,
  i.e. $\forall f \lessdot f^r : f \in (F^{\leq ex} \cup F^{\leq er} \cup F^{er}) \Rightarrow p(evt(f)) \neq undef$

Furthermore, we require that the value of a particular data object $o \in \mathcal{O}$ must not be changed within a decision problem (i.e. rule-based xor-split fragment) $f_r \in F^{rx}$,

- *if o impacts the decision of a data-based xor-split sub-fragment, i.e.:*
  $\exists f_{dx} \in F^{dx}, f_{dx} \lessdot f_r : o \in uses_O(grd(f_{dx}))$
  $\Rightarrow \forall f_a \in F^A, f_a \lessdot f_r : type(f_a) \notin chg(o)$

---

[1] In the context of uncertainty, the probability of each event is assumed to be unknown. We do not consider this as a prerequisite, but just ignore possibly known probabilities.

– *or if they impact KPIs that are used by the respective decision rule* $r = cnf(f_r)$, *i.e.:*

$$\exists k \in uses_K(r) \exists f_a, \in F^A, f_a \lessdot f_r : o \in imp(type(f_a), k)$$
$$\Rightarrow \forall f_{a'} \in F^A, f_{a'} \lessdot f_r : type(f_{a'}) \notin chg(o)$$

3.4 Execution Semantics of the r-Gateway

This section describes the application and evaluation of decision rules at run-time. Thereby, the application of decision rules requires KPI values for each alternative. Note that in the context of business process execution, alternatives may be composed of multiple activities and nested gateways. Thus, before applying the decision rules, we first discuss how to compute KPI values of the different alternatives. Then, we formally define the application of decision rules. Due to space limitations, we only consider decision problems under risk in this paper. In [10], we additionally address decision problems under certainty and uncertainty.

Computing KPI Values of Alternatives Under Risk. In this case, the probabilities of the events are known. Furthermore, only fragments of types $s, +, d\times, e\times, er$, and A may occur (cf. Definition 3). Thus, function vfr, which computes the expected KPI values of alternatives under risk, is composed out of six subfunctions:

$$vfr : F^{s,+,d\times,e\times,A} \times \mathcal{K} \times \mathbb{R}^O \to \mathbb{R} : (f, k, a) \mapsto vfc(f, k, a) := vfr_{type(f)}(f, k, a) \text{ with}$$
$$vfr_A(f, k, a) := val(class(f), k, a)$$
$$vfr_s(f, k, a) := Z^s(\{vfr(f', k, a) | f' \lessdot f\})$$
$$vfr_+(f, k, a) := Z^+(\{vfr(f', k, a) | f' \lessdot f\})$$
$$vfr_{d\times}(f, k, a) := Z^+(\{vfr(f', k, a) | f' \lessdot f \wedge grd(f')(a)\})$$
$$vfr_{e\times}(f, k, a) := \sum_{f' \lessdot f} p(evt(f')) \cdot vfr(f', k, a)$$
$$vfr_{er}(f, k, a) := \frac{1}{p(evt(f))} \cdot vfr(rf(f), k, a)$$

Application of Decision Rules. In this section, we formalize the application of decision rules during business process execution.

Decision rules under risk: Bayes Rule. Using function vfr, this rule determines the alternative with the maximum expected value of a particular KPI [14].

$$BY : \mathcal{K} \times \mathbb{R}^O \times 2^F \to F : (\lambda, k, a, F') \mapsto BY(k, a, F')$$
$$BY(k, a, F') := f, \text{ with } \forall f' \in F' : vfr(f, k, a) \geq vfr(f, k, a)$$

Figure 4 shows an example of the Bayes rule that comprises two alternatives. The first one contains an event-based loop, the second one leads to an event-based XOR-split. Based on the definition of vfr, the Bayes rule computes the expected value for both alternatives and then chooses the one with the highest expected value.

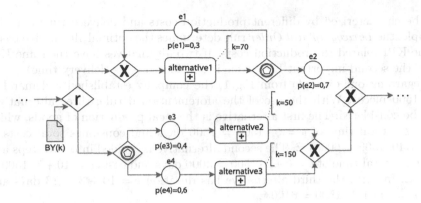

Fig. 4. Modelling of the Bayes Rule

$\mathcal{D} = (\mathcal{T}, \mathcal{A}, \mathcal{E}, \mathcal{O}, \mathcal{K}, chg, p, val, Z^s, Z^+, \epsilon_F)$ with $\quad$ $p(e1) := 0.3; p(e2) := 0.7; p(e3) := 0.4;$
$\mathcal{T} := \{s, +, dx, ex, rx, dr, er, \}$ $\qquad\qquad\qquad$ $p(e4) := 0.6; val(a1, k, 0) := 70;$
$\mathcal{A} := \{a1, a2, a3\}; \mathcal{E} := \{e1, e2, e3, e4\};$ $\qquad$ $val(a2, k, 0) := 50; val(a3, k, 0) := 150;$
$\mathcal{O} := \emptyset; \mathcal{K} := \{k\}; chg(o) := \emptyset;$ $\qquad\qquad\qquad$ $Z^s(k) := \sum; $ and $Z^+(k) := \sum;$

$P = (F, \lessdot, rf, type, class, evt, grd, cnf, f_{rx})$ with $\quad$ $type(f_{a2}) := A; type(f_{a3}) := A;$
$F := \{f_{rx}, f_{er}, f_{ex}, f_{a1}, f_{a2}, f_{a3}\};$ $\qquad\qquad\qquad$ $class(f_{a1}) := a1; class(f_{a2}) := a2;$
$f_{a1} \lessdot f_{er}; f_{a2}, f_{a3} \lessdot f_{ex}; f_{er}, f_{ex} \lessdot f_{rx};$ $\qquad$ $class(f_{a3}) := a3; evt(f_{er}) := e2; evt(f_{a1}) := e1;$
$rf(f_{ex}) := f_{a1}; grd := false;$ $\qquad\qquad\qquad\qquad$ $evt(f_{a2}) := e3; evt(f_{a3}) := e4;$
$type(f_{rx}) := rx; type(f_{er}) := er;$ $\qquad\qquad\qquad$ $cnf(f_{rx}) := BY(k);$ and $uses_K(BY(k)) := \{k\};$
$type(f_{ex}) := ex; type(f_{a1}) := A;$

Note that f_{rx} denotes a decision problem under risk:
$\forall f \lessdot f_{rx} : type(f) \in \{s, +, dx, ex, er, A\}$ and function p never returns $undef$.

$vfr(f_{a1}, k, 0) = val(class(f_{a1}), k, 0) = val(a1, k, 0) = 70;$

$vfr(f_{a2}, k, 0) = 50; vfr(f_{a3}, k, 0) = 150;$

$vfr(f_{er}, k, a) := \dfrac{1}{prop(evt(f_{er}))} \cdot vfr(rf(f_{er}), k, 0) = \dfrac{1}{prop(e2)} \cdot vfr(f_{a1}, k, 0) = \dfrac{1}{0.7} \cdot 70 = 100;$

$vfr(f_{ex}, k, 0) = \sum_{f' \lessdot f_{ex}} prop(evt(f')) \cdot vfr(f', k, 0)$

$\qquad = prop(evt(f_{a2})) \cdot vfr(f_{a2}, k, 0) + prop(evt(f_{a3})) \cdot vfr(f_{a3}, k, 0) = 0.4 \cdot 50 + 0.6 \cdot 150 = 110;$

$\Rightarrow BY(k, 0, \{f_{er}, f_{ex}\}) = f_{ex}$, because $vfr(f_{ex}, k, 0) \geq vfr(f_{er}, k, 0)$, i.e., the second alternative (f_{ex}) will be chosen.

4   Application Example

This section applies our approach to the example from Fig. 1. In this context note that Fig. 3 models the same make-or-by process. However, the latter comprises the rule-based XOR-split gateway introduced in Sect. 3.2. In this process, the decision maker must decide whether to produce goods locally or to outsource the production. In case of outsourcing, the goods may be produced by two different suppliers. Depending on the quantity of the ordered goods, in turn, the suppliers may be characterized by different production costs and delivery times. In this example, the *Lexicographical Order* rule determines the optimal alternative based on the KPI related to production costs. If two alternatives have the same KPI value, the second important KPI value is considered (e.g., delivery time).

Regarding our example from Fig. 1, the company established a demand of $n = 1500$ pieces. With the use of the aforementioned rule, three alternatives must be considered: The first alternative is the local production of goods, which requires a total time of $t = 5 \cdot 1500 = 7500$ days and consumes total costs of $c = 1 + 40 \cdot 1500 = 60001 \,€$. The second alternative is divided into two steps and requires a total time of $t = 6 + 2 \cdot 1500 = 3006$ days and costs $c = 10 + 7 \cdot 1500 = 10510 \,€$. In turn, the third alternative has duration $t = 10 + 3 = 13$ days and costs $c = 100 + 4 \cdot 1500 = 6100 \,€$.

Finally, as result of applying the Lexicographic Rule, we learn that the third alternative shall be taken. Of course, this simple example does not validate our approach, but just shall illustrate how the r-gateway works. A detailed evaluation is subject of future work.

5   Related Work

There exist several approaches that provide operational decision support in the context of process-aware information system (PAIS). For instance, [21,22] describe a simulation system for operational decision support in the context of workflow management. The approach combines and extends the workflow system YAWL and the process mining framework ProM. However, respective approaches do not offer methods for decision-making at run-time. In addition, they are not able to dynamically update the KPI values according to the current status of the company. The approaches presented in [23,24] provide operational decision support in terms of recommendations at run-time. However, these approaches do not provide a method for embedding decision rules in business process models. In our approach, we do not explicitly address the discovering of KPIs. In the context of process mining [6] and business intelligence (BI) [25], there exist approaches tackling this challenge. Knuplesch et al. [26] provides a framework for performance monitoring and analysis of WS-BPEL processes, which consolidates process events and KPI measurements. Additionally, [26] analyzes dependencies between KPIs by applying machine learning techniques. The approach described in [5] offers a toolbox of decision rules and methods to enable and ease the development of decision support systems.

Compared to this related work, our approach allows for the explicit specification of decision problems in business processes models. The use of KPIs as parameters for decision rules ensures that decisions will be made based on up-to-date values. Finally, it enables automated decision-making at run-time.

6   Conclusion

In this paper, we presented an approach for applying decision theory techniques to process models. For this purpose, we first outlined the adaptations to be made regarding the architecture of traditional PAIS. Then, we introduced the *(decision) rule-based XOR-split gateway (r-gateway)* to enrich current standards and notations for process modeling. The latter indicates the occurrence of a decision problem and must be configured with a particular decision rule. This rule shall be executed at run-time when enabling the respective r-gateway. To support an automated evaluation of decision rules, we formally described how to compute KPI values of alternatives composed out of multiple activities and nested gateways. Thereby, KPI values of single activities are discovered from process logs through the application of business intelligence tools.

Note that this paper only serves as a starting point for embedding decision theory concepts in business process management and process execution. Thus, our next steps will include a proof-of-concept implementation as well as a proper evaluation, including experimental results and the identification of potential drawbacks. Furthermore, we plan to consider properties of KPIs that depend on random distributions.

In general, the applicability of our approach will be highly dependent on the availability of accurate KPIs for each activity. Thereby, another challenge is to adapt current business intelligence technologies for optimizing our approach.

Finally, additional challenges emerge in the context of flexible processes [27,28] (e.g., regarding the dynamic addition of new activities and process fragments that might be relevant for decision making) and business process compliance [29–31] (e.g., regarding compliance rules that restrict alternatives in particular cases).

References

1. Lohrmann, M., Reichert, M.: Efficacy-aware business process modeling. In: Meersman, R., Panetto, H., Dillon, T., Rinderle-Ma, S., Dadam, P., Zhou, X., Pearson, S., Ferscha, A., Bergamaschi, S., Cruz, I.F. (eds.) OTM 2012, Part I. LNCS, vol. 7565, pp. 38–55. Springer, Heidelberg (2012)
2. Lohrmann, M., Reichert, M.: Modeling business objectives for business process management. In: Stary, C. (ed.) S-BPM ONE 2012. LNBIP, vol. 104, pp. 106–126. Springer, Heidelberg (2012)
3. Einhorn, H.J., Hogarth, R.M.: Behavioral decision theory: processes of judgment and choice. Acc. Res. **19**(1), 1–31 (1981)
4. Newell, A., Simon, H.A.: Human Problem Solving, vol. 14. Prentice-Hall, Englewood Cliffs (1972)
5. Worley, J.H., et al.: Adding decision support to workflow systems by reusable standard software components. Comput. Ind. **49**(1), 123–140 (2002)
6. van der Aalst, W.M.P.: Process Mining: Discovery Conformance and Enhancement of Business Processes. Springer, Heidelberg (2011)
7. Rozinat, A., Mans, R., van der Aalst, W.M.P.: Mining VPN models: discovering process models with data from event logs. In: CPN'06 (2006)
8. Joyce, J.M.: The Foundations of Causal Decision Theory. Cambridge University Press, Cambridge (1999)
9. Peterson, M.: An Introduction to Decision Theory. Cambridge University Press, Cambridge (1993)

10. Catalkaya, S., Knuplesch, D., Reichert, M.: Bringing more semantics to xor-split gateways in business process models based on decision rules. Technical report 2013-04, University of Ulm (2013)
11. Kahneman, D., Tversky, A.: Prospect theory: an analysis of decision under risk. Econometrica **47**, 263–291 (1979)
12. Peeta, S., Yu, J.W.: A hybrid model for driver route choice incorporating en-route attributes and real-time information effects. Netw. Spat. Econ. **5**(1), 21–40 (2005)
13. Wu, G., Zhang, J., Gonzalez, R.: Decision under risk. In: Koehler, D.J., Harvey, N. (eds.) Blackwell Handbook of Judgment and Decision Making, pp. 399–423. Blackwell, Oxford (2004)
14. Pawlak, Z.: Decision rules, Bayes' rule and rough sets. In: Zhong, N., Skowron, A., Ohsuga, S. (eds.) RSFDGrC 1999. LNCS (LNAI), vol. 1711, pp. 1–9. Springer, Heidelberg (1999)
15. Kartam, N.A., Tzeng, G.H., Teng, J.Y.: Robust contingency plans for transportation investment planning. IEEE Trans. Syst. Man Cybern. B Cybern. **23**(1), 5–13 (1993)
16. Dixit, A.: Entry and exit decisions under uncertainty. Polit. Econ. **97**, 620–638 (1989)
17. Arnold, B.F., Größl, I., Stahlecker, P.: The minimax, the minimin, and the hurwicz adjustment principle. Theor. Decis. **52**(3), 233–260 (2002)
18. Haimes, Y.Y., et al.: Risk of extreme events in a multiobjective framework. Am. Water Resour. Assoc. **28**(1), 201–209 (1992)
19. Rödder, W., Reucher, E.: A consensual peer-based DEA-model with optimized cross-efficiencies-input allocation instead of radial reduction. Oper. Res. Int. J. **212**(1), 148–154 (2011)
20. Vanhatalo, J., Völzer, H., Koehler, J.: The refined process structure tree. Data Knowl. Eng. **68**(9), 793–818 (2009)
21. Rozinat, A., et al.: Workflow simulation for operational decision support. Data Knowl. Eng. **68**(9), 834–850 (2009)
22. de Medeiros, A.K.A., van der Aalst, W.M.P., Pedrinaci, C.: Semantic process mining tools: core building blocks. In: ECIS'08 (2008)
23. Schonenberg, H., Weber, B., van Dongen, B.F., van der Aalst, W.M.P.: Supporting flexible processes through recommendations based on history. In: Dumas, M., Reichert, M., Shan, M.-C. (eds.) BPM 2008. LNCS, vol. 5240, pp. 51–66. Springer, Heidelberg (2008)
24. Vanderfeesten, I., Reijers, H.A., van der Aalst, W.M.P.: Product based workflow support: dynamic workflow execution. In: Bellahsène, Z., Léonard, M. (eds.) CAiSE 2008. LNCS, vol. 5074, pp. 571–574. Springer, Heidelberg (2008)
25. zur Mühlen, M., Shapiro, R.: Business process analytics. In: vom Brocke, J., Rosemann, M. (eds.) Handbook on Business Process Management 2, pp. 137–157. Springer, Heidelberg (2010)
26. Wetzstein, B., et al.: Monitoring and analyzing influential factors of business process performance. In: EDOC'09, pp. 141–150. IEEE (2009)
27. Reichert, M., Dadam, P.: ADEPT$_{flex}$ - supporting dynamic changes of workflows without losing control. Intell. Inf. Syst. (Special Issue on Workflow Management Systems) **10**(2), 93–129 (1998)
28. Reichert, M., Weber, B.: Enabling Flexibility in Process-Aware Information Systems. Springer, Heidelberg (2012)
29. Knuplesch, D., Reichert, M.: Ensuring business process compliance along the process life cycle. Technical report 2011-06, University of Ulm (2011)

30. Knuplesch, D., Reichert, M., Mangler, J., Rinderle-Ma, S., Fdhila, W.: Towards compliance of cross-organizational processes and their changes - research challenges and state of research. In: La Rosa, M., Soffer, P. (eds.) BPM Workshops 2012. LNBIP, vol. 132, pp. 649–661. Springer, Heidelberg (2013)
31. Knuplesch, D., Reichert, M., Fdhila, W., Rinderle-Ma, S.: On enabling compliance of cross-organizational business processes. In: Daniel, F., Wang, J., Weber, B. (eds.) BPM 2013. LNCS, vol. 8094, pp. 146–154. Springer, Heidelberg (2013)

Validating and Enhancing Declarative Business Process Models Based on Allowed and Non-occurring Past Behavior

Seppe K.L.M. vanden Broucke[1]([✉]), Filip Caron[1], Jan Vanthienen[1], and Bart Baesens[1,2]

[1] Department of Decision Sciences and Information Management, KU Leuven, Naamsestraat 69, 3000 Leuven, Belgium
[2] School of Management, University of Southampton, Highfield, Southampton SO17 1BJ, UK
seppe.vandenbroucke@kuleuven.be

Abstract. Contemporary organizations have been implementing a wide variety of process-aware information systems in order to streamline their operations. The current organizational environment is often characterized by a multitude of internal and external directives which impose restrictions through business rules on the operations and as such define declarative business process models. We present a twofold methodology which can be applied towards the validation and enhancement of process models which are expressed in a declarative form in order to improve their correctness and completeness. Our approach is based on validation of real-life behavior using rule property checking, and on allowed behavior by the process model which was not encountered in real-life cases by matching rule-generated rejected activity occurrences with absent behavior in the event log. Our methodology retains the ability to correspond retrieved findings to decision-makers in a clear and comprehensible manner (i.e. in the form of a new rule), rather than a formal revision of an implemented procedural model, which is a significant advantage when considering business-IT alignment concerns.

Keywords: Business rules · Business process models · Declarative process models · Correctness · Completeness

1 Introduction

Every organization executes a number of business processes in order to achieve its goals and to perform its day-to-day activities. The management of business processes has received a lot of attention from practitioners and academics alike, since the performance of an organization heavily depends on how effectively and efficiently it enacts its business processes. Modern organizations

N. Lohmann et al. (Eds.): BPM 2013 Workshops, LNBIP 171, pp. 212–223, 2014.
DOI: 10.1007/978-3-319-06257-0_17, © Springer International Publishing Switzerland 2014

are frequently confronted with a high degree of complexity, so that business processes often involve many people, activities and resources, making it hard to implement and automate them without some sort of information support system.

Recently, a new research field has sprung up which studies the problem of deriving knowledge from process event logs as recorded by these information systems. The field, denoted as "process mining", places itself at the intersection of the areas of data mining and Business Process Management [1]. Process mining is related to data mining because of the shared goal of learning from large data repositories [2]. Similarly, process mining can be associated with the field of Business Process Management as one of its major objectives is gaining insight into business operations based on recorded process data in so called event logs. As a result, process mining fits within the "diagnosis"-phase of the Business Process Management life cycle [3].

In this paper, we focus our attention to the validation and enhancement of process models. We present a methodology which can be applied on process models which are expressed in a declarative form, meaning in the form of rules, rather than a procedural construct such as a Petri net. Whereas other work targets the validation and enhancement of business processes in a procedural settings [4,5], we limit our scope towards declarative models due to two reasons. The first reason follows from a real-life aspect which comes into play when business processes are defined and developed in organizations. Oftentimes, two roles are involved in the management of organizational processes: domain experts, meaning business analysts or managers, and IT experts, who have the responsibility of translating business requirements to an effective implementation [6]. Two different perspectives can be identified between these complementary roles: while the IT expert often follows a procedural modeling style in order to better deal with implementation and execution aspects, the business analyst commonly applies a more declarative approach, describing business processes as a set of policies, rules and guidelines which guide the overall activity flow. When performing business process validation and enhancement tasks, the ability to correspond retrieved findings to decision-makers in a clear and comprehensible manner (e.g. in the form of a new rule), rather than a formal revision of an implemented procedural model is a significant advantage. The second reason follows from practicality concerns. Validating historic process cases on a procedural process model often involves some form of process trace replay (for example a token based replay on a Petri net [4]), which can rapidly become computationally hard in the presence of invisible or duplicate tasks. Similarly, analyzing if the process model allows for behavior which is not found in a given event log also proves difficult, often involving an extensive state space exploration. Our method deals with these concerns by using standard rule validation techniques on given process instances to detect real-life behavior which was rejected by one or multiple formulated rules. Additionally, behavior which is allowed by the set of given rules but not found in a given event log is derived by matching rule-generated forbidden activity executions with absent behavior in the event log.

2   Running Example

As a running example throughout the remainder of this paper, we will use an insurance claim handling process to illustrate the described methodology. Based on the Petri net model shown in Fig. 1, which was derived from a real-life environment, an event log was generated using CPNTools[1] containing twenty simulated process instances and 92 total events, denoting that a certain activity completed at a specific point in time within a process instance. Remark that the Petri net depicted in Fig. 1 will not be considered further throughout the remainder of this paper, as the focus of our methodology lies on the validation and enhancement of declarative, rule-based process models. The Petri net given below should thus only be used as a guidance in order to understand the possible flow of traces included in the simulated event log.

Fig. 1. Insurance claim handling process model used to generate example event log

3   Methodology

The process analysis tasks presented in this paper strive to validate and enhance declarative, rule-governed processes. Put broadly, we extract two types of behavior from a given event log in respect to an a-priori declarative process model in order to validate and enhance the current model:

1. Real-Life Behavior Which Is Rejected by the Process Model: *Correctness* **Perspective.** By validating current rules on historic process instances, deviating cases containing behavior that is explicitly disallowed by the given rules are detected, so that problematic or suspicious process instances can be identified and audited if necessary. However, it is possible that not all deviating instances should per definition be rejected, as it might be the case that some deviations are presenting allowed behavior after all, giving rise to process model enhancements in the form of the removal of restricting rules (decreasing the rule base). That is, instead of rejecting some deviating process cases which do not conform to a given model, it is also possible to modify the model to better represent the current real-life behavior. This type of behavior is thus applied to assess whether the given model is *correct* in accordance with observed, real life data.

2. Allowed Behavior Which Is Absent in Real-Life Instances: *Correctness* **Perspective.** Additional to investigating if the given declarative model supports the execution of process instances as they occurred in real-life, one can also check whether all allowed behavior by a process model can also be

---

[1] See: http://cpntools.org.

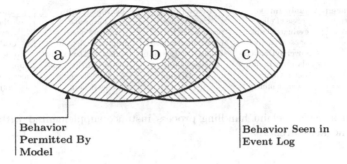

Behavior
Permitted By
Model

Behavior Seen in
Event Log

Area a: Allowed Superfluous Behavior: *Completeness* Issue
Area b: Normal, Allowed Behavior
Area c: Rejected Real-life Behavior: *Correctness* Issue

Fig. 2. Schematic overview of behavior found when comparing a declarative process model with real-life event log data. Permitted behavior is constrained by a declarative process model, which is then compared with the behavior seen in the event log. Area "a" then corresponds with behavior allowed by the process model but not evidenced by real-life data – indicating a completeness issue, whereas area "c" indicates real-life behavior which was rejected by the process model – indicating correctness issues. Area "b" corresponds with normal, allowed and seen behavior. Area "d" corresponds with rejected behavior, but which was also not observed in the event log.

found in an event log, or, put differently, if the process instances as they happen in real-life never exhibit certain behavior, although this behavior is nevertheless allowed by a given process model. This type of behavior is thus utilized to determine whether the given model is *complete* in accordance with observed, real life data. Figure 2 provides a schematic overview of these types of behavior.

Computing the complete set of allowed behavior from a declarative process model poses some specific difficulties, mainly following from the fact that the number of computations involved to generate all possible process traces from a given process model (either a procedural or declarative one) increases exponentially with the size and complexity of the process model. To deal with this problem, we apply an artificial negative event induction method as suggested in [7] to introduce negative examples in process instances. A brief overview of this technique is given below.

Negative events represent information about activities that were prevented from taking place. Such events are rarely logged in real-life logs [5], so that in [8], a generation algorithm is proposed to induce negative events in an artificial manner in an event log, which can be summarized as follows. Negative events record that at a given position in a trace, a particular event cannot occur. Thus, at each position in each trace in the event log, it is examined which negative events can be induced, by checking whether traces exist in the event log where the negative event under consideration does occur and was preceded with a

Positive Trace:	claimIntake	reviewPolicy	evaluateClaim	...	closeClaim
Negative Events:	reviewPolicy	claimIntake	claimIntake		claimIntake
	evaluateClaim	proposeSettlement	reviewPolicy		reviewPolicy
	proposeSettlement	approvePayDamages	proposeSettlement		evaluateClaim
	approvePayDamages	calculateNewPremium	approvePayDamages	...	proposeSettlement
	calculateNewPremium	closeClaim	calculateNewPremium		approvePayDamages
	closeClaim	rejectClaim	closeClaim		calculateNewPremium
	rejectClaim		rejectClaim		rejectClaim

Fig. 3. An insurance claim handling process instance supplemented with artificially generated negative events

similar execution history. If this check fails, no counter-evidence for the candidate negative event could be found in the event log, and the negative event is inserted in the original trace. The original version of the algorithm allows to configure the negative event generation procedure by means of a window size parameter and takes concurrent behavior into account as well when testing whether a negative event can be induced, whereas recent improvements [7] focus on better dealing with recurrent (looping) behavior.

As an example, consider an event execution trace from the running example as given in Fig. 3. After using the artificial negative event induction procedure, sets of negative events are inserted before the occurrence of each normal – positive – event, shown in Fig. 3 below each positive event. For example, after performing the activities of *claimIntake* and *reviewPolicy*, the real-data as it happened and was recorded in the event log rejects the occurrence of *claimIntake* (third column, i.e. before the occurrence of *evaluateClaim* in this trace). It is important to remark once more that the negative events are generated based on the behavior seen in real-life, i.e. as recorded in a running system.

Next, we compare this set of negative examples with the set of negative events as imposed by the current rule base, and apply common rule induction techniques in order to derive candidate-rules to extend the rule base, i.e. to increase its completeness.

We further outline our methodology below in the following sections. The first two steps briefly describe necessary pre-processing tasks. The last two steps then extract the two types of behavior described above in order to validate and extend a declarative process model on the perspectives of correctness and completeness based on an historic event log. We apply all steps on the insurance claim handling process used as a running example.

4 Steps 1 and 2: Pre-processing

4.1 Establish Current Process Model

In a first step, a declarative process model is established which describes the process in terms of rules as formulated or documented by managers and stake holders. In our methodology, we assume that all rules are formulated in such a way that they restrict the possible hypothesis space (that is, as constraints), which initially allows all activity sequences. This instead of rules that define allowed behavior, starting from an initial empty model where nothing is permitted. Furthermore, we limit our focus on control-flow constructs only.

We establish the current rule base for the insurance claim handling process as follows:

Rule 1. Claim evaluation (*evaluateClaim*) must be performed at least once.

Rule 2. Approval for pay of damages (*approvePayDamages*) and calculation of new premium (*calculateNewPremium*) are executed in parallel.

Rule 3. Claim evaluation (*evaluateClaim*) must precede a proposal for settlement (*proposeSettlement*).

Rule 4. Approval for pay of damages (*approvePayDamages*) must be preceded by claim evaluation (*evaluateClaim*).

Rule 5. Closing (*closeClaim*) and rejecting (*rejectClaim*) a claim are mutually exclusive.

In order to better automate the validation and extension tasks as described below, we convert the rule base from a natural language representation to a more formal representation. Declare [9], SCIFF [10,11], Linear Temporal Logic [12] and CONDEC [13] can all be applied towards this purpose. We will make use of Linear Temporal Logic (LTL) to represent the given constraints. LTL has a number of interesting advantages, the first being that it allows for an unambiguous interpretation of business rules. Secondly, many LTL "patterns" already exist in literature which are able to capture the multitude of given rules. For a detailed description of LTL semantics, we refer to [12]. The rule base is thus now represented as follows:

Rule 1. $\diamond(evaluateClaim)$
Rule 2. $\diamond(approvePayDamages) \Leftrightarrow \diamond(calculateNewPremium)$
Rule 3. $(evaluateClaim)W(\neg(proposeSettlement))$
Rule 4. $(evaluateClaim)W(\neg(approvePayDamages))$
Rule 5. $\neg(\diamond(closeClaim) \wedge \diamond(rejectClaim))$

4.2   Extract Event Log

In a second step, an event log is extracted from the process aware information system which implements the described process model. The following remarks should be taken into account when extracting an event log. First, one must assure that only finalized process instances (i.e. traces which have reached an end state) are included in the extracted event log, as running traces might be rejected on the basis of some rule (which is temporarily violated). Second, the time period under consideration is important as well. Longer time periods ensure the inclusion of a higher number of process traces, which leads to a more complete event log (i.e. more included distinct activity flow paths). On the other hand, if the process at hand is relatively volatile and changes frequently, one must take care not to include too many traces, as older traces might no longer correspond with the current reality.

In our running insurance claim handling process example, twenty random process instances were generated, containing 92 completion events, corresponding to the execution of a particular activity.

5   Step 3: Rejected Historic Logged Behavior – Correctness Perspective

Once a declarative process model and appropriate historic event log have been established, the two types of behavior as described above can be investigated.

First, real-life behavior which is rejected by the process model should be analyzed in order to assess the *correctness* of the declarative model. To do so, we perform a rule based property verification analysis by applying the "LTL Checker" plugin found in the ProM6 process mining toolkit [14] to validate our rule base against the traces found in the event log. Each rule in a declarative model can be either satisfied or unsatisfied when checked against an event log. Satisfied means that the rule holds valid on each trace contained in the given log, whereas an unsatisfied state denotes that "deviating traces" exist which break the rule.

Based on these deviating traces, it is possible to derive two types of conclusions. First, it may be the case that the declarative model is deemed incorrect based on real-life behavior (event log contains truth). That is, it may be that the model is outdated and does not reflect reality in a sufficient manner anymore, in which case the erroneous constraints should be removed or weakened in order to represent the current, valid behavior. Alternatively, implementation distortions can exist, causing a specified process model to be implemented in an incorrect manner, which is often due to the discrepancy between the declarative nature of the process model and the procedural nature of program code. Second, it may be the case that the event log is the source of the violation, so that the deviating traces indeed exhibit unwanted behavior (the process model contains truth). In this case, additional analysis should be performed in order to find the root cause for this deviation. Noise, for example, following from system downtime or data corruption could cause the faulty or partial logging of a process instance. Next, users can be responsible for the error as well, perhaps not knowing that a certain rule or policy was broken by undertaking a certain action.

6   Step 4: Superfluous Allowed Modeled Behavior – Completeness Perspective

6.1   Discovering Superfluous Modeled Behavior

Whereas rule based property verification as performed above has been well described in literature [14], the enhancement of declarative process models has received less attention[2]. Two reasons can be stated to provide an explanation. First, it follows from the nature of declarative models that over-specification is often (and willingly so) avoided, allowing to defer the exact control-flow sequence of activities until run-time. Second, computing all possible allowed paths from a given process model (either procedural or declarative) becomes increasingly more difficult when the size or complexity of the described process increases. Although we agree with the sentiment that the ability to generalize is one of the key benefits of declarative (process) models compared to procedural representations, we argue that investigating allowed behavior which never occurs in real-life is still valuable, for example to discover business rules which were never explicitly formulated, to discover behavior which is allowed by business and domain experts but which was not permitted in the running information system due to implementation distortions, or simply to gain insight in real-life processes. To deal with the second remark (computational difficulty), we apply the artificial negative event induction method as described above in order to introduce negative examples in historic process instances (non-occurring behavior), which are then compared with the set of negative events generated from the current rule base (model-rejected behavior). We then apply a rule induction technique in order to derive new candidate-rules.

We illustrate the intricacies of this step on the insurance claim handling example. First, since we are interested in constraining rules which restrict the possible flow between activities, we artificially induce negative events in historic process instances to capture which behavior did not occur during the actual, real-life execution of the process at hand (non-occurring, log-rejected behavior), as was described in Sect. 3.

Next, a second set of negative events is generated from the rule base (non-allowed, model-rejected behavior). To do so, we iterate over all events of all given traces and check which activity types other than the actually completed event could have occurred as well. Algorithm 1 describes this generation process.

Once the two sets (log-rejected and model-rejected) of negative events are constructed, a comparison operation is performed in order to find those negative events which are not yet imposed by one or multiple rules (unconstrained, non-occurring behavior)[3]. In our insurance claim handling example, the current rule base led to the induction of 102 model-rejected negative events, denoting that a certain activity could not occur. For example, Rule 3 – "Claim evaluation (*evaluateClaim*) must precede a proposal for settlement (*proposeSettlement*)" – introduces negative events with activity type *proposeSettlement* at every position of each trace as long as *evaluateClaim* was not completed at a previous

---

[2] Note that it is possible to relate the completeness of a declarative process model to the "precision" quality dimension as it is often described in the area or process conformance checking, i.e. does the model restrict unwanted, undesired behavior? The correctness perspective as described above would then fit with the "fitness" quality dimension.

[3] The actual comparison itself is exact and trivial, since the sets of negative events are inserted at the same positions in the same traces, so that comparison can be performed by iterating over each position in each event log trace.

Algorithm 1. Rule-based generation of negative events

Let L be the given event log, σ a trace containing completed events x_i at position i, let A be a set of all activity types in L, let $\mathcal{R}$ be a rule in process model M.

for each trace $\sigma \in L$ do
  for each event $\sigma_i \in \sigma$ with activity type a do
    for each activity type $b \in A \setminus \{a\}$ do
      let x_n be a negative event with activity type b
      for each rule $\mathcal{R} \in M$ which holds in trace σ do
        $\tau := \langle \sigma_1, \ldots, \sigma_{i-1}, x_n, \sigma_{i+1}, \ldots, \sigma_{|\sigma|} \rangle$
        if $\mathcal{R}$ does not hold in τ do
          x_n is a valid rule-induced negative event

position. These negative events are then removed from the log-rejected 593 negative events which were generated based on historic, logged information to derive unconstrained, non-occurring behavior.

Following this, the remaining set of negative events can then be analyzed in order to derive new domain knowledge. Note once more that these events describe behavior which did not occur in real-life, although the rule base does not explicitly prohibit this behavior from happening. Inspecting such cases can lead to new rules which extend the current model in order to improve its completeness, or can light up implementation distortions (something was permitted to occur by business conduct but prohibited by the implemented system).

6.2   Extending the Declarative Process Model

It is not always straightforward to propose or design new rules based only on absent behavior present in an event log. However, it is possible to apply the given positive and constructed negative events towards a rule induction technique in order to automate the process extension task. An example is provided to illustrate this technique. After inspecting the set of negative events which were not captured by one or multiple rules, it is found that the activity *reviewPolicy* is frequently rejected from completing based on actual logged behavior, although no single rule in the current process model constrains this activity in any way. Therefore, we are interested in deriving a new rule which does describe when a policy may be reviewed.

Based on the event log supplemented with the remaining negative events, a data set is constructed containing a discrete attribute for each activity type and a binary target variable denoting if the *reviewPolicy* activity type was completed (positive example) or rejected from completing (negative example). Next, for each positive or negative event in each trace with activity type *reviewPolicy*, its history θ is examined and an instance is added to the data set. Each such instance contains an attribute per activity type, denoting whether this activity was absent (attribute value equals "absent"), present (attribute value equals "present"), or present at the final position in history θ (attribute value equals "directly precedes"). Note that other input attributes can potentially be supplemented as well (e.g. to take into account case-related attributes), but for simple control-flow based rule discovery as described here, the set of properties as described above suffices. Once the data set is constructed, well-known rule induction techniques such as RIPPER [15] can be applied in order to derive a new rule. Maruster et al. [16] also derive control-flow based rules from a given process log using a similar rule induction methodology in order to discover a process model from a given event log. Contrary to our approach, however, the authors do not take into account natural or generated negative examples, so that the detection of non-occurring behavior becomes more troublesome. Furthermore, enhancing given declarative process models poses difficulties as well, since no comparison operation between model-rejected behavior and non-occurring behavior can be performed. Note that we target a perfect accuracy for the derivation of new rules. If misclassifications do occur, the data set can be supplemented with additional attributes which are able to perfectly distinguish between negative and positive examples in order to support the addition of a new rule to the process model. Finally, remark that we are mainly interested in deriving rules describing the occurrence of a negative event (i.e. the rejection of the execution of an activity), as the declarative model is formulated such that, by default (i.e. an empty model), all activity types are always allowed.

After having followed the steps above, the following rule for the *reviewPolicy* activity type is derived (depicted in conjunctive normal form):

Rule 6. IF (NOT claimIntake = "directly precedes")
        THEN reviewPolicy = 0

Or, stated otherwise: the *reviewPolicy* activity is rejected from being executed (value 0 corresponds with a negative event) if it is not directly preceded by a *claimIntake* activity. Domain experts can then decide if the rule "Reviewing insurance policy is optional but may only occur right after a new claim intake" should be added to the process model. The corresponding LTL representation for this rule would then read as:

Rule 6. $\Box(\bigcirc(reviewPolicy) \Rightarrow claimIntake) \lor \Box(\neg(reviewPolicy))$

Similarly, the *rejectClaim* activity type is also never executed at certain positions, even after taking the constraints imposed by the current rule base into account, so that the process model (Rule 5 in particular) can be made more strict. The following rules are derived and replace Rule 5:

Rule 7a. IF (evaluateClaim = "absent")
        THEN rejectClaim = 0
Rule 7b. IF (proposeSettlement = "present")
        THEN rejectClaim = 0

Our technique also deals with parallelism (AND-splits) in a correct manner. For example, the following rules are derived for *approvePayDamages*:

Rule 8a. IF (NOT proposeSettlement = "directly precedes")
        AND (NOT calculateNewPremium = "directly precedes")
        THEN approvePayDamages = 0
Rule 8b. IF (NOT proposeSettlement = "directly precedes")
        AND (approvePayDamages = "present")
        THEN approvePayDamages = 0

By following the technique as described above, the completeness of declarative process models can be improved in an automated manner by deriving new business rules based on the actual behavior of process instances.

7 Conclusion

In this paper, we have presented a methodology in order to validate and extend declarative process models based on the perspectives of correctness and completeness, using rejected historic behavior by a given rule base and allowed behavior which never occurred in real-life process cases.

In future work, we plan to extend the methodology presented here so that declarative models can also be enhanced on the basis of information other than control-flow constructs (i.e. "presence", "absence" and "precedence" information in the event history of process instances), so that the full flexibility of declarative process models can be leveraged. For example, by taking organizational and case data into account, more granular and refined business rules can be derived, revealing knowledge about the way people work together or how processes develop according to their specifics. Finally, our proposed methodology can also be developed into a complete recommendation engine, by ranking discovered rules according to their classification rate and how strongly they improve the model in accordance with real-life behavior.

Acknowledgment. We would like to thank the KU Leuven research council for financial support under grand OT/10/010 and the Flemish Research Council for financial support under Odysseus grant B.0915.09.

References

1. van der Aalst, W., Reijers, H., Weijters, A., van Dongen, B., Alves de Medeiros, A., Song, M., Verbeek, H.: Business process mining: an industrial application. Inf. Syst. **32**(5), 713–732 (2007)
2. Tan, P.N., Steinbach, M., Kumar, V.: Introduction to Data Mining. Addison-Wesley, Boston (2005)
3. vom Brocke, J., Rosemann, M.: Handbook on Business Process Management: Strategic Alignment, Governance, People and Culture. Springer, Heidelberg (2010)
4. Rozinat, A., van der Aalst, W.M.P.: Conformance testing: measuring the fit and appropriateness of event logs and process models. In: Bussler, C.J., Haller, A. (eds.) BPM 2005. LNCS, vol. 3812, pp. 163–176. Springer, Heidelberg (2006)

5. Rozinat, A., van der Aalst, W.: Conformance checking of processes based on monitoring real behavior. Inf. Syst. **33**(1), 64–95 (2008)
6. Chesani, F., Lamma, E., Mello, P., Montali, M., Riguzzi, F., Storari, S.: Exploiting inductive logic programming techniques for declarative process mining. In: Jensen, K., van der Aalst, W.M.P. (eds.) Transactions on Petri Nets and Other Models of Concurrency II. LNCS, vol. 5460, pp. 278–295. Springer, Heidelberg (2009)
7. vanden Broucke, S.K.L.M., De Weerdt, J., Baesens, B., Vanthienen, J.: Improved artificial negative event generation to enhance process event logs. In: Ralyté, J., Franch, X., Brinkkemper, S., Wrycza, S. (eds.) CAiSE 2012. LNCS, vol. 7328, pp. 254–269. Springer, Heidelberg (2012)
8. Goedertier, S., Martens, D., Vanthienen, J., Baesens, B.: Robust process discovery with artificial negative events. J. Mach. Learn. Res. **10**, 1305–1340 (2009)
9. Pesic, M., Schonenberg, H., van der Aalst, W.: Declare: full support for loosely-structured processes. In: 11th IEEE International Enterprise Distributed Object Computing Conference, 2007, EDOC 2007, pp. 287–287. IEEE (2007)
10. Alberti, M., Chesani, F., Gavanelli, M., Lamma, E., Mello, P., Torroni, P.: Verifiable agent interaction in abductive logic programming: the SCIFF framework. ACM Trans. Comput. Logic **9**(4), 1–43 (2008)
11. Chesani, F., Mello, P., Montali, M., Storari, S.: Towards a decserflow declarative semantics based on computational logic. Technical report (2007)
12. Clarke, E., Grumberg, O., Peled, D.: Model Checking. The MIT Press, Cambridge (1999)
13. Pesic, M., van der Aalst, W.M.P.: A declarative approach for flexible business processes management. In: Eder, J., Dustdar, S. (eds.) BPM Workshops 2006. LNCS, vol. 4103, pp. 169–180. Springer, Heidelberg (2006)
14. van der Aalst, W., De Beer, H., Van Dongen, B.: Process mining and verification of properties: an approach based on temporal logic. Inf. Syst. J. **3760**, 130–147 (2005)
15. Cohen, W.: Fast effective rule induction. In: Proceedings of the Twelfth International Conference on Machine Learning, ICML95 (1995)
16. Maruster, L., Weijters, A., van der Aalst, W., van den Bosch, A.: A rule-based approach for process discovery: dealing with noise and imbalance in process logs. Data Min. Knowl. Disc. **13**(1), 67–87 (2006)

Constructing Decision Trees from Process Logs for Performer Recommendation

Aekyung Kim, Josue Obregon, and Jae-Yoon Jung[⊠]

Department of Industrial and Management Systems Engineering,
Kyung Hee University, 1 Seochen-dong, Giheung-gu, Yongin, Gyeonggi,
Republic of Korea
{akiml007,jobregon,jyjung}@khu.ac.kr

Abstract. This paper demonstrates that the discovery technique using historical event logs can be extended to predict business performance and recommend performers for running instances. For the prediction and recommendation, we adopt decision trees, which is a decision support tool in management science. Decision trees are commonly used to help identify the most likely alternative to reach a goal. To provide effective performer recommendation, we use several filters with previous performers and key tasks to the decision tree. These filters allow for a suitable recommendation according to the characteristics of the processes. The proposed approach is implemented on ProM framework and it is then evaluated through an experiment using real-life event logs, taken from a Dutch Financial Institute. The main contribution of this paper is to provide a real-time decision support tool by recommendation of the best performer for a target performance indicator during process execution based on historical data.

Keywords: Process mining · Performer recommendation · Decision tree

1 Introduction

Process mining is the business analytical method that allows for the analysis of business processes based on event logs [1, 2]. The basic idea is to extract knowledge from event logs recorded by information systems to improve business performance [3]. Most process mining techniques work on "post mortem" event data in that they analyze events that belong to completed cases. However, huge data are being generated in executing business processes and they need to be analyzed in (near) real-time [4, 5]. Therefore, process mining should be extended to online operational support to include real-time decision support [6].

In this paper we introduce decision trees to process mining in order to deal with the recommendation of performers. Among decision support tools, decision trees have two advantages which can be applied to performer assignment. First, decision trees simplify decision making problems by evaluating performances of competing alternatives and pruning inferior alternatives from leaf nodes. Second, decision trees have two types of nodes, chance nodes and decision nodes, which are appropriate to represent scheduled tasks in a process model and possible performers based on historical

N. Lohmann et al. (Eds.): BPM 2013 Workshops, LNBIP 171, pp. 224–236, 2014.
DOI: 10.1007/978-3-319-06257-0_18, © Springer International Publishing Switzerland 2014

data, respectively. Furthermore, decision trees can reflect control-flow patterns such as sequence, AND-split, XOR-split and loop. We also define three filters which allow for a suitable recommendation depending on the characteristics of processes in the decision trees: *non-filter*, *k-recent performer filter* and *key-task performer filter*. Moreover, key performances of performers are predicted and the predicted performance values (e.g., the predicted remaining flow time or total labor cost according to performers) are projected onto the decision trees. The decision tree is then pruned with a running case and filter. Finally, best performers are recommended to minimize completion time or total labor cost.

The approach presented in this paper is implemented in the open-source process mining framework ProM and it is evaluated through an experiment using a real-life event log, taken from a Dutch Financial Institute. The proposed approach is also expected to be applied to manage business processes or projects in which performer assignment has a critical effect on business performance (e.g., software development project, troubleshooting process, and product repair process) [7]. The recommendation technique for performers presented in this paper can also be easily extended for business roles (e.g. skill levels of software engineers) and organizations (e.g. competitive teams).

2 Related Work

Process mining is a process management technique that allows for the analysis of business processes based on logs. van der Aalst categorized three types of process mining such as discovery, conformance and enhancement [3]. The last type is also regarded as operational support. He also suggests three ways of process mining to provide operational support: detect, predict and recommend. For the second type of operational support, van der Aalst et al. demonstrated that the discovered process models could be extended with information to predict the completion time of running instances [8]. For the third type of operational support, Schonenberg et al. proposed a recommendation service that could be used in combination with flexible process-aware information systems to support end users during process execution by giving recommendations on possible next steps [9].

There is also related work on job dispatching and task assigning to support decision making in business process management. Ha et al. devised process execution rules using individual worklists and proposed task assignment algorithms to maximize the overall process efficiency under the limitation of the agent's capacity [10].

The proposed approach in this paper differs from existing approaches. First of all, we predict performance indicators based on historical data. Second, we introduce a graph-based decision support tool (i.e. decision tree) to predict key performances by analyzing historical data. Finally, compared to existing process mining algorithms, the proposed approach can be applied to real-time decision support (i.e. filtered decision tree) to recommend the best performer to optimize the chosen performance indicator such as cost and time based on historical data.

3 Performer Recommendation Using Process Mining

This section describes the overall procedure of the proposed technique as shown in Fig. 1. There are information systems supporting and executing real operational processes. Events which occur in operational business processes are used to discover a process model. For process discovery, many process discovery algorithms have been proposed so far by many researchers. In our approach a decision tree is constructed from the given event log. Based on the historical data, performances are then predicted and annotated with information about times and costs (e.g., the average time and cost spent in a particular task) on the decision tree. Subsequently, the decision tree is matched with a running case and filtered according to process characteristics. Finally, the decision tree allows us to evaluate performances and recommend the best performer for the next possible tasks in terms of time and cost (e.g., the best performer in terms of completion time, or the best performer in terms of total cost).

4 Decision Tree Construction for Performance Prediction

In this section, we describe how to construct a decision tree for performance prediction based on an event log. To apply decision trees to the problem, tasks and performers are considered as environmental factors and decision factors, respectively. Therefore, in decision trees, tasks are represented by decision nodes which are depicted by squares while performers are represented by chance nodes which are depicted by circles. Then the information of predicted performances such as processing time and labor cost is annotated on the decision tree.

To explain how to predict performances, we first define the concept of a performer-oriented event log, a performer-oriented activity log and their annotation. Then we explain how to construct a decision tree from historical process data.

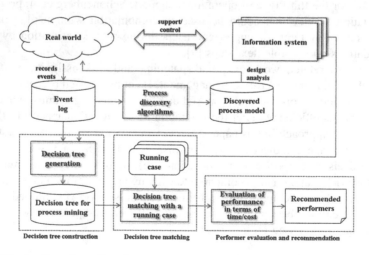

Fig. 1. Overview of performance recommendation based on historical data.

4.1   Historical Process Model

We first define the concept of a historical process data. To be able to reason about event logs and precisely specify the requirements for the logs, many researchers proposed their formal models of process mining. In this research, we adopt and extend the formal models presented by van der Aalst [3]. The performer-oriented event log in Definition 1 is described to define the performer-oriented event and case [11].

Definition 1 (Performer-oriented event log). Let $\mathscr{C}$ and $\mathscr{N}$ be the sets of all possible case identifiers and activity names, respectively. For any case $c \in \mathscr{C}$ and name $n \in \mathscr{N}$, $\#_n(c)$ is the value of attribute n for case c. Each case has a special mandatory attribute trace: $\#_{trace}(c) \in \mathscr{E}^*$ where $\mathscr{E}^*$ is the set of all finite sequences over the set of all possible event identifiers. $\hat{c} = \#_{trace}(c)$ is a shorthand for referring to the trace of a case. A *performer-oriented event $\underline{e}$* is an event which is characterized by a performer. A *performer-oriented trace* of case $\underline{\hat{c}}$ is a trace of a *performer-oriented event $\underline{e}$*, and a *performer-oriented event log $\underline{L} \subseteq \mathscr{C}$* is a bag of performer-oriented cases.

Performer-oriented events are identified by their activity names, performers, time and transactions, i.e., *performer-oriented event* $\underline{e} = (\#_{activity}(e), \#_{performer}(e), \#_{time}(e), \#_{trans}(e))$. Also, a *performer-oriented case* $\underline{\hat{c}} = <\underline{e_1}, \underline{e_2}, ... \underline{e_n}>$ and a *performer-oriented event log* $\underline{L} = [\underline{\hat{c}}]$. In this paper, we apply two following operators for considering processing time and labor cost: Given an activity identifier $a = \#activity(e)$, *operator1* is "$\#processingtime(a) = \#completetime(a) - \#starttime(a)$" and *operator2* is "$\#labor\_cost(a) = \#performer(a).unitcost \times \#processingime(a)$". Here $\#performer(a).unitcost$ means labor cost per an hour of $\#performer(a)$.

Definition 2 (Performer-oriented activity log). Let $\underline{L} \subseteq \mathscr{C}$ be a bag of *performer-oriented cases* as defined in Definition 1. If two operators are applied to a *performer-oriented event $\underline{e}$*, then a *performer-oriented activity model* (annotated with processing time and labor cost) $\underline{a} = (\#_{name}(a), \#_{performer}(a), \#_{processingtime}(a), \#_{laborcost}(a))$ and a *performer-oriented activity trace $\hat{m}_c = <\underline{a_1}, \underline{a_2}, \underline{a_3}, ...>$* i.e., sequence of $\underline{a}$, are obtained. Therefore a *performer-oriented activity log $\underline{M} = [\hat{m}_c]$*, i.e., a bag of *performer-oriented activity traces $\hat{m}_c$*, is defined.

4.2   Construction of Decision Tree

In this section we explain the procedure of creating a decision tree for performance prediction based on historical data. First we define formally the concept of performer-oriented decision tree.

Definition 3 (Performer-oriented decision tree). A *performer-oriented decision tree* is a tuple pDt $= (T, t_0, P, F, E)$ where T is the set of *task nodes*, $t_0 \in T$ is the *root node* of the *decision tree*, P is the set of *performer nodes*, F is the set of *final nodes* and $E \subseteq (T \times P) \cup (P \times T) \cup (P \times F)$ is the set of directed arcs that determines the flow direction of the tree. We assume that nodes are characterized for some attributes, e.g., *task nodes* have a label attribute and *performer nodes* have a label attribute and a processing time attribute. For any $t \in T$ and $p \in P$, $\#_n(t)$ or $\#_n(p)$ represent the value of attribute n for the node t or p. For example $\#_{label}(node)$ refers to the value of the attribute label of *node*.

Now let us define the procedure for constructing a *performer-oriented decision tree* pDt based on historical process data. Having a *performer-oriented activity log* $\underline{M}$ we define the steps for creating the decision tree as follows:

1. Create an empty *performer-oriented decision tree* pDt and a node called *current node* that will point to the current *task node* traversed on pDt.
2. Start traversing every $\hat{m}_c \in \underline{M}$ and every $\underline{a} \in \hat{m}_c$.
3. If t_0 is empty, it means that is the first activity read from the activity log therefore a new node is created and added as root of the decision tree i.e., t_0 of pDt. The creation of new nodes is as follows:

    a. Create a new task node *tnode* assigning $\#_{label}(tnode) = \#_{name}(a)$.
    b. Create a new performer node *pnode* assigning $\#_{label}(pnode) = \#_{performer}(a)$ and $\#_{processingtime}(pnode) = \#_{processingtime}(a)$.
    c. Assign *pnode* as child of *tnode*.
    d. Assign *tnode* as *current node*.
4. If t_0 is not empty, it means the tree is being traversed.

    a. Define a task node n that can take two possible values: the value of *current node* or the value of any task node connected to *current node* by means of its performer child node such that $\#_{label}(current\ node\text{-}child) = \#_{performer}(a)$. After that, three possible cases could occur

        i.   Node n such that $\#_{label}(n) = \#_{name}(a)$ does not exist. In this case the steps for new node creation are repeated (i.e., 3a, 3b, 3c and 3d) and the new node is added to pDt.
        ii. Node n such that $\#_{label}(n) = \#_{name}(a)$ already exists, but the node n does not have a child *nchild* that satisfy $\#_{label}(nchild) = \#_{performer}(a)$. In this case a new performer node is created assigning $\#_{label}(pnode) = \#_{performer}(a)$ and $\#_{processingtime}\ (pnode) = \#_{processingtime}(a)$. Then the new performer node is added as a child of the node n.
        iii. Node n such that $\#_{label}(n) = \#_{name}(a)$ already exists, and node n has a child *nchild* that satisfy $\#_{label}(nchild) = \#_{performer}(a)$. In this case add a new processing time to the bag of processing times $\mathbb{B}(pt)$ of *nchild* such as $\#_{processingtime}(nchild) = \#_{processingtime}(a)$.

After completing the steps given before, we have each performer node on the decision tree annotated with a bag of processing times $\mathbb{B}(pt)$. Thus each processing time $pt \in \mathbb{B}(pt)$ represents a specific case in which the performer appears into the *performer-oriented activity log $\underline{M}$*.

The next step is to calculate expected values of KPI, such as predicted processing time of individual performers, represented as *performer nodes* on the constructed *performer-oriented decision tree*. In this paper we combine the approach used in [8] with our approach as follows. First we have to convert the bag of processing times $\mathbb{B}(pt)$ into a single value. For this we use the same prediction function used in [8], in which the authors state that the bag of a chance node should be seen as a sample of

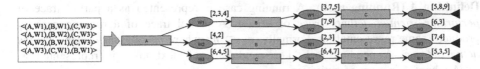

Fig. 2. A simple annotated decision tree with each chance node, representing a performer, annotated with processing times.

times. Based on this, the sample mean (i.e., $\overline{pt} = \sum_{i=1}^{n} pt_i/n$) is a good estimator of the population mean of processing times. Moreover, predicted processing times could be calculated independent or dependent on previous performers.

Let us define first how to calculate predicted processing time independently. If processing time is assumed to be independent on previous performers, the predicted processing time of the pending task by a particular performer is given by the average of the processing times contained in the union of bags $\mathbb{B}(pt)$ belonging to all the cases corresponding to the same performer, that have the same previous partial trace σ without taking in consideration the performer who executed each previous activity in σ. For example, in Fig. 2, if we want to calculate predicted processing time assuming independent of previous performers of $W1$ in task B in the first path of the decision tree, we have to take in consideration traces σ_1 <(A,W1) (B,W1) (C,W3)> and σ_3 <(A,W2) (B,W1) (C,W3)>. The bag of the first trace is $\mathbb{B}(\sigma_1) = [3, 5, 7]$ and the bag of the second trace is $\mathbb{B}(\sigma_3) = [2, 3]$. As we defined before, the predicted processing time of $W1$ on task B, assuming independent of previous performers, is calculated with the average of the union of bags of σ_1 and σ_3 ($\mathbb{B}(\sigma_1) \cup \mathbb{B}(\sigma_3) = [3, 7, 5, 2, 3]$). Therefore the predicted processing time of $W1$ in task B is 4 units of time. It is important to remark that the last trace of Fig. 2, σ_4 <(A,W1) (C,W1) (B,W1)> is not taken in consideration in the calculation of predicted processing time assuming independency of previous performers, although σ_4 has a performer $W1$ executing task B, the previous partial trace is not the same than σ_1 and σ_3.

Now we define how to calculate predicted processing time dependently. If processing time is assumed to be dependent on previous performers, the predicted processing time of the pending task by a particular performer is given by the average of the annotated processing times bag $\mathbb{B}(pt)$, belonging to the cases corresponding to the same performer, that have exactly the same previous partial trace σ, i.e. the task and the performer who executed each previous activity in σ should be the same.

5   Decision Tree Matching with Running Case

5.1   Running Process Case

We first present a model for running cases that can be monitored in process-aware information systems. During process execution, a partial trace can be captured through a running process. To represent the partial trace, the information of the running case is defined as a partial trace of a *performer-oriented activity trace* of case.

Definition 4 (Running case). A running case is represented as a partial trace of *performer-oriented activity trace* of a case. A partial trace of a running case σ_p produces some representation. Formally, $\sigma_p \subseteq \hat{m}_c$ where $\hat{m}_c$ is a *performer-oriented activity trace*. A pending task, i.e., candidates of next task, is represented as $t \in A$ where A is a set of activities.

5.2   Decision Tree Matching

We now explain how to match a constructed decision tree with a running case. The procedure of matching a decision tree with running cases is composed of three steps.

The first step is to select a filter and extract the subtrees from pDt according to the characteristics of the filter selected. Business processes include many tasks that do not affect the performance of performers because the tasks are not related between them. For this reason, we propose three kinds of filters that help to enhance the effectiveness of performance prediction. The filtering seeks to include only the tasks that have a considerable effect on predicting the value of KPI.

We propose three kinds of filters: *non-filter, k-recent performer filter* and *key-task performer filter*. The *non-filter* does not apply any special filtering over a decision tree and it considers all cases that have exactly the same partial trace σ than the running case. If the *non-filter* is selected, only a single subtree is extracted from the constructed decision tree. The *k-recent performer filter* filters a decision tree with k-recent performers. The filter considers that k-recent performers of a task affect the performance of the performer for a pending task. If the *k-recent performer filter* is selected, one or more subtrees are extracted from the constructed decision tree. The *key-task performer filter* filters a decision tree with the performers of the key tasks. It considers that the performers of important tasks affect the performance of the performer on a pending task. The extracted subtrees are merged into a single subtree. If one assumes independence on previous performers, the values of predicted processing time do not need to be updated, whereas if one assumes dependence on previous performers, the values of predicted processing time need to be recalculated and updated combining the bags of processing times $\mathbb{B}(pt)$ of the nodes merged corresponding to the same task and/or same performer depending on the filter selected.

Finally, we can evaluate and recommend performers using the performer-oriented decision tree. The procedure for recommendation of the best performer for a given a running case has two steps:

1. *Evaluate performer,* in this step performers are evaluated based on the predicted processing times calculated in previous steps. The filtered performer-oriented decision tree is traversed backwards. Starting from *final nodes*, a new attribute called *total remaining time* is calculated and added to the node being traversed. The attribute *total remaining time* is equal to the summation of the current node traversed *processing time* attribute value plus the minimum *total remaining time* attribute among its children nodes. From here it depends on which value of KPI we want to apply. If the KPI value concerns only on remaining time, we use the attribute *total remaining time* for evaluation. However, if the KPI value concerns about cost, the evaluation is based on the attribute *labor cost* defined in previous sections.

2. *Recommend the best performer*, the performer of the pending task who has the highest predicted value of performance indicator in the evaluation step is then recommended.

6   Implementation and Experiment

The technique presented in this paper was implemented as a plug-in for the ProM Framework. The ProM framework integrates the functionality of several existing process mining tools and provides additional process mining plug-ins [12, 13].

In this paper we implement the plug-in called *DTMiner* which takes an event log as an input. The plug-in constructs a *performer-oriented decision tree* based on an event log using the algorithm defined in previous sections. As an initial result, a *performer-oriented decision tree* is displayed on the screen as shown in Fig. 5. *Task nodes* are filled with blue color and *performer nodes* with green color. Node information such as processing time is displayed when the mouse pointer hovers on the node. The edge connection between task and performer nodes displays the predicted processing time taken by the performer to reach the next task.

The analysis section of the plug-in is displayed at the bottom of the screen as shown in Fig. 5. The completed activities of target running cases can be edited (i.e., added or removed) from here. Moreover different filter actions can be executed over the decision tree constructed as described in previous sections (e.g., *non-filter filter* or *k-recent performer filter*). Finally recommendation is provided to the user showing the recommended paths by means of filling nodes and coloring edges with color red as shown in Fig. 5. The predicted total remaining time (i.e. the predicted remaining time needed to finish the case) for each decision and chance node is calculated and showed when the mouse pointer hovers on the nodes.

We demonstrate the applicability of our approach using a real-life event log using *DTMiner* plug-in. For the experiment we used the real-life event log of a Dutch Financial Institute which was prepared by Business Process Intelligence Challenge (BPIC'12). We first explain the log and describe how to preprocess the log for experiment. Our approach is then validated and tested using the log.

6.1   Process Discovery from Event Log

As mentioned on the website[1] of BPIC, this log contains 13,087 cases and 262,200 events over a six month period from October 2011 to March 2012. The process represented in the event log is an application process for a personal loan or overdraft within a global financing organization.

To provide some insight into the structure of the process, we have used Disco which draws process models using the improved fuzzy algorithm. It also shows

---

[1] See http://www.win.tue.nl/bpi2012/doku.php?id=challenge

meaningful information such as variants, frequency, and duration and provides powerful filtering features. We found that the whole process could be split into three sub-processes by end events (i.e. *A_DECLINED, A_CANCELLED, A_ACTIVATED*). In the next subsection, we experiment using the three groups split from whole cases. The group that ends with *A_DECLINED* has 7,635 cases. The *A_CANCELLED* group has 2,807 cases and the *A_ACTIVATED* group has 2,246 cases.

Before testing our approach the log needs to be preprocessed, e.g., event and cases may be removed for various reasons. There are some events in the log where the resource information is missing. We first removed all the cases that have at least one event with NULL resource information because they cannot be used for the performer recommendation method. Also, we removed all cases which have at least one event with performers who have lower than 5 % of relative frequency. Second, we used only cases whose sequence of activities is shared by at least 10 cases using variation filtering functionality of Disco. Moreover, we consolidated all the resources performed in automatic activities which have zero duration into a resource called 'Automatic'. Finally, we split the filtered log into three sub-processes. As a result the group that ends with *A_DECLINED* has 5280 cases. The *A_CANCELLED* group has 1024 cases and *A_ACTIVATED* group has 534 cases after filtering. Figure 3 shows the process models of each group discovered by Disco.

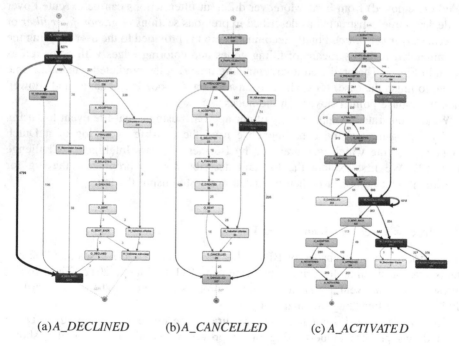

(a)*A_DECLINED*   (b)*A_CANCELLED*   (c) *A_ACTIVATED*

Fig. 3. The sub-process models discovered from Dutch Financial Institute's log

6.2   Performance Recommendation

In this subsection, we present an example scenario with the log of Dutch Financial Institute to describe how the proposed approach can be applied to performer's allocation problem with our plug-in for ProM. Using the plug-in with the example scenario, the historical process log of a business process was analyzed to construct the decision tree, which was used to recommend the best performers for an ongoing instance of the process.

To improve the quality of the customer loan service, the Dutch Financial Institute would want to reduce the lead time of their services. At the same time, they would want to decrease the cost of their processes. For this reason, the purpose of this experiment is to recommend the best performer who allows the remaining time and the total labor cost to be reduced for each possible next task.

As depicted in Fig. 1 the overall procedure of the proposed approach consists of three primary steps. Following these steps, we first constructed decision trees from the log using our *DTMiner* plug-in. In this step, we used three sub-logs and constructed decision trees separately. Figure 4 shows the decision trees constructed from the sub-process that ends with '*A_DECLINED*' and the annotated time is calculated by option of 'dependence'.

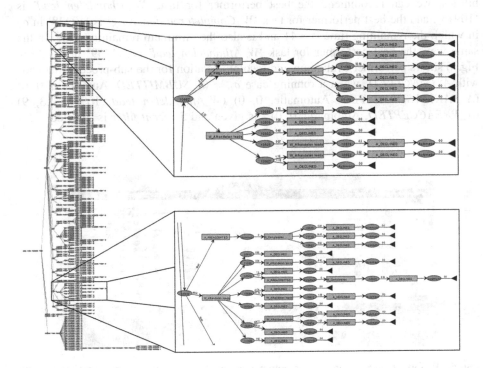

Fig. 4. The constructed decision tree from the sub-process that ends with '*A_DECLINED*'

In the second step, we considered that one running case $\sigma_p = (A\_SUBMITTED$, Automatic, 0, 0) $(A\_PARTLYSUBMITTED$, Automatic, 0, 0) $(W\_Afhandelen\ lead$, 11259, 3.8, 8)> was captured by information system. Also, we assumed that a manager did not want to filter with previous performers, and he wanted to obtain the recommended performers who can reduce the remaining time. Then, we set up the running case and filter options as shown in the bottom of Fig. 5.

In the last step, information about the running case was matched with the decision trees and its subtrees were extracted and merged. Also, the predicted KPIs were updated. Finally, we evaluated performance and recommended the best performer for each next possible task by means of reducing inferior performers from leaf nodes. Figure 5 shows the pruned decision tree and the best performer of each task in subprocess that ends with '$A\_DECLINED$'.

After executing the running case, the pruned decision tree showed two possible traces with different excution probabilities as shown in Fig. 5. The first trace $\sigma_1 = <A\_SUBMITTED$, $A\_PARTLYSUBMITTED$, $W\_Afhandelen\ lead$, $W\_Afhandelen\ lead$, $A\_PREACCEPTED$, $W\_Completeren\ aanvraag$, $A\_DECLINED$> had an execution probability of 40 % and the second trace $\sigma_2 = <A\_SUBMITTED$, $A\_PARTLYSUBMITTED$, $W\_Afhandelen\ lead$, $W\_Afhandelen\ lead$, $W\_Afhandelen\ lead$, $A\_DECLINED$> had an execution probability of 60 %. Based on this probabilities, we can recommend the best performer for task '$W\_Afhandelen\ lead$' is '10913', and the best performer for task '$W\_Completeren\ aanvraag$' is '10228' in σ_1 in which the remaining time is 3.41 and is also the minimum remaining time. In the same way, the best performer for task '$W\_Afhandelen\ lead$' is '11259' in σ_2. Also, Fig. 6 shows performer evaluation and recommendation for the sub-process that ends with '$A\_CANCLLED$' when a running case $\sigma_p = (A\_SUBMITTED$, Automatic, 0, 0) $(A\_PARTLYSUBMITTED$, Automatic, 0, 0) $(W\_Afhandelen\ lead$, 10982, 2.3, 9) $(A\_PREACCEPTED$, Automatic, 0, 0)> is given and *3-recent filter* is selected.

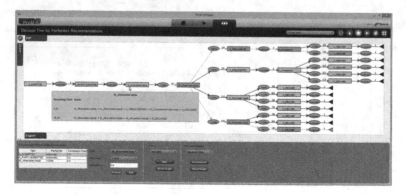

Fig. 5. Performer evaluation and recommendation for the sub-process that ends with '$A\_DECLINED$'

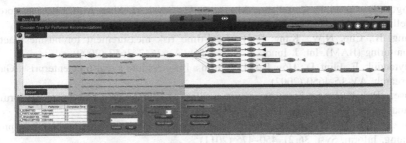

Fig. 6. Performer evaluation and recommendation for the sub-process that ends with '*A_CANCELLED*'

7 Conclusion

In this paper, we presented a new approach that constructs decision trees based on process event log for performer recommendation. Given a running case, our approach to performer recommendation allows answering questions such as "Who is the best performer to minimize remaining time until completion?" and "Who is the best performer to save additional labor costs?" Those questions are dependent on various aspects, e.g., orders or frequencies of performers. The solutions to the best performers are discovered by considering the predicted values of KPI based on historical data. To solve the problem, decision trees are constructed based on historical process events to support simple decision making for performance recommendation.

One of the main contributions of this paper lies in a real-time decision support technique for ongoing processes. Although existing decision support methods evaluate alternatives in run-time, the proposed technique can recommend an alternative of performers for every task in a running case during process execution based on the probabilistic data of historical events.

Acknowledgments. This work was supported by the National Research Foundation of Korea (NRF) grant funded by the Korea government (MSIP) (Nos. 2012R1A1B4003505 and 2013R1A2A2A03014718).

References

1. van der Aalst, W.M.P., Reijers, H.A., Weijters, A.J.M.M., van Dongen, B.F., de Medeiros, A.K.A., Song, M., Verbeek, H.M.W.: Business process mining: an industrial application. Inform. Syst. **32**(5), 713–732 (2007)
2. de Medeiros, A.K.A., Pedrinaci, C., van der Aalst, W.M., Domingue, J., Song, M., Rozinat, A., Norton, B., Cabral, L.: An outlook on semantic business process mining and monitoring. In: Meersman, R., Tari, Z. (eds.) OTM-WS 2007, Part II. LNCS, vol. 4806, pp. 1244–1255. Springer, Heidelberg (2007)
3. van der Aalst, W.M.P.: Process Mining: Discovery, Conformance and Enhancement of Business Processes. Springer, Heidelberg (2011)

4. Grigori, D., Casati, F., Castellanos, M., Dayal, U., Sayal, M., Shan, M.-C.: Business process intelligence. Comput. Ind. **53**(3), 321–343 (2004)
5. Kang, B., Cho, N.W., Kang, S.-H.: Real-time risk measurement for business activity monitoring (BAM). Int. J. Innov. Comp. I. **5**(11A), 3647–3657 (2009)
6. Buytendijk, F., Flint, D.: How BAM can turn a business into a real-time enterprise. Gartner Research, AV-15-4650 (2002)
7. Bose, R.: Understanding management data systems for enterprise performance management. Ind. Manage. Data Syst. **106**(1), 43–59 (2006)
8. van der Aalst, W.M.P., Schonenberg, M.H., Song, M.: Time prediction based on process mining. Inform. Syst. **36**(2), 450–475 (2011)
9. Schonenberg, H., Weber, B., van Dongen, B.F., van der Aalst, W.M.: Supporting flexible processes through recommendations based on history. In: Dumas, M., Reichert, M., Shan, M.-C. (eds.) BPM 2008. LNCS, vol. 5240, pp. 51–66. Springer, Heidelberg (2008)
10. Ha, B.-H., Bae, J., Park, Y.T., Kang, S.-H.: Development of process execution rules for workload balancing on agents. Data Knowl. Eng. **56**(1), 64–84 (2006)
11. Kim, A., Jung, J.-Y.: A process mining technique for performer recommendation using decision tree. In: Korean Institute of Industrial Engineers Conference (2012)
12. van Dongen, B.F., de Medeiros, A.K.A., Verbeek, H., Weijters, A., van der Aalst, W.M.: The ProM framework: a new era in process mining tool support. In: Ciardo, G., Darondeau, P. (eds.) ICATPN 2005. LNCS, vol. 3536, pp. 444–454. Springer, Heidelberg (2005)
13. Verbeek, H.M.W., Buijs, J.C.A.M., van Dongen, B.F., van der Aalst, W.M.P.: ProM 6: the process mining toolkit. BPM Demonstration Track **615**, 34–39 (2010)

An Exploratory Approach for Understanding Customer Behavior Processes Based on Clustering and Sequence Mining

Alex Seret[1]([⊠]), Seppe K.L.M. vanden Broucke[1], Bart Baesens[1,2],
and Jan Vanthienen[1]

[1] Department of Decision Sciences and Information Management, KU Leuven,
Naamsestraat 69, 3000 Leuven, Belgium
[2] School of Management, University of Southampton, Highfield,
Southampton SO17 1BJ, UK
`alex.seret@kuleuven.be`

Abstract. In this paper, a novel approach towards enabling the exploratory understanding of the dynamics inherent in the capture of customers' data at different points in time is outlined. The proposed methodology combines state-of-art data mining clustering techniques with a tuned sequence mining method to discover prominent customer behavior trajectories in data bases, which – when combined – represent the "behavior process" as it is followed by particular groups of customers. The framework is applied to a real-life case of an event organizer; it is shown how behavior trajectories can help to explain consumer decisions and to improve business processes that are influenced by customer actions.

Keywords: Clustering · Sequence mining · Business knowledge · Behavior process · Trajectories · Direct marketing

1 Introduction

Various data mining techniques have been proven to be a valuable approach in the quest for knowledge discovery in data from an exploratory point of view. Clustering techniques, for instance, combined with strong visualization techniques, allow analysts to get fast insights into the data they are confronted with. For these reasons, techniques such as k-means clustering and Self-Organizing Maps (SOM) have been widely and successfully applied in practice and extensively discussed in the literature [1].

When executed at one specific moment in time, however – as it often happens, the aforementioned techniques offer a static picture describing the composition of the data set at hand based on certain patterns derived from the attributes describing the instances in this data set. It would, however, be of great interest for the analyst to be able to understand the dynamics associated with the items

N. Lohmann et al. (Eds.): BPM 2013 Workshops, LNBIP 171, pp. 237–248, 2014.
DOI: 10.1007/978-3-319-06257-0_19, © Springer International Publishing Switzerland 2014

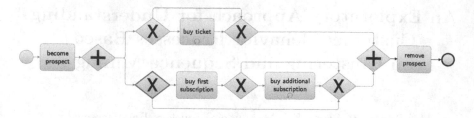

Fig. 1. High level process model of the customers decisions in a ticketing context.

represented in the data base, hence recording a "movie" of the data set instead of static pictures at specific points in time. In this paper, an approach enabling the exploratory understanding of the dynamics inherent in the capture of customers' data at different points in time is proposed. Broadly summarized, our novel approach is based on a two-step clustering approach, incorporating both self-organizing maps and sequence mining techniques. The proposed methodology combines these two methods to discover prominent customer behavior trajectories in data bases, which together help analysts to understand the behavior process as it is followed by particular groups of customers.

In this paper, a real-life ticketing context will be considered in order to illustrate the proposed methodology. The high level process model describing the evolution of the customers in such context is depicted in Fig. 1 and detailed as follows. A person first becomes a prospect of an event organizer and will be approached (using marketing campaigns) until a first purchase is registered. This purchase can consist of a normal ticket or a subscription. Continuing his relation with the organizer, incentives will be used in order to promote the subscription to different product categories. The process ends when the prospect is removed from the data base and not approached anymore. In general, from a marketing point of view, customers with a subscription (subscribers) are associated with the customers with the highest value for the company, as confirmed by the marketing manager of the organizer providing the data used in this paper. The goal of the organizer is thus not only to keep customers as subscribers as long as possible in order to maximize the total value of their customer base, but also to uncover the dynamics driving the decision behavior of customers opting to subscribe for the first time. Understanding consumer behavior as it dynamically changes through time is put forward as the topic of interest for this paper. We will hence zoom in to the shaded decision point as shown in Fig. 1, i.e. we aim to uncover what drives customers to "buy first subscription", as opposed to customers which do not do so. Contrary to related work as proposed in literature [2], this approach will be data driven using transactional data provided by an event organizer active in the Netherlands, meaning that no full event log data is required to utilize the outlined methodology. In addition, state-of-art clustering techniques are applied, allowing for the identification of different customer groups (based on the behavior patterns discovered in the data) behind the same decision outcome (e.g. opting for a subscription).

The remainder of the paper is structured as follows, in Sect. 2, the different techniques and approaches used in the remainder of the paper are introduced from a theoretical perspective. In Sect. 3, an application using real-life data from the concert industry is proposed and illustrates how the different concepts and techniques can be combined in order to answer an advanced business question. Section 4 concludes the paper.

2 Theoretical Approach

In this section, the different techniques supporting our novel dynamic clustering approach are discussed. References to related work are also described in this section. For the purpose of the application, a two-step clustering approach is considered, leading to clusters that will be used further on to generate trajectories summarized using a sequence mining approach.

2.1 Self-Organizing Maps

Self-organizing maps were introduced in 1981 by Kohonen; fields like data exploratory analysis, web usage mining [3], industrial and medical diagnostics [4], and corruption analysis [5] are contemporary examples of SOM analysis applications and successes. This section is based on [6] and aims at giving a theoretical background to the reader.

The two main objectives of the SOM algorithm are vector quantization and vector projection. Vector quantization aims at summarizing the data by dividing a large set of data points into groups having approximately the same number op points closest to them. The groups are then represented by their centroid points which typically are vectors obtained as the mean of the points of the respective groups (e.g. the k-means algorithm introduced in Sect. 2.4). A typical way to assess the quality of the resulting quantization is to calculate the mean quantization error (MQE) [1,7] by averaging all Euclidean distances between the different input vectors and their respective closest neurons. A low MQE value indicates that a good representation of the input by the SOM is achieved. The second objective is vector projection in which the dimensionality of the data points is reduced by projection onto lower dimensional maps (e.g. the PCA [8]). Typically, a projection to two-dimensional maps is performed in order to be able to visualize and represent the different variables on classical reporting supports. The projection is performed with the neurons obtained after the quantization phase. In a case of a good projection onto the two-dimensional maps, neurons close to each other in the high dimensional space should be mapped to position close to each other in the low dimensional space. The combination of vector quantization and projection enables to explore the data and to use techniques like visual correlation analysis or clustering analysis in an intuitive manner while keeping a mapping between the input vectors and the neurons in the low dimensional space. The different steps of the algorithm are briefly discussed in what follows. In the first step, a feed-forward Neural Network (NN) is trained on the input data. The output layer is a map with a lower dimensionality and a given number of neurons. During each iteration of the algorithm, an input data vector n_i, representing all the variables for the observation i, is compared with the neurons m_r of the output layer using Euclidean distances. Note that the quantization objective imposes both the input vectors n_i and neurons m_r to have the same dimensionality. m_r summarizes at the end of the algorithm a set of input vectors n_i. The neuron m_c with the smallest distance with regard to the input vector is identified as the Best Matching Unit (BMU):

$$\|n_i - m_c\| = \min_r\{\|n_i - m_r\|\}. \tag{1}$$

The weights of the BMU are then modified in the direction of the input vector, leading to a self-organizing structure of the neurons. A learning rate $\alpha(t)$ and a neighborhood function $h_{cr}(t)$ are defined as parameters of the learning function:

$$m_r(t + 1) = m_r(t) + \alpha(t)h_{cr}(t)[n_i(t) - m_r(t)]. \tag{2}$$

The learning-rate will influence the magnitude of the BMU's adaptation after matching with an input vector n_i, whereas the neighborhood function defines the range of influence of the adaptation. The obtained neurons are then projected on a two-dimensional map. Each neuron has then a representation in the high and low dimensional spaces. In Sect. 3 for instance, component planes are shown representing the relative values of the different neurons for the different variables on a two-dimensional map, providing the analyst with a powerful visualization facility. An exhaustive discussion of the projection approach and the influence of the parameters such as the number of neurons, the shape of the map, or the initial weights of the neurons is to be found in [6].

2.2 Knowledge-Based Constrained Clustering

In order to incorporate business knowledge in the segmentation exercise, the P-SOM algorithm proposed in [9] will be used in Sect. 3 to contrast the classical SOM algorithm. This algorithm is a modified version of the traditional SOM algorithm providing a mechanism which enables the prioritization of variables by modifying the BMU identification equation, hence guiding the clustering algorithm. To do so, the BMU identification (Eq. 1) of the SOM algorithm is modified, leading to the following equation:

$$\sqrt{\sum_{j=1}^{d} w_{d_j}(n_{id_j} - m_{cd_j})^2} = \min_r\{\sqrt{\sum_{j=1}^{d} w_{d_j}(n_{id_j} - m_{rd_j})^2}\}, \tag{3}$$

where w_{d_j} is a weight assigned to the variable d_j, n_{id_j} is the variable d_j of the training instance n_i, m_{rd_j} is the variable d_j of the neuron m_r and m_c is the BMU of n_i. The higher the value of w_{d_j}, the bigger is the impact of this variable in the resulting clustering as discussed in [9]. In order to fix the weights w_{d_j}, priorities are assigned to the different variables. p_{d_j} represents the priority of the jth dimension. A dimension d_j with $p_{d_j} = 1$ is considered as a dimension with the highest priority and has then a higher priority than a dimension d_o with $p_{d_o} = 2$, etc. A specific case of this approach is proposed in a setup involving only categorized variables represented by dummies, leading to a straightforward method proposed in [9] and applied in Sect. 3. In order to meet the requirements of this specific context, a qualitative variable with t different values should be transformed into t dummy variables. A value of 0 or 1 reflects whether or not the input vector is characterized by the value represented by the dummy variable, so that only one of the t dummy variables can be equal to 1. Concerning the quantitative variables, a categorization is possible using intervals represented by dummy variables as done for qualitative variables. Only one of the dummies obtained by the categorization can be equal to 1 if the intervals are not overlapping. Once this data preparation is performed, define a set $\mathcal{G}$ of g non overlapping groups g_k of dimensions of $\mathcal{D}$ so that there is no dimension of $\mathcal{D}$ not belonging to one group of $\mathcal{G}$ and no dimension of $\mathcal{D}$ belonging to two different groups of $\mathcal{G}$. The function $g(d_j)$ returns the group g_k such that $d_j \in g_k$. The notion of group is introduced in order to capture the fact that only one of the dummies obtained by the categorization of a variable can be equal to 1 if the categories are not overlapping. This information is used in what follows in order to fix the weights assigned to the different variables. An example of such a group could be the different dummies resulting from the categorization of a quantitative variable. For example, consider the initial variable Age, with $[18..25]$, $[26..35]$, $[36..50]$, $[51..65]$, and $[66..]$ the dimensions of the group represented by dummies. In order to complete the definition of a group, which is a real-world subdivision of the dimensions, the same priority should be assigned to all the dimensions of the same group, so that

$$\forall d_j \in g_k, p_{g_k} = p_{d_j}, \tag{4}$$

with g_k representing the kth group of $\mathcal{G}$ and p_{g_k} the priority assigned to it. Completing this context, a set $\mathcal{LP}^{g_k}$ is defined and gathers the groups g_l such that:

$$g_l \in \mathcal{LP}^{g_k}, \forall g_l : p_{g_l} > p_{g_k}. \tag{5}$$

Finally, given this context, the weights w_{d_j} can be obtained using the following equation:

$$w_{d_j} = 1 + \frac{|\mathcal{LP}^{g(d_j)}|}{\alpha}, \tag{6}$$

with $|\mathcal{LP}^{g(d_j)}|$ being the number of groups having a lower priority than the group of the variable d_j. The reader is referred to [9] for an exhaustive discussion of this prioritization strategy.

2.3 Contiguous Sequences Identification

We apply the generalized sequential pattern (GSP) algorithm proposed in [10] to extract customer behavior trajectories. The goal of the algorithm is to find contiguous sequential patterns by analyzing a sequence data set. The algorithm starts with a first pass over the data and will store the number of occurrences of each individual item forming the different sequences and knows at the end of this step which items are frequent using a minimum support. The identified frequent items are forming the frequent sequences of size 1. In a next pass, the algorithm will create candidate frequent sequences by combining the frequent sequences of the previous step, the seed sequences. Each candidate sequence has one more item than a seed sequence and its support is obtained during the pass over the data. The algorithm terminates when there are no frequent sequences at the end of a pass, or when there are no candidate sequences generated. The interested reader is referred to [10] for and exhaustive discussion of the strategies linked to the generation and the counting of the candidates.

2.4 Proposed Methodology

The main objective of the proposed methodology is to provide the analyst with a technique enabling the identification of frequent trajectories followed by items represented in a database and showing an evolution through time. In order to reduce the possible coordinates of the items and ease the description of their movements, a two-step clustering approach is used in order to capture the structure of the data. The first step consists of the application of the P-SOM algorithm, leading to a set a neurons summarizing the structure of the data while introducing some business-knowledge in the exercise. The neurons have the same dimensionality as the input data set and can be considered as prototypes of the items. Using the component planes as shown in Sect. 3, it is possible to visualize the structure of the data and to draw interesting conclusions. As will be seen in Fig. 3, some neurons are sharing the same characteristics and are grouped together on the output map, giving the analyst the possibility to identify areas having some specific properties. Although it is possible to visualize those areas and to make the analysis by only using the P-SOM output, a second k-means clustering step [11] is applied in order to capture substructures and to analyze them. The neurons resulting from the P-SOM algorithm are used as input and grouped using the k-means algorithm into a predefined number of clusters obtained using the Davies-Bouldin index as a measure of cluster quality [12]. The Davies-Bouldin index is calculated as:

$$index = \frac{1}{c} \sum_{i=1}^{c} \max_{i \neq j} \left(\frac{\sigma_i + \sigma_j}{d(c_i, c_j)} \right), \tag{7}$$

where c is the number of clusters, c_y is the centroid of cluster y, σ_y is the average distance of all elements of cluster y and $d(c_i, c_j)$ is the distance between the centroid of cluster i and cluster j. Since a good partitioning corresponds to a situation where the intra-cluster distances are low and the inter-cluster distances are high, the lower the Davies-Bouldin index, the better the partitioning obtained. The number of clusters leading to the best partitioning is thus chosen as a parameter of the k-means. The output of this step is a set of cluster centroids, which are averaged vectors characterizing the different clusters. Cluster characteristics can be initially derived from the weight vectors of the cluster centroids. Each weight vector has a length equal to the number of dimensions in the input space, where each weight corresponds to a specific dimension. For a cluster obtained using binary variables, a weight associated with a dimension portrays the degree to which that cluster is characterized by that dimension. High values are indicators of a high degree of characterization, as opposed to low values which correspond to a low degree of characterization.

Once the clusters are obtained, a mapping between the items and the neurons and between the neurons and the clusters allows the identification of trajectories followed by the items through time, i.e. items moving from cluster to cluster. The coordinates of the sequence of points forming the trajectory of each item can thus be represented by the clusters the item belongs to at different moment in time. Considering the coordinates $x_{n_i}^t$ of an input vector n_i in the original space $\mathcal{D}$ at the period $t : t \in [1..T]$, a function $\alpha(x_{n_i}^t)$ returning the BMU m_c corresponding to this input vector and a function $\beta(m_c)$ returning the cluster c_j corresponding to this neuron, the instance-level trajectory $ITr_{n_i} = \{x_{n_i}^{t=1}, x_{n_i}^{t=2}, ..., x_{n_i}^{t=T}\}$ of the input instance n_i can be transformed to the cluster-level trajectory $CTr_{n_i} = \{\beta(\alpha(x_{n_i}^{t=1})), \beta(\alpha(x_{n_i}^{t=2})), ..., \beta(\alpha(x_{n_i}^{t=T}))\}$. The CTr_{n_i} of the different input vectors n_i can thus be obtained and used as input for the GSP algorithm, leading to the generation of a set of frequent cluster-trajectories $\mathcal{FCT}$ with a minimum support m_{Sup}. The different steps of the proposed methodology are summarized in Fig. 2.

3   Application

An application of the proposed methodology in a ticketing context is reported in this section. The data consists of records about 67846 unique customers gathered during 66 months by a major event organizer based in the Netherlands. After preprocessing and transformation, 31 binary variables (D1 to D31) are representing the different customers. The 4 first variables represent the average number of days separating the purchase of a ticket and the event related to it; D1, D2, D3 and D4 representing respectively the categories 0, 1 to 6, 7 to 30 and more than 30 days. 4 variables represent the length of the relationship between the customer and the event organizer; D5, D6, D7 and D8 representing respectively a very short, a short, a long and a very long relationship. 5 variables represent the percentage of orders placed online; D9, D10, D11, D12 and D13 representing respectively 0 to 10, 11 to 40, 41 to 60, 61 to 90 and 91 to 100 percents of the orders. 3 variables represent the average number of tickets purchased for each event; D14, D15 and D16 representing respectively the categories 1, 2 and more than 2 tickets. 4 variables represent the category of the customers; D17, D18,

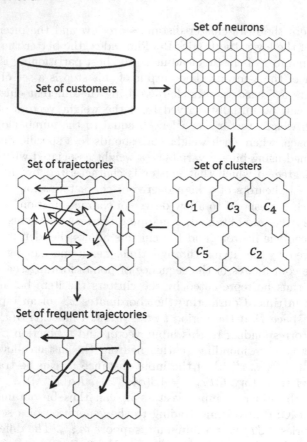

Fig. 2. Stepwise representation of the used methodology.

D19 and D20 representing respectively the males, females, families and companies. 4 variables represent the value of the customer for the event organizer; D21,
D22, D23 and D24 representing respectively the very bad, the bad, the good and
the very good customers. 6 variables represent the average distance separating
the booking computer from the event location; D25, D26, D27, D28, D29 and
D30 representing respectively the categories 0 to 5, 6 to 10, 11 to 15, 16 to 25, 26
to 50 and more than 50 kilometers. Finally the variable D31 captures whether
or not a customer already subscribed.

The objective of this application is to understand the decision behavior of
customers opting to subscribe for the first time. To do so, the 66 months of data
are divided into 66 periods l, with $l \in [1..66]$, respectively finishing at time l^t.
At the end of each period, a data set d_l is formed and gathers the 31 variables
D1 to D31 of each customer present at that moment l^t in the database. An
aggregated data set d^A is formed by consolidating all period data sets d_l in one
main data set. In this application, with 66 periods l, the aggregated data set
d^A contains 2764859 records. By definition, customers present in the database

at l^t will remain in the database at $(l + 1)^t$, hence being represented multiple times in d^A. Thanks to the unique identifiers of the different customers, it is thus possible to follow the evolution though time of the values of the 31 variables at a customer-level. In a first step, the P-SOM algorithm is applied to train a network of 25×20 neurons using the aggregated data set d^A as input. A higher priority is used for the variable D31 (subscription holders) in order to guide the clustering algorithm and obtain a partitioning mainly structured by this variable. To do so, a priority of 1 is given to D31 and a priority of 2 is given to the other variables. The output of this step is represented in Fig. 3 where the 31 component planes are represented. The color code used for the component planes is as follows. The neurons with the highest value for each specific variable are represented, in the respective component plane, in dark red while neurons with relatively low values are colored in dark blue. The color of the neurons with intermediate values is thus ranging from dark blue (low values) to dark red (high values). Thanks to the focus on the variable D31, the reader can see that this variable is effectively structuring the output, easing the remainder of the analysis.

In a second step, the k-means algorithm is applied on top of the P-SOM output, hence clustering neurons representing patterns in the customer base. A relatively high maximum number of clusters is used in order to allow a fine-grained analysis, leading to the 30 clusters represented in Fig. 4.

By comparing Figs. 4 and 3 or by analyzing the coordinates of the different clusters' centroids resulting from the k-means, 6 clusters, namely c_{23}, c_{10}, c_3, c_{24}, c_{19} and c_{14}, are identified as clusters of subscription holders and are shaded in Fig. 4. In order to understand the decision behavior of customers opting to subscribe for the first time, the cluster-level trajectories CTr_{n_i} are generated for all customers (3597) who subscribed in one of the 66 periods. To take into consideration the fact that we are interested in the first period of subscription, the constrained cluster-level trajectories $CTr_{n_i}^{D31}$ are defined and consist of the cluster-level trajectories truncated after the first period in which one of the clusters representing the subscription holders (clusters c_{23}, c_{10}, c_3, c_{24}, c_{19} and c_{14}) is encountered. After removing repetitions in $CTr_{n_i}^{D31}$ (as focus is put on movements rather than the duration of a particular item remaining in a certain cluster), the different trajectories are then used as input for the GSP algorithm with a minimum support set to 10. The set of frequent trajectories $\mathcal{FCT}$ obtained can provide the first insights concerning the decision behavior of customers opting to subscribe for the first time. As an illustration, Fig. 5 shows, for each cluster of subscription holders, the frequent trajectory of length 3 with the highest support.

A first visual analysis of, for example, the trajectory of Fig. 5 leading to the cluster c_3 of Fig. 4 can be done by referring to the component planes of Fig. 3. It can then be said that this trajectory, leading to the first subscription, is associated with an increase in the average number of days separating the purchase of the tickets and the event related to it (see Fig. 3, dimensions D3 and D4) and an increase in the customer value (see Fig. 3, dimensions D21 to D24). As a final step, although other visual explorations could lead to additional insights

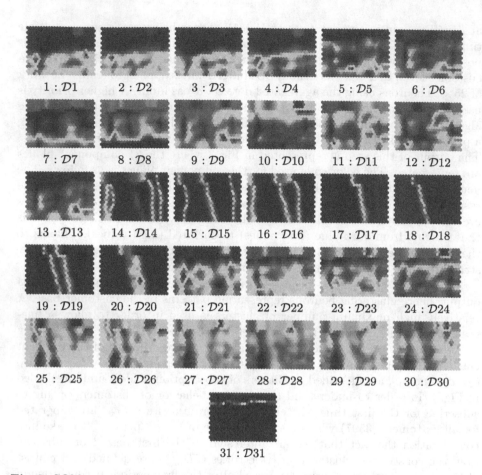

Fig. 3. SOM output obtained by using the prioritized SOM algorithm (Color figure online).

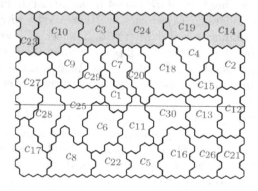

Fig. 4. Representation of the 30 clusters obtained by applying the k-means on top of the output of the P-SOM algorithm.

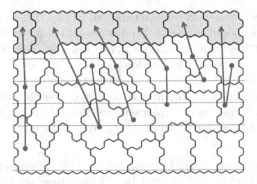

Fig. 5. Six frequent trajectories leading to the different clusters of subscription holders.

into the dynamics, a statistical approach is used in order to obtain an idea of the main trends in the steps preceding the first subscription. To do so, the different trajectories $CTr_{n_i}^{D31}$ previously obtained are used to calculate deltas, $\delta(CTr_{n_i}^{D31})$, resulting from the subtraction of the coordinates of the first period of each $CTr_{n_i}^{D31}$ from the coordinates of its last period, hence capturing the movement in the multidimensional space from the original cluster of each subscribing customer to the cluster representing subscription holders he belongs to. The obtained deltas are then clustered using the k-means algorithm in order to understand the main trends. With a k equal to 5, 5 clusters representing the main trends within the deltas are obtained and are further detailed by referring to their respective centroids. The main cluster, gathering 1712 deltas out of the 3597, represents customers not showing a significant increase in the value of any variable before reaching one of the clusters of subscription holders. The second cluster, gathering 1090 deltas, represents customers showing a strong increase in the value of variables D4 and D25, hence buying their tickets earlier and becoming customers with a higher value. The third cluster, gathering 389 deltas, represents customers showing an increase in the value of the variable D16, hence buying more tickets per event. The fourth cluster, gathering 244 deltas, represents customers showing an increase in the value of the variables D4, D15 and D25, hence buying their tickets earlier, being more and more used to buy pairs of tickets and becoming customers with a higher value. Finally, the fifth cluster, gathering 162 deltas, represents customers showing an increase in the value of the variables D4, D8, D16 and D25, hence buying their tickets earlier, becoming customers with a very long relationship with the organizer, buying more tickets per event and becoming better customers. These main trends combined with the different visual patterns provide the analyst with an exploratory approach for customers' dynamics.

4   Conclusion

In this paper, a novel approach enabling the exploratory analysis of the customer's dynamics is proposed. The first part of the paper introduced the different techniques required to achieve this goal from a theoretical point of view. The methodology proposed in Sect. 2.4 combines different techniques issued from the state-of-the-art in clustering and sequence mining. In Sect. 3, a case is presented in which the proposed methodology is applied in a ticketing context. The objective of this application is to understand the decision behavior of customers opting to subscribe for the first time. Using the different techniques and approaches of Sect. 2, a stepwise exploration of the data is conducted, leading to valuable insights into the dynamics of a large real data set.

Acknowledgment. We would like to thank the KU Leuven research council for financial support under grand OT/10/010 and the Flemish Research Council for financial support under Odysseus grant B.0915.09.

References

1. Kohonen, T.: Self-Organizing Maps. Springer Series in Information Sciences Series. Springer-Verlag GmbH, Heidelberg (2001)
2. Rozinat, A., van der Aalst, W.M.P.: Decision mining in ProM. In: Dustdar, S., Fiadeiro, J., Sheth, A.P. (eds.) BPM 2006. LNCS, vol. 4102, pp. 420–425. Springer, Heidelberg (2006)
3. Smith, K.A., Ng, A.: Web page clustering using a self-organizing map of user navigation patterns. Decis. Support Syst. **35**(2), 245–256 (2003)
4. Schwartz, D., Smith, K.A., Churilov, L., Dally, M., Weber, R.: Design and Application of Hybrid Intelligent Systems. Amsterdam, IOS Press (2003)
5. Huysmans, J., Martens, D., Baesens, B., Vanthienen, J., Van Gestel, T.: Country corruption analysis with self organizing maps and support vector machines. In: Chen, H., Wang, F.-Y., Yang, C.C., Zeng, D., Chau, M., Chang, K. (eds.) WISI 2006. LNCS, vol. 3917, pp. 103–114. Springer, Heidelberg (2006)
6. Kohonen, T.: Self-Organizing Maps. Springer, New York (1995)
7. Pölzlbauer, G.: Survey and comparison of quality measures for self-organizing maps. In: Paralič, J., Pölzlbauer, G., Rauber, A. (eds.) Proceedings of the Fifth Workshop on Data Analysis (WDA'04), Sliezsky dom, Vysoké Tatry, Slovakia, pp. 67–82. Elfa Academic Press, 24–27 June 2004
8. Jolliffe, I.: Principal Component Analysis. Wiley, New York (2005)
9. Seret, A., Verbraken, T., Versailles, S., Baesens, B.: A new knowledge-based constrained clustering approach: theory and application in direct marketing. Appl. Soft Comput. (under review)
10. Srikant, R., Agrawal, R.: Mining sequential patterns: generalizations and performance improvements. In: Apers, P.M.G., Bouzeghoub, M., Gardarin, G. (eds.) EDBT 1996. LNCS, vol. 1057, pp. 1–17. Springer, Heidelberg (1996)
11. Tan, P., Steinbach, M., Kumar, V., et al.: Introduction to Data Mining. Pearson Addison Wesley, Boston (2006)
12. Davies, D., Bouldin, D.: A cluster seperation measure. IEEE Trans. Pattern Anal. Mach. Intell. **PAMI-1**(2), 224–227 (1979)

1st Workshop on Emerging Topics in BPM (ETBPM 2013)

The Design of a Workflow Recommendation System for Workflow as a Service in the Cloud

Dingxian Wang[1], Xiao Liu[1(✉)], Zheng He[1], and Xiaoliang Fan[2]

[1] Software Engineering Institute, East China Normal University,
Shanghai, China
dingxianwang@gmail.com, xliu@sei.ecnu.edu.cn,
zhenghe_2006@hotmail.com
[2] School of Information Science and Engineering,
Lanzhou University, Lanzhou, Gansu, China
fanxiaoliang@lzu.edu.cn

Abstract. A cloud workflow system is designed to provide WaaS (Workflow as a Service) which harnesses the power of cloud computing for efficient and cost-effective workflow execution. The current cloud workflow systems are mainly used by people who possess the knowledge about the business processes such as the process structures and functional/non-functional requirements because they need to create the executable workflow applications by themselves. However, most end-users do not acquire such kind of knowledge and thus limits the system usability and hinders the implementation of complete WaaS. To address this problem, this paper proposes the design of a novel online workflow recommendation system which can help end-users to create their own executable workflow applications by only providing some keywords to describe their requirements without the specific workflow modeling process. The system framework and its core components are illustrated in this paper. A detailed case study on an online ordering business workflow is demonstrated to successfully prove the feasibility of our system design.

Keywords: Cloud workflow system · WaaS (Workflow as a Service) · Online workflow recommendation system

1 Introduction

Workflow systems have been widely used as software tools to support process automation, and also as middleware services for distributed high performance computing infrastructures such as cluster, peer-to-peer, and grid computing [10, 20]. In the upcoming few years, given the enormous market of cloud computing, there will be a rapid growth of SaaS (software as a service) [6], and we can envisage that cloud workflow system will be one of the competitive software platforms to support the design, development and running of cloud based software applications. The current cloud workflow systems take advantages of cloud computing [3] by employing cloud services, especially infrastructure services and software services. Before the running of a cloud workflow application, Cloud workflow users need to explicitly specify the

N. Lohmann et al. (Eds.): BPM 2013 Workshops, LNBIP 171, pp. 251–263, 2014.
DOI: 10.1007/978-3-319-06257-0_20, © Springer International Publishing Switzerland 2014

workflow application which includes the information such as the process structure, the functional requirements (such as what data and services are needed and their locations) and the non-functional requirements (such as QoS constraints on time, cost, security and reliability) [25]. However, such comprehensive workflow information usually can only be acquired by those who are very familiar with the business processes rather than the general end-users. For example, if a user wants to book a flight and then arrange her/his local travel, he/she must know the detailed process of booking a flight, reserving a local hotel and many other details such as how the payment will be handled and so on.

Therefore, to achieve the complete WaaS (Workflow as a Service), cloud workflow systems should be able to facilitate the creation of the workflow applications by providing some references such as related workflow information in the form of graph, text, or ready-to-use workflow applications. But such a facility is currently missing in most cloud workflow systems, which significantly affects the system usability for general end-users. To address this problem, we propose an online workflow recommendation system. This system can help general end-users to create their own executable workflow applications by only providing some keywords to describe their requirements without the efforts for detailed workflow modeling process.

This paper aims to present the design of a workflow recommendation system for workflow as a service to help solve the insufficiencies of current process and workflow systems. Workflow systems are good at saving time and efforts for those people who are doing researches and business based on computer programs but with limited computer programming knowledge. With the help of workflow systems, one can build a workflow application conveniently and promptly. Therefore, workflow systems can play a very important role in many fields. Many powerful workflow systems such as Kepler, Joget and Runmy offer comprehensive functions to specific fields. However, there are still some drawbacks. For example, reusing the workflows of others is difficult since the requirements, process structures, even contextual environment of different workflows are not the same, and even the process structures of the same workflows in the same organization may have some divergences. Compatibility is another key issue due to the fact that there are a lot of workflow systems nowadays but no unique data form is well adopted. It is hard to reuse the workflow application created by one workflow system with another workflow system. Lacking of workflow recommendation system is also a very critical problem because it is very time and efforts consuming to build a whole workflow application from scratch. If a recommendation system can provide all the necessary sub-workflows to the users, then the work can be done in a more efficient fashion. Therefore, a workflow recommendation system with the help of machine learning methods is proposed in this paper to solve the problems discussed above. Meanwhile, cloud computing is applied in our system design so as to take advantage of the unique characteristics of cloud computing such as its organization and delivery of computing resources. The recommendation system can provide information to the users sufficiently and efficiently.

The remainder of the paper is organized as follows. Section 2 presents the related work. Section 3 proposes the novel system design and illustrates its major components. Section 4 demonstrates a real-world example. Finally in Sect. 5, we address the conclusions and point out the future work.

2 Related Work

The cloud workflow system is becoming increasingly popular nowadays. However, the current cloud workflow systems are still at a preliminary stage. Cloud workflow systems are being widely used as platform software (or middleware services) to facilitate the use of cloud services by taking advantages of cloud computing. The cloud workflow systems can support many complex e-science applications such as climate modeling, earthquake modeling, weather forecast, astrophysics and high-energy physics. Cloud workflow systems have a lot of merits. Cloud computing brings workflow systems with a large number of easy access and powerful software and hardware services to support their extensive applications. The users can build up their applications with visual modeling (e.g. Petri Net or DAG based modeling tools) instead of sophisticated and time-consuming programming [3] Moreover, workflow systems bring cloud with a form of visual-programmable platform/middleware services to facilitate the easy use of cloud services [11, 13]. It provides programming like environments for the access and composition of cloud services and plays a significant role in cloud software development. However, most consumers in the cloud market are not IT professionals (e.g. scientists and businessmen in non-IT areas), and usually they do not acquire sufficient knowledge for sophisticated programming. Workflow systems, as a type of visual-programmable platform or middleware services, can relieve users from traditional programming with visual remodeling tools (or a little bit help of scripting language in some cases). Since the workflow systems are still at its preliminary stage, many drawbacks are still there [9, 19]. Among the others, the reusing of existing workflows and services is still limited and most platforms are still hard for people who don't have any programming background. There is also limited recommendation capability that can help users build their own workflow applications.

The recommendation systems [16] are highly developed in many fields. There are currently two major forms of workflow recommendation systems nowadays. One suggests task-specific information, and the other suggests process-oriented information. For task-specific systems, Abecker made an approach [1] and Stabb [24] proposed business-specific management workflow recommendation system towards integrating the semantics of semi-structured documents with task-support for (weakly structured) business processes and proactive inference capabilities of a desk support agent. Both methods achieve fair performance on business workflow data recommendation. Bowers offered an ontology-driven method providing data integration and transformation tools, allowing researchers to focus on "real science". A generic framework is defined for transforming heterogeneous data within scientific workflows [4]. For process-oriented based systems, Shen proposed a process view presenting system which is based on a quantitative method to evaluate the degree of relevance between the tasks and different organizational roles to recommend workflow information [23]. Zhang provided a method aiming to help domain scientists find interesting services and reuse matching processes to attain their research purposes in the form of workflows based on service usage history [26]. This approach is very helpful in making use of the service usage history to improve the recommendation. As introduced above, many existing workflow recommendation systems are domain specific. Therefore, it is very important to build a system integrating all the functions which can then be applied to general fields.

3   System Design

The framework of the proposed system is shown in Fig. 1. The basic idea of the system is to first collect data of workflow applications from all kinds of sources such as graph, text and xml data to build the workflow data corpus. Secondly, the workflow data will be analyzed and then segmented into meaningful sub-workflows. Thirdly, some types of features such as semantic features, statistical features and structure features for each sub-workflow from the workflows of interest will be extracted and fed to several classifiers by applying some recommendation models. Finally, according to user requirements, the recommendation system can help users find matching sub-workflows. The details of the framework will be introduced in the following sections.

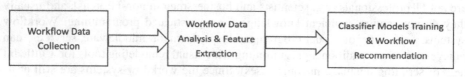

Fig. 1. System framework

3.1   Data Collection

The first component of the system is called Data Collection as shown in Fig. 2. The workflow data is very complex and it is difficult to find existing workflow corpus which suits the need of our system. Therefore, a well-defined workflow data collection system should be built. Meanwhile, our system will have the ability to handle different forms of data such as graph, text and xml. The corpus should be updated and enlarged to meet the needs of different users. Thus, it is very important to construct a reasonable mechanism to crawl and extract data from all kinds of sources and then convert them into the forms that can be dealt with in the next workflow data analysis and feature extraction phase.

First, the main data sources of our system are set to be web data and software generated data. The web data is the data crawling from the Internet and a web crawler [14] is constructed to crawl all the data concerning the workflow of interest. Usually the web crawler is based on search engines, after typing the keywords, several top searching results will be climbed down. Since the web data is so diverse and unstructured, it is difficult to classify and map. The software generated data is collected from various workflow systems and will output graph, text and xml data to help us mapping different data. After that, a rich workflow data corpus could be built.

Second, the workflow data are divided into graph, text and xml data so as to make the data analysis procedure convenient. The data crawled from Internet may include a

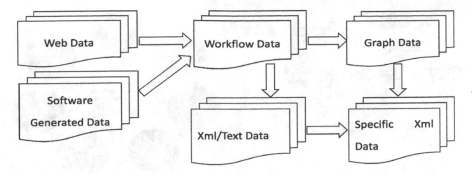

Fig. 2. Data collection

lot of unrelated data which must be removed from the corpus. A one-phase classifier [7] such as Support Vector Machine (SVM) [8] or a multi-phase classifier will be generated to extract the true workflow data. It will combine the advantages of several useful machine learning methods.

Finally, the workflow data corpus will be constructed and the corpus will be stored on the cloud so as to update the data efficiently and effectively.

3.2 Workflow Data Analysis and Feature Extraction

After constructing the workflow corpus on the cloud, then we come to the second part which is to analyze the corpus to extract the actual sub-workflows for domain specific processes and map them to different data forms such as graph, text, and xml to extract useful features.

Here, we take the purchase order business workflow as an example, three data forms including graph, text and xml are listed as shown in Figs. 3, 4 and 5. All the three data forms can display a complete purchase order workflow. As shown in Fig. 3, three different graphs are illustrated to show that even the structures of the graphs are different, the functions included are very similar. For text data, we can find that keywords such as 'first step' and 'priority' should be emphasized, while, tags such as '<purchase order>', '<name>' and '<product name>' should be highlighted in xml data. Therefore, different forms of data need to be treated accordingly. However, as depicted in Fig. 6, a general data analysis and feature extraction process can be applied similarly.

First, the workflow data is segmented by various methods according to its forms. Compared with xml and text data, the graph data is much more difficult to be processed. This is because even the structure of the graph can be viewed clearly by users, it is still very difficult for the computer to understand the graph and segment it into meaningful pieces. However, if the words and phrases in the graph could be comprehended by the computer, the segmentation work could be done more efficiently because similar pieces normally have similar names. Therefore, we can use some OCR techniques [21] and graph processing methods to help identify the words in the workflow so as to segment the graph as accurately as possible. The xml data should be

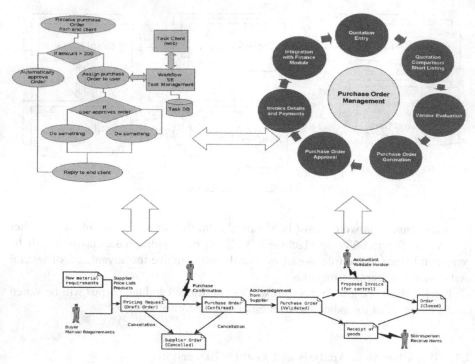

Fig. 3. Graph structures sample

A workflow process can be created to handle a work order. An enterprise has configured the system to route all new preventive maintenance work orders that are generated through the preventive maintenance work order generation cron task into a workflow process.

The first step is to evaluate the priority of the work order, as follows:

- If the preventive maintenance work order is high priority or has a null value in the **Priority** field, it is routed to a work planner for immediate review and approval.
- If the preventive maintenance work order has a low priority, it is routed to a Stop node and exits the process.

All preventive maintenance work orders then go through a financial approval process. Work orders with an estimated total cost of less than $500 are automatically approved. The maintenance supervisor must review and approve work orders with an estimated total cost of more than $500.

After a work order passes the financial approval process, it must be assigned to a work group, as follows:

- If the preventive maintenance work order is for a vehicle, the system assigns it to the fleet maintenance group.
- If the preventive maintenance work order is for a building or location, the system assigns it to the facilities maintenance group.
- The system assigns all other preventive maintenance work orders to the maintenance group.

After the system assigns the work order to a maintenance group, the work order exits the workflow process.

Fig. 4. Text structure sample

segmented based on the xml tags. According to the tag information, a segmentation program can be applied to extract different parts of workflows and classified them into different classes. The text data should be segmented by applying some methods as used in natural language processing. For example, several keyword lists can be built to help locate different parts of the workflows so as to extract the sub-workflows.

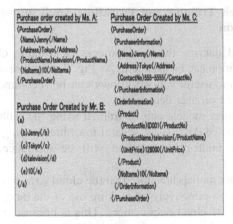

Fig. 5. Xml structure sample

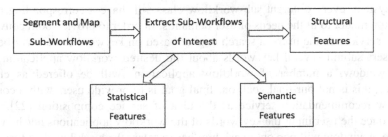

Fig. 6. Workflow data analysis and feature extraction

Second, sub-workflows of interest can be retrieved from the corpus. In this phase, useful sub-workflows are labeled according to their forms. The structural features such as position, tags and the number of tags including in the sub-workflows and the route from current tag to the root are considered in graph and xml data. The semantic features which include the semantic information contained in the xml nodes and the text are considered. Meanwhile, the statistical features consider the distribution of the nodes and tag information in graph, text and xml sub-workflows. Moreover, xml based workflow modeling language similar to XPDL or BEPL [15] is defined to convert all the possible forms of data into a unified data form so that it can be processed easily in our system. Moreover, once some new data forms are added to our system, all we have to do is adding a new interface to convert the new data source into our unified data form so as to save lots of data processing efforts.

Third, the graph, text and xml data can be mapped through the defined xml language and the extract features. Afterwards, the sub-workflows can be labeled incrementally. With these labeled dataset, a supervised learning classifier can be applied in the next classifier models training and workflow applications recommendation phase.

3.3 Classifier Models Training and Workflow Applications Recommendation

With the features and dataset, the final process of training classifier models and workflow recommendation can be executed. As Fig. 7 shows, several classifier models can be trained and some useful sub-workflows can be recommended by the recommendation system based on user demands.

First, several classifier models can be trained using the multi-class classification techniques with the labeled data. Thus, several machine learning methods are applied in our system and a multi-phase method will be introduced to achieve better performance.

Second, the classifier models are stored on the cloud so as to make the incremental update efficiently and cost-effectively by making use of the large capacity, high speed and stable platform of the cloud data centers. This is because the workflow data are increased all the time, so that a system based on cloud computing is needed to provide a reliable service.

Third, some useful sub-workflows are recommended based on user demands. In the system, every different sub-workflow class will have a corresponding recommendation model to fit the needs of user demands. In order to provide both convenient and fast services to the users, a search engine based on keyword search will be built. Once users submit several key words about the desired workflow application in the search window, a number of workflow applications will be offered as choices. However, this is not our final goal, our final goal is to provide users with a complete workflow recommendation service as the idea of service composition [22]. In our design, once the user input the key words of the workflow applications he/she want to generate, a window will pop out to ask him/her to select the workflow data forms such as graph, text or xml he/she prefers. Then, the system will combine the sub-workflows into some complete workflow applications. Several candidate workflows in different data forms will be supplied to the users so as to help them find the ideal workflow applications.

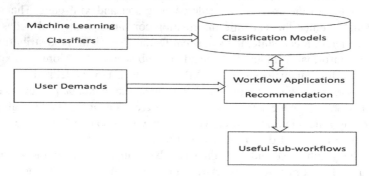

Fig. 7. Classifier models training and workflow applications recommendation

4 Case Study

In this section, a typical case about an online ordering workflow is studied so as to present a detailed view of our system. Since the ordering workflow is a very important part of many commercial applications, a large number of workflow examples can be acquired from the Internet by just searching with the keywords of "online ordering workflow" or "online ordering process", and most of them have very similar structures. An ordering workflow is generally used to describe the process such as picking, packing and delivery of the packed items to a shipping carrier[1,2]. The ordering workflow procedure starts with the acceptance of the order from the customer, and is considered as completed when the buyer has received the products. A successful ordering workflow procedure will make the order to be delivered accurately and completely. Companies often invest huge time and efforts in designing and implementation of an efficient ordering workflow, thus increasing the possibility of establishing a working relationship with its customers. Therefore, the ordering workflow plays a significant role.

In this section, a case study about mapping similar sub-workflows of different ordering workflows to help build an ordering workflow application is discussed. We mainly take the business order process depicted in Figs. 3, 4 and 5 as an example. However, due to the space limitation, only the most difficult graph data is displayed and processed in our paper as Fig. 8 shows. The processing methods on other forms will also be discussed.

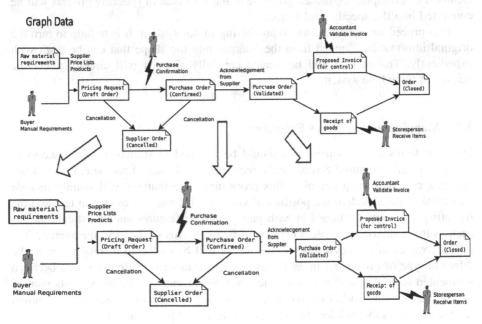

Fig. 8. Graph segmentation process

---

[1] http://www.wisegeek.com/what-is-order-processing.htm
[2] http://en.wikipedia.org/wiki/Order_processing

4.1 Data Collection and Preprocessing

To construct a both comprehensive and well-structured ordering workflow corpus, the ordering workflow data should first be crawled from the Internet or gained from some process software. Afterwards, a comprehensive data corpus which includes all kinds of ordering workflows can be built. Since there are various workflow data forms, it is critical to convert different data forms into a unified format to help system save both computing time and resources. The specific processes will be introduced in this section.

Firstly, graph, text and xml data should be segmented into small parts. Each part should provide a small and independent function to the whole process. The Fig. 8, has shown an example of the graph segmentation process. As can be seen, graph data of the ordering workflow are segmented into several phases according to their functions. The ordering workflow can be divided into several phases such as buyer presents manual requirements, purchase order confirmation and purchase order execution as Fig. 8 shows.

Secondly, a special xml language is defined to convert the different forms of segmented data into a unified form of expression. Therefore, one can easily retrieve the useful features which help to map the data. In the case of new workflow data forms, our system only need to provide an interface to help convert the new data forms into the xml style we defined. Then, the data can be processed by our system efficiently. For example, segmented graph, text and xml data of ordering process will be converted into the specific xml form.

This procedure is called data preprocessing in our system. It is to help to turn the original information climbed from the Internet into the shape that can be dealt with expediently. This step should be treated carefully since it will directly affect the quality of the whole system.

4.2 Mapping and Features Extraction

Different forms of segmented data should be mapped as shown in Fig. 9 shows to produce a well-structured corpus. Some recognizable features must be extracted from the data corpus to help complete this procedure. The features will mainly include structural features such as the position of xml tags, the number of tags in text and the repeating structures contained in each part, semantic features and statistical features such as the similarity of context between different forms of data [5], the average TF-IDF [2] values of the keywords (the keywords will be collected manually due to the different type of processes) in each part and the number of different words between segmented parts. For instance, graph, text and xml forms of "buyer presents manual requirements" sub-workflows are mapped as Fig. 9 presents. Therefore, common features of this sub-workflow in different forms could be extracted.

After getting the important features, a multi-phase classifier (such as SVM [8], Decision Tree [17], CRF [18] and Neural Network [11]) should be built up to distinguish different classes of the sub-workflow data. With the help of classifiers, many representative application areas of workflow systems can be covered so as to help to

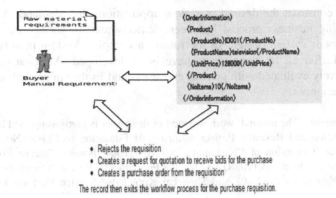

Fig. 9. Mapping procedure

construct the recommendation system. For example, a decision tree and SVM based two-phase classifier can be used to classify the different sub-workflows of the ordering workflow. In our system, a decision tree can be first used to filter those obviously irrelevant sub-workflows, and SVM can then be applied to handle those complicated sub-workflows. This is because decision tree is good at dealing with massive data while SVM is effective in coping with nonlinear and small-scale data.

4.3   Recommendation of Sub-Workflows to Users

After constructing a rich and well-formed data corpus, the information should first be converted into the special xml language as our targeted data form. Several recommendation models such as collaborative filtering recommendation [12] can be built on these data such as buyer presents manual requirements, purchase order confirmation and purchase order execution to help users find the sub-workflows they want. Then, if the user chooses the searching words as "order" in the searching window, several candidate sub-workflow will be listed and the user can choose any one he/she likes. Only if he/she selects one of the candidates, several composed workflow applications of that form will be offered to him/her to choose from. Thus, the user will find an ideal workflow application he/she wanted. It is very straightforward because the user can ignore a lot of details just focus on the key parts. It will also help us to reduce a lot of efforts and time.

5   Conclusions and Future Work

In this paper, to achieve the complete WaaS, the novel design of a machine learning based workflow recommendation system is proposed to solve the issues such as reuse, compatibility and recommendation of the current cloud workflow system. We have proposed a systematic framework which integrates data collection, data processing, features extraction and workflow recommendation. This system can help general end-users to construct the desired workflow applications they demand. A real-world online ordering business process has been demonstrated to successfully prove the feasibility of our system design. In the future, a complete system prototype will be implemented after all its components have been developed. Afterwards, it will be comprehensively evaluated with general end-users and further improved according to the user experiences.

Acknowledgement. The research work reported in this paper is partly supported by "Chunhui Plan" Cooperation and Research Project, Ministry of Education of China (No. Z2012114), Natural Science Foundation of China under No. 61021004, Natural Science Foundation of Gansu Province of China (No.1208RJZA278), the Fundamental Research Funds for the Central Universities (No.lzujbky-2013-40), and Shanghai Knowledge Service Platform Project under No. ZF1213.

References

1. Abecker, A., Bernardi, A., Maus, H., Sintek, M., Wenzel, C.: Information supply for business processes: coupling workflow with document analysis and information retrieval. Knowl.-Based Syst. **13**(5), 271–284 (2000)
2. Aizawa, A.: An information theoretic perspective of Tf-Idf mMasures. Inf. Process. Manage. **39**(1), 45–65 (2003)
3. Armbrust, M., Fox, A., Grith, R., Joseph, A.D., Katz, R., Konwinski, A., Lee, G., Patterson, D., Rabkin, A., Stoica, I.: View of cloud computing. Commun. ACM **53**(4), 50–58 (2010)
4. Bowers, S., Ludascher, B.: An ontology-driven framework for data transformation in scientific workflows. In: Rahm, E. (ed.) DILS 2004. LNBI, vol. 2994, pp. 1–16. Springer, Heidelberg (2009)
5. Brezillon, P.: Representation of procedures and practices in contextual graphs. Knowl. Eng. Rev. **18**(2), 147–174 (2003)
6. Buxmann, P., Hess, T., Lehmann, S.: Software as a service. Wirtschaftsinformatik **50**(6), 500–503 (2008)
7. Carpenter, G.A., Grossberg, S., Markuzon, N., Reynolds, J.H., Rosen, D.B.: Fuzzy ARTMAP: a neural network architecture for incremental supervised learning of analog multidimensional maps. IEEE Trans. Neural Netw. **3**(5), 698–713 (1992)
8. Cortes, C., Vapnik, V.: Support vector machine. Mach. Learn. **20**(3), 273–297 (1995)
9. Fan, X., Zhang, R., Brezillon, P.: Investigating the feasibility of making contexts explicit in designing cloud workflow. In: Proceedings of 2013 IEEE 27th International Parallel and Distributed Processing Symposium (IPDPS 13) Workshop on CloudFlow (2013)
10. Foster, I., Zhao, Y., Raicu, I., Lu, S.: Cloud computing and grid computing 360-degree compared. In: Grid Computing Environments Workshop, GCE'08, pp. 1–10 (2008)
11. Hagan, M.T., Demuth, H.B., Beale, M.H.: Neural Network Design. Pws Pub, Boston (1996)
12. Herlocker, J.L., Konstan, J.A., Riedl, J.: Explaining collaborative filtering recommendations. In: Proceedings of the 2000 ACM Conference on Computer Supported Cooperative Work, pp. 241–250 (2000)
13. Hess, A., Holt, J., Jacobson, J., Seamons, K.E.: Content-triggered trust negotiation. ACM Trans. Inf. Syst. Secur. (TISSEC) **7**(3), 428–456 (2004)
14. Heydon, A., Najork, M.: Mercator: a scalable, extensible web crawler. World Wide Web **2**(4), 219–229 (1999)

15. Hornung, T., Koschmider, A., Mendling, J.: Integration of heterogeneous BPM schemas: the case of XPDL and BPEL. In: CAISE Forum, CEUR Workshop Proceedings, vol. 231 (2006)
16. Kim, J.-g., Lee, E.-s.: Intelligent information recommend system on the internet. In: Proceedings of the 1999 International Workshops on Parallel Processing, 1999, pp. 376–380 (1999)
17. Kohavi, R.: Scaling up the accuracy of Naive-Bayes classifiers: a decision-tree hybrid. In: Proceedings of the 2nd International Conference on Knowledge Discovery and Data Mining, vol. 7 (1996)
18. Lafferty, J., McCallum, A., Pereira, F.C.: Conditional random fields: probabilistic models for segmenting and labeling sequence data. In: Proceedings of ICML (2001)
19. Liu, X., Chen, J., Yang, Y.: Temporal QOS Management in Scientific Cloud Workflow Systems. Elsevier (2012)
20. Liu, X., Yuan, D., Zhang, G., Zhang, G., Li, W., Cao, D., He, Q., Chen, J., Yang, Y.: The Design of Cloud Workflow Systems [M]. Springer, New York (2012)
21. Mori, S., Suen, C.Y., Yamamoto, K.: Historical review of OCR research and development. Proc. IEEE **80**(7), 1029–1058 (1992)
22. Ren, K., Liu, X., Chen, J., Xiao, N., Song, J., Zhang, W.: A QSQL-based efficient planning algorithm for fully-automated service composition in dynamic service environments. In: IEEE International Conference on Services Computing 2008, SCC'08, vol. 1, pp. 301–308 (2008)
23. Shen, M., Liu, D.-R.: Discovering role-relevant process-views for recommending workflow information. In: Mařík, V., Štěpánková, O., Retschitzegger, W. (eds.) DEXA 2003. LNCS, vol. 2736, pp. 836–845. Springer, Heidelberg (2003)
24. Staab, S., Schnurr, H.P.: Smart task support through proactive access to organizational memory. Knowl.-Based Syst. **13**(5), 251–260 (2000)
25. Van Der Aalst, W., Van Hee, K.M.: Workflow Management: Models, Methods, and Systems. The MIT Press, Cambridge (2004)
26. Zhang, J., Tan, W., Alexander, J., Foster, I., Madduri, R.: Recommend-as-you-go: a novel approach supporting services-oriented scientific workflow reuse. In: 2011 IEEE International Conference on Services Computing (SCC), pp. 48–55 (2011)

Business Process Assignment and Execution from Cloud to Mobile

Tao Peng[1,2], Marco Ronchetti[1] (✉), Jovan Stevovic[1,2], Annamaria Chiasera[2], and Giampaolo Armellin[2]

[1] University of Trento, Via Sommarive 5, 38123 Trento, Italy
{tao.peng,marco.ronchetti,jovan.stevovic}@disi.unitn.it
[2] Centro Ricerche GPI srl, Via Ragazzi del '99 nr.13, 38123 Trento, Italy
{annamaria.chiasera,giampaolo.armellin}@cr-gpi.it

Abstract. Connected to cloud, mobile devices enable workers to manage the business processes hosted on remote process engines. However, traditional business process execution is not tailored for mobile devices. Typically the business logic remains in the cloud, making the process execution on mobile devices vulnerable to unreliable network connection. In this paper, we propose a framework that assigns, deploys business process from cloud onto mobile devices and executes them in disconnected environments. To model the process assignment and execution on mobile devices, we extend BPMN with context constraints such as location and hardware resources. The proposed framework benefits from centralized process model management and the distributed process execution on mobile devices, regardless of the constant access to cloud. We implemented a prototype of mobile process engine with an application for blood pressure examination used by nurses in rural areas.

Keywords: Cloud · Mobile · Business process · Automatic assignment

1 Introduction

Mobile devices (e.g. smartphones) are emerging as working equipment for different industries [1]. They allow workers to manage the tasks execution at any time and from anywhere [2,3], thus are of great business potential. At the backend, cloud infrastructures, combined with the computational power and storage capacity of servers, can host the business process execution and expose unified service interfaces to distributed clients, including mobile clients. Such business process orchestration enables the centralized management of resources and eases the process design and deployment.

Despite their increasing capacity, mobile devices are connected to the cloud mainly as terminals, providing functions which are similar to desktop computers. For example, mobile users can design business processes, start an execution instance on a business process engine in the cloud, or accept a human task assigned by the process engine. Mobile devices are becoming more powerful not only because their CPU frequency and memory size increase, but also

N. Lohmann et al. (Eds.): BPM 2013 Workshops, LNBIP 171, pp. 264–276, 2014.
DOI: 10.1007/978-3-319-06257-0_21, © Springer International Publishing Switzerland 2014

because they are connected with different sensors and actuators and thus are able to detect and adapt to the execution context. Traditional cloud computing on mobile fails to utilize the full strength of mobile devices.

The recent trend in enabling the process execution on mobile devices, generating distributed implementation of business processes for mobile devices and enforcing context constraint on execution, have extended the utilization of mobile devices in business process management. These business process enabled systems either interact with mobile devices at single task level, or use mobile devices as a server to host process execution, failing to integrate centralized management in the cloud and distributed execution of business processes on mobile devices. More specifically, research questions remains on:

1. How to achieve the optimal assignment of tasks from cloud to mobile workers? The assignment can happen during process design phase or execution phase, but neither is trivial since the context information can affect the selection of mobile workers [4];
2. How to combine the capacity of cloud and pervasiveness of mobile devices to facilitate better reuse of the process models? Traditional business process models are typically designed for specific usage and deployed for pre-defined targeted organizations;
3. How to tolerate the unreliable connectivity? Mobile devices in some scenarios such as in rural areas lack of constant connection to the cloud, while traditional business process orchestration depends on reliable network to initiate tasks and receive execution results;

In this paper, we propose a framework that supports semi-automatic assignment and distributed execution of activities (i.e. single tasks or sub-processes) on mobile devices. The approach is based on four phases: service preparation, process design, activity assignment and activity execution. We extend Business Process Model and Notation (BPMN) 2.0 specification [5] to allow context-aware activity assignment, particularly to model context constraints on activity assignment and execution, and model invocations of services offered by mobile devices as part of business process models. As the prototype, we implement a mobile process engine and a UI Framework to execute business processes on Android smartphones, and a coordinator tool in the cloud that manages activity assignment.

2   Scenario

In our motivating project MOPAL [6], nurses deliver healthcare services at patients home with the assistance of mobile devices. A coordinator in the hospital schedules and assigns the healthcare services that nurses need to deliver. Task assignment considers criteria such as nurses qualifications, their location and service history, to obtain the most efficient task execution and meet the requirements of the healthcare service. The nurses receive the list of patients and the activities to perform through specific developed mobile applications. One of

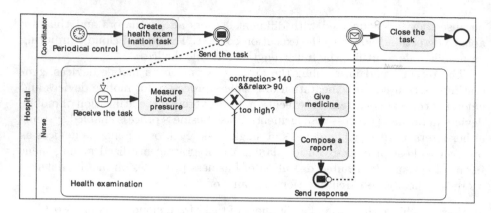

Fig. 1. Business process model of blood pressure examination

such mobile-assisted healthcare service is the blood pressure examination: the nurses use the mobile device to perform a set of tasks and collect patients blood pressure data through a sequence of steps.

Developing applications for such healthcare scenarios with high degree of customization is costly, due to: the demand of flexible task definition, assignment and execution; frequent updates of applications on all mobile devices. The task-intensive healthcare services require a more flexible assistance process definition approach using technologies such as BPMN, to adapt to fast changing contexts where the continuous evolution, monitoring and improvement of performed activities are crucial.

Figure 1 shows a process model of the described blood pressure measurement service. It comprises two lanes: coordinators lane defines the process of managing the health examination service, and it runs on the central process engine in the cloud; nurses lane defines the process of carrying out the health examination, and it runs on mobile devices used by nurses. Although this sample healthcare delivery process is not particularly complex, process assignment and distributed execution on mobile devices are challenging and still unsupported by current BPMN frameworks.

- Current BPMN 2.0 specification is inadequate to support process execution on mobile devices, as it does not exploit natively the functionalities offered by mobile devices, such as locations, network status, Short Message Service (SMS) or calls. The process execution on a mobile device needs a standard and lightweight library to provide a set of such basic services.
- To tolerate the unreliable connection, the mobile process engine should be able to execute process and related tasks in an offline modality. The mobile application should fetch the required data before disconnection and to synchronize with the cloud once finished.
- The modeling framework should support such mobile-specific context-aware constraints (e.g., current location of the nurse or required qualification) for smart and automatic activity assignment and execution on mobile device.

– The process models executed on mobile should be compatible with current BPMN 2.0 specification while supporting extra defined semantics of constraints and services present on mobile devices.

A cloud-based business process modeling framework and a mobile process engine can tackle these challenges: the business process orchestrator assigns processes from the cloud to mobile workers; the mobile process engine executes the assigned processes, interacting with mobile workers and invoking services on mobile devices or in the cloud.

3   Cloud-Based Mobile Process Management Approach

To tackle the challenges, we identify a methodology comprising a sequence of steps from requirements analysis to process execution performed by different participants having different competencies and using different tools: service preparation phase, in which the developers prepare the services following the requirement analysis; process design phase, in which the domain experts, with the help of developers, can compose and annotate processes on top of these services according to the business requirements; activity assignment phase, the semi-automated assignment of tasks from cloud to mobile devices; finally the process execution on mobile devices.

3.1   Services Preparation

To understand how to execute business processes on mobile devices, we need to analyze the implications of the shift of execution environment from desktop/server to mobile. We classify the services involved in the mobile business processes execution into two categories with respect to availability and location of the services invoked by the processes:

1. Services on mobile device: some mobile platforms (e.g. Android) allow cross-application invocations so that the mobile engine can easily invoke local services and applications available on the device. To facilitate such interaction we provide custom BPMN extensions that are executed on mobile process engine to support the execution of mobile specific tasks/events.
2. External services in the cloud: Web Services, or any other external resources that are published as services via predefined interfaces.. We provide the possibility to invoke such external resources from the mobile engine through the definition of specific modeling elements that are described later.

In service preparation phase, developers do not need to implement by themselves the required code to invoke the mobile specific services from the business processes. Our framework facilitates their invocation by providing a specific library, including email, calendar, browser, location sensor, motion sensor, etc. In particular, we have implemented the following components inside our process engine:

- FormService turns the process description into a form that shows predefined instructions to perform a task, accepts user input, and guides the task
  performer through the given process.
- EmailService composes an email draft and initializes the mandatory fields
  (e.g., receiver, subject, body) to incoming parameters.

We plan to publish our platform under an open source license and thus allow
developers to implement additional accesses to services available on the mobile
platforms and to share their services with others in need.

3.2 Process Design

Once the services have been prepared in the previous steps of our approach,
the business process modeling can take place. We do not provide at this stage
a specific process modeling framework allowing users to use any process editor
(e.g. Signavio [7]) that is compliant with BPMN 2.0 specification.

Figure 2 shows the sequence of steps that need to be performed to design the
process model and add additional custom extensions to execute it on the mobile
engine. The first step is to annotate the process models using our BPMN extension to support the automatic activity (simple tasks or sub-processes) assignment
and distributed execution on mobile engine. Our extensions of the BPMN 2.0
specification consist of:

1. **Constraints -** prerequisite situation for mobile process engine to execute the
   process. With the help of developers, domain experts are able to specify the
   context constraints on mobile devices (e.g. geolocation) and on task performers (e.g. nurse qualifications) for the coordinator in the cloud to assign the
   process and for mobile process engine to execute that process.

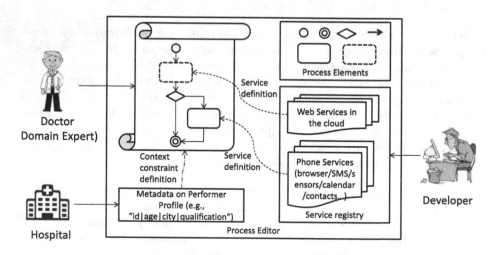

Fig. 2. Process design phase

2. **Services** - invocation definition. The list of available service is exposed through a developed library inside the mobile process engine. Domain experts only need to consider the business logic and the interaction between the process execution and task performers. Developers will take care of configuration details of the services, such as invocation and data exchange interfaces across services.

Once the process is designed and the process model is customized with annotations designed specially to exploit the characteristics of mobile devices, the process definition is published at a cloud-based repository for the coordinator.

3.3   Activity Assignment

With the assistance tool, the coordinator assigns the activities from cloud to mobile devices in four steps as (Fig. 3):

1. **Pre-assignment.** When the coordinator starts to schedule the process execution, the activity that is annotated with assignment constraint enters the state of *to-be-assigned*. Then the framework filters the list of available performers and recommends the best matching ones, and changes the state of the task to *pre-assigned*.
2. **Assignment confirmation.** By default, the *pre-assigned* tasks need to be confirmed by the coordinator to be *assigned*. Optionally, the task assignment tool can configured to by-pass the manual confirmation.
3. **Dispatching to mobile device.** When the framework sends the activity model to the mobile device successfully, the activity becomes *dispatched*.
4. **Result update.** A *dispatched* activity can either be *closed* upon successful execution, or return to the *to-be-assigned* state when the execution fails and automatic re-assignment is enabled.

Once assigned, the whole activity can be executed on mobile process engine and results committed and synchronized with the central engine.

3.4   Activity Execution on Mobile Devices

The activity (single task or sub-process) execution on mobile devices is performed by the process engine and the task performers.

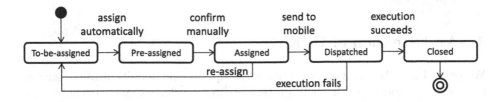

Fig. 3. Activity assignment

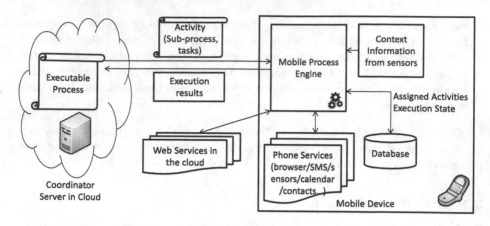

Fig. 4. Mobile process engine

Figure 4 shows the interaction between the central server in the cloud and mobile devices process engine. When the performer receives the process on her device, she can read the descriptions of the tasks assigned to her explaining when to start the tasks and how to execute them. When the performer starts the task execution, the mobile process engine checks if the execution constraint matches the task constrains and if the task can be executed under current context situation. If the execution constrains are satisfied, the performer can follow the instructions attached to the assigned tasks (e.g. FormService or EmailService) on the mobile device while the process engine will execute all the other service tasks such (e.g. SOAPService) or triggering of events.

When the process is deployed on the device, the engine parses the process definitions. It checks annotated execution constraints and verifies if their execution is supported on the current device. The contextual information is gathered from device sensors and saved in the process session or internal database. Data required for the process execution are loaded at deployment time from central server and saved on the device local database.

Current engine implementation does not enforce the returning of activity execution results and process state. The domain experts can decide when and how a process should return collected data to the central server. As it is shown in Fig. 1, it can be easily defined in the process model how to send back the execution result inside the Send Event elements that interacts with the central server in the cloud.

4   An Extension of BPMN

We extend the BPMN 2.0 specification to support the definition of constraint for assigning and executing sub-process on mobile device, and to enable the mapping of tasks and events to mobile specific services.

The extension is defined in the *extensionElements*, thus does not alter the predefined elements in process definitions. The traditional process editors and engines can still work with the process models that contains *extensionElements* defined by this extension, only that the extended semantics are ignored.

4.1   Context Constraints for Activity Assignment and Execution

We defined two categories of context constraints according to when the checking is performed: activity assignment and activity execution.

Assignment constraints. The task assignment tool matches the constraints against the profile and context information of mobile workers to suggest a binding between activity execution instance and the mobile worker. Such constraints can impose requirements on: mobile worker (e.g., roles, qualifications, affiliation), or mobile devices configuration (e.g., CPU capacity, free storage available, availability of specific APIs), or on any other context information (e.g., current geography location) available at the time of activity assignment. If there is no constraint to assign the activity, an assignment constraint with expression = true is defined to annotate that it is an activity to assign to mobile devices.

Execution constraints. Activity execution constraints are checked when the process engine on mobile device is going to start the execution of an activity. These execution constraints can impose requirements on context information available on mobile devices when starting the activity execution (e.g., current geography location, time).

Comparing these two categories of constraints, the assignment constrains are about relatively stable parameters characterizing the device and the user for process execution; while the execution constraints can be more transient parameters, since the mobile process engine verifies these conditions just before process execution.

It should be noted that conditional flows can also express the context constraints. However, we argue that it is better to detach those constraints that do not alter the structure of business process but only enable/disable the execution of the process, for reasons: the process structure is simpler and easier to evolve; it can exploit the rich context information available on mobile devices, and still remain interchangeable with traditional processes.

4.2   Services Provided on Mobile Devices

We define a *service* element to map tasks and events to mobile specific services. The *service* element can be inserted in *extensionElements* of tasks and events. An attribute *class* is defined in *service* element, which specifies the supporting component on mobile process engine. When the mobile process engine is finishing the execution of a task or event, the value of sub-elements in *service* will be passed to the next task or event.

Our BPMN extension syntax allows third-parties to define their own services. They can extend our mobile process engine or even implement their own engine to support the defined service. The XML schema of sub-elements for services is not restricted. It is up to the corresponding component on mobile process engine to consume the sub-elements of *service*. So far, our mobile process engine has provided *FormService*, *EmailService*, and *SOAPService*.

5 Mobile Process Engine and UI Framework

The framework that we have developed to support the mobile process definition, BPMN extensions to exploit mobile devices characteristics and the process execution includes the following components:

– A lightweight process engine for smartphones with Android operating system.
– A UI Framework that renders the user interfaces on mobile device according to the FormService definition. It manages also invocations of existing Android services such as mail service.
– A remote central server that hosts the process, checks the annotations, and assigns activities to the matched performers.

To test the process execution on mobile devices and to solve the identified challenges of process mobility under partially connected environment, we developed the mobile process engine for Android operating system. It uses XPath [8] library to parse the process definitions, and a SQLite instance [9] that is natively available on Android operating system to store the process execution state. When the performer starts the task execution, the mobile process engine checks if the execution constrains attached to the SubProcess, matches the current context information that is collected from the device sensors. If the execution constrains are satisfied, the performer can execute the process.

The mobile process engine provides an interactive form service to interact with activity performer and a email service to compose and send the email. Figures 5 and 6 show the usage of the FormService tasks to input patients data, administer the medicine, and confirm the measurement data before sending them with an email in Fig. 7 to the coordinator.

Fig. 5. Measure blood pressure

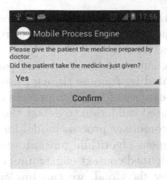

Fig. 6. Give medicine

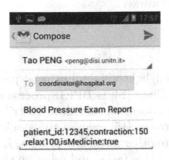

Fig. 7. Send response

The coordinator application runs on a central server on which an Activiti [10] process engine is deployed and exposed as a service in the cloud. The central process engine supports the process definition and it has been extended to support the parsing of context constraints by checking and automating the activity assignment. As previously mentioned, the supported context constraints include: constraints on environment such as time and geolocation; constraints on performer profile where any profile attributes defined by domain experts and coordinators can be used to match the activity assignment.

6   Discussion and Future Work

Although we have validated the first prototype in a simple nurse-visiting scenario, we need to test with more complex use cases. We are now adopting the framework in one project for children vaccine administration in Mozambique, and another project for personal lifestyle coaching. To assist the process designer to define the constraints and bind services, we are going to extend an available business process editor to allow domain experts to specify the context constraints and service endpoints.

Based on the formalization of representation and reasoning on process model [11,12], we can formalize the context constraint and process mobility to perform rigorous checking on process model.

Our current framework supports basic context constraints, i.e., attributes that can be directly evaluated by framework, e.g., user input, mobile server or mobile process engine. Researches of business process compliance checking [13], can provide more sophisticated validation to detect the violating process design, or even help to create the compliant process model for mobile execution.

Current activity assignment algorithm guarantees the result (task - worker tuple) is compliant to the defined context constraints of the processes, but may not be optimal. Powered by the cloud, we can implement more sophisticated algorithms to allocate tasks among available mobile workers and schedule the assigned tasks for a mobile worker.

7 Related Work

Researchers have developed light-weight business process engines to support mobile process execution. Sliver [14] is BPEL process engine for mobile device, but as it stated, the task allocation and data distribution challenges are not solved. The ROME4EU project [15] enables the single task assignment from a team leader's smartphone to other members' phones. It does not support assignment of process other than single tasks, and relies on the network during process deployment. Presto [16] is a pluggable platform that allows mobile users to perform different tasks depending on roles, physical environment, and process state. It focuses on process development on Internet of Things, and does not mention physical deployment of process on mobile device during run-time.

Tolerating the unreliability of mobile devices in business process execution is another related topic. Philips et al. designed a new workflow language NOW to support dynamic service discovery and communication to tolerate the communication or service failure in nomadic network [17]. Similarly, Mostarda et al. described an approach that can automatically generate a distributed choreographic implementation of a logically centralized orchestration process [18]. Different from these works, our focus is to enable dynamic activity assignment. Zaplata and Lamersdorf proposed a process management resource sharing and billing mechanism [19]. It still depends on connection, or even worse due to its peer-to-peer process engine sharing.

Our context constraints serve the similar purpose of activity assignment and execution, as other studies on business process task access control [20,21]. Our model of context constraints differs in the separation of assignment constraints and execution constraints. Under partially connected environment, this two-step control on constraints diminishes invalid activity assignment at early stage, and still enforces an accurate control of constraints on execution context.

8 Conclusion

Mobile devices and cloud infrastructure are becoming more powerful and more popular, and their integration is of great potential to extend the traditional business process management. Mobile devices include prevailing devices (e.g., smartphones) and new devices appearing (e.g., smart domestic electronics, embedded devices in vehicles). Their environmental contexts are becoming more complex, and connectivity to the cloud infrastructure remains a challenge for business process execution. In this paper, we proposed a framework to support the context-aware assignment and distributed execution of activities on mobile devices. The following research challenges are tackled:

1. The context constraint specification and mobile process engine allow the assignment of business processes from the orchestrator in the cloud to the mobile devices;
2. The UI and service components on the mobile process engine facilitate the execution of the process models with abstract service endpoints, allow the domain experts to focus on the business logic, and maximize the reuse of business process models;
3. By assigning and executing business process on the mobile process engine, constant connection to cloud is no longer mandatory to initiate the process execution. With complementary data prefetching mechanisms, the process execution on mobile devices gets higher success rate.

We demonstrated the deployment and execution of a business process for blood pressure examination. With the complete framework, the domain experts can design reusable business processes with less efforts, the coordinators get more efficient task allocation, and mobile workers can focus on the assigned work and worry less about the network disconnection. These benefits come from the join-force of cloud infrastructure and the mobile devices.

References

1. Hess, S., Kiefer, F., Carbon, R., Maier, A.: mConcAppt - a method for the conception of mobile business applications. In: Uhler, D., Mehta, K., Wong, J.L. (eds.) MobiCASE 2012. LNICST, vol. 110, pp. 1–20. Springer, Heidelberg (2013)
2. ActiveVos platform. http://www.activevos.com/
3. Pryss, R., Langer, D., Reichert, M., Hallerbach, A.: Mobile task management for medical ward rounds - the MEDo approach. In: La Rosa, M., Soffer, P. (eds.) BPM Workshops 2012. LNBIP, vol. 132, pp. 43–54. Springer, Heidelberg (2013)
4. Yuan, Y., Zheng, W.: Mobile task characteristics and the needs for mobile work support: a comparison between mobile knowledge workers and field workers. In: Eighth International Conference on Mobile Business 2009, pp. 7–11. IEEE (2009)
5. Object Management Group: Business Process Model and Notation (BPMN) Version 2.0. PDF (January 2011). http://www.omg.org/spec/BPMN/2.0/PDF (2011)
6. Corradi, M.: Design Collaborativo e Soluzioni Tecnologiche per lHealthcare: il caso MOPAL. Master Degree thesis, University of Trento (2010)

7. Signavio Process Editor. http://www.signavio.com/
8. W3C: XML Path Language. http://www.w3.org/TR/xpath20/ (2010)
9. SQLite database. http://www.sqlite.org/
10. Activiti BPM Platform. http://activiti.org/
11. Milner, R., Parrow, J., Walker, D.: A calculus of mobile processes, i. Inf. Comput. **100**(1), 1–40 (1992)
12. Cardelli, L., Gordon, A.D.: Mobile ambients. In: Nivat, M. (ed.) FOSSACS 1998. LNCS, vol. 1378, pp. 140–155. Springer, Heidelberg (1998)
13. van der Werf, J.M.E.M., Verbeek, H.M.W., van der Aalst, W.M.P.: Context-aware compliance checking. In: Barros, A., Gal, A., Kindler, E. (eds.) BPM 2012. LNCS, vol. 7481, pp. 98–113. Springer, Heidelberg (2012)
14. Hackmann, G., Haitjema, M., Gill, C., Roman, G.-C.: Sliver: a BPEL workflow process execution engine for mobile devices. In: Dan, A., Lamersdorf, W. (eds.) ICSOC 2006. LNCS, vol. 4294, pp. 503–508. Springer, Heidelberg (2006)
15. Russo, A., Mecella, M., Leoni, M.: Rome4eu-a service-oriented process-aware information system for mobile devices. Softw. Pract. Experience **42**(10), 1275–1314 (2012)
16. Giner, P., Cetina, C., Fons, J., Pelechano, V.: Presto: A pluggable platform for supporting user participation in smart workflows. In: MobiQuitous (2009)
17. Philips, E., Van Der Straeten, R., Jonckers, V.: NOW: orchestrating services in a nomadic network using a dedicated workflow language. Sci. Comput. Program. 1–27 (2011)
18. Mostarda, L., Marinovic, S., Dulay, N.: Distributed orchestration of pervasive services. In: Advanced Information Networking and Applications (AINA) (2010)
19. Zaplata, S., Lamersdorf, W.: Towards mobile process as a service. In: Proceedings of the 2010 ACM Symposium on Applied Computing, pp. 372–379 (2010)
20. Schefer-Wenzl, S., Strembeck, M.: Modeling context-aware RBAC models for business processes in ubiquitous computing environments. In: Mobile, Ubiquitous, and Intelligent, Computing (MUSIC) (2012)
21. Wolter, C., Schaad, A.: Modeling of task-based authorization constraints in BPMN. In: Alonso, G., Dadam, P., Rosemann, M. (eds.) BPM 2007. LNCS, vol. 4714, pp. 64–79. Springer, Heidelberg (2007)

Monitoring of Business Processes with Complex Event Processing

Susanne Bülow, Michael Backmann, Nico Herzberg$^{(\boxtimes)}$, Thomas Hille, Andreas Meyer, Benjamin Ulm, Tsun Yin Wong, and Mathias Weske

Hasso Plattner Institute at the University of Potsdam, Prof.-Dr.-Helmert-Str. 2-3, 14482 Potsdam, Germany

{nico.herzberg,andreas.meyer,mathias.weske}@hpi.uni-potsdam.de

Abstract. Business process monitoring enables a fast and specific overview of the process executions in an enterprise. Traditionally, this kind of monitoring requires a coherent event log. Yet, in reality, execution information is often heterogeneous and distributed. In this paper, we present an approach that enables monitoring of business processes with execution data, independently of the structure and source of the event information. We achieve this by implementing an open source event processing platform combining existing techniques from complex event processing and business process management. Event processing includes transformation for abstraction as well as correlation to process instances and BPMN elements. Monitoring rules are automatically created from BPMN models and executed by the platform.

Keywords: Business process intelligence · Complex event processing · BPMN · Event transformation · Event correlation

1 Introduction

The efficient and correct execution of business processes is essential for the success of an enterprise. Therefore, it is important to model and improve business processes as well as to monitor their executions [1]. Business process management systems (BPMS) control business processes and log the execution of process instances. These execution logs contain complete and structured information required for analysis and optimization of business processes. The information can be evaluated in the context of Business Activity Monitoring, for instance with process mining tools.

Yet in some cases, the use of a BPMS is not possible. Enterprises without a BPMS might still have large, complex processes that are executed distributed over several locations and are highly interesting to monitor. During process execution, there arises a lot of information in form of events. An event is the technical representation of a real world happening. In contrast to traditional execution logs, events cannot be analyzed as they are, since they might not be structured nor related to a process instance.

N. Lohmann et al. (Eds.): BPM 2013 Workshops, LNBIP 171, pp. 277–290, 2014.
DOI: 10.1007/978-3-319-06257-0_22, © Springer International Publishing Switzerland 2014

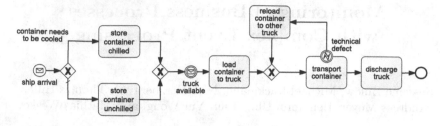

Fig. 1. Business process model of container transport process from harbor to destination in BPMN.

The goal of this paper is to enable business process monitoring with execution data, regardless of whether there are complete event logs or unstructured events. Therefore, we designed and implemented an open source event processing platform (EPP) combining existing techniques from complex event processing and business process management. The platform imports events from different sources, e.g., Excel lists or XML messages, and enriches them with information concerning the process, process instance, activity, and activity instance. In this approach, the methods of complex event processing are not only used for the actual monitoring but for the event enrichment as well. The system provides a high degree of flexibility and adaptability of those enrichment rules in order to make it configurable for different use cases.

The EPP presented in this paper builds upon a framework describing how to enrich raw events with context and process data via normalized and business events to process events [2]. There, raw events are the representation of real world happenings in information systems, normalized events have been put into a predefined structure based on the event type, business events contain contextual information existing orthogonally to business processes, and process events are correlated to specific process information, e.g., process instances. To allow monitoring of processes, we adapt the technique of event monitoring points [3], which are attached to specific state transitions of the life cycle of an activity [1] to signal the occurring of a specific event for a specific process instance.

The paper is structured as follows. Section 2 introduces a scenario that will be taken as a running example throughout the paper. Section 3 explains the developed techniques to enable monitoring without the existence of a BPMS. This includes transformation, correlation, and monitoring aspects as well as the architecture and implementation of the underlying platform realizing our concepts. Section 4 discusses related work before Sect. 5 concludes the paper.

2 Scenario

The scenario used as a running example in this paper addresses processes in logistics. Specifically, we want to examine a transport process of a container as it can be seen in Fig. 1 modeled in BPMN [4].

The container arrives on a ship at the harbor and is then stored at a warehouse. The storage is either chilled or unchilled depending on the goods stored in the container. As soon as a truck is available, the container is loaded to the truck and transported to the customer, where it is discharged. During the transport a technical defect might occur that turns it inevitable to reload the container to another truck.

There are a lot of events that occur during process execution. Some of these events can be seen in Fig. 2. A *ShipEvent* is sent from the ship containing information about the loaded containers, e.g., container id and storage hints, as well as arrival time. This event is in the EDIFACT format, which is the standard in technical business communication. The warehouse regularly sends Excel lists about the arrival of new goods or the sending of goods, which represents a *WarehouseEvent*. A *TruckReadyEvent* occurs when an empty truck is handed in at an in-house parking area. In our example, truck drivers are equipped with a mobile device that can send XML messages to the logistics headquarter. In this way a driver is able to send a message (*DriverReadyEvent*), when she is available for a new delivery. If a *TruckReadyEvent* and a *DriverReadyEvent* occur in the same area, driver and truck are available and can be used to transport the container to the customer. *DefectEvents* and *DeliveryEvents* are sent by the driver equally to a *DriverReadyEvent* informing the headquarter about a technical defect or updating the status of the delivery. Note that a *DefectEvent* is an unexpected event that does not need to occur for a successful process execution indicated by the dashed lines. Each type of event consists of different key-value pairs. Some example events can be seen in Fig. 3.

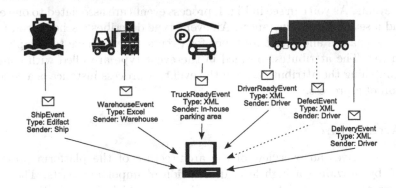

Fig. 2. Occuring events in container transport process

Event(1): WarehouseEvent	Event(2):TruckReadyEvent	Event(3): DriverReadyEvent
Timestamp: 17/04/2013 14:40	Timestamp: 17/04/2013 15:10	Timestamp: 17/04/2013 15:00
Container ID: AX23	Truck Number: 345	Driver Number: 987
Location: Rotterdam	Location: Rotterdam	Location: Rotterdam
Type: incoming		

Fig. 3. Examples for a *WarehouseEvent*, a *TruckReadyEvent*, and a *DriverReadyEvent*

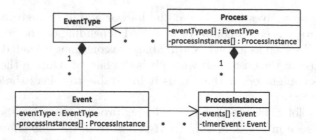

Fig. 4. Class diagram of the logical core classes for event processing.

The described process is not easy to monitor without software support, because these events are neither on the same abstraction hierarchy nor are they by content directly related to the process execution. However, with the approach described in this paper, it is possible to connect those events with the corresponding business process instances. Then, using the process model and some configuration rules, monitoring of the process execution is enabled.

3   Processing of Events and Monitoring

This chapter provides an overview of the platform's architecture and illustrates how correlation and transformation are used to enable the monitoring of process instances. It demonstrates the transformation from unstructured raw events to process events. As you can see in Fig. 4, process events are associated to one event type and a set of process instances. An event type describes a schema composed of attribute names and attribute types for events. Events have to comply with this schema. The attributes specified in the event type are filled with concrete values matching the attribute type in the event. A process instance is a concrete execution of a process.

3.1   Architecture

This section gives an overview of the architecture of the platform presented in Fig. 5 by providing a high level description of important parts. The *Event Producers* provide events to the *Event Receiver*, which forwards them to the *Correlation Processor*. Afterwards they are sent to the *Broker* that saves them via the *Persistence Layer* and passes them on to the *Query Processor* where the events are matched with the previously by the *Transformation Processor* and *Monitoring Processor* registered queries. The aforementioned important modules of the architecture are described in detail below.

Event Receiver. The *Event Receiver* is responsible for the import and normalization of events. It receives raw events from different external sources like

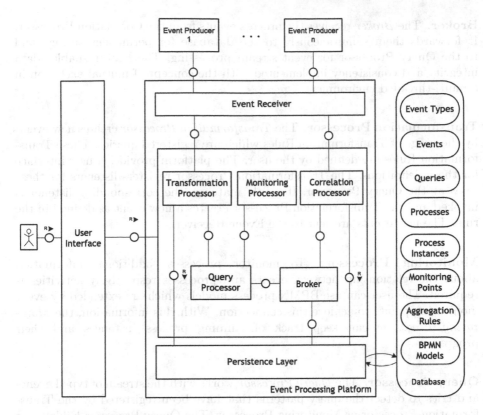

Fig. 5. Architectural overview of our event processing platform.

Excel (.xls/.xlsx), XML or EDIFACT files, and internally created events from transformation. The structure of raw events is undefined. Raw events and normalized events can be flat or hierarchical depending on the input. Based on the incoming events, the Event Receiver produces a normalized event stream. Normalized events are associated to an event type and contain at least a generated ID and a timestamp which can either be the import time or part of the incoming raw event. The remaining information is stored in the payload.

Correlation Processor. The *Correlation Processor* needs user defined rules to correlate events to process instances. Each event can be correlated to multiple process instances and each process instance contains a reference to one process. If there is no existing process instance representation in the EPP that fits to the incoming event, a new one is created. The correlation is executed on the normalized events from the event receiver and creates process events as output. Events which have no relation to any Correlation Rule are forwarded without modification.

Broker. The *Broker* receives the process events from the Correlation Processor. It forwards them simultaneously to the database for permanent storage and to the Query Processor for event stream processing. The Broker enables data integrity and consistency implemented with the concept of mutual exclusion in a multi-threaded environment.

Transformation Processor. The *Transformation Processor* creates new events by the usage of Transformation Rules which are registered queries. These Transformation Rules are defined by the user. The platform provides a user interface for these definitions. The Transformation Processor registers listeners for these rules at the Query Processor. If a rule matches, the corresponding listener is invoked and the Transformation Processor creates a new event as defined in the rule. The new events are sent to the Event Receiver.

Monitoring Processor. To monitor processes, additional information about the relationship between events and processes respectively activities is required. The user can use BPMN process models which are extended by event monitoring points to achieve this connection. With this information, the *Monitoring Processor* can keep track of running process instances and their progress.

Query Processor. The *Query Processor* works with the stream of typed events and tries to detect the query patterns that have been registered by the Transformation Processor or Monitoring Processor. The Query Processor holds these queries for monitoring and transformation. As soon as a query pattern matches, the Query Processor triggers the corresponding listener. The component that registered the query at the Query Processor can then react to the invoked listener. The Query Processor utilizes an event processing language (EPL), in our case the *Esper Query Language* [5].

Persistence Layer and Database. The *Persistence Layer* enables the connection of the platform to the *Database*. The database stores all relevant entities (processes, events, process instances, event types, etc.) and provides access to them. In our case, the database is realized with MySQL and the persistence layer connects the database to the platform implemented in Java via JPA, the Java persistence API.

In the following, we refer to the Transformation Processor in Sect. 3.2, the Correlation Processor in Sect. 3.3 and the Monitoring Processor in Sect. 3.4.

3.2   Transformation

Normalized events differ in quality since they originate from various business processes where events are captured with different techniques reaching from manual to fully-automated. Following the approach in [2], our Transformation Processor enables the creation of business events from normalized events and other business events by supporting the functionalities of *transformation event processing agents* described in [6] such as translation, aggregation, composition, enrichment and projection of events and the usage of context data that exists orthogonally to the business processes.

A Transformation Rule consists of a pattern that triggers the creation of a new event and the definition of the event that shall be created. The user has to define the pattern specifying conditions such as the execution order and filtering of events from different event streams. A Transformation Rule Editor abstracting from the Esper Query Language is provided to facilitate the creation of these patterns. The user can build a pattern by the usage of visual elements and suggestions with a preview illustrating the structure of the created pattern. Due to the graphical presentation and the input suggestions of the editor syntactical errors by the user can be avoided. To define the resulting business event, the attribute values have to be determined based on the selection of the event type for the event. These values are mapped by events included in the pattern definition or by context data pulled from the database. For unified access to the database, the context data is stored in an event structure. A query is derived from the Transformation Rule and registered at the Transformation Processor, which creates and activates a statement for the query. In the next step, the Transformation Processor registers a listener for the statement at the Query Processor. Once the events received from the Query Processor fulfill the defined pattern, the listener is invoked and the business event is created. If the type of this business event is referenced in another Transformation Rule, the creation of business events will cascade.

In the running example, events of the types *WarehouseEvent*, *TruckReadyEvent*, and *DriverReadyEvent*, e.g., Event(1), (2) and (3), as stated in Sect. 2 can be aggregated to a business event representing the information of an available driver with a truck assigned for the transport of a certain container. A *WarehouseEvent* expresses the arrival of a container in a warehouse and concurrently alerts the need for a transport via truck. Hence, a truck and a driver have to be available in the same region. This information is provided by events of the types *TruckReadyEvent* and *DriverReadyEvent*. The Transformation Rule defines a pattern matching on a *WarehouseEvent*, a *TruckEvent*, and a *DriverEvent* that occurred on the same location. If the events matching the pattern are received by the platform, the Transformation Rule is triggered, and the aggregated event is created as shown in Fig. 6. The transport planner can thus react to the aggregated event by assigning the driver to the truck and sending it on the road. In order to improve the location condition, a usage of context data referencing cities and container hubs to geospatial coordinates can be defined. By this means, the condition could be stated by defining a maximum distance of the locations and thereby enabling a more tolerant matching.

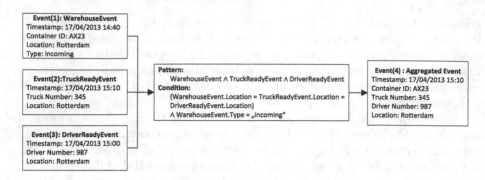

Fig. 6. Example of an event Transformation Rule creating a business event from normalized events.

3.3   Process Correlation

Every incoming event has to be assigned to a process instance to enable monitoring of processes. As already shown in Fig. 4, our events contain a list of process instances, where each process instance belongs to a process. *Correlation* is defined as "the relationship between two events and defines a collection of semantic rules to specify how certain events are related to each other" [7]. In our case, events are related to each other, if they contain equal values for certain attributes. These identifying correlation attributes define the relation of events to process instances as well. Thus, the Correlation Processor tries to correlate the events to a set of process instances.

In our approach, the *Correlation Rules* are defined by the user with suggestions from the *Correlation Processor*. The user has to determine a process for the Correlation Rule. Then he assigns a set of event types to the Correlation Rule. Every event type specifies a set of attributes. Out of these attributes, the user determines the identifying attributes for the Correlation Rule, the so called correlation attributes. The Correlation Processor uses the defined Correlation Rules during runtime in order to group matching events to process instances. The Correlation Processor groups all events from the database and new incoming events from external event sources that have an event type according to a Correlation Rule. Events belong to the same process instance, if they have the same value in the correlation attributes. Correspondingly, one process instance is created for every distinct value set of the correlation attributes.

In our example all events have an attribute which contains the identification number of the transported container (Container ID) (see Sect. 2). The Correlation Processor creates a process instance for every distinct identification number. This *single attribute correlation* is not sufficient for our use case as the process is intended to monitor a container from the arrival in the harbor until the discharge from the truck. Furthermore, one should consider that a container can be used several times. So if the container would arrive again some month later in the harbor, the event would be correlated to the same process instance as before. Therefore, it is possible to additionally correlate the events depending on their timestamp. One of the selected event types has to be determined as a timer and the user has to define a period of time starting or ending with the timer event. The timer can be seen as an additional Correlation Rule and if both rules (the single attribute and the timer rule) match, the event will be correlated to the process instance. In reference to the running example, the user determines the *ShipEvent* that indicates the arrival of the container in the harbor as timer event and defines the period of time as one week for the consecutive events. Therefore, the occurrence of an event of the type *ShipEvent* with the container ID *AX23* triggers the creation of a representation of the process instance in the platform. Event(2) as well as Event(4) from Sect. 3.2 are assigned to the same process instance. Events of the types *DefectEvent* and *DeliveryEvent* are treated the same way, if containing the same container ID and time frame. In consequence of enriching the Correlation Rule with the timer, a re-arrival of the container AX23 several months later, would result in an assignment of the new events to a second process instance.

3.4   Automatic Generation of Monitoring Queries

With complex event processing, it is possible to monitor the execution of processes and the analysis of finished process instances. Many users of process monitoring are more familiar with business process modeling languages than with an EPL like Esper Query Language in our case. Therefore, we decided to give the user the possibility to model a BPMN process and to upload it into the EPP. Afterwards, the Monitoring Processor derives queries from the BPMN process for the Query Processor. For automatic query generation, we assume, utilized BPMN process models are block-structured.

In order to create modular and independent queries, it is necessary to decompose the BPMN process in smaller components. We use the refined process structure tree (RPST) described in [8]. The RPST is an algorithm to decompose a workflow graph into smaller parts in a hierarchical structure. The elements of the RPST are *canonical* blocks with a single entry and a single exit. One advantage of a decomposition with the RPST is that the canonical blocks do not overlap, hence every edge of the model's graph is only considered in one query.

In the next step, we map every block of the tree to a specific pattern type which afterwards is used for the query creation. Possible pattern types for a block are:

- **Sequence:** all elements belong to a polygon of the RPST which indicates that they are in a sequential execution order.
- **Or:** the elements are located in a bond of the RPST on several paths (polygons), where only the elements of one path are executed.
- **And:** the elements are located in a bond of the RPST on several paths (polygons), where the elements of all paths are executed.
- **Loop:** the elements are located in a bond of the RPST and they belong to a loop.

- **Timer:** the polygon contains a sequence of elements that includes a boundary timer element which indicates the continuation of the process execution and interrupts the execution of the element with the attached timer after a specified time duration.

We generate a different query for each pattern type mentioned above. Additionally, there is a state transition query for each monitorable BPMN element. This state transition query represents the life cycle of a single element, therefore it is possible to monitor the different state transitions which an element passes through during its life cycle.

Figure 7a illustrates the three important canonical blocks for our scenario process. Due to the increased clarity, four smaller sequential blocks in the loop- and in the or-block are omitted. The canonical blocks have been enriched by their pattern types.

Besides, occurring events in the EPP need to be bound to the elements of the BPMN process. We enrich the BPMN process elements with event monitoring points as explained in [3]. A event monitoring point stores information concerning the different states of the element's life cycle. The state transitions within the event monitoring point can be bound to an event type via matching algorithms, e.g. string pattern matching or stemming. The matching is applied to the event type name and a certain value of the event monitoring point. Thus, it is possible to generate a query for every canonical block containing elements with event monitoring points. Only the elements with event monitoring points are monitorable and have to be considered whereas the remaining elements are ignored. In Fig. 7b the three generated pattern queries for the canonical blocks from Fig. 7a are depicted.

As mentioned above, the queries are written in the Esper Query Language [5]. This language provides patterns in order to query event streams. Every query is registered at the Query Processor, which provides a listener that then gives information about the query completion. The queries can be nested and also depend on the completion of other queries. The structure of the nested queries is closely related to the RPST-structure.

In our case, the Monitoring Processor is registered as a listener that collects the information about the execution status for every query. Through the assembly of the queries, it is possible to deduce the status of a process instance. The Monitoring Processor facilitates the monitoring of the running process instances and the detection of violations in the execution order. Furthermore, it gives possibilities to analyze finished process instances, e.g., the execution time or the frequency of execution paths.

In our scenario, the advancement and the status of containers can be pursued by means of this approach. Figure 7a illustrates how the event types introduced in Sect. 2 are bound to elements of the process model. If during process execution an event of the event type *ShipEvent* enters the Monitoring Processor, it is already correlated to a process instance. Then, the event is bound to the message start event of this process instance. The occurrence of an event of the type *WarehouseEvent* correlated to the same process instance will then indicate that

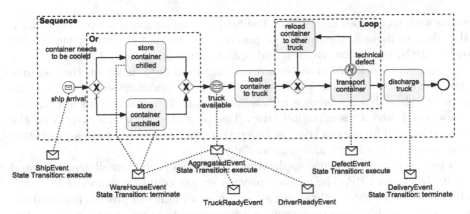

(a) BPMN process with canonical blocks and event types bound to process elements

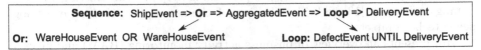

(b) Generated patterns for the BPMN process

Fig. 7. BPMN scenario process (a) with associated pattern queries (b)

the process instance is progressed to the waiting for a truck. Hence, through the binding of event types to process elements, e.g., activities, the progress of a process instance can be monitored in real-time with the arrival of the events.

3.5 Implementation

Our approach was implemented in a platform using the underlying EPL Esper and can be downloaded with test data and a screencast at http://bpt.hpi. uni-potsdam.de/Public/EPP. In the platform, event producers can be connected to the event receiver, who creates normalized events out of raw events. For event processing, transformation, and correlation rules can be configured. For monitoring, BPMN models annotated with event monitoring points can be uploaded to the platform and connected to business processes. A graphical Web interface is provided for usage of the system.

Summarizing, the users can configure and adapt the platform to monitor their processes with different event sources. Previously, process mining was not possible with heterogeneous and distributed raw events of process executions. With our platform, it is possible to deduce enough information to enable process mining and monitoring.

4 Related Work

The event processing platform (EPP) presented in this paper targets on an high-quality event basis for business process intelligence (BPI) by processing raw events with techniques known from the field is complex event processing (CEP). BPI aims to manage the quality of process executions by utilizing monitoring and analysis, prediction, control, and optimization [9,10]. [10–12] concerns the capturing and storing of business process execution data, however, they assume that every process step is recorded and thus, the resulting event log is complete. [9] describes a reference architecture for BPI, containing an integration, a functional, and a visualization layer. The presented approach targets on the integration and functional layer by integrating and combining process execution data, process knowledge, and context data.

Process mining [13] is one application of business process intelligence [14] and profits from the EPP. The created process events could be exported from the EPP to an event log to allow the extraction of all kinds of process information, e.g., execution times and conformance information to given process models. The presented EPP could be used as pre-processing step for the existing process mining techniques [13] to bridge the gap of the assumption that an event log needs to be complete.

[15] presents an overview of business activity monitoring (BAM) and gives a four class-categorization of BAM systems: pure BAM, discovery-oriented BAM, simulation-oriented BAM, and reporting-oriented BAM. As all of these classes base on events with high information content, the presented approach could be applied to enable BAM techniques and methods to provide valuable monitoring results by using the produced process events as input.

Del-Río-Ortega et al. [16] presents the concept of process performance indicators (PPI), the process related form of key performance indicators, to enable process evaluation. The presented EPP could provide the input for the so-called process measurements, e.g., time, costs, and occurrences and the concept of PPIs could be applied on top. Therewith, measurements can already be provided while process instance is still running. This enables that violations of tolerance thresholds can be mitigated before the process instance failed a PPI, for instance.

The first emphasis of the presented platform is set on the preparation of events for BPI. [17] explains an example of event preparation that creates structured event logs from static data tables. This is done without CEP context and therefore without hierarchical abstraction. In our approach, we use transformation as defined in [6] to abstract from low level events and create business events. Several works concentrate on the correlation of events to process instances. In [7], Correlation Rules are generated semi-automatically for various data sources. The Correlation Rules, we use, are determined by the user in our platform (with the guidance of the platform) and the corresponding procedure is manually configurable. Furthermore, our correlation is more flexible since it is not only dependable on correlation attributes but can be extended on time periods.

Secondly, we focused on automated BPI with the help of CEP. [18] introduces techniques to automatically generate Esper queries by taking a choreography model as a formalization of the process. We follow the same approach but with BPMN. In [19], BPMN models are taken as a basis to create EPL statements to monitor process violations but not to monitor the execution as it is our goal. [18] as well as [19] assume complete, structured event logs. Since we do not make the same precondition, the model in our approach must first be annotated with event monitoring points that bind events to states of the life cycle of BPMN elements as described in [3].

Our work supports and implements the framework introduced in [2]. We combine approaches to create queries from models with approaches concerning event preparation including normalization, transformation, and correlation to process instances and activity instances. Important terms related to CEP used in this paper are taken from [20].

5 Conclusion

In this paper, we have proposed an architecture for the approach to enable monitoring of business processes with execution data, independently of the structure and source of the obtainable events. We achieved this by using CEP with rules configurable by the user. Our approach supports business process models in BPMN, which is a well-known standard in process modeling. Furthermore, a graphical interface facilitates the usage of the system. Consequently, it can be used directly by managers without IT background. The developed platform can be easily configured for the user's own needs.

In future work, we intend to enhance our system to monitor process execution violations besides the actual instance monitoring. Beyond, the scalability and performance of our system has to be examined.

References

1. Weske, M.: Business Process Management: Concepts, Languages, Architectures, 2nd edn. Springer, Berlin (2012)
2. Herzberg, N., Weske, M.: Enriching raw events to enable process intelligence research challenges. Technical Report 73, Hasso Plattner Institute at the University of Potsdam (2013)
3. Herzberg, N., Kunze, M., Rogge-Solti, A.: Towards process evaluation in non-automated process execution environments. In: ZEUS, CEUR-WS, pp. 97–103 (2012)
4. OMG: Business Process Model and Notation (BPMN), Version 2.0 (2011)
5. Bernhardt, T., Vasseur, A.: Esper: event stream processing and correlation. http://onjava.com/pub/a/onjava/2007/03/07/esper-event-stream-processing-and-correlation.html, March 2007
6. Etzion, O., Niblett, P.: Event Processing in Action. Manning Publications Co, Stamford (2010)
7. Rozsnyai, S., Slominski, A., Lakshmanan, G.T.: Discovering event correlation rules for semi-structured business processes. In: Distributed event-based system, pp. 75–86. ACM (2011)
8. Vanhatalo, J., Völzer, H., Koehler, J.: The refined process structure tree. Data Knowl. Eng. 68(9), 793–818 (2009)

9. Mutschler, B., Reichert, M.: Aktuelles Schlagwort: business process intelligence. EMISA Forum **26**(1), 27–31 (2006)
10. Grigori, D., Casati, F., Castellanos, M., Dayal, U., Sayal, M., Shan, M.: Business process intelligence. Comput. Ind. **53**(3), 321–343 (2004)
11. Azvine, B., Cui, Z., Nauck, D., Majeed, B.: Real time business intelligence for the adaptive enterprise. In: CEC/EEE, p. 29. IEEE (2006)
12. Melchert, F., Winter, R., Klesse, M.: Aligning process automation and business intelligence to support corporate performance management. In: AMCIS, Association for Information Systems, pp. 4053–4063 (2004)
13. van der Aalst, W.M.P.: Process mining: overview and opportunities. ACM Trans. Manage. Inf. Syst. **3**(2), 7:1–7:17 (2012)
14. van der Aalst, W., et al.: Process Mining Manifesto. In: Daniel, F., Barkaoui, K., Dustdar, S. (eds.) BPM Workshops 2011, Part I. LNBIP, vol. 99, pp. 169–194. Springer, Heidelberg (2012)
15. Dahanayake, A., Welke, R., Cavalheiro, G.: Improving the understanding of BAM technology for real-time decision support. Int. J. Bus. Inf. Syst. **7**(1), 1–26 (2011)
16. del-Río-Ortega, A., Resinas, M., Ruiz-Cortés, A.: Defining process performance indicators: an ontological approach. In: Meersman, R., Dillon, T.S., Herrero, P. (eds.) OTM 2010, Part I. LNCS, vol. 6426, pp. 555–572. Springer, Heidelberg (2010)
17. Rodríguez, C., Engel, R., Kostoska, G., Daniel, F., Casati, F., Aimar, M.: Eventifier: Extracting process execution logs from operational databases. In: Demonstration Track of BPM Conference, CEUR-WS, pp. 17–22 (2012)
18. Baouab, A., Perrin, O., Godart, C.: An optimized derivation of event queries to monitor choreography violations. In: Liu, C., Ludwig, H., Toumani, F., Yu, Q. (eds.) CSOC 2012. LNCS, vol. 7636, pp. 222–236. Springer, Heidelberg (2012)
19. Weidlich, M., Ziekow, H., Mendling, J., Günther, O., Weske, M., Desai, N.: Event-based monitoring of process execution violations. In: Rinderle-Ma, S., Toumani, F., Wolf, K. (eds.) BPM 2011. LNCS, vol. 6896, pp. 182–198. Springer, Heidelberg (2011)
20. Luckham, D., Schulte, R.: Event processing glossary. http://www.complexevents.com/2011/08/23/event-processing-glossary-version-2-0/ (2011)

Bringing Semantics to Aspect-Oriented Business Process Management

Aldinei Bastos[(⊠)], Flávia Maria Santoro,
and Sean Wolfgand Matsui Siqueira

Programa de Pós-Graduação em Informática, Universidade Federal do Estado
do Rio de Janeiro (UNIRIO), Rio de Janeiro – RJ, Brazil
{aldinei.bastos,flavia.santoro,sean}@uniriotec.br

Abstract. In software development, crosscutting concerns, such as security, audit, access control, authentication, logging, persistence, transaction and error handling, can be modularized using aspect-oriented approaches, which can also benefit the business process from the reduction in complexity. Literature refers to techniques that address aspects on process implementation and modeling. However, they adopt different semantic representation of aspects and related elements, making it difficult to provide integration between these phases of the business process lifecycle. This paper aims at addressing the issue of cross-cutting concerns during the lifecycle of a business process with an approach based on an ontology for aspect-orientation and a semantic service invocation. Our main contribution is a bridge for the semantic gap between the modeling and implementation steps of aspect-oriented business processes.

Keywords: Aspect-oriented business process management · Semantics · Ontology

1 Introduction

Business processes consist of a set of coordinated activities performed within an organizational and technical environment [1]. They are described by business processes models, which should be simple enough to be understood by people, and at the same time, detailed enough to capture the complexity of the processes [2]. To deal with process models complexity, the strategy traditionally adopted is the decomposition in order to break business processes into sub-processes. However, there is a kind of complexity intrinsic to the business process requirements [2], such as security, audit, access control, authentication, logging, data flow and persistence, transaction and error handling, which can cross the modular structure of a process or of a set of processes. They are called crosscutting concerns.

These concerns appear tangled and scattered at several places of a same process or at different processes of a given model [3]. As the basic concepts of the process are mixed with the crosscutting concerns, the understandability of the process model is hampered. The maintainability of the process model is also compromised, since a change in a given concern might lead to changes in several places of the different process models where the concern is scattered. Furthermore, business process

N. Lohmann et al. (Eds.): BPM 2013 Workshops, LNBIP 171, pp. 291–302, 2014.
DOI: 10.1007/978-3-319-06257-0_23, © Springer International Publishing Switzerland 2014

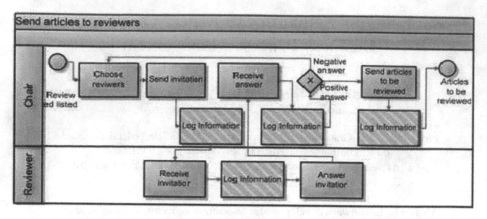

Fig. 1. Process model with the feature registration of transactions [3]

implementation should be based on a business process model, thus it could inherit the problems associated to the lack of crosscutting concerns modularity, also affecting its understandability and maintainability.

Figure 1 illustrates the representation of the requirement for registration of transactions (logging) scattered within the process model related to sending articles to reviewers. This kind of requirement is considered a crosscutting concern.

In software development, aspect-oriented approaches encapsulate crosscutting concerns as aspects and take them out of the core concerns in a given specification (requirements) or implementation (code) [4]. Applying the aspect concept can also benefit the business process from the reduction in complexity of the models by separating different concerns of the process. For instance, activities representing the *logging* concept could be modularized as an aspect.

To specify the composition of an aspect with the core process flow, an aspect contains pointcuts and advices. Pointcuts are the aspect elements that describe in which joint points of the process the aspect have to operate. Advices define the action which must be taken when a join point is reached. They can be configured to act before (before advice), after (after advice), or around (around advice) the join point. In the logging aspect case, the advice is the set of activities to log the core process.

Literature refers to two different, but complementary, tracks related to aspect-orientation in business processes, according to [5]: the first one is about techniques to address aspects on process implementation (e.g., [6]), and the second one uses the ideas of aspects in process modeling (e.g., [7]). Analyzing these approaches, we notice that they adopt different semantics in representation of aspects and related elements, making it difficult to provide integration between these phases of the business process lifecycle. While in process modeling the aspects and their elements are represented by visual elements as close as possible to what business experts and stakeholders already know, in process implementation the aspects are tied to technical solutions described by programming languages and software components.

This paper aims at addressing the issue of crosscutting concerns during the lifecycle of a business process through an approach based on an ontology for aspect-orientation and a semantic service invocation. The main contribution is a bridge for the semantic gap existing between the modeling and implementation steps of aspect-oriented business processes.

The paper is structured as follows: Sect. 2 discusses related work on aspect orientation in the different stages of business process; Sect. 3 describes the proposal, Sect. 4 illustrates a proof of concept, and Sect. 5 provides the conclusion and future work.

2 Aspect-Oriented Approaches for Business Process

2.1 Aspect-Oriented Business Process Modeling

In business processes modeling, as far as process models are built to represent different interests and perspectives of the business in a single view, the complexity of these models tends to increase [3].

The AOPML language [3] addresses the visual functionality for modularization of crosscutting concerns' representation and their relationships. Figure 2 illustrates the modularization of the requirement for registration of transactions. Notice that this proposal does not support characteristics related to the implementation or execution of the aspects. As well, other similar proposals found in literature are restricted to the modeling, such as [8] and [9].

2.2 Aspect-Oriented Business Process Implementation

Service orchestration languages allow describing executable business processes from interactions with Web Services. There are some languages proposed, but BPEL

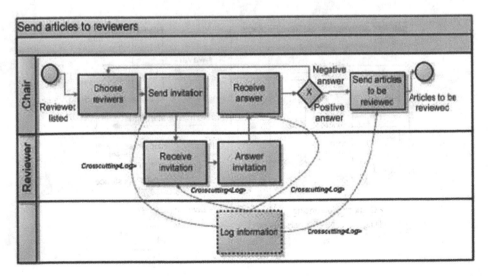

Fig. 2. Representation of a crosscutting concern as an aspect in a process model [3]

(Business Process Execution Language) has been considered as one of the most adopted by academia and market tools [10]. However, [6] argues that this language does not provide the means to modularize crosscutting concerns and does not provide appropriate support for dynamic adaptation of service composition.

To address these limitations, [6] proposes an BPEL execution engine adapted to handle the aspects at runtime, suggesting the use of Web Services for implementation of crosscutting concerns. Since [6] approach is restricted to the process execution phase, it is assumed that the identification and pre-configuration of services that will achieve the interests is previously made. Figure 3 shows an example of business processes and the crosscutting concerns audit and persistence, which are interpreted by the orchestration engine that invokes the services responsible for conducting interests.

The approaches found in literature for aspect orientation in business processes are bounded to only one stage of the lifecycle of business processes (either modeling or implementation). Furthermore, each approach has its particular goals, techniques and vocabulary; most often incompatible with each other, making it difficult to reuse and adapt aspects during the transition between modeling and execution.

3   Proposal Development

This paper proposes an Ontology for Aspect-Oriented Business Process Domain applied to business process management to enable the documentation, and development of the aspect all over the stages of processes modeling, configuration and implementation. Based on this ontology, we performed a proof of concept as a preliminarily evaluation of the proposal.

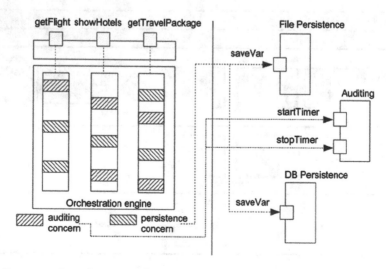

Fig. 3. Representation of a crosscutting concern as an aspect in a process implementation [6]

3.1   The Ontology for Aspect-Orientation in BPM

Ontology is a useful approach for the conceptualization of a domain, providing the unification of databases, knowledge bases, vocabularies, and for maintaining consistency in updating memories in knowledge management [11]. An ontology for aspect-oriented software development is already proposed in the literature, the AOSD Ontology [12]. We have extended this ontology for the domain of aspect oriented business processes, linking these with process model concepts and new aspect behavioral representations. The details of the business process concepts are not the focus of this ontology, because there are ontologies related to business process models already presented in the literature, as in [13]. Figure 4 shows an extract of the ontology, showing the relationship of the elements related to aspects with some crosscutting concerns samples.

During the modeling, a crosscutting concern can be identified and encapsulated as `Aspect`. In the ontology, `Security`, `Error Handling`, and `Logging` are samples of crosscutting concerns.

The `Pointcut` and `Advice` aspect elements can relate to any `ProcessElement` of a business process model, such as an activity or a sub-process.

The `Behavior` is the element of the `Aspect` that describes its performance for addressing the crosscutting concern. It can be represented by `BaseCode`, a model-based description of the process (`Process`), or an abstract definition of an objective (`Goal`). The goal concept represents an operational objective to express the desired behavior of a crosscutting concern within the business process. The concept is similar to that presented in [14], in which a procedure is proposed for the identification of aspects in processes based on the elicitation of operational goals of the process activities.

Using `Goal` as a description of the aspect behavior during the process modeling is appropriate, because usually during the process modeling phase the concrete implementation of the aspect is unknown; or flexibility in its implementation is desired. By extending the base ontology to a particular crosscutting concern domain, we extend

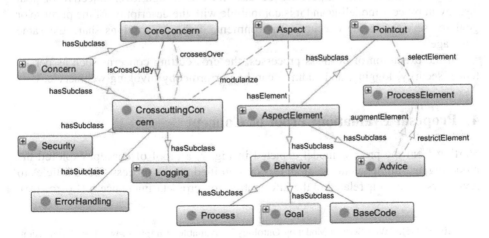

Fig. 4. Base ontology for Aspect-Oriented Business process domain

the Goal concept for the crosscutting concern characteristics to offer specific aspect settings to the process model.

In a traditional business process lifecycle where a software system is used to realize the business process, the business process model is enhanced at the configuration stage with technical information that facilitates the enactment of the process by the business process system [1]. In an aspect-oriented business process, the aspect elements and their settings, including goal definition, can be linked to the process configuration. This mechanism is known as aspect weaving and is explored in some works, such as [15].

In the next stage, to achieve the crosscutting concern implementation, we adopted the Web Service Modeling Ontology (WSMO) in a service architecture supported by the same conceptof Goal.

3.2   The Web Service Modeling Ontology Approach

A promising way of achieving a crosscutting concern at a business process run time is through the invocation of a Web Service. An approach for describing Web services suitable to the work presented here is the Web Service Modeling Ontology (WSMO).

The WSMO[1] provides a conceptual framework and a formal language for semantically describing all relevant aspects of Web service aimed at automation of discovery, invocation and dynamic combination of Web services. The framework is based on four pillars: Ontologies, Web Services, Goals and Mediators. Ontologies provide the terminology used by other WSMO elements to describe the relevant aspects of the domain. Web services are the functional parts, semantically described to allow semi-automatic use. Mediators are connectors that provide interoperability between the other components. Goals are objectives that the client have when accessing a Web Service.

The Goal here is equivalent to the same term of the ontology proposed in this paper. A Goal provides means to express the high-level description of a concrete task. Thus, the behavior of an aspect can be described as a high-level objective or goal already in process modeling and it is compatible with the description of the purpose or goal for services in the execution environment, if the descriptions share the same language.

In the execution of business processes, the crosscutting concerns such as persistence, security, logging, and auditing can be performedby invoking web services.

4   Proposal Evaluation: Proof of Concept

Starting from the process model depicted in Fig. 2, a proof of concept explored the modeling and implementation of an aspect identified on the process "Send articles to reviewers", which is related to the information log crosscutting concern (Logging).

---

[1] WSMO (2005), "Web Service Modeling Ontology", Available at http://www.w3.org/Submission/WSMO.

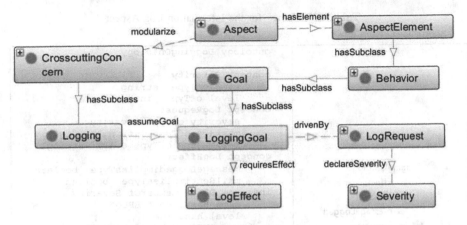

Fig. 5. An ontology extension for logging crosscutting concern domain

In order to address this aspect, we extended our base ontology to model a Logging Crosscutting Concern Domain, as shown in Fig. 5.

The description of the aspect behavior (`Behavior`) as an operational objective (`Goal`) needs the concepts related to logging, such as log request (`LogRequest`), effect/result of logging (`LogEffect`), severity of log information (`Severity`), and so on. Based on these concepts, we are able to configure our logging aspect in the process model for enabling implementation. We can use a specification language for this purpose.

Using WSML[2] specification language as entities of WSMO, we described these concepts in an ontology named *LoggingOntology* (see Table 1).

Using the ontology, a basic operational goal of information log is described as a Goal named *LoggingGoal* (see Table 2). The operational goal requires only some information as a precondition for implementation, which is the log severity, the log message and the message parameters.

A more restricting operational goal can specify that the information log is performed without communication by e-mail, as described by the `Goal` named *SilentLoggingGoal*, illustrated in Table 3.

From the description of operational goals, we can select and invoke services that meet the requirements of the aspect without prior knowledge of the location or implementation of these services. The service *MailAlertService* (see Table 4) serves the purpose of conducting further information log to an outgoing email. Thus, the service can carry out the implementation of the aspect with the *LoggingGoal* operational goal, but not of the aspect with goal of the *SilentLoggingGoal*.

A simple service that would meet the two goals is the *SimpleLogService* described in Table 5.

To effectively perform the services described based on operational goals instantiated, it is necessary an environment for executing the service models. For this proof

---

[2] WSML (2008), "Web Service Modeling Language", Available at http://www.wsmo.org/wsml/wsml-syntax.

Table 1. Ontology for the Information Log Aspect

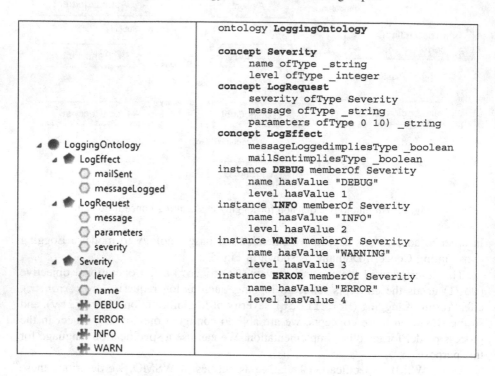

```
ontology LoggingOntology

concept Severity
    name ofType _string
    level ofType _integer
concept LogRequest
    severity ofType Severity
    message ofType _string
    parameters ofType 0 10) _string
concept LogEffect
    messageLoggedimpliesType _boolean
    mailSentimpliesType _boolean
instance DEBUG memberOf Severity
    name hasValue "DEBUG"
    level hasValue 1
instance INFO memberOf Severity
    name hasValue "INFO"
    level hasValue 2
instance WARN memberOf Severity
    name hasValue "WARNING"
    level hasValue 3
instance ERROR memberOf Severity
    name hasValue "ERROR"
    level hasValue 4
```

Table 2. Basic operational goal of the Information Log

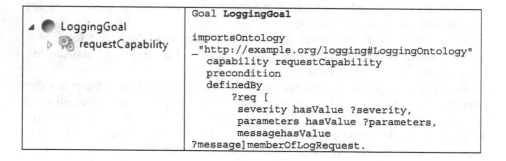

```
Goal LoggingGoal

importsOntology
_"http://example.org/logging#LoggingOntology"
    capability requestCapability
    precondition
    definedBy
        ?req [
        severity hasValue ?severity,
        parameters hasValue ?parameters,
        messagehasValue
?message] memberOfLogRequest.
```

of concept, we have chosen the Web Service Modeling eXecution environment
(WSMX). WSMX[3] enables discovery, selection, mediation, invocation and interoperation of Semantic Web Services (SWS). It implements a subset of WSMO and
contains repositories to maintain service entities, ontologies, goals, mediators and

---

[3] WSMX (2005), "Web Service Modeling Execution Environment", Available at http://www.w3.
org/Submission/WSMX/.

Table 3. Operational goal of the Information Log without communication by e-mail

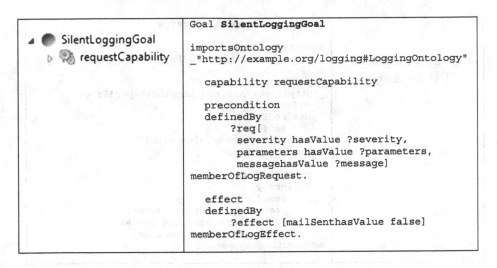

```
                            Goal SilentLoggingGoal

 ⊿ ● SilentLoggingGoal      importsOntology
   ▷ 🞕 requestCapability    _"http://example.org/logging#LoggingOntology"

                               capability requestCapability

                               precondition
                               definedBy
                                   ?req[
                                     severity hasValue ?severity,
                                     parameters hasValue ?parameters,
                                     messagehasValue ?message]
                            memberOfLogRequest.

                               effect
                               definedBy
                                   ?effect [mailSenthasValue false]
                            memberOfLogEffect.
```

Table 4. Information Log Service with communication by e-mail for severity >= WARN

```
                            webService MailAlertService

 ⊿ ● MailAlertService       importsOntology
   ▷ 🞕 capability              _"http://example.org/logging#LoggingOntology"
                            capability
                            _"http://examplo.org/logging#capability"
                               effect
                               definedBy
                                   ?effect[
                            messageLoggedhasValue true,
                            mailSenthasValue true] memberOfLogEffect.
                               precondition
                               definedBy
                                   ?req[
                                     parameters hasValue ?parameters,
                                     message hasValue ?message,
                                   severity hasValue ?severity]
                            memberOfLogRequest
                                   and
                                   ?severity[level hasValue ?level, name
                            hasValue ?name]
                               memberOf Severity
                                   and
                                   ?severityWARN[
                                     level hasValue ?levelWARN,
                                     name hasValue "WARNING"]
                                   and
                                   ?level >= ?levelWARN.
```

Table 5. Information Log Service with no restriction for communication by e-mail

▲ ● SimpleLogService
 ▷ 🧩 capability
	``
	webService SimpleLogService
	
	importsOntology
	 _"http://example.org/logging#LoggingOntology"
	
	capability
	_"http://example.org/logging#capability"
	  effect
	  definedBy
	      ?effect [
	  messageLoggedhasValue true]
	memberOfLogEffect.
	
	  precondition
	  definedBy
	      ?req [
	       severity hasValue ?severity,
	       parameters hasValue ?parameters,
	       messagehasValue?message]
	memberOfLogRequest.
	``

data. By combining the descriptions of Goals and Web services making use of inferences, the environment can perform discovery of the service implementation to be invoked to serve a given concern.

Web services that implement concrete crosscutting concern are implemented in a traditional manner, through a programming language, and are hosted on a Web server to be invoked.

Once WSMX was initialized, we recorded the entities of our proof of concept as statements of Ontologies, Goals and Web Services. The concrete Web Services were registered through their descriptors in Web Service Description Language (WSDL). The WSMX provides a mapping mechanism based on XSL transformation to relate our description of the semantic aspects of service with the descriptor of the concrete service specified in the WSDL. Once done this mapping, we could invoke the Web Service, providing as input to WSMX a request that is precondition for one or more operational goals representing the crosscutting concern of this business process, as shown in Table 6.

Table 6. Instantiating a log requisition to dynamically invoke a service

```
Instance logApproved memberOf LogRequest
Message hasValue "User %1 approved the ticket."
severity hasValue LoggingOntology#INFO
    parameters hasValue { "João" }
```

The proof of concept shows evidences of the viability to represent and document the behavior of an aspect at process modeling time through abstract goals without that implementation is previously known, allowing the desired behavior to be addressed at implementation time for services that are developed in compatibility with the described goals. Flexibility in the aspect implementation is noticed when we replace a service that meets the desired goal by another that fulfills the same goal.

5 Conclusions

The aspect orientation in business process modeling aims to reduce the complexity of the models. Literature has shown the advantages of this approach in different stages of the BPM cycle. However, in order to adopt a single aspect-oriented approach in all stages of business process management, it is necessary that the representations of aspects share a common vocabulary.

In this paper, we described a proposal to use an ontology for representing cross-cutting concerns, the aspects and their operational goals, allied with an execution environment that supports semantic services. The ontology can be extended for each type of crosscutting concern, enabling the process model to represent their aspects for later execution. The approach bridge the semantic gap between the modeling and implementation steps of aspect-oriented business processes.

A proof of concept highlighted the feasibility of the proposal, with the abstraction and adaptation of the aspect, besides automation while reducing the complexity of managing the process.

As future work, we plan to apply the concept to crosscutting concerns of various natures, enriching and extending the ontology of aspects, in addition seeking opportunities for benefits beyond the modeling and execution BPM phases. We plan to investigate whether known business process ontologies brings advantage to our base ontology. We should then bring analysts to evaluate our ontology, asking about its usefulness.

We also plan to perform a case study with an open-source workflow management tool, enabling this tool for aspects modeling, weaving and execution through the ontology and techniques presented in this paper.

References

1. Weske, M.: Business Process Management: Concepts, Languages, Architectures, 2nd edn., 407 p. Springer (2012)
2. Jalali, A.: Foundation of Aspect Oriented Business Process Management., Master Thesis, 98 p., Stockholm University (2011)
3. Cappelli, C., Leite, J.C.S.P., Batista, T., Silva, L.: An aspect-oriented approach to business process modeling. In: Proceedings of the 15th workshop on Early aspects EA 09, 7 (2009)
4. Kiczales, G., Lamping, J., Mendhekar, A., Maeda, C., Lopes, C.V., Loingtier, J., Irwin, J.: Aspect-oriented programming. In: Akşit, M., Matsuoka, S. (eds.) ECOOP 1997. LNCS, vol. 1241, pp. 220–242. Springer, Heidelberg (1997)

5. Santos, F.J.N., Cappelli, C., Santoro, F.M., Leite, J.C.S.P., Batista, T.V.: Aspect-oriented business process modeling: analyzing open issues. Bus. Process Manage. J. **18**(6), 964–991 (2012)
6. Charfi, A., Mezini, M.: AO4BPEL: An aspect-oriented extension to BPEL. World Wide Web Internet and Web Information Systems **10**, 309–344 (2007)
7. Cappelli, C., Santoro, F.M., Leite, J.C.S.P., Batista, T., Medeiros, A.L., Romeiro, C.C.: Reflections on the modularity of business process models: The case for introducing the aspect-oriented paradigm. Bus. Process Manage. J. **16**(4), 662–687 (2010)
8. Charfi, A., Müller, H., Mezini, M.: Aspect-oriented business process modeling with AO4BPMN. In: Kühne, T., Selic, B., Gervais, M.-P., Terrier, F. (eds.) ECMFA 2010. LNCS, vol. 6138, pp. 48–61. Springer, Heidelberg (2010)
9. Di Francescomarino, C., Tonella, P.: Crosscutting concern documentation by visual query of business processes. In: Ardagna, D., Mecella, M., Yang, J. (eds.) Business Process Management Workshops. LNBIP, vol. 17, pp. 18–31. Springer, Heidelberg (2009)
10. Andrews, T., Curbera, F., Goland, Y., Roller, D.: Business Process Execution Language for Web Services (2003). http://docs.oasis-open.org/wsbpel/2.0/OS/wsbpel-v2.0-OS.html
11. Gruber, T.R.: Towards Principles for the Design of Ontologies Used for Knowledge Sharing. In: Formal Ontology in Conceptual Analysis and Knowledge Representation 43, 907–928. (1993)
12. van den Berg, K., et al.: AOSD ontology 1.0 - public ontology of aspect-orientation. Technical report AOSD-Europe Deliverable D9, AOSD-Europe-UT (2005)
13. Nitzsche, J., Wutke, D., Van Lessen, T.: An ontology for executable business processes. In: Workshop on Semantic Business Process and Product Lifecycle Management (SBPM). CEUR Workshop Proceedings, vol. 251
14. Santos, F.G.N., Sampaio, J.C., Cappelli, C., Batista, T., Santoro, F.: Using goals to identify aspects in business process models. In: International Workshop on Early Aspects (EA '11), pp. 19–23. ACM, New York (2011)
15. Jalali, A., Wohed, P., Ouyang, C.: Dynamic weaving of aspects for business process management systems. In: Mendling, J., Weidlich, M. (eds.) Proceedings of the 4th International Workshop on the Business Process Model and Notation 2012, Vienna, Austria (2012)

3rd Workshop on Process-Aware Logistics Systems (PALS 2013)

3rd Workshop on Process-Aware Logistics Systems (PALS 2013)

Towards the Enhancement of Business Process Monitoring for Complex Logistics Chains

Cristina Cabanillas[1]([✉]), Anne Baumgrass[2], Jan Mendling[1], Patricia Rogetzer[3], and Bruno Bellovoda[3]

[1] Institute for Information Business, Vienna University of Economics and Business, Vienna, Austria
{cristina.cabanillas,jan.mendling}@wu.ac.at
[2] Hasso Plattner Institute, University of Potsdam, Potsdam, Germany
Anne.Baumgrass@hpi.uni-potsdam.de
[3] Institute for Production Management, Vienna University of Economics and Business, Vienna, Austria
{patricia.rogetzer,bruno.bellovoda}@wu.ac.at

Abstract. Logistics processes have some characteristics which are fundamentally challenging from a business process management perspective. Their execution usually involves multiple parties and information exchanges and has to ensure a certain level of flexibility in order to respond to unexpected events. On the level of monitoring, potential disruptions have to be detected and reactive measures be taken in order to avoid delays and contract penalties. However, current business process management systems do not exactly address these general requirements which call for the integration of techniques from event processing. Unfortunately, activity-based and event-based execution paradigms are not thoroughly in line. In this paper, we untangle conceptual issues in aligning both. We present a set of three challenges in the monitoring of process-oriented complex logistics chains identified based on a real-world scenario consisting of a three-leg intermodal logistics chain for the transportation of goods. Required features that such a monitoring system should provide, as well as related literature referring to these challenges, are also described.

Keywords: Business process management system · Process monitoring · Complex event processing · Information flow in international logistics · Logistics process

1 Introduction

The processes related to logistics chains have considerable differences with respect to processes realized in other domains. On the one hand, these processes

The research leading to these results has received funding from the European Union's Seventh Framework Programme (FP7/2007-2013) under grant agreement 318275 (GET Service).

N. Lohmann et al. (Eds.): BPM 2013 Workshops, LNBIP 171, pp. 305–317, 2014.
DOI: 10.1007/978-3-319-06257-0_24, © Springer International Publishing Switzerland 2014

are flexible, especially due to the fact that unexpected events can occur at any moment in the transportation process, e.g., due to accidents or to unfavorable weather conditions. On the other hand, logistics processes are often complex because of different means of transportation and/or various parties being involved, and a large amount of information being exchanged among the different parties. The resources involved are not only human resources (i.e., people), but also a variety of non-human resources are needed to assist in the transportation chain or in the exchange of information (e.g., cranes, Global Positioning System (GPS) devices, transponders). Specifically, the information exchange between dependent resources has to be ensured.

These special characteristics have an impact on the completion of all the phases of the business process lifecycle in the logistics domain. Grounding on the process lifecycle described by Dumas et al. [1], discovering and modeling such processes can be cumbersome: (i) expressive modeling notations supporting exception handling functionalities would be required; and (ii) the resulting process models could be large and difficult to read. Therefore, in order to implement and monitor the execution of logistics processes, special features are also required by the process engine and monitoring systems used. These features are mainly related to monitoring the collaboration among resources and handling of complex and unexpected events originating from different resources, so integrating functionality of Complex Event Processing (CEP) engines [2] into Business Process Management Systems (BPMSs) is required [3].

In this paper, we focus on the monitoring of complex logistics chains using process models as the mechanism for process execution, assuming that the previous lifecycle phases have already been addressed. Furthermore, we assume there is a system capable of capturing and processing events that occur during the transportation chain to monitor the information exchange among parties. Based on real processes discovered in the context of the EU-FP7 GET Service project[1], we describe a set of challenges to be faced for the monitoring of complex logistics processes. In particular, we look into monitoring from three perspectives, namely the monitoring of the status of the process, the monitoring of activities based on events, and the monitoring of the cargo being transported in the logistics chain. For each of these challenges, we provide an illustration and a conceptual description of the problem, a functional description referred to the monitoring system functionalities, and related work describing a similar problem in different application domains and solutions suggested.

In Sect. 2, we introduce the basic concepts handled in complex logistics chains by describing a real-world scenario. Section 3 describes the peculiarities of the monitoring of complex logistics processes. Section 4 presents the challenges identified, including the aforementioned information for each of them. Finally, conclusions and future work are summarized in Sect. 5.

---

[1] http://getservice-project.eu/

2 Introduction to Complex Logistics Chains

In the following, we describe a real scenario that allows us to define common terms in complex logistics chains and to study the requirements for monitoring the related processes. It consists of a logistics chain for the transportation of goods from the *client*'s warehouse in Austria to one of its distribution warehouses in Romania [4]. There is a *Third Party Logistics Provider (3PL)* in charge of organizing and controlling the whole transportation according to the *Service Level Objective (SLOs)* [5] defined by the client, which involve information such as the type of goods, amount, departure and delivery locations, and due time of arrival. Other *planners* participate in such a transportation too which is usually performed as depicted in Fig. 1.

Fig. 1. Inland waterway transportation from Austria to Romania

A train picks up the goods in the production warehouse and takes them to the port. At the *terminal* of the harbor, the *cargo* is loaded onto a vessel and transported to the port in Romania via the Danube river, traversing several countries (some of them not belonging to the EU customs, e.g., Serbia) and a total of ten locks. In each lock, the vessel must wait until the water level is regulated and the captain of the vessel receives permission to continue the transportation. Information about water level, traffic, opening and closing hours for locks, and updates on the *Estimated Time of Arrival (ETA)*can be received at any moment from an information and management technology service called River Information Services (RIS)[2]. Once in the port in Romania, a truck picks up the goods from the *terminal* and drives them to the distribution warehouse. In every *transportation leg*, the drivers of the vehicles and the captain of the vessel, must carry a set of

---

[2] RIS is a framework of compatible systems across Europe focusing on safety and traffic aspects of inland waterway transportation. Further information can be found here: http://www.ris.eu/.

documents called *waybills* [5] that contain the requirements and transportation information according to the contract for that specific transportation leg, also known as *forwarding instructions* [5]. These documents have to be presented upon request, e.g., in case of an inspection. The transportation chain finishes when an operator at the distribution warehouse reviews the freight and accepts the shipment. The process ends when payment and invoices are handled.

This logistics chain is complex and requires strong collaboration among all the parties involved due to several reasons. Firstly, it involves three transportation legs, that is, several well-limited steps in the transportation chain[3]. Secondly, there are different *transportation modes* (also called *means of transportation*) used throughout the process, namely railway, inland waterway, and road transportation. In particular, it is an *intermodal* logistics chain because there are several transportation modes involved but the *transportation unit* is not changed in the process, being it always units of goods. Lastly, more than thirty activities are performed by at least twelve different *stakeholders*, including the client, four *planners*, and seven *operators* belonging to different *shipping companies*, according to the process discovered [1].

Complex logistics chains involving many parties require much information exchange between different participants as well as punctual delivery for each transportation leg. The goal is to achieve the so-called Complete and On-Time Delivery (COTD) [6], that is, to transport the entire cargo from origin to destination, meeting the conditions agreed between *client* and *planner* in the SLOs. For that purpose, a number of systems must be used when required, e.g., Advanced Planning Systems (APSs), Transportation Management Systems (TMSs), and Intelligent Transport Systems (ITSs). In the case at hand, RIS is one of them. GPSs, transponders, and similar devices are also necessary. As a consequent, achieving reliable information exchange depends on the connection and collaboration between the parties and the systems involved. Thus, the events (e.g., positioning information) that are produced by the systems used in a logistics chain must be processed and appropriately distributed among the participants. Furthermore, proper reaction mechanisms to *disruptions* caused by unexpected events must be put into place and triggered when disruptions are detected. Altogether, reliable communication and reaction to disruptions in logistics chains depend on the identification and distribution of events as well as the correlation and aggregation of events to activities in the corresponding logistics process.

The business process for our logistics chain has been modeled in Business Process Model and Notation (BPMN) 2.0 [7], giving rise to the collaboration between participants represented in twelve pools, with more than thirty activities in total and plenty of messages exchanged. Figure 2 shows an abstract representation of such a BPMN model. We will use some of the activities there represented as example throughout this paper.

---

[3] Please note that *logistics chain* refers to technical and organizational activities, whereas *transportation chain* disregards the latter.

3   Process Monitoring in Logistics

Traditional BPMSs allow for modeling, executing, and analyzing business processes [1]. Each system requires an explicit business process model, e.g., modeled via BPMN, to enforce the execution of tasks by the right person at the right time using all necessary non-human resources. Our example in Sect. 2 shows that logistics chains demand information exchange among many parties since activities are executed across enterprise boundaries which in turn involve the need of having several different systems directly connected to a BPMS for controlling and monitoring the complete logistics chain. BPMSs are strong in coordinating and tracing discrete state changes of a business process. However, several logistics activities unfold in a continuous way, such as transportation which involves a continuous change of positions.

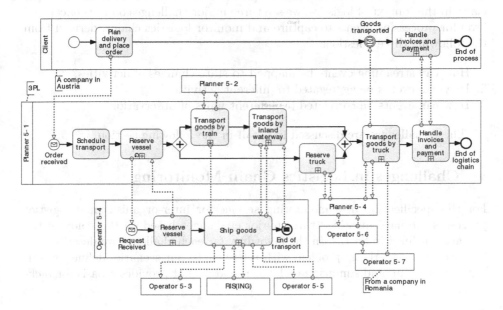

Fig. 2. Excerpt of the process model for inland waterway transportation

Recently, approaches have emerged that allow processing the great amount of events (e.g., positioning information) and at the same time permit using events as a basis for information exchange in inter-organizational processes (see, e.g., [3,8–10]). These approaches inspired our work to use events and derive information to manage, control, and monitor inter-organizational logistics chains.

The detection and processing of events originating from different systems can be handled by so-called CEP engines [11,12]. While BPMS operate on the basis of business process models, CEP engines process events based on event patterns. An event pattern describes the structure, causal dependencies, timing, data parameters, and context of events formalized via an Event Processing Language (EPL), e.g., Esper [13]. In the context of an Event-Driven Architecture (EDA), a CEP engine can consume, process, and publish/emit events from and to different systems, however, without controlling or monitoring the execution of a complete logistics chain. For logistics, a BPMS must be extended with CEP capabilities to allow the execution of logistics steps while managing the collaboration among different parties by integrating information coming from different systems. In other words, BPMS and CEP engines must be integrated to aggregate and correlate events to business process activities in order to enable the control and monitoring of a complete logistics chain.

In the context of CEP, the technical consumption, processing, and distribution of events in event-based systems has been discussed and is covered by existing approaches (see, e.g., [3,11,12]); however, less focus has been put on automated event handling in business processes in real-world scenarios. Especially in the context of logistics, we see three major challenges on the conceptual level for processing events to capture and monitor logistics chains, derived from the following three questions:

1. How can streaming events be mapped to state changes of activities?
2. How can events be aggregated to different activities?
3. How can events be correlated to different units of observation?

These challenges are discussed in detail in the following section.

4   Challenges in Logistics Chain Monitoring

For the specification of a monitoring service for inter-organizational logistics processes, we have identified three major challenges based on the study of the scenario outlined in Sect. 2. In the following, for each challenge we describe and illustrate the underlying problem with reference to our scenario, define its conceptual problem, and summarize related research that provides a basis for tackling it.

4.1   Discretization for Monitoring Status Based on Streaming Events

The first challenge relates to a gap between how transportation operations can be observed and how state changes are typically represented in business process models. Transportation operations unfold as a continuous movement of physical objects. In contrast to this, state transitions in a business process are discrete. For example, in subprocess "Railway transportation" in Fig. 2 there is an activity named "Take goods to port" in which the train driver performs the same activity during the entire activity execution, breaks to rest or put petrol apart. When we trace this activity, for instance using GPS sensor information, we receive a continuous stream of events related to geographic positions. This event stream per se does not inform us about the start and end of this activity, nor about exceptions related to potential problems occurred during the shipment.

The challenge is here to appropriately align continuous event streams with discretionary state changes. Specifically for monitoring, this entails the following problems of identifying start and end, as well as exceptions, as depicted in Fig. 3. First, additional information is required in order to measure the progress of a transportation activity. This requires traceability of where assets are at which moment in time (pos_i, t_i). Such information can be obtained from the GPS coordinates of the train (truck, or vessel) that are sent from some device attached to the vehicle or carried by the driver. Based on this type of data, a clear and explicit definition of start and end conditions have to be provided. In case such a definition is not possible, a human agent has to be involved in order to confirm start and end. Second, the event stream has to be continuously analyzed in order to notice exceptional behavioral or potential problems. Again, this requires the identification of exceptional events and corresponding conditions or patterns. If not all exceptional events can be defined in such a way, a human agent has to be involved.

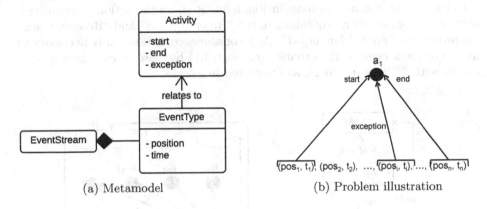

(a) Metamodel   (b) Problem illustration

Fig. 3. Monitoring status based on event streams

In order to avoid such problems, a discretization of the transportation chain is required. That means that criteria have to be established regarding the types of events that need to be received during continuous activities. Ideally, those types of events would refer to information of interest for the track and trace of the process execution, e.g., when a vehicle has achieved a percentage of the total distance, when the ETA has exceeded the due arrival time, or when the vehicle is stopped for an unexpected period of time. Therefore, the system should contain knowledge about the events to be taken into consideration and their potential consequences in the transportation process.

As aforementioned, the described challenge can be related to the problem of discretizing the transportation chain. In [14], Zaharia et al. introduce a new programming model called *Discretized streams (D-Streams)* that treats a streaming computation as a series of deterministic batch computation on small time intervals, thus lowering the event computation frequency of typical *record-at-a-time* processing models. The proposal by Appel et al. introduces event stream processing units as a conceptual frame for integrating complex event processing into BPMS [15]. In this concept, event streaming is a subordinate concept that can be started and completed within a classical workflow paradigm. Further modeling concepts are presented in [16,17].

4.2 Aggregation for Monitoring Activities Based on Fine-Granular Events

The second challenge relates to the fact that logistics operations provide an extensive amount of low-level event data. Therefore, activity monitoring requires the ability to automatically aggregate events to the activity instances of a business[4], in order to track and trace the process execution. Some logistics operations share part of the actions that are necessary to complete them, hence, there are events that can correspond to different process activities. For instance, several activities of the business process in Fig. 1 might share the action of creating a new order, e.g., activities contained in the "Reserve vessel" and "Reserve truck" subprocesses of pool "Planner 5-1". As a consequence, it is not only necessary to associate event types with activities (cf. Sect. 4.1) but also to associate specific events with activity instances, as illustrated in Fig. 4a.

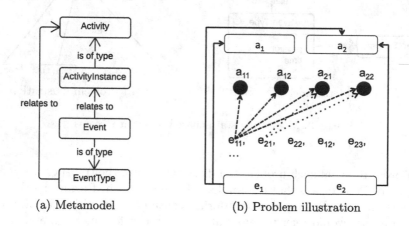

(a) Metamodel   (b) Problem illustration

Fig. 4. Monitoring coarse-granular activities based on fine-granular events

The challenge is here to deal with the different granularity levels between activities and events, i.e., activities provide less details than events. On the one

---

[4] In this paper, we define *aggregation* as a mapping of one or more events to one or more activity instances.

hand, an event type can be associated with several activities. On the other hand, an event can be associated with running instances of all the activities potentially related to this event type. Figure 4b contains an explicit representation of the problem. Events of type $e_1(e_{11}, e_{12})$ can occur during the execution of activities a_1 and a_2, and events of type $e_2(e_{21}, e_{22}, e_{23})$ are always related to instances of activity a_2. Thus, for each appearance in the event stream there are several aggregation options. In particular, e_{11} could refer to the four activity instances represented in the figure, e_{21} could be associated to the two instances of activity a_2, and so forth.

In order to deal with this issue, the system should support the cumbersome task of automatically aggregating events to activity instances during process execution. Sometimes, some events can be directly left aside for aggregation to an activity instance because of referring to a past state in the execution of the activity. For example, let us assume that we have three event types: e_1 indicates the start of an activity, e_2 the execution process, and e_3 its completion. Then, if we find an event e_{1i} that may be related to several activity instances, the activity instances a_{1i} for which an event of type e_1 has already been identified, can be disregarded, as event type e_2 is expected for them. Nonetheless, the problem persists for any other activity instance of type a_1 that has not yet started. In those occasions, decisions have to be made on how to associate events to activity instances. Appropriate heuristics are required in order to reduce the error margin in the aggregation.

Baier and Mendling state that an event to activity mapping is always a combination of both a mapping on type and a mapping on instance level [18]. They look at this challenge from the perspective of event logs. In particular, they assume the event logs contain specific information about each event, namely its name, the time when it occurred, and its transaction type in terms of whether the event has been completed or not; and they provide insights of all the possible mappings at type and instance level. For event to activity instance aggregation, they propose several heuristics for the definition of the *instance border conditions* such as the maximal distance between two events that belong to one activity instance. Clustering of events to activities is also discussed in other work. Günther, Rozinat and van der Aalst cluster events to activities based on time and position distance [19]. This approach is enhanced by considering co-occurrence of terms in [20].

4.3   Correlation for Monitoring Cargo Based on Events of Different Focus

The third challenge relates to the fact that cargo might be bundled, unbundled and rebundled during a *multimodal* transportation[5] activity, i.e., the so-called *focus shift* [21]. Goods are usually grouped and bundled into pallets, which are in turn distributed among containers, so the cargo cannot be considered as a single entity. Such bundling and unbundling tasks can be performed at different

---

[5] Use of two or more transportation modes changing the transportation unit.

stages of the transportation chain. It does not apply to our application scenario because it uses intermodal transportation.

The challenge in this case is to keep track of which *cargo unit* (*cu*) is loaded on which vehicle or vessel, which is outside the scope of process models, as they show an abstract representation of the general behavior of the process (i.e., for several executions) but cannot deal with such variability. Technically, this means that a multi-level containment hierarchy has to be stored for all legs of the transportation, as depicted in Fig. 5a. This also implies that there is potentially a 1:n relationship between process instance and transportation operations depending on the unit of observation (i.e., the *transportation unit* (*tu*)). If the vessel is the unit of observation, the transportation of the whole cargo from A to B relates to a single process instance. If each container is considered as a unit of observation, the same transportation relates to the process of each container (cf. Fig. 5b).

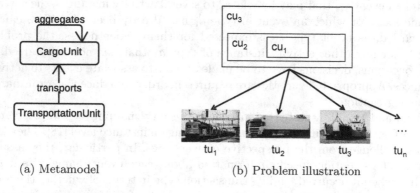

(a) Metamodel   (b) Problem illustration

Fig. 5. Monitoring cargo based on events of different focus

In order to address this problem, the different correlation levels at which cargo will be monitored must be defined, and the track and trace information must be updated after every bundling, unbundling or rebuilding operation. For instance, if bottle crates were the goods being transported in the scenario described in Sect. 2, in the production warehouse each bottle crate would be tracked and traced separately, i.e., the cargo unit would be a single bottle crate. Once several bottle crates were collected to be delivered as part of a transportation order, they would have to be considered as a whole, i.e., the cargo unit would be a group of bottle crates. Therefore, COTD would only be achieved if every single bottle crate belonging to that cargo unit, arrived at the destination point on time. Regarding the transportation unit to carry the freight in the as-is application scenario, it is likely to be a single train in the railway transportation leg. Similarly, the transportation unit in the inland waterway transportation is a unique vessel. However, if a large amount of cargo is being delivered, several trucks might be required to take the goods from the port to the destination warehouse. Thus, keeping track of every truck involved, is required.

As stated by Werner and Schill [5], modern Radio Frequency Identification (RFID) and sensor technologies enable the automatic identification of tagged items by eligible readers in combination with environmental information and thus can be used to monitor SLOs. Making use of this, they identify seven requirements for the monitoring of individual quality objectives for goods transportation using distributed event data, and describe the architecture of a corresponding monitoring system. However, the problem of focus shifts on cargo described above is not explicitly considered. Gerke et al. [21] investigate how the EPCglobal standard[6] for processing RFID can be utilized to construct supply chain case information from event logs, pointing out focus shift as key challenge in their approach. Besides such cargo monitoring mechanisms, some software must be implemented dealing with the monitoring of the transportation unit with which cargo is being transported. In [22], Patroumpas and Sellis define concepts for real-time traffic surveillance over densely congested road networks in large metropolitan areas. Their monitoring dashboards can also show current weather conditions, which may negatively affect the ETA. Further software solutions for the monitoring of events in logistics chains are, for instance, ProModel[7], TIBCO[8] and APAMA[9].

5 Conclusions and Future Work

Complex logistics processes require dedicated support of BPMS in order to monitor the expected execution and the occurrence of unexpected events. However, there are conceptual challenges for integrating event processing and business process management. This paper provides a basis for the conceptual enhancement of BPMS with CEP functionality for supporting logistics processes. Based on the case of a real-world logistics chain, we identified three major challenges that make the monitoring of such processes difficult. These include the discretization of streaming events, the aggregation of fine-granular event sets to activities, and the correlation of events that relate to the same cargo unit. For each of these challenges, we discussed related research contributions. This discussion reveals that there is currently no approach available that deals with these challenges in an integrated manner. In future work, we aim to address this research gap. More specifically, we will build a system that helps in discretizing, aggregating, and correlating events such that the overall business process can be traced.

References

1. Dumas, M., Rosa, M.L., Mendling, J., Reijers, H.A.: Fundamentals of Business Process Management. Springer, Heidelberg (2013)

---

[6] http://www.gs1.org/epcglobal
[7] http://www.promodel.com/solutions/logistics/
[8] http://www.tibco.com/industries/logistics/default.jsp
[9] http://www.progress.com/en/apama/apama-solutions.html

2. Mühl, G., Fiege, L., Pietzuch, P.: Distributed Event-Based Systems. Springer, Heidelberg (2006)
3. Daum, M., Götz, M., Domaschka, J.: Integrating CEP and BPM: how CEP realizes functional requirements of BPM applications (industry article). In: Proceedings of the 6th ACM International Conference on Distributed Event-Based Systems (DEBS) (2012)
4. Treitl, S., Rogetzer, P., Hrusovsky, M., Burkart, C., Bellovoda, B., Jammernegg, W., Mendling, J., Demir, E., van Woensel, T., Dijkman, R., van der Velde, M., Ernst, A.-C.: GET Service Project Deliverable 1.1: Use Cases, Success Criteria and Usage Scenarios (2013)
5. Werner, K., Schill, A.: Automatic monitoring of logistics processes using distributed RFID based event data. In: Proceedings of the Third International Workshop on RFID Technology (IWRT) (2009)
6. APQC: Blueprint for Success: Logistics, 2nd edn. APQC American Productivity and Quality Center, Houston (2011)
7. BPMN 2.0, Recommendation, OMG. http://www.omg.org/cgi-bin/doc?dtc/09-08-14.pdf (2011)
8. Rozsnyai, S., Lakshmanan, G.T., Muthusamy, V., Khalaf, R., Duftler, M.J.: Business process insight: an approach and platform for the discovery and analysis of end-to-end business processes. In: 2012 Annual SRII Global Conference. IEEE (2012)
9. Herzberg, N., Weske, M.: Enriching raw events to enable process intelligence - research challenges. Technical report 73, HPI at the University of Potsdam (2013)
10. Roth, M., Donath, S.: Applying complex event processing towards monitoring of multi-party contracts and services for logistics - a discussion. In: Daniel, F., Barkaoui, K., Dustdar, S. (eds.) BPM Workshops 2011, Part I. LNBIP, vol. 99, pp. 458–463. Springer, Heidelberg (2012)
11. Etzion, O., Niblett, P.: Event Processing in Action. Manning Publications Co., Stamford (2011)
12. Luckham, D.: The Power of Events: An Introduction to Complex Event Processing in Distributed Enterprise Systems. Addison-Wesley, Boston (2002)
13. EsperTech. Esper - Complex Event Processing, May 2013. http://esper.codehaus.org (2013)
14. Zaharia, M., Das, T., Li, H., Shenker, S., Stoica, I.: Discretized streams: an efficient and fault-tolerant model for stream processing on large clusters. In: Proceedings of the 4th USENIX Conference on Hot Topics in Cloud Computing (HotCloud), (Berkeley, CA, USA) (2012)
15. Appel, S., Frischbier, S., Freudenreich, T., Buchmann, A.: Event stream processing units in business processes. In: Daniel, F., Wang, J., Weber, B. (eds.) BPM 2013. LNCS, vol. 8094, pp. 187–202. Springer, Heidelberg (2013)
16. Kunz, S., Fickinger, T., Prescher, J., Spengler, K.: Managing complex event processes with business process modeling notation. In: Mendling, J., Weidlich, M., Weske, M. (eds.) BPMN 2010. LNBIP, vol. 67, pp. 78–90. Springer, Heidelberg (2010)
17. Caracaş, A., Kramp, T.: On the expressiveness of BPMN for modeling wireless sensor networks applications. In: Dijkman, R., Hofstetter, J., Koehler, J. (eds.) BPMN 2011. LNBIP, vol. 95, pp. 16–30. Springer, Heidelberg (2011)
18. Baier, T., Mendling, J.: Bridging abstraction layers in process mining by automated matching of events and activities. In: Daniel, F., Wang, J., Weber, B. (eds.) BPM 2013. LNCS, vol. 8094, pp. 17–32. Springer, Heidelberg (2013)

19. Günther, C.W., van der Aalst, W.M.P.: Mining activity clusters from low-level event logs. BETA Working Paper Series, WP 165, Eindhoven University of Technology (2006)
20. Günther, C.W., Rozinat, A., van der Aalst, W.M.P.: Activity mining by global trace segmentation. In: Rinderle-Ma, S., Sadiq, S., Leymann, F. (eds.) BPM 2009. LNBIP, vol. 43, pp. 128–139. Springer, Heidelberg (2010)
21. Gerke, K., Claus, A., Mendling, J.: Process mining of RFID-based supply chains. In: Proceedings of the 2009 IEEE Conference on Commerce and Enterprise Computing (CEC) (2009)
22. Patroumpas, K., Sellis, T.: Event processing and real-time monitoring over streaming traffic data. In: Di Martino, S., Peron, A., Tezuka, T. (eds.) W2GIS 2012. LNCS, vol. 7236, pp. 116–133. Springer, Heidelberg (2012)

Investigating Service Behavior Variance in Port Logistics from a Process Perspective

Ying Wang[1]($\boxtimes$), Filip Caron[2], Jan Vanthienen[2], Lei Huang[1], and Yi Guo[1]

[1] School of Economics and Management,
Beijing Jiaotong University, Beijing 100044, China
{ywang1,lhuang,11113164}@bjtu.edu.cn
[2] Department of Decision Sciences and Information Management, Faculty of Business
and Economics, KU Leuven, Naamsestraat 69, 3000 Leuven, Belgium
{filip.caron,jan.vanthienen}@kuleuven.be

Abstract. This paper presents an approach that explains the synergy between process mining and data mining for the investigation of the service behavior variances in the context of port logistics. The huge variances in service behaviors are identified and regrouped by the trace clustering technique applied to the operational processes. By incorporating domain information, the unsupervised process mining result is considerably improved in both accuracy and comprehensibility. Data mining techniques are then used for investigating the correlations between the variation in services and the contributing factors. The applicability of the proposed approach is demonstrated using an extensive case study carried out at an important Chinese port.

Keywords: Process-aware logistics systems · Service behavior · Port logistics · Process mining · Trace clustering · Data mining

1 Introduction

With the growing role of services in a service-oriented economy, there has been an increasing interest in the provision of better and innovative services to the clients [1]. Characterized as intangible, simultaneous production and consumption, heterogeneous, and perishable [2], a service can be defined as a series of activities for the delivery of a solution for a problem to the clients [3]. Therefore, special attention has been paid to the operational processes that deliver the services [4], which can be substantially different depending on the given context [5]. What's more, continuous service innovation has become the core capability of a service organization [6] within an intensified global competition. Consequently, the exponential growth of services considerably increases variances of the service behaviors as reflected by the operational processes.

This paper presents a comprehensive methodology for investigating the service behavior variances in port logistics from a process perspective. Considered as a classic example of service-oriented industry [7] with the abilities for the

N. Lohmann et al. (Eds.): BPM 2013 Workshops, LNBIP 171, pp. 318–329, 2014.
DOI: 10.1007/978-3-319-06257-0_25, © Springer International Publishing Switzerland 2014

provision of international value-adding logistics services, port logistics demonstrates a wide spectrum of potential process behaviors. A high emphasis has been placed upon the utilization of various knowledge elements as a vital intangible strategic resource [8] to achieve the enhanced port logistics service. This poses an interesting and very important research question as to obtaining port logistics service knowledge from the operational process variances: Which factors trigger changes in service behaviors? How do these factors influence the port logistics service behaviors?

The paper is structured as follows: Sect. 2 proposes the research objective through providing the necessary background on service behavior variance in port logistics as well as the techniques used for identifying the service behavior variances. The combination approach is presented in Sect. 3. Section 4 elaborates on the case study extensively and Sect. 5 gives the discussion. Finally, Sect. 6 concludes the paper.

2 Research Objective

Port logistics is a highly complex process involving numerous logistics activities dealing with voyage supporting, port entry, stevedoring, transit, storage, and inland transport connecting [9]. Considerable variances can be observed in the operational processes for delivering the port logistics services due to the numerous elements (e.g. the trade types, the inland transportation way) engaged. Take the cargo handling service as an example, though under normal circumstances rolled steel has to be weighed by the weigh bridge, some customers would prefer other cheaper methods (e.g. draught-based) to estimate the cargo weight. The knowledge in terms of these operational process variances constitutes a unique, inimitable, and non-transferable strategic asset [10] for the port companies in their efforts to deliver better and targeted services.

Process mining techniques have proved valuable for extracting non-trivial knowledge and interesting insights from operational processes [11]. For the real-life operational processes with a wide variety of potential behaviors, the results obtained by currently available process mining techniques often suffer from inaccuracy and incomprehensibility [12]. A divide-and-conquer approach was therefore proposed to partition the instances by trace clustering [13], which tries to split the event log into 'homogeneous subsets' each comprising instances with similar process behaviors.

The basis for measuring the similarity of cases in trace clustering technique is the concept of *trace profiles*. A *trace profile* is a set of items used to describe the trace from a specific perspective using information from the event log. The activity profile, for example, measures the activity item by counting the number of occurrences for each type of activity. Thus, an activity profile assigned to a trace is represented by a vector $< i_1, i_2, \ldots, i_n >$ with each item i_k indicating the number of occurrences for activity k for that case in the event log. The similarity between any two cases in the event log is accordingly calculated using a certain distance measure. For example, the Euclidean distance is the most popular metric for continuous features [14]. Various data clustering algorithms are then applied to regroup the log traces into subsets each composed of traces with a similar *trace profile*. As such, the unsupervised clustering methodology provides a viable way for regrouping the cases according to different service behaviors when little prior knowledge is available about the tacit process variables.

However, clusters obtained with little prior information available may have to be examined for their validity for the data [14]. In addition, there is an inherent difficulty with obtaining managerial insights from the process mining results within the context of unsupervised learning [15].

Aside from the control-flow perspective which records the existence and the ordering of tasks, the event logs can be augmented with the information about other perspectives for specific service industries where additional domain information (e.g. the customer region, the trade types) is available. This information can be related with the service behavior variance using a number of data mining techniques, which aim at deriving novel and useful patterns from large data repositories.

The research objective for this study is to provide a new method for investigating the service behavior variances in port logistics by a combination approach using process mining and data mining. The trace clustering technique is used to identify the different groups of service behaviors. Domain information is used to improve the accuracy and comprehensibility of process mining results. In addition, the service behavior variances are correlated with certain logistics elements using data mining techniques.

3   Methodology

In this section, we propose a formal roadmap and methodology which combines trace clustering and data mining techniques for investigating the service behavior variance. Figure 1 describes the proposed framework for implementing this approach as a series of sequential steps.

The underlying philosophy of the proposed combination approach is to apply the trace clustering technique for investigating service behaviors, whereas data mining techniques will be used to further analyze the contributing factors. The approach consists of five main steps as depicted in Fig. 1.

The first step involves investigating the case attributes and process events. Given an event log extracted from the information systems supporting the specific service operations, the service activities can be examined through the exploration of the events. Moreover, the event log can be extended with case attributes when the domain information (along with some derived information) is available for a specific service. This step will make the basis for the event log division in the next step.

During the second step, the complete event log is divided horizontally into case subgroups and vertically into event subgroups. The case attributes are used as the criteria for horizontal division, while the process events for vertical division. For example, the traces within the complete event log can be divided into subgroups each containing cases dealing with the same cargo types. In addition,

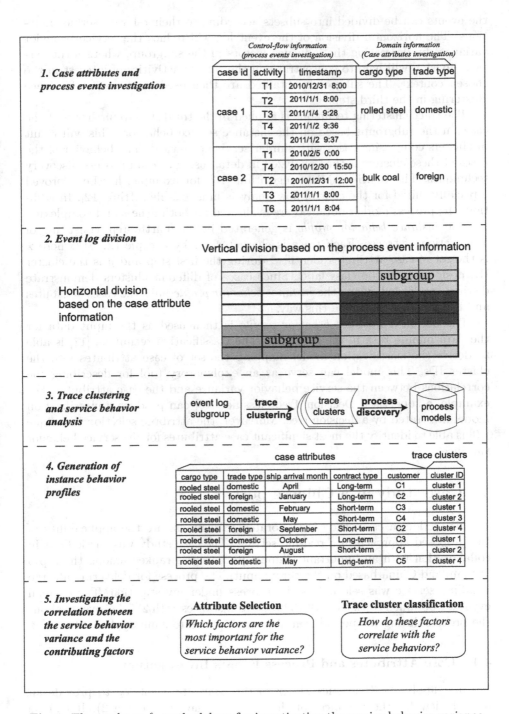

Fig. 1. The roadmap & methodology for investigating the service behavior variance

the events can be divided into subsets according to their relevant service functions. The horizontal division of the event log will reduce the service behavior variances by decreasing the influence factors in the subgroup, whereas the vertical division will help to concentrate on the service activities of interest in the chosen context. The subgroups obtained are then used as the input for trace clustering in the third step.

The trace clustering technique is applied in the third step to further split the cases in the subgroups based on the instance service behavior. This will result in clusters comprising cases with similar service behaviors. The behavior of the cases of these clusters is then analyzed in detail using a set of process discovery techniques. The HeuristicsMiner algorithm [16], for example, has been proved especially suited for the control-flow analysis in a real-life setting [12]. In addition, the process models obtained are evaluated for both fitness and complexity.

The *instance behavior profile* is generated in the fourth step, consisting of a collection of traces. Each trace is characterized by a tuple $(\mathbf{x}, y)$, where $\mathbf{x}$ is the set of case attributes identified during the first step and y is the cluster ID, designated as the class label. Since cases of different clusters demonstrate distinct service behaviors, the *instance behavior profile* links the cases attributes and the service behavior in this way.

The obtained *instance behavior profile* is then used as the input data for the data mining task in the fifth step. The classification technique [17] is able to derive the classification model mapping the set of case attributes into the cluster IDs. This model can serve as an explanatory tool for describing the correlations between the service behavior variance and the case attributes. For example, a supervised Decision Tree classifier [18] can produce a classification model illustrated by a decision tree. Moreover, the attribute selection technique [19] is able to identify the most significant case attributes for the service behavior variance.

4   Case study at a Chinese port

In this section, a case study is elaborated to demonstrate the applicability of the proposed approach in a real-life setting. The case study was carried out in collaboration with an important Chinese port that is ranked among the top 5 in mainland China based on the throughput. The process for delivering a cargo handling service was selected as the process under investigation. The original event log obtained consists of 10,752 process instances with 215,457 events about the process during the period from August 17, 2009 to January 4, 2012.

4.1   Case Attributes and Process Events Investigation

We first apply the Heuristics Miner to the complete event log to provide an overall view for the variances of the service behavior (see Fig. 2). It can be observed that the graph in Fig. 2 is of high complexity, consisting of 30 nodes and 252 arcs. This means that the process for delivering the service contains

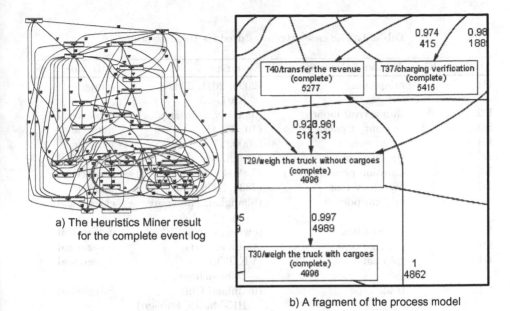

a) The Heuristics Miner result
for the complete event log

b) A fragment of the process model

Fig. 2. The discovered model for the whole process using the Heuristics Miner

30 types of service activities with huge variances for the service behaviors. These activities were then investigated for their functions in performing the service.

In total, the process traces contained in the event log deal with 67 types of cargoes carried by 760 different ships from 136 different ports all over the world. The domain information (e.g. the cargo type) is then obtained and used as the case attributes in the event log. In addition, some derived information (e.g. the information of case duration period) is added to the event log as extended attributes as well. Table 1 shows the case attributes used for the case study.

4.2 Event Log Division

We first apply the trace clustering technique to the complete event log. The activity profile is used to characterize the traces and the Euclidean distance metric is used to measure the similarity of cases. Table 2 shows the trace clustering results using SOM clustering algorithm, Density Based Clustering algorithm, and the K-means clustering algorithm respectively. Note that the degree of the graph complexity is measured by the arc-to-node ratios. On the whole, the heuristics nets resulting from these clusters are dense graphs that can hardly provide insights into the service behavior, with the huge amount of nodes and arcs as well as the high arc-to-node ratios. This indicates the necessity for event log division before applying clustering techniques in the "divide and conquer" strategy.

Table 1. The case attributes used for the case study

Attribute ID	Attribute Description	Examples	Attribute Type
D1	lump sum	(2096, 2041, 29426, 6801, ...)	numeric
D2	ship arrival month	(January, February, ...)	categorical
D3	amount of packages	(10, 23, 45, ...)	numeric
D4	cargo weight	(3000, 25000, ...)	numeric
D5	the customer	(c1, c2, c3, ...)	categorical
D6	duration period (days)	(3.89, 15.26, 123.32, ...)	numeric
D7	inventory cost	(7832, 9876, 0, ...)	numeric
D8	original port	(Shanghai, Singapore, ...)	categorical
D9	store or not	(owner, store)	categorical
D10	package type	(volume, parts, ...)	categorical
D11	ship name	(VICTORY, DonganJiang, ...)	categorical
D12	trade type	(mainland China, HK-Macao, Foreign)	categorical
D13	cargo distribution way	(truck, train, boat)	categorical
D14	cargo type	(rolled steel, coal, ...)	categorical
D15	contract type	(long-term, short-term)	categorical
D16	loading certificate type	(formal, temporary)	categorical

Table 2. A summary of the trace clustering result for the complete event log

Clustering	Cluster ID	#traces	Model fitness	#nodes	#arcs	Arc/node
SOM clustering algorithm	Cluster 1	10752	0	30	252	8.4
Density based clustering algorithm	Cluster 1	3072	0.35571247	29	129	4.45
	Cluster 2	5423	0.24995354	30	135	4.5
	Cluster 3	2257	0.43309698	30	104	3.47
K-means clustering algorithm	Cluster 1	541	0.6919859	29	61	2.1
	Cluster 2	2718	0.33425742	26	79	3.04
	Cluster 3	921	0.33847108	22	77	3.5
	Cluster 4	396	0.5087451	21	46	2.19
	Cluster 5	990	0.4468206	26	70	2.69
	Cluster 6	1519	0.36211777	28	132	4.71
	Cluster 7	406	0.37645078	23	68	2.96
	Cluster 8	1737	0.5797194	29	74	2.55
	Cluster 9	959	0.31511983	23	60	2.61
	Cluster 10	565	0.41708696	26	82	3.15

The complete event log is therefore divided before applying trace clustering using domain information both horizontally (based on the case attribute information) and vertically (based on the process event information). Since the cargo type would have a significant influence on the cargo handling service behavior, we first regroup the traces according to the cargo types. The traces of "rolled steel" are selected for the case study and the traces with short-term contract and temporary loading certificate are not included. What's more, we only focus on those dominant service activities dealing with contract signing (T1-1), ship arrival forecast (T4), tally book creation (T7), loading certificate creation (T16) and completion (T34), weighing (T23-2, T29, T30) and charging (T35). In total, we got a subgroup of the event log consisting of 2,813 instances and 16702 events as the input for the trace clustering.

4.3   Trace Clustering and Service Behavior Analysis

We then apply the K-means clustering algorithm to cluster the 2,813 cases according to the activity profile using Euclidean distance metric. Seven clusters are obtained and the three clusters containing more than 100 traces (see Table 3) are investigated. Significant improvement can be observed for this result in both model complexity and accuracy. More importantly, the heuristics nets (see Fig. 3) provide an explicit indication about the characteristics of service behaviors of each cluster. For example, there was no actual weighing activity for cases in cluster 0 and cluster 1 while both the weighing activities and the payment activities were carried out for all the cases in cluster 2.

Table 3. K-means clustering result for the subgroup of the event log

Cluster ID	Traces	Events	Nodes	Arcs	Arc\node ratio	Weighing (%)	Payment (%)	Model fitness
Cluster 0	1276	7656	6	7	1.17	0	100 %	0.8977077
Cluster 1	1181	5905	5	5	1	0	0	0.9871779
Cluster 2	324	2916	9	11	1.22	100 %	100 %	0.9031042

4.4   Relating Service Behavior Variances with the Case Attributes

The distinctive service behaviors are connected with the case attributes by generating an instance behavior profile which is composed of the case attributes and the cluster IDs (see Table 4).

We then apply the attribute selection algorithm CFS [20] to the data set and the attributes of 'D1' (the lump sum), 'D5' (the customer) and 'D12' (the trade type) are identified as the most significant factors contributing to the behavior variances. In addition, the decision tree classification algorithm J48 [21] is applied to *the instance behavior profile*. A decision tree model (see Fig. 4)

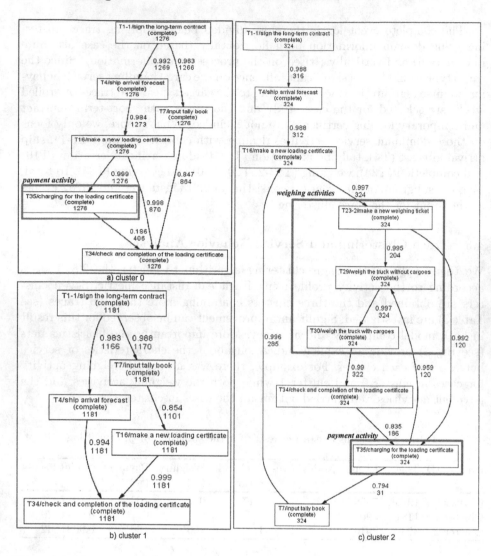

Fig. 3. The Heuristics Miner Result of the trace clusters resulting from applying K-means clustering algorithm to the event log subgroup

is derived and the classifier demonstrates a satisfactory performance. Note that traces of different clusters demonstrate distinct service behaviors (see Table 3). Some classification rules can be obtained accordingly as described in Table 5.

5   Discussion

Both technological and managerial implications can be obtained from the proposed method. On the one hand, the process mining result is significantly

Table 4. A fragment of the instance behavior profiles linking the cluster ID and the case attributes

D1	D2	D3	D4	D5	D6	D7	D8	D9	D10	D11	D12	D13	Cluster ID
4778	Jan	2		15860	C4	9.27	0	P5	Store	Volume	S4	F	Train Cluster 1
320	Dec	47		374030	C3	25.32	5905	P3	Store	Volume	S5	D	Train Cluster 1
112	Dec	14		231720	C2	9.27	260	P4	Owner	Volume	S4	H	Barge Cluster 1
254	Aug	150		399090	C5	9.27	58	P4	Owner	Volume	S3	D	Truck Cluster 2
1445	Dec	3		223635	C3	21.79	153	P3	Owner	Volume	S1	D	Truck Cluster 0
7586	Aug	5		135668	C2	36.68	0	P1	Store	Volume	S1	H	Barge Cluster 0
24421	Jan	31		204800	C1	6.06	59	P7	Store	Volume	S2	F	Truck Cluster 2

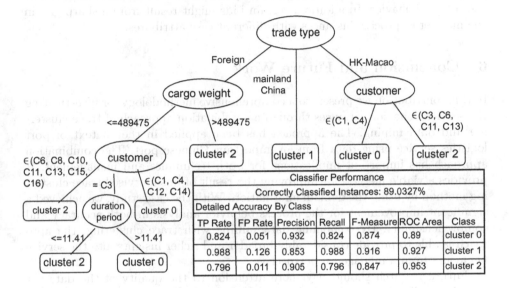

Fig. 4. Decision tree derived from the cluster classification according to the case properties

Table 5. The influence of "trade type" and "customer" on the process variances

Trade type	Cargo weight	Customer	Weighing	Payment
Mainland-China	-	(C2, C5, C7, C9, C17, C18)	No	No
Foreign	$(-\infty, 489475]$	(C6, C8, C10, C11, C13, C15, C16)	Yes	Yes
		C3	Yes or No	
	$(489475, \infty)$	(C1, C4, C12, C14)	No	
		(C1, C12, C13, C14, C15, C19, C3, C4, C6, C8)	Yes	
HK-Macao	-	(C1, C4)	No	Yes
	-	(C3, C6, C11, C13)	Yes	

improved both in the model accuracy and comprehensibility. By incorporating domain information, this approach effectively reduces the huge amount of variants hidden in the real-life processes. Consequently, the unsupervised trace clustering method is profitably modified making use of the domain information. On the other hand, the proposed approach provides managerial implications as well. By incorporating domain information with the unsupervised trace clustering method, process instances with similar service behaviors are regrouped into the same cluster, leading to a clear indication about the variances in service behaviors. In addition, the service behavior variance is correlated with the different domain elements through data mining techniques.

Challenges lie in extracting a suitable set of case attributes. An inappropriate set of case attributes may result in incomplete or inaccurate knowledge about the service behavior. In addition, certain bias might result from a sharp gap in the number of process instances with different case attributes.

6   Conclusion and Future Work

In this contribution we presented a comprehensive methodology for investigating the service behavior variances through a combination approach of trace clustering and data mining. The approach has been applied in the context of port logistics service using data from an important Chinese port. The combination approach has important implications for both techniques and management. It provides a viable method for improving the result of unsupervised trace clustering method by using the domain information. With the case study, we achieved a significant improvement for the process behavior analysis in both accuracy and comprehensibility. By combining data mining with trace clustering, the approach is able to provide considerably broader and richer insights into the service behaviors from a managerial perspective.

Future research should pay more attention to the quality of the data set and the application of other data mining techniques. Moreover, the comparison between this method and other approaches would be beneficial for the further improvement of this methodology.

Acknowledgements. This research is supported by the Natural Science Foundation of China under Grant Nos. 71132008.

References

1. Berry, L.L., Parish, J.T., Cadwallader, S., Shankar, V., Dotzel, T.: Creating new markets through service innovation. MIT Sloan Manag. Rev. **47**, 56–63 (2006)
2. Gallouj, F., Weinstein, O.: Innovation in services. Res. Policy **26**, 537–556 (1997)
3. Grönroos, C.: Service Management and Marketing, vol. 2. Wiley, New York (2001)
4. Reijers, H.A. (ed.): Design and Control of Workflow Processes. LNCS, vol. 2617. Springer, Heidelberg (2003)

5. De Brentani, U.: Success factors in developing new business services. Eur. J. Mark. **25**, 33–59 (1991)
6. Kandampully, J.: Innovation as the core competency of a service organisation: the role of technology, knowledge and networks. Eur. J. Innov. Manag. **5**, 18–26 (2002)
7. Chapman, R.L., Soosay, C., Kandampully, J.: Innovation in logistic services and the new business model: a conceptual framework. Int. J. Phys. Distrib. Logist. Manag. **33**, 630–650 (2003)
8. Siror, J.K., Huanye, S., Dong, W.: Rfid based model for an intelligent port. Comput. Ind. **62**, 795–810 (2011)
9. Roh, H.S., Lalwani, C.S., Naim, M.M.: Modelling a port logistics process using the structured analysis and design technique. Int. J. Logist. Res. Appl. **10**(3), 283–302 (2007)
10. Hult, G.T.M., Ketchen Jr, D.J., Cavusgil, S.T., Calantone, R.J.: Knowledge as a strategic resource in supply chains. J. Oper. Manag. **24**, 458–475 (2006)
11. van der Aalst, W.M., Reijers, H.A., Weijters, A.J., van Dongen, B.F., Alves de medeiros, A., Song, M., Verbeek, H.: Business process mining: an industrial application. Inf. Syst. **32**, 713–732 (2007)
12. De Weerdt, J., De Backer, M., Vanthienen, J., Baesens, B.: A multi-dimensional quality assessment of state-of-the-art process discovery algorithms using real-life event logs. Inf. Syst. **37**, 654–676 (2012)
13. Song, M., Günther, C.W., van der Aalst, W.M.P.: Trace Clustering in Process Mining. In: Ardagna, D., Mecella, M., Yang, J. (eds.) BPM 2008 Workshops. LNBIP, vol. 17, pp. 109–120. Springer, Heidelberg (2009)
14. Jain, A.K., Murty, M.N., Flynn, P.J.: Data clustering: a review. ACM Comput. Surv. (CSUR) **31**, 264–323 (1999)
15. Goedertier, S., De Weerdt, J., Martens, D., Vanthienen, J., Baesens, B.: Process discovery in event logs: an application in the telecom industry. Appl. Soft Comput. **11**, 1697–1710 (2011)
16. Weijters, A., van der Aalst, W.M., De Medeiros, A.A.: Process mining with the heuristics miner-algorithm. Technische Universiteit Eindhoven, Technical Report WP 166 (2006)
17. Kotsiantis, S., Zaharakis, I., Pintelas, P.: Supervised machine learning: a review of classification techniques. Front. Artif. Intell. Appl. **160**, 3 (2007)
18. Safavian, S.R., Landgrebe, D.: A survey of decision tree classifier methodology. IEEE Trans. Syst. Man Cybern. **21**, 660–674 (1991)
19. Hall, M.A., Holmes, G.: Benchmarking attribute selection techniques for discrete class data mining. IEEE Trans. Knowl. Data Eng. **15**, 1437–1447 (2003)
20. Hall, M.A.: Correlation-based feature selection for machine learning, Ph.D. thesis, The University of Waikato (1999)
21. Witten, I.H., Frank, E.: Data Mining: Practical Machine Learning Tools and Techniques. Morgan Kaufmann, San Fransisco (2005)

A Petri Net Approach for Green Supply Chain Network Modeling and Performance Analysis

Mi Pan and Weimin Wu[✉]

The State Key Laboratory of Industrial Control Technology & Institute
of Cyber-systems and Control, Zhejiang University, Hangzhou, China
lorna_pan@sina.com, wmwu@iipc.zju.edu.cn

Abstract. Green supply chain has become a promising and challenging field during the last decade driven by rising environmental conscious business and governmental legislation. In this paper, we develop a Petri-net based model to describe the green supply chain and to evaluate the essential performance. Generalized stochastic Petri nets (GSPN) are introduced to model the network of a general green supply chain with time characteristics. Performance analysis is carried out using the embedded Markov chain. Furthermore, we perform a comparison between green and normal supply chain to assert the superiority of the green supply chain in terms of profits.

Keywords: Green supply chain network · Generalized stochastic Petri net · PIPE2 · Modeling · Performance measures

1 Introduction

Under the global trend of circular economy and sustainable development, there is an increasing need for integrating energy-saving and environmental protection consciousness in business practice. As a consequence, green supply chain [7] becomes an attentive focus among researchers and industrial practitioners. According to the comprehensive reviews [16, 19], legions of relevant exiting studies are empirical and conceptual, while green supply chain modeling and network design is still a challenging and complicated issue in this area. Green supply chain network (GrSCN), known as closed-loop supply chain network, is the integration of the traditional forward supply chain process and reverse part. Forward chain has already been fully studied; reverse flow, namely recovery process, has been highly concerned and widely researched in recent years. Thierry et al. [12] distinguished three classes of activities for the returned products: direct reuse/resale without reprocessing; product recovery activities including repair, refurbishing, cannibalization, remanufacturing and recycling; and disposal. Fleischmann et al. [5] analyzed the general characteristics of recovery networks based on nine cases studies in different industries. Dowlatshahi [6] considered and analyzed the relevant literature in reverse logistics and generate a cost-benefit analysis regarding reverse logistics. Kumar et al. [17] explored a simple model for companies to understand and improve supply chain sustainability practices, and the model applied in two case studies proved that a green supply chain is a requirement for profitability. Even though the current achievement in GrSCN research is

N. Lohmann et al. (Eds.): BPM 2013 Workshops, LNBIP 171, pp. 330–341, 2014.
DOI: 10.1007/978-3-319-06257-0_26, © Springer International Publishing Switzerland 2014

encouraging, it seldom conducted in global business strategy. More research is necessitated in determining how green supply chain makes sense in different products. Besides, in terms of the methodology and approach adopted, Petri nets are seldom used.

Such a promising field is required for trying out new methodologies and using traditional techniques for overall design. In this respect, Petri net seems a novel method in GrSCN design. Moore et al. [11, 12] investigated a Petri net approach in making disassembly process plans automatically in product recycling or remanufacturing. Hanafi et al. [5] utilized a fuzzy colored Petri net in predicting the return of the end-of-life products in different locations for designing the collection strategies. However, these researches did not focus on integrity. Therefore, our work intends to study on the Petri net approach regarding the whole green supply chain network. It is also an encouraging area of trying out new applications of Petri nets.

In this paper, we view the green supply chain as a discrete event dynamic system and put forward a stochastic Petri net approach. Now that Petri net is such a perfect tool in system modeling and analysis, and less utilized in green supply chain area, our work is rewarding and innovated. More precisely, we aim at modeling the general GrSCN with Petri net, and then, analyzing the essential performance of the model.

The introduction of Petri net approach is presented in Sect. 2. Section 3 models the green supply chain network in a generalized stochastic Petri net. Performance analyses are discussed in Sect. 4 and 5. Section 6 draws conclusions.

2 An Overview of Petri Net Approach

Petri nets are used for modeling discrete event systems, first put forward by Carl Adam Petri [13] in 1962. As to its component, a Petri net consists of places, transitions, arcs and tokens. Places and transitions are model conditions and model activities respectively. They are connected by arcs. Tokens are in places, while a token transform from one place to another after firing the related transition.

Generalized Stochastic Petri nets (GSPNs), an extension of ordinary Petri nets with the additional behavior of timing, were originally proposed by G. Balbo and G. Conte [1] in order to better model, analysis and evaluate the real-life system with complexity and time-related features.

A GSPN [9] is a 6-tuple, $GSPN = \{P, T; F, W, M_0, \lambda\}$, where $P = \{P_0, P_1,...,P_m\}$ is a finite set of places; $T = \{T_0, T_1,...,T_n\}$ is a finite set of transitions, which can be divided into two types: timed transitions $T_i = \{T_0, T_1,...,T_k\}$, firing in exponentially distributed random times, which represent actions required some time to be completed, and immediate ones $T_i = \{T_{k+1},...,T_n\}$, firing in zero time, which represent logistical events; $F \subseteq (P \times T) \cup (T \times P)$ is a set of arcs associated with the firing relationship; Inhibitor arcs are additional in GSPN, which define that the appearance of tokens in the input places of inhibitor arcs will disenable the firing of the output transitions; W is the weight function, defining the weight of arcs, with $w_{ij}(T_i, P_j)$ is the weight of the arc from the transition T_i to its output place P_j and $w_{ij}(P_j, T_i)$ is the weight of the arc to the transition T_i from its input place P_j; M_0 is the initial marking of the Petri net; $\lambda = \{\lambda_0, \lambda_1...,\lambda_k\}$ is the array of firing rate of the corresponding timed transitions; $P \cap T = \emptyset$, $P \cup T \neq \emptyset$. Graphically, places are represented by circles, while transitions by rectangle boxes with immediate ones in black and timed ones in white. An inhibitor arc is drawn as a line with a small circle in end.

The behavior of the system can be described as the marking process. A marking in GSPN changed by the firing of the transitions according to the following firing rules:

1. *A transition T_i is enabled only when each input place P_j directing to T_i contains at least $w_{ij}(P_j, T_i)$ tokens. It fires by moving $w_{ij}(P_j, T_i)$ tokens from each input place node and depositing $w_{ij}(T_i, P_j)$ tokens in each output place node.*
2. *Immediate transitions have priority over timed transitions.*
3. *If more than one immediate transition is enabled at a marking M, which one can fired is based on the priorities and weights. The firing probability $P\{T_k\}$ can be illustrated in expression:*

$$P\{T_k\} = \frac{W(P_i, T_k)}{\sum_{j:T_j \in E(M)} W(P_i, T_j)} \tag{1}$$

where $E(M)$ is the set of enabled immediate transitions with the highest priority in marking M; $W\{P_i, T_j\}$ is the firing weight of transition T_j.

3 Modelling of the Green Supply Chain Network

Referring to the related literature, the general GrSCN is shown in Fig. 1. The raw materials gathered by the supplier are sent to the manufacturer for production, and then the finished products are delivered to the distributor and allocated to the retailer for selling. Used products from the customer are collected by the recycling collection center and detected for recovery process.

Fig. 1. A general green supply chain

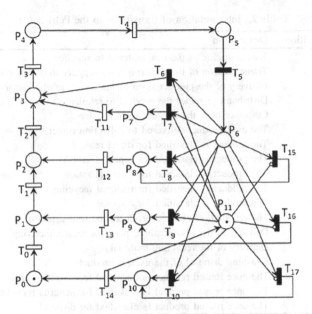

Fig. 2. GSPN model of green supply chain network

In this study, we model the GrSCN with the framework of GSPN (hereinafter referred to as GSPN-GrSCN). Figure 2 illustrates the GSPN model of the green supply chain network given in Fig. 1. Tables 1 and 2 give the description of each place and transition in the GSPN model respectively.

The token in place P_0 represents the initial state of the product, namely in raw material. And the flow of the token reveals the flow of the product in the GrSCN. The raw material is delivered to the supplier (P_1), and the manufacturer (P_2) obtains the material for production. The finishing product stored in distributor (P_3) is assigned to the retailer for selling (P_4). When the product is used out, it is collected (T_5) by the

Table 1. Interpretation of places in the Petri net

Places	Description
P_0	The raw material
P_1	Material stored in supplier
P_2	Manufacturer engages production
P_3	The product stored in distributor
P_4	Retailer sells the product
P_5	Customer uses the product
P_6	The recovery product inspected in collection center
P_7	Repair/Refurbish of the product
P_8	Cannibalization for remanufacturing of the product
P_9	Material recycling of the product
P_{10}	Disposal of the product
P_{11}	Assigning recovery mode

Table 2. Interpretation of transitions in the Petri net

Transitions	Description
T_0	Transportation of the raw material to supplier
T_1	Transportation of the material from supplier to manufacturer
T_2	Delivery of the product from manufacturer to distributor
T_3	Distributor provides the product to retailer
T_4	Customer buys the product from retailer
T_5	The used product delivered to collection center
T_6	The product is classified for direct reuse
T_7	The product is classified for repair/refurbish
T_8	The product is classified for cannibalization
T_9	The product is classified for material recycling
T_{10}	The product is classified for disposal
T_{11}	The repaired/refurbished product send to distributor
T_{12}	Delivery of the disassembled parts for remanufacturing
T_{13}	Delivery of the recycling material
T_{14}	Finishing disposal of the useless product
T_{15}	The once reused product is classified for cannibalization
T_{16}	The once reused product is classified for material recycling
T_{17}	The once reused product is classified for disposal

recycling collection center for detecting (P_5). Due to the fact that the customer using time of a product is much longer than other time consumption during the whole logistic flow, such as transporting time, manufacturing time, etc. We define T_5 as an immediate transition, not considered in performance evaluation. After the inspection, the collection center makes the decision of the recovery mode, including reuse (T_6), repair/refurbishing (T_7), cannibalization for remanufacturing (T_8), material recycling (T_9) and disposal (T_{10}). The function of the place P_{10} is to assign the recovery mode, that is the product only can be recovery through cannibalization (T_{15}) or material recycling (T_{16}) or disposal (T_{17}) if it has once be reused. We use an inhibitor arc to realize this. The token returns to place P_0 for another new recycling after material reclamation (T_{14}). Firing weight of immediate transitions T_6, T_7, T_8, T_9, T_{10}, T_{15}, T_{16}, T_{17} and firing rate of timed transitions T_0, T_1, T_2, T_3, T_4, T_{11}, T_{12}, T_{13}, T_{14} should be assigned according to the actual situations.

4 Stochastic Analysis

In this section, we show how the proposed model can be performed in performance analysis of green supply chain network. Note that the GSPN model is isomorphic with a semi-Markov process with a discrete state space, thus, performance analysis can be obtained by solving the underlying Markov chain problem. After generating the reachability tree, including tangible sates (the state only timed transitions are enable) and vanishing ones (the state at least one immediate transition is enable), the embedded Markov chain can be established, so does the calculation of stationary probabilities $P[M_i]$, equal to the steady state distribution of tangible states.

Various performance measures can be derived from the known stationary probability distribution as follow.

- The efficiency of each process e_i:
  This corresponds to the average number of tokens $\bar{u}_i$ in place P_i.

$$e_i = \bar{u}_i = \sum_j j \times P[M(P_i) = j] \tag{2}$$

  where $M(P_i)$ is the number of tokens in place when the marking is M, j is the probable number of tokens in P_i.
- The efficiency of the sub-procedure $E^{(l,k)}$:
  This corresponds to the sum of the average number of tokens $\bar{u}_i$ in the places of sub-system from place P_l to P_k.

$$E^{(l,k)} = \sum_{i:s_i \in S} \bar{u}_i = \sum_{i:s_j \in S} \sum_j j \times P[M(P_i) = j] \tag{3}$$

  where S is the sub-set starts from place P_l to P_k.
- Sojourn time for steady sate $\bar{\tau}[M_i]$:

$$\bar{\tau}[M_i] = \left(\sum_{T_j \in H} \lambda_j \right)^{-1} \tag{4}$$

  where H is the set of enabled transitions in M_i.
- The utilization of each workflow et_i:
  This corresponds to the transition utilization $U[T_i]$:

$$et_i = U(T_i) = \sum_{M_j \in E} P[M_j] \tag{5}$$

  where E is the set of markings where T_i is enabled.
- The throughput of each workflow r_i:
  This corresponds to the transition throughput $R(T_i)$:

$$r_i = R(T_i) = \sum_{P_j \in O} W(T_i, P_j) \times U(T_i) \times \lambda_i \tag{6}$$

  where O is the set of output places of T_i.
- Time consumption of sub-procedure $T^{(l,k)}$:

$$T^{(l,k)} = \overline{N}/\lambda = E^{(l,k)}/R(T_i) \tag{7}$$

The Little's Law [18] is used above, where $\overline{N}$ is the average number of tokens of the certain sub-system of the Petri net.

- Total time consumption T:

$$T = 1/R(T_{14}) \tag{8}$$

It reflects the efficiency of the whole system, and change in structure can promote the time performance.

- Manufacturing throughput $MT(P_2)$:

$$MT(P_2) = \bar{u}_2/\bar{u}_0 \tag{9}$$

This can be used for comparison. We define the average number of tokens in P_0 as the basic value, and thereby gaining the throughput as in (9). Variational parameters or different structures result in different manufacturing throughput.

With the above measures, we can also obtain the economic performance of the reclamation, which is discussed in the next section by considering the cost of each recovery process and the additional profit brought by reclamation.

5 Numerical Analysis

We use Platform Independent Petri net Editor 2 (PIPE 2) [8], a Java based editing and analysis software for Petri nets, as a tool for both model description and performance analysis. It is user-friendly and fully functional for this paper. It generates the reachability tree as seen in Fig. 3, where white ovals represent tangible (steady) sates and blue, vanishing (unstable) ones. Apparently, there are 13 stationary states and 4 vanishing ones in the GSPN-GrSCN model. Then, we have the embedded Markov chain (shown in Appendix A1).

To conduct a more visualized study, we first define the transition parameters. We assume the firing rate of timed transitions as $\lambda_{0,1,2,3,4,11,12,13,14} = [6, 3, 1.5, 6, 2, 6, 3, 2, 3]$ and firing weight of immediate ones as $W_{(P_6 \to T_6,T_7,T_8,T_9,T_{10},T_{15},T_{16},T_{17})} = [1,5,7,5,2,2,3,15]$. The Petri net state analysis shows it a bounded, safe and deadlock-free net.

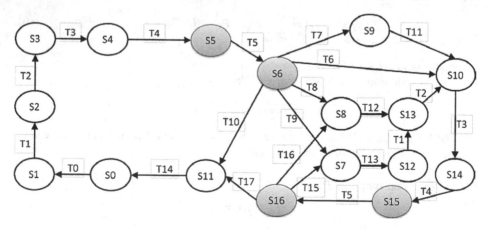

Fig. 3. The reachability graph of the GSPN model of GrSCN

The steady state probability of each state is illustrated in Table 3. Then we can compute the basic performance measures, including sojourn time, average tokens of places, transition utilization and transition throughput, of the GrSCN-GSPN model as indicated in Appendix A2, while Appendix A3 presents the results of the model when removing all the recovery parts (only remaining P_0, P_1, P_2, P_3, P_4, P_5, P_6, P_{10} and T_0, T_1, T_2, T_3, T_4, T_5, T_{10}, T_{14}).

Table 3. The steady probability of each state

State	Probability	State	Probability	State	Probability	State	Probability
M_0	0.04042	M_4	0.12126	M_8	0.038	M_{11}	0.14551
M_1	0.08084	M_5	0.08084	M_9	0.05214	M_{12}	0.03476
M_2	0.16168	M_6	0.0485	M_{10}	0.14551		
M_3	0.04042	M_7	0.01011				

The efficiency of each process can be attained in the light of (3) and (4). Specifically, Supplying efficiency contains material gathering and supplying process is 15.6 %; manufacturing efficiency is 30.7 %; product distribution efficiency is 8.9 %; retailer selling efficiency is 26.7 %; repair/refurbish efficiency is 1 %; disassembling efficiency is 3.8 %; material recycling efficiency is 5.2 % and disposal efficiency is 8.1 %. Supply managers can make wise decisions based on the above data, while arranging more staffs and more attentions to high-efficiency processes and reducing workers in low-efficiency processes for the maximization of the resource allocation. The utilization results show that the transportation of the product from manufacturer to distributor needs to be improved firstly. Besides, sales and material transportation are also two bottlenecks in the whole system, requiring attentions.

Manufacturing throughput of the GSPN-GrSCN model and the none-recovery one is 7.6 and 4, respectively. Obviously, recovery process nearly doubles the manufacturing performance, and enhances the manufacturing efficiency and utilization ratio.

Now we investigate the economic performance of green supply chain compared with traditional supply chain without recovery. Referring to [3], the values of the cost parameters for each process are given in Table 4.

Table 4. Value of the cost parameter for each process

Cost Parameter	Value (%)
Virgin unit price p_1	100
Second good's price p_2	80
Holding, Shortage and non-utilized capacity cost per unit per period c_1	10
Material cost per unit c_2	10
Manufacturing cost per unit c_3	10
Repairing cost c_4	5
Disassembly cost per unit c_5	3
Recycling cost per unit c_6	5
Disposal cost c_7	1

The economic benefit of none-recovery SCN per unit can be:

$$P_{n-recovery} = p_1 - c_1 \times \sum_{i=0}^{4} \tau[M_i] - c_2 - c_3 - c_7 = 60.67\,\%$$

and the additional profit brought by reclamation ΔP has:

$$\Delta P = p_2 - c_1 \times \sum_{i=5}^{11} \overline{\tau}[M_i] - c_4 \times \frac{U(T_{11})}{\sum_{k=11}^{14} U(T_k)} - (c_3 + c_5) \times \frac{U(T_{12})}{\sum_{k=11}^{14} U(T_k)}$$

$$- (c_3 + c_5 + c_6) \times \frac{U(T_{13})}{\sum_{k=11}^{14} U(T_k)} - c_7 \times \frac{U(T_{14})}{\sum_{k=11}^{14} U(T_k)} = 44.7\,\%$$

Then, the economic benefit of GrSCN per unit has:

$$P_{GrSCN} = P_{n-recovery} + \Delta P = 105.37\,\%$$

Clearly, reclamation increases the total profit more than half, bringing in great economic benefit to the company. This is also definitely a powerful proof of the necessity of green supply chain except its environmental factors.

6 Conclusions

This paper presents a Petri net approach for modeling and analyzing the green supply chain network, a promising research field both in academic and industrial area. The proposed model indicates the general green supply chain network pictorially and logically, consequently can be used in diverse industries in describing green supply chain. Base on the performance measures calculated by PIPE2, we put forward the approach to analyze the time performance, efficiency, manufacturing throughput and economic performance of the GSPN-GrSCN model. Results show that compared with traditional none-recovery supply chain, green supply chain improves the manufacturing throughput, drastically increasing the economic profit.

Green supply chain is not only a "hot" area under the global tendency of environmental business, but a promising field for trying out new application of Petri nets. This paper is just the first step towards a comprehensive research of green supply chain analysis, further work should extend to the following aspects: (1) discussing and analyzing more complex and realistic GrSCN; (2) applying Petri net approach in other fields of green supply chain, such as life-cycle analysis (LCA) of the product; (3) integrating Petri net with other tools to improve and optimize the proposed model.

Appendix

A1. Set of Steady States

State		P_0	P_1	P_2	P_3	P_4	P_5	P_6	P_7	P_8	P_9	P_{10}	P_{11}
S0	M_0	1	0	0	0	0	0	0	0	0	0	0	1
S1	M_1	0	1	0	0	0	0	0	0	0	0	0	1
S2	M_2	0	0	1	0	0	0	0	0	0	0	0	1
S3	M_3	0	0	0	1	0	0	0	0	0	0	0	1
S4	M_4	0	0	0	0	1	0	0	0	0	0	0	1
S11	M_5	0	0	0	0	0	0	0	0	0	0	1	0
S10	M_6	0	0	0	1	0	0	0	0	0	0	0	0
S9	M_7	0	0	0	0	0	0	0	1	0	0	0	0
S8	M_8	0	0	0	0	0	0	0	0	1	0	0	0
S7	M_9	0	0	0	0	0	0	0	0	0	1	0	0
S14	M_{10}	0	0	0	0	1	0	0	0	0	0	0	0
S13	M_{11}	0	0	1	0	0	0	0	0	0	0	0	0
S12	M_{12}	1	0	0	0	0	0	0	0	0	0	0	0

A2. Performance Measures of GSPN-GrSCN

Steady state M_i	Sojourn Time $\bar{\tau}[M_i]$	Place P_i	Average tokens $\bar{u}_i$	Transition T_i	Transition utilization $U(T_i)$	Transition T_i	Transition throughput $R(T_i)$
M_0	0.16667	P_0	0.04042	T_0	0.04042	T_0	0.24252
M_1	0.33333	P_1	0.1156	T_1	0.1156	T_1	0.34681
M_2	0.66667	P_2	0.30719	T_2	0.30719	T_2	0.46079
M_3	0.16667	P_3	0.08892	T_3	0.08893	T_3	0.53355
M_4	0.5	P_4	0.26677	T_4	0.26678	T_4	0.53355
M_5	0.33333	P_5	0	T_{11}	0.0101	T_{11}	0.06063
M_6	0.16667	P_6	0	T_{12}	0.038	T_{12}	0.11399
M_7	0.16667	P_7	0.01011	T_{13}	0.05214	T_{13}	0.10428
M_8	0.33333	P_8	0.038	T_{14}	0.08084	T_{14}	0.24252
M_9	0.5	P_9	0.05214				
M_{10}	0.5	P_{10}	0.08084				
M_{11}	0.66667	P_{11}	0.44462				
M_{12}	0.33333						

A3. Performance Measures of GSPN-SCN without Recovery

Place P_i	Average tokens $\bar{u}_i'$	Transition T_i'	Transition utilization $U(T_i)$	Transition T_i'	Transition throughput $R'(T_i)$
P_0	0.07692	T_0	0.07692	T_0	0.46153
P_1	0.15385	T_1	0.15384	T_1	0.46153
P_2	0.30769	T_2	0.30769	T_2	0.46153
P_3	0.07692	T_3	0.07692	T_3	0.46153
P_4	0.23077	T_4	0.23077	T_4	0.46153
P_5	0	T_{14}	0.15384	T_{14}	0.46153
P_6	0				
P_{10}	0.15385				

References

1. Ajmone Marsan, M., Balbo, G., Chiola, G., Conte, G.: Generalized stochastic petri nets revisited: random switches and prioritiesn. In: Proceedings of the International Workshop on Petri Nets and Performance Models, Madison (1987)
2. Dowlatshahi, S.: A cost-benefit analysis for the design and implementation of reverse logistics systems: case studies approach. Int. J. Prod. Res. **48**, 1361–1380 (2010)
3. El-Sayed, M., Afia, N., El-Kharbotly, A.: A stochastic model for forward-reverse logistics network design under risk. Comput. Ind. Eng. **58**, 423–431 (2010)
4. Fleischmann, M., Krikke, H.R., Dekker, R., Flapper, S.D.P.: A characterization of logistics networks for product recovery. Omega **28**, 653–666 (2000)
5. Hanafi, J., Kara, S., Kaebernick, H.: Generating fuzzy coloured petri net forecasting model to predict the return of products. In: IEEE International Symposium on Electronics and The Environment, vol. 245–250, pp. 7–10 (2007)
6. Hanafi, J., Kara, S., Kaebernick, H.: Reverse logistics strategies for end-of-life products. Int. J. Logistics Manag. **19**, 367–388 (2008)
7. Handfield, R.B.: Green supply chain: best practices from furniture industry. In: Proc 3th Annual Conference Decision Sciences Institute, New York, pp. 1295–1297 (1996)
8. http://pipe2.sourceforge.net/
9. Huang, Z.Q., Yi, R.H., Da, Q.L.: Study on the efficiency of the closed-loop supply chains with remanufacture based on third-party collecting. Chin. J. Manage. Sci. **3**, 73–77 (2008)
10. Lin, C.: Stochastic Petir Nets and System Performance Evaluation II. Tsinghua University Press, Beijing (2004)
11. Moore, K.E., Gungor, A.K., Gupta, S.M.: A petri net approach to disassembly process planning. Comput. Ind. Eng. **35**, 165–168 (1998)
12. Moore, K.E., Gungor, A.K., Gupta, S.M.: Petri net approach to disassembly process planning for products with complex AND/OR precedence relationships. Eur. J. Oper. Res. **135**, 428–449 (2001)
13. Petri, C.A.: Kommunikation mit Automaten. Thesis(PhD), Universität Bonn (1962)
14. Salema, M.I., Póvoa, A.P.B., Novais, A.Q.: Dynamic network design model with reverse flows. In: Sixteenth Annual Conference of POMS, Chicago, pp. 003–0036 (2005)

15. Kumar, S., Teichman, S., Timpernagel, T.: A green supply chain is a requirement for profitability. Int. J. Prod. Res. **50**, 1278–1296 (2012)
16. Samir, K.: Srivastava: green supply-chain management: a state-of- the-art literature review. Int. J. Manag. Rev. **9**, 53–80 (2007)
17. Thierry, M., van Wassenhove, L.N., van Nunen, J.A.E.E., Salomon, M.: Strategic issues in product recovery management. Calif. Manag. Rev. **37**, 114–135 (1995)
18. Travedi, K.S.: Probability and Statistics with Reliability, Queuing, and Computer Science Applications II. Wiley, New York (2001)
19. Zhang, X., Qiang, L., Teresa, W.: Petri-net based applications for supply chain management: an overview. Int. J. Prod. Res. **49**, 3939–3961 (2011)

Towards a DSL-Based Approach for Specifying and Monitoring Home Care Plans

K. Gani[✉], M. Bouet, M. Schneider, and F. Toumani

LIMOS, CNRS, Blaise Pascal University, Aubière, France
{gani,michel.schneider,ftoumani}@isima.fr,
marinette.bouet@univ-bpclermont.fr

Abstract. A (home) care plan defines the health cares or supportive cares delivered by health care professionals in patients' homes. Such a care plan is usually constructed through a complex process involving a comprehensive assessment of patient's needs as well as its social and physical environment. Managing home care plans is challenging because care plans are inherently non-structured processes which require complex interdisciplinary cooperation. This paper addresses the problems underlying the design and management of home care plans. First, we present a DSL (Domain Specific Language) based approach tailored to express home care plans using high level and user-oriented abstractions. Then, we describe and discuss preliminary results regarding formalization of the proposed DSL abstractions using timed automata in order to provide basic services to support analysis, verification, enactment and management of home care plans.

Keywords: Business process management · Domain specific language · Timed automata · Home care plan

1 Introduction

A business process is a collection of activities performed in coordination in order to achieve a particular business goal [8]. Current Business Process Management (BPM) landscape includes methods, techniques and tools developed over the last decades to support the design, analysis, enactment and management of operational business processes. BPM systems are *process-aware* in the sense that they require an explicit representation of business processes. This feature makes BPM systems very suited to handle structured processes where all the process execution paths are known in advance and captured in the process description. However, while many enterprise applications deal with structured processes, e.g., supply chain management, CRM, etc., there is an increasing number of applications where the underlying business process is unstructured or semi-structured. BPM models and concepts need to be extended to tackle such processes.

As part of the project Plas'O'Soins[1], we are interested by the problems underlying the design and management of home care plans. Home care refers to health

---

[1] http://plasosoins.univ-jfc.fr/

N. Lohmann et al. (Eds.): BPM 2013 Workshops, LNBIP 171, pp. 342–354, 2014.
DOI: 10.1007/978-3-319-06257-0_27, © Springer International Publishing Switzerland 2014

care or supportive care delivered by health care professionals in patients' homes. The target objective for social and economic reasons, is to enable people that require care to remain at home instead of having, long-term, stays in hospitals or health care facilities. Several types of care may be provided to persons in their own homes including health services, e.g., hospital-level care, and activity of daily living such as bathing, dressing, using the toilet, etc. These services are delivered by an interdisciplinary care team. A care plan defines all the services provided for a given person and coordinates the involved health care professionals. Such a plan is usually constructed through a complex process involving a comprehensive assessment of patient's needs (e.g., medical, nursing, social needs) as well as its social and physical environment.

Managing home care plans is challenging for several reasons. First, process modeling in the medical field is in general not an easy task [4]. Indeed, medical processes require usually complex coordination and interdisciplinary cooperation due to involvement of actors from various health care institutions. Moreover, home care plans display the following features that make them difficult to handle with traditional BPM technologies:

- A home care plan can be viewed as a collection of repetitive activities, (e.g., medical acts) which are repeated during a given period. The activities are however enacted according to an irregular schedule. The irregularities of an activity have two main causes. At first, the activity very often has to follow the evolution of the needs which is usually irregular. This type of irregularity is characterized by strengthening or weakening in the rhythm of realization. Then, an activity which requires human resources has to respect life cycles appropriate to this type of resources and in particular rest time of the weekend. This type of irregularity induces interruptions in the rhythm of the realization. Specification of irregular activities requires the use of suitable temporal constraints.
- Home care plans are essentially unstructured processes in the sense that each patient has its own specific care plan. Indeed, the care plan for each patient is developed on an individual basis because each patient is unique whether at its pathology or needs. Therefore, it is simply not possible to design a unique process capturing in advance the care plans of all the patients. In other words, a traditional approach *"model once, execute many times"* is not sustainable in our context.

To tackle the aforementioned problems, we aim in the Plas'O'Soins project at providing a high level specification environment that can be used by end users, in our case typically a medical coordinator, to design patient home care plans. The main features of our approach are described below.

- the cornerstone of our approach lies in the definition of a DSL (Domain Specific Language), or more specifically a business DSL, tailored to express home care plans using high level abstractions. The proposed DSL is a graphical language which provides basic constructs suitable for home care stakeholders.

- A supporting environment that enables to translate the produced specifications into a formal language, based on timed automata [2], and provides basic services to support analysis, verification, enactment and management of home care plans.

The paper is organized as follows. Section 2 discusses the difficulties underlying the design of care plans and presents the proposed DSL. Section 3 describes preliminary results regarding mapping of DSL-based specifications into timed automata and discusses automatic verification and monitoring of care plans in the proposed framework. We conclude and draw future research directions in Sect. 4.

2   A DSL-Based Approach for Specifying Care Plans

The design of a care plan is a complex collaborative process, managed by a primary medical coordinator and carried out by an interdisciplinary team. In order to understand such a design process and also to understand how a medical coordinator approaches the problem, we conducted in the context of the Plas'O'Soins project a thorough on-sites analysis of current practices in the field of home care. In particular, we carried out interviews with different professionals of home care institutions and we realized several analysis of key documents and procedures. This study showed the central role played by care plans as primary components of effective care coordination in patient's home. In a nutshell, a care plan encompasses all the services provided for a given patient and is essential to schedule the delivery of such services in the patient's home by health care professionals. More precisely, a care plan can be viewed as a collection of repetitive activities to be delivered to a given patient. An activity corresponds to a health care or a supportive care which is associated with temporal constraints (e.g., an *irregular* frequency) and to a required qualification (a nurse, a nurse auxiliary, etc). Table 1 shows a simple example of a content of a care plan for a given patient.

This example illustrates some important concepts of a care plan. The first column of Table 1 shows the period in which this plan is valid while the column Activity give the activities included in the plan (e.g., toilet, dress, injection). For each activity, the following information are given: (i) temporal constraints associated with the activity and expressed in terms of a Time slot (e.g., morning, afternoon or evening) and Repetition (e.g., every day except sunday), and (ii) the required qualification to carry out the activity (e.g., nurse auxiliary, nurse). Irregular activities are inherent to care plans. For example, a given activity, e.g., *"toilet"*, may be associated with complex temporal constraints, e.g., every two days except Sunday evening. Activities are then grouped together within interventions which are then performed in a rotating schedule in accordance with the specifications of the care plan.

From our analysis, it appears appropriate to provide tools to assist as much as possible the medical coordinator in the design of individual care plans as well as automated support for verification of the plans and monitoring of their executions. This is why in the Plas'O'Soins project, we propose a user-centeric approach based on a DSL.

2.1   A Domain Specific Language for Home Care Plans

A domain specific language (DSL) is a language designed to express a solution to a problem within a specific domain [7]. A DSL can be tailored to a business or industry domain. While DSLs have already been used to some extent in the fields of computer science and mathematics [6], their use in the health care domain is less widespread. We describe below the main concepts of a DSL tailored to express home care plans. The proposed DSL provides high level abstractions that can be used by a care coordinator to design a care plan for a given patient.

The main building block in a care plan is the notion of *activity*. An activity denotes a medical or a social service provided to persons in their own homes. The proposed DSL includes several predefined activities identified by our analysis of the application domain. Examples of predefined activities are:

- Health services: monitor medications, drug injection, aftercare, etc.
- Activities of daily living: bathing, assist with meal planning and preparation, dressing, maintain clean household, etc.

Each activity is associated with a description which provide additional information about the activity. In particular, a description of an activity includes the required qualification of the actors that are allowed to carry out the activity as well as the temporal constraints that specify when the activity must take place. More precisely, a temporal constraint is expressed as a triplet (Period, Days, Time ranges), where:

- Period specifies the time period during which the activity is defined.
- Days indicates the days within a period in which an activity must take place.
- Time ranges indicates the time slots in which the activity can occur.

Table 1. Excerpt of a care plan content.

Period	Time slot	Repetition	Activity	Required qualification
From		Every day	Toilet	Nurse auxiliary
01/01/2013	Morning	From Monday to Friday	Dress	
To		Tuesday, at 08 am	Injection	Nurse
03/31/2013	Evening	Every day except Sunday	Toilet	Nurse auxiliary
		Every day	Injection	Nurse

```
Period
<period> ::= <starting-date> "-"{<ending-date>}?
<starting-date> ::= "today"|<date>
<ending-date> ::= "today"|<date>

Days
<days> := {<date>}+ | {<day-of-week>}+ | <specific-day>
Where
<date> ::= /a date with the format dd/mm/yy/
<day-of-week> ::= "Monday"|"Tuesday"|"Wednesday"|"Thursday"|"Friday"|
"Saturday"|"Sunday"
<specific-day> ::= "odd-day"|"even-day"|"holiday"

Time ranges
<time-ranges> ::= (<integer> "times") |{<interval>}+ | "nothing"
Where
<integer> ::= /number of occurrences of the activity in the day/
<interval> ::= <string-form>|<pair-form>|<hour-form>
<string-form> ::= "morning"|"midday"|"afternoon"|"evening"|"night"
<pair-form> ::= <starting-hour>"-"<ending-hour>
<hour-form> ::= <hour>/an hour with the format hh/mm/
```

Fig. 1. Formal expression for temporal properties.

Predicted acts								
Act Id	Act	Temporalities			Main actor	Main actor	Number of	Int Id
		Days	Time ranges	Period	type	Name	actors	
A1 ⬚ ✎ ✖	Toilet	Monday-Saturday	morning evening	01/01/13-31/03/13	Nurse auxiliary		1	I1, I3
		Sunday	morning	01/01/13-31/03/13	Nurse auxiliary		1	
		...						
A2 ⬚ ✎ ✖	Injection	Everyday	evening	01/01/13-31/03/13	Nurse		1	I2, I4
		Monday-Wednesday	08h00	01/01/13-31/03/13	Nurse		1	
A3 ⬚ ✎ ✖	Dress	Monday-Friday	morning	01/01/13-31/03/13	Nurse auxiliary		1	I1
		...						
A4 ⬚ ✎ ✖	...	...						

Fig. 2. Example of the graphical user interface.

Figure 1 shows the formal expression of this triplet using the BNF (Backus-Naur Form). Several triplets can be associated to a same activity in order to permit the specification of irregularities and exceptions. Triplet is the basic component of a general declarative language that we have proposed for specifying near regular repetition of activities [3].

An appropriate external representation of the care plan is crucial to facilitate the work of the coordinator. Figure 2 shows the current GUI (Graphical User Interface) developed to support a coordinator in designing a care plan using the proposed DSL.

In addition to the notion of activity, another important concept of the DSL lies in the notion of Intervention. An intervention is a collection of activities that can be scheduled together. Interventions are defined by grouping together the

Predictive Interventions									
Int Id	Time range	Main actor type	Main actor name	Number of actors	Act Id	Act	Hours	Days	Period
I1	morning								
		Nurse auxiliary							
				1	A1	Toilet		Monday-Saturday	01/01/13..31/03/13
				1	A1	Toilet		Sunday	01/01/13..31/03/13
				1	A3	Dress		Monday-Friday	01/01/13..31/03/13
I2		Nurse							
				1	A2	Injection	08h00	Monday-Wednesday	01/01/13..31/03/13
I3	evening								
		Nurse auxiliary							
				1	A1	Toilet		Monday-Saturday	01/01/13..31/03/13
I4		Nurse							
				1	A2	Injection		Everyday	01/01/13..31/03/13

Fig. 3. GUI for predictive interventions.

activities that can be performed by a same professional and which occur in the same time range. Interventions may be specified manually by the coordinator or computed automatically from the specifications of the activities and then proposed to the coordinator for validation. Figure 3 shows the GUI corresponding to the interventions.

Besides the aforementioned concepts, the proposed DSL is enriched with additional constraints derived from the domain knowledge (e.g., medical knowledge represented in ontologies, etc). For example, various types of dependencies between activities may exist such as:

– *Obligation* to perform a given activity in a time period after a first one. For example, *"a Lovenox injection must be followed by a blood test within a time limit of one week"*.
– *Exclusion* of an activity in a given period. For example, *"a minimum of 12h is requested between two insulin injections"*.

2.2 Analysis and Monitoring of Care Plans

Once care plans are constructed using the DSL, they can be exploited for various purposes, as discussed below.

Static analysis of care plans. Such an analysis is performed at the design time, i.e., without actually executing the care plans, and targets the verification of various types of properties, such as:

– Care plans verification. This analysis takes place within a specific care plan and aims at checking all the possible run-time errors that may occur in the considered plan. For example, it is important to check the *realizability* of a care plan, i.e., to check whether or not the activities included in the plan can be effectively scheduled and performed according to the constraints specified in the plan.

- Interventions verification. This analysis takes into account interactions between the temporal constraints of an intervention and the constraints of the activities included in the considered intervention. For example, if an activity A appears in intervention I, then it is worth to check whether the temporal constraints of A are *compatible* with those of I.
- Consistency verification. In some cases a specification must satisfy some dependencies between activities. For example, *"a Lovenox injection must be followed by a blood test within a time limit of one week"* or *"a minimum of 12h is requested between two insulin injections"*. Indeed, a dependency between two activities entails dependencies between the corresponding Interventions. Hence, the verification of consistency must be extended to interventions.
- Compatibility verification. This analysis takes into account the patient agenda in order to avoid to schedule activities in time slots in which the patient is not available.

Monitoring of care plans executions. This analysis is performed at execution time. Note that most of the activities of a care plan are manual, i.e., performed manually by professionals. In current state of affairs, the activities that have been performed are often recorded manually on paper. Our goal is to enable electronic recording of executed activities in order to keep track of the execution traces of care plans. Such information can then be used to monitor care plans. For example, compliance of executions traces w.r.t. a care plan may be checked in order to detect the executions that do not satisfy the constraints specified in the considered care plan. For instance, checking that for every execution which contains an activity *Lovenox injection* there is also an activity *Blood test* which follows *Lovenox injection* activity after one week. Also, the monitoring system may be used to lunch alerts to avoid an actual executions to deviate from the specification. For example, in a running care plan, if the activity *Lovenox injection* is executed then the monitoring system may require the execution of the activity *Blood test* (e.g., an alert is lunched one week after the *Lovenox Injection* activity is executed).

Therefore, formal verification of care plans is a crucial problem. To enable automatic verification, it is then essential to map the DSL concepts into a formal model. In our approach we use timed automata [2] to formally describe care plan constructed using the DSL and then we rely on the large body of theoretical results and existing implemented systems for this class of automata in order to support verification and monitoring of care plans.

3   A Formal Framework Based on Timed Automata

This section first recalls some basic notion from the theory of timed automata then it illustrates the mapping of care plans into timed automata and discusses the benefits of the proposed approach.

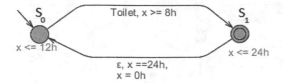

Fig. 4. Example of a timed automaton

3.1 Timed Automata: Basic Notions

Timed automata were introduced in [1,2] as an extension of finite state automata that enables explicit modeling of time. Informally, a timed automata is a finite state automaton enriched with *clock variables*. Moreover, transitions of timed automata are annotated with *guards*, expressed as time constraints, and *clock resets*. Several variants of timed automata have been proposed in the literature. We consider in this paper timed automata with ϵ-transition (i.e., silent transitions) and also guards on the states, also called *invariants*. As an example, Fig. 4 depicts timed automata that is made of two states s_0 and s_1 and the clock variable x. this automaton includes a transition labeled Toilet from state s_0 to s_1 which is guarded by the condition x >= 8h as well as ϵ-transition from state s_1 to s_0 which is guarded by condition x == 24h.

Definition 1 *(Timed automata). A timed automata is a tuple* $A = (S, s_0, \Sigma, X, Inv, T, F)$ *where:*

- *S is a finite set of locations or states of the automaton and $F \subseteq S$ is set of final states,*
- *$s_0 \subseteq S$ is a set of initial locations,*
- *Σ is a finite set of transition labels,*
- *X is a finite set of clocks,*
- *Inv: $S \to \phi(X)$ associates an invariant to each state of the automaton,*
- *$T \subseteq S \times \Sigma \cup \{\epsilon\} \times \phi(X) \times 2^X \times S$ is a set of transitions. A transition $(s, a, \phi, \lambda, s')$ represents an edge from location s to location s' on symbol a. ϕ is a clock constraint, and the set $\lambda \subseteq X$ gives the clocks to be reset after firing such a transition.*

A timed automaton recognizes *timed words*. Informally, given an alphabet Σ, a timed word is a sequence $(a_0, t_0), \ldots, (a_n, t_n)$ where the a_is belongs to Σ and the occurrence of times increase monotonically, i.e., $t_0 \leq t_1 \leq \ldots \leq t_n$. As an example, the sequence of activities $(Toilet, 10) \cdot (Toilet, 35) \cdot (Toilet, 59)$ is an execution which is accepted by the automata A_{Toilet} of Fig. 5 while the timed word $(Toilet, 6) \cdot (Toilet, 35) \cdot (Toilet, 59)$ is not recognized by this automaton.

3.2 Mapping Care Plans into Timed Automata

In this section we illustrate on an example our approach to map care plans constructed using the proposed DSL into timed automata. We propose a two

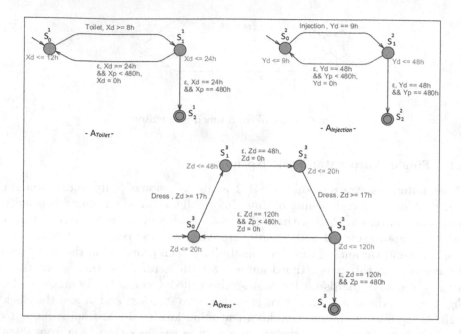

Fig. 5. The result of the mapping of the basic activities of the care plan

steps approach which works as follows: (i) first, basic activities of a care plan are translated into timed automata, then (ii) a global care plan is generated by composition of the components.

Mapping of basic activities. Each activity a of a care plan is mapped into a timed automaton A_a. The construction of A_a depends on the specification of the activity a and in particular its associated time constraints. We explain the mapping of a basic activity into a timed automaton using a simple example. Consider the following specification of a basic activity:

- Activity name: *Toilet*
- Days: *Everyday.*
- Time range: *Morning.*
- Period: $[06/10/2013 - 06/30/2013]$.

The corresponding timed automata $A_{Toilet} = (S, s_0, \Sigma, X, Inv, T, F)$, depicted at Fig. 5, is defined as follows:

- $S = \{s_0^1, s_1^1, s_2^1\}$ is the set of states with s_0^1 the initial state of A_{Toilet}.
- $F = \{s_2^1\}$ is the set of final states,
- $\Sigma = \{Toilet\} \cup \{\epsilon\}$ is the set of transition labels,
- $X = \{x_d, x_p\}$ is the set of variables where the variable x_d is used to measure the flow of time during a day and x_p is the variable used to control the whole period. The variables x_d and x_p are expressed using as time unit the *hour*,

- T is the set of the following transitions:
  - $(s_0^1, Toilet, x_d \geq 8, \emptyset, s_1^1)$, this transition specifies that when the automaton is at state s_0, it can moves to state s_1 upon the execution of the activity $Toilet$. The conjunction of the state invariant $x_d \leq 12$ at s_0^1 and the transition guard $x_d \geq 8$ ensure that the activity $Toilet$ can be performed only in the morning (i.e., when the value of x_d is between 8 and 12).
  - $(s_1^1, \epsilon, x_d == 24 \wedge x_p \leq 480, \{x_d\}, s_0^1)$, this transition enables the automaton to move back from s_1^1 to s_0^1, without performing any activity, at the end of the day (i.e., when x_d equals to 24) within the specified period (i.e., $x_p < 480$). Upon this transition, the variable x_d is reset to 0 to record the beginning of a new day.
  - $(s_1^1, \epsilon, x_p == 480, \emptyset, s_2^1)$, this transition is fired at the end of the period (i.e., when x_p equals to 480) and it enables the automaton to move to the final state s_2^1 and terminate the execution.

In addition to the automaton A_{Toilet}, Fig. 5 shows the following two additional automata constructed in a similar way:

- The timed automaton $A_{Injection}$ corresponding to the activity "Injection every two days at 9 am from 06/10/13 to 06/30/13", and
- The timed automaton A_{Dress} corresponding to the activity "Dress on Monday and Wednesday evening from 06/10/13 to 06/30/13".

Care plan generation from activities automata. The second step consists in generating automatically the whole care plan from the basic activities. Interestingly, the care plan can be also described by means of a timed automata which is obtained by composition of automata representing basic activities that have been generated in the first step. The composition is achieved using the asynchronous product of activities automata which allow us to recognize all possible configurations of the care plan. We recall below the definition of asynchronous product (or shuffle) of timed automata.

Definition 2 (Shuffle of timed automata). *Let $A_1 = (S_1, s_0^1, \Sigma_1, X_1, Inv_1, T_1)$ and $A_2 = (S_2, s_0^2, \Sigma_2, X_2, Inv_2, T_2)$ be two timed automata. The product of A_1 and A_2, denoted $A_1 \times A_2$, is the timed automata $(S_1 \times S_2, s_0^1 \times s_0^2, \Sigma_1 \cup \Sigma_2, X_1 \cup X_2, Inv, T)$, where Inv $(S_1, S_2) = Inv(S_1) \wedge$ Inv (S_2) and the transition function T is defined as follows: $T = \{((s_1, s_2), a, \phi, \lambda, (s_1', s_2')): ((s_1, a, \phi_1, \lambda_1, s_1') \in T_1 and s_2 = s_2')$ or $(s_2, a, \phi_2, \lambda_2, s_2') \in T_2 and s_1 = s_1')\}$.*

Figure 6 shows the product of the automata A_{Toilet} and $A_{Injection}$ of Fig. 5. The resulting automata encompasses all the possible schedules of the activities $Toilet$ and $Injection$.

3.3   Formal Aanalysis of Care Plans Using Timed Automata

With a formal model describing the behavior of care plans at hand, it becomes now possible to handle automatic verification and monitoring of care plans. We

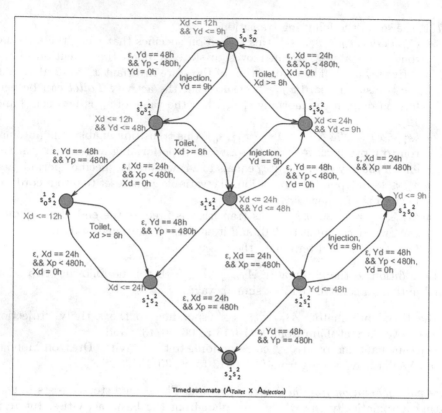

Fig. 6. Intervention of every day morning from 06/10/13 to 06/30/13"

discuss below how the proposed framework can be used to automate generation of Interventions and verification and monitoring of care plans.

– Automatic generation of candidate interventions automata. Given a time specification T, we may want to generate the interventions corresponding to T. The specification T may be defined as a precise time range (eg. Intervention of the morning, intervention of the evening, etc.), a combination of days and time ranges (eg. Intervention of the Monday morning, Wednesday afternoon, etc.) or a combination of time ranges, days and period (eg. Interventions of every Monday morning from 03/10/13 to 30/10/13, etc.). Candidate interventions are generated automatically using a composition of activity automata projected on the time specification T. For example, Fig. 6 depicts an automaton representing an intervention that is carried out *every day, morning, from 06/10/2013 to 06/30/2013*. This automaton is obtained by first projecting the activity automata A_{Toilet} and $A_{Injection}$ of Fig. 5 with respect the appropriate time specification (i.e., Time range = morning, Days = every day and Period =[06/10/2013-06/30/2013]) and then computing the asynchronous product of the result.

- Care plan verification. For example, checking *realizability* of a care plan can be reduced to the emptiness problem of the corresponding automaton.
- Intervention verification. Intervention are formally described as automata (in the same spirit of the previous mapping). Then intervention verification is achieved by checking the emptiness of the intersection of the activity automata with the intervention automata.
- Consistency verification. Dependencies are expressed as automata and then consistency checking is formulated as a composition of interventions automata with a dependency automata.
- Monitoring. Checking compliance of executions traces can be reduced to language recognition in timed automata. Moreover, it is possible to extend the proposed automata to manage alarms. For example, a care plan automata can be used to enforce that an alarm has to be activated one week after a *Lovenox Injection* has been performed.

4   Discussion

We described in this paper an ongoing research work devoted to the design of a DSL-based approach for specifying and monitoring (home) care plans. This work lies at the junction of two disciplines, computer science and medicine, and thereby it requires an active cooperation between the two communities. Care plans are inherently unstructured processes. This is due to the specificity of each patient, i.e., a specific care plan is required for each specific patient, as well as to the irregularity of repetitive activities within a plan. Nevertheless, we showed that using appropriate temporal expressions it is possible to specify the schedule of such activities. The obtained specification plays the role of a process model that must be enacted by a business process management or a workflow system. A detailed presentation of the temporal expressions used to specify the repetition of activities with irregularities is given in [3]. Curiously, few works were interested in this problem. A model closed to ours is proposed in [5]. However, in that model the repetitions are expressed trough a procedural language.

We rest on a formal framework based on timed automata to formally describe the care plans constructed using the proposed DSL. Our proposal includes in particular the representation of basic activities as timed automata and then the construction of a global care plan and specific interventions using operators, mainly composition and projection, on such automata. The paper discusses also how the proposed framework can be used for automatic verification of care plans and for monitoring their executions. Our future research directions will be devoted to the development of the theoretical framework based on timed automata. Our preliminary results pave the way for a more detailed exploration of the benefit of using formal verification and model checking techniques in our context.

References

1. Allur, R.: Timed automata. In: Halbwachs, N., Peled, D.A. (ed.) Proceedings of the 11th International Conference on Computer Aided Verification (1999)
2. Allur, R., Dill, D.L.: A theory of timed automata. Theor. Comput. Sci. **126**, 183–235 (1994)
3. Bouet, M., Gani, K., Schneider, M., Toumani, F.: A general model for specifying near periodic recurrent activities - application to home care activities. Technical report-LIMOS (2013)
4. Dadam, P., Reichertand, M., Kuhn, K.: Clinical workflows - the killer application for process-oriented information systems?. In: Business, pp. 1–15 (2000)
5. Fowler, M.: Recurring events for calendars. In: IEEE International Conference, vol. 2 (1997)
6. Fowler, M.: Domain Specific Languages. Addison-Wesley Professional, New York (2010)
7. Menezes, A.L., Cirilo, C.E., de Moraes, J.L.C. de Souza, W.L., do Prado, A. F.:.Using archetypes and domain specific languages on development of ubiquitous applications to pervasive healthcare. IEEE Computer Society (2010)
8. Weske, M.: Business Process Management: Concepts, Languages, Architectures. Springer-Verlag New York Inc, Secaucus (2012)

Urban Congestion: Arrangement Aamriw Intersection in Bejaia's City

N. Guerrouahane, S. Bouzouzou, L. Bouallouche-Medjkoune, and D. Aissani[✉]

Laboratory of Modeling and Optimization of Systems (LAMOS)
Department of Operational Research, University of Bejaia, Bejaia, Algeria
djamil_aissani@hotmail.com

Abstract. This study analyzes the traffic characteristics and management within Bejaia metropolis (Algeria). Large scale spatial and temporal land-use data were used to investigate the dynamics of land-use change in this area. In this paper, we considered the case of the intersection of Aamriw (Bejaia's city), using discrete event simulation. This allowed us to calculate the main performance of the system with traffic lights and with the construction of a hopper. We present simulation results that show the validity of the queueing models in the computation of average travel times. These results allowed us to make a comparison between different versions, with traffic lights or with hopper.

Keywords: Modeling and verification of processes in logistics-based systems · Urban congestion · Intersection · Traffic lights · Queueing Theory

1 Introduction

With the rapid increase in the transport demand in this last decade, congestion has become a mostly problem and frequently for the human mobility [18]. An effective policy of the transport is necessary to struggle against the urban congestion. Building infrastructure is one of the most important accompanying measure to reduce a road congestion. A question has been asked: the construction of the infrastructure should it be continue, or the growing demand for mobility should it be deplaced into public transport. Optimizing of the waiting time in the intersection have advantages: save time for drivers, reducing pollution and fuel use as well as through reducing congestion and improve the road safety [10,17]. The problem of congestion in an intersection persists and the construction of a new infrastructure was envisaged in this work. For this reasons we propose a study with the new situation. In this paper, we want to measure the traffic flow at the intersection of Aamriw in the Bejaia's city, using discrete event simulation. This allowed use to calculate the main performance of the system with traffic lights and with the construction of a hopper. Bejaia is one of the major towns of Algeria, located in the north to $180\,\mathrm{km}$ east of the capital Algiers, in edge Mediterranean sea. The density of Bejaia is a 481 inhabitants/km^2 in

N. Lohmann et al. (Eds.): BPM 2013 Workshops, LNBIP 171, pp. 355–364, 2014.
DOI: 10.1007/978-3-319-06257-0_28, © Springer International Publishing Switzerland 2014

2010, or in 1999 it was 276 inhabitants/km^2. This evolution that exceeds 80 % in this last decade reflect the society by any problems in particularly the urban congestion. The city have an international commercial port, whose principal activity is the transport of hydrocarbon. Moreover, for this year 2012, the port of Bejaia has become the first wearing of Algeria in term of transported goods. This city is one of the largest industrial centers due to its geographical location and most dynamic in Algeria; that is why a proper transport policy is neces-sary to struggle against the urban congestion and to answer at the request of displacement.

The intersection of Aamriw situated in north west of the Bejaia's city, is an important point of exchange and distribution at the center. This intersection is dense to traffic during the year, but the flows are different during the summer and the rest of the year, for this reasons we are interested in the arrangement to this intersection. The reasons of congestion in this intersection are:

– It is an important point to access at areas of Bejaia's city, center of city, OPOW stadium, Iheddaden's area and national road toward Boulimat,
– It is the transit point toward neighbor communes, and toward cities,
– Not conformity of existing indication,
– Insufficiency of the markings horizontal and vertical,
– The presence of anarchistic bus stops at the exit of the crossroads.

In order to cure the problem of urban congestion at this intersection, we used the modelilisation of the road traffic by queues, of which the goal is to calculate the average waiting time of a vehicle during a cycle. In practice, several solutions can be considered like the improvement of the system of road signs, construction of new roads, hoppers, etc. Because of the complexity of this problem, one solution is not effective but a combination of these alternatives allows us to minimize the problems of congestion. For this reason, we considered an arrangement of this intersection by a static control system which is the traffic lights and by construction of a hopper.

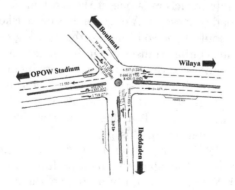

Fig. 1. Aamriw intersection

The remainder of this paper is organized as follows. In Sect. 2, we first present a brief review of the existing work on stochastic queueing models and the modeling of the traffic flow at signalized intersections. In this regards, we present the methodology to calculate the average waiting time at signalized intersections. The main performance of the system with signals timed and with the construction of a hopper is presented in Sects. 3 and 4. Finally, Sect. 5 gives the conclusion and future work of this paper.

2 Literature Review

Congestion leads to delays, decreasing flow rate, higher fuel consumption and thus has negative environmental effects. The issue of urban traffic control came with the exponential growth in the number of vehicles on the roads, and intersections are the points where traffic is dense [17,18]. Modeling the traffic flow at signalized and unsignalized intersections has been discussed in many works [3,5,7]. The arrival process in roadway traffic is modeled as singly arriving Poisson process [8,14] and as platoons to represent the behavior of the vehicles moving between traffic signals [1,7,9]. Daganzo [1] presented a cell transmission model, representing the traffic on a highway with a single entrance and exit, which can be used to predict the evolution of traffic over time and space. Deschutter and Demoor [3] minimized the waiting time in a continuous manner. Ahadar et al. [4] reduced the control system to a state of non-saturation while minimizing an optimality criterion (the sum of the queues, the quadratic form queues, etc). Cheah and Smith [12] explored the generality and usefulness of state-dependent $M/G/c/c$ queueing models for modeling pedestrian traffic flows. Jain and Smith [13] used $M/G/c/c$ state-dependent queueing models for modeling and analyzing vehicular traffic flow on a roadway segment which can accommodate a finite number of vehicles. Each vehicle space corresponds to a server, thus, the maximum number of vehicles that can be accommodated on the link provides the number of servers, c, in the queueing model. Heidemann [5,6] studied the signalized intersections, and presents an unifying approach to both signalized and unsignalized intersections. Vandaele et al. [16] used $M/M/1$, $M/G/1$ and $GI/G/1$ queues with or without state-dependent rates to model traffic flow. Van Woensel et al. [15] compared the queueing approach with other approaches and its potential benefits are described and quantified. Raheja [11] proposed an analytical model of uninterrupted single-lane traffic, using queuing analysis.

Olaleye et al. [19] examined the traffic characteristics and management within Abeokuta metropolis (Nigeria). Markov chain and descriptive analysis were used to analyse the traffic characteristic of the Lafenwa and Ibara intersections, and also to predict the short and long term daily traffic situation for the incoming and outgoing traffics. The results predicted that provision of terminal facilities, parking lots instead of on-street parking and adequate terminal facilities around the intersections are suggested traffic management options to reduce traffic congestion noticed at these intersections. Yonggang and Kyungyong [20] modeled the traffic at the intersection of Archer RD and SW 34 ST in Gainesville during busy hours by using $M/G/1$ model. Based on the collected data they proposed two approaches to make the system Ergodic, by increasing number of lanes or by adjusting green light time for each direction. From the results, they saw that increase of the number of lanes by 2 is optimal and increasing the green light duration is easy to implement but not feasible in the traffic of SW 34 ST. In our work, we examined the traffic characteristics and management within Bejaia metropolis (Algeria). We modeled the traffic at the intersection of Aamriw using discrete event simulation, and show the validity of the queueing models in the computation of average travel times. Because of the complexity of this problem, one solution is not effective. In this case we proposed a combination of two approaches to minimize the problems of congestion, by traffic lights and by the construction of a hopper. The results obtained from the simulation we make it clear that the traffic lights will not solve the congestion problems at the intersection of Aamriw and the construction of a hopper is necessary to cure this problem.

3   Methodology

It is more reasonable, before looking at extending the network to use wisely the existing infrastructure. As the use of road infrastructure controlled by a signaling system, the question is how to exploit the best control of the system to improve traffic flow. Modeling the traffic flow at signalized intersections has been discussed in many works [3,6–8].

The real situation is complicated compared to the classical model of queues [15,16]. The fact that during the red light, no departure is permitted and vehicles do not go necessarily in order of their arrival except in the case of the intersection that consists of a single road corridor. The establishment of a system of lights at an intersection makes a separation in time of admission to different schools of vehicles. We concerned with random variables:

– The average waiting time for a vehicle during a cycle,
– The average number of vehicles in the queue.

3.1   The Average Waiting Time in a Cycle

The average waiting time in a cycle can be found in Morris et al. [8] and is given by:

$$E[W_c] = E[W_R] + E[W_V], \tag{1}$$

where

$$E(W_R) = E[\int_0^R (N(0) + A(t))dt] = R.E[N(0)] + \frac{\lambda R^2}{2}, \tag{2}$$

and

$$E(W_V) = E[\int_R^C N(t)dt] = \frac{\lambda pR}{2(1-\lambda p)^2} + \frac{p(2\lambda R.E[N(0)] + (\lambda R)^2 + \lambda R)}{2(1-\lambda p)}. \tag{3}$$

in which $A(t)$ is the number of vehicles reaching the system at $[0, t]$, this interval starts at the red light. $N(0)$ is the length of queue at t = 0. W_R is the waiting time of any vehicle during the red light (R). W_V is the waiting time of any vehicle during the green light (V). W_c is the waiting time of any vehicle during a cycle (C = R + V). $N(t)$ is the number of vehicles in the queue at "t", p is the necessary period for a driver to cross the intersection (time service) and λ is the average number of arrivals per hour.

Remark 1. The necessary and sufficient condition for the queue is in equilibrium is that the average number of arrivals at cycle is less than the number of departures during the green. This means:

$$\lambda C < \frac{V}{p} \Rightarrow \lambda p < 1 - \frac{R}{C} \Rightarrow \quad \rho = \lambda p < 1 - \frac{R}{C}. \tag{4}$$

with the relations (1) and (2), the average waiting time during a cycle for any vehicle is:

$$E[W_c] = \frac{\lambda R}{2(1 - \lambda p)} (R + \frac{2E[N(0)]}{\lambda} + p(1 + \frac{1}{1 - \lambda p})). \tag{5}$$

Using Little's formula, we obtain the average waiting time during a cycle for one vehicle as:

$$E[d] = \frac{E[W_c]}{\lambda C} = \frac{\lambda R}{2C(1 - \rho)} (R + \frac{2E[N(0)]}{\lambda} + p(1 + \frac{1}{1 - \rho})). \tag{6}$$

Remark 2. If the traffic is fluid, $E[N(0)]$ can be negligible. Otherwise, calculate the value of $E[N(0)]$. Morris et al. [8] calculated the probability generating function of the initial size of the queue $(N(0))$.

3.2 The Directional Flow Analysis

According to the public works management 2010 [2], empirical observations of the road traffic at the intersection of Aamriw are referred to Fig. 1.

- **The channel 1** represents the flow from **Wilaya** on a global traffic of nearly 24 890 vehicles: 39 % for OPOW stadium, 35 % for Iheddaden and 26 % for Boulimat,
- **The channel 2** represents the flow from **Ihaddaden** on a global traffic of nearly 9950 vehicles: 56 % for Wilaya, 32 %for Boulimat and 12 % for OPOW stadium,
- **The channel 3** represents the flow from the **OPOW Stadium** on a global traffic of nearly 6170 vehicles: 65 % for Wilaya, 28 % for Iheddaden and 7 % for Boulimat,
- **The channel 4** represents the flow from **Boulimat** on a global traffic of nearly 3980 vehicles: 59 % for Iheddaden, 22 % for Wilaya and 19 % for OPOW stadium.

3.3   Statistical Analysis of Data

The adjustment of the probability laws of arrivals by theoretical laws was done with the statistical software R. This software allows us to test adjustments by different probability laws, discretes or continuous. Tests of Chi-square and Kolmogoriv-Smirnov are used in order to adjust the law of the arrivals. For that, each test is calculated in order to compare it with theoretical values and then decide the rejection or acceptance of the hypothesis (H) of the model of queues: H_0: "Arrivals$_i \longrightarrow$ Poisson (λ_i)" ons H_1: "Arrivals$_i \longrightarrow$ Not Poisson (λ_i)".

After trying several possibilities, the arrivals are Poisson at the crossroads for each destination of each channel. Indeed, the values of the Kolmogorov-Smirnov statistics (or Chi-square) calculated for the different destinations are all below the tabular value at a confidence level of 1%. This allows us to accept the hypothesis H_0.

For each destination of each channel, the arrival rates, λ_i, are estimated and given in Table 1.

Table 1. Arrival rate

Channel i	1	2	3	4
λ_i (veh/sec)	0.54	0.23	0.15	0.073

3.4   Discrete Event Simulation

The data from the whole year of 2010 was used in the MATLAB (MATrix Laboratory) to determine the performance of our system. MATLAB is an environment of calculation equipped with a language of very high level with an interactive interface and to apply in the fields of applied mathematics such as : numerical calculation and mathematical modeling, programming of the mathematical algorithms, etc. Simulation by discrete events indicates the modeling of a real system such as it evolves in time, by a representation in which the sizes characterizing the system change only into one finished or countable number of points isolated in time. These points are the moments when the events occur. The simulation queues allows us to calculate performances of our system (queue length, waiting time, etc.). The principle of a queueing system is, when a costumer arrives, it joins the queue if the server is busy, otherwise it immediately begins to be served. The events of a phenomenon waiting are:

1. The arrival of a customer in the system,
2. The customer access server (the start of service),
3. The output of a customer in the system (the end of service).

4   Comparison of Analytical Results with Signals Timed and with the Hopper

4.1   With Signals Timed and Without the Hopper

We consider a fixed cycle with 90 s, the green light is placed on the channels (1) and (3) and the necessary period for a driver to cross the intersection when the green light is on, is $p = 3$ s. The average waiting time when decreasing the green light period for the channels (1) and (3) (So the red light period for the channels (2) and (4) is also decreased) are shown in the Table 2.

Table 2. The average waiting time for motorist at each channel

Cycle (V, R) ⇓	Channel 1		Channel 2	
	Analytical	Simulate	Analytical	Simulate
(70,20)	Congested	-	Congested	-
(60,30)	Congested	-	Congested	-
(50,40)	Congested	-	Congested	-
(45,45)	Congested	-	Congested	-
(40,50)	Congested	-	Congested	-
(30,60)	Congested	-	Congested	-
(20,70)	Congested	-	61.8	75.23

Cycle (V, R) ⇓	Channel 3		Channel 4	
	Analytical	Simulate	Analytical	Simulate
(70,20)	30	33.9	20	29.03
(60,30)	46	29.34	26	39.56
(50,40)	50	57.61	28	22.50
(45,45)	70	85.09	30	15.64
(40,50)	90	107.61	28	22.50
(30,60)	Congested	-	26	39.56
(20,70)	Congested	-	25	29.03

Interpretation of Results
For channels 1 and 2 (resp. Wilaya, Ihedadden) the stability condition (3) is not checked for considered cycle, which means that both channels are congested. Note that for channel 2 (Ihedadden), the system will be stable if the red period for this channel is less than 27 s (according to (3)). But this will cause congestion of the channel 3 (OPOW Stadium). For channel 1, so that it is not congested it is necessary that the red period tends to zero and the service time is minimal. This clearly justifies the development of a new road.

4.2   With Signals Timed and With the Hopper

The governments has addressed the problem of congestion of the intersection of Aamriw. One of the solutions suggested in urgency is the construction of a

Table 3. Comparison of wait times for each variant of hopper and without hopper

Cycle (V, R) Channel 1	Variante 1 (Y) Analytical	Simulate	Variante 2 (arc) Analytical	Simulate	Without hopper Analytical	Simulate
(70,20)	Fluid	Fluid	26.32	28	Congested	-
(60,30)	Fluid	Fluid	20	18.12	Congested	-
(50,40)	Fluid	Fluid	Congested	-	Congested	-
(45,45)	Fluid	Fluid	Congested	-	Congested	-
(40,50)	Fluid	Fluid	Congested	-	Congested	-
(30,60)	Fluid	Fluid	Congested	-	Congested	-
(20,70)	Fluid	Fluid	Congested	-	Congested	-
Channel 2	Analytical	Simulate	Analytical	Simulate	Analytical	Simulate
(70,20)	Congested	-	Congested	-	Congested	-
(60,30)	Congested	-	Congested	-	Congested	-
(50,40)	35	33.83	Congested	-	Congested	-
(45,45)	23.15	29.25	Congested	-	Congested	-
(40,50)	26	28.45	Congested	-	Congested	-
(30,60)	20	25	Congested	-	Congested	-
(20,70)	11	10.22	62	75.23	61.8	75.23
Channel 3	Analytical	Simulate	Analytical	Simulate	Analytical	Simulate
(70,20)	20	18.51	30	33.9	30	33.9
(60,30)	40	35.98	46	39.34	46	29.34
(50,40)	48	50	48	50	50	57.61
(45,45)	33	38.05	33	40	70	85.09
(40,50)	58	61.82	58	61.82	90	107.61
(30,60)	Congested	-	Congested	-	Congested	-
(20,70)	Congested	-	Congested	-	Congested	-
Channel 4	Analytical	Simulate	Analytical	Simulate	Analytical	Simulate
(70,20)	40	47.64	40	47.64	20	29.03
(60,30)	38	45.77	38	45.77	26	39.56
(50,40)	30	30	30	30	28	22.50
(45,45)	28	28	28	28	30	15.64
(40,50)	28	30.40	28	30.40	28	22.50
(30,60)	20	26	20	26	26	39.56
(20,70)	15	11.18	15	11.18	25	29.03

hopper in order to increase the number of lanes (what reduces the arrival rate which pass by this intersection). Two variants are currently being discussed.

The first variant is a hopper 'Y', for the arrivals of channel 1 (Wilaya) towards channels 2 and 3 (resp. Ihedadden, OPOW Stadium), and the arrivals of channel 2(Ihedadden) towards channel 1 (Wilaya) (will have to go through the hopper). As for other locations, these drivers will go through the intersection (Arrivals channels 3 and 4 respectively, OPOW Stadium and Boulimat, will not change their habits). Hopper 'Y' increases the lane number by 2.

The second variant is a hopper 'arc', for the arrivals of channel 1 (Wilaya) towards the channel 2 (Ihedadden). Hopper 'arc' increases the lane number by 1.

In what follows, we will simulate the state of the intersection after the construction of the hopper, to determine the average waiting time for motorists entering the intersection. After an interpretation of the results, we will compare the two versions in terms of average waiting time.

The comparison of the average waiting time for each variant of hopper and without hopper is represented in Table 3.

Interpretation of Results

According to the simulation results of the two variants of the hopper, it is noted that with the second variant (arc), the congestion will not be eliminated, for channel 1 (Wilaya), traffic will be smooth for some cycles ((70,20), (60,30)) and congested for others, but the channel 2 (Ihedadden) will remain congested for some cycles (except the cycle (20,70)), so this hopper is not efficient in terms of waiting times for motorists from channels 1 and 2 (resp. Wilaya, Ihedadden). For the others channels 3 and 4 (resp. Boulimat, OPOW Stadium) there will be no improvement.

With the first variant (Y) traffic for channel 1 (Wilaya) will be fluid. For channel 2 (Ihedadden) traffic will remain congested only for two cycles (70,20) and (60,30). We can then conclude that the first variante (Y) is more appropriate to reduce congestion at the intersection of Aamriw.

5   Conclusion and Future Work

In this paper, we measured the traffic flow at the intersection of Aamriw (town of Bejaia, Algeria). We used discrete event simulation to calculate the main performance of the system with traffic lights and with the construction of a hopper. The results obtained from the simulation make it clear that the draft hopper is necessary to remedy of the congestion problems at this intersection, the traffic lights will not solve this problem.

Comparing the average waiting time, with both types of hopper : 'Y' and 'arc', it appears that the hopper 'Y' would be more beneficial to motorists in terms of saving time.

Our future work will include the extension of the current consideration with application of a dynamic control systems at signalized intersections which certainly captures more dynamics of traffic flow. At the same time, congestion level will be differentiated by peak, non-peak hour, and accidents to categorize the dynamics within different time periods.

Acknowledgments. The authors wish to thank the anonymous reviewers whose constructive suggestions helped improve the paper. The authors are especially thankful to Public Works Management of the town of Bejaia for providing accessibility to their vehicle data at the study intersection.

References

1. Daganzo, C.F.: The cell transmission model: a dynamic representation of highway traffic consistent with the hydrodynamic theory. Transp. Res. Part B **28**(4), 269–287 (1994)
2. Data on the road traffic on the level of the intersection of Aamriw, Public Works Management of the town of Bejaia (2010)
3. Demoor, B., Deschutter, B.: Optimal traffic light control for a single intersection. Eur. J. Control **4**(3), 260–276 (1998)
4. Elmoudni, R., Ahadar, Y.: R. Laboratoire SeT-Université de Technologie Belfort-Montbéliard UTBM, Bouyekh. Minimisation des files d'attente d'une intersection isolée (2003)
5. Heidemann, D.: Queueing at unsignalized intersections. Transp. Res. Part B **31**(3), 239–263 (1997)
6. Heidemann, D.: A queueing theory model of nonstationary traffic flow. Transp. Sci. **35**(4), 405–412 (2001)
7. Lehoczky, P.: Traffic intersection control and zero-switch queues. J. Appl. Probab. **9**(2), 382–395 (1972)
8. Morris, R.W., Darroch, J.N., Newell, G.F.: Queues for vehicle-actuated traffic light. Oper. Res. **12**(6), 882–895 (1964)
9. Neuts, M.F.: Modeling vehicular traffic using the discrete time Markovian arrival process. Transp. Sci. **29**(2), 109–117 (1999)
10. Pandian, S., Gokhale, S., Ghoshal, A.K.: Evaluating effects of traffic and vehicle characteristics on vehicular emissions near traffic intersections. Transp. Res. Part D **14**(3), 180–196 (2009)
11. Raheja, T.: Modelling traffic congestion using queuing networks. Indian Acad. Sci. Part 4 **35**, 427–431 (2010)
12. Smith, J.M., Cheah, J.Y.: Generalized M/G/C/C state dependent queuing models and pedestrian traffic flows. Queueing Syst. **15**, 365–385 (1994)
13. Smith, J.M., Jain, R.: Modeling vehicular traffic flow using M/G/C/C state dependent queueing models. Transp. Sci. **31**(4), 324–336 (1997)
14. Tanner, J.C.: A problem of interface between two queues. Biometrica **40**, 58–69 (1953)
15. Van Woensel, T., Kerbache, L., Peremans, H., Vandaele, N.: Vehicle routing with dynamic travel times: a queueing approach. Eur. J. Oper. Res. **186**(3), 990–1007 (2008)
16. Verbruggen, N., Vandaele, N., Van Woensel, T.: A queueing based traffic flow model. Transp. Environ. Transp. Res. Part D **5**(2), 121–135 (2000)
17. Wang, H., Rudy, K., Li, J., Ni, D.: Calculation of traffic flow breakdown probability to optimize link throughput. Appl. Math. Model. **34**, 3376–3389 (2010)
18. Wua, X., Liu, H.X.: A shockwave profile model for traffic flow on congested urban arterials. Transp. Res. Part B **45**, 1768–1786 (2011)
19. Olaleye, O.T., et al.: A Markov chain approach to the dynamics of vehicular traffic characteristics in Abeokuta metropolis. Res. J. Appl. Sci. Eng. Technol. **1**(3), 160–166 (2009)
20. Yonggang, L., Kyungyong, L.: Modeling Signalized Intersection Using Queueing Theory (2010)

Supply Chain Uncertainty Under ARIMA Demand Process

Mi Pan and Weimin Wu[(⊠)]

The State Key Laboratory of Industrial Control Technology,
Institute of Cyber-systems and Control, Zhejiang University, Hangzhou, China
lorna_pan@sina.com, wmwu@iipc.zju.edu.cn

Abstract. This paper discusses a typical supply chain system based on Auto-Regressive Integrated Moving Average (ARIMA) demand process. Minimum Mean Square Error principle and stochastic optimal control theory are introduced to build a new framework for supply chain uncertainty study under general ARIMA demand process. After formulating the order and inventory quantity at time period t, this paper analyzes the optimal order policy as to decrease the bullwhip effect and stock fluctuations under non-stationary demand. The theoretical analysis reveals that a reasonable order quantity can reduce the bullwhip effect generated by demand uncertainty. We also show the negative correlation between the bullwhip effect and inventory stability in the discussed supply chain model.

Keywords: Supply chain · Uncertainty · ARIMA · Bullwhip effect · Stochastic optimal control

1 Introduction

Supply chain is a hybrid system contains manufacturers, suppliers, distributors, retailers and customers. As a key determinant to enhance competitiveness of enterprises in the globalization, supply chain management plays a vital role in the equilibrium of customer demand and profit for supply chain partners. With the increasingly fierce market competition, customer demands become more diverse and fluctuate with time. Therefore, demand uncertainties become a pretty severe impediment in the effective supply chain management [18]. Specifically, the uncertainties is primarily characterized by customer demand variability, demand distribution difference and demand structure fluctuation, breeding a negative impact which is the so-called "bullwhip effect" [16], a phenomenon that the variation in demand grows from downstream members to upstream ones in the supply chain. Bullwhip effect can distort the demand information, cause the inventory backlog, and inflict big losses on upstream supply chain partners.

Therefore, how to analysis supply chain demand uncertainty and how to determine and combat the bullwhip effect are challenging problems in supply chain management area. Stationary time series, such as Auto-Regressive (AR) and Auto-Regressive Moving Average [2] (ARMA), are extensively introduced to address supply chain uncertainty problem and its bullwhip effect in many existing lecture

N. Lohmann et al. (Eds.): BPM 2013 Workshops, LNBIP 171, pp. 365–376, 2014.
DOI: 10.1007/978-3-319-06257-0_29, © Springer International Publishing Switzerland 2014

[2, 5–7, 11, 14, 19–21]. In particular, Lee *et al.* [16], Chen *et al.* [6] and Raghu-nathan [19] studied the stochastic properties in supply chain, demonstrating the effect of lead time, demand forecasting and information sharing on the bullwhip effect under an AR (1) demand process and order-up-to inventory policy separately. Gaalman et al. [11] and Xu et al. [20] addressed the supply chain uncertainty and the bullwhip effect using ARMA demand patterns. However, to the point of econometrics, the real market has a much more volatile customer demand which is often shown as unstable time series with "fat tail" property. Besides, non-stationary demand processes are not considered in most previous studies [1, 10, 12, 13, 15, 19]. Thus, Auto-Regressive Integrated Moving Average [2] (ARIMA) process, the model for unstable time series, has more practical value and meaning in the depiction of customer demand in the study of supply chain. Related works do not adequately consider the complicated and challenging general ARIMA models in demand uncertainty research of supply chain.

This paper addresses the design and analysis of labile demand model of supply chain. Referring to the analytical framework proposed in [19], the demand process is defined as ARIMA (p, d, q). Then we analyze the demand uncertainty and its resulting bullwhip effect in the supply chain. The contribution of this paper differs from the existing ones is twofold: a) to present detailed and direct description of the order and the inventory variance under the general ARIMA demand model with the stochastic optimal control theory; b) to demonstrate the bullwhip effect and inventory fluctuation for the non-stationary demand model and understand the observed differences driven by control policy.

The paper is structured as follows. In Sect. 2, we establish the two-stage supply chain model, as the analytical basis of the whole article. The demand model and optimal estimator are formulated in Sect. 3. Section 4 presents the two ordering policies through the view of stochastic optimal control. Extensive numerical experiments are performed in Sect. 5 to illustrate the supply chain demand uncertainty and its transmission. In Sect. 6, we make the final conclusion.

2 The Supply Chain Model

The system investigated in this paper is a two-stage supply chain model, presented in Fig. 1. In this model, the retailer estimates the customer demand under the historical data, placing orders O_t to its supplier in time period t based on the current inventory

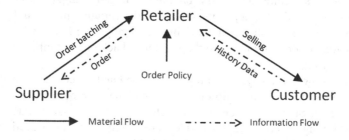

Fig. 1. A basic two-stage supply chain

and order policy. The products arrive in time period $t + L$, where L is the lead time. We assume L is constant.

The supply chain is regarded as a liner time invariant hybrid dynamic system driven by stochastic demand signal. We can obtain the following material balance equation as the mathematical model under the above assumption:

$$I_t = I_{t-1} + O_{t-L} - D_t \tag{1}$$

where I_t is the inventory of retailer in the end of time period t, O_t is the orders placed at the end of time period t, D_t is the customer demand in time period t.

With the time-series backward operator z^{-1}, we have:

$$z^{-1}I_t = I_{t-1} \tag{2}$$

$$O_{t-L} = O_{t-L} - O_{t-L-1} + O_{t-L-1} - O_{t-L-2} \cdots = (1 - z^{-1}) \sum_{m=-\infty}^{t-L} O_m \tag{3}$$

$$D_t = (1 - z^{-1}) \sum_{m=-\infty}^{t} D_m \tag{4}$$

Then (1) can be rewritten as follows:

$$I_t = \sum_{m=-\infty}^{t-L} O_m + \sum_{m=-\infty}^{t} D_m \tag{5}$$

Further (5) can be transformed to (6):

$$I_{t+L} = I_t + O_t + \sum_{m=t-L+1}^{t-1} O_m + \sum_{m=t+1}^{t+L} D_m \tag{6}$$

Where I_{t+L} is the target inventory of the retailer at time $t + L$; I_t is the inventory at time t; O_t is the orders placed at the end of time period t, depending on the order strategy; $\sum_{m=t-L+1}^{t-1} O_m$ is the delivers in transit placed in period m; $\sum_{m=t+1}^{t+L} D_m$ is the total estimated demand in the periods $[t + 1, t + L]$.

For the sake of the transmission analysis of demand information in the supply chain, two key questions should be discussed firstly, concerning the unknown $\sum_{m=t+1}^{t+L} D_m$ and O_t in Eq. (6):

- The demand model of the customer;
- The ordering policy of the retailer.

Deep discussion is in the sections below.

3   The Demand Model

3.1   ARIMA Model

In the above supply chain system, the ARIMA (p, d, q) demand model is as follows:

$$\Phi(z^{-1})(1 - z^{-1})^d (D_t - \mu) = \Theta(z^{-1}) e_t \tag{7}$$

$$\Phi(z^{-1}) = 1 + \varphi_1 z^{-1} + \ldots + \varphi_p z^{-p}$$

$$\Theta(z^{-1}) = 1 + \theta_1 z^{-1} + \ldots + \theta_q z^{-q}$$

Where D_t is the customer demand observed in cycle $t(1 - z^{-1})^d D_t$ represents the d-order difference of D_t, μ is the regressive mean, $\{e_t\}$ is random noise series that independent and normally distributed with zero mean and standard deviation σ. z^{-1} is time-series backward operator. $\Phi(z^{-1})$ and $\Theta(z^{-1})$ are polynomials p-step auto-regressive process and q-step moving average process respectively, d is the order of difference course. Only if $d = 0$, the process is stationary; when $d > 0$, unsteady [4].

From Eq. (7), we can obtain the expression of demand in the following form:

$$D_t = \frac{\Theta(z^{-1})}{\Phi(z^{-1})(1 - z^{-1})^d} e_t + \mu = \frac{\Theta(z^{-1})}{\Phi(z^{-1})(1 + \sum\limits_{i=1}^{d} c_i z^{-1})} e_t + \mu \tag{8}$$

$$= \frac{\Theta(z^{-1})}{\Psi(z^{-1})} e_t + \mu$$

Where

$$\Psi(z^{-1}) = \sum_{i=0}^{p+d} \psi_i z^{-i} = 1 + \psi_1 z^{-1} + \ldots + \psi_{p+d} z^{-(p+d)},$$

$$c_i = (-1)^i \frac{\prod\limits_{j=0}^{i=1} (d-j)}{i!}, \quad \psi_i = \sum_{j=0}^{i} (\phi_j c_{i-j})(i \geq 1)$$

with $\phi_0 = 1, c_0 = 1, \phi_j = 0(j > p), c_{i-j} = 0(i - j > d)$

Given $\mu = 0$, $n = \max\{p + d, q\}$, the ARIMA demand model can be written as follows:

$$D_t = \frac{\Theta(z^{-1})}{\Psi(z^{-1})} e_t \tag{9}$$

$$\Theta(z^{-1}) = 1 + \theta_1 z^{-1} + \ldots + \theta_n z^{-n}$$

$$\Psi(z^{-1}) = 1 + \psi_1 z^{-1} + \ldots + \psi_n z^{-n}$$

3.2 Demand Forecasting

On account of the characteristic of ARIMA process, we use Minimum Mean Square Error (MMSE) method for demand forecasting.

Firstly, we can obtain the expression of the future demand D_{t+k} at time period $t+k$ based on (9):

$$D_{t+k} = \frac{\Theta(z^{-1})}{\Psi(z^{-1})} e_{t+k} = W_k(z^{-1}) e_{t+k} + \frac{G_k(z^{-1})}{\Psi(z^{-1})} e_t \qquad (10)$$

The polynomials $W_k (z^{-1})$ and $G_k (z^{-1})$ can be calculated from the Diophantine equation as follows:

$$\Theta(z^{-1}) = \Psi(z^{-1}) W_k(z^{-1}) + z^{-k} G_k(z^{-1}) \qquad (11)$$

Demand D_{t+k} can be expanded to the following expression:

$$\begin{aligned} D_{t+k} &= e_{t+k} + w_1 e_{t+k-1} + \ldots w_{k-1} e_{t+1} \\ &+ g_0 e_t + (g_1 - g_0 \psi_1) e_{t-1} + \cdots \end{aligned} \qquad (12)$$

With the prediction properties of ARIMA time series, the demand forecasting of time $t + k$ from time t can be written as:

$$\hat{D}_{t+k/t} = d_0^* e_t + d_1^* e_{t-1} + \ldots \qquad (13)$$

From (12) and (13), the mean squares error can be obtained:

$$E[D_{t+k} - \hat{D}_{t+k/t}]^2 = (1 + w_1^2 + \cdots + w_{k-1}^2)\sigma^2 + [(g_1 - g_0\psi_1 - d_1^*)^2 + \cdots]\sigma^2 \qquad (14)$$

Under the principal of MMSE, we have:

$$\begin{aligned} d_0^* &= g_0 \\ d_1^* &= g_1 - g_0\psi_1 \\ &\cdots \end{aligned}$$

Hence, the optimal estimator of time $t + k$ at time t is given by:

$$\hat{D}_{t+k/t} = \frac{G_k(z^{-1})}{\Psi(z^{-1})} e_t \qquad (15)$$

The evaluated error is given by:

$$\tilde{D}_{t+k/t} = W_k(z^{-1}) e_t \qquad (16)$$

Moreover, the demand estimator is uncorrelated with its error, and then, the total future demand in cycle $[t + 1, t + L]$ can be expressed as the sum of estimator and error:

$$\sum_{m=1}^{L} D_{t+m} = \sum_{m=1}^{L} \hat{D}_{t+m/t} + \sum_{m=1}^{L} \tilde{D}_{t+m/t} \qquad (17)$$

4 The Ordering Model

4.1 Order-Up-To (OUT) Policy

The Order-Up-To (OUT) replenishment policy is a popular ordering approach as minimizing the stock holding and cost. Specifically, the retailer orders a quantity at time period t to bring the inventory to the order-up-to level, which has been calculated in advance.

The ordering criterion [9] in OUT policy is described as:

$$O_t = S_t - IP_t \qquad (18)$$

where O_t is the retailer orders, S_t is the OUT inventory level of the retailer, IP_t is the inventory position, the sum of in-hand stock and on-order stock:

$$IP_t = I_t + \sum_{m=t-L+1}^{t-1} O_m \qquad (19)$$

S_t is estimated from the observed demand:

$$S_t = m_t + z\sqrt{v_t} \qquad (20)$$

where $m_t = E\left(\sum_{m=1}^{L} D_{t+m}|D_t\right)$, $v_t = Var\left(\sum_{m=1}^{L} D_{t+m}|D_t\right)$, z is an constant related to service level. In practice, In practice, the value of z is typically set to zero, and increase the lead time L by one to replace the role of z in holding a desired safety stock. Then we have $S_t = m_t$, and the formula of the ordering quantity is:

$$O_t = \sum_{m=1}^{L} \hat{D}_{t+m/t} - \left(I_t + \sum_{m=t-L+1}^{t-1} O_m\right) \qquad (21)$$

Based on (21) and (6), the current stock is then given by:

$$I_t = \sum_{m=1}^{L} \hat{D}_{t+m/t} - \sum_{m=1}^{L} D_{t+m} = -\sum_{m=1}^{L} \tilde{D}_{t+m/t} \qquad (22)$$

By substituting (22) into (1), we can find the order expression in another way:

$$O_t = \sum_{m=1}^{L} \hat{D}_{t+m/t} - \sum_{m=1}^{L} \hat{D}_{t-1+m/t} + D_t \qquad (23)$$

4.2   Generalized Order-Up-To (G-OUT) Policy

In the previous section, the OUT policy only controls the inventory variance, ignoring the variance restrictions on the order quantity. Therefore, it always gives rise to variance amplification. From the view of stochastic optimal control theory [8], the performance indicator is formed by both inventory part and order part, producing the optimal order control policy.

To acquire the optimal order control policy, we select the objective function as:

$$J = \min_{O_t} E(I_{t+L}^2 + r_0^2 O_t^2) \tag{24}$$

Then, we have the following theorem.

Theorem 1. the optimal order quantity O_t is determined by the equation below:

$$O_t = \beta \left(\sum_{m=1}^{L} \hat{D}_{t+m} - IP_t \right) \tag{25}$$

Where $\beta = 1/(1 + r_0^2)$, then $0 < \beta \le 1$. IP_t is the inventory position at time t. Apparently, when $\beta = 1$, (25) is equal to OUT policy. It is known as Generalized Order-Up-To (G-OUT) policy.

Proof. First we combine (6) and (17) and rewrite (24) as:

$$J = E\left[\min_{O_t} \left(I_t + O_t + \sum_{m=t-L+1}^{t-1} O_m + \sum_{m=1}^{L} \hat{D}_{t+m} \right)^2 + r_0^2 O_t^2 \right]$$
$$+ E\left[\left(\sum_{m=1}^{L} \tilde{D}_{t+m/t} \right)^2 \right] \tag{26}$$

Based on the optimal replenishment rules, we can obtain:

$$O_t = \frac{1}{1 + r_0^2} \left(\sum_{m=1}^{L} \hat{D}_{t+m/t} - I_t - \sum_{m=t-L+1}^{t-1} O_m \right) \tag{27}$$

Let $\beta = 1/(1 + r_0^2)$, we get the Eq. (25).
Then the inventory can be expressed as follows:

$$I_t = \sum_{m=1}^{L} \hat{D}_{t+m/t} - \sum_{m=1}^{L} D_{t+m}$$
$$- \frac{1 - \beta}{1 - (1 - \beta)z^{-1}} \left(\sum_{m=1}^{L} \hat{D}_{t+m/t} - \sum_{m=1}^{L} \hat{D}_{t-1+m/t} + D_t \right) \tag{28}$$

Another mathematical expression of G-OUT policy is:

$$O_t = \frac{\beta}{1 - (1 - \beta)z^{-1}} \left(\sum_{m=1}^{L} \hat{D}_{t+m/t} - \sum_{m=1}^{L} \hat{D}_{t-1+m/t} + D_t \right) \tag{29}$$

Different values of β can produce different orders, affecting the ordering policy. It is apparent that the smaller the value of β is, the greater the factor of order can influence. A suitable value of β can eliminate the bullwhip effect. Consequently, the value should be determined according to the actual situation.

5 Numerical Investigation

5.1 The Definitions of Model Parameters

In this section, a numerical simulation is performed through Matlab 7.0 for a more intuitional analysis. First of all, we assume:

1. The retailer observes the following customer demand, an ARIMA (2, 1, 2) sto-chastic process: $(1 - z^{-1} + 0.41z^{-2})(1 - z^{-1})D_t = (1 - 0.4z^{-1} + 0.03z^{-2})e_t$
2. The lead time L = 3. Namely, the order is received 3 unit interval after it placed and then can be used to satisfy the customer immediately.
3. Only considering the influence caused by the customer demand uncertainty, without regard to other factors.

5.2 Experimental Results

Applying the prior model and order policy, we conduct the numerical simulations using Matlab.

Figure 2 shows the comparison between OUT policy and G-OUT policy with different β, from which we can see that G-OUT policy is much better in controlling bullwhip effect than OUT policy as a whole. In detail, we regard the OUT policy as a special G-OUT policy with $\beta = 1$. Then, Fig. 2 demonstrate the fluctuation of demand and order under G-OUT policy when $\beta = 1$, $\beta = 0.6$, $\beta = 0.3$ and $\beta = 0.15$ respectively. When order quantity is more variable than customer demand, it implies the existence of the bullwhip effect. And the larger the variance is, the bigger the bullwhip effect is. Clearly, we can observe that G-OUT policy improves the bullwhip effect with the diminution of the value of β. When $\beta = 0.3$, the bullwhip effect tends to disappear, as the order variance almost exactly tracks the demand variance. If the value of β is smaller, even anti-bullwhip effect will advent. This is consistent with the theoretical analysis above. We also plot the spectra of the demand and order series under signal spectrum analysis approach for LTI systems [17], as shown in Fig. 3. The area between the order curve and demand curve indicates the intensity of bullwhip effect. Thus, Fig. 3 also shows the controlling results of different order policy on bullwhip effect.

Figure 4 and Table 1 record the experimental results of the inventory variance under different ordering policies. The inventory under OUT policy fluctuates less than that under G-OUT policy. In addition, the smaller the β is, the severer the fluctuation is. From (15) and (21), we can see that the inventory under G-OUT has the additional inventory related to the value of parameter β, which creates the additional fluctuation.

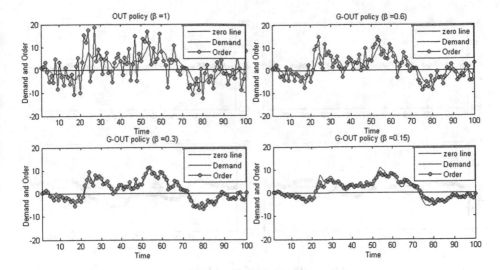

Fig. 2. The fluctuation of demand and order

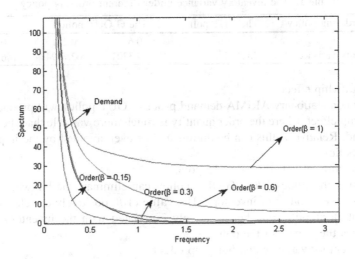

Fig. 3. Spectrum of the customer demand and the order series

Furthermore, when β has a relatively big value, the fluctuation under G-OUT is not necessarily more serious than OUT policy, which indicates that the additional inventory suppresses the inventory fluctuation. Since the inventory variance impacts the warehouse costs, it should be considered when making the order policy.

Several ARIMA demand models with different structure and parameters are experimented in Matlab. The results are in accord with each other. Therefore, we can have the following conclusions which gained by both theoretical analysis in the above section and numerical investigation in this part:

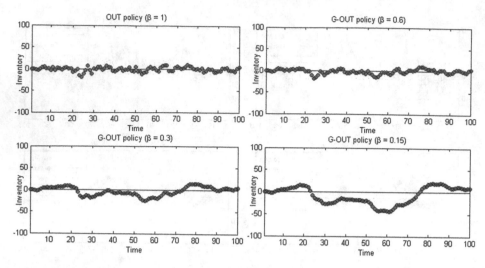

Fig. 4. The fluctuation of Inventory

Table 1. The inventory variance under different ordering policy

The ordering policy	The OUT policy	The G-OUT policy		
β	1	0.6	0.25	0.15
Inventory variance	20.8327	19.3701	62.7194	146.5725

1. The bullwhip effect
   Under non-stationary ARIMA demand process, OUT policy will produce serious bullwhip effect, where the order quantity is much more variable than the customer demand. Relatively, this can be diminished or even avoided by the improved G-OUT policy.
2. The function of generalized OUT policy
   Adjusting the value of β of G-OUT policy can eliminate the bullwhip effect but sacrifice the stability of inventory. The value of β, positively correlated with the fluctuation amplification but negatively correlated with the inventory variance, concerns the impact of the policy.
3. The inventory variance and bullwhip effect
   Theoretically, there is a negative correlation between the fluctuation of inventory and bullwhip effect under Order-Up-To replenishment rule. Experimental simulations also illustrate this phenomenon. It is thereby absolutely essential to strike an appropriate balance between them.

6   Conclusions

In this paper, we discussed the demand uncertainty and its bullwhip effect under the general ARIMA demand process through both theoretical analyses and experimental simulations. Demand predictions are made by MMSE rule. The ordering policies are expressed by optimal control theory. We can theoretically conclude that the bullwhip effect can be avoided by proper generalized order-up-to policy, which also can be experimentally proved. Moreover, the inventory variance opposites the bullwhip effect intension under the ARIMA demands, which should be carefully considered in the practice.

In the future, the following issues will be addressed: (1) The quantization method for bullwhip effect under non-stationary demand process should be investigated. (2) The model can be extended to multi-stage cases and its fluctuation of the inventory and the order can be discussed. (3) Other ordering policies can be employed in ARIMA demand cases. (4) More complicated and practical non-stationary time series, such as ARCH model, can be analyzed in the supply chain.

References

1. Babaia M.Z., Alic M.M., Boylanc J.E., Syntetosd A.A.: Forecasting and inventory performance in a two-stage supply chain with ARIMA (0,1,1) demand: theory and empirical analysis. Int. J. Prod. Econ. http://dx.doi.org/10.1016/j.ijpe.2011.09.004
2. Balakrishnan, A., Geunes, J., Pangburn, M.S.: Coordinating supply chains by controlling upstream variability propagation. Manuf. Serv. Oper. Manage. **6**, 163–183 (2004)
3. Box, G.E.P., Jenkins, G.M.: Time Series Analysis, Forecasting and Control. Holden Day, San Francisco (1970)
4. Brockwell, P.J., Davis, R.A.: Time Series: Theory and Methods, 2nd edn. Springer, New York (1996)
5. Cheng, Y.S., Tang, B.Y., Ling, D.S.: Research on ARMA supply chain model. J. Syst. Eng. Electron. **29**, 753–755 (2007)
6. Chen, F., Drezner, Z., Ryan, J.K., Simchi-Levi, D.: Quantifying the bullwhip effect in a simple supply chain: the impact of forecasting, lead times and information. Manage. Sci. **46**, 436–443 (2000)
7. Chen, Y.F., Disney, S.M.: The myopic Order-UP-To policy with a proportional feedback controller. Int. J. Prod. Res. **45**, 351–368 (2007)
8. Dejonckheere, J., Disney, S.M., Lambrecht, M.R., Towill, D.R.: Measuring the bullwhip effect: a control theoretic approach to analyse forecasting induced bullwhip in order-up-to policies. Eur. J. Oper. Res. **147**, 567–590 (2003)
9. Dejonckheere, J., Disney, S.M., Lambrecht, M.R., Towill, D.R.: The impact of information enrichment on the bullwhip effect in supply chains: a control engineering perspective. Eur. J. Oper. Res. **153**, 727–750 (2004)
10. Dong, H., Li, Y.P.: Dynamic simulation and optimal control strategy of a decentralized supply chain system. In: ICMSE, Moscow, Russia, pp. 419–424 (2009)
11. Gaalman, G., Disney, S.M.: State space investigation of the bullwhip problem with ARMA(1,1) demand process. Int. J. Prod. Econ. **104**, 327–339 (2006)
12. Gilbert, K.: An ARIMA supply chain model. Manage. Sci. **51**, 305–310 (2005)
13. Graves, S.C.: A single-item inventory model for a nonstationary demand process. Manuf. Serv. Oper. Manage. **1**, 50–61 (1999)
14. Hosoda, T., Disney, S.M.: On variance amplification in a three-echelon supply chain with minimum mean square error forecasting. Omega **34**, 344–358 (2006)
15. Hsiao, J.M., Shieh, C.J.: Evaluating the value of information sharing in a supply chain using an ARIMA model. Int. J. Adv. Manuf. Technol. **27**, 604–609 (2006)

16. Lee, H.L., Padmanabhan, V., Whang, S.: Information distortion in a supply chain: the bullwhip effect. Manage. Sci. **43**, 546–558 (1997)
17. Ljung, L.: System Identification: Theory for the User, 2nd edn. Prentice Hall, Upper Saddle River (1999)
18. Petrovic, D., Roy, R., Petrovic, R.: Modelling and simulation of a supply chain in an uncertain environment. Eur. J. Oper. Res. **109**, 299–309 (1998)
19. Raghunathan, S.: Information sharing in a supply chain: a note on its value when demand is nonstationary. Manage. Sci. **47**, 605–610 (2001)
20. Xu, H., Rong, G., Feng, Y.P., Wu, Y.C.: Control variance amplification in linear time invariant decentralized supply chains: a minimum variance control perspective. Ind. Eng. Chem. Res. **49**, 8644–8656 (2010)
21. Zhang, X.L.: The impact of forecasting methods on the bullwhip effect. Int. J. Prod. Econ. **88**, 15–27 (2004)

4th Workshop on Process Model Collections: Management and Reuse (PMC-MR 2013)

Methods for Evaluating Process Model Search

Matthias Kunze(✉) and Mathias Weske

Hasso-Plattner-Institute, University of Potsdam,
Prof.-Dr.-Helmert-Str. 2-3, 14482 Potsdam, Germany
{matthias.kunze,mathias.weske}@hpi.uni-potsdam.de

Abstract. Process model search has received significant interest in the scientific community, recently, due to its precursory role for process model reuse. An abundance of diverse techniques has been proposed. Yet, few of them have been evaluated thoroughly, and a commonly agreed evaluation method is missing. Based on a literature review, we present measures and propose methods for evaluating the quality and performance of process model search techniques, and discuss their relevance and suitability by a case study. This work aims at improving the analysis of future process model search techniques and comparability between them.

Keywords: Process model search · Evaluation · Quality · Performance

1 Introduction

Business process models capture the operations an organization carries out in order to create business value. Used not only for documentation and communication, but also for analysis, process implementation, and certification, process models play a central role to sustain an organization's competitiveness. Therefore, modern organizations maintain hundreds and thousands of process models in process model repositories [21]. Their reuse requires effective and efficient means to find them.

Research in that field has created an abundance of promising techniques toward discovering commonalities and equivalences among process models, quantifying them, and applying them to process model search [3,24]. In order to transfer these into practice, they need to be evaluated with respect to their quality and performance. Such evaluation also offers the opportunity to compare different techniques with each other, to identify strengths and weaknesses, and to assist developers in choosing the technique most appropriate to solving their problem. However, only few authors evaluated their techniques and different approaches are not comparable. We observed that the reason for this is a lack of commonly agreed evaluation measures and methods for process model search.

In our work, we borrowed fundamental evaluation measures from information retrieval [2,4,10], extended them, and applied them to process model search. We propose a comprehensive methodology to evaluate the quality and performance of a process model search technique, and thereby, strive to spark a practice

N. Lohmann et al. (Eds.): BPM 2013 Workshops, LNBIP 171, pp. 379–391, 2014.
DOI: 10.1007/978-3-319-06257-0_30, © Springer International Publishing Switzerland 2014

of process model search evaluation in the scientific community that facilitates knowledge transfer and enables comparability of innovative techniques.

The remainder of this paper is structured as follows. In Sect. 2, we briefly introduce the conceptual background of process model search and present the running examples used throughout the paper. Methods to evaluate process model search techniques toward their quality are presented in Sect. 3, and toward their performance in Sect. 4. Section 5 examines literature on process model search techniques that provide an evaluation and discusses further related work, before the paper is concluded in Sect. 6.

2 Background

Searching for process models takes a search question, i.e., a *query*, as input and retrieves all models from a collection of *candidates* that satisfy the query. These are called *matches*. We observe two search strategies in the literature, *similarity search* and *querying*, that differ essentially in the way the query is compared with a candidate.

In process model similarity search, the query is a regular process model of the same type as the candidates and their comparison yields a measure that quantifies the resemblance between two models, e.g., by the share of common behavior [17] or graph-edit-distances [6]. Similarity search is well suited to find duplicates and redundancies in a collection of process models, e.g., to merge process model repositories. Querying, in contrast, supports cases where few yet essential aspects of a search question must be met precisely by a match. Here, the query can be expressed in any structured form, e.g., using a textual or visual query language [1], or with an incomplete process model itself [19]. Despite its focus on approximate matching, similarity search is not suited for these cases, as a matching model must supersede the query in all requested features and will therefore show only low similarity.

2.1 Searching in Process Model Collections

Process model search is comprised of several steps to retrieve process models from the repository that match the given query model, depicted in Fig. 1. (1) The first step of search consists of processing the input query, i.e., extracting the features that compose the search question. Based on these features and an index,

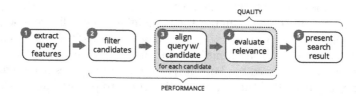

Fig. 1. Steps comprising process model search and their evaluation.

(2) a set of candidate models that may be relevant to the query are obtained. Here, the index allows for efficient search, if irrelevant models can be excluded from the remaining search process. For each candidate, (3) an alignment with the query must be constructed, i.e., the features requested in the query must be mapped to corresponding features in the candidate process model, cf. [8,25]. (4) Based on the alignment, the relevance of the candidate with regard to the query can be computed and irrelevant candidates excluded. As a result of steps 3 and 4, a set of relevant process models is proposed as search result for the query. (5) In the final step, these models are ranked such that the most relevant results are presented first to the user.

Evaluation of a particular search technique addresses assessing the performance of these steps and the quality of their result. Here, performance refers to the time required to return a search result and the scalability to large process model collections. Quality generally assesses the relevance of search results and their ranking.

2.2   Similarity Measures and Data Set

The evaluation methods presented in this paper can be applied to similarity search and querying, likewise. To illustrate and discuss them in the following sections, we present results obtained from experiments for two similarity measures. The *structural* measure computes similarity by the graph-edit-distance of canonical process model graphs, i.e., the minimal number of inserting, updating, or deleting nodes and edges to transform the query model into the candidate model. It is based upon [6], but uses a binary alignment as input and therefore provides different results. The *behavioral* similarity measure, introduced in [17] quantifies the amount of common behavior by means of ordering relations between pairs of activities. In both cases, we use the string-edit-distance and a simple threshold matcher to compute the process alignment.

Since the evaluation of quality measures requires a reference to compare experimental results with, we resorted to a data set provided by [6]. In this data set, the pairwise similarity of 10 queries and 100 candidate process models from the SAP reference model [5] has been assessed manually in a survey with business process experts. These measures and their evaluation are primary objectives of this paper, and they are rather used to explain the proposed evaluation methods.

3   Quality

Evaluating the quality of a process model search technique requires a *reference* to be compared with, also referred to as standard in information retrieval [2,10]. Such a reference defines which candidate models ideally match a given query. Quality measures evaluate the difference of an actual search result and the provided reference and, hence, assess how well the search technique complies with the reference. These measures allow for direct comparison of the strengths and weaknesses of various process model search techniques with regard to a given reference.

We distinguish quality measures by three categories: *Effectiveness* addresses evaluation measures adopted from information retrieval, whereas *robustness* and *ranking* are introduced for process model search.

3.1 Effectiveness

Effectiveness measures quantify the accuracy of a search technique by the correlation of its output with the reference. Precision and recall, introduced in [23], are probably the most prominent of these measures. Figure 2 illustrates the underlying concepts. Given a process model collection C and a process model query, a particular search technique will propose A as a search result. In contrast, R represents the ideal search result defined by the reference, which we refer to hereafter as relevant search results. Effectiveness measures quantify the agreement between these two sets. $A \cap R$ denotes the subset of matches provided correctly by the search technique with respect to the reference R, and therefore, $A \setminus R$ are considered false positives: matches that are not confirmed by R.

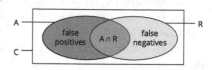

Fig. 2. Effectiveness of search result.

Precision, p, assesses the amount of false positives in the search result A. The less false positives are contained, the higher the precision of a search result.

$$p = \frac{|A \cap R|}{|A|}$$

Recall, r, evaluates the amount of completeness of a search result, i.e., how many relevant search results are contained in A.

$$r = \frac{|A \cap R|}{|R|}$$

k-precision, $p(k)$, and k-recall, $r(k)$ requires the result set to be ranked. $p(k)$ and $r(k)$ then compute the precision and recall of the first k models of the result set, respectively. Precision and recall are of limited use to compare the effectiveness of several search techniques, as either may have a higher recall and a lower precision than the other, such that no clear preference can be obtained. Therefore, evaluation measures that combine precision and recall provide better comparability.

The **f-score** [10], f, computes the harmonic mean between precision and recall. It is typically used to evaluate different configurations of a system, where the highest produced f-score indicates the best configuration.

$$f = 2 \cdot \frac{p \cdot r}{p + r}$$

The **overall** measure [10], o, evaluates the effort to correct a search result so that it resembles the reference. If more relevant models must be added than are already contained, it will provide a negative value.

$$o = r \cdot \left(2 - \frac{1}{p} \right)$$

All of the above measures can only be computed for a result set A of fixed size. This is straightforward in the case of querying process models, as the result set is strictly constrained by the query. In case of similarity search, the result set is typically only limited by the number of the models presented to the user or a minimal similarity threshold. Hence, the size of the result set needs to be chosen a priori. On the other hand, similarity search offers the opportunity to expand the search result by adding process models with lower similarity to the query. While this will include more false positives in the result set, it will also add true positives and, hence, increase the recall of a search result. This particularity of similarity search can be used for a very insightful method to present effectiveness.

Precision-recall curve diagrams depict the precision of a search result at increasing recall levels. As more irrelevant models are added, the precision typically declines. In an ideal case, precision remains high over large recall levels, whereas inferior cases are identified by an early and gradual decline. Figure 3 shows a diagram for the similarity measures introduced above. Here, the behavioral measure outperforms the structural. Besides a generally lower precision, the structural curve also declines earlier than the behavioral.

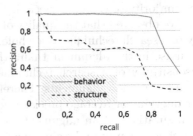

Fig. 3. Precision-recall curve.

A performance indicator for the effectiveness of a similarity search query, in the same fashion as the f-score or overall for querying, is the **average precision**, p_{avg}, which denotes the average precision of a search result, after all relevant models have been included in the result set [4] and approximates the area under the precision-recall curve.

$$p_{avg} = \frac{\sum_{k=1}^{|C|} (p(k) \cdot rel(k))}{|R|}$$

The effectiveness measures presented above are computed for a single query only; a thorough evaluation, however, must consider a diversity of independent queries addressing many aspects of matching. Hence, these measures are often aggregated over a set of queries. For example, aggregation of the average precision over all queries yields the **mean average precision**, which is useful to assess the effectiveness of a similarity search technique in a single figure. In our examples, mean average precision of the structural similarity is 0.37, and of the behavioral similarity 0.78. Aggregation, however, hides interesting outliers that should be rather highlighted and critically discussed as specific aspects of a search technique.

Plotting the individual performance of queries in a coordinate space spanned by precision and recall offers insights into outliers and provides a basis to discuss their relative impact on the effectiveness. An example is illustrated in Fig. 4, where we computed precision and recall for a result set comprised of 10 matches, i.e., $p(10)$ and $r(10)$, for each query and located the resulting data point in the given coordinate system. Data points in the lower left quadrant, $(p < 0.5, r < 0.5)$, should be discussed for apparent issues.

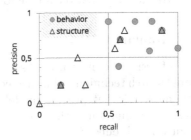

Fig. 4. Precision/recall values for individual queries.

3.2 Robustness

One particular aspect of process model search is the computation of a process alignment, before a match is decided, cf. Sect. 2. Although this does not necessarily apply to all process model search techniques, we observed that it holds for the majority of them, cf. Sect. 5.

We observed that the quality of an alignment has a major impact on the quality of a search technique as a whole. However, some techniques are more resistant to noise in the alignment than others. To this end, **robustness** expresses the insensitivity of a search technique to noise, i.e., reliable results are provided even for inferior alignments. Therefore, an effectiveness measure, e.g., the f-score for querying or average precision for similarity search, is computed over various configurations of an alignment. In our example, we leverage a threshold-based matcher to compute the alignment, i.e., only if the string-edit-distance of a pair of activities is higher than the threshold, they will be considered for an alignment. To evaluate our similarity search techniques, we computed the mean average precision for various alignment threshold values between 0.4 and 1. The results are depicted in Fig. 5.

The curves show the impact of the alignment on the overall effectiveness of a similarity measure. By increasing the threshold and, thereby, eliminating falsely identified correspondences, the mean average precision for the structural similarity rises. In comparison, the behavioral similarity is less sensitive to that bias indicated by an flat progress of the mean average precision. The decline for high threshold values is caused by missing correspondences, that are not found if the labels need to be close to identical.

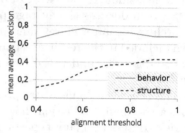

Fig. 5. Robustness over an increasing alignment quality.

Whereas effectiveness measures evaluate the overall quality of a search technique with particular data sets, robustness discloses valuable insights into the very aspect of process matching. Similar evaluations of robustness are possible over all configuration parameters and can be used to tune a search technique for optimal quality.

3.3 Ranking

The effectiveness measures discussed above evaluate the accuracy of process model search techniques, but neglect any ordering of matches in the search result. Yet, more relevant process models should be ranked higher than less relevant ones. An evaluation of the search result ranking is rare, since attention is rather spent on high effectiveness of search results in related work, cf. Sect. 5.

One meaningful measure is the **overlap**, $l(k)$. Here, A_k represents the subset of A that contains the k highest ranked process models; the same holds for R_k.

$$l(k) = \frac{|A_k \cap R_k|}{k}$$

The overlap measure assesses the agreement of the reference with the actual search result on the k most relevant process models in the search. In practice, k should be chosen such that it represents the number of process models that are presented to a user on the first result page [2], i.e., between 5 and 10.

We illustrate the overlap over an increasing k for our exemplary similarity measures aggregated over all 10 queries, in Fig. 6. For the first 3 models, structural similarity supersedes behavioral with respect to human assessment. For increasing k, the overlap converges to 1, as more and more process models are common in A_k and R_k.

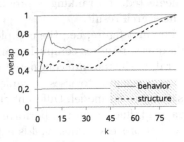

Fig. 6. Overlap over growing k.

More intricate measures have been proposed to evaluate the ranking correlation between ordered lists, e.g., the Spearman coefficient and Kendall's Tau, see [2], and the ranking agreement measure [12] for process model similarity. To keep the paper concise, we do not repeat their definitions here.

4   Performance

Quality measures evaluate the agreement of a search technique with a reference, obtained from human feedback. In contrast, performance measures address the practical applicability of a technique in terms of resource consumption; typical measures are speed and memory consumption [10]. The performance of a search technique can be measured and evaluated without human reference data. However, for the purpose of comparability, such measures need to be computed on the same set of queries and process model collection across various search techniques, referred to as benchmarks.

In related work, we observed that performance evaluations are typically provided in absolute values, e.g., fractions of a second it takes in average to return a search result, cf. Sect. 5. As such values depend significantly on the runtime environment, authors often provide information about the used operating system, CPU speed, and available memory. Still, these evaluations are of limited use, as they cannot be directly compared with each other. Implementations may not be publicly available or incompatible in their assumption of the runtime environment. Therefore, relative measures and trend analyses are more useful, because they show the scalability of the approach in a practical setting.

4.1   Algorithmic Complexity

The computational complexity of a search technique is a theoretic measure, yet essential, and can be determined purely by examining the algorithms employed for search. Following our discussion in Sect. 2.1, the time to obtain matches for a given process model query results from the time to compare a query with a candidate multiplied with the number of such comparison operations required to obtain relevant matches, plus the time to rank process models. The latter can be neglected, if a ranking is provided implicitly by the similarity of the models in the search result.

The first figure, i.e., the complexity to evaluate the relevance of a candidate for a query, requires computing an alignment and deciding a match thereon. In general, both steps are conducted with regard to activities in the process model, so it is reasonable to assess complexity as a function of the number of the activities of a process model. Different classes of process models may have a positive or negative influence on the performance of search. For instance, comparing state spaces of process models yields exponential complexity for time and space, due to the state space explosion problem for concurrent behavior [22]. If, in practice, process models show close to no concurrent behavior, this decreases significantly.

The second figure, the number of comparison operations required for search, is largely influenced by index data structures and algorithms that make search efficient, i.e., avoid the comparison of the query with each process model in the collection. In earlier work [18], we showed that hierarchical indexes can be used to reduce the number of comparison operations significantly. A well-established approach is the usage of an inverted index that allows early exclusion of models that cannot match a query, and therefore, reduces the number of comparison operations.

4.2   Efficiency

Algorithmic complexity often provides a worst-case evaluation of performance as it needs to acknowledge edge cases, whereas, in practice, search techniques perform more encouragingly. The efficiency of a search technique can be estimated by means of a benchmark, i.e., a collection of candidates and queries that are searched and for which performance figures are recorded. Efficiency refers to relative measures with respect to resource consumption or computational complexity that are independent of the actual processing environment. These measures address the optimization of the overall search performance achieved by optimizations, estimations and heuristics, and additional data structures, e.g., indexes. Here, we focus on the latter.

Saved comparison operations, c, is a relative measure that evaluates the performance improvement gained from an index, i.e., the actual number of comparisons, $|C|$,

$$c = 1 - \frac{n}{|C|}$$

required for search in relation to sequential search, where a query is compared against each candidate, with n being the number of candidates. Again, this measure can be aggregated over a set of queries to be more expressive, and a quantitative evaluation of the distribution, e.g., using box-plots, yields valuable insights. For instance, a mean value that is significantly larger than the median over the set of candidates and queries indicates that there exist considerably poor cases that show low efficiency of the indexing approach. Such cases should be examined. Also, variance and standard deviation provide a well-established means to judge on the distribution of values.

Memory consumption depends largely on the employed index and characteristics of the search approach. For instance, an inverted index that maps activity labels to process models, which contain that activity stores up to n entries, where n is the number of distinct activities in all process models in the collection. If, instead, the index stores relations between pairs of activities, e.g., control flow edges, up to n^2 entries must be stored. With respect to evaluating scalability, the memory consumed by an index should be quantified as ratio of the memory required to store all process models of a collection [16].

4.3   Trend Analysis

The **scalability** of a particular search technique can be evaluated by comparing performance figures, both absolute and relative, over an increasing size of the process model collection considered for search. The progression of the resulting curve gives an insight into the capacity of the approach to cope with large process model collections. This type of analysis is common in related work, cf. Sect. 5, although it is provided almost exclusively for absolute search times.

The exemplary search techniques introduced earlier can be optimized by a metric index as their similarity measures can be translated into proper metrics, cf. [17, 18]. Figure 7 visualizes their scalability in terms of required comparison operations over an increasing process model collection; lower values are better. The dotted curve represents the number of comparison operations for sequential search for reference. Approaches that show a linear increase should remain below sequential search to be considered efficient. From Fig. 7 it becomes

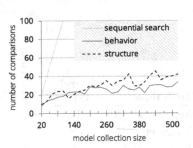

Fig. 7. Scalability of saved comparison operations.

apparent that the index provides even better efficiency, because both curves show a logarithmic trend, i.e., efficiency increases for growing model collections. This is explained in more detail in [18].

5   Related Work

Despite the plethora of different techniques proposed for process model search [3, 24], only few recent contributions include an evaluation of their approaches. We first characterize these techniques and show that evaluation is still a major issue in the field, and then turn to related that discusses evaluation measures and methods, and compare it with our work.

Table 1 gives an overview of the different evaluation criteria that have been applied to process model search techniques. All criteria used in these approaches have been presented above. With regard to the completeness of evaluation, it becomes obvious that search techniques have been evaluated rather sparsely and the majority of authors who evaluate the effectiveness of their approaches resort to precision and recall.

The SAP reference model collection with a human similarity assessment, introduced in Sect. 2.2, has been used as an evaluation reference by [6,9,17,26]. In comparison, [11,20,27] used a rather small set of process models and provided a reference on their own, to evaluate effectiveness. A more detailed analysis for effectiveness is provided in [7,17] that leverage precision-recall curves. The authors of [9] discuss the distribution of effectiveness values using basic statistic measures, minimum, maximum, arithmetic mean, and standard deviation. It is worth mentioning that both robustness and ranking have not yet been evaluated in the literature. We articulate this to two reasons: (a) the focus of research has been on high performance or good effectiveness, and (b) there is no agreed corpus of evaluation methods in the area of process model search, yet.

As mentioned earlier, performance has largely been measured in terms of average runtime for a search, complemented with trend diagrams to visualize

Table 1. Overview of related work that evaluates process model search techniques.

Technique	Search type	precision	recall	f-measure	overall	avg. precision	robustness	ranking	complexity	efficiency	speed	memory
Nejati et al. [20]	sim	mean	mean	–	–	–	–	–	–	–	–	–
Kunze et al. [18]	sim	–	–	–	–	–	–	–	–	%	–	–
Jin et al. [16]	query	–	–	–	–	–	–	–	–	–	s	%
Grigori et al. [11]	sim	yes	yes	–	yes	–	–	–	–	–	s	–
Kunze et al. [17]	sim	mean	mean	–	–	mean	–	–	–	–	–	–
Jin et al. [14]	sim	–	–	–	–	–	–	–	–	–	s	%
Dijkman et al. [6]	sim	mean	mean	–	–	mean	–	–	yes	–	s	–
Yan et al. [26]	sim	yes	–	–	–	–	–	–	–	%	s	–
Jin et al. [15]	sim	–	–	–	–	–	–	–	–	–	s	%
Yan et al. [27]	query	mean	mean	–	–	–	–	–	–	–	s	–
Humm et al. [13]	sim	mean	mean	mean	–	–	–	–	–	–	–	–
Ekanayake et al. [9]	sim	min mean max std	min mean max std	min mean max std	–	–	–	–	–	–	–	–

scalability in [11,14–16]. In earlier work [18], we proposed measuring efficiency of a process model search technique by the saved comparison operations. This has been adopted in [26]. In [14–16] relative measures for memory consumption were proposed.

From these figures, it becomes obvious that comprehensive evaluations are still missing in scientific publications that address process model search, and authors either focus on quality or performance. This is, at least in part, due to the lack of references to evaluate the quality of an approach and benchmarks to have a common data set for performance evaluations. In this regard, the SAP reference model [5] and the human assessment of similarity introduced in [6] gained considerable interest. Yet, they are not suited for all use cases, e.g., querying.

This paper is the first to propose a comprehensive set of methods to evaluate techniques for process model search. Some proposed measures, in particular effectiveness and performance measures, are already well established in information retrieval [2] and ontology matching [10]. However, particular aspects in process model search, e.g., the dependency on a process alignment, and the produced ranking of search results, require additional consideration. In [3], a comparative survey of process model similarity measures identifies desirable properties of such measures, and compares the measures by their mutual agreement on matches for a set of queries. While this is related to the effectiveness measures, the authors do not address evaluation and assess the effectiveness of these approaches in comparison of a reference standard.

6 Conclusion

We motivated the need for a thorough evaluation of process model search techniques to make them comparable and to contribute to their transfer into practice. A review of related literature has disclosed that the research community did not yet agree on a corpus of evaluation measures and methods. To tackle this shortcoming, we studied established evaluation measures from the fields of information retrieval and ontology matching and applied them to process model search.

With the help of a case study, we illustrated particular evaluation aspects with respect to quality and performance. Quality addresses the effectiveness, robustness, and ranking of a search result; performance considers not only resource consumption but also focuses on their scalability. Furthermore, we put these evaluation measures in a methodical context to examine and present evaluation results in an informative and unbiased fashion. The evaluation measures proposed in this paper have been implemented as a small Java library and are available at https://github.com/mtkunze/evaluation.

With regard to future work, we perceive the development of reference standards and benchmarks as the most pressing issue. Without such references, there is no common ground to evaluate and compare a technique with. The data set mentioned in Sect. 2.2 is a very helpful resource, but restricted to similarity search and a comparably homogeneous collection of models and terminology. More heterogeneous reference collections are required to evaluate both quality and performance of a search technique, and to make them comparable.

References

1. Awad. A.: BPMN-Q: a language to query business processes. In: EMISA, pp. 115–128 (2007)
2. Baeza-Yates, R., Ribeiro-Neto, B.: Modern Information Retrieval - The Concepts and Technology Behind Search, 2nd edn. Pearson Education Ltd., Harlow (2011)
3. Becker, M., Laue, R.: A comparative survey of business process similarity measures. Comput. Ind. **63**(2), 148–167 (2012)
4. Buckley, C., Voorhees, E.: Evaluating evaluation measure stability. In: SIGIR '00, pp. 33–40. ACM, New York (2000)
5. Curran, T., Keller, G., Ladd, A.: SAP R/3 Business Blueprint: Understanding the Business Process Reference Model. Prentice-Hall Inc., Upper Saddle River (1997)
6. Dijkman, R., Dumas, M., Dongen, B., Käärik, R., Mendling, J.: Similarity of business process models: metrics and evaluation. Inform. Syst. **36**(2), 498–516 (2011)
7. Dijkman, R., Rosa, M., Reijers, H.: Managing large collections of business process models - current techniques and challenges. Comput. Ind. **63**(2), 91–97 (2012)
8. Dumas, M., García-Bañuelos, L., Dijkman, R.: Similarity search of business process models. IEEE Data Eng. Bull. **32**(3), 23–28 (2009)
9. Ekanayake, C.C., Dumas, M., García-Bañuelos, L., La Rosa, M., ter Hofstede, A.H.M.: Approximate clone detection in repositories of business process models. In: Barros, A., Gal, A., Kindler, E. (eds.) BPM 2012. LNCS, vol. 7481, pp. 302–318. Springer, Heidelberg (2012)
10. Euzenat, J., Shvaiko, P.: Ontology Matching. Springer, Heidelberg (2007)
11. Grigori, D., Corrales, J., Bouzeghoub, M., Gater, A.: Ranking BPEL processes for service discovery. IEEE TSC **3**, 178–192 (2010)
12. Guentert, M., Kunze, M., Weske, M.: Evaluation measures for similarity search results in process model repositories. In: Atzeni, P., Cheung, D., Ram, S. (eds.) ER 2012 Main Conference 2012. LNCS, vol. 7532, pp. 214–227. Springer, Heidelberg (2012)
13. Humm, B.G., Fengel, J.: Semantics-based business process model similarity. In: Abramowicz, W., Kriksciuniene, D., Sakalauskas, V. (eds.) BIS 2012. LNBIP, vol. 117, pp. 36–47. Springer, Heidelberg (2012)
14. Jin, T., Wang, J., Wen, L.: Efficient retrieval of similar business process models based on structure. In: Meersman, R., et al. (eds.) OTM 2011, Part I. LNCS, vol. 7044, pp. 56–63. Springer, Heidelberg (2011)
15. Jin, T., Wang, J., Wen, L.: Efficient retrieval of similar workflow models based on behavior. In: Sheng, Q.Z., Wang, G., Jensen, C.S., Xu, G. (eds.) APWeb 2012. LNCS, vol. 7235, pp. 677–684. Springer, Heidelberg (2012)
16. Jin, T., Wang, J., Wu, N., La Rosa, M., ter Hofstede, A.H.M.: Efficient and accurate retrieval of business process models through indexing. In: Meersman, R., Dillon, T.S., Herrero, P. (eds.) OTM 2010. LNCS, vol. 6426, pp. 402–409. Springer, Heidelberg (2010)
17. Kunze, M., Weidlich, M., Weske, M.: Behavioral similarity – a proper metric. In: Rinderle-Ma, S., Toumani, F., Wolf, K. (eds.) BPM 2011. LNCS, vol. 6896, pp. 166–181. Springer, Heidelberg (2011)

18. Kunze, M., Weske, M.: Metric trees for efficient similarity search in process model repositories. In: IW-PL '10, Hoboken, USA (2010)
19. Kunze, M., Weske, M.: Local behavior similarity. In: Bider, I., Halpin, T., Krogstie, J., Nurcan, S., Proper, E., Schmidt, R., Soffer, P., Wrycza, S. (eds.) EMMSAD 2012 and BPMDS 2012. LNBIP, vol. 113, pp. 107–120. Springer, Heidelberg (2012)
20. Nejati, S., Sabetzadeh, M., Chechik, M., Easterbrook, S., Zave, P.: Matching and merging of statecharts specifications. In: ICSE '07, pp. 54–64. IEEE (2007)
21. Rosemann, M.: Potential pitfalls of process modeling. BPMJ **12**(3), 377–384 (2006)
22. Valmari, A.: The state explosion problem. In: Reisig, W., Rozenberg, G. (eds.) APN 1998. LNCS, vol. 1491. Springer, Heidelberg (1998)
23. Rijsbergen, C.: Information Retrieval. Butterworth, London (1979)
24. Wang, J., Jin, T., Wong, R., Wen, L.: Querying business process model repositories. World Wide Web **17**(3), 427–454 (2014)
25. Weidlich, M., Dijkman, R., Mendling, J.: The ICoP framework: identification of correspondences between process models. In: Pernici, B. (ed.) CAiSE 2010. LNCS, vol. 6051, pp. 483–498. Springer, Heidelberg (2010)
26. Yan, Z., Dijkman, R., Grefen, P.: Fast business process similarity search. Distrib. Parallel Dat. **30**, 105–144 (2012)
27. Yan, Z., Dijkman, R., Grefen, P.: FNet: an index for advanced business process querying. In: Barros, A., Gal, A., Kindler, E. (eds.) BPM 2012. LNCS, vol. 7481, pp. 246–261. Springer, Heidelberg (2012)

Decomposition and Hierarchization of EPCs: A Case Study

Jürgen Walter[✉], Peter Fettke, and Peter Loos

Institute for Information Systems (IWi), German Research Center for Artificial Intelligence (DFKI) and Saarland University, Campus, Building D32 66123 Saarbrücken, Germany
{Juergen.Walter,Peter.Fettke,Peter.Loos}@iwi.dfki.de

Abstract. Nowadays, organizations utilize process model collections with several hundreds or thousands of models. To reduce model complexity, large process models are typically decomposed into smaller ones. Moreover, processes are modeled at different levels of abstraction by means of hierarchization. Although the hierarchization and decomposition concepts result in a reuse of processes and foster a better understanding, their applications can lead to various syntactic and semantic issues concerning the concatenation of the resulting processes. In this article, the decomposition of event-driven process chains (EPCs) is examined by an analysis of an established reference model as well as the hierarchization concept. Furthermore, a classification of the identified issues will be presented. The awareness about these issues can be used to avoid modeling weaknesses of new models or for the evaluation of other (reference) models.

Keywords: Business process modeling · Decomposition · Hierarchization

1 Introduction

Many organizations maintain large process model collections, which consist of several hundreds or thousands of models. For clarity and reuse purposes, the concept of decomposition is applied to larger process models. This results in smaller sub-processes. Depending on stakeholders needs, hierarchization can be used to detail individual process model components on a lower level of abstraction. Both concepts are extensively used within the 55 EPCs of the Retail-H reference model [1], with the event-driven process chains (EPCs) [2] as modeling language. The decomposition concept is supported in EPC by process interfaces. A *decomposition* [1, 3] is understood as a splitting of an EPC into smaller EPCs by the use of such process interfaces, whereby these EPCs remain at the same level of abstraction as the original EPC [1]. The concept of hierarchization in the reference model provides three levels of abstraction [1]: A framework on the top level (the H of the Retail-H), function blocks at the second level and process models and data models at the third level. In this work, a *hierarchization* refers to a refinement of an EPC-function at the third level by another EPC (refined EPC). Thus, the refined EPC has a lower level of abstraction.

N. Lohmann et al. (Eds.): BPM 2013 Workshops, LNBIP 171, pp. 392–404, 2014.
DOI: 10.1007/978-3-319-06257-0_31, © Springer International Publishing Switzerland 2014

Generally, certain syntactic rules must be met so that the content and semantics of a model are equal before and after the application of the concepts of decomposition and hierarchization. The objectives of this article are to analyze these concepts and focus on identifying and classifying possible modeling weaknesses. The first step was a manual digitization of a model collection, the Retail-H reference model [1]. Several syntactic and semantic issues occurred. To solve them always in the same manner, they were systematically logged and analyzed. To understand the nature of the identified issues, the syntactic rules given by the authors have been considered. Moreover, formalizations of EPCs were taken into account. The one with the most extensive coverage, with regard to both concepts, was introduced by Mendling [4]. According to several semantic rules, all process interfaces and all refined functions within the process models were analyzed as well as all events contained in the presets and postsets of these elements. The results of the analyses shed light on previously unknown relationships within the scope of the science of information systems. This enables a description of similar issues on a higher level of abstraction ("generalization"). The findings can be used for the creation and evaluation of further reference models [5].

The rest of the article is organized as followed: Section 2 starts with a related work part and an introduction to event-driven process chains (EPCs). Furthermore, an intuitive semantics of EPCs is outlined. In Sect. 3, the Retail-H reference model is analyzed in detail. There, an analysis of the levels of abstraction of EPCs as well as the results of the analysis of decomposition and hierarchization concepts are presented. Finally, Sect. 4 summarizes the findings and gives an outlook on future research.

2   Related Work and Basics

2.1   Related Work

The concepts of decomposition and hierarchization are already known in the context of event-driven process chains [1, 3, 4, 6, 7]. Basic requirements for models in terms of these concepts have been mentioned in the guidelines of modeling [6]. These guidelines consider different aspects of modeling: Correctness, Relevance, Economic efficiency, Clarity, Comparability and Systematic design [6]. In this work, the first aspect is especially relevant because it is assumed that the correctness of a model is a precondition for its meaningful interpretation by a user. In [6], a distinction between syntactic and semantic correctness is made. The former is ensured by the syntactic rules of a modeling language. A model has to met them if it should be regarded as syntactically correct [6]. Semantic correctness refers to the structure and behavior of a model that should be consistent with the relevant snippet of reality. The topic of syntax and semantics is addressed by several approaches [4, 7–10], but the concepts of decomposition and hierarchization of EPCs have not yet been analyzed in depth. A reason for this could be the assumption, that any decomposed and/or refined EPC can be reintegrated into a single EPC. Colloquially, this is called flattening of EPCs [1, 4]. This assumption will be evaluated in this work. For this purpose, the established modeling guidelines and syntactical rules provided by the authors of the Retail-H and the formalization given in [4] are examined for their usefulness for flattening of an EPC.

2.2 Event-Driven Process Chains

An EPC in [1] consists of a set of events, functions, connectors and directed arcs. Connectors are distinguished into conjunctive, disjunctive and adjunctive connectors as well as split and join connectors. The sequence operator is omitted here for simplicity as well as process objects, organizational units and application systems, which can be annotated to functions. A decomposition of an EPC is realized through process interfaces and hierarchization through a refinement of a function (c.f. Fig. 2). Furthermore, several syntactical constraints for EPCs were outlined informally. With regard to process interfaces, no specific constraints were provided by the authors. For the hierarchization, two constraints [1] were mentioned: (1) The preceding event of a refined function must be contained in the set of start events of the referenced model and (2) the succeeding event must be contained in the set of end events.

In literature, various formalizations for the syntax and semantics of event-driven process chains [3, 4, 8, 9, 11–16] do exist. In [4], a summary of [3, 12, 14–16] as well as a further formalization of EPCs are presented. There, syntactical constraints for EPCs are also stressed. In this work, the analysis is based on the informal descriptions of EPCs presented in [1] and the formalization given in [4]. However, a reproduction of the formalization of [4] is omitted for simplicity, except for two relevant notions. In our work, the definition of an *Upper Corona* and *Lower Corona* is of special interest (c.f. Definition 2.5 in [4]): Informally, the upper corona includes those non-connector nodes of the transitive preset of a node n of an EPC that reach n via a connector chain. The lower corona is defined analogously.

For the following considerations, a simplified and informal description of the semantics of EPCs will be sufficient. For this reason, a differentiation between the various formalizations of semantics of EPCs is omitted. An EPC starts with at least one start node and ends with at least one end node. These nodes are connected via a control flow represented by directed arcs. Start and end nodes are either events or process interfaces. Functions contained in a control flow will be "processed". The control flow can be splitted and joined via different types of connectors. Process interfaces are used for the decomposition of larger EPCs, whereby the control flow continues in the referenced EPCs. A hierarchization is realized through a refinement of a function by another EPC. Once a refined function is reached, the control flow continues in the referenced EPC and returns when the referenced EPC is executed.

3 Exemplarily Analysis of a Reference Model

3.1 Levels of Abstraction in the Retail-H model

For the analysis of the Retail-H reference model [1] an abstract overview was created (cf. Fig. 1). It covers all EPCs and their correlations. Different sub-clusters are marked

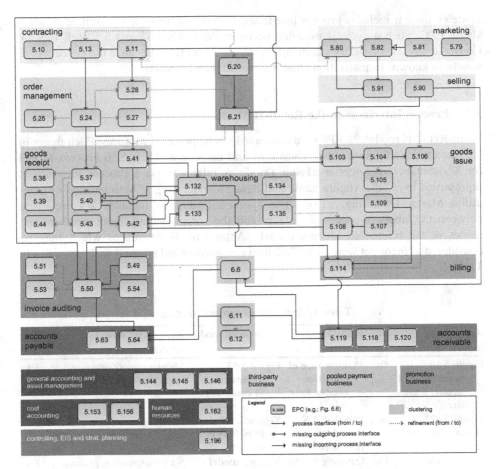

Fig. 1. Relations of EPCs in the Retail-H reference model

with color gradations (e.g., cluster "procurement" with sub-clusters "contracting", "order management", etc.). EPCs are represented by rounded rectangles (e.g., 5.10 refer to "Fig. 5.10" in [1]). A black arc represents a reference induced by a process interface and a red dotted arc implies a reference induced by a refined function.

The simultaneous application of both concepts can lead to a hierarchy clash, implying that different level of abstraction can be assigned to one EPC. As illustration: the EPC 5.80 references the EPCs 5.82 and 5.91 via process interfaces. Thus, they have the same level of abstraction. At the same time, EPC 5.80 references EPC 5.82 via a refined function, implying a hierarchy clash because a lower level of abstraction is now assigned and this contradicts the level implied via the process interface. So far, in literature no explicit rules have been mentioned regarding the compliance of the level of abstraction. But they can still be derived implicitly from the proposed directed and acyclic hierarchy graph (cf. Definition 2.9/2.10 in [4]). Generally, a node of a directed acyclic graph can only have one level of abstraction. The proposed hierarchy graph prohibits loops that pass over several EPCs. This unnecessarily restricts a modeler since it includes process interfaces. In contrast, loops are permitted inside a single EPC. Such a cycle is modeled between the EPCs 5.42 and 5.50 (cf. Fig. 1). Consequently, two contrary statements were given in [1, 4]. Because the concepts are scholarly known, formalization should cover them adequately.

3.2 Process Interfaces in the Retail-H Model

In the Retail-H model, 32 EPCs are connected via 82 process interfaces. Each figure in [1] has a unique figure number, chart type and name, e.g., "Fig. 5.10 Process Model for Maintenance of Supplier Master Data". A reference via a process interface is represented by a label (figure name and figure number), e.g., "Maintenance of Condition Master Data (Fig. 5.13)". The systematic analysis includes a comparison between the labels of process interfaces and the corresponding figure numbers and names of the referenced process models. A total of 43 references which may be considered as incorrect were identified, then categorized and covered with examples in Table 1.

Table 1. Inconsistent process interfaces

Referencing model	i/o	Process interface	Referenced model	Referenced process interface	Cat.
Figure 5.10 maintenance of supplier master data	Out	**Maintenance of condition master data** (Fig. 5.13)	Figure 5.13 **maintenance of conditions**	Maintenance of supplier master data (Fig. 5.10)	1.1
Figure 5.42 Goods assessment	In	**POS/FWWS upload (Fig. 5.102)**	**Figure 5.108 POS-/FWWS- upload**	Goods assessment (Fig. 5.42)	1.3
Figure 5.132 Stock transfer	Out	Outgoing goods warehouse (???)	**Missing model**	No corresponding process interface	1.3 2.2
Figure 5.40 Goods putaway	In	Stock transfer **(Fig. 5.131)**	**Figure 5.132** Stock transfer	**Missing process interface**: Figure 5.37 Goods receipt warehouse (unclear, if this is the corresponding process interface; succeeding event match)	1.2 2.1
Figure 5.13 maintenance of condition master data	In	**Action planning** (Fig. 6.20)	Figure 6.20 **process model of operational action planning**	**Missing process interface:** it was modeled as refined function	2.1 2.2
Figure 6.20 **process model of operational action planning**	Out	Action processing (Fig. 6.21)	Figure 6.21 Action processing	**Action planning** (Fig. 6.20)	2.1

Category 1: A Process Interface does not Match a Referenced Figure. This type of incorrect referencing occurs most in the reference model. The 30 occurrences can be divided into three cases: In the first two cases, (1.1) where the figure number does not match and (1.2) where the figure name does not match, incorrect numbers and names can be exchanged for correction purposes. In the third case (1.3), neither the figure number nor the figure name matches. Thus, a corresponding process model must be identified, by using for example similarity approaches for the affected labels. It can also be checked if a corresponding process interface exists, which references the current model. The preceding or succeeding events must occur in the referenced model (cf. corona 2.2) so they can be used for identification. If no corresponding process model can be found, a technical discussion is required.

Category 2: No Corresponding Process Interface Exists in the Referenced Model. In 21 EPCs, a process interface references a process model in which no corresponding process interface exists. Two cases are distinguished: Firstly (2.1), the figure number or name does not match, i.e., a corresponding process interface exists in the referenced model but itself references a wrong process model. Secondly (2.2), a corresponding process interface is missing in the referenced model, i.e., either a corresponding process interface cannot be identified or it simply does not exist. A new process interface can be introduced by identifying a preceding or succeeding event of the referencing process interface. Otherwise, a technical discussion is required.

Table 1 shows several examples for both categories. Inconsistencies are printed bold. The example in row five shows the necessity for the check if a corresponding process interface exists in the referenced model. A simple check whether all existing process interfaces reference a different model (cf. Definition 2.10 Point 3 in [4]) is not sufficient, because missing process interfaces cannot be detected in that way.

3.3 Hierarchization in the Retail-H Model

Generally, a refined function is rather labeled with a reference to another process model than to a task description. All 28 refined functions found in the reference model were analyzed analogous to the process interfaces. An analysis of the preceding and succeeding events (cf. corona) was taken into account as well as the preceding and succeeding connectors of a refined function. If these connectors do not match the connectors in the referenced model, semantic issues can occur. In 19 refined functions 23 deviations were observed. These deviations are divided into three categories.

Category 1: A Refined Function does not Match a Referenced Figure. In the Retail-H model the labels of three refined functions do not match the labels of the referenced models. A differentiation like in 1.1 and 1.2 of Sect. 3.2 was not carried out.

Category 2: Preceding Events were Modeled Differently in the Referenced Model. In this category, four cases can be distinguished: In the first two cases, (2.1) none or (2.2) not all of the preceding events exist in the referenced model. The cause can be traced back to two occurrences of deviating labels or at least one of the preceding events could not be identified in the referenced model. In the third case (2.3), preceding events do not appear in the set of start events in the referenced model. This case was identified twice. There, the events are available but not as end events as it is claimed in Sect. 2.2 (cf. Definition 2.10 point 4 and 5 in [4]). In the forth case (2.4), preceding events are connected differently as in the referenced model. This case occurred once. Succeeding connectors of the start events in the referenced model do not match with the preceding connectors of refined function in the referencing model. This can raise semantic issues that will be discussed later in Sect. 3.4.

Category 3: Succeeding Events were Modeled Differently in the Referenced Model. This category is analogous to category 2, whereby here the succeeding events and connectors are considered. For reason of space, the precise enumeration is omitted.

In Fig. 2a, "Fig. 6.21 Action Processing" [1], the function "Picking Planning (Fig. 5.103)" is refined. The succeeding event is "Inventory variation is posted". According to constraint 2 in Sect. 2.2, this event must occur as an end event in the references model in Fig. 2b. Instead, Fig. 2b references the model in Fig. 2c via a process interface. There, the expected event occurs not as an end event. It is followed by a process interface that references the model in Fig. 2d. This example shows that a referenced EPC can be decomposed in such a way that the expected end events of a refined function do not appear in the referenced model. This violates the mentioned constraint. Since decompositions are adequate instruments for the reduction of model complexity, are the given constraints useful? If so, they should be adapted.

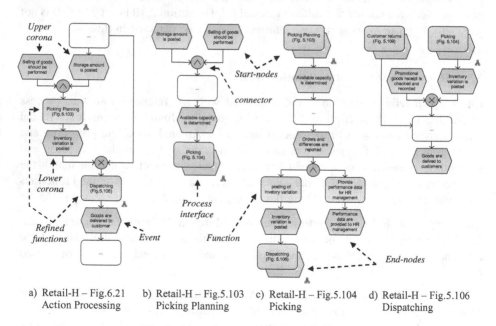

a) Retail-H – Fig.6.21   b) Retail-H – Fig.5.103   c) Retail-H – Fig.5.104   d) Retail-H – Fig.5.106
    Action Processing   Picking Planning   Picking   Dispatching

Fig. 2. Inconsistencies of refined functions

3.4 Semantic Analysis

Inconsistencies Implied by Different Connectors in a Referenced Model.

As already mentioned in Sect. 3.3, the case 2.4 can raise semantic issues. The model in Fig. 3a is an abstract of Fig. 6.6 [1]. There, the first two events are connected by an and-connector. In the referenced EPC in Fig. 3b, the constraint 1 in 2.2 is certainly respected, but the events are connected by a xor-connector (marked red). Therefore, which of the connectors is the correct one with respect to the desired intention of the modeler? Generally, no constraints concerning preceding or succeeding connectors of process interfaces or refined functions are known to the authors. To avoid such inconsistencies, new syntactic rules must be taken into account in formalizations. The idea of the repetition of events in a referenced process can also be questioned. Both possibilities should be analyzed in further approaches.

Succeeding Events are not Part of the End Events in a Referenced Model.

According to constraint 2 in Sect. 2.2, the succeeding events of the refined function "Billing (Fig. 5.114)" in Fig. 3a must occur as end events in the referenced model in Fig. 3b. Instead, further process fragments follow the events. The red dotted process fragment appears twice in Fig. 3b and in Fig. 3a, so it is redundant. What happens if these events occur? Does the control flow remains in the referenced process, so that the succeeding fragments will be executed or does it returns to the referencing model?

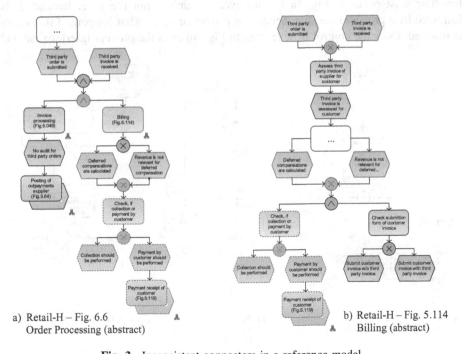

a) Retail-H – Fig. 6.6
   Order Processing (abstract)

b) Retail-H – Fig. 5.114
   Billing (abstract)

Fig. 3. Inconsistent connectors in a reference model

Another possibility is that the events are triggered like in event-driven-architectures, so that the control flow is splitted indirectly? In the example, the last assumption would lead to a redundant execution of the mentioned process fragments. However, these questions are not discussed in literature so far.

According to Definition 2.10 in [4] (Syntactically Correct Hierarchical EPC), the EPCs in this example are not syntactically correct, because the events do not correspond to the end events in the referenced process. Furthermore, if the redundant parts are executed twice, the process model of Fig. 5.119 [1] will also be executed twice. In this model, two separate incoming process interfaces were modeled. One of it references Fig. 3a, the other Fig. 3b. To avoid this, the redundant part in the model in Fig. 3a should be omitted and the refined function, that references Fig. 5.119, can be replaced by a process interface that references Fig. 3b.

Unintended Multiple Executions of Processes or Process Fragments.

In the example presented in Fig. 4, a multiple execution of process fragments is possible. There, only the relevant parts of the models are shown. The process model in Fig. 4b references the process models in Fig. 4a and Fig. 4b by refined functions. The model in Fig. 4c is referenced twice from Fig. 4b by two redundant refined functions. This can simply be corrected by placing the succeeding xor-connector before the refined function, so that the redundant part can be omitted. But there is still a possible multiple execution of the model in Fig. 4c. This is due to the fact that the model in Fig. 4a also references Fig. 4c by a process interface. Here, several issues occur at once. First, Fig. 4a is referenced by Fig. 4b, so the succeeding event of the refined function must occur in Fig. 4a as end event, which is not the case. Instead, it is followed by a process interface. Second, it is unclear again what happens if this event is reached. Does the control flow returns to Fig. 4b or is the process interface called?

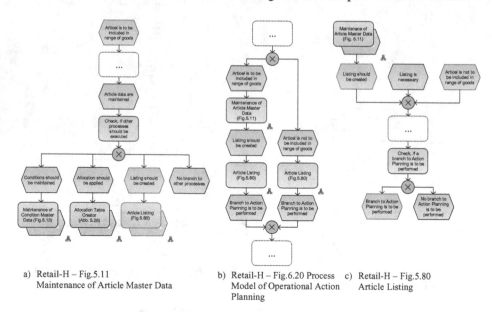

a) Retail-H – Fig.5.11
   Maintenance of Article Master Data

b) Retail-H – Fig.6.20 Process
   Model of Operational Action
   Planning

c) Retail-H – Fig.5.80
   Article Listing

Fig. 4. Multiple executions of processes or process fragments.

Third, the control flow of the model in Fig. 4a must not return to Fig. 4b at all, because of multiple end nodes (outgoing process interfaces or end events). A solution for the first two cases would be that corresponding process interfaces in model. Figure 4a and 4c are omitted. A simple solution for the third case is not obvious and needs further analysis.

In Sect. 3.3, a process model was identified that utilizes a refined function that references a model which is decomposed. According to this decomposition, semantic issues occur. In detail: the model in Fig. 2a references Fig. 2b by a refined function. There, the expected end event do not occurs. Instead, a process interface is used for a decomposition of the referenced model. The referenced model is shown in Fig. 2c. Now, in this model, the previously expected event occurs. But again, not as an end event because it is followed by a further process interface which references the model given in Fig. 2d. Here again, the same question as above occurs, what happens if an event is reached in the referenced process? This will be discussed in the next subsection.

This model shows a further issue. Through the decomposition of the referenced model, it was not obvious to the modeler that the process model in Fig. 2d is refer-enced twice. First, it is referenced indirectly by the decomposed referenced model via Fig. 2a → Fig. 2b → Fig. 2c → Fig. 2d. Second, it is referenced by a refined function that references Fig. 2d directly.

A simple solution to avoid the multiple execution of the model in Fig. 2d would be that the process interface in Fig. 2c, which references the model in Fig. 2d, is omitted. This is possible due to the fact that the refined function in the model Fig. 2a references the model in Fig. 2d. Thus, there would be no change in the semantic of the models, except that the second reference is omitted.

Unclear Continuation of Processes.

Several semantic issues can occur if an event is reached in a referenced model. What happens if the end event in Fig. 2d is reached, if the model was referenced by Fig. 2c? Does the control flow returns to the model in Fig. 2c, then to Fig. 2b and finally to Fig. 2a? Several answers to this question are possible. First, if events are treated like events in an event-driven-architecture of an information system, then each event is unique in a system, independently of the number of occurrences in different models. If such an event occurs, then all connected functions are triggered. This corresponds to an indirect split of the control flow, contradicting the concept of connectors, which are explicitly used to split or join the control flow. However, this kind of interpretation of events needs an adaptation of current existing constraints for the syntactical correctness of EPCs; otherwise, the mentioned issues cannot be avoided.

A second interpretation could be that equally labeled events are independent of each other. But if they are independent, why are they labeled equally? This assumption contradicts the constraints for the syntactical correctness of EPCs.

A third interpretation is very special. What happens if the model in Fig. 2d was called through the second process interface (Fig. 5.109)? Does the control flow returns to Fig. 2a as in the first example or does the process really ends there? If the control flow returns to Fig. 2a, then the processes of Fig. 5.109 and the model in Fig. 2a will be interconnected. Such a connection was surely not intended by the modeler. Contrarily, if the control flow should end if the end event is reached, then a semantic is implicitly applied as for function calls in programming languages. This is implied by the dependencies of end event from the start node. For EPCs, this interpretation was explicitly excluded [17]. In addition, such a semantic implies the existence of a global system state. If a global system state would exist, the discussion about the semantics of the or-connector would be more or less superfluous.

This example shows that semantic issues can occur if the decomposition concept and hierarchization concepts are simultaneously applied to EPCs.

Refined Function with Multiple End Events.

Semantic issues can also occur, if a refined function is followed by an amount of events (cf. lower corona) differing from the amount of end events in the referenced model. Firstly, if the amount of succeeding events is greater than the amount of end events in the referenced model, it is impossible to decide how the process has to be further executed. This refers to a modeling error, which should be eliminated to realize the intended model semantic. In the reference model, such an error occurred three times. Secondly, the amount of succeeding events is lower (cf. Fig. 4). What happens if an event is reached that does not occur in the referencing process? Possibly, the referenced process does not return to the referencing process. This can be seen as a "silent" exit of the referencing process, which is invisible in the referencing model. In contrast, if the referenced model is reintegrated into the referencing model, this exit is obvious. To avoid discrepancy, the number of the events should be equal. This constraint is mentioned for syntactically correctness of EPCs in definition 2.10 in [4]. Nevertheless, a refined function can be exited by a process interface. Thus, a model can be syntactically correct according to this definition while the same semantic issue occurs. The second case occurs in 18 models of the Retail-H reference model.

4   Conclusion and Outlook

In this work, the concepts of decomposition and hierarchization of event-driven process chains (EPC) have been analyzed. Starting point was a reference model for the retail market, the Retail-H reference model of Becker and Schütte [1]. This model was chosen, because both concepts were extensively used.

In general, for decomposition of larger EPCs, process interfaces are used. Refined functions are used for a more detailed description of selected parts of a model. Thus, both EPC elements reference further EPCs. For the systematical analysis of the reference model, all contained process interfaces, refined functions as well as preceding and succeeding events and connectors of these elements have been evaluated.

The following list summarizes the result of the analyses:

- In literature, no concrete specifications for references implied by process interfaces or refined functions are outlined. This concerns in particular the labels of these elements, as well as the labels of models. A correction of those labels must take place, if necessary, manually at a technical-conceptual level.

- Implicitly, a level of abstraction can be assigned to each model. The simultaneous use of both concepts can lead to a contradiction of assigned levels.
- A syntactical requirement regarding the existence of corresponding process interfaces in referenced models does not exist in literature so far. In some models, process interfaces are missing or they refer to non-existent models.
- Preceding or succeeding events of process interfaces and refined functions are not or only partially included in the referenced model. This can lead to semantic issues.
- In literature, preceding and succeeding connectors of process interfaces or refined functions are not considered so far. To avoid semantic issues, syntactical constraints should be established.
- Any model can be decomposed, even a referenced model. But some syntactic rules that are given in literature cannot be applied to such models, then.
- Further semantic issues can occur if a model that is referenced by a refined function can be exited through process interfaces or end events that are not specified in the referencing process. This has also not been considered in literature so far.
- Sometimes, flow-controlling functions are modeled in decomposed or hierarchical models, such as "check, if it must be branched backward into process x or y". These require knowledge of a global system state, which does not exist in EPCs. Such a modeling indicates an unfavorable decomposition or hierarchization of process models, which should be manually corrected at technical-conceptual level.

As shown, the existing syntactical rules allow different ways of model decomposition and hierarchization. This has lead to several syntactic and semantic issues in the analyzed reference model. Accordingly, there is a need for a consistent definition how to apply the concepts of decomposition and hierarchization in EPCs. This would also be helpful for a better intuitive interpretation of process models. Generally, there are three ways to solve the identified issues in future work: (1) Adaptation of the models, (2) adaptation of syntactical rules for EPCs, (3) a new definition of EPCs.

References

1. Becker, J., Schütte, R.: Handelsinformationssysteme. Domänenorientierte Einführung in die Wirtschaftsinformatik. Redline Wirtschaft, Frankfurt am Main (2004)
2. Keller, G., Nüttgens, M., Scheer, A.-W.: Semantische Prozeßmodellierung auf der Grundlage "Ereignisgesteuerter Prozeßketten (EPK)". Arbeitsbericht, Institut für Wirtschaftsinformatik, Universität Saarbrücken (1992)
3. Keller, G., Teufel, T.: SAP R/3 Process Oriented Implementation - Iterative Process Prototyping. Addison-Wesley, Reading (1998)
4. Mendling, J.: Metrics for Process Models: Empirical Foundations of Verification, Error Prediction, and Guidelines for Correctness. Springer, Heidelberg (2008)
5. Frank, U.: Evaluation of reference models. In: Fettke, P., Loos, P. (eds.) Reference Modeling for Business Systems Analysis, pp. 118–140. Idea Group Inc., London (2007)
6. Becker, J., Rosemann, M., von Uthmann, C.: Guidelines of business process modeling. In: van der Aalst, W., Desel, J., Oberweis, A. (eds.) Business Process Management - Models, Techniques, and Empirical Studies. LNCS, 1806th edn, pp. 30–49. Springer, Heidelberg (2000)

7. Mendling, J., Reijers, H.A., van der Aalst, W.M.P.: Seven process modeling guidelines (7PMG). Inf. Softw. Technol. **52**, 127–136 (2009)
8. Nüttgens, M., Rump, F.J.: Syntax und Semantik Ereignisgesteuerter Prozessketten (EPK). In: Desel, J., Weske, M. (eds.) Prozessorientierte Methoden und Werkzeuge für die Entwicklung von Informationssystemen - Promise 2002 – 9–11 Oktober 2002 in Potsdam, pp. 64–77, Bonn (2002)
9. van der Aalst, W.M.P., Desel, J., Kindler, E.: On the semantics of EPCs: a vicious circle. In: Nüttgens, M., Rump, F.J. (eds.) EPK 2002 - Geschäftsprozessmanagement mit Ereignisgesteuerten Prozessketten, Proceedings des GI-Workshops und Arbeitskreis-treffens, pp. 71–79, Trier (2002)
10. Kindler, E.: On the semantics of EPCs: a framework for resolving the vicious circle. In: Desel, J., Pernici, B., Weske, M. (eds.) BPM 2004. LNCS, vol. 3080, pp. 82–97. Springer, Heidelberg (2004)
11. Chen, R., Scheer, A.-W.: Modellierung von Prozeßketten mittels Petri-Netz Theorie. Arbeitsbericht, Institut für Wirtschaftsinformatik, Universität Saarbrücken (1994)
12. Langner, P., Schneider, C., Wehler, J.: Prozeßmodellierung mit ereignisgesteuerten Prozeßketten (EPKs und Petri-Netzen). Wirtschaftsinformatik **39**, 479–489 (1997)
13. Langner, P., Schneider, C., Wehler, J.: Petri net based certification of event-driven process chains. In: Desel, J., Silva, M. (eds.) ICATPN 1998. LNCS, vol. 1420, pp. 286–305. Springer, Heidelberg (1998)
14. van der Aalst, W.M.P.: Formalization and verification of event-driven process chains. Inf. Softw. Technol. **41**, 639–650 (1999)
15. Rump, F.J.: Geschäftsprozeßmanagement auf der Basis ereignisgesteuerter Prozeßketten.: Formalisierung, Analyse und Ausführung von EPKs. Teubner B.G. GmbH (1999)
16. Mendling, J., Nüttgens, M.: EPC modelling based on implicit arc types. In: Godlevsky, M., Liddle, S.W., Mayr, H.C. (eds.) Information Systems Technology and its Applications, International Conference ISTA'2003, 19–21 June 2003, Kharkiv, Ukraine, Proceedings. LNI, pp. 131–142 (2003)
17. Scheer, A.-W.: Business Process Engineering - Reference Models for Industrial Enterprises. Springer, Heidelberg (1998)

Process Model Fragmentization, Clustering and Merging: An Empirical Study

Xiang Gao[1], Yurong Chen[1], Zizhe Ding[1]([✉]), Meng Wang[1], Xiaonan Zhang[1],
Zhiqiang Yan[2], Lijie Wen[2], Qinlong Guo[2], and Ran Chen[2]

[1] Department of Management Information System,
China Mobile Communications Corporation, Beijing 100033, China
[2] School of Software, Tsinghua University, Beijing 100084, China
{gaoxiang,chenyurong,dingzizhe,wangmeng,zhangxiaonan}@chinamobile.com
zhiqiang.yan.1983@gmail.com, {wenlj00,gql12,r-chen09}@mails.thu.edu.cn

Abstract. Nowadays, it is common for an organization to maintain thousands of business processes. Technologies that provide automatic management for such amount of models are required. The objective of this paper is to deal with the problem of process model fragmentization, clustering and merging for the consolidation of Office Automation (OA) systems in China Mobile Communications Corporation (CMCC). After investigating the structural statistics of real-life process model samples, we propose an approach, based on the refined process structure tree (RPST) and software product line (SPL), to automatically identify reusable process fragments and merge similar ones into master fragments. These fragments can, for example, be used to facilitate the (re)design of numerous process models. Special attention is paid to the empirical study and statistics from the experiment on a sample set of 37 real-life OA processes. Lesson learned and problems to be further considered are also proposed.

Keywords: Process model fragmentization · Clustering · Merging · OA

1 Introduction

With the development and profound impact of business process management (BPM) technology, more and more organizations start to recognize it as a holistic approach that promotes business effectiveness and efficiency while striving for innovation, flexibility, and integration with technology [1]. Therefore, the number of process models increases rapidly in these organizations. Especially for large enterprises, more than thousands of process models are being managed and maintained for daily work.

China Mobile Communications Corporation (CMCC) is one of the world leading mobile services providers. Its Office Automation (OA) systems[1] have been

---

[1] Office Automation (OA) is one of the most important management information systems (MIS) for large enterprises in China, to process the information of daily office work for all staffs. It fundamentally refers to supporting enterprise general management business processes in offices, e.g., document flow, approval, transfer, and archive.

N. Lohmann et al. (Eds.): BPM 2013 Workshops, LNBIP 171, pp. 405–416, 2014.
DOI: 10.1007/978-3-319-06257-0_32, © Springer International Publishing Switzerland 2014

independently built by each subsidiary organization[2] and used for more than 10 years. There are totally more than 8000 processes running in these systems, independently maintained and evolved by subsidiary organizations themselves. It causes increasing architecture heterogeneity, high integration complexity and especially high construction and maintenance cost. In order to alleviate the previous drawbacks, CMCC is committing itself to the consolidation, aiming at building one centralized OA system supporting all the business processes of subsidiary organizations. Obviously, such a large number of business processes must be elaborately "consolidated" first in the context of system consolidation.

There are several challenges in attempts to achieve such an objective.

- Different subsidiary organizations follow unified business specifications and design their own processes. Due to individual management requirements, their processes, even expressing the same business behavior, are usually not exactly the same while having a high degree of similarity. That is the essential reason why the number of processes is up to more than 8000. In the context of consolidation, re-designing these processes one by one will be an arduous task. The technology to reduce duplications and make the differences between process models explicit is really important.
- The OA processes contain plentiful complex business logics. For example, "countersign" is a common part within most of document approval processes. It includes one distribution activity and several implementation activities, frequently applied in the scenario that the superior simultaneously asks subordinates for comments concerning certain business. The feedback from subordinates to the superior can be asynchronous. After the last feedback, the superior collects all the comments and makes the decision. The whole procedure can also be nested and recursively called, since countersign is always consecutively exploited in different organizational levels. It can be modeled as a parallel multi-instance with recursive sub-process. Formal design of these business units should be of much consideration.
- There is always a big gap: business analysts have deep understanding of business but cannot design the process models independently without the support of IT staffs, even though notation based modeling language is exploited. We expect them to complete the most part of modeling, maybe in a configurable way. It is really important to provide an efficient approach to assist flexible and agile design of process models for business analysts with the least IT efforts.

From the above challenges, we summarize that it is required to identify the common fragments that preferably express specific business behavior with complex logics. Then the process modeling can be mostly realized by combining the fragments instead of activities, which provides support for business analysts to design process models more independently and efficiently.

---

[2] The subsidiary organizations include 31 provincial companies, 1 design institute, and several specialized companies.

To reach this aim, automatic fragmentization of process models and identification of highly reusable fragments are required. The contribution of this paper is as follows. Firstly, we summarize the structural features of 37 real-life OA processes in CMCC. Secondly, we outline an approach to implement process model consolidation by applying existing technologies. Thirdly, we apply the approach to the 37 models and show the statistics of the fragment reuse and merging, where we emphasize the findings and problems to be further considered.

The rest of the paper is organized as follows. The next section provides the statistical features of OA process models. In Sect. 3, complete process models consolidation approach (including fragmentization, clustering and merging) is proposed. The section following that investigates the empirical findings. Section 5 introduces the related work and Sect. 6 concludes the paper.

2 Sampling and Statistics of OA Process Models

In this section, we explain how we get our sampling process models and then show the characteristics of these models.

As mentioned above, there are more than 8000 existing processes in all the OA systems. However, these processes are described differently and each subsidiary may have its own description, mainly based on informal user-definition or natural-language text documents. It makes the process consolidation more challenging. As a first attempt, the consolidation starts from 3 small-scaled subsidiary organizations maintaining totally 216 processes. A business analyst of each subsidiary models about 10 of the processes in its OA system and together we get 37 models in BPMN 2.0 notation. The sample contains 4 categories of typical and most frequently used processes, which are sending documents, receiving documents, summarizing meetings and asking for instructions.

As an example, the process model of "Xizang Provincial Company Receiving Document", is shown in Fig. 1 (the figure also shows the RPST decomposition of the process model, denoted by dotted box, for later reference). It describes the scenario that there is a document of new regulations from a higher-up organization (e.g., the headquarters of CMCC), required to be implemented in the Xizang provincial company. The process consists of the following steps. (1) It starts with the document registration by the secretary of Department of General Affairs (DGA). (2) The document is transferred to the DGA manager, who selects a responding department or a co-responding department. (3) If the regulations are very crucial to the subsidiary, it is sent to the company VP first for review and approval and then distributed to departments. (4) The document with comments from DGA is distributed to the responding department or the co-responding department in case that the responding department is not available. (5) In selected department, the document is first sent to the manager for review and approval, and then carried out by staffs.

Next, the structural statistics on the selected 37 models is shown by using the 24 features adapted and extended from [8]. These features include important information such as the number of transitions, number of and-splits, edge

408   X. Gao et al.

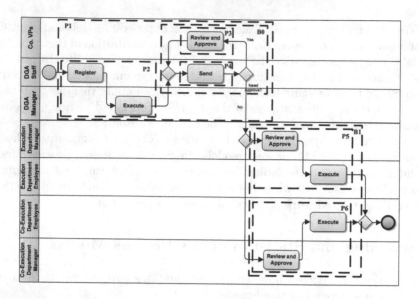

Fig. 1. RPST decomposition of "Xizang Provincial Company Receiving Document"

density, etc. Since the features are originally defined by Petri Net [8], a model transformation is applied to convert the existing BPMN 2.0 models to Petri Net. The *task* and *event* are treated as *transition*. The *gateway* is treated as *place* and the *edges* remain the same. Moreover, additional places and silent transitions are inserted in order to maintain the bipartite graph of Petri Net. Table 1 shows the model structural statistics based on provincial companies, with 14 models in the Hainan subsidiary, 7 models in the Ningxia subsidiary, and 16 models in the Xizang subsidiary. The rows of the table list the selected features and the columns of the table list the average value (μ) and the standard deviation (σ) of each feature in different subsidiaries.

Investigating the eight values of each feature as listed in the columns of Table 1 thoroughly, we can find that process models belonging to different provincial companies have almost the same average feature value and a bit different standard deviation. The number of transitions in each model ranges from 9 to 64 and each model is an extremely sparse graph (edge density = 0.07). There is no gateway with AND and OR types because these OA process models conform to the normal routines of handling paper documents, which leads to connector heterogeneity be 0. About 13 XOR gateways are used to jump between different points in each model for redoing and skipping specific tasks by means of about 14 invisible tasks. The XOR-split and XOR-join do not match each other perfectly (mismatch = 3). The average diameter (i.e., the length of the longest path from the start node to the end node, which consists of both transitions and places) is 26.65. There are about 6 duplicate tasks in each model because these tasks with the same labels will be executed by different departments or roles.

Table 1. Structural statistics of process models in CMCC: μ for the average and σ for the standard deviation

Feature	Hainan		Ningxia		Xizang		ALL	
	μ	σ	μ	σ	μ	σ	μ	σ
Number of transitions	25.07	12.94	23.14	5.98	24.13	9.64	24.30	10.28
Number of places	18.07	9.47	16.00	3.61	16.69	5.44	17.08	6.90
Number of arcs	50.14	25.88	46.29	11.97	48.25	19.28	48.59	20.56
Edge density	0.06	0.02	0.07	0.01	0.07	0.03	0.07	0.02
Number of and-split	0.00	0.00	0.00	0.00	0.00	0.00	0.00	0.00
Number of or-split	0.00	0.00	0.00	0.00	0.00	0.00	0.00	0.00
Number of xor-split	7.93	4.21	5.71	1.98	8.50	4.13	7.76	3.90
Number of xor-join	4.93	2.34	4.71	1.98	4.63	1.54	4.76	1.91
AND-XOR mismatch	3.00	2.25	1.00	1.00	3.88	2.85	3.00	2.55
Sequentiality	0.74	0.02	0.78	0.04	0.73	0.02	0.75	0.03
Connector heterogeneity	0.00	0.00	0.00	0.00	0.00	0.00	0.00	0.00
Control-flow complexity	16.64	9.48	14.00	5.20	17.25	8.35	16.41	8.21
Ratio of nodes in cycle	0.83	0.22	0.56	0.37	0.74	0.37	0.74	0.33
Diameter	26.43	5.67	25.71	6.58	27.25	11.40	26.65	8.56
Separability	0.24	0.12	0.36	0.37	0.22	0.15	0.25	0.20
Structuredness	0.63	0.28	0.79	0.27	0.53	0.28	0.61	0.29
Coefficient of connectivity	1.16	0.03	1.18	0.07	1.17	0.06	1.16	0.05
Max degree of connector	3.71	0.91	4.29	1.25	4.19	1.33	4.03	1.17
Depth	1.43	0.51	1.86	0.90	1.19	0.54	1.41	0.64
Number of invisible tasks	13.93	7.11	12.43	4.83	14.25	8.36	13.78	7.19
Number of duplicate tasks	6.64	6.83	7.57	3.15	5.50	1.83	6.32	4.53
Number of non-free-choice	0.00	0.00	0.00	0.00	0.00	0.00	0.00	0.00
Number of arbitrary cycles	5.64	2.79	3.14	3.18	6.25	4.19	5.43	3.63
Number of nested loops	1.43	1.16	0.86	0.69	1.75	1.39	1.46	1.22

Also we can find a serious problem that these process models are not that structured (structuredness = 0.61) and have more than 5 arbitrary cycles. For more details about the meaning of each feature, readers can refer to [8].

3   Approach for OA Process Model Consolidation

The overview of our approach for OA process model consolidation is shown in Fig. 2. Taking a set of process models as input, our approach will generate a set of master fragments as output through three successive steps, i.e., fragmentization, clustering, and merging. All process models and fragments conform to BPMN 2.0 specification. The steps involved in our approach will be introduced in the following paragraphs.

We take a process model as an example to describe its fragmentization based on the refined process structure tree (RPST) [11,16]. We notice that in the process model that we have studied and other process models of CMCC, an activity may have more than one input or output edges. To make a process model more structured and readable, gateways are added automatically before/after

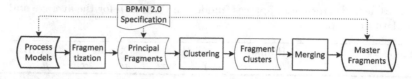

Fig. 2. Overview of the approach for OA process model consolidation

the activity that is detected with multiple inputs/outputs. The modified process model is then transformed into a directed graph as the input of the RPST algorithm (activities and gateways are considered as nodes, and sequence-flows are considered as edges). The corresponding output process model of "Xizang Provincial Company Receiving Document" after fragmentization is shown in Fig. 1. From the figure, we know that the model is well structured and decomposed into fragments that can be reused afterwards.

Process models are decomposed into many fragments of different granularity, e.g., one process model in Fig. 1 already has 8 fragments after fragmentization. We decide to select some of the fragments that are suitable for reuse instead of storing them all. The selection can be made either manually or automatically. On one hand, business analysts can go through these fragments one by one and decide which one to be selected for reuse. On the other hand, business analysts can also check a part of these fragments and then set thresholds by size. For example, in the case of CMCC, we can select fragments with more than 2 nodes, and no more than 7 nodes. Then fragments $P1$ and $B1$ in Fig. 1 are selected for reuse. The size may vary in different situations because of the different properties of process models in a collection. More explanation and analysis about the fragmentization of the 37 models and the selection of fragments will be given in the next section.

There are fragments that are very similar to each other after fragmentization. They have similar structure, and very few differences. When considering more process models apart from these 37, there would be more similar fragments. In practice, we'd like to use one or two representatives, named master fragments, to express similar behavior. Therefore, we need a function to distribute fragments into clusters based on their similarity. We assume that the same task in different process models has an identical label and the similarity between process models are measured based on their structure. This is because in CMCC we have standard terminologies, but tasks of the same process model in different subsidiaries are usually organized differently in structure. We apply the technique in [17] to compute the similarities of process fragments and then a hierarchical clustering algorithm [7] to distribute these fragments into clusters based on the similarities. The produced cluster tree is encoded in the Newick format[3]. An example of clustering based on our dataset will be given in the next section.

The results of hierarchical clustering are usually presented in a dendrogram. Therefore, we need to decide on which hierarchical level, fragments are to be

---

[3] http://evolution.genetics.washington.edu/phylip/newicktree.html

merged into a master fragment. This can be done by setting a threshold of similarity between fragments. We will explain more about this in the next section. The merging operation converts a set of similar fragments into one merged fragment (also referred as master fragment). Variation points in the merged diagrams represent locations where the input models disagree in their behavior. That is, a variation point occurs when several alternative flows that belong to different input processes go out from a common activity. We borrow some basic ideas from the software product line (SPL) [10] and design a procedure which deals with input fragments incrementally, in a pairwise manner. An example of merging based on our dataset will also be given in the next section.

4 Empirical Findings

The 37 process models of CMCC are decomposed into 429 fragments using RPST, which is implemented as part of the jBPT project[4]. On average, each model consists of 11.6 fragments. To reduce the amount of fragments to be stored, a selection is made based on the number of nodes in a fragment. After going through these fragments, the ones containing more than 2 nodes and no more than 7 nodes are selected (start and end events are not counted). Fragments, containing only 2 nodes, are discarded because of the following two reasons. On one hand, these fragments can be easily modeled by a business modeler and do not add too much value to be reused [6]. On the other hand, the number of this type of fragments is large, 288 out of 429, which adds the difficulty for users to locate the fragment they are looking for if they are also stored. Fragments, containing more than 7 nodes, are also discarded because they are barely reused. In the experiments we run, 90 out of 429 fragments contain more than 7 nodes, all of which are distinct from each other. Ultimately, only 51 fragments are selected.

Figure 3 shows the BPMN 2.0 models of reused fragments, which are almost in accord with business understanding. (Start and end events are added to indicate the entry and exit points of the fragments). There are basically four types of process behavior captured in these ten fragments. (1) Fragments 42, 108, 140, 144 and 181 express the processing conducted by DGA. They usually exist in the final part of a document process. These 5 fragments partially or fully contain assigning ID, typesetting, reading, printing and distribution activities, since for different documents the DGA takes different processing ways. For example, fragment 42 is usually used for meeting summary, which needs to be distributed. Fragment 108 exists in most contract related processes, where the contract after approval should be printed. Fragment 144 contains the most activities, which means the document should be strictly processed step by step, and thus, is used for preparing some formal reports. (2) Fragment 64 and 136 have the same style, but with different activities. Fragment 64 represents the scenario that a department is asked for instruction about a certain document. The department manager reviews and approves it, and then transfers it to the next department.

---

[4] http://code.google.com/p/jbpt/

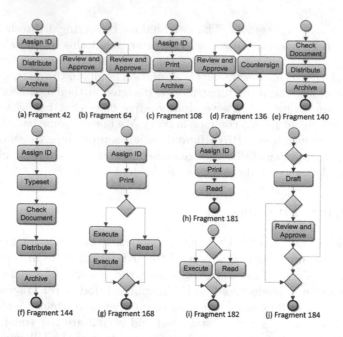

Fig. 3. All fragments with IDs that have been reused

He can also transfer it to his subordinate, who will review and approve the request before further instruction collection. Differently, fragment 136 changes asking one subordinate to asking for countersign within a division. (3) Both of fragment 168 and 182 contain exclusive-choice control flow. It means that a document is selectively transferred to someone for further execution (i.e., need to complete sth.) or notification (i.e., just need to know). (4) Fragment 184 may be the most commonly used one in the beginning of a document process, expressing the document preparation. That is, employee makes the draft, and then delivers it to his manager for review and approval or directly delivers it to the next department if the draft is all right. The manager can return the draft back to the employee for revision or transfer it to the next department if there is no problem. Table 2 shows the statistics of the fragment reuse. The columns of the table list fragments that are reused. The rows of the table list the ID of each fragment, the number of nodes' size of each fragment (start and end events are not counted), the reuse frequency of each fragment, and whether the fragment appears in the process models of different subsidiaries. From the table we can find that most of the fragments are reused from 2 to 7 times. This is because the numbers of models and fragments are relatively small. We can also know that only two of these fragments appear in process models from different subsidiaries. This is because models of different subsidiaries are designed by different business analysts separately, and two process models of the same behavior could be different. These issues can be mostly resolved after merging reused fragments into master fragments, which will be shown in the following.

Table 2. Fragment reuse statistics

Fragment ID	42	64	108	136	140	144	168	181	182	184
Number of nodes	3	4	3	4	3	5	7	3	4	6
Reuse frequency	3	2	3	2	3	2	2	3	2	7
Across subsidiaries	No	Yes	No	No	No	Yes	No	No	No	No

By applying the similarity analysis to these reused fragments, we can get a similarity matrix consisting of the similarity of each pair of these fragments. Furthermore, a cluster tree encoded in Newick format is obtained to organize these fragments into hierarchical clusters, as shown in Fig. 4. The distance labeled on each branch between fragments equals to one minus their similarity degree, i.e., two fragments are closer if they are more similar. A threshold of similarity should be set by business analysts to divide fragments into clusters. For example, in our experiment 0.75 is used as our threshold, and then these fragments are divided into four clusters: fragment 42, 108, 140, 144, and 181; fragment 64 and 136; fragment 168 and 182; fragment 184. These are the exact four types of business behavior we observe when analyzing these ten fragments of Fig. 3.

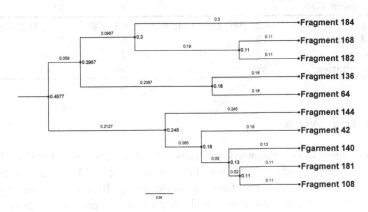

Fig. 4. FigTree representation of clustering result of fragments

Table 3 shows the reuse statistics of the master fragments. The setup of the table is similar to Table 2 (with one more row to show which master fragment consists of which fragments). As expected, most master fragments are reused frequently and by different subsidiaries. Figure 5 shows the merging result of fragment 42, 108, 140, 144 and 181. The master fragment covers all the possible activities and carrying out procedures of the cluster. Business analysts can easily use it to design process models by necessary configuration. However, the complexity of master fragment grows with the number of fragments merged, which will decrease its readability.

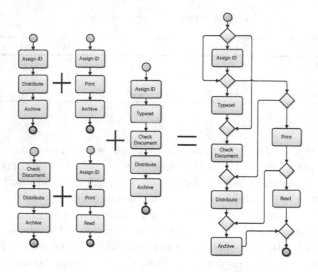

Fig. 5. Merging of fragments concerning DGA process

Table 3. Master fragment reuse statistics

Master fragment ID	1	2	3	4
Consisting of fragments	42, 108, 140, 144, 181	64, 136	168, 182	184
Number of nodes	15	5	7	6
Reuse frequency	14	4	4	7
Across subsidiaries	Yes	Yes	Yes	No

5   Related Work

To our best knowledge, the work presented in this paper is related to business process model reuse and merging model components [2–4,14]. Gschwind et al. [15] also propose an efficient method for process modeling. It provides users with basic workflow patterns for control flows, such that modelers can apply these patterns directly instead of constructing these patterns by themselves. Compared with [15], our work finds reused fragments in real-life models instead of abstract patterns to make modeling more efficient. Ekanayake et al. [6] provide an technique to detect approximate clones of business process models. This work [6] and our work share the fragmentization and clustering steps, while the difference is that our work further merges fragments of a cluster into a master fragment.

The following work is the basis of our approach: fragmentization, similarity search, and clustering. Vanhatalo et al. [16] provide an algorithm, RPST, which decomposes a well-structured process model uniquely. Polyvyanyy et al. [11] enhance the algorithm, which makes RPST capable of decomposing models with multiple entries and multiple exits (MEME). Dijkman et al. [5] summarize methods of computing similarity between two models. Kaufman et al. [7] introduce the clustering technology.

6 Conclusions

The paper focuses on an empirical study of process model fragmentization, clustering and merging, in the real scenario of CMCC OA consolidation. One of the main issues involved in such work is to elaborately analyze the features of OA processes, and take sufficient consideration of applying RPST technology combined with process fragment clustering and merging by borrowing basic idea from SPL. The objective is to build a bridge to let the business analysts design complete processes by just using fragment with exact and distinct business logic, instead of BPMN elements. The approach is applied to 37 real-life OA process models to run an experiment. Among the process fragments 10 reused ones are selected, which are further merged into 4 master fragments. These fragments describe typical business behavior in the OA systems of CMCC, which are suitable to be reused for business analysts during modeling.

There are several drawbacks of the current procedure. Lessons learned and directions for future work are summarized as follows.

- Firstly, the fragmentization is done by RPST, which decomposes process models only based on the structure instead of business logics. This may suggest that business behavior cannot be well represented by a certain fragment[5], so that business analysts cannot easily use them for modeling. Therefore, involving business semantics into the fragmentization algorithm should be a further research direction.
- Secondly, the fragmentization considers only one process model at a time instead of the collection together as a whole. This may cause a problem that some fragments are similar with most part in common but could not be reused. Therefore, a fragmentization method, considering the characteristics of the whole collection of process models, is required.
- Thirdly, techniques are further required to manage these fragments, for example, maintaining the relationships between similar fragments or fragments of different versions using change operations [12].

Acknowledgments. This work is supported by the Ministry of Education & China Mobile Research Foundation (no.MCM20123011).

References

1. van der Aalst, W.M.P.: A decade of business process management conferences: personal reflections on a developing discipline. In: Barros, A., Gal, A., Kindler, E. (eds.) BPM 2012. LNCS, vol. 7481, pp. 1–16. Springer, Heidelberg (2012)
2. Awad, A., Sakr, S., Kunze, M., Weske, M.: Design by selection: a reuse-based approach for business process modeling. In: Jeusfeld, M., Delcambre, L., Ling, T.-W. (eds.) ER 2011. LNCS, vol. 6998, pp. 332–345. Springer, Heidelberg (2011)

---

[5] Maybe specific business behavior is divided into different pieces, or a fragment is a composite of some business behavior.

3. Pascalau, E., Awad, A., Sakr, S., Weske, M.: On maintaining consistency of process model variants. In: Muehlen, M., Su, J. (eds.) BPM 2010 Workshops. LNBIP, vol. 66, pp. 289–300. Springer, Heidelberg (2011)

4. Emilian, P., Ahmed, A., Sherif, S., Mathias, W.: Partial process models to manage business process variants. Spec. Issue Int. J. Bus. Process Integr. Manage. (IJBPIM) 5(3), 240–256 (2011)

5. Dijkman, R.M., Dumas, M., van Dongen, B., Uba, R., Mendling, J.: Similarity of business process models: metrics and evaluation. Inf. Syst. 36(2), 498–516 (2011)

6. Ekanayake, C.C., Dumas, M., García-Bañuelos, L., La Rosa, M., ter Hofstede, A.H.M.: Approximate clone detection in repositories of business process models. In: Barros, A., Gal, A., Kindler, E. (eds.) BPM 2012. LNCS, vol. 7481, pp. 302–318. Springer, Heidelberg (2012)

7. Kaufman, L., Rousseeuw, P.J.: Finding Groups in Data: An Introduction to Cluster Analysis. Wiley, New York (1990)

8. Mendling, J.: Metrics for Process Models. LNBIP, vol. 6. Springer, Heidelberg (2008)

9. Hepp, M., Leymann, F., Bussler, C., Domingue, J., Wahler, A., Fensel, D.,: Semantic business process management: a vision towards using semantic web services for business process management. In: Proceedings of IEEE International Conference on e Business Engineering, pp. 535–540 (2005)

10. Rubin, J., Chechik, M.: Combining related products into product lines. In: de Lara, J., Zisman, A. (eds.) FASE 2012. LNCS, vol. 7212, pp. 285–300. Springer, Heidelberg (2012)

11. Polyvyanyy, A., Vanhatalo, J., Völzer, H.: Simplified computation and generalization of the refined process structure tree. In: Bravetti, M. (ed.) WS-FM 2010. LNCS, vol. 6551, pp. 25–41. Springer, Heidelberg (2011)

12. Reichert, M., Dadam, P.: ADEPT$_{flex}$-supporting dynamic changes of workflows without losing control. J. Intell. Inf. Syst. 10(2), 93–129 (1998)

13. SAP, IDS, OU, PUE: Project IST 026850 SUPER: Semantics utilized for process management within and between enterprises (2008)

14. Sakr, S., Awad, A., Kunze, M.: Querying process models repositories by aggregated graph search. In: La Rosa, M., Soffer, P. (eds.) BPM Workshops 2012. LNBIP, vol. 132, pp. 573–585. Springer, Heidelberg (2013)

15. Gschwind, T., Koehler, J., Wong, J.: Applying patterns during business process modeling. In: Dumas, M., Reichert, M., Shan, M.-C. (eds.) BPM 2008. LNCS, vol. 5240, pp. 4–19. Springer, Heidelberg (2008)

16. Vanhatalo, J., Völzer, H., Koehler, J.: The refined process structure tree. In: Dumas, M., Reichert, M., Shan, M.-C. (eds.) BPM 2008. LNCS, vol. 5240, pp. 100–115. Springer, Heidelberg (2008)

17. Yan, Z., Dijkman, R.M., Grefen, P.W.P.J.: Fast business process similarity search. Distrib. Parallal Databases 30(2), 105–144 (2012)

Towards Measuring Process Model Granularity via Natural Language Analysis

Henrik Leopold[1]($\boxtimes$), Fabian Pittke[1], and Jan Mendling[2]

[1] Humboldt-Universität zu Berlin, Unter den Linden 6, 10099 Berlin, Germany
{henrik.leopold,fabian.pittke}@wiwi.hu-berlin.de
[2] WU Vienna, Welthandelsplatz 1, 1020 Vienna, Austria
jan.mendling@wu.ac.at

Abstract. Nowadays business process modeling is an integral part of many organizations to document and redesign complex organizational processes. Particularly due to the large number of process models, quality assurance represents an important issue in many organizations. While many quality aspects are well understood and can be automatically checked with existing tools, there is currently no possibility to support modelers in maintaining a consistent degree of granularity. In this paper, we leverage natural language analysis in process models to introduce a novel set of metrics that indicate the granularity of process models. We evaluate the proposed metrics using two hierarchically organized process model collections from practice. Statistical tests demonstrate the expressive power of the proposed metrics.

Keywords: Process modeling · Model granularity · Granularity metrics

1 Introduction

Nowadays business process modeling is an integral part of many organizations. The use cases of business process modeling range from documentation to the redesign of complex organizational operations [1]. As a result of such initiatives, many companies face huge process model repositories, including, in extreme cases, up to thousands of models [2]. The sheer amount of process models motivates the need for techniques and concepts that ensure the efficient management and organization of these repositories.

One of the key concepts to keep track of the large number of process models is the introduction of a process architecture [3]. Such a process architecture represents an organized overview of the company's business process models and their interrelations [4]. Therefore, process architectures typically define a hierarchy with different levels of granularity. While models on higher levels represent processes on a rather abstract level, models on lower levels illustrate fine-grained process details. A driving issue in this context is to define, to identify, and to maintain a consistent degree of detail on each level of a process architecture [5]. Although there exist several guidelines on the proper design of process models

N. Lohmann et al. (Eds.): BPM 2013 Workshops, LNBIP 171, pp. 417–429, 2014.
DOI: 10.1007/978-3-319-06257-0_33, © Springer International Publishing Switzerland 2014

[6–8], the provided recommendations on process model granularity are not very specific and do not support process modelers in deciding on the appropriate level of detail. As there is currently no sufficiently effective possibility of measuring the granularity of a process model, the decision about the appropriate level of detail is purely based on the subjective assessment of the modelers.

In this paper, we address the problem of measuring the granularity of process models. Our contribution is twofold: first, we propose a set of metrics that operationalize the concept of granularity for process models from a natural language perspective, and second, we evaluate the statistical power of each metric to indicate process model granularity. As a result, a modeler can be supported and guided during the modeling process in order to create models with consistent granularity.

The remainder of the paper is structured accordingly. Section 2 reflects upon the concept of granularity in related research streams and proposes several perspectives for measuring process model granularity. Then, Sect. 3 introduces a set of granularity metrics based on these perspectives. Subsequently, Sect. 4 challenges these metrics against two model repositories from practice and evaluates their statistical significance. Finally, Sect. 5 concludes the paper.

2   Background

This section introduces the concept of granularity and relates it to the context of this paper. First, we provide a generic perspective on granularity before discuss other approaches to granularity from a variety of research streams. Finally, we discuss granularity in the context of process models and the associated perspectives.

2.1   On the Concept of Granularity

Granularity is one of the most basic concepts of human cognition that decomposes a whole into smaller parts of it. The term granularity originates from the Latin word *granus* and refers to the property of being granular and consisting of smaller grains or particles[1]. Zadeh [9] defines this concept as construction, interpretation, and representation of granules, i.e., a clump of objects drawn together by indistinguishably, similarity, proximity, or functionality.

We can distinguish three different interpretations of the granularity of a system composed of a number of entities [10]. First, granularity is interpreted in terms of the *gestalt effect*. This theory states that human cognition of concepts is highly narrow and causes the effect that a collection of entities is perceived as a whole rather than a set of individual parts. Second, granularity can be interpreted in terms of generality and specificity which typically leads to a number of hierarchical levels of granularity used for classification purposes. Third, granularity can be perceived by instantiation relationships. This is the case, when

---

[1] see Oxford Online Dictionary for *granularity* and *granular*.

an object is created from another object by adding detail or, from the opposite viewpoint, when an object is linked to another by removing detail. Considering the different interpretations of the granularity concept, a variety of approaches exist that apply the granularity concept on different subjects.

2.2 Operationalizations of Granularity

The concept of granularity has been recognized in various research fields such as granular computing, information retrieval, service-oriented architectures, software and application design, text and language processing, and conceptual modeling. However, only a part of these works define metrics that operationalize granularity.

Particularly in the field of service-oriented architectures, many authors proposed strategies to measure granularity. This is due to the fundamental importance of granularity in this context. Many of these approaches consider the scope of a service by referring to its lines of code (LOC) or its function points [11–14]. Krammer et al. [11] as well as Heinrich and Zimmermann [12] extend these approaches by a distance-oriented metric that explicitly considers the hierarchical position of a service in an architecture and by a size-oriented metric that considers the amount of directly and indirectly included services. This idea is also applied by Wang et al. to decompose software components into different layers [15].

In information retrieval, granularity is concerned by two subjects, namely queries that retrieve documents and the documents themselves which are the result of a given query. The approaches defined in [16,17] adhere to the second interpretation of granularity and formalize the specificity of a query in terms of the amount of retrieved documents and their size. In contrast to this syntactic approach, Yan et al. [18] combine syntactic and semantic aspects of the document content. Specifically, the topical coverage of a document and its semantic associations among the domain concepts are used as an indicator for granularity.

Another research stream that applies the granularity concept is natural language processing (NLP). The main focus of NLP is the automated analysis of large natural language texts, which are also referred to as corpora. In this context, granularity is concerned with predicting the scope of a corpus, i.e. its topical coverage, or the specificity of a given text. In order to predict text specificity, Allen and Wu [19] propose a set of predictors, such as entropy and word co-occurence, to determine the specificity of input terms with respect to a list of general and specific terms. To decide on the collection scope, Allen and Wu combine a semantic relatedness measure and the co-occurrence of words [20].

In accordance with prior research from other fields, granularity metrics are also adapted in the domain of process modeling. The need for embracing this concept arises from the hierarchical organization of process models in many process model collections. Typically, such a hierarchy contains coarse-grained models on the top level and more fine-granular models on the lower levels. Hence, the granularity of a process model is indicated by its position in the level hierarchy. To measure process model granularity, different metrics have been introduced. Similarly to approaches from other fields, Holschke et al. use the number of model elements to discuss granularity [21]. Other authors make use of the number of meronymic relationships in a model [10]. Nevertheless, these approaches do not consider the special characteristics of process models provided by the combination of modeling elements and natural language elements. Therefore, such metrics are not sufficient to effectively guide modelers in reaching a consistent level of granularity.

2.3 Perspectives on Process Model Granularity

Aiming at measuring the granularity of process models, it is necessary to investigate the characteristics of process models in more detail. In particular, it is essential to understand process models as a combination of modeling language and natural language. Thus, both perspectives should be considered for process model granularity. Therefore, we follow a systematic approach and explore how process models convey real-world semantics.

Looking at a typical process model, we observe that it is composed of two basic elements. First, we identify different constructs from modeling languages such as BPMN or EPC. Generally, we can distinguish modeling constructs like activities, events, gateways, flow relations, and roles. In addition, these constructs are combined according to certain modeling language rules. Second, we identify natural language text labels that enrich the model constructs with necessary information to fully capture real world-semantics. Therefore, both elements are required as modeling constructs without a natural language text label would ignore necessary details.

Following this line of argumentation, a process model combines two types of languages: a modeling language and a natural language. Both languages have a syntactic dimension and a semantic dimension. The syntactic dimension defines how the constructs of the modeling language or the words of the natural language can be combined. The semantic dimension specifies the meaning of the constructs of the modeling language or the meaning of the words of the natural language. The overall semantics of the model is thus given by combining the semantics of both languages as depicted in Fig. 1. Accordingly, we can assess the granularity from four perspectives: the syntax of the modeling language, the semantics of the modeling language, the syntax of the natural language, and the semantics of the natural language.

As shown in the literature review, prior work on process model granularity primarily focused on syntactic and semantic perspective of the modeling language in process models [10,21]. In this context, the number of process model nodes represents a syntactic aspect and the number of different constructs a semantic aspect. Obviously, the adequate consideration of natural language is missing. As natural language, however, represents an important share of the overall model semantics, it can be expected to represent an informing source for assessing process model granularity. Therefore, we aim at levering the potential

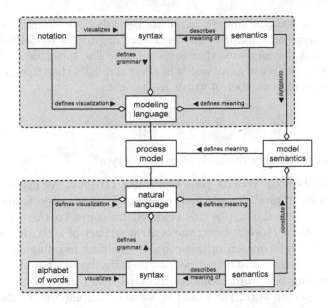

Fig. 1. Perspectives on a process model, adapted from [22]

of natural language and focus on the syntactic and the semantic dimension of natural language.

3 Conceptual Approach

In this section, we introduce a set of metrics indicating the granularity of a process model. Therefore, we consider a process model P containing a set of activities A. Each activity $a \in A$ consists of three components: an action a^a, a business object a^{bo}, and an addition a^{add}. As example, consider the activity *Notify customer of problem* consisting of the action *notify*, the business object *customer*, and the addition *of problem*. Note that the business object and the addition of an activity can be empty. The automatic annotation of activities with these components can be accomplished with the technique defined in [23].

In the following, we define two classes of metrics. First, we specify metrics operationalizing the syntactic dimension of natural language. This includes aspects like the number of words per label, but also more informed characteristics as for instance the usage of label components. Second, we introduce metrics operationalizing the semantic dimension of natural language. Hence, we consider aspects like the specificity of words. The following subsections introduce each metric in detail.

3.1 Metrics Building on Natural Language Syntax

Average Number of Words. As discussed by several works from prior research (e.g. [11,12]), size is a commonly applied indicator for the granularity of an object. With the average number of words per label, we directly address this basic characteristic and adapt it to the nature of process model labels. Thus, we explicitly consider all words that form a label. The rationale is that coarse-grained process models use more words in their activities than fine-grained ones. We define the average number of words as follows:

$$NoW = \frac{\sum_{a \in A} |a|}{|A|},$$ (1)

with $|a|$ being the number of words of the activity a.

Average Number of Words per Business Object. As discussed earlier, activity labels are typically composed of action, business object, and addition. Conceivably, we can also apply size oriented measures to these components. Particularly business objects, being the central artifact of activities, represent a valuable source of information in this context. Looking into linguistic literature how complex words are constructed, we can identify the concept of *compounding* [24]. Compounding is a word formation process that combines two words to a new and more specific word. For example, we can combine the words *order* and *purchase* to form the more specific word *purchase order*. Inspired by this concept, we consider the number of words of a business object as an indicator for word specificity. Accordingly, we introduce the following metric:

$$NoW^{bo} = \frac{\sum_{a \in A} |a^{bo}|}{|A^{bo}|},$$ (2)

with $|a^{bo}|$ being the number of words of the business object and A^{bo} representing all activities having a business object.

Average Number of Components. We already discussed that the activities tend to become more specific with an increasing number of words. Using the label annotation technique [23], we have another syntactic perspective on activity labels because we can explicitly distinguish between the three different components. Assuming that fine-granular models tend to include more components than activities from coarser grained models, we can define the following metric:

$$NoC = \frac{\sum_{a \in A} cov(a)}{|A|}$$ (3)

with $cov(a)$ being the number of components of activity a.

Maximum Business Object Count. In [25], the authors introduce the notion of a *dominating business object* representing a business object that is, due to its importance for the process, mentioned more often than other business objects. As a result, this particular business object is apparently discussed in more detail. Hence, we may conclude that models containing a dominating business object are more specific than models including a different business object in each activity.

Following this line of argumentation, we introduce a measure that considers the maximal number of business objects in a process model:

$$MaxC^{bo} = arg\ max\ \{count(a^{bo}, A)|a^{bo} \in A\} \tag{4}$$

where the function *count* returns the number of occurrences of the business object a^{bo} in the model A.

Share of Business Objects or Additions. As we can distinguish between different components, we can analyze the contribution of each component to the label as a whole. Since we require activity labels to have at least one action, we restrict ourselves to business objects and additions. Similar to the compounding approach, a label that encompasses business objects or additional fragments is more specific than one that does not. Accordingly, process models with a considerably higher share of labels with business objects or additional fragments are more fine-grained and vice versa. Thus, we can define the following two metrics:

$$SoC^{bo} = \frac{|\{a^{bo} \in A|a^{bo} \neq \emptyset\}|}{|A|} \tag{5}$$

$$SoC^{add} = \frac{|\{a^{add} \in A|a^{add} \neq \emptyset\}|}{|A|} \tag{6}$$

3.2 Metrics Building on Natural Language Semantics

Intrinsic Information Content of Business Objects and Actions. In the context of process model specificity, Friedrich [26] identified the taxonomy depth as an indicator for specificity. We seize this indication and extend it with the concept of *information content* [27]. More specifically, we use the intrinsic information content, which is based on the number of hyponyms (more abstract concepts) of a term in a taxonomy [28]. Since the addition of an activity does not represent a term, but a phrase, we calculate the intrinsic information content for actions and business objects:

$$IIC^{bo} = \frac{\sum_{a^{bo} \in A} IIC_{seco}(a^{bo})}{|A|} \tag{7}$$

$$IIC^a = \frac{\sum_{a^a \in A} IIC_{seco}(a^a)}{|A|} \tag{8}$$

where the function IIC_{seco} represents the intrinsic information content as defined in [28].

WordNet Coverage of Business Objects and Actions. The last set of metrics is motivated by work from information retrieval, in which the authors explicitly consider the scope of a query to decide on the granularity [16,17]. Similar to these approaches, we measure the amount of words that is retrievable in a lexical database. We assume that specific words, such as compounding words, are not covered and therefore can give valuable clues about the granularity of process models. Accordingly, we define:

$$WNC^{bo} = |\{a^{bo} \in A | a^{bo} \notin WordNet\}| \tag{9}$$

$$WNC^a = |\{a^a \in A_p | a^a \notin WordNet\}| \tag{10}$$

4   Evaluation

In this section, we evaluate the applicability of the introduced metrics for measuring process model granularity. We use two hierarchically organized process model collections from practice and evaluate the statistical power of the metrics to indicate the hierarchy level of the considered process models. First, Sect. 4.1 gives a brief overview of the evaluation setup. Then, Sect. 4.2 introduces the process model collections we utilize. Finally, Sect. 4.3 presents the evaluation results.

4.1   Setup

To evaluate the proposed metrics, we implemented them in the context of a Java prototype. For the metrics WNC^{bo} and WNC^a, we accordingly employed the WordNet database [29]. To determine whether the metrics have sufficient statistical power to indicate the hierarchy level of a process model, we conducted a statistical test. Specifically, we first used the Kolmogorov-Smirnov test to evaluate whether the metric values are normally distributed. As this is not the case, we employed the Kruskal-Wallis test for determining the statistical significance. In particular, this test is suited for comparing the means of two or more nonnormally distributed and independent samples. For these reasons, we preferred this test over other statistical tests, such as the Mann-Whitney or the t-test.

4.2   Test Collection Demographics

In order to demonstrate the applicability of the presented metrics, we employ two process model collections differing with respect to important characteristics including domain, model size, and the number of hierarchy levels:

- **SAP Reference Model**: The SAP Reference Model (SRM) captures the business processes of the SAP R/3 system in its version from the year 2000 [30, pp. 145–164]. It comprises 604 Event-driven Process Chains with in total 2433 activities covering 29 functional branches such as sales and accounting. The SAP Reference Model organizes the included process models in a hierarchy of two levels.

Table 1. Characteristics of employed model collections

Property	SRM	IMC
No. of models	604	349
No. of hierarchy levels	2	3
No of models on level 1	102	22
No of models on level 2	502	89
No of models on level 3	-	238
No. of activities	2433	1840
Average no. of activities per model	4.03	5.27

- **Insurance Model Collection**: The Insurance Model Collection (IMC) contains 349 EPCs dealing with the claims handling activities of a large insurance company. In total, the models include 1840 activities and hence are slightly bigger than the models from the SRM. The models are organized in a hierarchy of three different hierarchy levels.

Table 1 gives a summarizing overview of the characteristics of both process model collections.

4.3 Evaluation Results

Table 2 gives an overview of the obtained results. It shows the arithmetic mean of the metrics for each hierarchy level (AM), the respective standard deviation (STD), and the p-value from the statistical test. From the table, we can classify the introduced metrics into three categories: (1) metrics being statistically significant for both collections, (2) metrics being statistically significant for one collection, and (3) metrics that are not significant for any of the collections.

Metrics falling into the first category include the total number of words (NoW), the number of words of the business object (NoW^{bo}), the number of components (NoC), and the share of additions (SoC^{add}). The fact that these metrics are significant for both collections emphasizes that the degree of linguistic detail is a good indicator for the hierarchy level. Apparently, fine-granular models use more words to describe the process semantics. Interestingly, this cannot only be derived from the total number of words, but also from the label components. In particular additions are more frequently used in models from the lower levels of the hierarchy (level $\geq$ 2). The significance of the metric NoW^{bo} also emphasizes that models from lower levels use more specific business objects. As an example, consider the business object *customer service request* consisting of three words. Such a business object is typically only used in models belonging to lower hierarchy levels.

Metrics belonging to the second category include the share of business objects (SoC^{bo}), the intrinsic information content of actions (IIC^a), the wordnet coverage of business objects (WNC^{bo}), and the maximum number of business objects ($MaxC^{bo}$). In general, these differences can be explained by different styles of

Table 2. Evaluation results

	Metric	Level 1 AM	STD	Level 2 AM	STD	Level 3 AM	STD	p-value
SRM	NoW	2.73	1.12	3.66	1.31	-	-	<0.01**
	NoW^{bo}	1.46	0.57	1.86	0.79	-	-	<0.01**
	NoC	1.83	0.32	2.07	0.32	-	-	<0.01**
	$MaxC^{bo}$	1.39	0.68	1.4	0.74	-	-	0.88
	SoC^{bo}	0.73	0.25	0.89	0.22	-	-	<0.01**
	SoC^{add}	0.07	0.15	0.14	0.27	-	-	<0.05*
	IIC^{bo}	0.55	0.30	0.57	0.28	-	-	0.55
	IIC^{a}	0.51	0.25	0.51	0.22	-	-	0.81
	WNC^{bo}	0.37	0.89	0.36	0.85	-	-	0.88
	WNC^{a}	0.04	0.20	0.04	0.21	-	-	0.77
IMC	NoW	3.58	1.07	3.94	1.05	4.98	1.27	<0.01**
	NoW^{bo}	2.56	1.03	2.28	0.90	2.52	0.95	<0.01**
	NoC	1.98	0.11	2.17	0.22	2.35	0.29	<0.01**
	$MaxC^{bo}$	1.06	0.21	1.37	0.61	1.38	0.91	0.04*
	SoC^{bo}	0.98	0.11	0.98	0.07	0.98	0.93	0.66
	SoC^{add}	0.00	0.00	0.18	0.22	0.38	0.29	<0.01**
	IIC^{bo}	0.61	0.41	0.69	0.20	0.65	0.20	0.13
	IIC^{a}	0.97	0.16	0.52	0.26	0.46	0.24	<0.01**
	WNC^{bo}	0.18	0.39	0.82	1.22	1.03	1.65	<0.01**
	WNC^{a}	0.00	0.00	0.00	0.00	0.01	0.09	0.63

* Metric is significant at the 0.05 level (2-tailed)
** Metric is significant at the 0.01 level (2-tailed).

modeling. For the two semantic metrics IIC^{a} and WNC^{bo}, we obtain significant results for the three layered IMC. Apparently, the IMC models consistently use more specific words on the lower hierarchy levels. Further, they use a higher number of business objects on higher levels. Hence, the metric $MaxC^{bo}$ is significant as well. For the SRM collection, only the share of business objects SoC^{bo} obtains significant results. From this constellation we may conclude that the SRM models rather use no business objects on the lower levels than using less specific ones. Nevertheless, these results still emphasize that these metrics may represent valuable indicators for the granularity of a process model.

Although many metrics turned out to be relevant indicators for at least one collection, we did not obtain significant results for the wordnet coverage of actions (WNC^{a}) and the intrinsic information content of business objects (IIC^{bo}). These results can be explained by having a closer look at the WordNet dictionary. The non-significance of the metric WNC^{a} results from the fact that WordNet covers almost all verbs of the English language. Hence, non-covered actions represent an exception and cannot be used as granularity indicator. The non-significance of the metric IIC^{bo} suffers from the opposite problem. As many business objects are compounded by two or more words and thus rather specific, they are not part of the WordNet dictionary. As a result, it is not possible to employ WordNet to calculate useful specificity values for business objects from a semantic perspective.

All in all, the evaluation highlights that many of the introduced metrics have the statistical power to explain the hierarchy level of a process model. This has two important implications for maintaining a consistent quality of process model collections. First, the introduced metrics can be used to evaluate the consistency of existing process model collections, and second, they can support modelers to achieve an adequate level of detail right from the start. Depending on the goals of an organization, modeling tools could be configured to indicate the desired characteristics. This may include syntactic aspects as the existence of an addition, or semantic aspects as the specificity of actions and business objects.

5   Conclusion

In this paper, we introduced a novel set of metrics to measure the granularity of a process model. Specifically, we used natural language analysis techniques and exploited syntactic and semantic aspects of natural language to operationalize process model granularity. The evaluation with two hierarchically organized process model collection from practice illustrated that a major share of the metrics have a statistically significant power to explain the hierarchy level of a process model. We highlighted that these results pave the way for evaluating and ensuring an adequate level of detail of process models. Considering the increasing size of process model collection in practice, this work represents an important contribution for the automated quality insurance of process models.

As this work is, to our knowledge, the first endeavour aiming at measuring process model granularity via natural language analysis, there are several directions for future work. First, we aim at investigating whether the proposed metrics can be combined to a single granularity indicator. Second, we plan to evaluate how the granularity assessment can support other process model techniques. For instance, process model matching could benefit from determining regions of differing granularity in the matching candidates. Finally, we plan to study in how far the metrics can effectively guide users to create models with an adequate level of granularity.

References

1. Kettinger, W., Teng, J., Guha, S.: Business process change: a study of methodologies, techniques, and tools. MIS Quarterly **21**, 55–80 (1997)
2. Rosemann, M.: Potential pitfalls of process modeling: part A. Bus. Process Manage. J. **12**(2), 249–254 (2006)
3. Malinova, M., Leopold, H., Mendling, J.: An empirical investigation on the design of process architectures. In: Wirtschaftsinformatik, p. 75 (2013)
4. Dijkman, R., Vanderfeesten, I., Reijers, H.A.: The road to a business process architecture: an overview of approaches and their use. Technical report, Working Paper WP-350, Eindhoven University of Technology (2011)

5. Becker, J., Mühlen, M.: Towards a classification framework for application granularity in workflow management systems. In: Jarke, M., Oberweis, A. (eds.) CAiSE 1999. LNCS, vol. 1626, pp. 411–416. Springer, Heidelberg (1999)
6. Becker, J., Rosemann, M., Uthmann, C.: Guidelines of business process modeling. In: van der Aalst, W.M.P., Desel, J., Oberweis, A. (eds.) Business Process Management. LNCS, vol. 1806, pp. 30–49. Springer, Heidelberg (2000)
7. Mendling, J., Reijers, H.A., van der Aalst, W.M.P.: Seven process modeling guidelines (7PMG). Inf. Softw. Technol. **52**(2), 127–136 (2010)
8. Krogstie, J., Sindre, G., Jørgensen, H.: Process models representing knowledge for action: a revised quality framework. Eur. J. Inf. Syst. **15**(1), 91–102 (2006)
9. Zadeh, L.A.: Toward a theory of fuzzy information granulation and its centrality in human reasoning and fuzzy logic. Fuzzy Sets Syst. **90**(2), 111–127 (1997)
10. Henderson-Sellers, B., Gonzalez-Perez, C.: Granularity in conceptual modelling: application to metamodels. In: Parsons, J., Saeki, M., Shoval, P., Woo, C., Wand, Y. (eds.) ER 2010. LNCS, vol. 6412, pp. 219–232. Springer, Heidelberg (2010)
11. Krammer, A., Heinrich, B., Henneberger, M., Lautenbacher, F.: Granularity of services. Bus. Inf. Syst. Eng. **3**(6), 345–358 (2011)
12. Heinrich, B., Zimmermann, S.: Granularity metrics for it services. In: ICIS'12, pp. 1–19 (2012)
13. Kulkarni, N., Dwivedi, V.: The role of service granularity in a successful soa realization - a case study. In: SERVICES '08, pp. 423–430 (2008)
14. Ma, Q., Zhou, N., Zhu, Y., Wang, H.: Evaluating service identification with design metrics on business process decomposition. In: SCC '09, pp. 160–167 (2009)
15. Wang, Z.J., Zhan, D.C., Xu, X.F.: STCIM: a dynamic granularity oriented and stability based component identification method. SIGSOFT Softw. Eng. Notes **31**(3), 1–14 (2006)
16. He, B., Ounis, I.: Inferring query performance using pre-retrieval predictors. In: Apostolico, A., Melucci, M. (eds.) SPIRE 2004. LNCS, vol. 3246, pp. 43–54. Springer, Heidelberg (2004)
17. Plachouras, V., Cacheda, F., Ounis, I., Rijsbergen, C.J.V.: University of glasgow at the web track: dynamic application of hyperlink analysis using the query scope. In: TREC'03, pp. 636–642 (2003)
18. Yan, X., Lau, R.Y., Song, D., Li, X., Ma, J.: Toward a semantic granularity model for domain-specific information retrieval. ACM Trans. Inf. Syst. **29**(3), 1–46 (2011)
19. Allen, R.B., Wu, Y.: Generality of texts. In: Lim, E., Foo, S.S.-B., Khoo, Ch., Chen, H., Fox, E., Urs, S.R., Costantino, T. (eds.) ICADL 2002. LNCS, vol. 2555, pp. 111–116. Springer, Heidelberg (2002)
20. Allen, R.B., Wu, Y.: Metrics for the scope of a collection: research articles. J. Am. Soc. Inf. Sci. Technol. **56**(12), 1243–1249 (2005)
21. Holschke, O., Rake, J., Levina, O.: Granularity as a cognitive factor in the effectiveness of business process model reuse. In: Dayal, U., Eder, J., Koehler, J., Reijers, H.A. (eds.) BPM 2009. LNCS, vol. 5701, pp. 245–260. Springer, Heidelberg (2009)
22. Leopold, H.: Natural language in business process models. Ph.D. thesis, Humboldt Universität zu Berlin (2013)
23. Leopold, H., Smirnov, S., Mendling, J.: On the refactoring of activity labels in business process models. Inf. Syst. **37**(5), 443–459 (2012)
24. Bieswanger, M., Becker, A.: Introduction to English Linguistics. UTB für Wissenschaft: Uni-Taschenbücher. Francke (2010)
25. Leopold, H., Mendling, J., Reijers, H.A.: On the automatic labeling of process models. In: Mouratidis, H., Rolland, C. (eds.) CAiSE 2011. LNCS, vol. 6741, pp. 512–520. Springer, Heidelberg (2011)

26. Friedrich, F.: Measuring semantic label quality using wordnet. In: EPK, pp. 7–21 (2009)
27. Resnik, P.: Using information content to evaluate semantic similarity in a taxonomy. In: IJCAI'95, pp. 448–453 (1995)
28. Seco, N., Veale, T., Hayes, J.: An intrinsic information content metric for semantic similarity in WordNet. Proc. of ECAI **4**, 1089–1090 (2004)
29. Miller, G.A.: WordNet: a lexical database for english. Commun. ACM **38**(11), 39–41 (1995)
30. Keller, G., Teufel, T.: SAP(R) R/3 process oriented implementation: iterative process prototyping. Addison-Wesley, Boston (1998)

Automatic Extraction of Process Categories from Process Model Collections

Monika Malinova[1(⊠)], Remco Dijkman[2], and Jan Mendling[1]

[1] Institute for Information Business, Wirtschaftsuniversität Wien,
Vienna, Austria
{monika.malinova,jan.mendling}@wu.ac.at
[2] Eindhoven University of Technology, Eindhoven, The Netherlands
r.m.dijkman@tue.nl

Abstract. Many organizations build up their business process management activities in an incremental way. As a result, there is no overarching structure defined at the beginning. However, as business process modeling initiatives often yield hundreds to thousands of process models, there is a growing need for such a structure. This challenge calls for a technique to extract process categories from a set of process models automatically which yields an up-to-date view of the structure of a collection of process models. It also provides a means to check whether pre-defined process categories are still reasonable. In this paper, we introduce a technique for automatically extracting process categories from process model collections and test it using a collection from industry. The results demonstrate the usefulness of the technique by revealing issues of the pre-existing process categories. In this way, we contribute to the field of process model management and quality assurance.

Keywords: Clustering · Process model collection · Process architecture · Process category

1 Introduction

Business process management initiatives are confronted with an extensive number of process models, often ranging in thousands of models. A key challenge in handling such a number of models is to define a suitable structure for organizing them and to provide useful techniques for abstracting from individual models to develop an understanding at a higher level of abstraction [1]. A structure for a process model collection is often referred to as *process architecture*. We define a process architecture as an overview of the processes that exist in an organization as well as the relations between these processes. Typical relations that are covered include input/output and decomposition relationships. The term process category is used to refer to coherent groups of processes that exist in the most abstract model of a process architecture. Defining a process architecture is especially problematic for modeling initiatives that have grown over time without a predefined or outdated structure. But also process model collections that have been well organized at a certain point in time might have evolved in such a way that the structure has become obsolete.

N. Lohmann et al. (Eds.): BPM 2013 Workshops, LNBIP 171, pp. 430–441, 2014.
DOI: 10.1007/978-3-319-06257-0_34, © Springer International Publishing Switzerland 2014

The definition of a process architecture is a problem that relates to the research area of quality management for process model collections. While there are various works that help to verify a single process model [2], to restructure it [3], or to rework labels [4], there is little research on the automatic identification of relationships between multiple process models. The need for such techniques is emphasized by papers on process model refactoring [5, 6]. The works by [1, 7] belong to the few examples that aim to extract decomposition relationships. There is a research gap in this area regarding techniques that help to organize a process model collection in terms of a process architecture.

In this paper, we address this research gap by translating the problem of constructing a process architecture into a clustering problem. To this end, we define a technique for extracting process categories from a collection of process models. Our technique builds on the concept of a document vector representation of process models. We use classical K-means clustering on these vectors in order to build process categories. We test the technique using a process model collection from industry. The results demonstrate the usefulness of the technique by revealing quality issues of the pre-existing process categories. In this way, we contribute to the field of process model management and quality assurance.

Against this background, the remainder of the paper is structured as follows. Section 2 summarizes essential concepts of process architecture and illustrates our research problem. Section 3 defines our technique for process category extraction based on deriving document vectors and clustering them. Section 4 presents and discusses the results of applying our technique to an industry collection of process models. Section 5 states the implications for research and practice before Sect. 6 concludes the paper.

2   Background

In this section, we discuss the background of our work and formalize the notions of process model collection and process architecture.

2.1   Process Architecture

Process architecture is used by organizations as a means for understanding the organization from a business process perspective [8]. Prior studies have pointed out that many organizations fail to look at their processes as an integrated collection, and rather focus on singular processes [9]. A process architecture is of good help in this regard, as it explicates the relations between the different processes of an organization [10]. Typically, the relations between processes are defined in two directions: input/output and decomposition. Input/output relationships can be defined between processes belonging to the same category [11, 12]. In the simplest case, such a relationship shows that one process provides an output which is used as an input by another one. In the general case, also n:m relationships can occur. Decomposition relationships can be defined between process models at different levels of granularity.

Typically, decomposition is defined in a hierarchical way where elements of a process are decomposed into more fine-grained sub-processes [10, 12].

In this line, process architecture can be described as a process model collection that is systematically organized in terms of explicit relations between the processes [10]. A process category refers to an element of the most abstract model, which is the root of the decomposition tree of the process architecture. More precisely, we define a process architecture as follows:

Definition 1. Process Architecture. *A process architecture is a tuple (P, T, R), in which: P is a set of business processes; T is a set of relationship types; and R: P × P × T is a set of relations between processes.*

In a concrete architecture, the set T defines concrete relationship types and their graphical representation (e.g. ArchiMate [13]). The different relations that can be defined between processes partially relate to relationships that are typically described between activities. The control relation defines that the completion of one process triggers the execution of another one. The data flow relation can indicate such a trigger relation as well. The decomposition relation describes that subordinate processes might be required to complete before a superordinate process can complete. This relation is discussed in various works on process modeling, e.g. in [14, 15]. However, the research focus so far has been on how a single activity relates to a sub-process. Some empirical works in this area exist [7, 16]. What is missing at this stage is an appropriate coverage of the overall set of decomposition relations in a process architecture.

2.2   Process Categories

From the perspective of process architecture, the decomposition relation relates a business process to a business process that is a part of it. Figure 1 shows an example where a *Sales* process relates to a *Billing* process in a decompositional way. Processes like *Sales, Procurement* and *Human Resource Management* in this example can be abstract process categories. Such process categories are typically defined at the top level of a process architecture for structuring the whole organization from a process perspective. The root element of the decomposition graph of a process architecture is often referred to as a process map or process landscape. Throughout this paper, we consider it in an abstract way and define the elements on the level below this root element as process categories. Therefore, the set of process categories in Fig. 1 contains the elements *Sales, Procurement* and *HRM*.

Fig. 1. Decomposition of Processes in a Process Architecture

Definition 2. Process Category. *Given a process architecture* (P, T, R), *the set of process categories PC refers to the top-level elements of the decomposition relation such that* $PC = \{ p \in P \mid (root, p, decomposition) \in R\}$.

There are various challenges associated with process categories. First, a hierarchical decomposition defines a classification problem. In practice, organizations often establish their process categories based on organizational units. Such a case is apparent in Fig. 1 where among others the category *Sales* has been defined based on the Sales department. A strict decomposition based on such categories often leads to classification problems for more fine-grained processes that are shared between departments. Second, a set of process categories might be appropriate at a certain point in time. However, organizations evolve over time, partially organic, but also disruptively when divisions are sold or outsourced, or when other companies are acquired. Third, many companies build up their BPM activities in an incremental way. As a result, there is no overarching process architecture defined in the beginning. While an increasing number of smaller or bigger sets of models from various projects are stored, there is a growing need for structure. All these challenges call for a technique to extract process categories from the set of process models automatically. Thus, such a technique yields an up-to-date view on the process models. Furthermore, it provides a means to check whether the pre-defined process categories are still reasonable.

3 Conceptual Approach

In this section, we describe our technique for automatically extracting process categories from a collection of process models. Our technique could be applied on process collections with no pre-defined categories. In this study we use a process collection with a pre-existing list of process categories, and aim to check its plausibility.

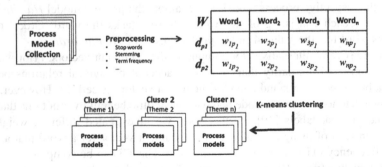

Fig. 2. Technique for extracting process categories

An overview of our technique is shown in Fig. 2. As a first step, we apply preprocessing filters on a process model collection, such as the removal of stop words, stemming, etc. Each process model is then mapped to a vector space based on frequency. We apply the K-means clustering method to the set of vectors. Process models are placed in the same cluster if there is a co-occurrence relationship between them. Each cluster is furthermore defined in terms of themes which stem from their most frequent words [17].

3.1 Document Vectors of a Business Process

To be able to apply K-means clustering, it is necessary to represent business processes in a vector space. To this end, we will rely on a notion of similarity in the vector space of which task labels encode each business process as a corresponding document vector.

Definition 3. Document Vector of a Business Process. Let $\mathcal{W}$ be a set of words, P be a set of processes and $w(p) = (W, m)$ be the function that returns the bag of words that appear in a process $p \in P$, where $W \subseteq \mathcal{W}$ and $m\colon W \rightarrow \mathbf{N}$. $d_p = (w_{1p}, w_{2p}, \ldots, w_{np})$ is the document vector of process $p \in P$, in which each index i represents a word from the set of all words in the collection $\bigcup\{W \mid (W, m) = w(p), p \in P\}$ and $w_{ip} = 1$ if $w \in w(p)$ for the word w represented by i, $w_{ip} = 0$ otherwise.

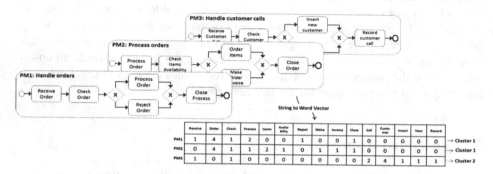

Fig. 3. Vector generation of business process models

	Receive	Order	Check	Process	Items	Availability	Reject	Make	Invoice	Close	Call	Customer	Insert	New	Record	
PM1	1	4	1	2	0	0	1	0	0	1	0	0	0	0	0	→ Cluster 1
PM2	0	4	1	1	2	1	0	1	1	1	0	0	0	0	0	→ Cluster 1
PM3	1	0	1	0	0	0	0	0	0	0	2	4	1	1	1	→ Cluster 2

In Fig. 3 we illustrate the vector generation for business process models. Here we see that the values in each vector encode the word presence and frequency of the words in the respective process model. For example the process model *Handle orders* has five tasks each consisting of two words. In four tasks the word 'Order' occurs, hence this word has the value 4 in the vector space for *Handle orders*.

There are several alternatives for computing the document vectors. Prior work has defined a notion of similarity that takes into account behavioral relations between tasks in a business process and encodes them in a vector space [18]. However, it has been shown that notions that encode behavior have little benefit over notions that work only based on task labels [19]. Furthermore, we investigated different weights. In particular, instead of using the value 1 in a document vector for a word that appears, the term frequency (TF) of the word can be used. The TF can be computed in various ways (e.g.: given $w(p) = (W, m)$, $w_{ip} = m(w)$ for a word $w \in W$ represented by i) [20]. Also, TF divided by the inverse document frequency (IDF) can be used. There are also different options for computing the IDF (e.g.: for a word w the IDF is $log \, |P| \, / \, |\{p \mid p \in P, w \in w(p)\}|$) [20]. Another variation that can be applied is that words can be removed from the collection of words that is to be considered. Common preprocessing that is applied to reduce the total number of words is to remove 'stop words', which are frequently occurring words that do not bear any relevant meaning, such as 'the' and 'a'. Also frequently applied is 'stemming', which is the action of reducing words to the stem form. For example, stemming would reduce 'stemming', 'stemmed', and 'stemmer' to 'stem' [21]. Given the document vectors of a collection of business process models, the clustering method can now be applied.

3.2   Clustering

The K-means clustering method assumes that elements exist in a vector space. It will create K clusters in that space, corresponding to K points that are at the center of each cluster, also called centroids. These clusters are created by determining the centroids in such a way that, if each element is assigned to its closest centroid, the total distance from elements to their centroids is minimal. An algorithm to compute such a clustering is developed by [22].

Definition 4. Clustering. *Given a set of p document vectors d_p and a number of clusters K, we define clustering as a technique to group similar document vectors together by finding a classification C of d_p into K classes $\{C_1, C_2, ..., C_K\}$. There exists a distance function that evaluates the quality of a clustering, which is minimized.*

The distance measure between the document vectors that we use is the Euclidean distance, which finds the co-occurrence relationship between process models based on how many words the process models have in common.

Definition 5. Euclidean Distance. *Euclidean distance of two document vectors d_1 and d_2 is defined as $dis(d_1, d_2) = d_1 - d_2$. The smaller the (dissimilarity) value of $dis(d_1 d_2)$ is, the more similar the two document vectors are.*

We can use the Euclidian distance to define the cluster quality function, which is needed to find the optimal clustering, as follows:

Definition 6. Clustering quality. *Given a clustering C and a distance function dis: $d_p \times d_p \rightarrow \mathbb{R}$ the clustering quality is: $\sum_{c \in C} \sum_{d_1, d_2 \in c, d_1 \neq d_2} -dis(d_1, d_2)$*

For example, in Fig. 3, the process models *Handle orders* and *Process orders* are placed in cluster 1 because of their similarity. On the other hand, the process model *Handle customer calls* is placed in cluster 2, as a result of the low co-occurrence relationship with the process models in cluster 1. Accordingly, cluster 1 is characterized in terms of words such as *order*, *check* and *process*, because they appear often in both process models. Cluster 2 covers words like *customer* and *call*.

The cluster goodness can be additionally evaluated through measuring the purity, entropy and F-Measure [23–25]. In the case of pre-existing classes of process models, these measures show how representative the derived clusters to the pre-existing classes are. Thus, a cluster would be ideal if it contains processes from a single class (purity = 1), the distribution of the classes within a given cluster is low (entropy = 0), and it contains processes from one class and processes from one class have been placed in only one cluster (F-Measure = 1).

Definition 7. Entropy. *Given a cluster j and a class i, the entropy of a cluster is $e_j = -\sum_j^L p_{ij} \log_2 p_{ij}$, where L is the number of classes and p_{ij} is the probability that*

member of cluster j belongs to class i. The total entropy of the clustering is
$E = -\sum_i^K \frac{m_i}{m} e_i$, *where m is the number of data points and K is the number of clusters.*

Definition 8. Purity. *Given a cluster j and a class i, the purity of a cluster is*
$p_i = \max_j p_{ij}$. *The total purity of the clustering is* $P = \sum_i^K \frac{m_{ij}}{m_j} p_i$, *where m is the number of data points and K is the number of clusters.*

Definition 9. F-Measure. *Given a cluster j and a class i, the F-Measure of a cluster is*
$F(i,j) = \frac{2R(i,j)P(i,j)}{R(i,j)+P(i,j)}$, *where* $R(i,j) = \frac{m_{ij}}{m_i}$ *is the recall of class i with respect to cluster j*
and $P(i,j) = \frac{m_{ij}}{m_i}$ *is the precision of class i with respect to cluster j. The total F-measure*
for the entire data set of size p is given by $F = \sum_i \frac{m_i}{m} [F(i,j)]$.

4   Evaluation

In this section we test our technique on the SAP process model collection. To begin with, we describe the preprocessing filters we apply to the data. Then we present the results of the process clusters we extracted comparing to the pre-existing classes.

4.1   Experiment Input

We use the SAP process collection consisting of 604 process models grouped in 29 process categories as shown in Table 1. Each SAP process category corresponds to a functional block of the SAP system and consists of those business process models this block is dedicated to. We disregard duplicate process models within one SAP process category, but leave those that have the same label but belong to different categories. Hence, we apply the clustering method to the remaining 453 SAP process models.

4.2   Data Preprocessing

Before we start with the clustering method, we first preprocess the data and map each process model to a vector space. We apply several transformations on the vector representation. First, we remove the stop words. Second, we use a stemmer in order to map words with different endings into a single word. Third, we discard words that appear with less than a given threshold frequency because they make little contribution to the similarity between two process models [26] We select words ranked by their weights appearing at least 10 times. The most frequent words are however not necessarily the most important ones. Words which appear frequently in a small number of process models, but rarely in the other, tend to be more relevant and specific for that particular group of process models. Thus, we transform the basic term frequencies TF and TF-IDF weighting scheme and we use the TF-IDF value instead of the absolute term frequency of each term to build the vector for each process model. We normalize the process models on their length, as to avoid giving advantages to larger process models over smaller ones. The rationale behind this is that words in large process models will appear more frequently which will lead to these being

Table 1. Clusters

SAP Process Category (number of processes)	1	2	3	4	5	6	7	8	9	10	11	12	13	14	15	16	17	18	19	20	21	22	23	24	25	26	27	28	29
Financial Accounting (53)				1	12			12			1	12		3						3			2	7					
Sales and Distrib. (36)	1						1	2				9						1				2	1	1	10	8			
Project Mngm (34)								1				9					2		13			1	2		1			4	1
Asset Accounting (32)											9	8			3	6				4								2	
Customer Service (25)	1						2					8		1				1	1	5					3	3			
Treasury (24)									3			8															13		
Procurement (20)	1				1		3					2		2					2			9		2					
Reven.&Cost Control. (19)												2	4						2		1							10	
Enterprise Controlling (19)						2						6	2						3					4				2	
Quality Management (18)												3		12					1	2									
Compensation Mngm (17)										16	1																		
Production (16)						8						3							5										
Plant Maintenance (32)	1						2					3							1	8									
Envir. Health and Saf. (15)					1							13									1								
Produc.&Procur.Plan. (14)												8							6										
Train.&Event Mngm (12)		12																											
Personnel Time Mngm (11)										11																			
Personnel Develop. (10)										10																			
Recruitment (9)										8			1																
Payroll (7)									7																				
Benefits Admin. (6)									2	4																			
Real Estate Mngm (6)								3	1		1																	1	
Organizational Mngm (5)										4							1												
Personnel Admin. (4)										4																			
Invent. Mngm&Transp. (3)				3																									
Product Data Mngm (3)													3																
Travel Management (1)									1																				
Retail (1)					1																								
null (1)												1																	
Total in cluster	2	2	12	4	3	14	17	27	43	20	9	98	9	15	3	6	3	4	32	15	8	11	9	12	13	12	13	19	1
Entropy$_j$ (E=1,98)	1,0	1,0	0,0	0,8	1,6	0,6	2,2	2,0	2,1	2,3	0,0	3,8	1,5	0,9	0,0	0,0	0,9	1,5	2,4	1,4	1,4	0,7	2,1	1,6	0,8	1,2	0,0	1,9	0,0
Purity$_j$ (P=0,49)	0,5	0,5	1,0	0,8	0,3	0,9	0,5	0,4	0,4	0,4	1,0	0,1	0,4	0,8	1,0	1,0	0,7	0,5	0,4	0,5	0,5	0,8	0,4	0,6	0,8	0,7	1,0	0,5	1,0
F-Measure$_{ij}$ (F=0,21)	0,1	0,1	1,0	0,9	0,1	0,4	0,5	0,3	0,5	0,6	0,4	0,2	0,3	0,7	0,2	0,3	0,1	0,2	0,4	0,3	0,2	0,6	0,3	0,2	0,4	0,3	0,7	0,5	0,1

ranked above smaller ones. We also make sure that the maximum number of words and the minimum term frequency is not enforced on a per-class basis, but based on the process models in all the categories. As a result of the data preprocessing, the initial set of 2351 words was reduced to 422. Finally, clustering is performed by measuring the distance between the vectors.

4.3 Clustering

We apply K-means clustering to the SAP process collection with its 29 pre-existing process categories. In case that the categories perfectly reflect the words and themes, the clustering would be expected to output 29 clusters with purity of 1, entropy of 0 and F-Measure of 1. In this case, each cluster should contain process models from one single SAP process category, and processes from one SAP process category are placed in only one cluster. For this reason we set K to be 29.

4.4 Results and Discussion

Clustering in general is not straightforward to evaluate, especially when a large set of data has been used. However, based on Tables 1 and 2 we are able to derive some insights into the benefits the clustering solution brings when used to organize a large set of process models.

Table 1 summarizes the clustering of the SAP process models and shows the values for the *entropy, purity* and *F-Measure*. The total entropy measure for all 29 clusters (E = 1.98) shows that processes from one category have been dispersed to several clusters. On the other hand, the total purity measure (P = 0.49) tells us that in average all clusters contain almost 50 % processes coming from the same category. Whereas the total F-Measure (F = 0.21) specifies that in average 21 % of the retrieved relevant processes within one cluster are in fact relevant.

We use color scaling to highlight the dominance of an SAP process category in each cluster. The darker the shade the more dominant the process category in the respective cluster, whereas the brighter the shade the less processes from that category have been placed in that particular cluster. Therefore, when we look at each cluster individually, we derive somewhat different and more revealing insights than the overall clustering quality values. Based on Table 1 and the quality measures, we can essentially distinguish between three types of clusters. The first type (several categories – one cluster) typically have high values for entropy, while low values for purity and F-Measure (e.g. clusters 7, 8, 9, 10, 12, 18, 19, etc). Accordingly, these clusters contain processes from different process categories. The second type (one category – several clusters) has entropy of 0 and purity of 1 (e.g. clusters 11, 15, 16, 27 and 29) indicating that in these clusters processes from a single category have been stored. Yet, for all these clusters the F-Measure is low, which assesses the tradeoff of recall and precision. Hence, whereas processes from a single category have been placed in these clusters, also other clusters contain processes from the same category. Lastly, the third type (one category - one cluster) is when all process models from one SAP process category have been placed in only one cluster (e.g. Cluster 3). According to the cluster quality measures, this cluster is ideal because it has entropy of 1, purity of 0 and F-Measure of 1.

Nonetheless we find that the underlying reason for such process distribution amongst the clusters occur because each resultant cluster consists of those processes that relate to one theme [26]. Table 2 illustrates each cluster theme and its most frequent words. Tables 1 and 2 indeed show a different, yet meaningful categorization of the SAP process models. For example, in the first type of clusters (several categories – one cluster) although the processes come from different SAP categories, they do in fact deal with the same theme. Such as, in Cluster 8, (C8): *Manage accounts and payment*, all process models that relate to accounts and payment have been stored (e.g. process models coming from SAP *Financial Accounting*, SAP *Payroll, etc*). As a result, all process models being placed in C8 will in turn be used by all these SAP functional areas. On the other hand, clusters from the second type (one category – several clusters) suggest that one SAP category holds processes that deal with different aspects of the same or similar entity. Accordingly, these processes have been spread out to more clusters, each addressing a different aspect of an entity (e.g. *C11: Manage assets, C15: Acquire assets, C16: Analyze investments*). Lastly, Cluster 3 apparently is not associated with any other cluster, because the most frequent words for this cluster are distinctive and do not appear in the other clusters.

Table 2. Cluster theme and word frequency for each cluster

ID	Cluster theme (most frequent words in cluster)	ID		ID	
C1	**Post goods receipt** (goods, receipt, delivery, post, inbound, receive)	C11	**Manage assets** (asset, depreciation, carry, accounting, year, cost)	C21	**Manage budget** (budget, funds, carry, cost, assign, order, payment, activity)
C2	**Measure work hours** (time, sheet, measurement, order, data, hour)	C12	**Process data** (process, create, data, plan, budget, material, product)	C22	**Handle purchase requisition** (purchase, requisition, order, release, create, schedule)
C3	**Plan business events** (event, business, exist, need, order, resource, plan)	C13	**Plan profit** (profit, center, plan, data, prepare, transfer, copy)	C23	**Specify basic data** (data, specify, basic, information, system, price, define, function)
C4	**Perform inventory** (inventory, physical, perform, count, management, storage)	C14	**Manage quality** (inspection, quality, notification, defect, update, maintenance)	C24	**Handle customer payments** (payment, down, vendor, invoice, customer, clear, request, credit)
C5	**Enter protocol** (service, protocol, medical, entry, enter, sheet)	C15	**Acquire assets** (asset, post, acquisition, fix, master, record, group, lease)	C25	**Process order delivery** (create, order, document, sales, block, due, credit, delivery, quotation)
C6	**Transfer financial data** (company, carry, enter, data, transfer, currency, financial)	C16	**Analyze investments** (order, investment, measure, analysis, settlement, complete)	C26	**Manage credit and billing** (create, bill, memo, credit, service, good, process, contract, request)
C7	**Produce and deliver goods** (goods, material, order, production, create, delivery)	C17	**Manage project personnel** (exist, personnel, need, project, change, approval, plan, internal)	C27	**Handle payment transactions** (currency, generate, transaction, payment, valuation,
C8	**Manage accounts and payment** (account, payment, calculation, carry, bill, exchange, balance)	C18	**Manage stock items** (item, difference, transfer, order, confirm, process, stock, management)	C28	**Handle cost overhead** (cost, plan, order, overhead, actual, settlement, calculate)
C9	**Plan personnel** (personnel, need, plan, time, exist, employee, specification)	C19	**Plan production** (plan, create, order, require, maintenance, cost, production)	C29	**Manage activity time** (time, activity, confirmation, data, sheet, working, hours)
C10	**Employ personnel** (benefit, employee, applicant, trip, process, offer, contract)	C20	**Maintain orders** (order, maintenance, create, material, service, capacity)		

Based on this, we find that those clusters that contain processes from the same SAP process category are by some means related to each other (e.g. (C11, C15 and C16) or (C6, C8, C12 and C24)). Because, when processes are decomposed based on departments, it is usually not visible how the process models of these units relate to each other. We also observed process redundancies within the same cluster, which was in fact the same process model coming from a different SAP process category. Thus, our clustering solution helps in avoiding process redundancies among the different SAP functional areas.

5   Implications

Our study offers three main implications for research and practice, namely the quality check of pre-existing process categories, process category extraction from a process model collection, and naming activities in process models.

First of all, by clustering process models from a process model collection we yield an up-to-date view of the structure of a collection of process models. Accordingly we evaluate the plausibility of pre-existing process categories. Our findings show that categorizing processes based on organizational units is not such a good criterion. In fact, due to the unclear relations between the process models belonging to different organizational units, this type of classification yields process redundancies. Yet, when the process models are categorized according to themes, an organizational unit eventually (depending on the value that needs to be created) uses processes that belong to different themes and are necessary for the value-creation. This would help increase the correlation between the process categories and in turn cause process reuse among departments. In addition, this will assist organizations use a single process for more purposes, instead of using one process for a single purpose within one department.

We also identify the significance of assigning meaningful labels to process model activities. This is because useful information should be deduced from the process activity names in order for them to be correctly clustered. Accordingly, process activities should be appropriately labeled. Each activity label should relate to one entity and the different aspects associated with this entity.

6 Conclusions

In this paper we presented a technique for extracting process categories from process model collections. We applied this technique to a process model collection from industry with pre-existing process categories. This enabled us to gain insights into the quality of the pre-defined categories and the usefulness of the technique. When applying the technique to the process model collection, we revealed several quality issues with the pre-existing process categories, thus demonstrating the usefulness of the technique. We find that a strict decomposition of processes based on organizational units often leads to classification problems for processes on more detailed levels that are shared between departments. Rather, categorizing process models according to themes, where process models that pertain to the same theme belong to the same category, causes process reuse among organizational units. We prove that categorization based on themes does indeed reflect processes and process dependencies in industry.

In future work we will complement this study by adapting our technique by using various clustering methods in order to extract process categories from a process model collection with no pre-existing categories. We will also focus on positioning the extracted process categories in a process architecture and validating the process architecture with the respective organization.

References

1. Smirnov, S., Reijers, H.A., Weske, M., Nugteren, T.: Business process model abstraction: a definition, catalog, and survey. Distrib. Parallel Databases 3, 63–99 (2012)
2. van Dongen, B.F. Mendling, J., van der Aalst, W.M.: Structural patterns for soundness of business process models. In: Enterprise Distributed Object Somputing Conference (2006)
3. Polyvyanyy, A., García-Bañuelos, L., Dumas, M.: Structuring acyclic process models. In: Hull, R., Mendling, J., Tai, S. (eds.) BPM 2010. LNCS, vol. 6336, pp. 276–293. Springer, Heidelberg (2010)
4. Leopold, H., Smirnov, S., Mendling, J.: On the refactoring of activity labels in business process models. Inf. Syst. 37(5), 443–459 (2012)
5. La Rosa, M., Wohed, P., Mendling, J., ter Hofstede, A., Reijers, H.A., van der Aalst, W.M.: Managing process model coplexity via abstact syntax modifications. IEEE Trans. Ind. Informatics. 7–4, 614–629 (2011)
6. Weber, B., Reichert, M., Mendling, J., Reijers, H.A.: Refactoring large process model repositories. Comput. Ind. 5–62, 467–486 (2011)
7. Reijers, H.A., Mendling, J., Dijkman, R.M.: Human and automatic modularizations of process models to enhance their comprehension. Inf. Syst. 5–36, 881–897 (2011)

8. Pritchard, J.P., Armistead, C.: Business process management - lessons from European business. Bus. Process Manag. J. (BPMJ). **1–5**, 10–35 (1999)
9. Armistead, C.: Principles of business process management. Emerald Manag. Rev. **6–6**, 48–52 (1996)
10. Malinova, M., Leopold, H., Mendling, J.: An Empirical Investigation on the Design of Process Architectures. Wirtschaftsinformatik, Leipzig (2013)
11. Dijkman, R.M., Vanderfeesten, I., Reijers, H.A.: The Road to a Business Process Architecture: An Overview of Approaches and their Use. Einhoven University of Technology, The Nederlands (2011)
12. Dumas, M., La Rosa, M., Mendling, J., Reijers, H.A.: Fundamentals of Business Process Management, pp. 42–43. Springer, Berlin (2013)
13. Lankhorst, M.: Enterprise Architecture at Work: Modelling, Communication and Analysis. Springer, Berlin (2009)
14. Davis, R.: Business Process Modelling with ARIS: A Practical Guide. Springer, London (2001)
15. Mendling, J.: Metrics for Process Models: Empirical Foundations of Verification, Error Prediction, and Guidelines for Correctness. LNBIP, vol. 6. Springer, Heidelberg (2008)
16. Smirnov, S., Reijers, H.A., Weske, M.: From fine-grained to abstract process models: a semantic approach. Inf. Syst. **8–37**, 784–797 (2012)
17. Kim, S., Wilbur, J.W.: Thematic clustering of text documents using an EM-based approach. J. Biomed. Semant. **3** (2012)
18. van Dongen, B.F., Dijkman, R., Mendling, J.: Measuring Similarity between Business Process Models. In: Bellahsène, Z., Léonard, M. (eds.) CAiSE 2008. LNCS, vol. 5074, pp. 450–464. Springer, Heidelberg (2008)
19. Dijkman, R.M., Dumas, M., van Dongen, B., Käärik, R., Mendling, J.: Similarity of business process models: metrics and evaluation. Inf. Syst. **2**, 498–516 (2011)
20. Wu, H.C., Luk, R.W.P., Wong, K.F., Kwok, K.L.: Interpreting tf-idf term weights as making relevance decisions. ACM Trans. Inf. Syst. **26**(3), 1–37 (2008)
21. Porter, M.: An algorithm for suffix stripping. Program **14**(3), 130–137 (1980)
22. Lloyd, S.P.: Least squares quantization in PCM. IEEE Trans. Inf. Theory. **28**(2), 129–137 (1982)
23. Wu, J., Xiong, H., Chen, J.: Adapting the right measures for k-means clustering. In: Proceedings of the 15th ACM SIGKDD International Conference on Knowledge Discovery and Data Mining (2009)
24. Xiong, H., Wu, J., Chen, J.: K-means clustering versus validation measures: a data-distribution perspective. IEEE Trans. Syst. Man Cybern. Part B Cybern. **39**(2), 318–331 (2009)
25. Huang, A.: Similarity measures for text document clustering. In: Proceedings of the 6th New Zealand Computer Science Research Student Conference (NZCSRSC2008), Christchurch. pp. 49–56 (2008)
26. Huang, A., Milne, D., Frank, E., Witten, I.H.: Clustering documents using a wikipedia-based concept representation. In: Theeramunkong, T., Kijsirikul, B., Cercone, N., Ho, T.-B. (eds.) PAKDD 2009. LNCS, vol. 5476, pp. 628–636. Springer, Heidelberg (2009)
27. Eid-Sabbagh, R.-H., Dijkman, R., Weske, M.: Business process architecture: use and correctness. In: Barros, A., Gal, A., Kindler, E. (eds.) BPM 2012. LNCS, vol. 7481, pp. 65–81. Springer, Heidelberg (2012)
28. Huang, Y.J., Powers, R., Montelione, G.T.: Protein NMR recall, precision, and F-measure scores (RPF scores): structure quality assessment measures based on information retrieval statistics. J. Am. Chem. Soc. **127**, 1665–1674 (2005)

Report: The Process Model Matching Contest 2013

Ugur Cayoglu[1]([⊠]), Remco Dijkman[2], Marlon Dumas[3], Peter Fettke[4,5],
Luciano García-Bañuelos[3], Philip Hake[4,5], Christopher Klinkmüller[6],
Henrik Leopold[7], André Ludwig[6], Peter Loos[4,5], Jan Mendling[8],
Andreas Oberweis[1], Andreas Schoknecht[1], Eitam Sheetrit[9], Tom Thaler[4,5],
Meike Ullrich[1], Ingo Weber[10,11], and Matthias Weidlich[9]

[1] Institute of AppliedInformatics and Formal Description Methods (AIFB),
Karlsruhe Institute of Technology (KIT), Karlsruhe, Germany
ugur.cayoglu@kit.edu
[2] Eindhoven University of Technology, Eindhoven, The Netherlands
r.m.dijkman@tue.nl
[3] University of Tartu, Tartu, Estonia
{marlon.dumas,luciano.garcia}@ut.ee
[4] Institute for Information Systems (IWi), DFKI, Saarbrücken, Germany
{Tom.Thaler,Philip.Hake,Peter.Fettke,Peter.Loos}@iwi.dfki.de
[5] Saarland University, Saarbrücken, Germany
[6] Information Systems Institute, University of Leipzig, Leipzig, Germany
{klinkmueller,ludwig}@wifa.uni-leipzig.de
[7] Humboldt-Universität zu Berlin, Arcata, Germany
henrik.leopold@wiwi.hu-berlin.de
[8] Wirtschaftsuniversität Wien, Vienna, Austria
jan.mendling@wu.ac.at
[9] Technion - Israel Institute of Technology, Haifa, Israel
{eitams,weidlich}@tx.technion.ac.il
[10] Software Systems Research Group, NICTA, Sydney, Australia
ingo.weber@nicta.com.au
[11] School of Computer Science & Engineering, University of New South Wales,
Kensington, Australia

Abstract. Process model matching refers to the creation of correspondences between activities of process models. Applications of process model matching are manifold, reaching from model validation over harmonization of process variants to effective management of process model collections. Recently, this demand led to the development of different techniques for process model matching. Yet, these techniques are heuristics and, thus, their results are inherently uncertain and need to be evaluated on a common basis. Currently, however, the BPM community lacks established data sets and frameworks for evaluation. The Process Model Matching Contest 2013 aimed at addressing the need for effective evaluation by defining process model matching problems over published data sets.

This paper summarizes the setup and the results of the contest. Besides a description of the contest matching problems, the paper comprises short descriptions of all matching techniques that have been

N. Lohmann et al. (Eds.): BPM 2013 Workshops, LNBIP 171, pp. 442–463, 2014.
DOI: 10.1007/978-3-319-06257-0_35, © Springer International Publishing Switzerland 2014

submitted for participation. In addition, we present and discuss the evaluation results and outline directions for future work in this field of research

Keywords: Process matching · Model alignment · Contest · Matching evaluation

1   Introduction

Business process models allow for managing the lifecycle of a business process, from its identification over its analysis, design, implementation, and monitoring [1]. A process model captures the activities of a business process along with their execution dependencies. Process model matching is concerned with supporting the creation of an alignment between process models, i.e., the identification of correspondences between their activities.

In recent years, many techniques building on process model matching have been proposed. Examples include techniques for the validation of a technical implementation of a business process against a business-centered specification model [2], delta-analysis of process implementations and a reference model [3], harmonization of process variants [4,5], process model search [6–8], and clone detection [9]. Inspired by the field of schema matching and ontology alignment, cf., [10,11], this demand led to the development of different techniques for process model matching. Yet, these techniques are heuristics and, thus, their results are inherently uncertain and need to be evaluated on a common basis. Currently, the BPM community lacks established data sets and frameworks for evaluation.

In this paper, we report on the setup and results of the Process Model Matching Contest 2013. It was organized as part of the 4th International Workshop on Process Model Collections: Management and Reuse (PMC-RM 13) that took place on August 26, 2013, at the 11th International Conference on Business Process Management in Beijing, China. The Contest Co-Chairs were Henrik Leopold and Matthias Weidlich.

The Process Model Matching Contest (PMMC) 2013 addresses the need for effective evaluation of process model matching techniques. The main goal of the PMMC is the comparative analysis of the results of different techniques. By doing so, it further aims at providing an angle to assess strengths and weaknesses of particular techniques and at outlining directions for improving process model matching. Inspired by the Ontology Alignment Evaluation Initiative (OAEI)[1], the PMMC was organized as a controlled, experimental evaluation. Two process model matching problems were defined and published with respective data sets. Then, participants were asked to send in their result files with the identified correspondences along with a short description of the matching technique. The evaluation of these results was conducted by the Contest Co-Chairs.

There have been seven submission to the contest covering diverse techniques for addressing the problem of process model matching. All submissions provided

---

[1] http://oaei.ontologymatching.org

U. Cayoglu et al.

reasonable results and could, therefore, be included in the evaluation and this paper. For each submitted matching technique, this paper contains an overview of the matching approach, details on the specific techniques applied, and pointers to related implementations and evaluations.

We are glad that the contest attracted interest and submissions from a variety of research groups. We would like to thank all of them for their participation.

The remainder of this paper is structured as follows. The next section gives details on the process model matching problems of the PMMC 2013. Section 3 features the short descriptions of the submitted matching approaches. Section 4 presents the evaluation results. Based on these results, Sect. 5 outlines directions for future work in process model matching before Sect. 6 concludes the paper.

2   Data Sets

The contest includes two sets of process model matching problems:

- **University Admission Processes (UA):** This set contains process models representing the admission processes of nine German universities. All models contain English text only. The models have been created by different modelers using varying terminology and capturing activities at different levels of granularity. All models are available as Petri-nets in the PNML format and shall be matched pairwise. Further, for eight out of the 36 model pairs, we also provide a gold standard alignment for initial evaluation.
- **Birth Registration Processes (BR):** This set comprises nine models of birth registration processes in Germany, Russia, South Africa, and the Netherlands. Four models were created by graduate students at the HU Berlin and five of the models stem from a process analysis in Dutch municipalities. Again, all models contain only English text, are available as Petri-nets in the PNML format, and shall be matched pairwise to obtain 36 alignments.

Table 1 gives an overview of the main characteristics of the two data sets. In addition to the minimum, maximum, and average number of labeled transitions per model, it shows the total and average number of simple and complex

Table 1. Characteristics of test data sets

Characteristic	UA	BR
No. of labeled Transitions (min)	11	9
No. of labeled Transitions (max)	44	25
No. of labeled Transitions (avg)	22	17.9
No. of 1:1 Correspondences (total)	345	348
No. of 1:1 Correspondences (avg)	9.6	9.7
No. of 1:n Correspondences (total)	83	171
No. of 1:n Correspondences (avg)	2.3	4.75

correspondences. From the numbers, we can learn that both model sets particularly differ with regard to the number of complex correspondences. While the admission models only contain an average of 2.3 complex correspondences per model, the birth certificate models contain 4.75. Consequently, we expect the birth certificate set to represent the more challenging sample.

3   Matching Approaches

In this section, we give an overview of the participating process model matching approaches. In total, seven matching techniques participated in the process model matching contest. Table 2 gives an overview of the participating approaches and the respective authors. In the following subsections, we provide a brief technical overview of each matching approach.

Table 2. Overview of participating approaches

No.	Approach	Authors
1	Triple-S: A Matching Approach for Petri Nets on Syntactic, Semantic and Structural Level	Cayoglu, Oberweis, Schoknecht, Ullrich
2	Business Process Graph Matching	Dijkman, Dumas, García-Bañuelos
3	RefMod-Mine/NSCM - N-Ary Semantic Cluster Matching	Thaler, Hake, Fettke, Loos
4	RefMod-Mine/ESGM - Extended Semantic Greedy Matching	Hake, Thaler, Fettke, Loos
5	Bag-of-Words Similarity with Label Pruning	Klinkmüller, Weber, Mendling, Leopold, Ludwig
6	PMLM - Process Matching Using Positional Language Models	Weidlich, Sheetrit
7	The ICoP Framework: Identification of Correspondences between Process Models	Weidlich, Dijkman, Mendling

3.1   Triple-S: A Matching Approach for Petri Nets on Syntactic, Semantic and Structural Level

Overview. So far, a handful contributions have been made to the problem of process model matching. The Triple-S matching approach adheres to the KISS principle by avoiding complexity and *keeping it simple and stupid*. It combines similarity scores of independent levels as basis for a well-founded decision about matching transition pairs of different process models. The following three levels and scores are considered:

- **Syntactic level - $SIM_{syn}(a,b)$:** For the syntactic analysis of transition labels we perform two preprocessing steps: (1) tokenization and (2) stop word elimination. The actual analysis is based on the calculation of Levenshtein distances between each combination of tokens (i.e. words) from the labels of transitions a and b. The final syntactic score is the minimum distance over all tokens divided by the number of tokens, i.e. the minimum average distance between each token.
- **Semantic level - $SIM_{sem}(a,b)$:** Prior to analysis, we perform the same preprocessing steps as above mentioned. Subsequently, we apply the approach of Wu & Palmer [12] to calculate the semantic similarity between each token of labels of transitions a and b based on path length between the corresponding concepts. The final semantic score is the maximum average similarity, i.e. it is calculated in an analogous manner to the final syntactic score.
- **Structural level - $SIM_{sem}(a,b)$:** Here, we investigate the similarity of transitions a and b through a comparison of (i) the ratio of their in- and outgoing arcs and (ii) their relative position in the complete net.

These three scores are combined to the final score $SIM_{total}(a,b)$ which represents the matching degree between two transitions a and b from different process models. It is calculated according to the following formula:

$$SIM_{total}(a,b) = \omega_1 * SIM_{syn}(a,b) + \omega_2 * SIM_{sem}(a,b) + \omega_3 * SIM_{struc}(a,b)$$

The three parameters ω_1, ω_2 and ω_3 define the weight of each similarity level. A threshold value θ is used to determine whether transitions actually match, i.e. iff $SIM_{total} \geq \theta$, two transitions positively match.

Specific Techniques. Compared to [13], the Triple-S approach makes several adjustments. Firstly, stop words are eliminated and the Levenshtein distance is calculated on the level of single tokens instead of complete sentences. Secondly, for the semantic level an established NLP approach is introduced. Finally, on the structural level TripleS performs contextual analysis by investigating local similarity only.

Implementation. The Triple-S approach has been implemented using Java. For the calculation of the semantic score with the approach of Wu & Palmer, the *WS4J Java API*[2] has been used to query Princeton's English *WordNet* 3.0 lexical database [14]. Relative positions of transitions are calculated using the implementation of Dijkstra's algorithm by Vogella[3]. The code can be obtained from http://code.google.com/p/bpmodelmatching/wiki/Download?tm=4 under *GNU GPL v3* license.

---

[2] https://code.google.com/p/ws4j/
[3] http://www.vogella.com/articles/JavaAlgorithmsDijkstra/article.html

Evaluations. During our experiments we tried to approximate optimal results based on the gold standard examples. For the contest, we have used the following values: $\omega_1 = 0.45$, $\omega_2 = 0.3$, $\omega_3 = 0.25$ and $\theta = 0.6$. The Triple-S approach is currently developed as part of the ongoing SemReuse research project addressing business process model reuse. This contest on business process similarity presents a welcome possibility for first experiments. We are planning on refining the current measures for the individual levels, especially the semantic and structural level and improved detection of 1:n matches.

3.2   Business Process Graph Matching

Overview. Business process graph matching works by considering a business process as a labeled graph, wherein nodes correspond to tasks, events or gateways, and edges capture the flow of control between nodes in the process. Nodes are generally assumed to have a label, although gateways may be unlabeled.

Graph matching aims at computing a mapping between the nodes in the input graphs. In its most common form, the mapping relates one node in a graph to at most one node in the another graph (partial inductive mapping). The mapping induces a distance between the two graphs, which is usually calculated by adding the following components:

- the number of inserted nodes: nodes that appear in one graph, but not in the other (i.e.: nodes that are not part of the mapping);
- the sum of the distances between nodes that *are* part of the mapping based on their labels (e.g.: the nodes labeled 'receive request' and 'receiving request' are closer than the nodes labeled 'receive request' and 'reject request'); and
- the number of inserted edges: edges that appear in one graph, but not in the other.

The goal of a typical graph matching algorithm is to find the mapping with the smallest possible distance, also called as the graph-edit distance [15]. This is a computationally complex problem, because the space of possible mappings that need to be explored. Thus in practice, some pruning technique must be employed.

Specific Techniques. Graph matching algorithm can primarily be varied with respect to two points. The first variation point is the metric that is used for computing the weight of mapped nodes. The second variation point is the algorithm that is used to explore the space of possible mappings.

The two main classes of metrics to compute the weight of mapped nodes are syntactic metrics and semantic metrics. Syntactic metrics look at the label as a string of characters. For example, a typical syntactic metric between two labels is string-edit distance, which is the minimum number of character insertions, deletions and substitutions that must be performed to transform one string into another. Semantic metrics treat the label as a list or bag of words. A typical semantic similarity metric is based on matching the words of two given labels and defining a distance based on this matching. Words that are closer semantically (e.g. they are synonyms or share a hypernym) are more likely to be matched. The number of matches found and the strength of the matches then determines the similarity between the labels. Additional tweaks may be applied to deal with unlabeled nodes such as gateways.

Several algorithms can be envisioned to explore the space of possible mappings between two business process graphs. One is a greedy algorithm that, in each iteration, adds a mapping between two nodes that decreases the distance the most, until no such mapping can be found anymore. Another is based on search of the space of mappings based on the so-called A-star heuristics. We have investigated these alternatives in a number of papers [16,17].

Implementation. The graph matching approach to business process matching has been implemented both as part of the ICoP framework [18] and as part of version 5 of the tool ProM[4]. ProM is open source. ICoP is available on request. The tool uses WordNet to compute the semantic weights of node mappings.

Evaluations. We have evaluated several graph matching techniques on a collection of models extracted from the SAP R/3 reference model. The extracted collection consists of 100 so-called "document" models that simulate a repository of process models, and 10 so-called "query" models that simulate business process graphs that a user would be looking for. The goal is, given a query model, to rank the document models according to their similarity to the query model.

In this experiment, the aim was to test how close different techniques correspond to the "perceived similarity" of models as determined by a golden standard. The golden standard was constructed by asking a number of individuals to rate the similarity between pairs of process models in the collection (query model, document model) on a scale of 1 to 7.

In this respect, we found that a technique based on A-star achieves a higher mean average precision, which is a measure of ranking accuracy commonly used in information retrieval. The greedy algorithm comes relatively close to the A-star algorithm, while being faster.

3.3 RefMod-Mine/NSCM - N-Ary Semantic Cluster Matching

Overview. The approach for clustering business process model nodes consists of four components which are executed sequentially. First of all it conducts a *semantic error detection (1)*, where defects of modeling are being identified and automatically handled. After that, it uses all models as input for an *n-ary cluster matcher (2)*, which uses a *semantic similarity measure (3)* for pairwise node comparison. As a result of that cluster matching we get a set of clusters containing nodes of all considered models, which are being *extracted* to *binary complex matchings (4)*.

---

[4] http://www.processmining.org

Specific Techniques. *Semantic error detection.* While analyzing different business process models, we recognized the existence of model failures which leads to a misinterpretation of nodes during a process matching. Against that background, the main function of semantic error detection is the identification of wrong modeled transition nodes. Since the algorithm as well as the gold standard only matches transitions, this functionality checks whether the label suggests a node being a place or confirms it being a transition. Therefore the form and order of nouns and verbs of a label are being analyzed, which leads to the applicability only to English language models. The identified transitions are being marked as "ignore" and will not be considered in the following matching components.

N-Ary cluster matching. In contrast to existing matching techniques, the authors use an n-ary clustering instead of a binary matching. The nodes of all models are being pairwise compared using a semantic similarity measure. Since the cluster algorithm is agglomerative [1], it starts with clusters of size 1 (= transitions) and consolidates two transitions to a cluster if their similarity value passes a user-defined threshold. If two nodes are being clustered and both are already part of different clusters, the two clusters are being merged. Thus, the resulting clusters are hard and not fuzzy [19].

Semantic similarity measure. The used similarity measure consists of three phases. The first phase splits node labels L into single words w_{i_L}, so that $split(L) = \{w_{1_L}, ..., w_{n_L}\}$. Stop words, like *the, is, at* as well as waste characters like additional spaces are being removed. The second phase computes the Porter Stem [20] $stem(w_{i_L})$ for each word and compares the stem sets of both labels. The number of stem matchings is being divided by the sum of all words.

$$sim(L_1, L_2) = \frac{|\{stem(w_{1_{L_1}}), ..., stem(w_{n_{L_1}})\} \cap \{stem(w_{1_{L_2}}), ..., stem(w_{m_{L_2}})\}|}{|split(L_1) + split(L_2)|}$$

If the resulting similarity value passes a user-defined threshold, the third phase checks the labels for antonyms using the lexical database WordNet [21] and checking the occurrence of negation words like not. Thus, that phase decides the similarity being 0 or $sim(L_1, L_2)$.

Binary matching extraction. The last component extracts binary matchings from the node clusters calculated by the n-ary cluster matcher. For each model pair all clusters are being scanned for the occurrence of nodes of both models. The containing node set of the first model is then being matched to the node set of the second model. Thus, the component returns a binary complex (N:M) matching for each model pair.

Implementation. The mentioned technique has been implemented in form of a php command line tool and can publicly checked out[5]. Next to the n-ary semantic cluster matching and other matching techniques, the research prototype is able to calculate node and process similarities from recent literature as well as analyzing models and matchings.

---

[5] https://refmodmine.googlecode.com/svn

Evaluations. To evaluate the approach, the authors analyzed the precision and recall values in case of the delivered admission models with the corresponding gold standard. After justifying the algorithm, the results leaded to a precision of 67 % and a recall of 34 %. Thereby, the threshold for semantic similarity was set to 60 %.

3.4 RefMod-Mine/ESGM - Extended Semantic Greedy Matching

Overview. In a first attempt dealing with the matching problem, a greedy matching [17] was implemented and evaluated based on precision and recall. Though a considerably high precision is achieved by this approach, only a low degree of recall is reached due to neglect of potential complex matches. To attain a higher recall and meet the demands of complex matches, the approach is extended.

The approach introduced here matches business process models pair-wisely based on the similarities of the process models' transitions. The result of the matching algorithm is a set of complex (N:M) transition matches between two process models. The matching is subdivided into three steps.

In the first step, a *pre-processing* of data is applied to the models. The second step consists in computing the similarity of all potential 1:1 transition matches of two models using a *word matching* technique. In a final step, a *heuristic grouping* of similar transitions from step 2 is conducted.

Specific Techniques. *Pre-Processing.* While evaluating precision and recall, the authors noticed that some transitions which seemed to represent process events rather than activities, had not been matched with regard to the gold-standard. Hence one step of the pre-processing is a heuristic filter which excludes such transitions from further matching steps.

Moreover, the labels of the transitions are split up into word sets according to split characters like whitespace or hyphen. After all non-word characters[6] have been removed from the word sets, stop words like *to*, *the*, and *is* are removed from the word sets.

Word Matching. Unlike most approaches, the computation of the transitions' similarity is accomplished applying the greedy matching technique [17] on business process models to transition labels. Therefore, at first, the similarity of the words of two labels is determined.

The computation of the similarity score sim_w of two words is based on dictionary lookups and a syntactic similarity measure [16]. In case the words represent synonyms or it exists a nominalization of one word that is synonymic to the other or vice versa, they receive a similarity score of 1. If the words or their nominalizations are considered antonyms, a similarity score of -1 is returned, otherwise they receive a syntactic similarity score based on Levenshtein's edit distance.

Let L be a label of Transition T that belongs to process model M and W a set of words of a label L. $sim_w(w_1, w_2)$ denotes the similarity of two words

---

[6] http://docs.oracle.com/javase/1.4.2/docs/api/java/util/regex/Pattern.html

$w_1 \in W_1$ and $w_2 \in W_2$. Furthermore, let $M_W : W_1 \rightarrow W_2$ be a partial injective mapping on the word sets W_1, W_2. Then $sim_L(L_1, L_2)$ denotes the similarity of two labels L_1, L_2.

$$sim_L(L_1, L_2) = \frac{\sum_{(w_1,w_2) \in M_W} sim_w(w_1, w_2)}{max(|W_1|, |W_2|)} \tag{1}$$

Heuristic Grouping. The subsequent grouping of transitions consists in adding all pairs which do not fall below a predefined similarity threshold t to the result. The following rules depict the heuristic grouping technique.

Let G be a set of transitions representing a group of transitions. Given a pair of transitions (T_1, T_2), which satisfies the threshold criterion $(sim_L(L_i, L_j) \geq t)$, a new group $G = \{T_1, T_2\}$ is added to the result set if neither T_1 nor T_2 belongs to any group. In case only one transition, either T_1 or T_2, is not represented in any group, this transition is added to the group the other transition belongs to. If T_1 belongs to group G_i and T_2 to group G_j, the groups G_i, G_j are replaced by the new group $G_n = G_i \cup G_j$.

Implementation. The matching approach is implemented in Java (jre6) and is embedded in RefMod-Mine, which is a tool set dedicated to the mining of reference models. The computation of the labels similarity largely relies on dictionary lookups. The underlying dictionary is the WordNet [21] database (v 3.0) and it is accessed via the RiTa.WordNet Java/Javascript API[7], which is free and open-source licensed under GPL.

Evaluations. The approach has been evaluated based on the partial gold standard provided. Therefore, the threshold for the grouping was set to 65 %.

3.5 Bag-of-Words Similarity with Label Pruning

Overview. The approach to process model matching discussed here is a subset of our previous paper [22]. While we explored various options before, herein we focus on the matching strategy that provided the most significant increase in match quality in our experiments. This technique solely considers activity labels, disregarding other information present in the process models such as events, process structure or behavior.

In a nutshell, the approach computes label similarity by (i) treating each label as a *bag of words* (a multi-set of words), (ii) applying word stemming (to transform, e.g., "evaluating" into "evaluate") for better comparability, (iii) computing the similarity scores as per Levenshtein [23] and Lin [24] for each pair of words, (iv) pruning the multi-sets for both activity labels under comparison to be equal in the number of words, (v) computing an overall matching score for each activity pair, and (vi) selecting all activity pairs whose score is above a given threshold.

---

[7] RiTa.WordNet, http://www.rednoise.org/rita/wordnet/documentation/

Specific Techniques. For a detailed introduction of the overall approach we refer the reader to [22]. In the following we explain specific aspects of it and the configuration used in this paper.

One characteristic of the bag-of-words similarity is that it neglects the grammatical structure of the label. This is in contrast to [25] where the individual words of the labels are assigned with types; and words will only be compared if they belong to the same type. The rationale for neglecting label structure is that the brevity of labels makes it hard to deduce information like word forms. In this way, the bag-of-words similarity aims to offer a means to find matches like "reject applicant" vs. "send letter of rejection".

Furthermore, in case the two bags-of-words under comparison are different in size, the larger one is pruned to the size of the smaller one. Therefore, words with a small similarity score are removed from the larger set. This is done to better capture activity labels with a strong difference in specificity. For instance, "rank case" vs. "rank application on scale of 1 to 10" may have a very low average word similarity as the second label also contains information about a condition not present in the first label.

Finally, the decision to rely on a syntactical (Levenshtein) as well as a semantic (Lin) word similarity notion tries to lessen the weaknesses of both notions. While syntactical notions cannot account for a strong conceptual similarity of two words, a semantic notion struggles when spelling errors are present. However, there are still cases where this combination struggles.

Implementation. The technique is implemented in Java and part of the *Process Model Matching Tools for Java* (jpmmt)-project which aims at providing algorithms and measures for process model matching. The project is publicly available[8] under the terms of the MIT License[9].

Evaluations. In [22] we evaluated various configurations of the bag-of-words similarity with label pruning and its basic variant the bag-of-words similarity. These configurations included different pruning criteria and word similarity functions. In order to achieve comparability, we used the data set from [25] which includes the university admission processes and the corresponding matching standard also part of the data set of this matching contest. The evaluation showed that the technique has the potential to increase recall of process model matching compared to results yielded by the approaches introduced in [18, 25].

Furthermore, we applied the technique in the context of *Business Process Querying* (BPQ). In [26] an approach to BPQ is presented that decomposes a BPMN-Q query [27] into a set of sub-queries. For these sub-queries corresponding process model fragments are determined within a process collection. Finally, these fragments are aggregated in order to provide a list of process model fragments that provide answers to the whole query. Our technique constitutes the

---

[8] http://code.google.com/p/jpmmt/
[9] http://opensource.org/licenses/mit-license.php

base for an extension of this approach. Instead of relying on 1:1 matches for the activities in the query this assumption is relaxed and more complex matching constellations are allowed. An evaluation which also relies on the university admission processes shows that the technique in combination with the approach from [26] yields promising results. However, the size of the collection and queries is relatively small, and further experiments need to be conducted.

3.6 PMLM - Process Matching Using Positional Language Model

Overview. This matching technique is tailored towards process models that feature textual descriptions of activities, introduced in detail in [28]. Using ideas from language modeling in Information Retrieval, the approach leverages those descriptions to identify correspondences between activities. More precisely, we combine two different streams of work on probabilistic language modeling. First, we adopt passage-based modeling such that activities are passages of a document representing a process model. Second, we consider structural features of process models by positional language modeling. While using those probabilistic language models, we create a similarity matrix between the activities and derive correspondences using second line matching.

Specific Techniques. *Activities as Passages.* Let $\mathcal{T}$ be a corpus of terms. For a process model P, we create a document $d = \langle T_1, \ldots, T_n \rangle$ as a sequence of length $n \in \mathbb{N}$ of passages, where each passage is a set of terms $d(i) = T \subseteq \mathcal{T}, 1 \leq i \leq n$. The set $d(i) = T$ comprises all terms that occur in the label or description of the activity at position i. The length of d is denoted by $|d|$. We denote by $\mathcal{D}$ a set of processes, represented as documents.

Our model is built on a cardinality function $c : (\mathcal{T} \times \mathcal{D} \times \mathbb{N}) \rightarrow \{0,1\}$, such that $c(t, d, i) = 1$ if $t \in T = d(i)$ (term t occurs in the i-th passage of d) and $c(t, d, i) = 0$ otherwise. To realize term propagation to close-by positions, a proximity-based density function $k : (\mathbb{N} \times \mathbb{N}) \rightarrow [0, 1]$ is used to assign a discounting factor to pairs of positions. Then, $k(i, j)$ represents how much of the occurrence of a term at position j is propagated to position i. We rely on the Gaussian Kernel $k^g(i, j) = e^{(-(i-j)^2)/(2\sigma^2)}$, defined with a spread parameter $\sigma \in \mathbb{R}^+$ [29]. Adapting function c with term propagation, we obtain a function $c' : (\mathcal{T} \times \mathcal{D} \times \mathbb{N}) \rightarrow [0, 1]$, such that $c'(t, d, i) = \sum_{j=1}^{n} c(t, d, j) \cdot k^g(i, j)$. Then, our positional, passage-based language model $p(t|d, i)$ captures the probability of term t occurring in the i-th passage of document d ($\mu \in \mathbb{R}$, $\mu > 0$, is a weighting factor):

$$p_\mu(t|d, i) = \frac{c'(t, d, i) + \mu \cdot p(t|d)}{\sum_{t' \in \mathcal{T}} c'(t', d, i) + \mu}. \tag{2}$$

Derivation of Passage Positions. To instantiate the positional language model for process models, we need to specify how to order the passages in the document to represent the order of activities in a process. In this matching contest, we chose to use a Breadth-First Traversal over the process model graph starting from an initial activity that creates the process instance (we insert a dummy node connect to all initial activities if needed).

Similarity of Language Models. Using the language models, we measure the similarity for document positions and, thus, activities of the process models, with the Jensen-Shannon divergence (JSD) [30]. Let $p_\mu(t|d, i)$ and $p_\mu(t|d', j)$ be the smoothed language models of two process model documents. Then, the probabilistic divergence of position i in d with position j in d' is:

$$jsd(d, d', i, j) = \frac{1}{2} \sum_{t \in T} p_\mu(t|d, i) \lg \frac{p_\mu(t|d, i)}{p^+(t)} + \frac{1}{2} \sum_{t \in T} p_\mu(t|d', j) \lg \frac{p_\mu(t|d', j)}{p^+(t)} \quad (3)$$

$$\text{with} \quad p^+(t) = \frac{1}{2}(p_\mu(t|d, i) + p_\mu(t|d', j))$$

When using the binary logarithm, the JSD is bound to the unit interval $[0, 1]$, so that $sim(d, d', i, j) = 1 - jsd(d, d', i, j)$ can be used as a similarity measure.

Derivation of Correspondences. Finally, we derive correspondences from a similarity matrix over activities, which is known as second line matching. Here, we rely on two strategies, i.e., *dominants* and *top-k*, see [31]. The former selects pairs of activities that share the maximum similarity value in their row and column in the similarity matrix. The latter selects for each activity in one model, the k activities of the other process that have the highest similarity values.

Implementation. The application was built in C#, and uses the Lemur ToolKit for stemming terms, and calculating the probability of each term to be relevant given a certain passage and position in a document. In our implementation, we first read the XML files representing the process models, transform each element into an object according to its type (transition, place or arc) and order the transitions. In the first phase, we create an ordered document containing only the activity labels (with no propagation), create a similarity matrix using the Lemur ToolKit and find correspondences using *dominants* approach. In the second phase, we create another ordered document with activity labels, descriptions and term propagation, create a similarity matrix using the Lemur ToolKit and find correspondences using *top-3* approach. Finally, we choose matches according to the *dominants* result and add the selected *top-3* if their similarity score is no less then 80 % of the highest similarity value in their row.

The implementation is still in development stage, so for the time being it is not available for a public use.

Evaluations. We conducted experiments with several real-world model collections. First, we used models from the Bank of Northeast of Brazil (BNB) that capture business processes on three levels: business perspective, technical perspective, or executable process specification, also used in [2]. Second, we used models from an electronics company and from municipalities in the Netherlands, described and used for evaluation in [32]. All sets include textual annotations for at least some of the activities. Our results indicate that this matching technique is geared towards high recall, increasing it up to a factor of 5 over existing work [28]. While average precision is rather low, we observe k-precision values (k-precision extends precision to top-k lists, where a match is a top-k list where a correct pair is found) above 60 %. Hence, correct correspondences can be extracted by an expert with reasonable effort, thereby supporting semi-automated matching.

3.7   The ICoP Framework: Identification of Correspondences between Process Models

Overview. The ICoP framework [32] aims at solving the problem of matching process models with a particular focus on complex correspondences that are defined between sets of activities instead of single activities. Towards this end, the framework proposes an architecture and a set of re-usable components for assembling concrete matchers.

The ICoP architecture defines process model matching as a multi-step approach involving four different types of components.

Searchers try to cope with the combinatorial challenges induced by potentially complex correspondences by applying heuristics to search the space of possible matches. Here, different strategies are first applied for group activities and, second, for assessing the similarity of these groups of activities. Searchers return a set of candidate correspondences with assigned confidence scores.

Boosters aggregate candidate correspondences and adapt their scores. On the one hand, the multiset of matches returned by the searchers is aggregated to obtain a set of candidate correspondences. Also, scores are adapted, e.g., based on subsumption of candidate correspondences.

Selectors build up the actual final set of correspondences from the set of candidate correspondences, by selecting the best candidates that are non-overlapping in their sets of activities. Here, selection is guided by the scores of the candidates as well as an evaluation score computed by an evaluator (see below). Then, selection of correspondences is done iteratively. Yet, exhaustive search for the best selection is typically not possible, so that a greedy strategy or an approach with a certain lookahead is followed.

Evaluators assign a score to a set of correspondences. Computation of this score is typically based on the original process models, such that the consistency of certain structural or behavioural properties of the process models under the given correspondences is assessed.

In addition to this architecture, the ICoP framework provides different implementations of these four components that may be used to assemble matchers. Examples include searchers that rely on vector space scoring, different aggregation boosters, evaluators based on the graph edit distance, and selectors that implement different strategies for combining scores of individual candidates and the evaluation scores for sets of correspondences.

Specific Techniques. We want to highlight two specific techniques that are used in components of the ICoP framework:

Virtual Document Searchers. Searchers implement heuristics to first group activities in either process model and then assess the similarity of these groups to derive candidate correspondences. Given a set of activities groups in either model (e.g., derived based on proximity in terms of graph distance or by structural decomposition), searchers in the ICoP framework exploit virtual documents for similarity assessment. Here, the notion of a virtual document is inspired by work on ontology alignment [33] where a virtual document of a node consists of all textual information in an ontology that is related to that node. Then, two virtual documents are scored based their Cosine similarity in a vector space that is spanned by the terms that appear in the documents. In the ICoP searchers, a virtual document for a group of activities consists of the terms of the activity label and any additional textual information related to the activity, such as an activity description, data input and output artefacts, and names and descriptions of related roles and information systems. Combined with common techniques from information retrieval, e.g., stop-word filtering and term-frequency based weighting, this technique provides a means to consider not only activity labels, but a broad spectrum of textual information related to an activity for the matching.

Execution Semantics Evaluator. An evaluator scores a set of correspondences, typically based on the original process models. The ICoP framework defines an evaluator that exploits the execution semantics of the process models for scoring a set of correspondences. To this end, it relies on the relations of the behavioural profile of a process model, cf., [34]. Such a profile abstracts trace semantics of a process by a set of binary behavioural relations defined over its activities: two activities are ordered (if one can occur before the other but not vice versa), exclusive (if they cannot occur jointly in an execution sequence), or interleaved (if they can occur in either order). This information is used for assigning a score to a set of correspondences by checking for each pairs of activities of distinct correspondences in one model, whether their behavioural relation is mirrored by all the corresponding activities in the other model. Then, the ratio of consistent pairs and all investigated pairs provides us with a score that captures the extent to which the behavioural characteristics of one model are preserved in the other model under the given correspondences.

Implementation. The ICoP framework has been implemented in Java and is available upon request from the authors of [32]. Currently, process models are expected to be given as Petri nets in the PNML format.

A major revision of the framework is under way. By building upon the jBPT library [35], this new implementation will support a broader class of process model descriptions and serialization formats.

Evaluations. The ICoP framework has been designed with a particular focus on the identification of complex correspondences. An evaluation of the framework can be found in [32]. It illustrates that the ICoP architecture allows for the creation of matchers that find a significant share of complex correspondences. Yet, it also shows that a certain homogeneity of the process model vocabulary is required for the identification of complex correspondences.

4 Results

For assessing the submitted process model matching techniques, we compare the computed matches against a manually created gold standard. Using the gold standard, we classify each computed activity match as either true-positive (TP), true-negative (TN), false-positive (FP) or false-negative (FN). Based on this classification, we calculate the precision (TP/(TP+FP)), the recall (TP/(TP+FN)), and the f-measure, which is the harmonic mean of precision and recall (2*precision*recall/(precision+recall)). Table 3 gives an overview of the results for the university admission data set and Table 4 presents the results for the birth certificate data set. For getting a better understanding of the result details, we report the average (AVG) and the standard deviation (STD) for each metric. The highest value for each metric is marked using bold font.

Table 3. Results of university admission matching

No.	Approach	Precision		Recall		F-Measure	
		AVG	STD	AVG	STD	AVG	STD
1	Triple-S	0.31	0.19	0.36	0.26	0.33	0.12
2	BP Graph Matching	**0.60**	0.45	0.19	0.30	0.29	0.29
3	RefMod-Mine/NSCM	0.37	0.22	0.39	0.27	0.38	0.19
4	RefMod-Mine/ESGM	0.16	0.26	0.12	0.21	0.14	0.17
5	Bag-of-Words Similarity	0.56	0.23	0.32	0.28	**0.41**	0.20
6	PMLM	0.12	0.05	**0.58**	0.20	0.20	0.08
7	ICoP	0.36	0.24	0.37	0.26	0.36	0.23

Table 4. Results of birth certificate matching

No.	Approach	Precision		Recall		F-Measure	
		AVG	STD	AVG	STD	AVG	STD
1	Triple-S	0.19	0.21	0.25	0.33	0.22	0.23
2	BP Graph Matching	0.55	0.48	0.19	0.28	0.28	0.30
3	RefMod-Mine/NSCM	**0.68**	0.19	0.33	0.22	**0.45**	0.18
4	RefMod-Mine/ESGM	0.25	0.28	0.18	0.26	0.21	0.23
5	Bag-of-Words Similarity	0.29	0.35	0.22	0.30	0.25	0.31
6	PMLM	0.19	0.09	**0.60**	0.20	0.29	0.12
7	ICoP	0.42	0.27	0.28	0.23	0.33	0.24

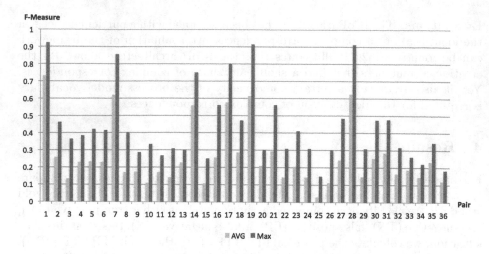

Fig. 1. Detailed results of admission data set

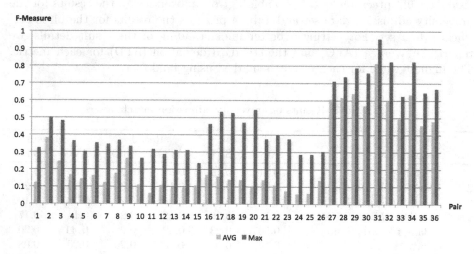

Fig. 2. Detailed results of birth certificate data set

From the results presented in Table 3 and Table 4, we can draw the following conclusions. Most importantly, it has to be noted there is no clear winner. As the employed data sets are different with respect to characteristics such as the number of complex correspondences and the linguistic consistency, different capabilities are required to come up with a good matching result. Apparently, no technique can perfectly deal with both data sets. However, there are a couple of interesting observations.

Focussing on the f-measure, the bag-of-words similarity approach yields the best result for the university admission set (0.41) and the RefMod-Mine/NSCM approach yields the best result for the birth certificate set (0.45). However, it should be noted that the RefMod-Mine/NSCM approach is quite close to the f-measure of the bag-of-words similarity approach for the university admission set (0.38) while the bag-of-words approach has a rather average result quality for the birth certificate models (0.25). Interestingly, the best f-measure is not necessarily associated with the best recall and precision. The PMLM approach yields the best recall (0.60 and 0.58) for both sets. Nevertheless, due to its rather low precision, it only yields average f-measures. The opposite situation can be observed for the BP Graph Matching approach. While it has rather low recall values, it yields top precision values (0.48 and 0.60). Apparently, the trade-off between precision and recall is still a major issue in the context of process model matching.

Looking at the standard deviation, we can see that many approaches suffer from quite unstable results. A detailed consideration of the results for individual model pairs reveals that there are some model pairs that are matched well, while others represent a considerable challenge for all participating techniques. Figures 1 and 2 illustrate this fact by showing the average and maximum f-measure among all techniques for each matching pair. In the admission set, we observe particular high results for the pairs 1,7, 14, 17, 19, and 28. The pairs 25 and 36 apparently represent complex matching problems. For the birth certificate data set, we observe a quite similar constellation. While the techniques yield good results for the pairs 31, 32, and 34, they fail to adequately match the pairs 10 and 15. Having a closer look into these extreme cases, we can identify two main characteristics that influence the result quality for a matching pair: the similarity of labels and the number of complex matches.

The more *similar* the labels of the matching pair, the better the matching result. By contrast, if many business objects are different or even missing, the identification of the matches may represent a serious challenge. As example, consider the match between *Checking if complete* and *Check documents*. Here, the rather unspecific verb *check* is the only connection between the labels. The second characteristic indicating the hardness of the matching challenge is the *the number of complex matches*. As such matches often require a semantic grouping of activities, their identification is a complicated and error-prone task. The identification of complex matches is often further aggravated by the fact that the connection between actions and business objects is hard to detect. As example, consider the complex match between the activity *Clarify name* and the activities *Consult mother* and *Consult father*. Taking a standard semantic similarity measure such as the Lin metric, the similarity between these labels is close to zero. In order to adequately address such problems, more sophisticated approaches are required.

Besides this comparative discussion, the obtained precision and recall values indicate that matching techniques cannot yet be expected to provide an out-of-the-box solution for fully automated matching. However, the detailed analysis of individual model pairs reveals that very good results can be obtained for a certain setting. Also, the variability of the techniques in terms of their preference for either precision or recall outlines potential for further improvements.

5 Future Directions

Based on the results and the observations from the Process Model Matching Contest 2013, we use this section to outline major directions for future work in the field of process model matching. In particular, we discuss strategies to address the overall matching result quality, the need for addressing semantics, the applicability of push-button approaches, and the question of how process model matching can be evaluated.

The results from this contest highlight that the *overall result quality* still needs to improved. Still, the differences between the employed data sets also indicate that many techniques can properly match a particular set of models. This raises the question whether appropriate matchers can be automatically selected based on the matching problem at hand. This, however, requires a precise understanding of the capabilities of the different matchers and an accurate selection algorithm. A promising strategy to address this problem might be the incorporation of prediction techniques as they have been recently proposed in the area of schema matching [36]. If the quality of the result of a matching technique can be predicted based on certain characteristics of the model or the match constellation, the best matching technique can be selected in an automated fashion. In this context, it could be also a promising strategy to determine a set of matchers that jointly address the given matching problem.

The detailed consideration of the matching results revealed that particular *semantic* relationships are hard to detect. Hence, we are convinced that semantic technologies need to be explored in more detail. While it turned out to be helpful to differentiate between label components such as action and business object, the simple comparison with semantic similarity measures is not sufficient. In order to detect more complex semantic relationships, it might be necessary to include ontologies or additional information such as textual descriptions of the models.

Most of the currently existing process model matching techniques represent *push-button approaches* that compute results without any user interaction. Thus, matching shall be considered as an iterative process that includes feedback cycles with human experts, a process known as reconciliation in data integration [37,38]. Given the general complexity of the matching task, such a semi-automated technique could still provide significant support to the user. By collecting feedback from the user, important decisions during the construction of a matching can be validated, leading to a better overall result.

So far, many matching techniques *evaluate* the result quality using precision, recall, and f-measure. However, considering the complexity of the matching setting, it can be doubted that these simplistic metrics are appropriate. In many cases, a match constellation is not necessarily true or false and the decision is even hard for humans. Against this background, it might be worth to pursue different evaluation strategies, such as non-binary evaluation [39]. Also, one shall consider the actual benefit achieved by (semi-) automated matching. However, measuring the post-match effort turned out to be challenging and is also not well understood for related matching problems [40]. Further work is needed to understand how tool-supported matching compares to manual matching in terms of time and quality.

Altogether, it must be stated that there are many directions for future research. Many of them are concerned with improving existing techniques. However, acknowledging that process model matching is not a simple task with a single correct result, it is also important to focus on alternative evaluation strategies.

6 Conclusion

In this paper, we reported on the setup and the results of the Process Model Matching Contest 2013. This contest addressed the need for effective evaluation of process model matching techniques. We provided two different process model matching problems and received automatically generated results of 7 different techniques. The evaluation of the results showed that their is no clear winner of the contest since no approach yielded the best performance for both data sets. We learned that there is still a huge trade-off between precision and recall, and that semantic and complex correspondences represent considerable challenges.

For future work, we highlighted that it is important to further improve the result quality achieved by the matching techniques. This may be accomplished by automatically selecting the best matcher based on the matching problem at hand, by exploiting semantics in a more elaborated way, or by incorporating user feedback. Further, we emphasized the importance of proper evaluation. As precision, recall, and f-measure are overly simplistic and only allow matches do be true or false, it might be worth to consider alternative evaluation strategies. This may, for instance, include the comparison of a matching technique with a human matching in terms of time and quality.

Acknowledgement. This work has been developed with the support of DFG (German Research Foundation) under the project SemReuse OB 97/9-1.

References

1. Dumas, M., La Rosa, M., Mendling, J., Reijers, H.: Fundamentals of Business Process Management. Springer, Berlin (2012)
2. Castelo Branco, M., Troya, J., Czarnecki, K., Küster, J., Völzer, H.: Matching business process workflows across abstraction levels. In: France, R.B., Kazmeier, J., Breu, R., Atkinson, C. (eds.) MODELS 2012. LNCS, vol. 7590, pp. 626–641. Springer, Heidelberg (2012)
3. Küster, J.M., Koehler, J., Ryndina, K.: Improving business process models with reference models in business-driven development. In: Eder, J., Dustdar, S. (eds.) BPM Workshops 2006. LNCS, vol. 4103, pp. 35–44. Springer, Heidelberg (2006)
4. Weidlich, M., Mendling, J., Weske, M.: A foundational approach for managing process variability. In: Mouratidis, H., Rolland, C. (eds.) CAiSE 2011. LNCS, vol. 6741, pp. 267–282. Springer, Heidelberg (2011)

5. La Rosa, M., Dumas, M., Uba, R., Dijkman, R.: Business process model merging: An approach to business process consolidation. ACM Trans. Softw. Eng. Methodol. **22**(2), 11:1–11:42 (2013)
6. Dumas, M., García-Bañuelos, L., Dijkman, R.M.: Similarity search of business process models. IEEE Data Eng. Bull. **32**(3), 23–28 (2009)
7. Kunze, M., Weidlich, M., Weske, M.: Behavioral similarity – a proper metric. In: Rinderle-Ma, S., Toumani, F., Wolf, K. (eds.) BPM 2011. LNCS, vol. 6896, pp. 166–181. Springer, Heidelberg (2011)
8. Jin, T., Wang, J., Rosa, M.L., ter Hofstede, A.H., Wen, L.: Efficient querying of large process model repositories. Comput. Ind. **64**(1), 41–49 (2013)
9. Ekanayake, C.C., Dumas, M., García-Bañuelos, L., La Rosa, M., ter Hofstede, A.H.M.: Approximate clone detection in repositories of business process models. In: Barros, A., Gal, A., Kindler, E. (eds.) BPM 2012. LNCS, vol. 7481, pp. 302–318. Springer, Heidelberg (2012)
10. Euzenat, J., Shvaiko, P.: Ontology Matching. Springer, Heidelberg (DE) (2007)
11. Bellahsene, Z., Bonifati, A., Rahm, E. (eds.): Schema Matching and Mapping. Springer, Heidelberg (2011)
12. Wu, Z., Palmer, M.: Verbs semantics and lexical selection. In: Proceedings of the 32nd annual meeting on Association for Computational Linguistics, ACL '94, pp. 133–138, Stroudsburg, PA, USA. Association for Computational Linguistics (1994)
13. Ehrig, M., Koschmider, A., Oberweis, A.: Measuring similarity between semantic business process models. In: Roddick, J.F., Hinze, A. (eds.) Proceedings of the 4th Asia-Pacific Conference on Conceptual Modelling. Australian Computer Science Communications, vol. 67, pp. 71–80 (2007)
14. Miller, G., Fellbaum, C.: WordNet: An Electronic Lexical Database. MIT Press, Cambridge (1998)
15. Bunke, H.: On a relation between graph edit distance and maximum common subgraph. Pattern Recogn. Lett. **18**(8), 689–694 (1997)
16. Dijkman, R.M., Dumas, M., van Dongen, B.F., Käärik, R., Mendling, J.: Similarity of business process models: metrics and evaluation. Inf. Syst. **36**(2), 498–516 (2011)
17. Dijkman, R., Dumas, M., García-Bañuelos, L.: Graph matching algorithms for business process model similarity search. In: Dayal, U., Eder, J., Koehler, J., Reijers, H.A. (eds.) BPM 2009. LNCS, vol. 5701, pp. 48–63. Springer, Heidelberg (2009)
18. Weidlich, M., Dijkman, R., Mendling, J.: The ICoP framework: identification of correspondences between process models. In: Pernici, B. (ed.) CAiSE 2010. LNCS, vol. 6051, pp. 483–498. Springer, Heidelberg (2010)
19. Jain, A.K., Murty, M.N., Flynn, P.J.: Data clustering: a review. ACM Comput. Surv. **31**(3), 264–323 (1999)
20. Porter, M.F.: Readings in Information Retrieval. Morgan Kaufmann Publishers Inc., San Francisco (1997)
21. Miller, G.A.: WordNet: a Lexical database for english. Commun. ACM **38**(11), 39–41 (1995)
22. Klinkmüller, C., Weber, I., Mendling, J., Leopold, H., Ludwig, A.: Increasing recall of process model matching by improved activity label matching. In: Daniel, F., Wang, J., Weber, B. (eds.) BPM 2013. LNCS, vol. 8094, pp. 211–218. Springer, Heidelberg (2013)
23. Levenshtein, V.I.: Binary codes capable of correcting deletions, insertions, and reversals. Sov. Phys. Dokl. **10**(8), 707–710 (1966)

24. Lin, D.: An information-theoretic definition of similarity. In. In Proceedings of the 15th International Conference on Machine Learning, pp. 296–304. Morgan Kaufmann (1998)
25. Leopold, H., Smirnov, S., Mendling, J.: On the refactoring of activity labels in business process models. Inf. Syst. **37**(5), 443–459 (2012)
26. Sakr, S., Awad, A., Kunze, M.: Querying process models repositories by aggregated graph search. In: La Rosa, M., Soffer, P. (eds.) BPM 2012 Workshops. LNBIP, vol. 132, pp. 573–585. Springer, Heidelberg (2013)
27. Awad, A.: BPMN-Q: A language to query business processes. In: Reichert, M., Strecker, S., Turowski, K. (eds.) EMISA. LNI, vol. P-119, pp. 115–128 St. Goar, Germany, GI (2007)
28. Weidlich, M., Sheetrit, E., Branco, M., Gal, A.: Matching business process models using positional passage-based language models. In: Ng, W., Storey, V.C., Trujillo, J.C. (eds.) ER 2013. LNCS, vol. 8217, pp. 130–137. Springer, Heidelberg (2013)
29. Lv, Y., Zhai, C.: Positional language models for information retrieval. In: Allan, J., Aslam, J.A., Sanderson, M., Zhai, C., Zobel, J. (eds.) SIGIR, pp. 299–306. ACM, New York (2009)
30. Lin, J.: Divergence measures based on the shannon entropy. IEEE Trans. Inf. Theory **37**(1), 145–151 (1991)
31. Gal, A., Sagi, T.: Tuning the ensemble selection process of schema matchers. Inf. Syst. **35**(8), 845–859 (2010)
32. Weidlich, M., Dijkman, R., Mendling, J.: The ICoP framework: identification of correspondences between process models. In: Pernici, B. (ed.) CAiSE 2010. LNCS, vol. 6051, pp. 483–498. Springer, Heidelberg (2010)
33. Qu, Y., Hu, W., Cheng, G.: Constructing virtual documents for ontology matching. In: Carr, L., Roure, D.D., Iyengar, A., Goble, C.A., Dahlin, M. (eds.) WWW, pp. 23–31. ACM, New York (2006)
34. Weidlich, M., Mendling, J., Weske, M.: Efficient consistency measurement based on behavioral profiles of process models. IEEE Trans. Softw. Eng. **37**(3), 410–429 (2011)
35. Polyvyanyy, A., Weidlich, M.: Towards a compendium of process technologies - the jbpt library for process model analysis. In: Deneckère, R., Proper, H.A. (eds.) CAiSE Forum. CEUR Workshop Proceedings, vol. 998, pp. 106–113. www. CEUR-WS.org (2013)
36. Sagi, T., Gal, A.: Schema matching prediction with applications to data source discovery and dynamic ensembling. VLDB J. **22**(5), 689–710 (2013)
37. Belhajjame, K., Paton, N.W., Fernandes, A.A.A., Hedeler, C., Embury, S.M.: User feedback as a first class citizen in information integration systems. In: CIDR, pp. 175–183. www.cidrdb.org (2011)
38. Quoc Viet Nguyen, H., Wijaya, T.K., Miklós, Z., Aberer, K., Levy, E., Shafran, V., Gal, A., Weidlich, M.: Minimizing human effort in reconciling match networks. In: Ng, W., Storey, V.C., Trujillo, J.C. (eds.) ER 2013. LNCS, vol. 8217, pp. 212–226. Springer, Heidelberg (2013)
39. Sagi, T., Gal, A.: Non-binary evaluation for schema matching. In: Atzeni, P., Cheung, D., Ram, S. (eds.) ER 2012. LNCS, vol. 7532, pp. 477–486. Springer, Heidelberg (2012)
40. Duchateau, F., Bellahsene, Z., Coletta, R.: Matching and alignment: what is the cost of user post-match effort? In: Meersman, R., et al. (eds.) OTM 2011, Part I. LNCS, vol. 7044, pp. 421–428. Springer, Heidelberg (2011)

2nd Workshop on Security in Business Processes (SBP 2013)

Keynote: Specification and Conflict Detection for GTRBAC in Multi-domain Environment

Ning Bao, Hejiao Huang[✉], and Hongwei Du

Shenzhen Key Laboratory of Internet Information Collaboration,
Harbin Institute of Technology Shenzhen Graduate School, Shenzhen, China
bn_china@163.com, {hjhuang,hwdu}@hitsz.edu.cn

Abstract. Although the development and expansion for the time-based RBAC policy has enhanced the security greatly, there are hardly any paper paying attention to the conflicts that produced by the time feature in multi-domain RBAC model. In this paper, we focus on temporal constraints and the role inheritance constraints that occurred in the interoperation domains based on Petri nets. The approach can check whether an inter-domain access requirement has violated its local RBAC policy or the inter-domain access control policy has improper temporal constraints. In order to illustrate this approach, an applicable example is shown for the specification and conflict detection.

Keywords: Multi-domain · RBAC · Time-based · Colored Petri net (CPN) · Conflict detection

1 Introduction

Nowadays, how to achieve safe and reliable cross-domain resource sharing in the multiple heterogeneous systems has became much more important. What's more, in order to meet the needs of a variety of real world applications, time constrained information sharing between different systems is becoming a common phenomenon too. To address these problems, formal methods and logical approaches already provide some help. The RBAC policy was verified in [1] by Basit Shafiq and his teamwork in 2005. In 2009, Hind Rakkay and Hanifa Boucheneb [2] improved Shafiqs work with CPN-Tool, they built a detailed structure for the policy and gave a practical example to verify the correctness of the policy. However, they didn't take temporal factor into account. In [3], the conditions of inheritance violation for secure interoperation were detailed described. However, just like the previous work, the temporal factor was not considered in this

This work was financially supported by National Natural Science Foundation of China with Grants No. 61370216, No. 11071271, No. 11371004 and No. 61100191, and Shenzhen Strategic Emerging Industries Program with Grants No. ZDSY20120613125016389, No. JCYJ20120613151201451 and No. JCYJ20130329153215152. And also Natural Scientific Research Innovation Foundation in Harbin Institute of Technology under project HIT.NSFIR.2011128.

N. Lohmann et al. (Eds.): BPM 2013 Workshops, LNBIP 171, pp. 467–472, 2014.
DOI: 10.1007/978-3-319-06257-0_36, © Springer International Publishing Switzerland 2014

paper. In [4], Kadloul, L., et al. used CPN-Tool to model and verify the TRABC model. Although they proposed some effective methods for the building of the model, their work based only on the local domain. In [5,6], although these papers didn't take the temporal factor into consideration, we could draw on the basic idea about the secure interoperation design.

Notice that, there are some new conflicts in the multi-domain environment while take the temporal factor into consideration. In this paper, we intend to model and verify the GTRBAC [7] policy in the multi-domain environment, propose some new conflicts and present a formal approach for the structured description and collision detection using color Petri net (CPN) [8]. The conflicts that we mainly deal with in this paper are the temporal constraint and the role inheritance constraint. The temporal constraints could be further divided into the duration constraint and the periodicity constraint. In Sect. 3, a scenario example is shown to describe the conflicts in detail.

2   CPN Model of GTRBAC in the Multi-domain Environment

In this section, we will introduce part of the basic constraint modules that used for the overall structure of the model using the CPN-tool, more information about CPN can be found in [8]. The detailed structured description of the two modules is listed as follows.

2.1   Color Set

For instance, the colset *Role* could be defined as
  colset Role = index R with 0..RoleNum timed;
  This color set declares a sequence of roles and the number of the sequence is *RoleNum* which is a constant integer declared in the initialization. As most of the properties of the color set could be found in the place definition and the arc expression, we will not repeat here. All of the color sets are shown in Fig. 1.

2.2   Place

Place *EPE* contains three kinds of tokens: the tokens for the periodical requesting events that contain the enabling/disabling request event, the tokens for the persistent requesting events.

The tokens in the place *Rallowed* stand for the initial request events in the assignment module.

The place *DR_allow* stores a list of tokens that used as the initialization of the inter-domain assignment module.

Tokens in *RH* record the hierarchy relationships from the high to low level while tokens in *R_RH* record the hierarchy relationships from the low to high level.

```
▼Declarations
 ►Standard priorities
 ▼Standard declarations
  ▼colset UNIT = unit timed;
  ▼colset INT = int;
  ▼colset DurTime = product INT*INT ;
  ▼colset STRING = string;
  ▼colset BOOL = bool;
  ▼colset IntString = list INT;
  ▼colset Role = index R with 0..RoleNum timed;
  ▼colset DomainRole = product INT*Role;
  ▼colset DomainRList = list DomainRole;
  ▼colset User = index U with 0..UserNum;
  ▼colset Domain_Role = product INT*DomainRList;
  ▼colset Permission = index P with 0..PerNum;
  ▼colset DomainUser = product INT*User;
  ▼colset DomainUList = list DomainUser;
  ▼colset Domain_User = product INT*DomainUList;
  ▼colset RoleList = list Role;
  ▼colset UserList = list User;
  ▼colset PermissionList = list Permission;
  ▼colset DomainPermission = product INT*Permission;
  ▼colset TimeR = product INT*DurTime *DomainRole ;
  ▼colset DomainPList = list DomainPermission;
  ▼colset DUsers = product DomainUser*INT*INT;
  ▼colset RH = product DomainRole*DomainRList;
  ▼colset DRoles = product DomainRole*INT*INT;
  ▼colset Roles = product Role*INT*INT;
  ▼colset User_assign = product DomainRole*DomainUList;
  ▼colset Role_assign = product DomainUser*DomainRList;
  ▼colset RSSoD = product DomainRole*DomainRList;
  ▼colset RDSoD = product DomainRole*DomainRList;
  ▼colset RactiveU = product DomainUser*DomainRList;
  ▼colset USSoD = product DomainUser*DomainRole*DomainUList;
  ▼colset UDSoD = product DomainUser*DomainRole*DomainUList;
  ▼colset UactiveR = product DomainRole*DomainUList;
  ▼colset Role_allowed = product DomainUser*DomainRList;
  ▼colset Role_Permission = product DomainRole*DomainPList;
  ▼colset DomainR_allowed = product DomainUser*DomainRole*DomainRList;
  ▼colset User_PermissionList = product DomainUser*DomainPList;
  ▼colset DR_DRL = product DomainRole*DomainRList;
  ▼colset Domain_Map = list DR_DRL;
  ▼colset ChargeEvent =
   product STRING*INT*DurTime*DomainRole;
  ▼colset ReqE = product INT*Role;
  ▼colset ReqEvent =
   product INT*DurTime*DomainRole timed;
  ▼colset ReqPerEvent =
   product INT*DurTime*INT*INT*ReqE timed;
```

Fig. 1. The definitions of the color sets

The place *DRassign* mainly stores the tokens that dealing with the inter-domain request events. The roles and the users that the roles tend to be assigned to are from different domains.

The place *DMap* stores the tokens that used to record the role mapping relationship between the interoperation domains.

The place *D_conflict* stores the tokens that used to record the conflicts that occur in the *interdomain* assignment module.

2.3 The Arc Expression, the Guard Function, and the Modeling Description

In this section, we list the basic definitions for variables in Fig. 2. And some of the functions used in the transitions is shown in the Fig. 3. Two modules of the whole structure are listed in Figs. 4 and 5. The enable/disable module is used to simulate the initialization about the request events which could easily describe the temporal constraints. The inter-domain assignment module is used to simulate the conflict detection about the inter-domain environment.

```
▼var Tbegin,Tend,per,Etime,pri,t,domain,domain1: INT;
▼var Tbegin1,Tend1,pri1,USC,UDC:INT;
▼var Tbegin2,Tend2,pri2,RSC,RDC:INT;
▼var role_test :STRING ;
▼var int_string : IntString;
▼var DMap_list : Domain_Map;
▼var user,user1,user2 : User;
▼var dr_drl : DR_DRL;
▼var domainR1,domainR,domainR2: DomainRole;
▼var domainU,domainU1,domainU2:DomainUser;
▼var role_list,role_list1 ,domainR_list,RSSoD_list,ReqR_list,RDSoD_list,
 RH_list,RH_list1,R_RH_list,R_RH_list1,rl_allowed,rl_assign: DomainRList;
▼var user_list ,domainU_list,USSoD_list,UDSoD_list: DomainUList;
▼var per_list,per_list1 : DomainPList;
▼var role ,role1,role2,role3: Role;
▼var E,D : STRING;
```

Fig. 2. Variables description

E3(domain,Tbegin,Tend,per,Etime,pri,role)	Used to periodically decrease the temporal interval of the tokens
E4(domain,Tbegin,Tend,per,Etime,pri,role)	used to send out the disabling request event periodically
E5(domain,domain1,pri1,pri,Tbegin1,Tend1, Tbegin2,Tend2,role1,role2)	used to choose the proper request event when there is a conflict
dealDR((a:DR_DRL),(l:Domain_Map), (dr1:DomainRole))	used to record the role mapping information between the interoperation domaisns
check_loop(x:Domain_Map,y:DomainRList,i:INT,d :INT,z:DomainRList,dr:DomainRole, dr1:DomainRole)	use iterative query to find out whether there is a directed cycle in the inheritance relationship between domains

Fig. 3. Functions description

The guard functions $[Tbegin1 = Tbegin2, role1 = role2, domain = domain1]$ is used to make sure that the two events happen at the same time. The guard function [$memrl\_alloweddomainR$] is mainly to specify that the third element of the tokens in place ER should be the member of the roles that the initial request events for the inter-domain assignment module tend to obtain($rl\_allowed$). The guard function [$length\ role\_list <= USC$] is used to specify whether the number of the roles that the corresponding user has obtained is larger than the cardinality constraint of the user. The guard function [$intersect\ USSoD\_listuser\_list = []$] is used to check whether there is a user that has user static SoD constraint with the user which is currently being processed.

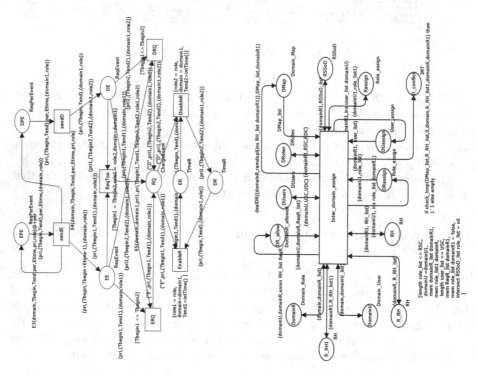

Fig. 4. Enable/Disable module   **Fig. 5.** Inter-domain assignment module

3   The Verification for the Model

3.1   A Scenario Example

In this section, a representative example is used for illustrating the correctness of the model as shown in Fig. 6. In the domain 1, there is $DSoC$ between $courier1(R(2))$ and $courier2(R(2))$, the role static/dynamic cardinality constraints are (2,2), (2,2), (3,2), (2,3) for the $R(1)$, $R(2)$, $R(3)$, $R(4)$ respectively. There are three users: $U1$, $U2$, $U3$. The user static/dynamic cardinality constraints are (2,2), (2,2), (3,2) respectively. In the domain 2, the cashier and buyer have static SoD conflict and the role static/dynamic cardinality constraints are

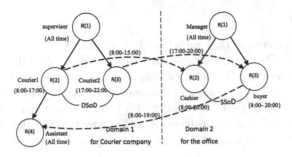

Fig. 6. A scenario example

(2,2), (2,2), (2, 2) for the $R(1)$, $R(2)$, $R(3)$ respectively. There are two users : $U1$ and $U2$. The user static/dynamic cardinality constraints are (2,2), (2,2) respectively. The temporal constraints for the two domains are: *courier*1 {8:00-17:00}, *courier*2 {17:00-22:00}, *cashier* {8:00-20:00}, *buyer* {8:00-20:00}.

The initial tokens for the enable/disable module could be described as: (*pri*, (*Tbegin, Tend*),*per,Etime*,(*domain, role*)). *pri* stands for the priority of the request event. *Per* stands for the execution cycle of the corresponding request event. *Etime* stands for the duration of the corresponding event. Thus, using appropriate initialization tokens could easily describe the duration constraint and the periodicity constraint. For instance, the tokens for $R(3)$ in domain 1 could be described as:

(1, (17, 24 * 7), 24, 5, (1, R(3)))@ + 17

The initial tokens for the enable/disable module could be described as: (*domainU*, (*Tbegin1, Tend1*)*domainR, ReqR_list*). *domainU* stands for the user that tends to obtain the roles that in the different domain. *domainR* stands for the role that the corresponding user has already obtained in the local domain. *ReqR_list* stands for the list of roles that the user tends to obtain by role Inheritance though *domainR* in a different domain. We list some of the initial tokens for this module:

h: ((1, U(1)), (20, 22), (1, R(3)),[(2, R(3))])
i: ((1, U(2)), (18, 20), (1, R(2)),[(2, R(2))])
j: ((2, U(1)), (8, 19), (2, R(3)),[(1, R(4))])
k: ((1, U(1)), (17, 20), (1, R(3)),[(2, R(3))])

There are some obvious constraints in the tokens mentioned above:

- In the token h, the request temporal interval is (20, 22) which is conflict with the temporal interval for $R(3)$ (8, 20) in the domain 2.
- In the token i, the request temporal interval is (18, 20) which is conflict with the temporal interval for $R(2)$ (8, 17) in the domain 1.
- The token k and j make up a road from (1, $R(3)$) to the local domain again (1, $R(4)$). What's more, the life cycle for the arc from (1, $R(3)$) to (2, $R(3)$) is (17,20) and the life cycle for the arc from (2, $R(3)$) to (1, $R(4)$) is (8, 19), so the intersection of the two life cycles are not null. The role inheritance conflict occurs.

3.2 Analysis

For the scenario example that mentioned above, the CPN tool generates a full state space with 17966 nodes and 57429 arcs, which is difficult to be described with the state space tree. To deal with this problem, we split the whole model into the separate modules. There are no infinite occurrence sequences, all places in all states are bounded. What's more, the graph terminates in the dead marking, so the scenario specified has no problem. Another way is using the query functions to find out the bad markings, this part is not repeated here.

4 Conclusion

We tended to avoid the conflicts between the interoperation domains with the temporal constraints in this paper. We listed two modules to specify the time constrained secure interoperation policy. Verification for the model was shown at last. For further details, please refer to our journal version published later.

References

1. Shafiq, B., Masood, A., Joshi, J., Ghafoor, A.: A role-based access control policy verification framework for real-time systems. In: Proceedings of the 10th IEEE International Workshop on Object-Oriented Real-Time Dependable Systems (2005)
2. Rakkay, H., Boucheneb, H.: Security analysis of role based access control models using colored Petri nets and CPNtools. In: Gavrilova, M.L., Tan, C.J.K., Moreno, E.D. (eds.) Transactions on Computational Science IV. LNCS, vol. 5430, pp. 149–176. Springer, Heidelberg (2009)
3. Huang, H.J., Kirchner, H., Liu, S.Y., Wu, W.L.: Handling inheritance violation for secure interoperation of heterogeneous systems. Int. J. Secure. Network. 9(4), 223–233 (2009)
4. Kadloul, L., Djouani, K., Tfaili, W.: Using timed colored Petri nets and CPN-tool to model and verify TRBAC security policies. In: Fourth International Workshop on Verification and Evaluation of Computer and Communication Systems, VECoS 2010 (2010)
5. Shafiq, B., Joshi, B.D., Bertino, E., Ghafoor, A.: Secure interoperation in a multi domain environment employing RBAC policies. IEEE Trans. Knowl. Data Eng. 12(3), 203–210 (2010)
6. Huang, H.J., Kirchner, H.: Secure interoperation design in multi-domains environments based on colored Petri nets. Inf. Sci. 221, 591–606 (2013)
7. Joshi, J.B.D., Bertino, E., Latif, U.: Generalized temporal role-based access control model. IEEE Trans. Knowl. Data Eng. 17(1), 4–23 (2005)
8. Jensen, K.: Coloured Petri Nets: Basic Concepts, Analysis Methods and Practical Use. Springer, Heidelberg (1997)

Multi-dimensional Secure Service Orchestration

Gabriele Costa[1], Fabio Martinelli[2](✉), and Artsiom Yautsiukhin[2]

[1] Dipartimento di Informatica, Bioingegneria, Robotica e Ingegneria dei Sistemi,
Universitá di Genova, Genova, Italy
gabriele.costa@unige.it
[2] Istituto di Informatica e Telematica Consiglio Nazionale delle Ricerche, Pisa, Italy
{fabio.martinelli,artsiom.yautsiukhin}@iit.cnr.it

Abstract. Web services composition allows a software designer for combining atomic services, for instance taken from a marketplace, in a complex business process fulfilling a desired functional goal. Moreover, among a large number of possible compositions, the designer may want to consider only those which satisfy specific non-functional requirements.

In our work we consider verification of security properties and evaluation quantitative security metrics in a single framework. The main focus of this article is the verification of a composition with several security metrics at once. We provide a general solution for the problem and show how such verification can be made more efficient in specific cases (e.g., when a metric is an abstraction of another one). We employ a mathematical structure called c-semirings granting the generality of our approach.

1 Introduction

Service composition allows a service designer to create a new complex service out of a set of available services (announced in a Marketplace). Often the result of such process is a set of alternative compositions, which fulfil the same functional goal but have different Quality of Service (QoS). Providers of complex services want to obtain the highest quality services and to guarantee this quality even if some problems with components arise. Naturally, security is one of such qualities.

A number of techniques were provided to obtain the evidences whether the service composition satisfies some security properties [1–5]. Many of these techniques use formal methods to model a complex service and to proof the compliance of this model with a security specification. First, it is important to model services in a "safe" way in order not to miss any security-relevant behaviour. Secondly, the actual service implementation must comply with its specification to assure that the results of the analysis are valid.

Some security properties are of quantitative nature and a decision about whether they are satisfied depends on the concrete requirements of the customer [6]. Thus, when a service provider advertises the QoS of its service it

This work was partly supported by EU-FP7-ICT NESSoS, EU-FP7-ICT ANIKETOS and EU-FP7-ICT SPaCIoS projects.

N. Lohmann et al. (Eds.): BPM 2013 Workshops, LNBIP 171, pp. 473–485, 2014.
DOI: 10.1007/978-3-319-06257-0_37, © Springer International Publishing Switzerland 2014

needs to specify the values of security metrics for the service. Some mathematical models were proposed to analyse service composition with security metric [7,8].

Since, there is no one reliable security metric which completely and unambiguously describes the security level provided by a service [9,10] several quantitative security requirements could be considered by a service orchestrator at once [8,11]. Moreover, the same security qualities may be expressed in a slightly different manner. Therefore, there is a need for a framework which not only evaluates a service composition using several metrics, but also works with different types of similar metrics.

In this paper we extend our previous work [12,13] (based on a type and effect system of Bartoletti et al. [3]) on secure service orchestration in which we provided a single framework for analysis of security properties and security metrics. In this article we show how multi-dimensional security metrics can be incorporated into our framework without violating a safety property. We apply n-dimensional c-semirings to preserve generality of our approach. Although we may not always choose the best/worst option, we show that metric abstraction can help to do this in some cases. In this paper we focus on security metrics but the approach may be generalised for other quantitative qualities of services.

This paper is organised as follows. We start with a running example (Sect. 2). Then, we recall some features from our previous work (Sect. 3). Section 4 contains the core ideas on aggregation of different security metrics. We finish the paper with related work (Sect. 5) and conclusions (Sect. 6).

2   Running Example

A travel agency BestTravel, which offers a travel planning service, moves a part of its business to the web. BestTravel exploits existing services for implementing its process, which includes three sub-processes: (i) find_a_connection, (ii) find_a_hotel, (iii) prepare_invoice. A service developer starts with creation of an abstract workflow, which defines the general process but does not assign concrete services to the defined tasks (e.g., see Fig. 1 represented using BPMN [14]).

Reading Fig. 1 (from left to right) a process of BestTravel works as follows. First, BestTravel finds_a_connection and finds_a_hotel in parallel (rooted in $\oplus$). The find_a_connection sub-process consists of searching_for_a_direct_flight and booking_the_direct_flight. If the cheap direct flight was not found the service searches_for_an_itinerary and books_the_itinerary. An itinerary also may be a direct flight but it costs more than the direct option considered before. In parallel BestTravel searches_for_a_hotel and books_the_hotel. Finally, BestTravel signs_the_receipt.

There are 10 concrete services found in a marketplace suitable for the defined tasks. Table 1 displays these concrete services and their mapping to the abstract services. All services specify values of several security-relevant parameters. Note, that sometimes parameters are of different kind. For example, trust value for Windjet and Ryanair are discrete values from a set $\{1, 2, 3, 4, 5\}$, when other

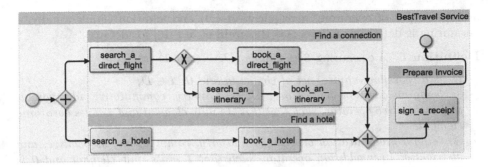

Fig. 1. Abstract workflow for BestTravel.

Table 1. Abstract and concrete services

Abstract	Index	Concrete	Risk	Trust	Recovery time
Search a direct flight	1	Windjet	10	5	75
	2	Ryanair	20	4	45
Search an itinerary	3	Lufthansa	5	0.98	fast
	4	Airfrance	8	0,95	normal
Booking service	5	Paypal	5	0.95	30
	6	Ripplepay	15	0.89	60
Search a hotel	7	HotelBooker	40	0.93	60
	8	HotelClub	30	0.92	90
Sign a receipt	9	ESignForms	0.3; 0.6; 0.9	0.73	150
	10	VeriSign	0.4; 0.5; 0.8	0.87	200

trust values are from [0;1] interval. In contrast to other services, Lufthansa and AirFrance express the recovery time as qualitative values. Finally, risk values of ESignForms and VeriSign represented as triples containing the probability of not violating integrity, confidentiality and availability.

BestTravel has several security requirements for the created process. First, BestTravel wants to have *risk* level of find_a_flight and find_a_hotel reservation sub-processes less than *75* euro (measured as Annualised Loss Expectancy (ALE) [15]). Furthermore, the two sub-processes must have the overall *trust* rating not lower than *0.8* (or not lower than 5 for a discrete scale). The *time of recovery* of the sub-processes should not be more than *120* min. Finally, the risk value for sign_a_receipt must be *medium* or smaller.

3   Background

3.1   C-Semirings

We exploits the notion of *c-semiring* [16] for the abstraction of metrics and operators over metrics to provide a generic framework for all metrics which could be considered as c-semirings. A c-semiring consists of a domain of values D, and two types of operators: multiplication ($\otimes$) and addition ($\oplus$). Formally, a c-semiring is defined as follows (see Bistarelli et al., [16] for details).

Definition 1. *A c-semiring S is a tuple $\langle D, \oplus, \otimes, \mathbf{0}, \mathbf{1} \rangle$ where*

- *D is a (possibly infinite) set of elements and $\mathbf{0}$, $\mathbf{1} \in D$;*
- *$\oplus$, being an addition defined over D, is a binary, commutative, idempotent, and associative operator, such that $\mathbf{0}$ is its unit element and $\mathbf{1}$ is its absorbing element;*
- *$\otimes$, being a multiplication over D, is a binary, commutative, associative, and distributive over addition operator, such that $\mathbf{1}$ is its unit element and $\mathbf{0}$ is its absorbing element;*

Definition 2. *$\leq_S$ is a partial order relation over D: $d_1 \leq_S d_2$ iff $d_1 \oplus d_2 = d_2$.*

In this work we need a reverse operation, which returns the worst possible value for summation $\oplus^{-1}$ which is defined as follows.

Definition 3. *$d_1 \oplus^{-1} d_2 = glb(d_1, d_2)$;*

where $glb(d_1, d_2) = d$ if and only if (i) $d \leq_S d_1 \wedge d \leq_S d_2$, and (ii) $\forall\, d'\,.\, d' \leq_S d_1 \wedge d' \leq_S d_2 \rightarrow d' \leq_S d$

The definition of the reverse operation returns the opposite value of direct addition operation when the operation is defined. For the cases in which the addition operation is undefined, the greatest lower bound (glb) is returned[1].

Property 1. Operation $\oplus^{-1}$ is associative, commutative, idempotent, distributive over $\otimes$, monotone[2].

Example 1. Regarding to the security targets BestTravel is going to use three metrics: trust, risk, and recovery time. Trust is often seen as a probability that a provider behaves according to the contract, i.e., for majority of services in the marketplace (see Table 1) trust has a value between 0 and 1. The values are aggregated by multiplication, and the highest values is preferable. Thus, c-semiring for trust formally is defined as follows: $S^1 = \langle [0, 1], max, \times, 0, 1 \rangle$.

Risk is often considered as possible losses and has the domain of positive natural numbers. Aggregation of risk values is summation of losses, and a lower risk is better than a higher one. Thus, c-semiring for risk is $S^2 = \langle \mathbb{N}^+ \cup \{\infty\}, min, +, \infty, 0 \rangle$.

Recovery time denotes the time required for the service to recover after an incident (e.g., after a successful DOS attack). For majority of services in the marketplace (see Table 1) time has domain of positive real numbers. Aggregation of recovery time values is a maximising operation, while a lower time of recovery is considered better than a higher one. Thus, c-semiring for recovery time is $S^3 = \langle \mathbb{N}^+ \cup \{\infty\}, min, max, \infty, 0 \rangle$.

---

[1] Note that the existence of glb is granted by the presence of top element in our domains.

[2] A link with proofs: http://wwwold.iit.cnr.it/staff/artsiom.yautsiukhin/Resources/Proofs-SBP.pdf.

Table 2. Syntax of history expressions.

$$H, H' ::= \varepsilon \mid h \mid \alpha(r) \mid H \cdot H' \mid H + H' \mid H \mid H' \mid \bar{d}\#H \mid \varphi[H] \mid \gamma\langle H \rangle \mid \mu h.H$$

$$H_{BT} = \left(\gamma \left\langle (H_1 + H_2) \cdot \left(\begin{array}{c} (H_5 + H_6) \\ + \\ ((H_3 + H_4) \cdot (H_5 + H_6)) \end{array} \right) \right\rangle \middle| \gamma \left\langle \begin{array}{c} (H_5 + H_6) \\ \cdot \\ (H_7 + H_8) \end{array} \right\rangle \right)$$
$$\cdot \gamma \langle \mu h.((H_9 + H_{10}) \cdot h + \varepsilon) \rangle$$

Fig. 2. History expression for BestTravel.

3.2 History Expressions and Services

In our previous paper [12] we have described how history expressions, originally proposed to model the behaviour of complex services [17], can be suitably
enriched with metric annotations. Also, History expressions can be adopted for
verification of temporal properties by checking whether they satisfy a corresponding specification (e.g., a LTL formula or a security automaton). History
expressions can be inferred from service implementation by means of a suitable
type and effect system which grants the soundness, namely *type safety*, of the
resulting expressions. Here we do not detail the type and effect inference process
and we refer the interested reader to [12] and to [17].

In this paper we assume the history expression inference process for service
implementation as given. We only recall the inference rule for access events
below. Also, we (informally) recall the type safety theorem stated in [12].

Theorem 1. *If the type and effect system infers a history expression H from a
service e, then every possible execution trace of e is denoted by H.*

The syntax of the history expression is shown in Table 2. Intuitively, history
expressions can be empty (i.e. ε), variables (ranged over by h, h') or access
operations (access α to a resource r, in symbols $\alpha(r)$). Also, a history expression
can be a sequence $H \cdot H'$, a choice $H + H'$, a parallel composition $H \mid H'$
or a recursion $\mu h.H$. Finally, history expressions can be annotated with metric
vectors, e.g., $\bar{d}\#H$, security framings, e.g., $\varphi[H]$, and metric framings, e.g., $\gamma\langle H \rangle$.
Their meaning is straightforward. The annotation[3] $\bar{d}\#H$ says that (the service
associated to the history expression) H can originate metric vectors which are
bounded by $\bar{d}$. A security framing $\varphi[H]$ says that, over the execution histories
produced by H, the security policy φ holds. Similarly, $\gamma\langle H \rangle$ applies a metric
policy γ to H.

---

[3] Here we go ahead a bit and use vectors of values instead of simple values. In the
following we show that such substitution is just.

Example 2. Using the type and effect inference presented in [12], we associate the history expression of Fig. 2 to the BestTravel service (see Fig. 1) and in Example 3 we will add metric values to these expressions.

We proposed to aggregate metrics (specified as c-semirings) according to the business process of complex web services using equational rules (see Table 3). In short, security and trust metrics are expressed as c-semirings and assigned to specific history expressions (i.e., $\bar{d}\#H$, called metric normal form (MNF)) in the history expression for the composite service (similar to Fig. 2). Then the equational rules are consequently applied to find the values of metrics for the complete process. In fact, Table 3 states, that multiplication operator is used for aggregation of values for parallel $(\bar{d}_1\#H_1 \mid \bar{d}_2\#H_2)$, sequential $(\bar{d}_1\#H_1 \cdot \bar{d}_2\#H_2)$ and cyclic $(\mu h.H)$ execution of services, while reverse addition is used for non-deterministic choice $(\bar{d}_1\#H_1 + \bar{d}_2\#H_2)$ and selection of the worst alternative [12]. Such an aggregation process results can be used to advertise the level of security provided by the composite web service. Also, in [12] we proved that $\equiv$ is an equivalence relation for history expressions semantics. Hence, although security is not a compositional property in general, security analysis can be safely carried out on the aggregation of history expressions.

Table 3. Equational rules.

$$H \equiv \mathbf{1}\#H \quad \bar{d}_1\#\bar{d}_2\#H \equiv \bar{d}_2\#\bar{d}_1\#H \equiv \bar{d}_1 \otimes \bar{d}_2\#H$$

$$\bar{d}_1\#H_1 \cdot \bar{d}_2\#H_2 \equiv \bar{d}_1 \otimes \bar{d}_2\#(H_1 \cdot H_2) \quad \varphi[\bar{d}\#H] \equiv \bar{d}\#\varphi[H]$$

$$\bar{d}_1\#H_1 + \bar{d}_2\#H_2 \equiv \bar{d}_1 \oplus^{-1} \bar{d}_2\#(H_1 + H_2) \quad \bar{d}_1\#H_1 \mid \bar{d}_2\#H_2 \equiv \bar{d}_1 \otimes \bar{d}_2\#(H_1 \mid H_2)$$

$$\gamma\langle\bar{d}\#H\rangle \equiv \bar{d}'\#\gamma\langle H\rangle \quad \text{where } \gamma = T \geq_T \bar{d}'' \text{ and } \bar{d}' = \bar{d} \oplus^{-1} \bar{d}''$$

$$\mu h.H \equiv \bar{d}''\#\mu h.H' \quad \text{where } \bar{d}'' = \bigoplus_n {}^{-1}\Phi^n(\mathbf{0}) \text{ and } \Phi(\bar{d}) = \bar{d}' \Leftrightarrow \begin{cases} H[\bar{d}\#h/h] \equiv \bar{d}'\#H' \\ \wedge \\ \bar{d}'\#H' \text{ is in MNF} \end{cases}$$

4   Aggregation of Several Security Metrics with C-Semirings

In practice, several security parameters are required to assess a service. In this case we should use an n-dimensional c-semiring [18]:

Definition 4. *Assume that we have n c-semirings $\mathbf{S}^i$, $0 < i \leq n$ (we also add upper index i to every parameter of a semiring, i.e., $\mathbf{S}^i = \langle D^i, \oplus^i, \otimes^i, \mathbf{0}^i, \mathbf{1}^i\rangle$). An n-dimensional c-semiring is $\bar{S} = \langle \bar{D}, \oplus, \otimes, \bar{\mathbf{0}}, \bar{\mathbf{1}}\rangle$, where $\bar{D} = (D^1, ..., D^n)$, including $\bar{\mathbf{0}} = (\mathbf{0}^1, ..., \mathbf{0}^n)$ and $\bar{\mathbf{1}} = (\mathbf{1}^1, ..., \mathbf{1}^n)$. For any two vectors of values $\bar{d}_1$ and $\bar{d}_2$ of $\bar{S}$ the multiplication operations is defined as follows: $\bar{d}_1 \otimes \bar{d}_2 = (d_1^1 \otimes^1 d_2^1, ..., d_1^n \otimes^n d_2^n)$. The additional operation is defined using Pareto-optimality: $\bar{d}_1 \oplus \bar{d}_2 = \bar{d}_2 \; iff \; \forall i \; d_1^i \oplus^i d_2^i = d_2^i$.*

Table 4. Metric annotation of concrete sub-services.

$H_1 = \bar{d}_1 \# H_1' = (10, 5, 75) \# H_1'$	$H_6 = \bar{d}_6 \# H_6' = (15, 0.89, 60) \# H_6'$
$H_2 = \bar{d}_2 \# H_2' = (20, 4, 45) \# H_2'$	$H_7 = \bar{d}_7 \# H_7' = (40, 0.93, 60) \# H_7'$
$H_3 = \bar{d}_3 \# H_3' = (5, 0.98, \text{fast}) \# H_3'$	$H_8 = \bar{d}_8 \# H_8' = (30, 0.92, 90) \# H_8'$
$H_4 = \bar{d}_4 \# H_4' = (8, 0.95, \text{normal}) \# H_4'$	$H_9 = \bar{d}_9 \# H_9' = ((0.3; 0.6; 0.9), 0.73, 150) \# H_9'$
$H_5 = \bar{d}_5 \# H_5' = (5, 0.95, 30) \# H_5'$	$H_{10} = \bar{d}_{10} \# H_{10}' = ((0.4; 0.5; 0.8), 0.87, 200) \# H_{10}'$

In the article we use upper indexes to denote different c-semirings, which compose an n-dimensional c-semiring, while the lower indexes denote different instances of a c-semiring. For the sake of presentation, we also specify an n-dimensional c-semiring as a vector of c-semirings, e.g., $\bar{S} = (S^1, S^2, ..., S^n)$. Note, that n-dimensional c-semiring is a c-semiring as well [16]. This means that all our formulas written for the quantitative analysis of a composite service presented in [12] are relevant for the new c-semiring structure.

A crucial property we want to prove is that usage of n-dimensional c-semirings does not invalidate the semantics of history expressions, i.e., it does not affect the safety property stated by Theorem 1.

Property 2. For all history expressions H and H' if $H \equiv H'$ then each execution trace is denoted by H if and only if it is also denoted by H'.

In general, we know that all history expressions can be reduced to a corresponding MNF as stated by the following property.

Property 3. For each history expression H there exists H' such that $H \equiv H'$ and H' is in MNF.

The last property we recall from [12] is *metric safety*, which characterises one of the main aspects of the metric annotations we generate.

Theorem 2. *If the type and effects system infers H from a service e and $H \equiv \bar{d} \# H'$ such that $\bar{d} \# H'$ is in MNF, then for each execution of e starting from vector $\bar{d}'$ and generating $\bar{d}''$ holds that $\bar{d}'' \leq_S \bar{d}' \otimes \bar{d}$.*

Similarly to type safety, this theorem guarantees that metric annotations produced by our equational theory provide an upper bound to the metric values generated by the execution of a term. As each of them has a corresponding MNF, this theorem can be universally applied to any history expression. Referring to our working example, the theorem above guarantees that we can always build a table like Table 1 starting from the implementation of the involved services (see [12] for details about the automatic assignment of metric annotations to history expressions).

Example 3. In Fig. 2, H_{BT} denotes the behaviour of BestTravel. In particular, we use H_i as an abbreviation for the history expression of sub-service i and $\bar{d}_i$ for the annotating metric. The structure of each history expression H_i is reported in Table 4. Each history expression H_i has the form $\bar{d}_i \# H_i'$ where H_i' has no further metric annotations, that is, H_i is in *metric normal form*.

Example 4. In our running example the n-dimensional c-semiring for the find_a_hotel sub-process, can be specified as follows: $\bar{S} = (S^1, S^2, S^3)$ (see Example 1) We have two alternatives for search_a_hotel (see Table 1): $(40, 0.93, 60) \# H'_7 + (30, 0.92, 90) \# H'_8$, and two alternatives for book_a_hotel: $(5, 0.95, 30) \# H'_5 + (15, 0.89, 60) \# H'_6$. We see that $\bar{d}_5 \oplus^{-1} \bar{d}_6 = \bar{d}_6$ and these values $(\bar{d}_6)$ the BestTravel is able to guarantee if at least one of the two services is available. Unfortunately, $\bar{d}_7 \oplus^{-1} \bar{d}_8$ cannot be solved, since $40 > 30$, but $0.93 > 0.92$ and $60 < 90$ and we have to propagate the glb for search_a_hotel activity further. The whole find_a_hotel sub-process has (H_{f_h}) the result $(55, 0.8188, 90) \# H'_{f\_h}$. Note, that the result satisfies0 the requirements specified in Sect. 2.

4.1 Aggregation of Similar Metrics

Sometimes the same property is measured in different ways. For example, security risk level is measured by quantitative (e.g., using natural numbers) and qualitative (e.g., using high, medium, and low levels) methods. Also trust may be computed either as a values in [0;1] interval (similar to eBay reputation system) or as a discrete value (e.g., {-1, 0, 1, 2, 3, 4} [19]).

In order to make our analysis work with different types of metrics we first need to link a more concrete metric and a more abstract one. Such a link must satisfy the conditions for *Galois insertion* to correctly approximate a concrete metric in abstract domain and vice versa (see [16] for details):

Definition 5. *Let we have two sets D^c and D^a and two operations $\sqsubseteq_s$ and $\leq_s$ which define the order in the two sets correspondingly (we write $(D^c, \sqsubseteq_s)$ and $(D^a, \leq_s)$ to denote these posets). A Galois insertion $\langle \alpha, \gamma \rangle : (D^c, \sqsubseteq_s) \rightleftharpoons (D^a, \leq_s)$ is a pair of mapping functions: $\alpha : D^c \to D^a$ and $\gamma : D^a \to D^c$ such that:*

1. *α and γ are monotone,*
2. *$\forall d^c \in D^c,\ d^c \sqsubseteq_s \gamma(\alpha(d^c))$, and*
3. *$\forall d^a \in D^a,\ \alpha(\gamma(d^a)) = d^a$*

If we can prove that α abstraction satisfies the order-preserving property [18], we can transform all concrete metrics to abstract ones and find the optimal solutions using only one (abstract) set of metrics (see [18] for the proof). Note, that in this case the optimal solution for a more abstract metric may be referred to several concrete solutions.

Definition 6. *The abstraction α is order-preserving if for any two sets D_1^c and D_2^c of concrete elements the following observation holds:*

$$\tilde{\bigotimes}_{d \in D_1^c} \alpha(d) \sqsubseteq_s \tilde{\bigotimes}_{d \in D_2^c} \alpha(d) \implies \bigotimes_{d \in D_1^c} d \leq_s \bigotimes_{d \in D_2^c} d$$

where $\tilde{\bigotimes}$ and $\bigotimes$ are multiplicative operations for abstract and concrete c-semirings correspondingly.

Example 5. Without loss of generality we consider recovery time metric in isolation. In the marketplace (see Table 1) there are two alternatives for search_for_an_itinerary (Lufthansa and AirFrance) which have values *fast* and *medium* from c-semiring $\langle \{very\ fast, fast, normal, slow, very\ slow\}, min,$ $max, very\ slow, very\ fast \rangle$. Note, that booking_services (PayPal and Ripplepay) have values 30 and 60 from a different c-semiring $\langle N^+ \cup \{\infty\}, min, max, \infty, 0 \rangle$. The α abstraction in this case is defined as the following mapping: $[0, 15] \mapsto very\,fast,\ (15, 50] \mapsto fast,\ (50, 100] \mapsto normal,\ (100, 300] \mapsto slow,\ [300, +\infty] \mapsto veryslow$. The backward transformation γ: $very\ fast \mapsto 15;\ fast \mapsto 50;\ normal \mapsto 100;\ slow \mapsto 300;$ $very\ slow \mapsto +\infty$.

Thus, the value of the first option for booking activity (PayPal) is mapped to *fast* in the more abstract c-semiring, when the second option (Ripplepay) has *medium* value. To be in a safe position we consider the worst case, getting *medium* value for the sub-process.

Unfortunately, many abstractions do not have such property and we have to use glb for aggregation.

In many cases a service may define a metric only in one c-semiring, while another service defines a similar metric with another c-semiring. In order to aggregate or select a value in such situation we can assign the best value (i.e., $\mathbf{1}$) to the undefined c-semiring without changing the result. We can do this, since $\mathbf{1}$ is a unit element for $\otimes$ and $\oplus^{-1}$, i.e., $\forall d\ \mathbf{1} \otimes d = d$ and $\mathbf{1} \oplus^{-1} d = d$.

Example 6. The trust metric for search_a_direct_flight services is of a different c-semiring than others: $S^4 = \langle \{1, 2, 3, 4, 5\}, max, min, 1, 5 \rangle$. The Galois insertions between S^4 and S^3 we used for trust so far (see Example 1) is defined as follows: α: $[0, 0.2) \mapsto 1;\ [0.2, 0.4) \mapsto 2;\ [0.4, 0.6) \mapsto 3;\ [0.6, 0.8) \mapsto 4;\ [0.8, 1] \mapsto 5;$ and γ: $1 \mapsto 0;\ 2 \mapsto 0.2;\ 3 \mapsto 0.4;\ 4 \mapsto 0.6;\ 5 \mapsto 0.8$.

Since, we cannot make a final choice about the selected candidate for search_a_direct_flight subprocess H_{12} we should propagate the glb of them $(10, 5, 75)\#H'_1$ and $(20, 4, 45)\#H'_2$, which is $(20, 4, 75)\#H'_{12}$. The result of the check for the following non-deterministic choice (H_{11}) is equal to $(23, 0.8455, normal)\#H'_{11}$: the branch of booking an itinerary has the worst value (after aggregation of the worst alternatives for search_an_itinerary $(8, 0.95, normal)\#H'_4$ and book_an_itinerary $(15, 0.89, fast)\#H'_6$). In order to aggregate values of $\bar{d}_{12}$ and $\bar{d}_{11}$ we need to have two dimensions for two types of trust metrics. Thus, our n-dimensional c-semiring transforms to $\bar{s}' = (S^1, S^2, S^4, S^3)$. The c-semirings under consideration are transformed to $(20, 1, 4, 75)'\#H'_{12}$, and $(23, 0.8455, 5, normal)'\#H'_{11}$. Now, we can easily aggregate the c-semirings. The result for find_a_flight sub-process (H_{f_f}) is $(43, 0.8455, 4, normal)'\#H'_{f\_f}$.

Finally, at the end of the aggregation process we can use abstraction to a metric common for different components of n-dimensional c-semiring for selecting the worst alternative. Note, that adding $\mathbf{1}$ at a place of an absent component does not change the result of the aggregation at the abstract level. First, such addition does not change the result of aggregation and selection, as shown above. Second, even if no aggregation or selection is needed, abstraction maps **1** in a concrete c-semiring to **1** in an abstract c-semiring (see [18]) and thus, does not affect the result of aggregation on the abstract level.

Example 7. We continue Example 6. Now we can transform the more concrete value to the abstract one using α: $0.8455 \mapsto 5$, and aggregate the values of trust c-semirings S^2 and S^4 using aggregation operation of abstract metric: $min(4,5) = 4$. Thus, the result is $(43, 4, normal)\#H'_{f-f}$. We see, that this sub-process may violate the policy of having the trust value at least 5. On the other hand, for order-preserving abstractions we may do the backward mapping γ to find the lowest bound for recovery time and, this means, that the final value of the recovery time metric does not violate the policy (see Example 5): $normal \mapsto 100 < 120$.

Finally, the abstraction may be used to compare metrics even if an abstract metric is not a component of the n-dimensional c-semiring at all.

Example 8. Now, consider the prepare_invoice sub-process, which consists of one activity only, i.e., sign_a_receipt. For the sake of simplicity, we consider only risk metric, since there are no other requirements for this sub-process.

There are two concrete services with assigned 3-dimensional c-semirings. The metrics of the 3-dimensional c-semiring denote the probability of not violating of integrity, confidentiality and availability, which could be seen as probabilistic semirings: $\mathbf{S}^5 = \langle [0; 1]; max; \times; 0; 1 \rangle$. We have 2 alternatives with the $(\mathbf{S}^5, \mathbf{S}^5, \mathbf{S}^5)$ c-semirings: $(0.3, 0.6, 0.9)\#H'_9 + (0.7, 0.9, 0.6)\#H'_{10}$. These values cannot be simply compared, but we can use an abstractions to qualitative risk value: for integrity α^{int}:$[0, 0.333) \mapsto high$, $[0.333, 0.666) \mapsto medium$, $[0.666, 1] \mapsto low$; for confidentiality α^{conf}: $[0, 0.666) \mapsto medium$, $[0.6661] \mapsto low$; for availability α^{av}: $[0, 0.666) \mapsto medium$, $[0.666, 1] \mapsto low$. Here we assumed, that integrity has high impact, while confidentiality and availability - medium impact and used the Risk-Level Matrix from [20][4].

Now, we are able to compare the alternatives using a c-semiring for qualitative risk: $\mathbf{S}^r = \langle \{low, medium, high\}, min, max, low, high \rangle$. The results of the abstraction are: $(high, medium, low)^r\#H'_9 + (low, low, medium)^r\#H'_{10}$ ($\bar{d}^r_9, \bar{d}^r_{10} \in (\mathbf{S}^r, \mathbf{S}^r, \mathbf{S}^r)$). We aggregate values for every c-semiring separately and see that the risk value for ESignForms is *high* and violates the requirement.

5   Related Work

Many authors proposed formal languages for specifying and verifying agreements, also called *contracts*, between a service provider and a customer. Some authors [5,21] propose formal languages for defining service contracts. Such languages rely on process algebra-like syntax and exploit automatic verification

---

[4] In this example, we also assume, that security breaches are independent.

techniques for generating service orchestrations. In [22] Martinelli and Matteucci describe how to synthesise a secure orchestrator, i.e., an agent which drives the interaction between two services respects a certain security policy. History expressions have been applied to model and verify service compositions by Bartoletti et al. [3]. They apply local policies through a security framing operator and find service orchestrations respecting all of them. Although, the proposals described above use contracts for the specification and analysis of history-based service properties, none of them allow for the definition of security metrics and restrictions on them as we do in this work.

Jaeger et al. [23] proposed to aggregate quantitative service qualities taking into account workflow of services. Such metrics as mean cost and mean reputation were considered. Yu et al. [8] extended the application of the ideas of Jaeger at. al. to select a composition with the best values of a considered quantitative metric. The authors also defined a set of aggregation functions for some specific metrics and applied algorithms for solving multidimensional multiple choice knapsack problem to find the best alternative which satisfies the considered constraints. Security specific metrics were taken into account by Massacci and Yautsiukhin [7]. The authors created a directed graph using the workflow of a process and defined the aggregation algorithm for monotonic metrics.

All these methods lack of generality since the algorithms should be changed when a new metric is considered. Moreover, most of these proposals consider a single metric at a time. Yu et al. [8] proposed a specific weighted function in order to compute a single combined metric and then use it for service selection. Massacci and Yautsiukhin also extended their framework to perform the analysis with several metrics using Pareto-optimality principle [11]. Although, our work uses the same principle, we also have shown that we can apply abstraction to combine similar metrics more efficiently and without using weighted functions, which are hard to define precisely. Moreover, our metric analysis is merged in a unique framework with security property checks and can be preformed at the same time. Finally, our framework determines the values of QoS the service developer may guarantee even if all best services are not available at the moment.

6   Conclusion

In the paper we provided a framework which allows for checking several quantitative security requirements at the same time. We have found that few changes are required to extend our framework for multidimensional analysis. We also found that when metrics satisfy the order-preserving property we are able to use only the abstract metric for analysis. In case this property fails, we still are able the lower value we can guarantee. In both cases, the proposed method allows eliminating alternatives from the consideration in one run avoiding unnecessary aggregation of these values, making the analysis more efficient. Naturally, the proposed method depends on the correct definitions of c-semirings and abstraction functions. Since both definitions are metric-specific, it is enough to specify them once and reuse them in any scenario afterwards. As a future work, we consider implementation of our framework and testing it in a real scenario.

References

1. Nielson, H.R., Nielson, F.: A flow-sensitive analysis of privacy properties. In: Proceedings of the CSF-07 (2007)
2. Rossi, S., Macedonio, D.: Information flow security for service compositions. In: Proceedings of the ICUMT-09 (2009)
3. Bartoletti, M., Degano, P., Ferrari, G.L.: Planning and verifying service composition. J. Comput. Secur. 17(5), 799–837 (2009)
4. Bravetti, M., Lanese, I., Zavattaro, G.: Contract-driven implementation of choreographies. In: Kaklamanis, C., Nielson, F. (eds.) TGC 2008. LNCS, vol. 5474, pp. 1–18. Springer, Heidelberg (2009)
5. Padovani, L.: Contract-directed synthesis of simple orchestrators. In: van Breugel, F., Chechik, M. (eds.) CONCUR 2008. LNCS, vol. 5201, pp. 131–146. Springer, Heidelberg (2008)
6. Karabulut, Y., et al.: Security and trust in it business outsourcing: a manifesto. ENTCS, vol. 179. Elsevier, Amsterdam (2006)
7. Massacci, F., Yautsiukhin, A.: Modelling of quality of protection in outsourced business processes. In: Proceedings of the IAS-07. IEEE (2007)
8. Yu, T., Zhang, Y., Lin, K.J.: Efficient algorithms for web services selection with end-to-end qos constraints. ACM Trans. Web 1, 1–26 (2007)
9. Krautsevich, L., et al.: Formal approach to security metrics. what does "more secure" mean for you? In: Proceedings of the MESSA-10. ACM Press (2010)
10. Jaquith, A.: Security Metrics: Replacing Fear, Uncertainty, and Doubt. Addison-Wesley, Upper Saddle River (2007)
11. Innerhofer-Oberperfler, F., Massacci, F., Yautsiukhin, A.: Pareto-optimal architecture according to assurance indicators. In: Proceedings of the 13th Nordic Workshop on Secure IT Systems (2008)
12. Costa, G., Martinelli, F., Yautsiukhin, A.: Metric-aware secure service orchestration. In: Proceedings of the ICE-12. EPTCS (2012)
13. Costa, G., Degano, P., Martinelli, F.: Modular plans for secure service composition. J. Comput. Secur. 20(1), 81–117 (2012)
14. OMG: Business Process Model and Notation (BPMN). version 2.0 edn.
15. Gordon, L.A., Loeb, M.P.: Managing Cybersecurity Resources: A Cost-Benefit Analysis. McGraw Hill, New York (2006)
16. Bistarelli, S., Montanari, U., Rossi, F.: Semiring-based constraint satisfaction and optimization. J. ACM 44, 201–236 (1997)
17. Bartoletti, M., Degano, P., Ferrari, G.-L., Zunino, R.: Secure service orchestration. In: Aldini, A., Gorrieri, R. (eds.) FOSAD 2006/2007. LNCS, vol. 4677, pp. 24–74. Springer, Heidelberg (2007)
18. Bistarelli, S., Codognet, P., Rossi, F.: Abstracting soft constraints: framework, properties, examples. Artif. Intell. 139, 175–211 (2002)
19. Abdul-Rahman, A., Hailes, S.: A distributed trust model. In: Proceedings of the NSPW. ACM (1997)
20. Stoneburner, G., Goguen, A., Feringa, A.: Risk management guide for information technology systems. Technical, report 800–30, NIST

21. Bravetti, M., Zavattaro, G.: Towards a unifying theory for choreography conformance and contract compliance. In: Lumpe, M., Vanderperren, W. (eds.) SC 2007. LNCS, vol. 4829, pp. 34–50. Springer, Heidelberg (2007)
22. Martinelli, F., Matteucci, I.: Synthesis of web services orchestrators in a timed setting. In: Dumas, M., Heckel, R. (eds.) WS-FM 2007. LNCS, vol. 4937, pp. 124–138. Springer, Heidelberg (2008)
23. Jaeger, M.C., Rojec-Goldmann, G., Muhl, G.: QoS aggregation in web service compositions. In: Proceedings of the CEC-05 (2005)

Explication of Termination Semantics as a Security-Relevant Feature in Business Process Modeling Languages

Jens Gulden[✉]

IT Security Management, University of Siegen, Hölderlinstr. 3, 57068
Siegen, Germany
gulden@wiwi.uni-siegen.de

Abstract. Some business process modeling languages offer explicit constructs for expressing time-out conditions and other termination semantics with regard to process execution. However, the use of these language elements is usually optional, and most languages allow to model business processes without any time-outs or other termination conditions at all. This leads to an underspecification of execution semantics with negative impact on execution safety and security, because it remains open how processes will behave, if some of the involved process steps terminate other than expected, or do not terminate at all. The work presented in this article motivates the obligatory use of termination semantics in business process models and newly created business process modeling languages, especially in domain-specific process modeling languages.

Keywords: Business process modeling · Security · Termination semantics · Time-out · Cancellation

1 Motivation

Diverse process modeling approaches claim to provide means for modeling business processes. Business processes are processes which at some points relate to situations originating from an outer environment beyond any processing system, the "real world", they are not purely algorithmic and are typically not solely performed by an automatic processing mechanism such as a computer. Instead, they come into existence as a whole process by the interaction of individually acting entities. When modeling such processes, visual diagram languages are typically used.

While the way BPMLs describe the interaction among multiple process steps has undergone extensive research in the past [6, 11–13], less considerations have been performed with regard to the question what it means to execute a single individual process step in a business process, and how model elements representing individual process steps should be semantically treated in a BPML. Due to their relationship to real-world goals and tasks, process steps in BPMLs share

N. Lohmann et al. (Eds.): BPM 2013 Workshops, LNBIP 171, pp. 486–497, 2014.
DOI: 10.1007/978-3-319-06257-0_38, © Springer International Publishing Switzerland 2014

some common properties with regard to their embedding into an entire process. One of these properties is the idea, that a process step should always finish with a specified exit state. This means it is typically assumed, that a hypothetical orchestration mechanism is able to derive the termination state of an individual process step, and an orchestration mechanism will always be able to continue process execution invoking subsequent process steps. When looking closer at this assumption, it turns out that it unleashes an underspecification of formal process step execution semantics in available BPMLs compared to possible real-world situations that may occur during non-automatic, non-algorithmic parts of the execution of modeled process steps. The impact of possible deviations from the default assumed termination semantics may vary widely, depending on the real-world domain referred to by business process models. In security relevant contexts, e.g., when processes for risky environments are modeled, or processes which affect human health or lives, it can be dangerous to specify business processes with modeling languages and techniques that do not allow to cover possible exceptional behavior of individual process steps in the model.

As a consequence, the research question arises, how language means for expressing the termination semantics of individual process steps from an entire process's orchestration point of view can be incorporated into business process modeling languages. This is especially important in those cases, where deviations from the default assumed process behavior are likely to be of high impact. The upcoming article looks deeper at the semantic constellations related to process step termination, and theoretically argues for designing higher expressive BPMLs which account for specifying process step termination semantics as inherent part of process step modeling.

Section 2 introduces related approaches in scientific research and discusses some available process modeling languages. In Sect. 3, a variety of possible semantic constellations is described and discussed, to form a terminological framework for describing ways of process step termination. Section 4 derives recommendations for designing new business process modeling languages, especially domain-specific process modeling languages, from the considerations given in the section before. With the presentation of two prototypically developed domain-specific business process modeling languages in Sect. 5, a practical evaluation of the presented theoretic considerations is given. Section 6 closes with concluding remarks and notes about possible future research.

2   Related Work

For the purpose of semantically analyzing business process models, some fundamental research has been carried out about deriving structural and semantic properties from given model instances. Most of these approaches have in common that their primary objects of interest are business processes in their entirety, i.e., they analyze structural properties of processes and the semantics of their execution [6], rather than looking at individual process steps. Individual process steps are merely treated as black boxes in most of the available research work, which makes the work at hand a contribution which complements these existing approaches with the orthogonal perspective on single individual process steps.

In [1,13] and others, the property of soundness is discussed. For a process model to be sound means that no deadlocks can occur during runtime execution, and that no runtime instances can reach an endless loop. It should be noted that the soundness property exclusively refers to the orchestration of entire processes and does not consider different termination semantics of individual process steps. This means, the soundness property is blind towards possible blockings or non-termination of individual steps.

Additional semantic properties of process models, which can be derived via analysis of model instances, e.g., reachability and executability, are discussed in [14]. In combination with these considerations, quantitative means for measuring structural properties of business process models [3] have been examined.

Specific meta-properties, such as the possibility for conflicts of mutual exclusion, which is a generalization of the idea of deadlocks, are taken into focus by [10]. A general notion of "forbidden behavior" is consulted in [11], to gain a theoretical grip on how correctness of process models can be defined. The proposed approach consists of a stricter notion of how to define correctness, compared to the notion of soundness.

Some existing business process modeling languages and workflow modeling languages support to specify a subset of the possible range of termination semantics. In BPMN 2.0, e.g., event types for interrupting process steps are part of the language. These cover message events, time-outs and time-related events, error catching, compensation handlers, and others [4]. While these language constructs allow to express many relevant termination conditions on the conceptual modeling level, they do not inherently belong to the notion of process steps, but remain independent language elements which can be related to several different model element constellations apart from process steps, too. The use of event types for specifying process step termination conditions is purely optional in BPMN 2.0, and their extensive use results in models with high complexity, if multiple termination conditions are specified for all process step elements in a model. This makes BPMN 2.0 applicable for modeling secure workflow processes on an implementation level of abstraction, but not suitable for conceptually specifying secure business processes from a non-technical business modeling perspective.

A number of extensions to the BPMN language have been suggested, which can be considered as alternative ways of expressing termination conditions and other security constraints. Some of the approaches suggest to include runtime expressions based on process performance measurements into the process execution, which allow to model alternative process flows depending on time-out values and other measurements derived from a process instance [2].

Implementation-level workflow modeling languages offer time-out constructs, although their use cannot be understood as an explicit conceptual specification of termination semantics. E.g., the BPEL language uses `<bpel:invoke>` and `<bpel:receive>` language elements [8] to synchronously invoke a web-service as a process step implementation, or to receive results from an asynchronously invoked web-service, respectively. However, both of these language primitives rely on externally specified time-outs provided by the execution interpreter configuration, and cannot be changed as part of the semantics of the BPEL workflow. Instead, to incorporate time-out semantics inside a BPEL workflow model, the invocation of synchronous web-services has to be surrounded by a `<bpel:scope>` block with a `<bpel:onAlert>` event handler inside its `<bpel:eventHandlers>` section. To realize an asynchronous receive operation using an explicitly specified time-out, BPEL requires to use a `<bpel:pick>` operation instead of a `<bpel:receive>` operation, which can specify an inner `<bpel:onAlert>` branch that is executed if no message is received by the pick operation in between a specified amount of time of until a given point in time.

The inconsistent syntax constructs used in BPEL for reflecting the notion of time-outs in different contexts show that the BPEL language design does not reflect the notion of termination semantics of invoked web-services on a general level of abstraction, but that the language elements used for realizing time-outs in BPEL originate from implementation-driven, technological requirements.

3   Termination Semantics of Process Steps

Theoretic reflection on business process modeling languages mostly puts focus on language constructs that bind together individual steps of action in a process, to form an entire process out of multiple individual pieces. Such language elements are, e.g., sequence elements which express a follower relationship among different individual steps of action, or conditional constructs which mark some branches of modeled process as being optionally executed. Depending on how these constructs are applied, structural properties of the resulting processes, e.g., their soundness [1], or the possible flow of information, can then be subject to theoretical research.

The notion of individual steps of action in a process, which has different names in different BPMLs, such as "action" or simply "process", is uniformly called "process steps" in the subsequent elaboration.

During the operation of process steps, the relevant work in a process is done. This is reflected by the assumption most BPMLs make, that state changes of the process are caused exclusively by the process step execution. Despite this important role of process steps concerning the semantics of the overall processes they are embedded in, the conceptual notion of process steps is mostly not elaborated in depth in BPML specifications, and from the point of view offered by a BPML, process steps are often only atomistic black boxes, which are executed separately from the overall process orchestration semantics.

As the previous considerations have shown, the notion of process steps in business process models is kept very general, to cover a wide range of possible concrete realizations. This means in turn for the termination semantics of process steps, that almost any possible kind of behavior with respect to termination of a single step can possibly occur in general purpose business process modeling languages.

Multiple different kinds of conditions under which a process step may terminate are identified in the following. Some of these conditions can be combined, to form a set of more complex conditions to be differentiated when talking about a process step's termination.

Some BPMLs, such as the business process modeling notation (BPMN) language [4], make use of block-oriented semantics to specify different types of process flows, e.g., sequential, parallel, or random execution of process steps inside a specified block. Other languages use the notion of sequences for specifying the possible execution order of process steps. The considerations made here are independent from how process step execution orders are explicated, and can be applied to both to BPMLs which use a graph-oriented or a block oriented mode. This is the case, because the considerations in this article primarily focus on the execution semantics of individual process step elements, not on the orchestration semantics provided by the dynamics of a BPML.

To form a terminological framework for describing possible alternative ways of process step termination, a variety of possible semantic constellations for process step termination inside business processes is discussed in the following.

(1) Termination with a valid result. The default termination behavior of a process step, as it is typically assumed by the notion of process steps used in business process models, is a regular termination with a defined kind of result. Results can be physical entities, e.g., in process steps where physical objects are created from raw material. Results may also be documents or state changes in computer systems involved in performing the process.

In the most general case, a process step's result is represented by a state change in the assumed execution logic of an orchestration instance that schedules individual process steps to form coherent process instances. Such state changes can consist of information passed as return values to the orchestration logic, but may also be restricted to the fact that an invocation has occurred. In this sense, all process steps may possibly terminate with a valid result from the point of view of the orchestration logic, even steps which are considered to be triggered in a one-way fashion without returning any explicit result value, or without throwing any exceptions, etc., to the orchestration logic. Such steps still cause a state change in the orchestration logic when invoked, and triggering them without error during the invocation itself can be considered to fall into the category of terminating with a valid result.

(2) Termination with an invalid result. The question whether a result is valid or invalid depends on the semantics of the process step in the context of the entire business process. This means, a process orchestration mechanism cannot know by itself whether a result is valid or not, and the process model itself must contain mechanisms in the further described course of the process to test for the validity of a result. Results are thus not valid or invalid by themselves, but become declared as such by the process semantics.

BPMLs typically do not allow to distinguish between the cases of valid or invalid results already when modeling the integration of a process into the overall process orchestration. Instead, a result provided by a process step needs to be explicitly tested for its validity using according evaluation and branching operations provided by the modeling language.

(3) Termination with an undefined result. When conceptualizing process steps on a general abstraction level, an informal logic must be assumed which is not bound to a "tertium non datur" notion. That means, to realistically model termination semantics in which a result of any kind is expected, the alternative of a "not there" for results in a physical sense, or a "don't know" for information results, must be considered.

Most of the existing general purpose BPMLs do not offer implicit language constructs to cope with this kind of process step termination semantics. Comparable to handling the case of invalid results, modeling constructs for explicitly testing results for being properly defined or not have to be used.

(4) Termination with a non-fatal error. When process steps fail with a non-fatal error, they unintentionally produce an undefined result due to erroneous conditions, but the mistakes that lead to the error do not have destructive consequences for the interaction functionality of the entire distributed process system. The error remains local to entities which have been involved in performing the process step, but the integrity of the entire process orchestration is not affected.

From the point of view of an orchestrating instance, this case can be treated in the same way as an undefined result. Other than in the undefined case, however, the notion of an error indicates that the realization of the process step did not occur in a planned or in any way sound matter. This means that apart from treating the result as undefined, other mechanisms such as error reporting of invocations of recovery procedures should be initiated, which are orthogonal to the process orchestration task.

The characterization of being "non-fatal" refers to the effects the error has on the overall process orchestration. It is not an internal characterization of the process step's realization regarding how the error was produced.

(5) Termination with a fatal error. When process steps terminate with a fatal error, they produce an undefined result, and the conditions that lead to the error do not allow to continue with the entire process orchestration. The error has destructive consequences for the interaction of the distributed actors of the process, and the process integrity is hurt in a way that typically does not allow to continue with the process.

(6) No termination. This condition at first appears to be unrealistic, because in the modeled real-world domain, no possible realization of a process step can be imagined, which practically never terminates. However, from the point of view of a process orchestration mechanism, the situation of no termination at all is more likely to occur than it seems at first sight. This is because the "no termination" condition applies to a process step from the point of view of an orchestration mechanism in several cases, which can either be caused by the realization of the process step itself, or by outer circumstances that influence the flow of information required for the orchestration mechanism to detect a process step's termination.

The idea that process steps might never complete is contradictory to the way process steps are embedded in process models, because every process model assumes an execution logic, which continues performing the overall process step scheduling, or finishes off the process if indeed the last process steps has been performed. The entire idea of executing a process composed of multiple steps would not make sense, if during the execution of the process, a process step would be able to prevent any further modeled process steps from execution by not completing at all. It thus must be understood as inherent to the notion of process steps that they return to a completed state (successfully or unsuccessfully) after some time of execution. Any process modeling language, which does allow to specify process steps as parts of processes without any time-out, thus allows for creating process model instances with underspecified semantics. A solution to this would be to accompany the language documentation with a default time-out to be assumed by automatic execution engines when process steps without explicit time-out are executed as part of a process execution. This leaves it to the documented convention and the implementation in process execution engines, whether modeled processes can be executed semantically valid way.

(7) Unknown termination. Another kind of termination semantics, which at first sight appears useless, but occurs quite often in practice, are process step terminations which do not matter for the orchestration engine to continue with the process flow. This is the case when two sub-conditions match, first, there is no result expected from the process step, and second, the start of the process step is triggered once, without making use of a synchronization mechanism that would cause the invoking orchestration instance to wait until the process step signalizes back some kind of termination notification.

In technical terms, this situation occurs whenever asynchronous web-service invocations are realized to services, which do not provide a result message and thus do not require an asynchronous callback from the service to the orchestration instance after termination.

Some BPMLs provide means to model different termination conditions at least as explicit language constructs. The BPMN language [4] allows to use a time-out event handler combined with a message event handler, which both provide means to express different termination conditions in BPMN.

While the given examples show some attempts to locate the notion of cancellation conditions on the conceptional language level, none of these languages requires to declare cancellation conditions. This shows that the underlying notion of steps in a process still stems from a technical, synchronous workflow understanding, in which process steps are deterministic in their behavior and can be expected to terminate after a predictable duration. From a conceptual view, it cannot be reasonable to offer BPMLs which support such an unrealistic notion of process steps. The more abstract the conceptual level of a BPMLs is regarded, the more likely it becomes that the actual realization of a process steps occurs in a non-deterministic, non-automatizable way, which is surrounded by a multitude of possible cancellation conditions determined by the real-world setting a business process is executed in.

4   Design Recommendation for Creating Domain-Specific Business Process Modeling Languages

As a consequence of the prior consideration, it turns out that it is of high value to conceptually bear in mind the notion of termination semantics inseparable from the notion of process steps in business process modeling languages. Whenever process modeling languages are designed, language engineers should consider to include language constructs which are directly bound to process step modeling elements, e.g., as attribute values, or as inherent child elements of process step modeling elements.

Since the use of domain-specific modeling and development methods typically includes creating a new domain specific modeling language at the beginning of a project [5], this recommendation can generally be applied to all domain specific modeling projects, in which language constructs for modeling process perspectives on real-world incidents, are included.

Due to the manifold nature of possible termination conditions in the conceptualizations of general purpose BPMLs, it turns out to be a recommendation to make use of domain-specific process modeling languages in cases, where termination semantics of process steps are of high interest with respect to the modeling purpose. If, e.g., a security relevant software system is to be derived from process model specifications, a more detailed focus needs to be put on process steps' termination semantics. To allow the specification of termination characteristics and possible process orchestration behavior on the process model level, a general purpose BPML can be expected to not offer enough expressiveness. As a consequence, the cost for creating a domain specific language or for adapting an existing one may be justified with respect to the gain in possibly derived functionality, e.g., in the field of software security.

5   Prototypical Implementation in Secured Food Supply Chain Process Modeling Languages

To demonstrate the previous considerations on the background of a real-world modeling and software development project, two examples of domain specific process modeling languages for securing the food supply chain domain are shown in this section.[1]

The economic sector of food production, supply, and retail, faces a high degree of complexity in size and dynamics, with a large number of market participants acting to a great extent independently. While the traded goods involve an increased level of risks connected to health and other security issues, the products and their distribution processes currently are mostly unprotected along the supply chain, and exposed to potential vulnerabilities, either by intended threats

---

[1] The work presented in this section has flown into the project RESCUEIT, funded by the German Federal Ministry of Education and Research (Bundesministerium für Bildung und Forschung, BMBF) under support code no. 13N10963 – 13N10968.

or unintended disasters. Risks in the food supply chain can potentially range from quality leaks and recipe manipulations, to disease infections or poisonings. To reduce the threats along the food supply chain, it is desirable to introduce mechanisms that allow for an IT-supported usage control and a more reliable risk management along the supply chain [9].

In current food supply chain realizations, the electronic communication between the participants is not necessarily secured, and the overall flow of the supply chain process is not coordinated and controlled, because no joint overview on the overall supply chain process is available from any of the involved systems. Individual supply chain activities thus cannot be controlled for validity in the overall process flow, which makes it possible to accidentally or intentionally manipulate supply chain processes in a way it cannot be noticed by any of the involved supply chain members or further parties. These fundamental vulnerabilities of supply chain processes, as they are currently present in the food industry sector, can be overcome by taking in a comprehensive overview perspective on supply chains and the actions performed during their execution. Achieving a bird's-eye-view on all involved activities, acting entities, and resources, allows to perform checks for validity and consistency of exchanged documents and executed process activities along the overall supply chain.

A suitable modeling language for creating a supply chain model can be composed of domain-specific model elements for expressing involved actors, action steps in the supply chain, and elements to express resources, physical as well as immaterial ones. As argued in the previous sections, to reflect possible vulnerabilities resulting from irregular process step termination, the model elements representing process steps are equipped with domain-specific attributes to configure the process behavior in case of deviating process step terminations.

A domain-specific business modeling language with corresponding model editor tooling support has been developed as a research prototype together with partners in the RESCUEIT project [7]. The model excerpt in Fig. 1 shows an abstraction of a food supply chain, in which different steps of actions performed by a retailer, a food manufacturer, and a logistician, are represented with corresponding security configuration attributes. Figure 2 zooms into one individual process step model element in the model, which makes use of a time-out construct included in the domain-specific model, to specify a time-based termination condition on the conceptual modeling level.

For cases of deviations of a realized process instance from the modeled main supply chain process, reaction processes can be prepared which describe steps to execute in cases of emergencies. Reaction process models are created in a separate reaction process modeling language, which incorporates the specification of time-outs for process steps as a mandatory semantic feature attached to process elements. Figure 3 shows an example excerpt of a reaction process model. The relevance of the time-out specification is stressed by including this model attribute into the visual diagram representation of reaction process models.

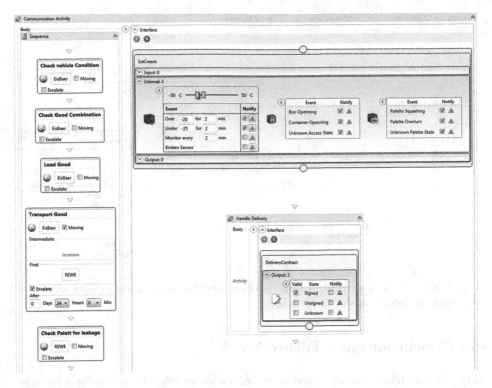

Fig. 1. Excerpt of an example food supply chain model in a domain-specific modeling language based on [7].

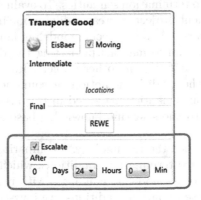

Fig. 2. Focus on a domain-specific process step model element with a time-out construct.

The conceptually modeled time-outs in the domain-specific language are implemented by a model-transformation, which converts parts of the conceptual model to a machine executable BPEL workflow process.

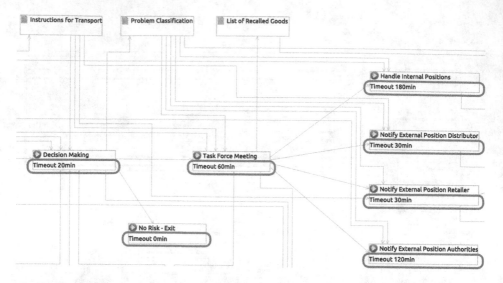

Fig. 3. Excerpt of an example reaction process model to recover from emergency cases in a domain-specific modeling language.

6   Conclusions and Future Work

The work at hand has presented an examination of what it means for a process step modeled as part of a business process model to terminate. As a theoretical contribution, it has established a terminological framework for describing multiple facets of process step termination semantics. To evaluate these considerations in a practical development project, corresponding modeling language constructs have been integrated in two domain-specific modeling languages, and have been implemented by model transformations projecting the domain specific models into executable BPEL semantics and other implementation artifacts.

An integration of the traditional notion of soundness with the notion of process step termination semantics suggested in this article might be a fruitful theoretic contribution to the scientific knowledge base about business process semantics.

After having established the terminology, a comparison framework could be derived from the identified termination conditions, which would allow to evaluate existing business process modeling languages with respect to their semantic expressiveness covering termination conditions. An investigation with this scope, however, would exceed the available range of this paper.

References

1. Fahland, D., Favre, C., Koehler, J., Lohmann, N., Völzer, H., Wolf, K.: Analysis on demand: instantaneous soundness checking of industrial business process models. Data Knowl. Eng. **70**(5), 448–466 (2011)

2. Friedenstab, J.-P., Janiesch, C., Matzner, M., Müller, O.: Extending BPMN for business activity monitoring. In: Proceedings of the 45th Hawai'i International Conference on System Sciences (HICSS), Maui, HI, pp. 1–10 (2012)
3. Gruhn, V., Laue, R.: Complexity metrics for business process models. In: 9th International Conference on Business Information Systems (BIS 2006). LNI, vol. 85, pp. 1–12 (2006)
4. Business Process Management Initiative. Business process modeling notation 2.0 (BPMN 2.0) (2011)
5. Kelly, S., Tolvanen, J.-P.: Domain Specific Modeling: Enabling Full Code-Generation. Wiley, New York (2008)
6. Mendling, J., Lassen, K.B., Zdun, U.: On the transformation of control flow between block-oriented and graph-oriented process modeling languages. Int. J. Bus. Process Integr. Manage. (IJBPIM). Special Issue on Model-Driven Engineering of Executable Business Process Models 3(2), 96–108 (2008)
7. Monakova, G., Schaad, A.: Visualizing security in business processes. In: SAC-MAT '11 Proceedings of the 16th ACM Symposium on Access Control Models and Technologies, pp. 147–148. ACM, New York (2011)
8. OASIS Web Services Business Process Execution Language (WSBPEL) Technical Committee. Web services business process execution language version 2.0. http://docs.oasis-open.org/wsbpel/2.0/OS/wsbpel-v2.0-OS.html (2007)
9. Pretschner, A., Hilty, M., Basin, D.: Distributed usage control. Commun. ACM - Priv. Secur. Highly Dyn. Syst. 49, 39–44 (2006)
10. Schefer, S., Strembeck, M., Mendling, J., Baumgrass, A.: Detecting and resolving conflicts of mutual-exclusion and binding constraints in a business process context. In: 19th International Conference on Cooperative Information Systems (CoopIS 2011), Crete, Greece (2011)
11. Simon, C., Mendling, J.: Verification of forbidden behavior in EPCS. In: Mayr, H.C., Brey, R. (eds) Modellierung 2006. LNI, vol. P-82, pp. 233–242 (2006)
12. van der Aalst, W.M.P., Ter Hofstede, A.H.M., Kiepuszewski, B., Barros, A.P.: Workflow patterns. Distrib. Parallel Databases 3(14), 5–51 (2003)
13. van Dongen, B.F., Mendling, J., van der Aalst, W.M.P.: Structural patterns for soundness of business process models. In: Proceedings of the Tenth IEEE International Enterprise Computing Conference (EDOC 2006), Hong Kong, China, pp. 116–128. IEEE Computer Society, Washington, D.C., 16–20 Oct. 2006
14. Weber, I., Hoffmann, J., Mendling, J.: Beyond soundness: on the verification of semantic business process models. Distrib. Parallel Databases (DAPD) 27(3), 271–343 (2008)

Supporting Domain Experts to Select and Configure Precise Compliance Rules

Elham Ramezani[✉], Dirk Fahland, and Wil M.P. van der Aalst

Eindhoven University of Technology, Eindhoven, The Netherlands
{e.ramezani,d.fahland,w.m.p.v.d.aalst}@tue.nl

Abstract. Compliance specifications concisely describe selected aspects of what a business operation should adhere to. To enable automated techniques for compliance checking, it is important that these requirements are specified correctly and precisely, describing exactly the behavior intended. Although there are rigorous mathematical formalisms for representing compliance rules, these are often perceived to be difficult to use for business users. Regardless of notation, however, there are often subtle but important details in compliance requirements that need to be considered. The main challenge in compliance checking is to bridge the gap between informal description and a precise specification of all requirements. In this paper, we present an approach which aims to facilitate creating and understanding formal compliance requirements by providing configurable templates that capture these details as options for commonly-required compliance requirements. These options are configured interactively with end-users, using question trees and natural language. The approach is implemented in the Process Mining Toolkit ProM.

Keywords: Compliance specification · Compliance checking · Configurable compliance rules · Auditing · Question tree

1 Introduction

Compliance checking techniques determine if business operations are within the boundaries set by law, managers and other stakeholders or obey security requirements set by the company. Such constraints can be formalized using different specification formalisms such as temporal logic [14] or deontic logic [30] depending on the compliance checking technique that is being employed. A problem often encountered in practise [19], however, is specifying precisely the behavior intended.

Many practitioners prefer capturing compliance requirements using informal notations, such as natural language, instead of formal specification languages. These representations are more accessible but often imprecise and of less value when doing automated compliance checking. Since domain experts usually describe informally a compliance requirement, technical experts may invest considerable effort formalizing it and check if the recorded process executions conform with it, only to later determine that the property has been

N. Lohmann et al. (Eds.): BPM 2013 Workshops, LNBIP 171, pp. 498–512, 2014.
DOI: 10.1007/978-3-319-06257-0_39, © Springer International Publishing Switzerland 2014

specified incorrectly. Whereas if domain experts are involved in the specification process, the intended behavior with all its subtle aspects can be specified directly and thus avoiding ambiguities.

Numerous researchers have developed specification patterns to facilitate construction of formal specification of compliance requirements. Feedback indicates [16] that these patterns are considered helpful but they fail to capture subtle aspects of a specific requirement. In addition, adaption and application of these patterns are not trivial for many practitioners as they are less familiar with the underlying formalization.

This paper describes an approach that addresses the gap between informal requirements and formal compliance specifications. We introduce an interactive approach for using tacit knowledge of domain experts to specify compliance requirements. Our approach aims at (i) enabling business users and compliance experts to specify compliance constraints and (ii) encouraging them to think about the subtle aspects of their intended behavior when specifying a constraint. The key components of this process are *question trees*, and *configurable generic compliance patterns* pre-formalized in configurable Petri nets that capture common compliance requirements. We have developed a repository of configurable compliance patterns. Every pattern allows for alternative variations of a compliant behavior. Selecting an appropriate configurable pattern and configuring a pattern for its configuration options are done interactively with user. A questionnaire consisting of two question trees asks users about their intended compliant behavior. The first question tree helps the user selecting a general compliance requirement, i.e., a configurable pattern. The second tree helps the user configuring a general requirement w.r.t. various subtle semantic aspects. The approach is implemented and a case study is being prepared to evaluate the approach.

The remainder of this paper is organized as follows. Section 2 explains a compliance management life cycle. An overview of the methodology and notions that our work is built on are discussed in Sect. 3. Section 4 introduces the repository of configurable compliance patterns. Section 5 describes how this approach facilitates compliance specification for domain experts and showcases implementation of the technique in ProM. We will review the related work in Sect. 6 and finally Sect. 7 concludes the paper and motivates future work.

2   Compliance Management

Organizations are confronted with an ever growing set of laws and regulations to comply to. Failing to comply to regulations can impose severe risks such as penal consequences on management level or lost contracts with clients. *Compliance Management* (CM) within an organization comprises the design, implementation, maintenance, verification and reporting of compliance requirements and it calls for a structured methodology. We proposed a compliance management life cycle in [23] as a methodology to elicit, formalize, implement, check, and optimize compliance requirements in organizations. As is shown in Fig. 1, compliance management activities can be identified as:

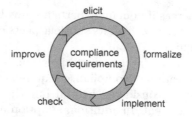

Fig. 1. Compliance management life cycle

- *Compliance Elicitation*: determine the compliance requirements that need to be satisfied. (i.e., rules defining the boundaries of compliant behavior).
- *Compliance Formalization*: specify formally compliance requirements originating from laws and regulations derived in the compliance elicitation phase.
- *Compliance Implementation*: enforce specified compliance requirements in business operation.
- *Compliance Checking*: investigate whether the constraints will be met (forward compliance checking) or have been met (backward compliance checking).
- *Compliance Optimization*: improve business processes and their underlying information systems based on the diagnostic information gained from compliance checking.

In the following we will elaborate on elicitation and formalization and briefly discuss compliance checking.

Compliance Elicitation and Formalization. Specifying precise compliance requirements spans over *Compliance Elicitation* and *Compliance Formalization* phases of the CM life cycle and introduces many challenges. It calls for combination of different knowledge areas such as compliance expertise, formalization skills, and domain specific knowledge.

Regulations are usually presented informally and described in an abstract way because they need to be independent from implementation. Moreover, the writers and users of regulations are lawyers or business users, their instrument of work uses natural language. This language is non-formalized and incorporates domain specific terminology, as well as structure and definitions. Therefore enforcing and checking a compliance requirement requires a precise formalization of this requirement. *In the step from natural language to precise formalization many subtle aspects of the requirement have to be considered.*

For instance, consider a compliance requirement we obtained from internal policies of a specialized hospital that accepts only patients requiring a specific medical treatment: "For every patient registered in the hospital an X-ray must be taken". This compliance requirement enforces that *patient registration* must be followed by activity *X-ray*. The requirement seems very straightforward but no matter which formalism is chosen for this simple requirement, while formalizing, it is important to decide about some details e.g.,: (1) whether *patient registration* should be directly followed by *X-ray* or other activities may occur in between the specified sequence; (2) whether it is allowed that other activities occur before

patient registration or a patient cannot receive any treatment without registration; (3) whether a patient can be registered several times (for instance in
different departments) and if yes; (4) should the specified sequence be followed
every time; (5) whether it is allowed that the specified sequence never occurs
i.e., if it is allowed that a patient is never registered. Interpreting an informal
rule with all its details can be surprisingly difficult and must be done by domain
experts who are usually less familiar with different formalisms. Therefore an
approach is required to hide the complexity of formalization from business user
and at the same time support automated compliance checking. In this context
an interactive *'question and answer'* approach based on "disciplined" natural
language seems promising. Such an approach is used in property specification
for software development in [8, 19, 28] and is a suitable candidate for compliance
specification. However, compliance specification is more challenging as, unlike in
software development, the formalized requirement is not inspected again by an
expert in formal techniques and immediately used to check compliance.

Compliance Checking. Precisely formulated compliance requirements derived
from previous phases in CM life cycle are used for verification, monitoring and
auditing of business processes. There are two basic types of compliance checking:
(1) forward compliance checking aims to design and implement processes where
compliant behavior is enforced [6, 12, 13, 18, 26] and (2) backward compliance
checking aims at detecting and localizing non-compliant behavior [2, 5, 17, 25]
that happened in the past. Regardless of which analysis technique is used, automated compliance checking can only be applied if a compliance requirement has
been specified precisely.

Compliance Rule Repository. In [2, 23] we have shown that compliance
requirements (originating from legislations) restrict one or several perspectives
of a process including control flow, data flow, process time or organizational
aspects. In [20, 22] we have shown how a complex compliance requirement covering several perspectives of a process can be decomposed into smaller compliance
rules which can be formalized as parameterized compliance patterns in terms of
Petri nets. These Petri nets then can be used in backward compliance checking
to provide diagnostic information about compliance violations.

This approach is supported by a repository of more than 50 compliance
patterns covering a majority of the compliance rules found in literature [21]. In
this paper we present an approach to consolidate this repository and *to select
and configure the right rule to precisely express a given informal description.*

3   Methodology

As is motivated in Sect. 2, compliance requirement specification calls for an approach that allows for defining different variations of a compliance requirement,
and is accessible in order to benefit from the compliance expertise of business
users and mathematically precise to enable automated compliance checking.
That is, it needs to offer variations of a specified behavior, hide complexity

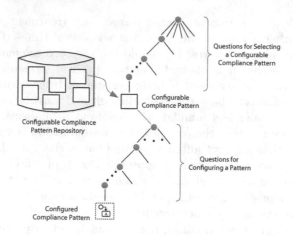

Fig. 2. Compliance specification overview

of formalization from business users and at the same time produce a formal definition of the compliance requirement.

In this section, we explain how our approach can help practitioners elucidate a compliance requirement by making informed choices between different variations of a compliance rule. Figure 2 gives an overview of our approach for compliance specification. This approach is built upon a repository of configurable compliance patterns.

Configurable Compliance Pattern Repository. Although the collection of compliance rules in [21] is comprehensive, there are subtle variations of a compliance requirement which cannot be expressed only by selecting a compliance rule from the rule repository and instantiating it for its parameters, rather slight modification in the underlying formalization may be necessary. Therefore one would like to see a general rule which allows to define all possible variations.

In addition there are over 50 compliance rules (only for control-flow perspective) in the rule repository which makes the choice of appropriate compliance rule cumbersome and error prone if the user is not familiar with the underlying formalization. To help the user selecting the right rule, we consolidated the compliance rules by merging similar rules (that differ in variations of subtle semantic aspects) into one configurable compliance pattern that is easier to describe in general terms. Consolidating similar rules into a configurable pattern is done manually following a generic approach. We first define a core behavior for the configurable pattern and then extend the core behavior with all possible configuration options. These configuration options allow to define different variations of a compliance requirement. The idea is that a user first picks a general configurable pattern with all its configuration options and then configures it w.r.t. various subtle aspects. Details of the repository of configurable patterns are given in Sect. 4.

Question Tree. In order to enable domain experts to specify the intended behavior of a compliance requirement, we apply an interactive question and answer based approach. We aim to guide users to select an appropriate configurable compliance pattern and elaborate on how to configure its configuration options such that it represents intended behavior. Thus we apply a Question Tree (QT) representation which is basically a decision tree and its content is based on disciplined natural language.

We apply *two* distinct question trees; a set of questions which guide the user to *select a specific configurable compliance pattern* and a set of questions which are asked to resolve different configuration options of a chosen configurable pattern in order to specify details of intended admissible behavior.

Questions to Select a Configurable Compliance Pattern. The QT of the first phase breaks the problem of deciding which configurable pattern is most appropriate by asking users to consider only one differentiating attribute at a time. In this phase, QT has a hierarchical structure and this structure supports the isolation of concerns, only presenting a question to the user that is relevant in context of their previous answer. A new question that can be revealed after answering a given question is a child question of that previous answer; the previous question is the parent question of that child question. By selecting a different answer to a parent question, the user will explore a different set of child questions that are relevant to that answer and will arrive at a different configurable pattern. Figure 3 QT-phase1 (left) presents the question tree for selecting a configurable pattern in the example discussed earlier in Sect. 2.

Questions to Configure a Configurable Compliance Pattern. Questions in the second phase concern configuring subtle behavioral aspects of a specific

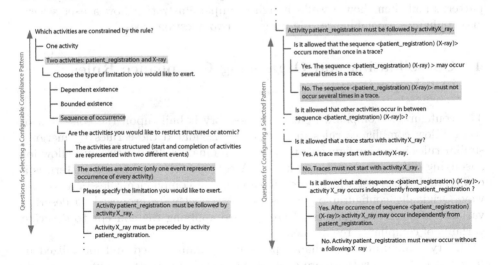

Fig. 3. QT-phase1 (left), QT-phase2 (right)

pattern. Not all questions in this phase have a hierarchical structure. That is, many questions in this phase can be asked in any order, since there are some options in each of configurable patterns which are conceptually orthogonal to each other. These questions will be presented to the user together and s/he may answer them in any order based on personal preferences and understanding. However, some options are not orthogonal e.g., a question whether a sequence of repeated events may occur several times is only meaningful if the user first answers that a sequence of repeated events is allowed. In such cases, the former question is only asked if a certain pre-configuration holds for it. Please note that the configurable pattern i.e., the underlying Petri net and its configuration options are *not shown* to the end user and user only deals with textual descriptions of rules in terms of questions and answers. In the back-end, every *answer node* of QT in the second phase is mapped to a configuration option in a configurable pattern and configures the pattern based on choices user makes. The configuration process is continued until all details of a compliant behavior is decided. Figure 3 QT-phase2 (right) presents partially the question tree of the second phase for the example of Sect. 2.

Illustrating a Compliance Rule to a Domain Expert. The configurable compliance pattern is hidden from user and s/he is only represented with questions and answers which are designed in a simple hence structured and clear text. In order to remove any ambiguity for the user while answering questions of subtle behavioral aspects, there are several compliant and non-compliant sample traces given for every answer. That is, a user can easily see how a certain choice can impact (i.e., limit or extend) admissible behavior. The configured compliance pattern determined in the second phase is a Petri net that can be used for automated compliance checking applying the techniques in [20,22].

In the following we will first discuss the repository of configurable compliance patterns and then show a walk-though example illustrating how a user selects and configures a compliance rule using the two question trees.

4   Consolidating and Organizing Compliance Rules in a Repository

The configurable compliance pattern repository is built upon the collection of control-flow compliance rules in [21]. We consolidated these rules by merging similar rules into a configurable pattern to eliminate redundancies and allow for specifying different variations of a rule. A configurable compliance pattern is a configurable Petri net which describes a group of compliance rules in a concise way. Originally configurable process models [3,24] were proposed to describe variants of a reference process. Here, we are applying the concept to describe variants of compliance requirements.

Every configurable compliance pattern is parameterized and formalized in terms of Petri nets with a core component. This core structure enforces a core behavior (e.g., a sequence). In addition a pattern has several other components

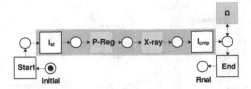

Fig. 4. Sequence of *P-Reg* and *X-ray*

which determine variations of core behavior. Core behavior enables a clear distinction between commonalities shared among compliance rules in one category and variability.

To consolidate the rules in [21], we studied rules which share a common behavior. We kept the core component in a configurable pattern and added all possible configuration options to it. The resulting configurable pattern can describe all the original rules it is derived from, and many more because of the new possible combination of different configuration options. The configurable patterns are sound be design. Please recall the example given earlier in Sect. 2. The Petri net pattern shown in Fig. 4 formalizes the core behavior of the requirement of this example.

The compliance pattern starts by firing transition *Start* and a token in place *Final* represents a completed case. The core of the rule is formalized in the grey-shaded part between transitions I_{st} and I_{cmp} which represents an instance of the compliance rule. The rule becomes active when I_{st} fires and it is satisfied when I_{cmp} fires. The hollow transitions (*Start*, I_{st}, I_{cmp}, and *End*) are invisible. The core structure of the pattern enforces; if *patient registration* (*P-Reg*) occurs then it must be followed by *X-ray*. Every compliance pattern allows to focus on activities restricted by the corresponding compliance rule and abstract from all other activities in a process. The Ω activity after I_{cmp} represents any other activity in a process apart from *P-Reg* and *X-ray*. If we want to add other options to the behavior specified in the Petri net pattern in Fig. 4, we need to add some more components to the pattern and build a configurable pattern out of it.

The configurable pattern shown in Fig. 5 is parameterized over the activity names such that activity $A = P\text{-}Reg$ and activity $B = X\text{-}ray$. The configurable pattern allows for defining variations of the core behavior and by blocking or activating a component we can extend or limit admissible behavior. In the following we will explain the components of the configurable pattern in Fig. 5 and explain how blocking or activating a component can change the behavior of the pattern.

- *Comp.1-Ω*: Activating this component allows for occurrence of arbitrary other activities in between the sequence $\langle (P\text{-}Reg)(X\text{-}ray) \rangle$ and blocking this component enforces that activity *P-Reg* must be followed directly by *X-ray*.
- *Comp.2-Ω*: Activating or blocking this component, enforces that other activities may occur before *P-Reg* or not.

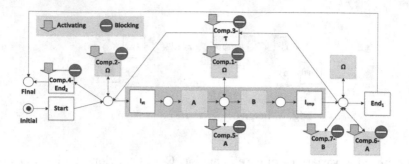

Fig. 5. Configurable sequence of *P-Reg* and *X-ray*

- *Comp.3-τ*: Activating or blocking this component allows that the sequence $\langle(P\text{-}Reg)(X\text{-}ray)\rangle$ occurs multiple times in a trace or not.
- *Comp.4-End₂*: Activating or blocking this component allows that a patient, would never get registered or not.
- *Comp.5-A*: Activating or blocking this component allows that several registrations of a patient can be followed by one execution of activity *X-ray* or not.
- *Comp.6-A*: Activating or blocking this component allows that after occurrence of the sequence $\langle(P\text{-}Reg)(X\text{-}ray)\rangle$ a patient gets registered without a following *X-ray* or not.
- *Comp.7-B*: Activating or blocking this component allows that activity *X-ray* occurs independently from the specified sequence of $\langle(P\text{-}Reg)(X\text{-}ray)\rangle$ or not.

When designing a configurable compliance pattern, we abstract from concrete examples and consider all possible configuration options. The configuration options we address in our approach include: *activating*, *blocking*, and *hiding/skipping* a transition, an arc or a group of transitions and arcs. In addition we consider configuring *arc weights*.

By developing configurable patterns, we could eliminate redundancies in a compliance rule family and reuse the commonalities, thus decreasing the number of patterns to 22 configurable compliance patterns having 0–38 configuration options each. This way, over 1000 different compliance patterns can be derived (including the original 50 patterns) though picking different configuration options.

5   Supporting Domain Experts to Specify Compliance Constraints

In this section we will elaborate our methodology and its implementation by going through a real life example step by step and showcase how a user who is not familiar with any formalism specifies his/her admissible behavior considering its detailed aspects.

The technique is implemented in the *Compliance* package of the Process Mining Toolkit ProM6, available from http://www.processmining.org. The package contains the repository of all configurable compliance patterns. The *Elicit Compliance Rule* plug-in takes a log as input and returns a compliance rule using the approach of Sect. 3. The returned rule can be used for compliance checking using the *Check Compliance of a Log* plug-in. In the following we show how a user can use this implementation to select and configure a compliance rule.

We chose the event log taken from *BPI Challenge 2011* available from [1]. The log is taken from a Dutch Academic Hospital. This log contains some 150.000 events in over 1100 cases. Apart from some anonymization, the log contains all data as it came from the hospital's systems. Each case corresponds a patient of the hospital's Gynaecology department. The log contains information about when certain activities took place, which group performed the activity and so on. Many attributes have been recorded that are relevant to the process.

To demonstrate the approach, we chose to formalize a rule that captures the following behavior observed on the event log [7]: *Glucose level must be estimated 4 times repetitively if a patient diagnosed for cervical cancer of uterus (diagnosis code M13) and classified as an urgent case*[1]. We have preprocessed this log for patients who are suffering from cervical cancer of uterus. Urgent patients are those cases where at least one activity of type urgent is manifested. A very common activity representing an urgent case is *'haemoglobin photoelectric-urgent'*. If we rephrase the constraint and substitute the activity names with corresponding event names in the log, the rule states: *In case of patients diagnosed for code M13, activity 'haemoglobin-photoelectric-urgent' must be followed 4 times by activity 'glucose-urgent'*.

We take this log as input and run the *Elicit Compliance Rule* plug-in that implements the approach of Sect. 3. The very first question of the questionnaire always asks the user to specify the number of activities of primary interest. For this a list of available activities in log is shown to user and the user can choose the activities s/he wants to restrict from this list. Depending on the number of activities chosen different sets of questions will be triggered. For instance if the user chooses one activity of primary interest, the next question will ask about the number of times a specified activity is allowed to occur. If more than one activity (e.g., in case of our example two activities) is chosen, the questions related to relationships between chosen activities will be asked. In our example:

- Which type of limitation you would like to exert?
  - Dependent Existence; define whether the occurrence or non-occurrence of an activity imposes an obligation on occurrence or non-occurrence of another activity, e.g., define an inclusive relation between two activities.

---

[1] Please note that the observed behavior does not indicate a medical rule but we chose this observation to show how we can specify a behavior using *Elicit Compliance Rule* plug-in.

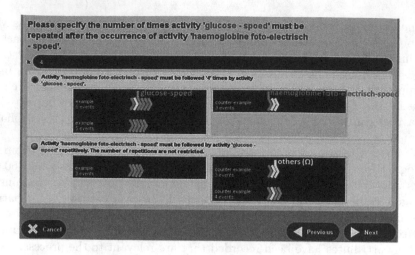

Fig. 6. Elicit compliance rule plug-in

- Bounded Existence; define whether number of occurrences of one activity is dependent to number of occurrences of the other activity.
- Sequence of Occurrence; define whether there should be a sequential relation between occurrence of two activities, e.g., define a precedence or simultaneous relation between two activities.
- Bounded Sequence of Occurrence; define whether a specified sequence must be repeated.

We choose *Bounded Sequence of Occurrence* from the list of alternative answers. As the result of this choice, a configurable pattern is selected in the back-end and questions to configure the selected pattern are presented.

The first question from the second phase will ask whether the user wants to limit the repetition of activity *'glucose-urgent'* after activity *'haemoglobin-photoelectric-urgent'* and if yes how many times *'glucose-urgent'* must occur after *'haemoglobin-photoelectric-urgent'*. Figure 6 illustrates this step in *'Elicit Compliance Rule'* plug-in in ProM where we chose: 4 times repetition of *'glucose-urgent'* after *'haemoglobin-photoelectric-urgent'*.

In order to support the user to make informed choices, for every answer a sample compliant trace and non-compliant trace is given as shown in Fig. 6. Additionally, the outcome of the currently chosen configuration is visualized to the user: the selected and partially configured rule is used to check compliance of the log w.r.t. this preliminary rule using the technique of [20]. The screen in Fig. 6 shows several compliant and non-compliant traces by which the user can use her domain knowledge to assess which answer translates her intention best.

Subsequent questions assist the user in deciding about details of the intended behavior. These questions concern configuration options which are orthogonal to each other, hence they can be resolved in any order. These questions include:

- Is it allowed that other activities occur between occurrences of activity *'haemoglobin-photoelectric-urgent'* and *'glucose-urgent'*?
- Is it allowed that other activities occur between occurrences of activity *'glucose-urgent'*?
- Is it allowed that several occurrences of activity *'haemoglobin-photoelectric-urgent'* be followed by specified repetitions of activity *'glucose-urgent'*?
- Is it allowed that activity *'glucose-urgent'* occurs before activity *'haemoglobin-photoelectric-urgent'* independently from the defined sequence?
- Is it allowed that the specified sequence of $\langle(haemoglobin\text{-}photoelectric\text{-}urgent)$ $\underbrace{(glucose-urgent)\dots(glucose-urgent)}_{4}\rangle$ occurs multiple times?
- Is it allowed that the specified sequence of $\langle(haemoglobin\text{-}photoelectric\text{-}urgent)$ $\underbrace{(glucose-urgent)\dots(glucose-urgent)}_{4}\rangle$ never occurs?
- Is it allowed that after the specified sequence $\langle(haemoglobin\text{-}photoelectric\text{-}urgent)\underbrace{(glucose-urgent)\dots(glucose-urgent)}_{4}\rangle$, activity *'haemoglobin-photoelectric-urgent'* occurs without being followed by repetitions of *'glucose-urgent'*?

Resolving these questions yields a *configured pattern* which describes precisely the intended behavior. This Petri net can be used further for automated compliance checking.

6   Related Work

Informal description of compliance requirements can be interpreted differently in context of different business operations. Therefore precise specification of them is necessary [15]. Specification patterns are extensively used in software development [4,8,9,16,28] and also in formulating compliance requirements [10–12,27,29]. Most of these approaches use some type of structured natural language and pre-formulated templates to construct formal specifications that can then be analyzed. Often, these informal specifications are initially mapped to an intermediate representation (e.g., model-driven patterns), at which point context dependencies and ambiguities are resolved. The result is then further refined into a targeted formalism. In [10,11,29] Elgammal et al. introduce a pattern-based approach for capturing compliance requirements. Their patterns are parameterized and formalized in LTL. In order to make the approach usable for business users, they developed a tool-set where user can define compliance requirements using a specialized version of declare modeling notation. A common problem in most of above mentioned works is that pre-formulated patterns are limited and hard coded; hence they fail to capture subtle aspects of different compliance requirements. In addition in most of the approaches, mapping and adapting patterns in a specific context requires extensive knowledge in specification languages. Our approach aims to allow compliance specification for end users without such extensive knowledge.

7   Conclusion and Future Work

The *Compliance* plug-in of ProM supports the capabilities described in this paper. The configurable compliance pattern repository is comprehensive and allows for specifying different types of compliance requirements we found in literature and many more. However, an accurate evaluation of the tool and approach is required. In future we would like to evaluate how effective the approach and tool are in practise involving business users. In the presented approach, we focused on control-flow compliance rules. We would like to investigate similar approaches for formalizing requirements restricting other perspectives of processes such as time, data, and resource. In addition we would like to check the scalability of configurable compliance patterns by applying our approach in different domains and identify compliance requirements that we are not able to specify using our current set of configurable compliance patterns.

References

1. http://dx.doi.org/10.4121/uuid:d9769f3d-0ab0-4fb8-803b-0d1120ffcf54
2. van der Aalst, W.M.P., Adriansyah, A., van Dongen, B.F.: Replaying history on process models for conformance checking and performance analysis. Wiley Interdisc. Rew.: Data Min. Knowl. Disc. 2(2), 182–192 (2012)
3. van der Aalst, W.M.P., Dreiling, A., Gottschalk, F., Rosemann, M., Jansen-Vullers, M.H.: Configurable process models as a basis for reference modeling. In: Bussler, ChJ, Haller, A. (eds.) BPM 2005. LNCS, vol. 3812, pp. 512–518. Springer, Heidelberg (2006)
4. Abid, N., Dal Zilio, S., Le Botlan, D.: Real-time specification patterns and tools. In: Stoelinga, M., Pinger, R. (eds.) FMICS 2012. LNCS, vol. 7437, pp. 1–15. Springer, Heidelberg (2012)
5. Adriansyah, A., van Dongen, B., van der Aalst, W.M.: Conformance checking using cost-based fitness, analysis. In: EDOC'11, pp. 55–64 (2011)
6. Awad, A., Weidlich, M., Weske, M.: Visually specifying compliance rules and explaining their violations for business processes. J. Vis. Lang. Comput. 22(1), 30–55 (2011)
7. Bose, R.P.J.C., van der Aalst, W.M.P.: Analysis of Patient Treatment Procedures. In: Daniel, F., Barkaoui, K., Dustdar, S. (eds.) BPM Workshops 2011, Part I. LNBIP, vol. 99, pp. 165–166. Springer, Heidelberg (2012)
8. Cobleigh, R.L., Avrunin, G.S., Clarke, L.A.: User guidance for creating precise and accessible property specifications. In: SIGSOFT FSE, pp. 208–218. ACM (2006)
9. Dwyer, M.B., Avrunin, G.S., Corbett, J.C.: Property specification patterns for finite-state verification. In: FMSP. pp. 7–15. ACM (1998)

10. Elgammal, A., Türetken, O., van den Heuvel, W.J.: Using patterns for the analysis and resolution of compliance violations. Int. J. Coop. Inf. Syst. **21**(1), 31–54 (2012)
11. Elgammal, A., Turetken, O., van den Heuvel, W.-J., Papazoglou, M.: Root-cause analysis of design-time compliance violations on the basis of property patterns. In: Maglio, P.P., Weske, M., Yang, J., Fantinato, M. (eds.) ICSOC 2010. LNCS, vol. 6470, pp. 17–31. Springer, Heidelberg (2010)
12. Fötsch, D., Pulvermüller, E., Rossak, W.: Modeling and verifying workflow-based regulations. In: ReMo2V. CEUR Workshop Proceedings, vol. 241. CEUR-WS.org (2006)
13. Ghose, A.K., Koliadis, G.: Auditing business process compliance. In: Krämer, B.J., Lin, K.-J., Narasimhan, P. (eds.) ICSOC 2007. LNCS, vol. 4749, pp. 169–180. Springer, Heidelberg (2007)
14. Governatori, G., Milosevic, Z., Sadiq, S.W.: Compliance checking between business processes and business contracts. In: Hung, P.C.K. (ed.) EDOC, pp. 221–232. IEEE Computer Society, Los Alamitos (2006)
15. Koliadis, G., Desai, N., Narendra, N.C., Ghose, A.K.: Analyst-mediated contextualization of regulatory policies. In: IEEE SCC, pp. 281–288. IEEE Computer Society (2010)
16. Konrad, S., Cheng, B.H.C.: Facilitating the construction of specification pattern-based properties. In: RE, pp. 329–338. IEEE Computer Society (2005)
17. de Leoni, M., van der Aalst, W.M.P., van Dongen, B.F.: Data- and resource-aware conformance checking of business processes. In: Abramowicz, W., Kriksciuniene, D., Sakalauskas, V. (eds.) BIS 2012. LNBIP, vol. 117, pp. 48–59. Springer, Heidelberg (2012)
18. Lu, R., Sadiq, S.K., Governatori, G.: Compliance aware business process design. In: ter Hofstede, A.H.M., Benatallah, B., Paik, H.-Y. (eds.) BPM Workshops 2007. LNCS, vol. 4928, pp. 120–131. Springer, Heidelberg (2008)
19. Smith, R.L., Avrunin, G.S., Clarke, L.A.: From natural language requirements to rigorous property specifications. In: Monterey Workshop 2003 (SEES 2003), No. UM-CS-2004-019, Chicago, IL, pp. 40–46, September 2003
20. Ramezani, E., Fahland, D., van der Aalst, W.M.P.: Where did I Misbehave? diagnostic information in compliance checking. In: Barros, A., Gal, A., Kindler, E. (eds.) BPM 2012. LNCS, vol. 7481, pp. 262–278. Springer, Heidelberg (2012)
21. Ramezani, E., Fahland, D., van Dongen, B., van der Aalst, W.: Diagnostic information in temporal compliance checking. Technical report, BPM Center Rep. BPM-12-17 (2012)
22. Ramezani Taghiabadi, E., Fahland, D., van Dongen, B.F., van der Aalst, W.M.P.: Diagnostic information for compliance checking of temporal compliance requirements. In: Salinesi, C., Norrie, M.C., Pastor, Ó. (eds.) CAiSE 2013. LNCS, vol. 7908, pp. 304–320. Springer, Heidelberg (2013)
23. Ramezani, E., Fahland, D., van der Werf, J.M., Mattheis, P.: Separating compliance management and business process management. In: Daniel, F., Barkaoui, K., Dustdar, S. (eds.) BPM Workshops 2011, Part II. LNBIP, vol. 100, pp. 459–464. Springer, Heidelberg (2012)
24. Rosemann, M., van der Aalst, W.M.P.: A configurable reference modelling language. Inf. Syst. **32**(1), 1–23 (2007)
25. Rozinat, A., van der Aalst, W.M.P.: Conformance checking of processes based on monitoring real behavior. Inf. Syst. **33**(1), 64–95 (2008)
26. Sadiq, W., Governatori, G., Namiri, K.: Modeling control objectives for business process compliance. In: Alonso, G., Dadam, P., Rosemann, M. (eds.) BPM 2007. LNCS, vol. 4714, pp. 149–164. Springer, Heidelberg (2007)

27. Schumm, D., Turetken, O., Kokash, N., Elgammal, A., Leymann, F., van den Heuvel, W.-J.: Business process compliance through reusable units of compliant processes. In: Daniel, F., Facca, F.M. (eds.) ICWE 2010. LNCS, vol. 6385, pp. 325–337. Springer, Heidelberg (2010)
28. Smith, R.L., Avrunin, G.S., Clarke, L.A., Osterweil, L.J.: Propel: an approach supporting property elucidation. In: ICSE, pp. 11–21. ACM (2002)
29. Türetken, O., Elgammal, A., van den Heuvel, W.J., Papazoglou, M.P.: Enforcing compliance on business processes through the use of patterns. In: ECIS (2011)
30. Liu, Y., Muller, S., Xu, K.: A static compliance-checking framework for business process models. IBM Syst. J. **46**(2), 335–361 (2007)

Short Paper: A Framework for the Privacy Access Control Model

Sandugash Askarova[1(✉)], Darkhan Mukhatov[2],
Altynbek Sharipbayev[1], and Dina Satybaldina[1]

[1] L.N. Gumilyov Eurasian National University, Astana 010000, Kazakhstan
sandugash.kz@gmail.com, sharalt@mail.ru,
satybaldina_dzh@enu.kz
[2] "Zerde" Holding JSC, Astana 010000, Kazakhstan
dmukhatov@zerde.gov.kz

Abstract. Today privacy is a key issue when securing business processes. It has received increasing attention from consumers, companies, researchers and legislators. Organizations claim to have their own privacy policy as well as guarantee its proper enforcement. In this work we consider privacy features at the early stages of the systems development and specifically focus on modelling and analysis of the system requirements. A framework for modelling privacy access control policies was created through (i) defining access control policies that satisfy privacy requirements (ii) verification of designed privacy access control policy, and (iii) a set of heuristics for defining policy.

Keywords: Security management · Access control · Privacy policy modelling languages · Information systems

1 Introduction

Privacy is an increasingly important business concern in health care, financial services, and other organizations. Organizations that collect and use personal information face the growing challenge of conducting their business effectively while managing privacy risks and compliance requirements [1]. Organizations have adopted various strategies to protect personal data privacy. In particular, in the financial sector laws and regulations have been created to protect privacy data such as Basel II, Sarbanes-Oxley Act (SOX), Gramm-Leach-Bliley Act (GLBA) [2].

Access control policies are defined as rules, which regulate how users can access resources [3]. These access control policies are created based on models. The classical models are Mandatory Access Control, Discretionary Access Control and Role Based Access Control [4]. Access control models cannot enforce privacy policies and designed access control policies do not include privacy requirements such as purpose binding, conditions and obligations [5].

In order to enforce privacy policies in organizations, access control policies satisfying the privacy requirements in the requirements engineering should be formally identified [6]. Existing privacy policy languages such as P3P [7], APPEAL [9], E-P3P [8], EPAL [10] and XACML [4] do not completely solve privacy issues, and they are

N. Lohmann et al. (Eds.): BPM 2013 Workshops, LNBIP 171, pp. 513–519, 2014.
DOI: 10.1007/978-3-319-06257-0_40, © Springer International Publishing Switzerland 2014

isolated from requirements analysis. As a result, defined privacy policies do not comply with system requirements. There are many frameworks for access control requirements modelling such as i^* framework [12], GBRAM and its extension [13], analytical role modelling framework (ARMF) [14], and Knowledge Acquisition in Automated Specification [15].

The focus of this research study is to model privacy requirements into access control policies. Our research is aimed at delivering a model of designing privacy aware systems by incorporating privacy requirements into access control policy. The framework for modelling privacy access control policies was created. This framework is developed by extending ARMF [14]. Sections 2 and 3 present our framework for modelling privacy access control policies and its heuristics for defining and verifying these policies. In Sect. 4 we summarize the findings by focusing on the aim and objectives of study and provide future work.

2   A Framework for Modelling Privacy Access Control Policies

The framework was developed based on ARMF [14], by adding the purpose meta-concept and corresponding relations. Purpose specification principle has been selected to investigate how access control policies can be defined and how it can be enforced during the requirements modelling. It also has been selected as the only principle stated in the Law of the Republic of Kazakhstan [6]. The framework uses notations of Z language [16].

Policies define restrictions to access valuable assets (privacy data). Such an access is required to carry out tasks. The tasks cannot be processed in a way that may be incompatible with the purposes for which the data have been collected. To include these notion into the framework the following meta-concepts are needed:

[Asset] – represents privacy data that we wish to protect;

[Task] – the activities that an organizational unit or individual carries out;

[Purpose] – personal data that shall be collected for specified, lawful and legitimate purpose or purposes and not processed in ways that are incompatible with the purposes for which data have been collected.

The meta-concepts of an agent and role are identified as follow:

[Agent] – represents a physical person;

[Role] – an assignment of an obligation, of performing some function, which is a composite element representing the organisational function, organisational domain, and authority. Three types of roles are defined according to organizational structures: roles based on seniority, roles based on function, and roles based on market. The meta-concepts are as following:

[Authority] – represents the seniority of a role;

[Org_Function] – a functional grouping within an organisation;

[Org_Domain] – represents a "market based" grouping i.e. a grouping that is delegated a market to serve such as a set of clients in a specific geographic location.

The meta-concept role is a composite of authority, organizational function, and organizational domain and is defined formally as follows:

Role ≜ [authority: Authority; org_function: Org_Function; org_domain: Org_Domain]

The inheritance between organizational functions is formally defined as follows:
Inheritance_f ≜ {inhf: Org_Function↠ Org_Function; org_function: P Org_Function| (∀of: org_function • of ∉ inhf⁺ (|{of}|))}.

The inheritance of roles is formally defined as follows:
Inheritance_r ≜ {inhr: Role↠ Role; role: P Role| (∀r: role •r∉ inhr⁺ (|{r}|))}.

The aggregation hierarchy for organizational domain is formally identified as follows:
Aggregation_d ≜ {aggd: Org_domain ↠ Org_domain; org_domain: P Org_domain| (∀od: org_domain • od ∉ aggd⁺ (|{od}|))}

Formally the task aggregation is defined as follows:
Aggregation_t ≜ {aggt: Task↠ Task; task: P Task|(∀t: task • t ∉ aggt⁺ (|{t}|))}.

Purpose aggregation is defined as follows:
Aggregation_p ≜ {aggp: Purpose↠ Purpose; purpose: P Purpose| (∀p: purpose • p ∉ aggt⁺ (|{p}|))}.

The relationship between tasks and purposes is represented by a task purpose dependency relation as follow:
Task_purpose_dependency ≜ {task_purpose_dependency: Task →Purpose |(∀t: Task. ∃₁p: Purpose • (t, p) ∈ task_purpose_dependency) ∧ (∀t: aggt⁺(|{t}|). ∃₁p:aggp⁺(|{p}|) • (t, p) ∈ task_purpose_dependency)}.

The relation between purpose and asset or assets is represented by purpose asset dependency as follow:
Purpose_asset_dependency ≜ {purpose_asset_dependency: Purpose →P Asset; purpose: P Purpose; asset: P Asset| (∀p: purpose. ∃a: asset • (p, a) ∈ purpose_asset_dependency)}.

The relationship between asset and organizational domain is formally identified as:
Asset_domain ≜ {asset_domain: Asset → Org_Domain| (∀a: Asset. ∃₁od: Org_domain • (a, od) ∈ asset_domain)}.

Policies will be defined using the following composite type:
Authorization_Policy ≜ {role: Role; task: Task}

There are implicit assumptions in this defined policy: firstly, the policy applies to any subtask if the task in the policy; secondly the organizational domain in the role of the policy applies to all assets associated with the task through the following relations:
Task_purpose_dependency ≜ {task_purpose_dependency: Task →Purpose |(∀t: Task. ∃₁p: Purpose • (t, p) ∈ task_purpose_dependency) ∧ (∀t: aggt⁺(|{t}|). ∃₁p:aggp⁺(|{p}|) • (t, p) ∈ task_purpose_dependency)};

Purpose_asset_dependency $\triangleq$ {purpose_asset_dependency: Purpose →P Asset; purpose: P Purpose; asset: P Asset| ($\forall$p: purpose. $\exists$a: asset • (p, a) ∈ purpose_asset_dependency)}.

3 Heuristics for Defining and Verifying Policies

Application of ARMF extensions is applied through six steps: (*i*) identifying organizational groups (*ii*) identifying level of authority (*iii*) defining roles (*iv*) identifying tasks, assets, purposes (*v*) defining policies, and (*vi*) verifying policies.

Once we have identified organizational functions, we need to show specialization hierarchy using the principle of inheritance as follow: **Definition**: inhf: Org_Function ↠ Org_Function; **Constraint**: org_function: P Org_Function•($\forall$of: org_function• of $\notin$ *inhf*$^+$ (|{of}|)).

Similarly, once we have identified organizational domains, we need to show them in aggregation hierarchy as follow: **Definition**: aggd: Org_domain↠ Org_domain; **Constraint**: org_domain: P Org_domain • ($\forall$od: org_domain • od $\notin$ *aggd*$^+$ (|{od}|).

Levels of authority need to be assigned to groups. Once we have identified authority's levels we need to show their seniority as follow:

Definition: senior: Authority ↠ Authority; **Constraint**: authority: P Authority • ($\forall$a: authority • a$\notin$ *senior*$^+$(|{a}|)).

In next step we need to identify tasks and their associated purposes and then assets related to purposes in the organization: **Definition:** aggt: Task↠ Task; **Constraint:** task: P Task • ($\forall$t: task • t $\notin$ aggt$^+$ (|{t}|)).

Next, we need to identify purposes for defined tasks, which enable tasks to have access to asset or group of assets. Identified purposes are needed to be organized in hierarchical structure. It can be done by aggregation hierarchy as follow:

Definition: aggp: Purpose↠ Purpose; **Constraint:** purpose: P Purpose • ($\forall$p: purpose•p $\notin$ aggt$^+$ (|{p}|)).

After that we need to show task purpose dependency as follow:

Definition: task_purpose_dependency: Task →Purpose: **Constraint:** ($\forall$t: Task. $\exists$p: Purpose • (t, p) ∈ task_purpose_dependency) ∧ ($\forall$t: aggt$^+$(|{t}|). $\exists_1$p:aggp$^+$(|{p}|) • (t, p) ∈ task_purpose_dependency).

The relation between purpose and asset or assets is represented by purpose asset dependency: **Definition:** purpose_asset_dependency: Purpose →P Asset; **Constraint:** no constraint.

The relationship between asset and organizational domain is formally identified as follow: **Definition:** asset_domain: Asset → Org_Domain; **Constraint:** no constraint.

Once we have identified organizational context, roles and tasks we now define policies as follow: **Definition:** Authorization_Policy $\triangleq$ {role: Role; task: Task}; **Constraint:** no constraint.

The final step is to verify policies through scenarios. In creation scenario the following domain concepts should be instantiated. Instantiation of domain:

Definition: insd: Org_Domain $\rightarrowtail$ Org_Domain; **Constraint:** org_domain: P Org_Domain $\bullet$ ($\forall$od$_1$; od$_2$: org_domain $\bullet$ od$_2 \in$ insd ($|\{$od$_1\}|$) $\implies$ insd ($|\{$od$_2\}|$)=$\varnothing$); **Constraint:** $\forall$ od$_1$; od$_2$: Org_Domain $\bullet$ od$_1 \in$ aggd ($|\{$od$_2\}|$) $\implies$ (insd ($|\{$od$_1\}|$)$\neq\varnothing$ $\wedge$ insd ($|\{$od$_2\}|$)$\neq\varnothing$) $\vee$ (insd ($|\{$od$_1\}|$)= $\varnothing$ $\wedge$ insd ($|\{$od$_2\}|$)= $\varnothing$).

Instantiation of role: **Definition:** insr: Role $\rightarrowtail$ Role; **Constraint:** role: P Role $\bullet$ ($\forall$r$_1$; r$_2$: role $\bullet$ r$_2 \in$ insr ($|\{$r$_1\}|$) $\implies$ insr ($|\{$r$_2\}|$)=$\varnothing$); **Constraint:** $\nexists$ role: Role $\bullet$ (insr ($|\{$role$\}|$) = $\varnothing$ $\wedge$ insd ($|\{$role.org_domain$\}|$) $\neq\varnothing$) $\vee$ (insr ($|\{$role$\}|$) $\neq\varnothing$ $\wedge$ insd ($|\{$role.org_domain$\}|$) = $\varnothing$); **Constraint:** $\nexists$ policy: Authorization_Policy $\bullet$ insr($|\{$policy.role$\}|$) $\neq\varnothing$.

Instantiation of task: **Definition:** inst: Task $\rightarrowtail$ Task; **Constraint:** task: P Task $\bullet$ ($\forall$t$_1$; t$_2$: task $\bullet$ t$_2 \in$ inst ($|\{$t$_1\}|$) $\implies$ inst ($|\{$t$_2\}|$)=$\varnothing$)

Instantiation of purpose: **Definition:** insp: Purpose $\rightarrowtail$ Purpose; **Constraint:** purpose: P Purpose$\bullet$($\forall$p$_1$; p$_2$:purpose$\bullet$p$_2 \in$ insp($|\{$p$_1\}|$)$\implies$ insp ($|\{$p$_2\}|$)=$\varnothing$)

Instantiation of asset: **Definition:** insa: Asset $\rightarrowtail$ Asset; **Constraint:** asset: P Asset $\bullet$ ($\forall$a$_1$; a$_2$: asset $\bullet$ a$_2 \in$ insa ($|\{$a$_1\}|$) $\implies$ insa ($|\{$a$_2\}|$)=$\varnothing$)

Instantiated roles are assigned to agents as follow: **Definition:** role_assignement: Agent $\leftrightarrow$ Role. **Constraint:** no constraint.

There is needed to model the carrying out of a task by an agent. This will be represented by relation performs, which defines an agent performing a task:

Definition: performs: Agent $\leftrightarrow$Task; **Constraint:** $\forall$ p: perform $\bullet$ $\forall$task: ran performs $\bullet$ inst($|\{$task$\}|$) $\neq$ $\varnothing$. **Constraint:** $\forall$p: performs $\bullet$ $\forall$task : ran performs $\bullet\forall$ ins_purpose: task_purpose_dependency ($|\{$task$\}|$) $\bullet$ $\exists$ purpose: task_purpose_dependency ($|$inst($|\{$task$\}|$)$|$) $\bullet$ purpose$\in$ insp($|\{$ins_purpose$\}|$).

Constraint: $\forall$p: performs $\bullet$ $\forall$task : ran performs $\bullet\forall$ ins_asset: purpose_asset_dependency ($|\{$purpose$\}|$)$\bullet$ $\exists$ asset: purpose_asset_dependency ($|$insp($|\{$purpose$\}|$)$|$) $\bullet$ asset$\in$ insa($|\{$ins_asset$\}|$).

After identifying a scenario, we determine relation performs between specific agent and corresponding instantiated task. It can be done by using elimination rules and substituting instantiated elements, which was used in creating performs relation.

4 Conclusion

This paper has addressed the problem of modelling access policies in order to ensure that security goals can be achieved and that operational requirements are consistent with access policies. The framework includes a meta-model and a set of heuristics.

The meta-model represented a link between organizational context and privacy enforcement in order to capture the whole privacy domain. Heuristics were determined for defining policies and scenarios.

The limitation of this research is that proposed framework was created in Z language. This language requires a special knowledge in a set theory and mathematical logic. In addition, heuristics for defining and verifying policy were not illustrated by any example. The future research for this research study is implementation of the proposed framework in banks. In addition the future research can be done by considering other policies and validating them in the case studies.

References

1. Barth, A., Datta, A., Mitchell, J.C., Sundaram, S.: Privacy and utility in business processes. In: Proceedings of 20th IEEE Computer Security Foundations Symposium, pp. 279–294 (2007)
2. Anton, A.I., Earp, J.B., Potts, C., Alspaugh, T.A.: The role of policy and privacy values in requirements engineering. In: Proceedings of the 5th IEEE International Symposium on Requirements Engineering (RE'01), Toronto, Canada, pp.138–145 (2001)
3. Sandhu, R., Samarati, R.: Access control: principles and practice. IEEE Commun. Mag. 32(9), 40–48 (1994)
4. Ni, Q., Trombetta, A., Bertino, E., Lobo, J.: Privacy-aware role based access control. In: Proceedings of SACMAT'07, Sophia Antipolis, France (2007)
5. Ferraiolo, D.F., Kuhn, D.R., Chandramouli, R.: Role-Based Access Control, 2nd edn. Artech House, London (2007)
6. Law of the Republic of Kazakhstan "On informatization", Astana (2007)
7. Lu, C.: Powerful Privacy Potential: P3P in the Context of Legislation and Education (2003)
8. Stufflebeam, W., Antón, A.I., He, Q., Jain, N.: Specifying privacy policies with P3P and EPAL: lessons learned. In: Proceedings of the Workshop on Privacy in the Electronic Society, Washington (2004)
9. Anton, A.I., Earp, B., Bolchini, D., He, Q., Jensen, C., Stufflebeam, W.: The lack of clarity in financial privacy policies and the need for standardization. IEEE Secur. Priv. 2(2), 36–45 (2003)
10. Ashley, P., Hada, S., Karjoth, G., Schunter, M.: E-P3P privacy policies and privacy authorization. In: Proceedings of the Workshop on Privacy in the Electronic Society (WPES'02), Washington (2002)
11. Karjoth, G., Schunter, M., Waidner, M.: Platform for enterprise privacy practices: privacy-enabled management of customer data. In: Dingledine, R., Syverson, P.F. (eds.) PET 2002. LNCS, vol. 2482, pp. 69–84. Springer, Heidelberg (2003)
12. Liu, L., Yu, E.S.K., Mylopoulos, J.: Security and privacy requirements analysis within a social setting. In: Proceedings of 11th IEEE International Conference on Requirements Engineering (RE'03), Monterrey, USA, pp. 151–61 (2003)
13. He, Q., Anton, A.I.: A framework for modelling privacy requirements in role engineering. In: Proceedings of 9th International Workshop on Requirements Engineering – Foundation for Software Quality (REFSQ'03), pp. 137–146, Klagenfurt/Velden, Austria (2003)
14. Crook, R., Ince, D., Nuseibeh, B.: On modelling access policies: relating roles to their organisational context. In: Proceedings of 13th IEEE International Requirements Engineering Conference (RE'05), Paris, France (2005)

15. van Lamsweerde, A.: Requirements Engineering: From System Goals to UML Models to Software Specifications. Wiley, England (2009)
16. ISO/IEC 13568:2002. Information Technology – Z Formal Specification Notation – Syntax, Type System and Semantics (2002)

Short Paper: Role-Based Access Control for Securing Dynamically Created Documents

Kaarel Tark[1] and Raimundas Matulevičius[2(✉)]

[1] Nortal AS, Lõõtsa 6C 11415 Tallinn, Estonia
kaarel.tark@nortal.com
[2] Institute of Computer Science, University of Tartu,
J. Liivi 2 50409 Tartu, Estonia
rma@ut.ee

Abstract. Nowadays most of documents are held in digital form and stored in document repositories or databases. The documents can contain delicate information such that not all the actors on the partner side should see and edit. This leads to the necessity to restrict the actions that users could perform with the document content. In this work we research a possibility to integrate existing technologies in order to dynamically define forms and their security permissions. As the solution to the problem we introduce a dynamic way to define security permissions on the XML documents. We propose to use a role-based access control application on the document structure components and introduce a merging strategy to maintain the document's integrity.

Keywords: Role-based access control · XML · XML schema · SecureUML

1 Introduction

Extensible Mark-up Language (XML) (www.w3.org/XML/) helps to describe content and structure of documents, which potentially contain a vast amount of information. Since the XML document structure could be defined dynamically, it becomes rather difficult to apply access restriction rules for the different parts of the document content. Role-based Access Control (RBAC) [10] is a method to define user assignments to roles and role assignments to permissions in order to authorize policies over the protected resources. In this paper we illustrate how the nowadays existing technology could be integrated with XML documents and RBAC. We also propose how to dynamically define document structure and the security policy over the documents without losing context-based information. As a solution we apply the SecureUML language [1] to dynamically define RBAC policy on the XML documents together with XML Schema based form building (DynaForm [8]). This combination allows developers to create and update document structure and its security concerns not when implementing but when designing the document itself.

The structure of this paper is as follows: In Sect. 2 we will use the illustrative example to present both the architecture and security modelling approach to secure dynamically created documents. In Sect. 3 we will discuss some related work. We will conclude our discussion in Sect. 4.

N. Lohmann et al. (Eds.): BPM 2013 Workshops, LNBIP 171, pp. 520–525, 2014.
DOI: 10.1007/978-3-319-06257-0_41, © Springer International Publishing Switzerland 2014

2   Securing XML-Based Documents

2.1   Running Example

To illustrate our proposal we will use the extract of the *patient's ambulatory treatment record* taken from the medical domain. The lifecycle of this document (see Fig. 1) includes three actors: receptionist, nurse and doctor. Firstly, the receptionist registers a patient (see action Register patient) by adding his/her data. After the patient is invited to the doctor's cabinet, a nurse collects the patient's complaints and observations (see action Collect complains and observations). The doctor is, then, able to read the diary records (see action Read diary record) and to register the diagnosis about the illness (see action Propose diagnosis).

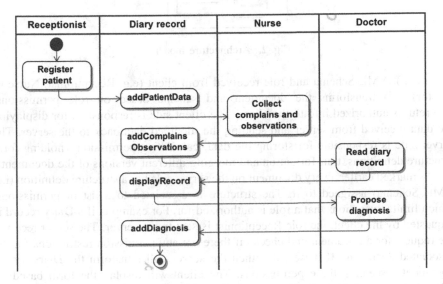

Fig. 1. Extract of the ambulatory treatment record

As different actors need to see and modify the diary data (i.e., add PatientData, addComplainsObservations, displayRecord, and addDiagnosis), the security restrictions on the document content needs to be applied so that only the authorized users would be able to see their relevant information. In the next section we will illustrate the architectural solution used to solve the above problem.

2.2   Architecture

In Fig. 2 we propose the architectural solution consisting of two parts: *modelling* and *application*. In this section we present the application part consisting of *server* and a *client* machines. The *server* machine contains information about the structure of the documents and data. The server (i) combines XML document (e.g., Diary record

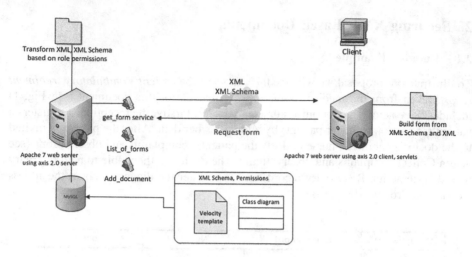

Fig. 2. Architecture model

document), XML Schema and role received from client (e.g. Receptionist, Nurse or Doctor); (ii) transforms the document and schema based on role permissions; (iii) returns authorized info to the client. The client side is responsible for displaying the data received from server and sending the modified data back to the server. The server side is responsible for storing the data, calculating permissions, holding form structure definitions, transformation and merging different versions of the documents.

As marked earlier, every document on the server side has a structure definition (i.e. XML Schema) assigned to it. The structure is associated to a list of permissions, which limits the actions that a role is authorized for. For example, if a Diary record is requested by the client, the role Receptionist is sent to the server. The server receives the request for a document and checks if there are any permission restrictions for the associated document. If these exist, then the server will transform the Diary record document respecting these permissions. The client will display the form based on XML Schema and fill it in with data from XML, so that receptionist will only see authorized information. For example, the Receptionist would be able to edit the patient's public data: name, legal code, and age, but will be restricted to see patient's treatment information.

Role permissions can be defined at the level of the document's structure component, for example, patient, primaryDiagnosis etc. To apply RBAC restrictions, we introduce a domain specific language, which contains the following syntax structure: `{Role} <> {element} ≫ {permissions} <break>`.

The `{element}` field name has to match the local name of the field. For `{permissions}` we can define four security actions: *read* ("R" – element value is visible), *write* ("W" – if the element is visible then it is allowed to change the element's value; this also implies that the "R" permission is granted), *insert* ("I" – if multiple sections allowed, then allows adding another section) and *delete* ("D" – allowed removing elements appearing more, than in the XML Schema definition). For example a permission to read and write *patientName* field can be defined as:

```
Receptionist <> patientName ≫ R, W, -, - <break>
```

2.3 Security Modelling

As described in [1], SecureUML uses stereotypes to characterise the RBAC resources, roles and permissions (see Fig. 3):

- ≪*secuml.resource*≫ – a class that defines the protected resource (e.g., DiaryRecord);
- ≪*secuml.role*≫– a class that specifies user's role (e.g., Receptionist, Nurse, and Doctor). The role name must match the role requesting document.
- ≪*secuml.permission*≫ - an association class that defines the security permission given to the role regarding the protected resource (e.g., Receptionist-FormPermissions, NurseFormPermissions, and DoctorFormPermissions).

For XML Schema we introduce an additional stereotype - ≪*xml.schema*≫. This stereotype is applied to a class that defines the main document structure class (*i.e.* DiaryRecord).

Permissions in SecureUML resources are given through association classes with stereotype ≪*secuml.permission*≫. The security actions (e.g., Insert, Write, Read) are specified as attributes. The authorisation constraint between the permission and form field (e.g., patient, primaryDiagnosis, and complainsObeservations) is defined via abstract association between a certain permission attribute (e.g., regis-terPatient: Insert) and form attribute (e.g., patient: Patient).

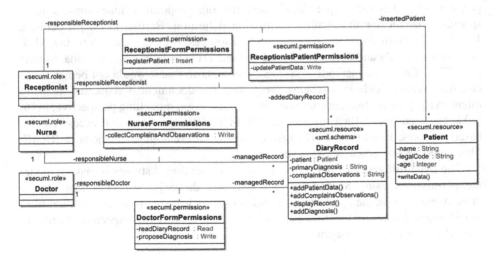

Fig. 3. SecureUML class diagram

In addition to the constraints regarding the ≪xml.schema≫ class, one could also specify the security restriction between any defined roles and any other secured resource (e.g., Patient). For instance in our example, the Receptionist potentially should have a permission to *write* Patient's name, legalCode, and age (see ReceptionistPatientPermissions).

To generate security permissions from the SecureUML model we have developed Velocity-based (velocity.apache.org) templates, which transform the diagrams into SQL update sentences. Additionally we developed Velocity-based templates to generate the XML Schema from the SecureUML class diagram. The main benefit from modelling XML schema and their security permissions in SecureUML is that the same tool (in our case MagicDraw: www.magicdraw.com) could be used to change the rules and structure, and could move the security development complexity from the code to system design level.

3 Related Work

There exist few studies related to our work. For instance, extensible access control language [9] (XACML) similarly allow developers to define rules on XML elements level. However, we are using a targeted access control model, like RBAC, to secure our resources; in XACML the specific access control model is not supported. On another hand the XACML supports definition of the permission delegations, which is not supported in our solution.

Zhang *et al.* [10] define RBAC on Document Type Definition and XML Schema. The work is similar to ours: they have four main actions and they calculate permissions on elements' level, but this study assumes that the output XML Schema is known, thus it does not support transformation of the XML Schemas together with XML document. Damiani *et al.* [4, 5] define access control on the document type definition (DTD) level. They propose to use XML access control list to specify the permissions and X-path expressions. Contrarily our proposal includes some domain specific language for the security permission definition. Bertino *et al.* [3] define a Java-based system for access control to XML sources. It can be used to secure XML documents directly and documents based on their DTD and not XML Schema. Murata *et al.* [7] define static methods to secure documents so that it would not be needed to calculate visible fields in a schema every time the document is requested, as there might exists policies that are common for all roles. From modelling perspective, in [6] Lakk has used SecureUML to generate PL/SQL database views and access control based on roles. Elsewhere, in [2] Brucker defines a break-glass methods in RBAC. This could be one potential extensions to our work.

The main difference of our proposal from the mentioned studies is that we model the permissions using SecureUML and generate the SQL sentences that can be directly executed in the application. Additionally, we have analysed the solution from modifying and merging the documents in the business process perspective in order to keep the information's integrity.

4 Conclusion

In this paper we have considered how existing technologies could be dynamically combined to define security constraints on the XML forms and their content elements. As the result we created solution that:

- has RBAC policies applied on the dynamically created documents;
- generates code dynamically for forms and permissions from SecureUML model;
- transforms documents based on the role permissions;
- is able to manage simple XML Schema (the ones that does not contain complex attribute types).

We have performed some limited validation study to verify that we are able to generate correct XML Schemas and capture all permissions from SecureUML models. Our observations indicate potential usefulness of our solution.

As a future work, we could extend the XML Schema to be able to hold information on the visual output of the fields: *i.e.* field length, where to get data and field titles in multiple languages.

References

1. Basin, D., Doser, J., Lodderstedt, T.: Model driven security: from UML models to access control infrastructure. ACM Trans. Softw. Eng. Methodol. (TOSEM) **15**(1), 39–91 (2006)
2. Brucker, D.A., Petritsch, H.: Extending access control models with break-glass. In: Proceedings of the 14th ACM Symposium on Access Control Models and Technologies, pp. 197–206. ACM (2009)
3. Bertino, E., Braun, M, Castano, S., Ferrari E., Mesiti, M.: Author-X: a Java-based system for XML data protection. In: IFIP Workshop on Database Security, pp. 15–26, (2000)
4. Damiani, E., Vimercati, S.C., Paraboschi, S., Samarati, P.: A fine-grained access control system for XML documents. ACM Trans. Inf. Syst. Secur. (TISSEC) **5**(2), 169–202 (2002)
5. Damiani, E., De Capitani di Vimercati, S., Paraboschi, S., Samarati, P.: Securing XML documents. In: Zaniolo, C., Grust, T., Scholl, M.H., Lockemann, P.C. (eds.) EDBT 2000. LNCS, vol. 1777, pp. 121–135. Springer, Heidelberg (2000)
6. Lakk H.: Model-driven role-based access control for databases. Master thesis, University of Tartu (2012)
7. Murata, M., Tozawa, A., Kudo, M., Hada, S.: XML access control using static analysis. ACM Trans. Inf. Syst. Secur. **9**(3), 292–324 (2006). ACM
8. Raudjärv, R.: Dynamic schema-based web forms generation in Java. Master thesis, University of Tartu (2010)
9. Seitz, L., Rissanen, E., Sandholm, T., Firozabadi B. S., Mulmo O.: Policy administration control and delegation using XACML and delegent. In: Proceedings of the 6th IEEE/ACM International Workshop on Grid Computing, pp. 49–54. IEEE (2005)
10. Zhang, X., Park, J., Sandhu, R.: Schema based XML security: RBAC approach. In: De Capitani di Vimercati, S., Ray, I., Ray, I. (eds.) Data and Applications Security XVII. IFIP, vol. 142, pp. 330–343. Springer, New York (2004)

2nd Workshop on Theory and Applications of Process Visualization (TAProVis 2013)

Short Paper: Towards Enhancing Business Process Monitoring with Sonification

Tobias Hildebrandt(✉)

Faculty of Computer Science, University of Vienna, Vienna, Austria
Tobias.Hildebrandt@univie.ac.at

Abstract. State-of-the-art business process monitoring systems usually base on different types of real-time visualizations, in which data is typically presented using various graphical elements such as speedometers. However, these systems have several drawbacks, such as the inability to constantly monitor process executions while at the same time working on other things. This is why this paper proposes to enhance visual process monitoring with techniques from the area of sonification (the presentation of data using sound). Even though sonification has already successfully been evaluated in several domains for real-time monitoring, there is so far no comprehensive research for its usage in business process monitoring. This paper proposes sonification techniques and user interactions that can be implemented in future applications.

Keywords: Business process management · Business process monitoring · Process visualization and sonification · Multi-modal displays

1 Introduction

For most of today's businesses, it is very important to be able to monitor their process executions in real-time in order to be able to quickly adapt to arising problems or deviations during execution to obtain a current overview over their processes', and subsequently their businesses' performance. Current state-of-the art business process monitoring applications (such as e.g. ARIS Process Performance Manager or IBM business activity monitoring) base on dashboard and cockpit views that aggregate single process execution events and present them in real time, using visualization techniques such as speedometers [1]. Users who have an interest in monitoring process executions (such as technicians or managers) usually pay attention to these dashboard overviews periodically, while at the same time interrupting other activities they are working on. This has the drawback that users only learn about possibly time critical process events when they next look at their monitoring application or, in case users are constantly monitoring their dashboard application, that they cannot effectively perform other tasks while at the same time getting informed about occurring process events.

N. Lohmann et al. (Eds.): BPM 2013 Workshops, LNBIP 171, pp. 529–536, 2014.
DOI: 10.1007/978-3-319-06257-0_42, © Springer International Publishing Switzerland 2014

Process monitoring is typically a passive activity, which is usually being performed while concentrating mainly on another task (in contrast to e.g. process analysis, a task that users typically dedicate their full attention to). However, visual means are often not ideal for areas in which monitoring occurs in parallel to other activities, as they require our visual focus and thus make it difficult to work on another task at the same time. Therefore, this paper suggests to combine existing visual process monitoring techniques with methods from the area of sonification in order to tackle some of the mentioned drawbacks of current process monitoring. Sonification is "the use of non-speech audio to convey information" [2] and has a few characteristics that make it especially suitable for process monitoring:

- It allows the visual focus to be elsewhere, allowing users to work on another task while getting informed about process performances.
- Humans are very sensitive to even small changes in rhythms and sequences because sound is inherently a temporal medium, while visualization is primarily a spatial medium. This makes sonification very suitable to convey information that changes over time, such as process execution events or KPIs (Key Performance Indicators).
- Sound is very suitable for attracting attention in possibly time-critical situations, which is why sound is typically preferred over visual means for alarms and alerts.

Due to these characteristics, several researchers (such as [3]) argue that audio is more useful than video in cases of peripheral monitoring activities which are performed as background tasks. Studies, such as e.g. conducted by [4], suggest, that while only under certain conditions are sonifications better suited to convey data than visualizations, in a majority of cases multi-modal displays combining visual and auditory elements yield better results than each modality alone.

Thus, even though it seems natural to complement current visual business process monitoring systems with methods from sonification, there exist only a few first approaches into this direction ([5,6]).

The paper at hand paper complements a previously published paper [7], which introduces the peculiarities of business process execution data and the tasks that are typically involved in process monitoring. It also analyzes in detail the different sonification techniques and methods that have already successfully been applied for monitoring applications which base on similar tasks and data structures as business process execution data. This paper, on the other hand, focuses on giving a more general introduction into the strengths and weaknesses of sonification for process monitoring as well as on introducing an initial suggestion for a mapping of process execution data to sound, as well as possible user interfaces to control the sonifications.

2   Sonification in Process Monitoring

Due to the specific characteristics of sound and our listening capabilities that have been presented in the introduction, sonification has been researched and applied in various disciplines, especially for purposes of real-time monitoring. Application areas of sonification in monitoring are e.g. industrial production processes (e.g. [8]), network and web-server behavior (e.g. [9]) or computer program execution and debugging (e.g. [10]). Several conducted studies proved the effectiveness of sonification for monitoring purposes. In [11] sonification has been applied for the monitoring of an assembly line. The authors concluded that users who had visual as well as auditory feedback were able to perceive more information than those who had visual information alone. Experiments conducted by [10,12] indicate that a developed musical sonification of program executions was useful for bug location and detection tasks.

Concluding, sonification has already successfully been applied to several application domains that have similar challenges and data structures as business process monitoring. It has however, apart from a few first considerations ([5,6]), so far not been applied specifically to this task. Gaver et al. [8] sonified the events that occurred at a factories' individual work stations, which successfully helped users to monitor the status of ongoing processes. However, their sonification does not consider business-process-related constructs such as process models and -instances or KPIs. What is therefore missing is research concerning the domain-independent usage of sonification for business process monitoring. Such a sonification should not only consider the single events that occur during instance executions, but should also enable a sonification of continuously updated KPIs.

3   Business Process Monitoring Using Sonification

During business process monitoring, companies want to keep informed about the performances of currently executed process instances and critical events that occur during the execution. Sub domains that could specifically benefit from novel monitoring techniques are probably manufacturing and logistics processes. When executing complex, company-spanning production processes across the whole supply chain it is essential, both for suppliers and customers, to obtain real-time information concerning status of production and logistics as well as being informed about situations that might delay the final delivery date (such as delays in transport or stock shortages). Therefore, it is planned to evaluate prototypical multi-modal monitoring systems in the context of the Adventure project (http://www.fp7-adventure.eu/), which focuses on creating a framework to combine and monitor virtual factories in a pluggable way.

One aspect that will be considered when developing the system is that not every user is interested in the same process information. Technicians or people working on concrete process activities are typically more interested in low-level information, such as individual events that occur or specific error or warning messages. Managers on the other hand are often less interested in the individual events, but want high-level overviews over process performances. In order to address the information needs of the different users groups, the users should be able to adjust the data granularity level of the sonification.

This paper proposes a multi-modal solution that combines visualization and sonification. During normal operation, the sonification will sonify occurring events (for which users will be able to specify the level of detail and types of events they are interested in) and notifications and alerts as *sound events* whenever they occur. KPIs on the other hand are being sonified by continuously updated *sound streams*. In general, the sonification should distract the users as little as possible from their main work. Different types of events (such as the starting or stopping of activities, variables changing their values or occurrences of notifications and alerts) will be sonified with different sounds, enabling the users to decide if they direct their immediate attention to their process monitoring application in order to take respective actions. If e.g. certain notifications or alerts are sonified, a KPI suddenly changes its value, or other peculiarities occur, the users attention is attracted. They can then use the visual dashboard of their engine to e.g. search for the root cause of an error or read the detailed text of a notification. Users will not only be able to react to occurring problems in real-time, but in certain cases might even be able to anticipate such situations before they occur (e.g. if an activity takes substantially longer than usually, or if the value of a KPI is constantly rising). Other positive effects might include e.g. that when the activities of a process are usually executed in the same order, a user might get used to hearing the respective acoustic events in that order and might immediately notice it if that execution order is different than usual.

A first prototype has been developed that sonifies execution events as they occur. The sonification bases on the principle of Earcons, where each event type is assigned to a different sound event. In this case, the sound events are short melodic sequences that are based on the principles of musical contour (the direction and shape musical notes move in) in order to increase recognizability, as previous research (like presented in the previous section) successfully applied melodic Earcons for event-based sonifications. However, for further prototypes, sonifications based on different techniques (such as Auditory Icons or non-musical Earcons) will be developed as well. Example recordings of this prototype can be found under:

https://soundcloud.com/tobias_hildebrandt/

The recording "Event types"[1] contains a sonification of five different event types in sequential order ("activity started", "variable changed", "warning occurred", "error occurred" and "activity finished"). Most melodies in this example have been played in the same instrument (piano), except for "variable changed" and "error occurred". The developed prototype uses different instruments in order to convey the information in which activity the respective events occurred (or, in the case of events of the type "variable changed", which variable is concerned). Thus, if two events are being sonified using the same instrument, it means that they both occurred while executing the same activity. The second example "Activities"[2] shows different events of the same type ("activity started") that are all

---

[1] direct link: https://soundcloud.com/tobias_hildebrandt/event-types-contour-1
[2] direct link: https://soundcloud.com/tobias_hildebrandt/event-types-contour

played with different instruments, meaning that these events are related to different activities. The "Event sonification examples" 1, 2 and 3 (https://soundcloud. com/tobias_hildebrandt/event-sonification-example-1, http://soundcloud.com/ tobias_hildebrandt/event-sonification-example-2, http://soundcloud.com/tobias_ hildebrandt/event-sonification-example-3) show different sonifications of a sample processes' execution. The first example contains a warning in the second activity. In the second example, an error occurs instead of the warning and therefore the second activity does not finish. In the third example, no errors or warnings are occurring, and subsequently the second activity is finished before the first one. First informal user evaluations suggest, that if always the same instrument is used, the different event types can be distinguished and memorized very well, even after only rudimentary instructions. However, especially with a high frequency of occurring events, the telling-apart of the different event types becomes more difficult as soon as different activities (and thus different instruments) are involved. However, it seems that user performance increases with training time.

In general, it can be expected that in companies that run processes in which a high number of events occur, a sonification of all individual events (as presented in the example recordings) would not be very helpful and probably also annoying and distracting. On the other hand, for processes in which only a few events per day occur (such as for processes whose tasks are mainly executed manually) such a sonification might be beneficial. However, even for cases that are suitable to convey individual event occurrences using e.g. Earcons based on musical contour, it probably makes sense in terms of perception to only play a very limited number of notes simultaneously (if any). What this paper proposes instead is to queue occurring events in order to play them sequentially, perhaps starting with urgent events such as alarms. Therefore, not only the level of detail should be adjustable and filterable in real-time, but also how the individual events and KPIs are mapped to sound, thus e.g. taking into consideration aesthetical preferences of the users as well as data density. The system will thus be built in such a way as that it enables the exchange different modular Sonification Components, which can base on different sonification techniques and methods. Therefore it will be possible to flexibly select the sonification techniques that are best suited for a specific company and its individual users.

Figure 1 shows a conceptual view of the proposed system architecture. The central component will be the Monitoring Component, which collects occurring process events from different sources, pre-processes and sends them, according to the users' settings, over the messaging protocol OSC (Open Sound Control) to different Sonification Components. Each user can access a customized web interface where he or she can adjust the mappings from data to sound, filters and other settings that will directly effect his or her personal sonification.

Figure 2 shows a mock-up of how a part of such a customization interface might look like. The user interface should allow to adjust the way process events are sonified as well as to customize what is conveyed in what detail during run time. These settings will apply to what is being sonified, as well as what is displayed in the graphical user interface. Thus, if users e.g. hear an auditory

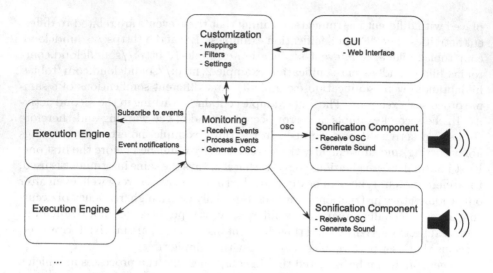

Fig. 1. Architecture proposal for multi-modal process monitoring

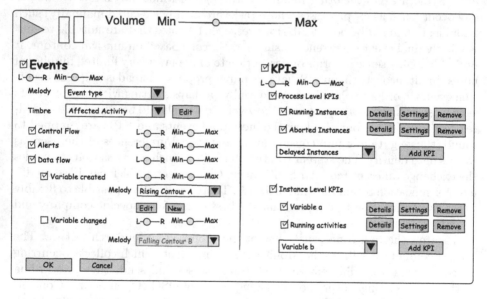

Fig. 2. Possible menu options for multi-modal process monitoring

event that sonifies the occurrence of an event of a specific type, they directly can read the detailed event description when they open their GUI.

The left side of the screen shows how detailed settings for the event sonifications (in this case specifically events related to the data flow) could look like. On the right side, the overview for the settings for the KPI sonifications can be found.

4   Conclusion and Future Work

Applications that enable real-time business process monitoring usually are built around different types of visualization, which do not in all cases enable optimal user performance. Visual monitoring applications are e.g. often not suitable for time critical notifications and in general do not allow users to effectively work on parallel tasks while monitoring process executions. Sonification, the presentation of data using sound, offers certain characteristics (such as the ability to perceive sound passively while concentrating on other things) that make it seem extremely suitable to enhance visualization in business process monitoring. As sonification has already successfully been evaluated for the purpose of monitoring in different application domains, it seems plausible that some of those results can be transferred to business process monitoring. This paper therefore tries to lay the foundation for such a multi-modal process monitoring system by suggesting sonification techniques and a user interface that will be implemented in the near future. The next steps are comprehensive user evaluations for the proposed sonification techniques as well as for the user interface and the user interaction. An important aspect to consider when conducting these evaluations will be to recreate conditions that are as life-like as possible, meaning that it should be taken into account that users typically will perform other tasks in parallel to monitoring.

Acknowledgment. This work was partially supported by the Commission of the European Union within the ADVENTURE FP7-ICT project (Grant agreement no. 285220).

References

1. Eckerson, W.W.: Performance Dashboards: Measuring, Monitoring, and Managing Your Business. Wiley, Hoboken (2010)
2. Kramer, G., Walker, B., Bonebright, T., Cook, P., Flowers, J., Miner, N.: Sonification Report: Status of the Field and Research Agenda - Report prepared for the National Science Foundation by members of the International Community for Auditory Display. International Conference on Auditory Display (1999)
3. Schmandt, C., Vallejo, G.: "Listenin" to domestic enviroments from remote locations. In: Brazil, E., Shinn-Cunningham, B. (eds.) Proceedings of the 9th International Conference on Auditory Display (ICAD2003), pp. 220–223. Boston University Publications Production Department, Boston (2003)
4. Salvador, V., Minghim, R., Levkowitz, H.: User evaluations of interactive multi-modal data presentation. In: 2005 Proceedings of the Ninth International Conference on Information Visualisation, pp. 11–16. IEEE, July 2005

5. Hildebrandt, T., Kriglstein, S., Rinderle-Ma, S.: Beyond visualization: on using sonification methods to make business processes more accessible to users. In: 18th International Conference on Auditory Display (ICAD 2012), pp. 248–249. Georgia Institute of Technology, June 2012
6. Hildebrandt, T., Kriglstein, S., Rinderle-Ma, S.: On applying sonification methods to convey business process data. In: CaISE 2012 Forum. CaISE Forum, CEUR (2012)
7. Hildebrandt, T., Rinderle-Ma, S.: Toward a sonification concept for business process monitoring. In: 19th International Conference on Auditory Display (ICAD 2013), Lodz, Poland, July 2013
8. Gaver, W.W., Smith, R.B., O'Shea, T.: Effective sounds in complex systems: the ARKOLA simulation. In: Proceedings of the SIGCHI Conference on Human Factors in Computing Systems: Reaching through Technology (CHI'91), pp. 85–90. ACM (1991)
9. Ballora, M., Panulla, B., Gourley, M., Hall, D.L.: Preliminary steps in sonifying web log data. International Community for Auditory Display, Washington, D.C. (2010)
10. Vickers, P., Alty, J.L.: Siren songs and swan songs debugging with music. Commun. ACM **46**(7), 86–93 (2003)
11. Rauterberg, M., Styger, E.: Positive effects of sound feedback during the operation of a plant simulator. Selected papers from the 4th International Conference on Human-Computer Interaction, EWHCI '94, pp. 35–44. Springer, London (1994)
12. Vickers, P., Alty, J.L.: Musical program auralisation: a structured approach to motif design. Interact. Comput. **14**(5), 457–485 (2002)

A Navigation Metaphor to Support Mobile Workflow Systems

Jorge Cardoso[1,2](✉), Stefan Jablonski[3], and Bernhard Volz[3]

[1] Karlsruhe Service Research Institute,
Karlsruhe Institute of Technology, Karlsruhe, Germany
jorge.cardoso@kit.edu
[2] CISUC/Department of Informatics Engineering,
University of Coimbra, Coimbra, Portugal
jcardoso@dei.uc.pt
[3] Database and Information Systems Group,
University of Bayreuth, Bayreuth, Germany
{stefan.jablonski,bernhard.volz}@uni-bayreuth.de

Abstract. Mobile devices have enabled the development of a new breed of enterprise solutions. Oracle, SAP, IBM, and others are offering mobile clients (e.g. ERP, BI, CRM) for iPhone and Android devices. Nonetheless, in the field of workflow management systems (WfMS) the progresses do not support well mobile workers. In this paper we explore how metaphors can be used to drive the development of mobile workflow systems. Our approach relies on the use of the TomTom metaphor to establish an *isomorphism* between car navigation systems and WfMS. Based on the isomorphism, we used the Technology Acceptance Model (TAM) to provide a first validation of the approach. The positive results led us to implement an early prototype to be used as a proof of concept and to identify important requirements such as context information.

Keywords: Metaphors · Workflow management · Navigation systems · Mobile workers · Process models

1 Introduction

The last decade has seen substantial progresses in the development of workflow management systems (WfMS). Nonetheless, mobility was overlooked. Systems were mainly confined to organizational 'firewalls'. IBM WebSphere MQ Workflow, Oracle BPM Suite, SAP NetWeaver BPM, etc. are all major enterprise systems which function in hermetic organizational ecosystems (see [1]).

To address this gap in the field of mobility, our approach consisted on finding a metaphor to derive new paradigms for WfMS to support mobility. The importance of metaphors in systems development has long been identified as a catalyst for the success of information systems [9]. In our work, we argue that the use of a TomTom-like interface will encourage users to transfer knowledge about

N. Lohmann et al. (Eds.): BPM 2013 Workshops, LNBIP 171, pp. 537–548, 2014.
DOI: 10.1007/978-3-319-06257-0_43, © Springer International Publishing Switzerland 2014

this familiar system of everyday experience to the operation of mobile workflow management systems to ease understanding of its structure and functionality [8]. More precisely, we explore the familiar features of car navigation systems as a catalyst to foster process navigation by establishing an analogy between networks of roads and the graph structure of a process. For instance, we map the well-known situation of driving into a dead-end road with the existence of a logical deadlock in a process instance. The need for more TomTom-like functionalities for WfMS to make systems more user-friendly was first identified in [12]. Many mappings between TomTom and workflow management systems may be derived, e.g., by creating interpretations of traffic symbols in the context of workflow management - some of which will be shown in Sect. 2.1. It became clear that it was a benefit to think about metaphors rather than to simply follow the more traditional approach and create formal requirements specifications [15].

To better convey our goal, Fig. 1 shows a mockup of a car navigation system which was adapted to include several information elements related to process models and instances (labeled with 1–5) rather than to travels and trips. It is for this type of navigation applications that we concentrate our attention on. We contend that symbolism holds the promise to develop a new wave of workflow systems (c.f. [8]). In this particular example, the name of the highway, on the top of the figure and marked with (1), was replaced by the name of the currently executing process and its process identifier (i.e. 'Request Quote' and 'P3'); the number of remaining kilometers to reach the destination has been replaced by a process Key Performance Indicator (KPI) (see label (2)); label (3) indicates at what time the instance is expected to be completed; the speedometer was replaced by the current cost of the process (see label (4)); and label (5) marks a road selection in a highway which indicates a path selection (i.e. an XOR-split) in the process model. Naturally, the design of a high-fidelity prototype for the mockup of Fig. 1 would not include all graphical elements. For example, the skyline may not find a correspondence in mobile workflow applications.

Fig. 1. The use of the car navigation metaphor to inspire process model navigation

This paper is structured as follows. Section 2 describes an isomorphism between the elements present in car navigation systems and workflow systems.

Section 3 describes the use of the Technology Acceptance Model [4] to provide a first validation of our approach. Section 4 describes the implementation of a running prototype which provides a proof of concept for the metaphor. Section 5 provides the related work in this field. Finally, Sect. 6 presents our conclusions.

2 Process Model Navigation

Most traditional process models are based on a graph-based representation for specifying how a business process or workflow operates. Let us use Petri nets to model processes. The question to be asked is *"how can we establish an analogy between a Petri net and a geographic map in the context of a car navigation metaphor?"*. We established the following fundamental mappings:

- Process models correspond to geographic maps
- Process instances correspond to moving vehicles
- Process places correspond to route sections and intersections
- Process transitions correspond to routes

In other words, a process model (i.e. a graph) which links places with transitions, defining a more or less ordered pattern, is describable in terms of a network of streets, roads and highways. Two streets are linked, if the transitions they represent lead to the same place. Since processes are essentially planar structures, the corresponding route network has a two-dimensional structure. We use the term *route* as an abstraction concept to refer to a street, highway, road, etc.

By analyzing the features that can be implemented for process navigation using a car navigation metaphor, we created a taxonomy of three important concepts to be considered: topology, connectivity, and landmarks.

2.1 Topology

The topology, or structure, of a process contains specific elements (such as splits and joins) which can find a mapping counterpart in a car navigation metaphor. Let us use the workflow patterns identified in [13] as a starting point and analyze how they can be matched to a split road, a road junction, a traffic light, a dead end, a roundabout and the notion of distance.

- *Split road.* An exclusive choice (XOR-split) and a multi-choice (OR-split) can be represented with a split road, i.e. a point where a flow of traffic splits. See Fig. 2(a)) for a possible road sign to use to represent a process split. A parallel split (AND-split) can be represented with various parallel lanes running in the same direction (see Fig. 1, label (5)).
- *Road junction.* The process synchronization pattern (AND-join) and the simple merge (XOR-join) can all be represented with a road junction, i.e. a place where two or more roads meet.
- *Traffic light.* The structured synchronizing merge (OR-join sync) can be effectively illustrated with a traffic light. When an instance stops at a traffic light, users can immediately understand that a synchronization point has been reached (see Fig. 2(b)).

- *Dead end.* A process with a deadlock, i.e. a situation where an instance cannot continue to be executed anymore, can be made graphically visible in a navigation system using the road dead end sign (see Fig. 2(c)).
- *Roundabout.* Many cyclic process models include small repetitive cycles for error checking or quality improvements. These small cycles composed of a few transitions can be made explicit and be represented using a roundabout sign (see Fig. 2(d)).
- *Distance.* Route networks are spatially extended webs. It is possible to work with two types of distance measures: topological and geometrical. Topological route length is computed from the number of nodes (i.e. transitions or places) of a path; while the geometrical length is the sum of the lengths of all transitions of a path.

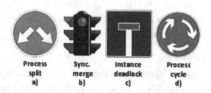

Process split a)   Sync. merge b)   Instance deadlock c)   Process cycle d)

Fig. 2. Using road signs to express process and instance structures and behaviors.

2.2 Connectivity

Connectivity explores process transitions (i.e. tasks) that connect places. In geographical maps, connectivity is expressed using streets, avenues, highways, walking paths, etc. Routes can be used to portray the static nature of process models and the dynamic behavior of process instances. For example,

- *Route type.* The frequency a transition is executed in the context of a process instance or in the context of several instances can be represented using different types of routes. For example, a transition which is rarely executed can be represented using a dirty road; a transition with an average number of invocations can be represented with a lane; and a highway can be used to indicate frequently executed transitions.
- *Route failure.* Often a process transition can stop functioning due to an underlying problem in the information system that supports it (e.g. database failure, incorrect login/password, Web service invocation error, etc.). In such a case, the failure can be illustrated in real-time as a route being interrupted by landslides.
- *Multiple lanes.* The workflow parallel split pattern (i.e. an AND-split) introduces the concurrent execution of two of more instances which were split at some point. This concurrent execution can be visualized using additional routes which are parallel to the one followed by an instance.

- *Route names.* Since routes represent transitions, a route inherits its name from the transition it represents (see Fig. 1, label (1)). This is static information associated with a process model, rather than with dynamic instances.
- *Route duration/cost.* For the duration of routes (i.e. transitions), the research done in the context of Workflow QoS (Quality of Service) [2] can be applied to enable each route to have a duration model. Quantitatively, the elapsed time or remaining duration of a route can be mapped to a concept similar to the one of physical distance in kilometers.

In these five examples, transitions and routes represent the static nature of design time processes. While routes characteristics represent the dynamic nature of processes instances.

2.3 Landmark

In a map some aspects are more relevant than others. For example, Points Of Interests (POI) indicate places which are worth visiting. The notion of landmark brings the notion of frequency, clustering, and containment for process navigation.

- *Frequency.* To express the importance of a place, which is often visited by process instances, a POI can be used. For example, an airport can illustrate a busy place where many instances flow.
- *Clustering.* Navigation maps identify areas which aggregate similar elements. For example, a city clusters similar roads (usually streets). In the same way, the elements of a process can also be clustered based, for example, on the similarity of transitions. The size of clusters can then be represented differently to express their relevance.
- *Containment.* Processes are often built by relying on subprocesses which define containment relationships. The notion of a process which contains subprocesses, which in turn contains yet another subprocess, can be expressed by using a linear hierarchy of city → town → village or alternatively, country → state → county. As instances 'travel' from a process to a subprocess, the navigation system can change the visualization context.

Implementing frequency, clustering, and containment using a semantic layer of information can provide environments characterized by intuitive clues (e.g. POI, cities, and towns) to the static and dynamic structure of processes.

2.4 Limitations

On the one hand, the use of metaphors has the advantage of enabling users to reapply the knowledge they already have from a domain. On the other hand, a metaphor might involve the danger that it does not go far enough and that certain characteristics cannot be well supported. For example, while Sect. 2.1 suggests multiple lanes to be interpreted as a parallel split, the analogy maybe hard to understand and implement. Since there are multiple lanes, one needs to be selected. It is not possible to drive on multiple lines in parallel. One solution can be to duplicate the "car" in different lanes simultaneously. Naturally, this scenario does not typically happens in real life. In a parallel split, the need to represent activities executing asynchronously is also a requirement.

To reduce complexity, navigation can be combined with process view mechanisms to enable, e.g., zooming in/out by aggregating/removing parts of the process. Similarly, views can be used to provide personalized versions of a process omitting activities not relevant to the current "driver" (see Sect. 2.3).

3 Prevalidation of the Approach

The validation of the proposed process model navigation metaphor, as with most information systems, can be subdivided into prevalidation, primary validation, and post validation. In this paper, we will be concerned with prevalidation. This first phase is carried out before implementing any prototype or running system [3].

We have used the Technology Acceptance Model (TAM) [4] for empirically prevalidating the navigation metaphor. TAM has been used successfully in many studies for more than two decades to test the potential adoption of new information systems by end users. Despite the fact that several other models have also been proposed to predict the future use of a system, TAM has captured most attention from the information systems community.

TAM suggests that *perceived usefulness* (PU) and *perceived ease of use* (PEOU) are beliefs about a new technology that influence an individual's *attitude toward use* (ATU) of that technology. In addition, the model postulates that the attitude toward using a new technology has a mediating effect on *behavioral intention* (BI) to use.

TAM uses a survey method to inquire end users about their perception levels (see Sects. 3.1 and 3.2). Afterwards, survey data is collected (Sect. 3.3) and descriptive and inferential analysis techniques are performed, typically, using software packages for statistical analysis such as SPSS or SAS (Sect. 3.4). The final step is to interpret statistical results to determine if a constructed model can predict that a new technology will be adopted, or not, by end users (Sect. 3.4).

3.1 Instrument Development

We constructed a survey (presented in Table 1) to measure perception levels. The table lists the four general constructs (PU, PEOU, ATU, and BI) and the 13 items/questions that were part of the survey. These items were recommended in TAM's original article [4]. The items were validated in a pilot study involving two researchers and some wording was changed to make the survey specific for process navigation. All items were measured using a seven-point Likert-type scale with anchors from "Strongly disagree"(which mapped to 1) to "Strongly agree" (which mapped to 7). The survey included one item worded with proper negation. Items were shuffled to reduce monotony of questions measuring the same construct.

Table 1. The TAM-based survey students took (M = median)

Construct/Item & Measure	M
Perceived Usefulness (PU)	
PU1 I would find Navigation useful for business process management.	6
PU2 Using Navigation would enable to accomplish the task of process management more quickly.	6
PU3 Using process navigation would increase my productivity.	6
PU4 Using Navigation would make it easier to do my job to manage business processes.	6
Perceived Ease Of Use (PEOU)	
PEOU1 My interaction with the Navigation system would be clear and understandable.	6
PEOU2 It would be easy for me to become skillful at using the system.	5
PEOU3 I would find Navigation easy to use.	6
PEOU4 Learning to operate the Navigation system would be easy for me.	6
Attitude Toward Using Technology (ATU)	
ATU1 Using business process navigation is a bad idea (negative).	2
ATU2 Navigation makes business process management more interesting.	6
ATU3 Working with a business process navigation is fun.	6
ATU4 I would like working with a process navigation system.	6
Behavioral intention (BI)	
BI1 Assuming business process navigation would be available, I predict I would use it.	6

3.2 Setup and Procedure

The subjects were students of the Department of Informatics Engineering, University of Coimbra. Before the experiment, subjects had a one semester introductory course on *Information Systems Management*. In the last week of classes, subjects were asked to give their opinion on the use of process navigation as a way to help them manage process models in the future.

The concept of a process navigation system was described to subjects using user interface (UI) mockups of the system drawn with Microsoft Powerpoint. The experimenter administered the survey to the subjects in class. Four UI mockups were shown to subjects (Fig. 3 illustrates an example). One mockup was shown per slide. The functionality of the system was explained. The explanations given lasted 10 min in total.

After all participants had listen and understood the UI mockups, the experimenter shortly introduced the format of the survey and the survey was handed out. The survey was identical for all subjects. The subjects did not receive any textual description of the mockups.

As soon as every subject received the survey, they were asked to start filling out the questionnaire. The experimenter stayed in the room for the whole experiment assuring there was no collaboration among the subjects. Subjects could

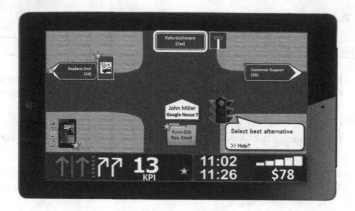

Fig. 3. Example of a mockup shown to subjects based on the prototype implemented (see Sect. 4). Compared to the prototype, the mockups had additional elements which are marked with a star in the Figure; e.g. a bar showing KPIs, icons, and the visual outline of the signs for next steps was improved.

leave the room as soon as they were finished and every subject finished within 15 min. There were no limits on time.

3.3 Subjects Characteristics

A total of 14 Master degree students participated in the survey. It was held at the end of a 14 weeks semester. During the first four weeks of the semester, students were taught Business Process Management (e.g. state diagrams, workflow nets, Petri nets, tasks, activities, cases, control-flow, etc.). During the reminding of the semester, process models from ITIL (Information Technology Infrastructure Library) were also covered. At the time the survey was completed, students had a good knowledge of (business) process modeling and management. The sample consisted of 7 % female and 93 % male students with an age between 22 and 26 years. All the students (100 %) were from Computer Science. No tests for colour blindness or visual acuity were conducted.

3.4 Analysis and Findings

Prior to the assessment of the survey, guidelines for screening missing data and outliers were followed. The 14 usable questionnaires were examined for missing data. They showed a few missing values and the mean of existing values was used to generate replacement values for all the missing data. Due to the reduced number of subjects, no other tests were carried out.

Descriptive statistics showed that subjects have ranked the process navigation approach high in the items PU, PEOU, ATU, and BI. Most common answers to the questions pertaining these items included *I strongly agree*, *I agree*, *I somewhat agree*. Table 1 shows the median of the answers. Results suggest that subjects agree with the usefulness and perceived use of the metaphor since the median for most questions was 6, i.e. subjects have given the answer *I agree*. Subjects have also a positive attitude toward using a system implementing the metaphor, and believe that if such a system would exist they would use it.

We believe that these insights on the navigation metaphor are a good starting point to exploit its practical use by developing a first prototype. Nonetheless, this preliminary study needs to be replicated involving a larger number of subjects to be more statistically significant.

4   First Prototype

The main objective of the prototype was to further study how mobile workers perceive a navigation system for processes. While in the TAM survey, the results were significantly influenced by the interpretation of the meaning of the navigation metaphor by subjects, the prototype allows us to study how the metaphor is perceived. For instance, we can visualize arbitrary cases to process workers on their Android powered device (cf. Figure 3) and study their reaction on it. Furthermore, we can show or hide context information, e.g. about the availability of data or the current 'traffic', and investigate the effect of its absence or presence on mobile workers. Different scenarios may be specified with a desktop application and sent on demand to connected Android front-ends. Consequently, all front-ends report the reaction of users (e.g. a direction sign was touched) back to the desktop application. However, since we first wanted to further investigate the effects of applying the navigation metaphor to process management on mobile devices, the desktop controller application does not (yet) comprise a workflow engine that automatically derives the next situation to be shown to users. Instead, the simulation is manually controlled and situations may be either defined dynamically or loaded from configuration files.

This basic simulation process is shown in Fig. 4. It starts with the launch of the controller application on a PC which needs to be connected to the same network as the mobile devices (or which is reachable from the internet via its IP address). Then, the simulation front-end is started on Android powered mobile devices. Upon its start, the simulation front-end will try to establish a connection to the controller. Afterwards, the simulation supervisor may load a specific workflow case, update it to its specific needs and transmit it to connected front-ends. If a completely new situation is to be created, this may also be achieved by the supervisor using the controller application. It is important to note that the controller itself is not meant to be used as a solution for process modeling; instead, it allows for creating single tasks with a graphical user interface.

Upon receiving a specific case, the front-ends will set up the corresponding visualization. Subjects can introspect it, interpret the labels and descriptions, and make a decision about what to do next by interacting with their device (e.g. by touching the label of one of the alternatives shown on screen). This decision is then send back to the controller and visualized to the supervisor. It is then his responsibility to switch to the next situation in the workflow.

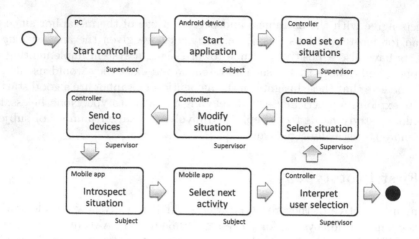

Fig. 4. Basic steps of the simulation as implemented by the prototype.

Even though both, architecture and the basic simulation process, were implemented in a very simple manner, they allow for studying the first important results relevant to the interaction of agents within a distributed, mobile workflow execution environment. First, the prototype shows our concept of how a workflow instance may be visualized following the navigation metaphor as described in earlier sections. It has some limited flexibility because of its current status, such as it only provides a detailed view on a specific case but not (yet) an overview of the whole process instance such that it supports taking single decisions but does not outline the route up to the destination. Second, it shows that the interaction between concurrently acting workflow agents need to be considered more closely. Even though agent selection and notification may be considered a standard feature of modern workflow management systems, the mobile scenario adds another level of complexity to the underlying problem in which agents may be temporarily disconnected from a central server instance. Work may be started and finished without being able to notify a server. Last but not least, the front-end only provides information about tasks to users. Real data is not yet transmitted. Accordingly, the controller receives notifications about the selection of a following task but no updates on the status of data or other workflow resources.

5 Related Work

The applicability of the car navigation metaphor to workflow systems has been first discussed in [12]. In our work, we take one step forward and explore how it can be used to guide the development of mobile workflow solutions.

Hipp et al. [7] suggest to navigate through large process models using Google Earth. Compared to our work, the navigation is static. In other words, process instances are not visualized. The approach sees large processes as maps and the proposed system adds zooming functionalities. Effinger [5] developed a 3D Flight

Navigator for visualizing process models. While the idea is interesting, so far, it only enables to represent models using a 3D view. Since process models are conceptual and logical representations, it is not clear what are the direct benefits of a 3D representation, except, possibly, the hierarchical visualization of sub-processes. Poppe and et al. [11] constructed a prototype for remote collaborative process modeling using virtual environments. The system relies on Second Life, a head mounted display, and enables the modeling of processes using BPMN. While this work contrasts with ours since we target the navigation of process models and instances, the results are relevant since preliminary data indicates that users interact well with virtual environments. Vankipuram et al. [14] rely on virtual world replay to visualize critical care environments. Our approach is distinct since we target the use of metaphors with a high degree of acceptance among end users for navigation applied to mobile devices.

Hackmann et al. [6] present a BPEL execution engine (called Sliver) which supports a wide variety of devices ranging from mobile phones to desktop PCs. The challenge of the work done was to demonstrate that mobile devices are capable of hosting sophisticated workflow/groupware applications. Leoni and Mecela [10], in contrast, describe a distributed workflow management system that runs on mobile devices (in this case on the Windows Mobile platform), that relies on BPEL for its execution logics. Following the traditional task list behaviour, the application only provides a screen for managing an assigned task.

6 Conclusion

Research indicates that new workflow paradigms for mobile devices can be inspired from the TomTom metaphor. Therefore, we have established an isomorphism between navigation and workflow systems which aggregates mappings in three categories: (1) topology of route networks, (2) the connectivity of maps, and (3) landmarks. Afterwards, we have conducted an acceptance evaluation to determine if end users would use a workflow system implementing a car navigation metaphor. The results were encouraging and led to the implementation of a first prototype. We believe that the isomorphism will enable users to reapply their knowledge from the domain of driving to the domain of workflow management and, thus, will facilitate the navigation of process models and instances. Our future work will focus on the implementation of additional features and to carry out a more complete system evaluation.

Acknowledgements. This work was partially funded by iCIS (CENTRO-07-ST24-FEDER-002003).

References

1. Cardoso, J., Van Der Aalst, W.: Handbook of Research on Business Process Modeling. Information Science Reference, Hershey (2009)
2. Cardoso, J., Miller, J.A., Sheth, A., Arnold, J., Kochut, K.: Quality of service for workflows and web service processes. J. Web Semant. 1(3), 281–308 (2004)

3. Carter, W.C., Dunham, J.R., Laprie, J.-C., Williams, T., Howden, W., Smith, B., Lewis, C.M.: Design for validation: an approach to systems validation. Technical report NASA-181835, NASA - National Aeronautics and Space Administration (1989)
4. Davis, F.: Perceived usefulness, perceived ease of use, and user acceptance of information technology. MIS Quarterly **13**, 319–340 (1989)
5. Effinger, P.: A 3d-navigator for business process models. In: La Rosa, M., Soffer, P. (eds.) BPM Workshops 2012. LNBIP, vol. 132, pp. 737–743. Springer, Heidelberg (2013)
6. Hackmann, G., Haitjema, M., Gill, ChD, Roman, G.-C.: Sliver: a bpel workflow process execution engine for mobile devices. In: Dan, A., Lamersdorf, W. (eds.) ICSOC 2006. LNCS, vol. 4294, pp. 503–508. Springer, Heidelberg (2006)
7. Hipp, M., Mutschler, B., Reichert, M.: Navigating in process model collections: a new approach inspired by google earth. In: Daniel, F., Barkaoui, K., Dustdar, S. (eds.) BPM Workshops 2011, Part II. LNBIP, vol. 100, pp. 87–98. Springer, Heidelberg (2012)
8. Hirschheim, R., Newman, M.: Symbolism and information systems development: myth, metaphor and magic. Infor. Syst. Res. **2**(1), 29–62 (1991)
9. Kendall, J.E., Kendall, K.E.: Metaphors and their meaning for information systems development. Eur. J. Inf. Syst. **3**(5), 37–47 (1994)
10. de Leoni, M., Mecella, M.: Mobile process management through web services. In: 2010 IEEE International Conference on Services Computing (SCC), pp. 378–385. IEEE, Piscataway (2010)
11. Poppe, E., Brown, R.A., Recker, J.C., Johnson, D.M.: A prototype augmented reality collaborative process modelling tool. In: 9th Interantional Conference on Business Process Management, Clermont-Ferrand, France (2011)
12. van der Aalst, W.M.P.: Tomtom for business process management (tomtom4bpm). In: van Eck, P., Gordijn, J., Wieringa, R. (eds.) CAiSE 2009. LNCS, vol. 5565, pp. 2–5. Springer, Heidelberg (2009)
13. Van Der Aalst, W., Ter Hofstede, A., Kiepuszewski, B., Barros, A.: Workflow patterns. Distrib. Parallel Databases **14**(1), 5–51 (2003)
14. Vankipuram, M., Kahol, K., Cohen, T., Patel, V.L.: Visualization and analysis of activities in critical care environments. In: AMIA Annual Symposium Proceedings, pp. 662–666 (2009)
15. Walsham, G.: Organizational metaphors and information systems research. Eur. J. Inf. Sys. **1**(2), 83–94 (1991)

Evaluating KIPN for Modeling KIP

Joanne Manhães Netto[✉], Flávia Maria Santoro[✉],
and Fernanda Araujo Baião[✉]

Research and Practice Group in Information Architecture (NP2Tec)
Department of Applied Informatics Federal, University of the State of
Rio de Janeiro (UNIRIO), Janeiro, Brazil
{joanne.netto, flavia.santoro,
fernanda.baiao}@uniriotec.br

Abstract. Modeling Knowledge-Intensive Processes (KIP) is not an easy task due to its essential characteristics: unstructured, based on social interactions, experience and intentions of the actors involved. The previously developed Knowledge Intensive Process Ontology (KIPO) proposed all the concepts (and relationships among them) to make a KIP explicit. However, KIPO does not provide a graphical notation, which is crucial for the stakeholders to reach a common understanding about it. This paper presents the Knowledge Intensive Process Notation (KIPN), a notation for building knowledge-intensive processes graphical models. We discuss the results of an exploratory study where a KIP was modeled by its participants. The goal was to explore the use of the notation as a basis for identifying the elements within the process modeling.

Keywords: Visualizing process designs · Process design in collaborative environments · Linking process design to organizational strategy and goals

1 Introduction

Process modeling is essential for the systematization and management of organizational knowledge artifacts [26]. However, this is not an easy task, especially when it comes to the so-called Knowledge-Intensive Processes [15].

A Knowledge-Intensive Process (KIP) involves many subjective and complex concepts, typically tacit for from their stakeholders' minds. Additionally, a KIP usually comprises activities based on acquisition, sharing, storage, (re)use of knowledge, and collaboration among participants, so that the amount of value added to the organization depends on the knowledge of the process agents. They deal with unpredictable decisions, creativity-oriented tasks, and dynamic execution that evolves based on the experience acquired by the agents. All those issues hinder their representation, and make them subject to different interpretations.

Abecker [1] affirms that the representation of knowledge-intensive business activities helps to reach understanding to support business management. Research on KIP points out its essential characteristics [9, 11]. However, it is difficult to find out an approach that addresses all or at least most of these characteristics in the representation of their processes, mainly due to the lack of proper modeling strategies, as

N. Lohmann et al. (Eds.): BPM 2013 Workshops, LNBIP 171, pp. 549–561, 2014.
DOI: 10.1007/978-3-319-06257-0_44, © Springer International Publishing Switzerland 2014

discussed in [12, 13]. Additionally, the Object Management Group (OMG) [24] states that, in addition to underlining the concepts inherent to a domain, a notation enhances the models' clarityand allows communicating the concepts uniformly.

The literature discusses how a KIP can be better understood and managed, particularly regarding representation [2, 7, 14, 15, 17, 23, 24, 27]. However, none of them captures all essential KIP characteristics, as shown in [11, 13], and most approaches do not provide special attention to the notation applied in KIP representation. Considerations on these approaches are presented in Sect. 2.

The Knowledge Intensive Process Ontology (KIPO) [11] was developed, from an extensive literature review, with the target to comprise all the elements to make a KIP explicit. KIPO comprises concepts from several perspectives that are crucial for a complete understanding and representation of a KIP, namely: the Business Process perspective, the Business Rules perspective, the Decision-Making Rationale perspective, and the Collaboration perspective. Nevertheless, KIPO does not include a specific graphical notation for representing processes, requiring the instantiation of the ontology to make this process explicit. Based on the potential of KIPO to portray the essential features of KIP, this paper presents a notation for building KIP graphical models: the Knowledge Intensive Process Notation – KIPN.

The paper is organized as follows. Section 2 describes current approaches for knowledge intensive processes representation. Section 3 presents the ontology KIP, Sect. 4 presents the Knowledge Intensive Process Notation (KIPN) and specifies its diagrams and core symbols. Section 5 discusses the case study executed to evaluate the proposal. Section 6 concludes this paper.

2 State of the Art in Representing KIP

KIP has its own characteristics that distinguish it from conventional structured processes, such as socialization and collaboration, the dynamics and the influence of intentions and experiences of the agents in decision making. Some traditional process modeling graphic approaches, such as Event Driven Process Chain (EPC) [17] and Business Process Modeling Notation (BPMN) [18, 24] have been adapted to allow the representation of the intrinsic elements of knowledge within business processes, but these methods do not include all the required features to describe a KIP [13].

Besides, the literature shows approaches dedicated to highly-intensive knowledge processes representation. Among them, we highlight three, whose primary focus is on the graphical notation. The Knowledge Modeling Description Language (KMDL) [14] represents both tacit and explicit knowledge of the process. Thus, the different possibilities of knowledge conversion can be modeled and the flow of knowledge between actors is depicted. The Oliveira's methodology [23] is an extension of Ericsson et al. [10] for business process modeling that is composed of diagrams representing a hierarchy of models. It uses constructs adapted from KMDL [14] to model business processes, considering Knowledge Management aspects. Supulniece et al. [27] extended BPMN incorporating concepts also defined in [14], where three different objects: knowledge objects, information objects and data objects were used. The authors observed in [3] that the relationship between the phenomena behind the symbols is unclear in the modeling process. The evaluation in [13] concluded that current process modeling representation languages are not adequate for the representation of KIPs, since relevant information about the KIP dynamics is lost.

Other approaches are also related to KIP, despite their different terminology. According to Van der Aaslt et al. [2], Case Management (or Case Handling) deals with instances (cases) of processes with little or no structure at all, in which non-atomic activities predominantly take place without a predefined order. In such cases, interaction among agents is not restricted to data and knowledge exchange, but it is supported by collaborative tools. Man [19] points two perspectives of Case Handling representation: communication-based and artifact-based process control. He states that these approaches [2, 28], despite representing a sequence of activities with flexibility, do not include human aspects, such as collaboration and decision-making.

The definition provided by Hill et al. [16] to an "Artful" process is also very similar to a KIP, in the sense that an artful process is a dynamic process that depends on agents skills and experience in challenging activities, and requires quick complex decisions among many possible alternatives. Di Ciccio et al. [7] discuss two proposals for graphically modeling a KIP, named DCR Graphs [15] and MailofMine [6]. While the first attempts to show the implementation state of activities and interdependencies to ease the flow, the second intends to model an artful process by mining elements from emails exchanged during the accomplishment of the knowledge workers' activities. We note that such approaches represent the flow and performance of activities dynamically, without considering the characteristics related to collaboration. Although the focus of artful process is on agents and their knowledge, the proposals do not represent specific characteristics that led to the decision making, knowledge building, improvements in activities, and influence of external events.

3 The Knowledge-Intensive Process Ontology (KIPO)

França et al. [11] designed KIPO, a formal ontology comprising the key concepts and relationships involved in the conceptualization of knowledge-intensive processes. KIPO aims at providing a common, domain-independent understanding of KIPs and, as such, it may be used as a meta-model for a KIP representation language. The first column of Table 1 lists some of the generic concepts from KIPO. It includes tacit elements linked to the process, such as Belief, Desire, Intention and Perception, which have a role in building the foundation of intentions and objectives to be achieved by

Table 1. KIPN graphical symbols and descriptions.

Symbol	Description	Symbol	Description
Agent	An agent in the process, free from his acting role.	External Agent	Someone who contibutes with knowledge to a Socialization, but does not participate in the process.
Impact Agent	Someone who is responsible for the execution of the process.	Innovation Agent	Someone who is responsible for solving issues of the process with innovation and creativity.

Table 1. (*Continued*)

Process Goal	An expected objective for executing the process.	**Goal**	A goal that is pursued by an agent and motivates his/her actions.
Association	The association between information and artifacts.	**Message Flow**	Communication between agents during an informal exchange.
Knowledge-Intensive Process	Represented as a pool, the execution of the process depends on the knowledge requirements of its participants.	**Socialization**	Socialization that occurs on the activities. Represented as a swimlane.
Knowledge-intensive Activity	An activity of a KIP that involves Socialization among Agents.	**Activity**	A conventional activity of a KIP.
Assertion	A formally specified piece of knowledge within a KIP.	**Mental Image**	Interpretation and mental organization of information that creates knowledge.
Innovation	Innovation or renewal incorporated by the innovation agent during an knowledge intensive activity.	**Data Object**	A relevant information required by an activity.
Experience	A previous circumstance or issue known by an Agent that may influence a decision.	**Speciality**	An academic or professional competence of an Agent that may influence a decision.
Desire	Something that the agent desires.	**Intention**	Something that the agent intends to achieve when performing an activity. It is the agent's commitment to reach a goal.
Belief	Something that the agent believes at any given time, and can become an intention. It is not necessarily the truth.	**Feeling**	A feeling of the agent that may influence his/her decision.
Decision	The result of a decision-making process.	**Question**	Some issue considered by the agent when making a decision.
Chosen Alternative	Selected alternative to address issues of a decision.	**Discarded Alternative**	Excluded alternatives that were not enough to solve the issues of the decision.
Advantage	Advantage related to an alternative.	**Disadvantage**	Disadvantage related to an alternative.
Risk	Some possible result that may represent a threaten for a decision.	**Restriction**	Something (a law, a rule, or any known circumstance) that may restrict or limitate the decision making.
Evidence	A proof, a sign that something exists.	**Fact**	Fact in reality, some occurrence in the KIP scenario.
Contingency	External event to the process, considered during the socialization agents.	**Criterion**	Established criteria for analyzing advantages and disadvantages of alternatives.

Table 1. *(Continued)*

Integrity Rule	A statement that should be kept true regarding the domain concepts and their relationships. It is a structural business rule.	Derivation Rule	A statement of knowledge derived from other existing knowledge from the domain. As a conclusion, it defines domain concepts with regard to other concepts. It is a derivation business rule.
Reaction Rule	A statements specifying an activity that should be carried out on the occurrence of an specific event and condition. It is a reaction business rule.	Informal Exchange	An informal (either face to face, or based in documentation) exchange of knowledge among agents during a socialization.

the process, as discussed in [5, 25]. Usually this type of process is guided by agent's intentions in achieving the process objective. Thus, the representation of these concepts allows the tracking of what motivated the decision makings and the outcomes achieved through the process execution.

KIPO also addresses collaborative aspects, which are essential due to the high degree of tacit knowledge exchanged among agents and to the frequent process evolution along time. The loss of this information decreases the awareness of when and how a collective action is performed, thus compromising a common understanding and collaboration among agents. Our evaluation of the proposals and notations from the literature showed that they do not represent all the characteristics and dimensions proposed in KIPO. However, KIPO does not provide a graphical notation. So far, Moody [20] argues that visual notations are effective because they provide powerful resources for the human visual system and are transmitted in a more concise and precise manner than ordinary text-based language. Although KIPO does not address the problem of representing KIP graphically, it opens a way to explore the potential of a visual notation for KIPs proposal. We address this potential by proposing KIPN – A Knowledge Intensive Process Notation.

4 The Knowledge-Intensive Process Notation (KIPN)

This section presents KIPN, a graphical notation developed to promote a cognitively-effective understanding of a KIP. KIPN covers all characteristics defined by KIPO.

The objective of this proposal is to represent the concepts defined by KIPO in a clear, intuitive and easy to understand manner, so that the resulting graphical model of the process is precisely understood by users of the domain. These requirements suggest the concept of Cognitive Effectiveness, defined by Moody [20] as the speed, ease and accuracy with which a representation can be processed by the human mind.

Moody [20] defined nine principles for high-quality design of visual languages from a cognitive viewpoint that should be followed when proposing a graphical notation for conceptual modeling: semiotic clarity, graphic economy, perceptual discriminability, visual expressiveness, dual coding, semantic transparency, cognitive fit, complexity management and cognitive integration. In [21], we describe in details how these principles were applied while building KIPN.

According to Moody [20], the "anatomy" of a visual notation is composed by: a set of graphical symbols, forming the graphic vocabulary; a set of compositional rules, forming the visual grammar; and the semantic concepts, forming the visual semantics. In our proposal, the visual semantics is defined by KIPO. The visual syntax (the graphic vocabulary and rules of the visual grammar) comprises a set of diagrams that are related to each other in order to represent the main perspectives within a KIP. Since a KIP is a specific subtype of a business process, our proposed set of diagrams work together as a breakdown of the components of a process diagram. Therefore, some existing approaches (BPMN[25], i*[29] and Mind Maps[4]) were reused from literature to represent certain aspects of the KIP. The diagrams that represent the KIP dimensions are described as follows, and Table 1 shows the KIPN symbols proposed.

KIP Diagram. The first and main KIPN diagram is the KIP Diagram. It depicts a comprehensive overview of the processes and activities using BPMN-based elements. However, different from a standard BPMN process representation, the control-flow among KIP activities is not determined; rather, there is no predefined order of execution for the activities. Moreover, processes can be modeled in different levels of abstraction, which means building a hierarchy of models. In this approach, a model in one level abstracts details from the models in the next level anytime they get too complex to be understood (due to the number of activities or to the relationships with other processes/sub-processes, for example).

Socialization Diagram. The Socialization diagram is at the core of a KIP, where swimlanes highlight how communication happens among agents, what are the messages exchanged, and which pieces of knowledge are acquired and shared. This diagram shows socialization and contingency events that influence decisions, as well as which elements are produced and handled. Knowledge structures may result from the socialization among agents. These may be formal structures (such as Data Objects or Assertions) or informal and thus unstructured artifacts (a Mental Image). To highlight these interactions between agents, each Socialization is represented by a swimlane including informal knowledge exchanges, innovations proposals, external events (contingencies) and decision activities. In particular, decisions in a Socialization diagram represent the final result of a decision-making process (which is in turn detailed in the Decision Diagram, presented next).

Decision Diagram. The Decision Diagram details all relevant elements involved in a decision-making process that may occur during the KIP, and its corresponding result. This diagram focuses on showing the process of decision making, unlike most previously discussed that represent this step with a symbol gateway. Elements may include real facts and evidences observed by the agent, a set of proposed alternatives (even those that were discarded by the agent). Each alternative is described through its evaluation criteria, the set of advantages and disadvantages it raises, and which are the risks of following this alternative. Moreover, the KIP modeler should also register the chosen alternative as the final decision result, and possibly some restrictions that may have influenced the agent's choice (such as an organizational business rule, for example), as well as mention his/her experience applied or expertise produced while solving a problem. The Decision Diagram follows a Mind Mapping notation focusing on explicating the rationale followed by an agent until he/she gets to a final Chosen Alternative. Mind Mapping [4] is used to represent semantic or other connections among portions of learned material in a creative and seamless manner [9], making it easier to explicit decision making processes. The aspects that influence a decision-making process are associated in a radial way to the centered icon of the chosen alternative, giving an objective and concise view about the process.

Agent Diagram. The socialization and decision activities ultimately promote new experiences, and even expertise gain to agents. To map the expertise and experience of those agents, we suggest the Agent Diagram. A (generic) agent keeps previous experiences on its work; and an innovation agent also has specific expertise that contributes to innovation and decision-making. In this diagram, it is possible to associate the expertise and experience with their corresponding agent in order to illustrate a competence matrix that maps the skills of those involved.

Intention Diagram. The intrinsic characteristics of agents that mainly influence his/her activities are shown in the Intention Diagram. This includes desires, feelings and beliefs that motivate an agent to execute an activity in order to reach a goal. In the Intention Diagram, all elements related to the KIP Goal should be carefully disposed. The Agent should be vertically connected to his/her intentions, desires, beliefs and feelings. The visual disposition of elements in this diagram follow the Intentionality Panel proposed in the ERi*c method [22]. This Intentionality panel is based on the concept of intention applied by the i* framework [29] to represent intentions when identifying software requirements.

Business-Rules Diagram. The Business Rules Diagram represents documented business rules that restrict a decision during a KIP. This may include organizational rules and procedures, contracts, and laws. For each decision, a business rule diagram must be created to include all business rules that were considered when analyzing alternatives. Each business rule is an assertion, and is ideally described in a formal language so as to avoid misinterpretations.

Next section presents a case study executed in order to explore the application of KIPN in modeling real processes.

5 Exploratory Case Study

In a case study approach [30], exploratory studies are suggested to conduct initial investigations over a phenomenon in order to build or refine a hypothesis or a theory; explanatory studies, on the other hand, are then applied to confirm or deny the hypothesis or theory [8]. In this work, we conducted an exploratory case study in order to investigate the KIPN [21] with regard to two perspectives: (i) adequacy for modeling a real KIP, more specifically how well the proposed symbols and diagrams suffice to represent a KIP in a real scenario; and (ii) comprehensibility by the stakeholders involved in the KIP execution.

The case study was conducted by two analysts with different levels of experience in the KIP domain. The first analyst is an actor in the process with little knowledge about KIPO, while the second analyst has already completed his/her Master's degree and is an expert on KIPO. Different experiences in the same process were important to evaluate both perspectives. Moreover, exploring levels of knowledge about KIPO enabled us to assess the correct use of symbols to represent KIPO concepts.

Since the focus of the exploratory study was on the notation itself, each analyst created the model using the tool of his/her choice, as long as it could incorporate the proposed KIPN graphic symbols. The analysts received a document describing KIPN rules (as discussed in Sect. 3) and the set of symbols, so that they could import them into a tool. The chosen KIP was "Build Master Thesis". The analysts should create the proposed KIPN diagrams according to her/his experience with this process.

After the modeling phase, the analysts were interviewed about their impressions regarding KIPN. A list of topics helped to conduct the interview, but the analysts were free to expose their difficulties and suggestions. The main topics were (i) difficulty in modeling or understand some diagram; (ii) difficulty in associating some KIPO concept to its KIPN symbol; (iii) all domain known concepts were represented in KIPN diagrams and (iv) diagram became overwhelmed by symbols.

A common difficulty that was reported by the analysts was how to distinguish between the model-level versus the instance-level when representing a KIP. KIPO (and consequently our proposed subjacent notation) does not differentiate concepts (and symbols) of the KIP model from its individual instances representations. Analyst 1 experienced some difficulty to create a model for each decision process because she believes that all decisions would have identical models (i.e., the same concepts and relationships). Also, none included innovation in their Socialization diagrams (where it was supposed to be represented) because Innovation is a symbol that would typically appear at the instance-level of a KIP. Moreover, analyst 2 struggled to define the Agents Matrix, while both analysts reported difficulties with the Intentionality panel, because in their opinion these diagrams are at the instance-level of a KIP.

Although the previous comments from analysts contribute to evidence the relevance and occurrence of several KIPO concepts in the studied scenario and no problems were reported to the notation itself, solving the difficulty of distinguishing a model from its instances was out of the scope of our evaluation. Figure 1 shows the modeled decision making in the domain for Analyst 1.

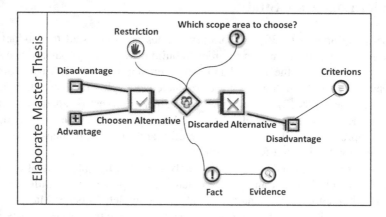

Fig. 1. Decision Diagram modeled by Analyst 1.

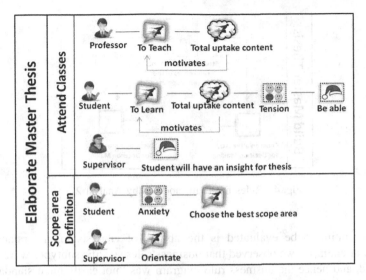

Fig. 2. Intention Diagram modeled by Analyst 1.

With regard to the Socialization Diagram, the analysts used swimlanes to organize symbols of the Intention Diagram, with no previous instructions for doing it that way. During the interview, one analyst reported that activities and process would be better organized this way. This may have occurred because the diagram specification was not complete. Moreover, the use of a modeling tool with no structural rules enforced allowed analysts to modify the design as their own perspective, thus incurring in some deviations from the KIPO specification, as showed in Fig. 2.

In the Agents Matrix the analysts reported issues linked to the dynamics of a PIC, such as when they represented agents' specialties and experiences acquired during the process. The Agent Matrix modeled for the domain is shown in Fig. 3.

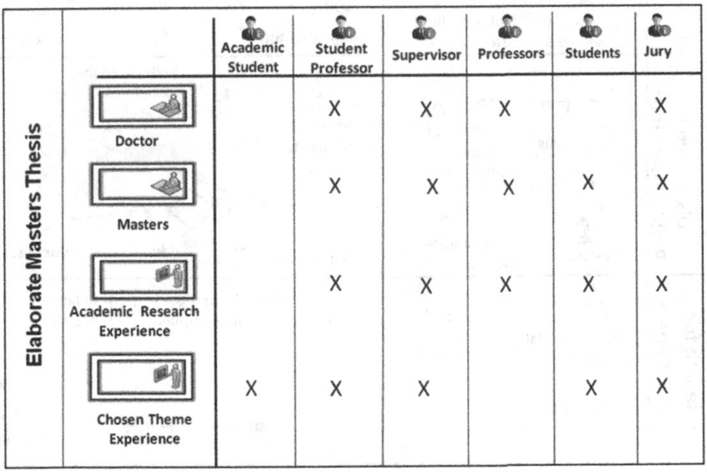

		Academic Student	Student Professor	Supervisor	Professors	Students	Jury
Elaborate Masters Thesis	Doctor		X	X	X		X
	Masters		X	X	X	X	X
	Academic Research Experience		X	X	X	X	X
	Chosen Theme Experience	X	X	X		X	X

Fig. 3. Agent Matrix modeled by Analyst 2.

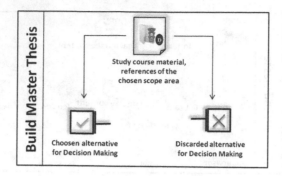

Fig. 4. Rules Diagram modeled by Analyst 2.

Another point to be evaluated is the ability of analysts to understand KIPN symbols. For example, we observed that business rules specific subtypes were not well understood, and hence the business rule diagram was "not easily understandable", in his/her opinion. Figure 4 shows an example from Analyst 2 model. The lack of knowledge about these concepts surely restricts the understanding of the notation, since the concepts are not clear for the modeler.

Regarding the models design, one analyst thought the Socialization diagram can become overwhelmed by symbols, in scenarios where agents interact intensively. This could limit the ability of reading and understanding this diagram. She/he suggested

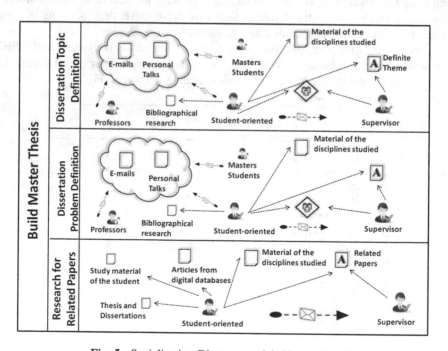

Fig. 5. Socialization Diagram modeled by Analyst 2.

that a specific KIP modeling tool might probably solve this constraint. Figure 5 shows the visual disposition of elements in this diagram.

About the scope of KIPN, both analysts agreed that, even though the number of concepts in KIPO is greater than the number of symbols defined by KIPN, all relevant information about the studied KIP could be represented. Some KIPO concepts may be inferred within the models, such as communication between the agents, the messages exchanged in a message flow during an informal exchange of knowledge, the agent that sends and receives a message in a socialization, and the socialization itself (which is represented in the swimlanes of the socialization diagram). Concerning to the analysis of symbols, both analysts reported no difficulties in associating domain concepts to the proposed KIPN symbols.

6 Conclusions

The paper presented KIPN, a notation for modeling knowledge-intensive processes, and a discussion about its use in an exploratory study.

This notation represents concepts defined in the knowledge-intensive processes ontology (KIPO) using a set of proposed symbols and diagrams. KIPN proposes the integration of different approaches to represent concepts of one single semantic metamodel. This is perhaps the main challenge of our proposal, making the resulting model an "organized mix of concepts" that can be understood and managed by domain experts.

The results from the exploratory evaluation pointed out issues to be improved in the notation, such as the arrangement of symbols in the Intention Diagram and the need for a closer look in the Business-rule diagram. But it is important to note that the analysts had no difficult in using KIPN to model the proposed KIP, considering their experience in this domain and their level of knowledge of the KIPO concepts.

Future work includes the development of a modeling tool that supports KIPN, as well as a methodology for mapping, analyzing and representing KIP. A further issue that also deserves attention is a deeper analysis about model-level versus instance-level representation of KIPs. This issue, in fact, involves theoretical definitions that are beyond the scope of the notation *per se* and are already under investigation.

References

1. Abecker, A.: DECOR Consortium: DECOR – Delivery of context-sensitive organizational knowledge. E-Work and E-Commerce. IOS Press, Amsterdam (2001)
2. Aalst, W.M.P., Weske, M., Grünbauer, D.: Case handling: a new paradigm for business process support. Data Knowl. Eng. **53**(2), 129–162 (2005)
3. Businska, L., Kirikova, M.: Knowledge dimension in business process modeling. In: Nurcan, S. (ed.) CAiSE Forum 2011. LNBIP, vol. 107, pp. 186–201. Springer, Heidelberg (2012)
4. Buzan, T.: The Mind Map Book, 2nd edn. BBC Books, London (1995)

5. Cardoso, E.C.S., Santos Jr., P.S., Almeida, J.P.A., Guizzardi, R.S.S., Guizzardi, G.: Semantic integration of goal and business process modeling. In: International Conference on Research and Practical Issues of Enterprise Information Systems, Brasil (2010)
6. Di Ciccio, C., Mecella, M., Catarci, T.: Representing and visualizing mined artful processes in MailOfMine. In: Holzinger, A., Simonic, K.-M. (eds.) USAB 2011. LNCS, vol. 7058, pp. 83–94. Springer, Heidelberg (2011)
7. Di Ciccio, C., Marrella, A., Russo, A.: Knowledge-intensive processes: an overview of contemporary approaches. In: International workshop on Knowledge-intense Business Processes, Italy, pp. 32–47 (2012)
8. Easterbrook, S.M., Singer, J., Storey, M., Damian, D.: Selecting empirical methods for software engineering research. In: Shull, F., Singer, J. (eds.) Guide to Advanced Empirical Software Engineering. Springer, London (2007)
9. Eppler, M.J., Seifried, P.M., Ropnack, A.: Improving knowledge intensive processes through an enterprise knowledge medium. In: ACM Special Interest Group on Computer Personnel Research, USA, pp. 222–230 (1999)
10. Eriksson, H.-E., Penker, M.: Business Modeling with UML: Business Patterns at Work. E.U.A. Wiley, Somerset (2000)
11. França, J.B.S., Santoro, F.M., Baião, F.A.: Towards characterizing knowledge intensive processes. In: International Conference on Computer-Supported Cooperative Work in Design, China , vol. 113, pp. 497–504 (2012a)
12. dos França, J.B.S., Netto, J., Carvalho, J.E.S., Santoro, F., Baião, F.A., Pimentel, M.: An exploratory study on collaboratively conceptualizing knowledge intensive processes. In: Bider, I., Halpin, T., Krogstie, J., Nurcan, S., Proper, E., Schmidt, R., Soffer, P., Wrycza, S. (eds.) EMMSAD 2012 and BPMDS 2012. LNBIP, vol. 113, pp. 46–60. Springer, Heidelberg (2012)
13. dos França, J.B.S., Netto, J., Barradas, R.G., Santoro, F., Baião, F.A.: Towards knowledge-intensive processes representation. In: La Rosa, M., Soffer, P. (eds.) BPM Workshops 2012. LNBIP, vol. 132, pp. 126–136. Springer, Heidelberg (2013)
14. Gronau, N., Muller, C., Korf, R.: KMDL - capturing, analyzing and improving knowledge intensive business process. J. Univ. Comput. Sci. 11(4), 452–472 (2005)
15. Hildebrandt, T.T., Mukkamala, R.R.: Declarative event-based workflow as distributed dynamic condition response graphs. In: Programming Languages Approaches to Concurrency and Communication-cEntric Software, Cyprus, pp. 59–73 (2010)
16. Hill, C., Yates, R., Jones, C., Kogan, S.L.: Beyond predictable workflows: enhancing productivity in artful business processes. IBM Syst. J. 45(4), 663–682 (2006)
17. Korherr, B., List, B.: A UML 2 profile for event driven process chains. In: Proceedings of International Conference on Research and Practical Issues of Enterprise Information Systems, Springer (2006)
18. Korherr, B., List, B.: Extending the EPC and the BPMN with business goals and performance measures. In: http://www.wit.at/people/korherr/publications/iceis2007.pdf Accessed in: 23 Sep 2011
19. Man, H.: Case management: a review of modeling approaches. In: BPTrends, January 2009
20. Moody, D.: The physics of notations: toward a scientific basis for constructing visual notations in software engineering. IEEE Trans. Software Eng. 35(6), 756–779 (2009)
21. Netto, J.M.; França, J.B.S.; Santoro, F.M.; Baião, F.A.: A notation for knowledge-intensive processes. In: 17th IEEE International Conference on Computer Supported Cooperative Work in Design, Canada , pp. 190–195 (2013)
22. Oliveira, A.P.A.: Intentional requirements engineering: a method of elicitation, modeling and analysis of requirements. D.Sc. Thesis, PUC, Rio de Janeiro, Brazil (2008) (In Portuguese)

23. Oliveira, F.F.: A collaboration ontology and its applications. M.Sc. Dissertation. Federal University of Espírito Santo, Brazil (2009) (In Portuguese)
24. OMG: Business Process Modeling and Notation (BPMN). Version 2.0 (2011). In: http://www.bpmn.org/ Accessed in: 26 June 2011
25. Rao, A.S., Georgeff, M.P.: BDI agents: from theory to practice. In: First International Conference on Multiagent Systems, USA, pp. 312–319 (1995)
26. Schreiber, G., Akkermans, H., Anjewierden, A., Hoog, R., Shadbolt, N., De Velde, W.V., Wielinga, B.: Knowledge Engineering and Management: The CommonKADS Methedology. MIT Press, Cambridge (2002)
27. Supulniece, I., Businska, L., Kirikova, M.: Towards extending BPMN with the knowledge dimension. In: Bider, I., Halpin, T., Krogstie, J., Nurcan, S., Proper, E., Schmidt, R., Ukor, R. (eds.) BPMDS 2010 and EMMSAD 2010. LNBIP, vol. 50, pp. 69–81. Springer, Heidelberg (2010)
28. Wang, J., Kumar, A.: A Framework for Document-Driven Workflow Systems. In: van der Aalst, W.M., Benatallah, B., Casati, F., Curbera, F. (eds.) BPM 2005. LNCS, vol. 3649, pp. 285–301. Springer, Heidelberg (2005)
29. Yu, E.: Towards modelling and reasoning support for early-phase requirements engineering. In: Proceedings of the 3rd IEEE International Symposium on Requirements Engineering, USA, pp. 226–235 (1997)
30. Yin, R.K.: Case Study Research: Design and Methods, 3rd edn. Sage Publications Inc, Thousand Oaks (2003)

Author Index